Book No._____   Cost_____

Property of
RIDGEFIELD HIGH SCHOOL
(Name of School)

INSTRUCTIONS: The pupil to whom this book is loaned will sign in space provided below. He or she will be required to pay to this school the cost price of this book if it is lost or damaged during the period for which it is loaned. Allowance will be made for wear caused by careful use.

Signature of Pupil	Condition	Date Loaned	Date Returned
Jim Morelli	New	'80	

FUNDAMENTALS OF DATA PROCESSING

S. J. WANOUS
Professor of Education/University of California/Los Angeles, California

E. E. WANOUS
South-Western Publishing Company/Cincinnati, Ohio

GERALD E. WAGNER
Chairman, Data Processing Department/School of Business Administration.
California State Polytechnic College/Pomona, California

Published by
J50   **SOUTH-WESTERN PUBLISHING CO.**
Cincinnati   Chicago   Dallas

Pelham Manor, N.Y.   Palo Alto, Calif.   Brighton, England

COBOL

ACKNOWLEDGEMENT

Any organization interested in reproducing the COBOL report and specifications (of the Conference on Data Systems Language) in whole or in part, using ideas taken from this report as the basis for an instructional manual or for any other purpose is free to do so. However, all such organizations are requested to reproduce this section as part of the introduction to the document. Those using a short passage, as in a book review, are requested to mention "COBOL" in acknowledgement of the source, but need not quote this entire section.

COBOL is an industry language and is not the property of any company or group of companies, or of any organization or group of organizations.

No warranty, expressed or implied, is made by any contributor or by the COBOL committee as to the accuracy and functioning of the programming system and language. Moreover, no responsibility is assumed by any contributor, or by the committee, in connection therewith.

Procedures have been established for the maintenance of COBOL. Inquiries concerning the procedures for proposing changes should be directed to the Executive Committee of the Conference on Data Systems Languages.

The authors and copyright holders of the copyright material used herein

FLOW-MATIC (Trademark of Sperry Rand Corporation), Programming for the UNIVAC (R) I and II, Data Automation Systems copyright 1958, 1959, by Sperry Rand Corporation; IBM Commercial Translator Form No. F28-8013, copyrighted 1959 by IBM; FACT, DS127A5260-2760, copyrighted 1960 by Minneapolis-Honeywell

have specifically authorized the use of their material in whole or in part, in the COBOL specifications. Such authorization extends to the reproduction and use of COBOL specifications in programming manuals or similar publications.

Copyright © 1971
Philippine Copyright 1971
by South-Western Publishing Co.
Cincinnati, Ohio

All Rights Reserved

The text of this publication, or any part thereof, may not be reproduced or transmitted in any form or by any means, electronic or mechanical, including photocopying, recording, storage in an information retrieval system, or otherwise, without the prior written permission of the publisher.

Standard Book Number: 0-538-10500-3

Library of Congress Catalog Card Number: 77-139157

7 8 H 8

Printed in the United States of America

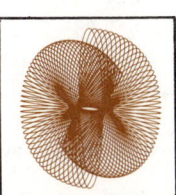

ON THE COVER—A COSMOGRAPH

The design on the cover of this book is called a *Cosmograph* and is a unique graphic arts innovation. It unerringly reflects the spirit of the present electronic era in that the design is free-form art, unencumbered by traditional patterns. Cosmographs are the products of an invention by a physicist in sound, Edward Lias, and copies are distributed by Photo-Lettering, Inc. of New York. The lines represent harmonious musical tones. The sounds are converted electronically to images that are displayed on an X-Y plotter and then photographed. The adjustment of tones to different ratios produces an almost limitless variety of formations. The designs are a result of science, art, and music merging capabilities to produce dramatic visual harmony that truly portrays the age of electronic computers.

PREFACE

Purpose of this book

1. To satisfy the curiosity of students who want to know how data are processed by electronic computers.
2. To acquaint students with the changes that have taken place in processing data because of electronic computers.
3. To develop, through the unfailing logic required by the computer, experience and skill in analyzing problems and laying out logical, step-by-step solutions.
4. To help prepare students for careers in which they need to understand automated data processing, even though their jobs may not be directly connected with electronic computers.
5. To acquaint students with the job openings in data processing and the qualifications needed to fill them.
6. To give students a basic foundation on which they can build in order to prepare themselves for careers in electronic data processing.

Specialized equipment not needed

This text can be used with or without specialized equipment. The availability of punched card machines and an electronic computer would definitely aid teachers and students in meeting the above goals. It is equally true, however, that the goals can be met without any specialized equipment. The book describes and illustrates in complete detail the form in which data must be prepared for the computer. Further, the text explains and illustrates the different kinds of instructions that can be carried out by the computer and the code in which these instructions must be written.

The problems used as illustrations, while simple, were solved with a computer, using the programs explained in the text. However, the students can get the same experience in writing programs without using a computer, as all essential steps are presented. Although the experience of pushing the proper control buttons is lacking, the emphasis is on the development of logic rather than the use of machinery.

Safeguards observed in preparing the text

Because the computer is a fantastic tool, the course can be interesting and challenging; but it need not be impossible. A study of automated data processing can be based on sophisticated technical theories that can be understood by only a handful of students. An introductory course need not be over the heads of most students, however, as long as it is based on practical problems and adequate safeguards are kept in mind in organizing it.

The safeguards observed in preparing this course are summarized as follows:

1. A number of manual data processing methods are reviewed at the outset. Some shortcuts in these methods are explained. Finally, a number of practical problems are solved using these methods.
2. The punched card, as a medium of communication between man and machine, is illustrated and explained. The operations performed by the unit-record system are discussed and illustrated. Using flow charts, the students lay out plans for solutions to the problems solved earlier by the manual method. The two methods are then compared.
3. The unique features of the electronic computer are explored. The students learn how the computer uses electronic impulses to represent data. They also learn how these impulses can be stored and manipulated to obtain a desired answer and how the computer makes the answers available to the user.
4. The students learn to write programs for the computer by first writing them in English, then in machine language, and finally in **COBOL**, a commonly used symbolic language. The problems solved earlier by manual and unit-record systems are now solved by the computer. Frequently a single problem is modified and expanded until a number of basic program instructions are explained.
5. A limited number of computer instructions are presented, but these are sufficient to enable the students to write a variety of programs, including storage of data, looping, branching, calculating, decision-making, and printing processed data.
6. The material is presented one step at a time, and all essential concepts are clearly illustrated. There is sound logic in the order in which concepts are presented.
7. The examples used are drawn from common business transactions and from those encountered by students in the conduct of actual school activities. The decision-making capabilities of the computer are illustrated by these programs. By providing the students with relevant problems, the study of data processing becomes more realistic and meaningful, and the students are made aware of the role the computer plays in their lives.

Teaching materials available

Color is used in the book to stress important points and to enhance its appearance. The size of the book permits the use of large illustrations. At the same time, the lines are of such length that they are easy to read.

Review questions are placed in the textbook at points at which the students should stop reading to check their understanding of the material they have covered before proceeding further. A comprehensive glossary helps the students to master the necessary technical vocabulary.

The text is self-contained and can be used without additional materials. For the teacher desiring a complete instructional package, however, a kit of correlating materials is available. The kit contains study guides, projects, working papers, and a flow charting template. Transparencies may also be obtained. With the study guides, a student can check his understanding of material covered. The guides are designed so that the learner may check his work and reread appropriate parts of the book when questions are missed.

A number of practical projects and working papers are included in the kit of materials. The working papers give the learner an opportunity to use some of the tools of automation, such as punched cards, source documents, program sheets, flow charts, and templates.

Many teachers, students, and data processing specialists have helped in writing this book. The authors wish to express their appreciation to them and to the organizations that generously provided many of the illustrations.

S. J. Wanous / E. E. Wanous / Gerald E. Wagner

CONTENTS

PART 1   GROWTH AND IMPORTANCE OF DATA PROCESSING

    Chapter 1 Data Processing Functions, 3

    Chapter 2 Development of Data Processing Tools, 13

    Chapter 3 Manual Data Processing, 31

    Chapter 4 Automated Data Processing, 43

PART 2   BASIC COMPONENTS OF AUTOMATED SYSTEMS

    Chapter 5 The Punched Card, 61

    Chapter 6 Card Planning and Layout, 71

    Chapter 7 Recording Information in Cards, 87

    Chapter 8 Sorting and Classifying Data in Cards, 111

PART 3   UNIT-RECORD SYSTEM

    Chapter 9 Printing, Calculating, and Preparing Reports, 133

    Chapter 10 The Control Panel, 151

PART 4 THE ELECTRONIC COMPUTER SYSTEM

      Chapter 11 The Electronic Computer, 167

      Chapter 12 Language and Computing Systems, 201

      Chapter 13 Internal Storage of Information, 215

      Chapter 14 Human Language Programs and Block Diagrams, 229

      Chapter 15 Machine Language Instructions, 253

      Chapter 16 Introduction to COBOL, 291

      Chapter 17 COBOL Applications, 333

      Chapter 18 Jobs and Careers in Automated Data Processing, 375

GLOSSARY, 385

INDEX, 401

PART 1

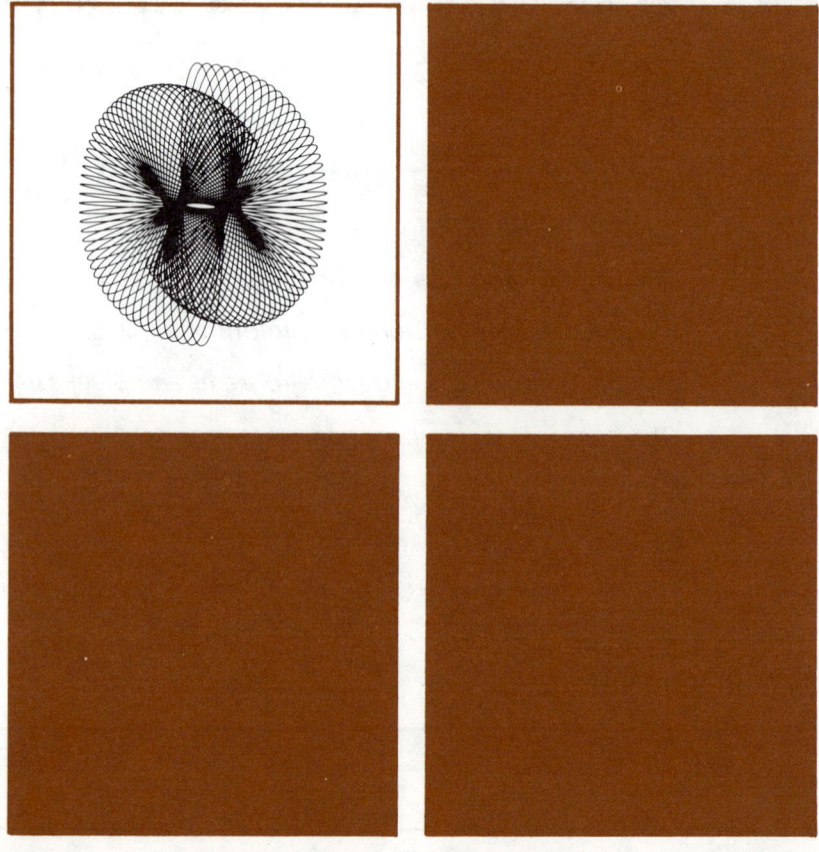

GROWTH AND IMPORTANCE OF DATA PROCESSING

Chapter	1	DATA PROCESSING FUNCTIONS
Chapter	2	DEVELOPMENT OF DATA PROCESSING TOOLS
Chapter	3	MANUAL DATA PROCESSING
Chapter	4	AUTOMATED DATA PROCESSING

CHAPTER 1

DATA PROCESSING FUNCTIONS

Men have always been challenged by problems that needed solutions. The tons of steel required for the San Francisco Bay Bridge, the best route to lay railroad tracks through the Colorado Rockies, or the man-hours of labor necessary to erect the Empire State Building were problems that fascinated men in the past. However, hundreds upon hundreds of routine computations essential to arrive at solutions to these problems were drudgery and were done with little enthusiasm. Often the collection and computation of data for a project proved to be so time-consuming and troublesome that the project was forgotten entirely. As a result, men throughout the ages have attempted to devise tools to make computing easier.

FANTASTIC SPEED OF ELECTRONIC COMPUTER

The electronic computer is but the latest in the long list of tools developed by man to aid him in making computations. Here, finally, is a machine that can make routine computations with little assistance from man. The computer makes the computations so rapidly that most people cannot comprehend its speed, which is measured in the nano-second (1/1,000,000,000 of a second). A large computer is capable of making six million calculations per second. In its main memory of over 500,000 characters, the computer can locate a number in one-millionth of a second. Reports say that a large computer can operate faster than 500,000 men with desk calculators.

SOME OF THE COMPUTER'S MANY USES

Aids space exploration

The computer is considered by many as the most remarkable invention of this decade. Some say that it will take a place, along with fire, the wheel, and the steam engine, as one of the great inventions of man. Others say that the computer and automation will bring about the greatest change in the entire history of humanity. As the most powerful and sophisticated tool devised by mankind, the computer is already touching the lives of all persons, opening a wide new range of discoveries. Without the computer, the Space Age would not be possible. When a space ship is launched, thousands of calculations must be made in a few seconds to make sure that it goes into proper orbit. Entire armies of men cannot make the calculations and coordinate them fast enough to handle such a complex problem. Because of the computer, man-made satellites are circling the earth and sun. Man has already set foot on the moon. What started as an attempt to project man beyond counting on his fingers will one day propel him far into the solar system.

From counting to poetry

Computers are being used today to compose music, write poetry, play chess or tic-tac-toe, match men and women on the basis of similar tastes and interests, arrange class schedules, keep airline reservations in order, teach boys and girls how to read, sort and route mail, and assist doctors in the diagnosis and control of diseases. Computers also control the flow of electric power for much of the nation, route long-distance calls, set newspaper type, and navigate ships.

Processes business data

Computers are used to keep records in banks, insurance companies, business offices, and government agencies. Computers prepare payrolls, maintain inventory records, check on the credit status of customers, send out statements of account, verify income tax returns, and handle every conceivable bookkeeping job. They are widely used by banks to keep depositors' accounts in proper order. The computer does the data-processing jobs that man can do, but it does them faster.

Controls production

The computer can handle large amounts of information. Because it has this ability, it can regulate production of a steel mill, bake bread, refine petroleum, or handle other similar processes. The factors that enter into the production of steel, bread, or gasoline, for example, are controlled by the computer on the basis of a set of directions prepared in advance and stored in the computer. Thereafter, all factors from the amount of heat to the mixture of ingredients are carefully supervised and regulated by the computer.

An oil refinery, with its maze of vats and vessels interconnected by miles of spaghetti-like pipes, is an ideal work place for the computer. Dials and sensors monitor intricate chemical processes inside furnaces, separators, and treaters and feed back impulses to the computer. Valves are turned, temperatures are regulated, and gases are mixed in exactly the right proportion as the computer interprets and reacts to the information admitted to it from a variety of sources.

Aids decision making

Computers also have the ability to work with statistical "models." For example, since there can be put into the computer detailed data on the batting, fielding, and pitching capabilities of the baseball players in a league, the computer can often tell us at the beginning of the season which team is most likely to win the pennant. It can often tell us what candidate will win an election on the basis of early returns. In the same way, the computer can predict whether a new store location or a new method of making a product should return a profit to its owners. It can make this prediction without the store's being built or the method's being tried out.

The accuracy of the computer in giving answers depends entirely upon the accuracy of the information put into it. The computer does only what it is told to do. On the other hand, the computer does force its users to think logically about the various factors having a bearing on solutions to their problems and about the relative importance of these factors. It makes them consider the questions that should be raised before arriving at a decision. In the same way that steam, gasoline, and electric motors have relieved people of the drudgery of doing work by hand, the computer has taken from decision making much of the drudgery associated with making routine computations. The computer, rightly used, can extend man's ability to find solutions to problems that formerly were impossible to solve.

Touches everyone

At this point, it must be concluded that the computer is something more than a machine that will add columns of figures, turn out a payroll, or keep customers' accounts straight. It does these jobs, of course, and with amazing speed and accuracy. In a larger sense, however, it processes information wherever information is needed. Because the rapid communication of information is so important in the modern world, the computer touches the lives of everyone in some manner.

DATA PROCESSING OPERATIONS

What is data processing? *Data* can be defined generally as detailed or factual material of any kind. There is a tendency to think of data as the factual material appearing on business forms that is used only in bookkeeping and accounting jobs. This is a misconception. To be sure, there are accounting data; but also included in data are facts, figures, letters, words, charts, maps, tables, and other basic elements of information. Thus, data may consist of scores on tests, enrollment figures in classes, salaries paid to employees, sales made to customers, and weather reports. The list could be expanded almost indefinitely. The data used in this book to illustrate a process or principle are obtained from many fields. However, the basic techniques of processing remain fairly constant regardless of the field from which the data are drawn.

Data and *information* are used more or less interchangeably. If a distinction is made, data are generally referred to as raw figures and facts to which meaning may or may not have been ascribed. Information, on the other hand, is the knowledge that grows out of data when they have been processed. Thus, if one accepts this distinction, the chief goal of data processing is the conversion of raw data into useful information.

A broadly-accepted definition of *data processing* is that it is the manipulation of factual matter of all kinds for the purpose of producing a desired answer or result. It includes one or more of the following operations: recording, classifying, sorting, calculating, summarizing, communicating, and storing. The term applies whether the work is done by hand or by machine.

Recording

Recording is the process of writing, rewriting, or reproducing data by hand or by machine. In a manual system, data are recorded in human language on a wide variety of forms. In the unit-record and electronic computer systems, data are also recorded on these forms in human language. Thereafter, they are recorded in some code form acceptable to the system being used.

Classifying (coding)

Classifying is the systematic assigning of similar data into categories according to established rules. A code, in the form of an alphabetic or numeric abbreviation, is then assigned to each category of data in order to facilitate processing. For example, the names of customers, names of states, and names of divisions of a company are frequently designated by code number. Once data have been identified by means of a code, that code must be used without exception throughout the entire processing routine if confusion is to be avoided.

Chapter 1   Data processing functions

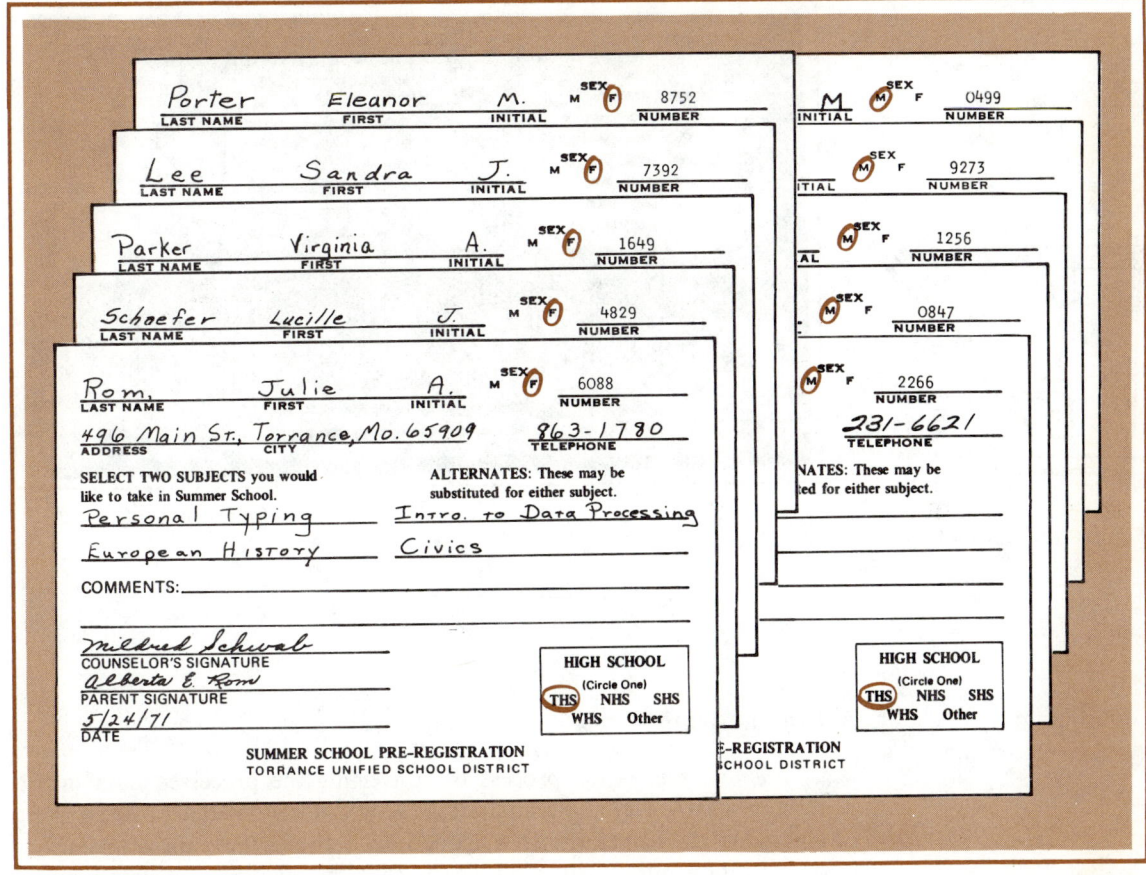

Figure 1-1. Sorting according to sex

Sorting

Sorting is the process of separating data into similar groups. Enrollment data, for example, may be separated according to subjects, teachers, rooms, grades, ages, sex, and other categories. Sorting is a function that facilitates further processing. Frequently, however, the sole objective of data processing is the grouping of information according to some plan. The sorting of data by manual or automatic methods is quite common.

Calculating

Calculating is the process of computing in order to arrive at a mathematical result. It usually results in the creation of new information. A wide variety of calculating machines has been developed to speed up mental and manual computations.

Courtesy of The National Cash Register Co.

Figure 1-2. Calculating

Summarizing

Summarizing is the process of converting the processed data into a concise, usable form. Summarizing is very closely related to the sorting and calculating operations. Distinctions between these three operations do exist, however. Sorting is accomplished by separating information into similar groups or categories. The grouped data may be quite useless, however, until they have been calculated or summarized. A student's report card received at the end of a school year is a summary of his scholastic evaluation, supported by many types of calculations.

REPORT OF ENROLLMENTS IN SELECTED COURSES	
DATA PROCESSING	121
TYPEWRITING	145
BOOKKEEPING	73
MATHEMATICS	55
ENGLISH	160
TOTAL ENROLLMENTS	554

Figure 1-3. Summarizing

Communicating

Communicating is the process of transmitting information to the point of use. The process covers both oral and written communication. Frequently, the operation includes nothing more than the transfer of reports from one desk to another. Communicating can also include processes such as transmission of information by mail, telephone, telegraph, radio, and closed-circuit television.

Storing

Storing is the orderly filing of information so that it may be used when it is needed. The files of an enterprise may be compared in function to the reference books in a library. Stored data provide the background against which many of the decisions important to the operation of an enterprise are made. Incomplete, badly managed files are among the chief causes of mismanagement and administrative confusion.

SCOPE OF THIS BOOK

This book describes the manual, unit-record, and electronic computer systems of processing information. Major emphasis is placed on the last two of the three systems. Occasional reference is made to the manual system, using traditional office machines for the purpose of comparing and contrasting the manual system with the newer systems.

The student will discover the many ways in which man can communicate with machines. Card fields will be planned for recording information, and the data that have been punched into the cards in code will be interpreted. The different methods by which punched cards, punched paper tape, magnetic tape, and mark-sensed cards are used in processing data will be explored. Directions will be written to solve problems, and the student will discover the various ways in which computers can be programmed to make decisions. Arithmetic problems will be solved in binary code — the code used by computers.

Finally, the student will learn to speak and read the language of automation. Not only is this language used in business, but it is becoming popular in the vocabulary of the layman. Examples of these terms are *input, input media, loop, branch, program, flow chart,* and *computer logic*.

The principal goal of this book is a basic introduction to the automated data processing field and the variety of ways in which information is processed automatically. The process can be understood without becoming concerned with the internal design of the machines used. The machines can be regarded only as metal boxes that obey commands to process information after the information has been prepared in proper form. Viewed in this light, the machines are only incidental to the process itself.

Many of the fine points of automatic processing are omitted for the sake of simplicity and clarity. Basic understandings are emphasized, nevertheless, and will serve as stepping stones to further study for those who desire to become specialists in this field.

PLAN FOR LEARNING

The principles and procedures leading to an understanding of automated data processing are explained and illustrated in detail. These principles and procedures are then applied to the solution of typical problems. The illustrations and solutions to these problems should be studied carefully. A search should be made for meaningful relationships between principles and practices while working through the book.

Review questions and problems appear throughout the chapters. These aids should be used to help check the understanding of the material covered. If the questions and problems seem difficult, it is recommended that the student reread the chapter.

The text comes with a set of jobs or projects to be worked, as well as the necessary papers and forms for their completion. The student will thus be brought into close contact with some of the special tools used in automated data processing. In addition to the projects, study guides for each chapter are included to check understanding of the important points covered.

SUMMARY

Over the centuries, men have sought new and faster ways of making computations. The computer, which is considered by many as the most important invention of this era, is the latest in the long list of tools developed to make computing easier. It has already opened a whole new range of discoveries. Without the computer, the Space Age would not be possible. In addition, the computer is being used to prepare payrolls, keep bank accounts, check on the credit standing of customers, verify income tax returns, and to handle hundreds of similar jobs.

The computer is also being used in factories to control the production of everything from bread to steel. Moreover, because it can work with statistical models, it is being used to help make decisions on such matters as locating new schools, predicting winners of elections, and determining the selling price of products.

Data is a general term denoting detailed information of any kind. *Data processing* is the manipulation of factual matter of all kinds in order to produce a desired answer or result and the processing consists of one or more of the following operations: recording, classifying, sorting, summarizing, calculating, communicating, and storing.

Chapter 1   Data processing functions

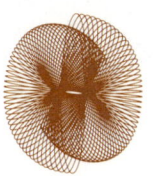

REVIEW QUESTIONS

1. What length of time does a nano-second represent?
2. What are some of the ways in which the electronic computer is being used?
3. Why are computers necessary to the space exploration program of this country?
4. How does the electronic computer aid in decision making?
5. What are some of the ways in which the computer is touching or affecting human lives?
6. What is meant by the term *data*?
7. What is *data processing*?
8. What are the seven operations included in processing data?
9. Define sorting; summarizing.
10. What is the difference between classifying (coding) and sorting?
11. What is the purpose of these review questions?
12. What is the primary purpose of this book?

STUDY GUIDE 1

Complete Study Guide 1 by following the instructions in your **STUDY GUIDES** booklet.

PROJECT

Complete Project 1-1 by following the instructions in your **PROJECTS** booklet.

CHAPTER 2

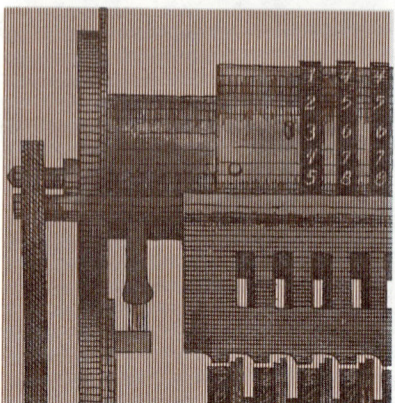

DEVELOPMENT OF DATA PROCESSING TOOLS

FROM FINGER COUNTING TO ELECTRONIC COMPUTERS

The *Mark I*, known as the first successful general-purpose digital computer, was not built until 1944. Although slow compared to today's computers, it made computations automatically and rapidly. What did man do before that date to speed up his calculating jobs and make them less boresome?

Finger counting

Before the nineteenth century, most calculations were made in a man's brain. His first computations were simple counting; and no doubt he used his ten fingers to help him — an aid that is not exactly foreign to young learners today. The early Roman schools actually taught finger counting and devised a method of multiplying and dividing on the fingers.

Abacus

From the use of his fingers, man moved to aids such as pebbles, sticks, and beads for his computations. More than 3,000 years ago, the *abacus*, the first counting machine, was invented. It consists of a frame in which rods strung with beads are set. The beads represent digits and the rods represent places — units, tens, hundreds, and higher multiples of ten. In the abacus illustrated in Figure 2-1, each bead in the top compartment has an assigned value of five; each in the bottom compartment, a value of one. The beads in both compartments have a counting value when they are

Figure 2-1. Abacus

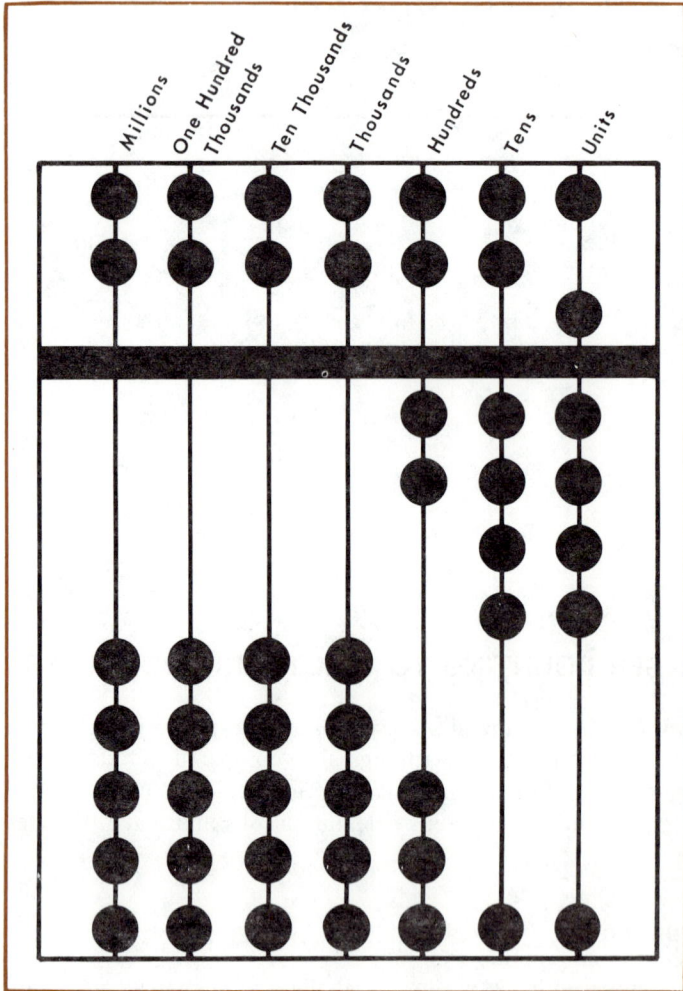

pushed toward the board that separates the two compartments. In the illustration, the beads represent a total of 249.

The origin of the abacus is uncertain. Some say it is a product of the ancient Hindu civilization. Others say it came from Babylon or Egypt. Some believe that the Chinese invented it. The Chinese modified and adopted it early in their history; and it has, therefore, become known generally as a Chinese invention.

The Japanese also modified and adopted the abacus. The Japanese model is known as the *soroban*. It differs from the abacus in that it has only one bead on each rod in the upper compartment and five beads in the lower compartment. You will note in Figure 2-1 that the abacus has two beads on each rod in the upper compartment and five in the lower compartment. Both devices are still widely used in some countries. In skilled hands, they are amazingly rapid and efficient in making computations.

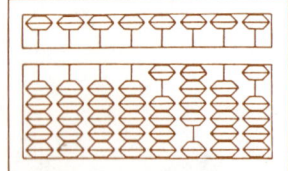

Figure 2-2. Soroban

Chapter 2   Development of data processing tools   15

Stonehenge

North of Salisbury, in Wiltshire, England, there is evidence that early man was able to record with great accuracy the seasons and possibly even the eclipses and significant risings and settings of the sun and moon. Stonehenge was believed to have been constructed in various stages between 1800 and 1400 B.C. It was apparently a place of religious worship and sacrifice. The correlation with the seasons was probably based upon the primitive seasons of worship. Consisting of a circular arrangement of pillars and stones circumscribed by an earthwork, the ruins of Stonehenge would indicate that man, during the Late Neolithic and Early Bronze ages, was attempting to keep records and to make predictions based upon these records.

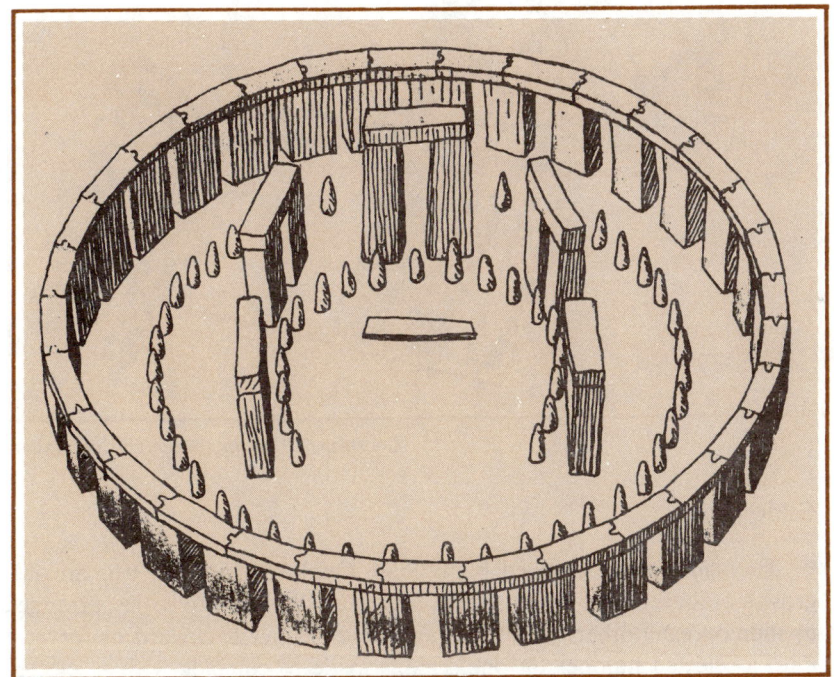

Courtesy of Planning Research Corporation

Figure 2-3. Stonehenge

Figure 2-4. Leonardo da Vinci's hodometer

Hodometer

Leonardo da Vinci, in the late fifteenth century, invented a device for computing distances by dropping pebbles into a box for counting. This device, although never widely accepted, did utilize the same principle of analogous comparison that is used in an analog computer.

Logarithms

John Napier gave to the world in 1614 his famous invention of *logarithms*. Tables of logarithms were used to simplify computations requiring multiplication and division. Napier later invented a device consisting of rods or strips of bone on which numbers were printed. The device became known as "Napier's bones." By means of these rods or bones, computations could be performed, including the extraction of square and cube roots. See Figure 2-5.

Figure 2-5. Napier's Bones

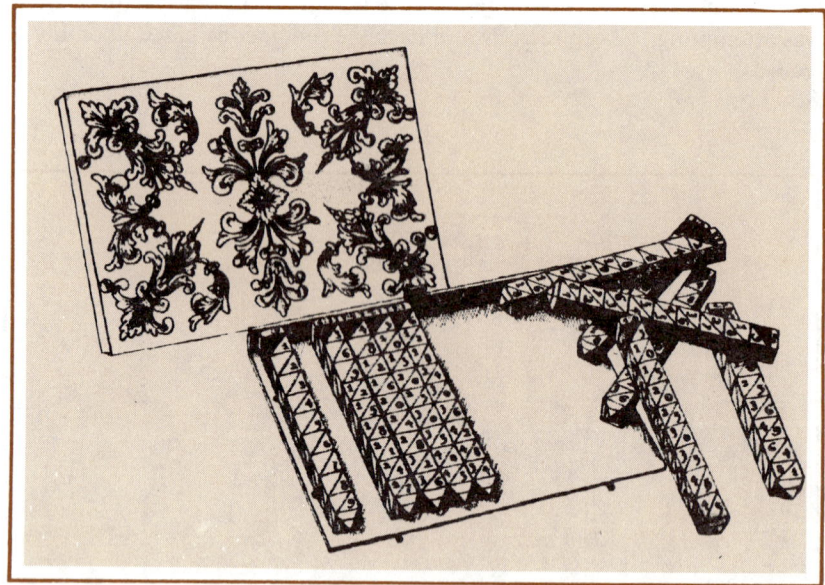

Courtesy of Planning Research Corporation

Slide rule

The *slide rule*, conceived by William Oughtred in 1622, was an outgrowth of logarithms. It consists of two rules, divided into scales, arranged to slide on each other. The rules are moved either backward or forward until a selected number on one scale is made to coincide with a selected number on the other. The desired result is then read from a third scale. The slide rule, sometimes referred to as our first practical analog computer, is widely used today by engineers and scientists. It is suitable for many rough calculations. Its accuracy is limited by the ability of the naked eye. Its user can make an accurate reading only to one or two decimal places unless he works with a very large slide rule. Even then, he cannot be accurate beyond four decimal places.

All slide rules depend upon the mechanical use of logarithms, and the scales appearing on the rules are graduated on a logarithmic basis. Generally, all problems involving multiplication and division, including

Chapter 2   Development of data processing tools   17

powers, roots, and proportions, may be solved by adjusting the rules and reading the result. See Figure 2-6.

Early calculators

Blaise Pascal. In 1642, Blaise Pascal invented the first mechanical adding machine. It was capable of carrying tens automatically. His machine consisted of wheels with cogs or teeth, on which were engraved the numbers from 0 to 9. The first wheel on the right represented units; the second, tens; the third, hundreds; and so on. As the wheels were turned, the numbers would appear in a window at the top of the machine. When the units wheel was turned beyond the Digit 9, the tens wheel at the left would reflect the carry. For example, to add 7 and 4, the 7 was stored on the first wheel by turning the wheel until the 7 appeared in the window. Then the wheel was turned again through 4 places. This procedure resulted in a carry, which was accomplished by a series of gears arranged in such a way that they turned the next wheel. As a result, 1's appeared in the windows above the tens and units wheels.

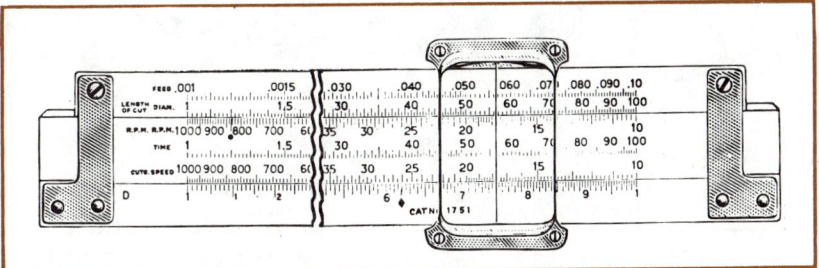

Figure 2-6. Slide rule

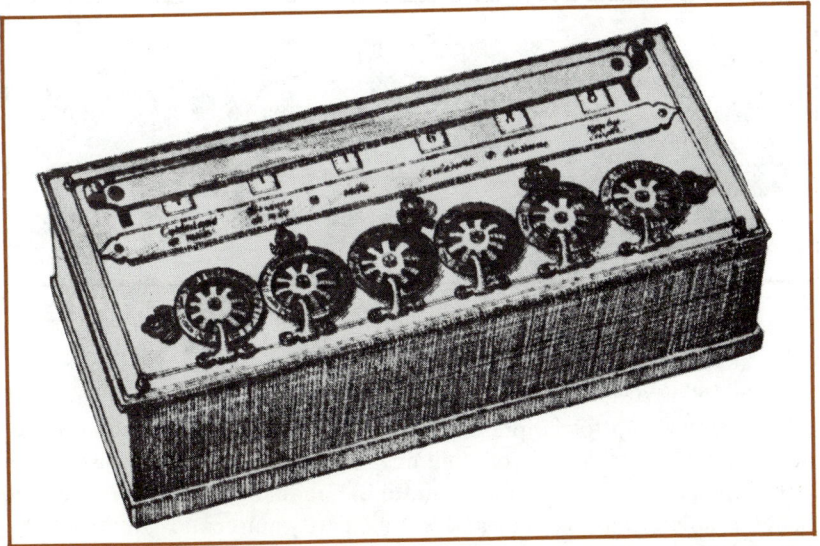

Courtesy of Planning Research Corporation

Figure 2-7. First mechanical adding machine

Samuel Morland. In 1666, Samuel Morland developed an adding machine, in an attempt to speed up and simplify the accounting of English currency. See Figure 2-8.

Gottfried von Leibnitz. Gottfried von Leibnitz drew the plans in 1671 for a calculator that could multiply and divide as well as count, add, and subtract. In 1694, a machine was actually built using his plans, but it did not work very well. The plans were all right, but the art had not yet been developed for making parts to the high precision required. See Figure 2-9.

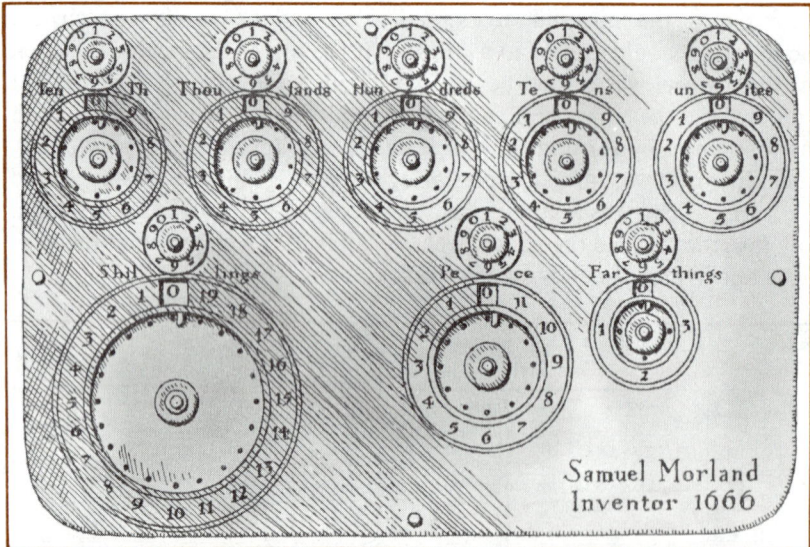

Figure 2-8. Morland's adding machine

Courtesy of Planning Research Corporation

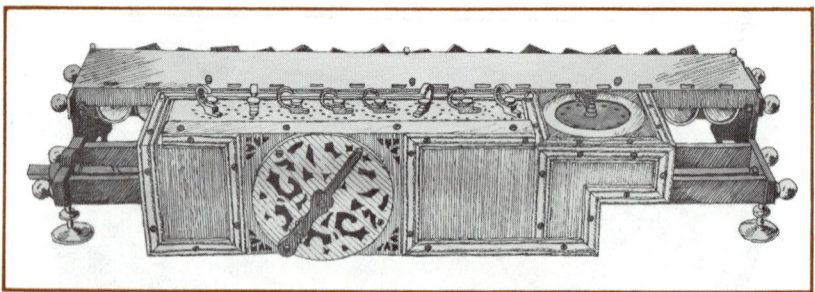

Figure 2-9. Von Leibnitz's calculator.

Courtesy of Planning Research Corporation

Charles Xavier Thomas. For the next two hundred years, and, of course, leading up to the present time, many attempts were made to improve on the Pascal and von Leibnitz inventions. Progress was made, although slow and sometimes painful. Gradually, calculators became faster, smaller, more reliable, and at least partly automatic. In the 1820's, Charles Xavier Thomas invented a calculator that was the first to add, subtract, divide, and multiply accurately. It was widely copied by other

Chapter 2 Development of data processing tools 19

inventors and was thus considered to be the ancestor of present-day desk calculators. Figure 2-10 is a typical 1880 machine, capable of performing the four principal arithmetic operations.

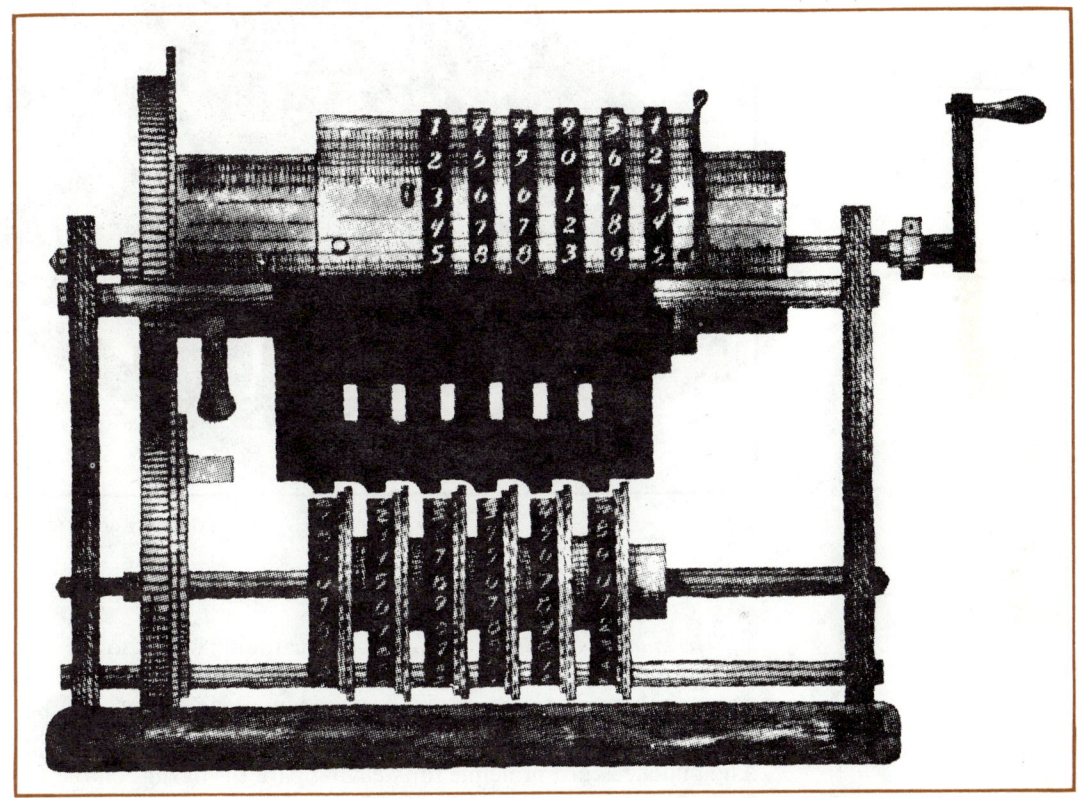

Figure 2-10. Grant's calculator — a typical 1880 machine similar to the first calculator invented by Charles Xavier Thomas

Courtesy of Planning Research Corporation

Early American inventors. All early calculator inventors were Europeans. In 1872, however, Frank S. Baldwin invented the first calculator in the United States. The event marked the beginning of a rapidly growing calculator industry in this country. See Figure 2-11. The first practical adding machines which listed amounts and sums on paper were invented in the late 1800's by Dorr Eugene Felt and William S. Burroughs.

Oscar and David Sundstrand invented the 10-key adding-listing machine in 1914. Ten-key adding machines have since become the most commonly used calculators in modern business offices. During the same period, Jay R. Monroe and Frank S. Baldwin invented a calculator that could multiply and divide automatically. A new era in the development of calculators was underway. The magic words of the era were to become "speed" and "automatic."

Figure 2-11. First U.S. Calculator

Courtesy of Burroughs Corp.

Punched card machines

Herman Hollerith. Using punched cards in which to record factual information, Herman Hollerith developed an entirely new system of processing data. Punched paper tape and punched cards had been used as early as 1728 by Bouchon and Falcon to control a weaving machine. The punched-card principle for weaving patterns in rugs on the first automatic loom was perfected in 1801 by Joseph Jacquard. See Figure 2-12.

Figure 2-12. Jacquard's cards

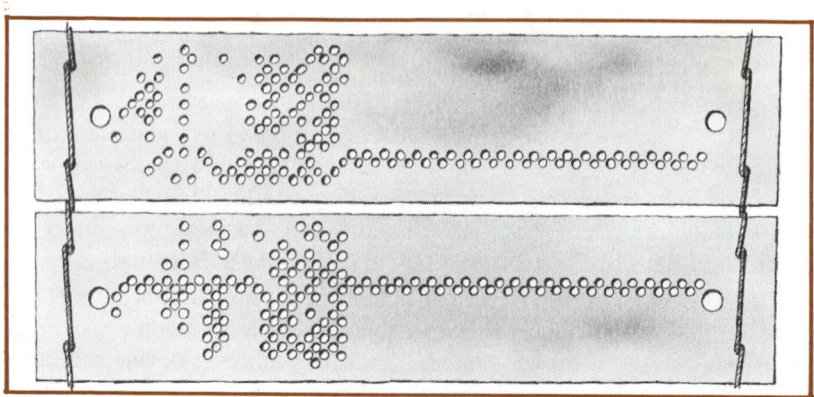

Courtesy of Planning Research Corporation

Chapter 2 Development of data processing tools

The pattern of punches in a paper card determined which threads would be woven into a rug at each pass of the shuttle, thus determining the pattern for a rug. The process was based on the use of rods in the Jacquard loom which did or did not encounter punches in the paper cards.

In 1880, Hollerith was employed by the U.S. Census Bureau to expedite the sorting and tabulating of census data, because it became apparent that it would take over ten years to tabulate the next census figures. By 1887, he had worked out a code of representing census information through a system of punched holes in paper strips, later changed to a standard-sized card because the paper strips did not work very well. Thus, Hollerith developed the first machine capable of processing statistical information from punched cards. The system included the cards, a card punch, a sorting box, and a tabulator equipped with electromagnetic counters. With this equipment, cards could be sorted at the rate of about 80 a minute. Data appearing in them could be tabulated and counted at the rate of 50 to 75 cards per minute.

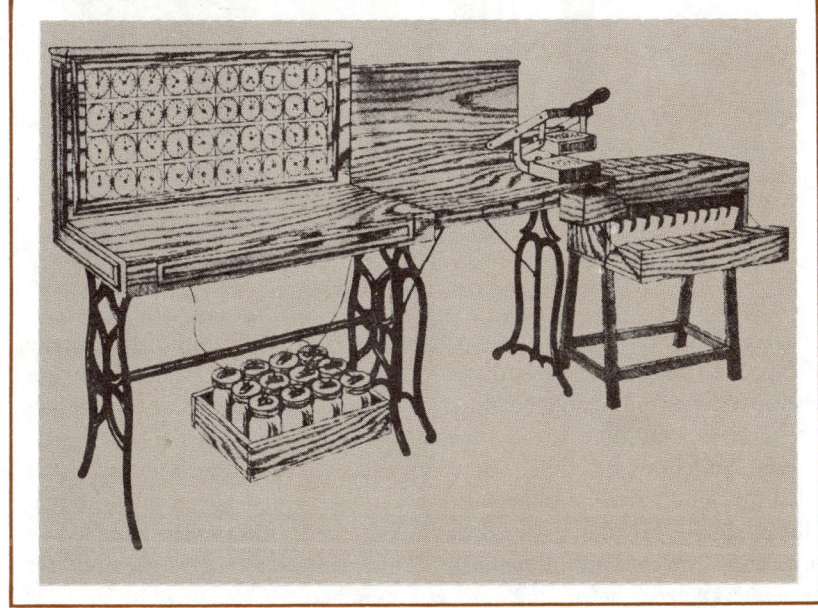

Figure 2-13. Hollerith's punched card machine

Courtesy of Planning Research Corporation

The Hollerith System was used to process the 1890 Census. As a result, the 1890 Census was completed in one-fourth the time needed to compile the 1880 Census. Hollerith then organized a company to manufacture and market his system. This company later came to be known as the International Business Machines Corporation (IBM).

Figure 2-14. Powers' punching machine

Courtesy of Univac Division, Sperry Rand Corporation

James Powers. James Powers was employed by the U.S. Census Bureau to improve further the methods for processing the 1910 Census. Powers developed a new punching machine, sorter, and tabulator. These machines were said at that time to be superior to those developed by Hollerith. Powers' punching machine, for example, used the die-set principle in which all the data to be punched in a card were first keyed into the machine correctly. By depressing a single key, the operator then punched all the holes in the card simultaneously. This method permitted the operator to correct an error before the card was punched.

Like Hollerith, Powers later organized a company to make and sell his machines. These machines were later acquired by the Remington Rand Corporation, now the Univac Division of the Sperry Rand Corporation.

Punched card era. Many improvements have been made on the original Hollerith and Powers machines. Punched cards were developed in which could be recorded 80 columns of information. The machines for punching holes in the cards were equipped with a number of automatic devices and improved. Moreover, machines were introduced that could

Chapter 2   Development of data processing tools   23

Figure 2-15. Improved punched card machine

Courtesy of IBM Corporation

add, subtract, and multiply, giving them the ability to handle most of the record-keeping jobs in business. Eventually, a punched-card calculator was developed that could divide. In addition, provision was made for processing alphabetic as well as numeric information and for printing the results. The speed and versatility of the machines were increased. As a result, punched card data processing was widely adopted in the 1920's and 1930's. It is widely used today, either as an independent system of data processing or in conjunction with the electronic computer.

Cards are punched manually by an operator on a card punch machine with a keyboard similar to that found on a typewriter. The sorting function in a punched card system is controlled by a dial or crank on a sorting machine. The operator merely turns the dial to the column on which the sorting is to take place. The tabulating, calculating, and printing functions, however, are regulated by control panels attached to certain tabulating machines. Before one can tabulate, calculate, or print the data punched into cards, he must first hook up appropriate circuits in the control panel by hand — an operation that is similar to plugging in the connections on a telephone switchboard. Once the circuits are connected and the board is attached to the proper machine, many cards can be processed without further human intervention.

Many of the data processing functions in the punched card system are performed automatically. While the machines in the system are electrically powered, they operate mechanically. Calculating, for example, is accomplished through a system of cogwheels and gears, the same system used in the more common adding machines. For this reason, the speed of the machines is limited when compared with the speed of the more modern electronic computers.

The punched card system is sometimes referred to as an electromechanical system. It is also known as the tab or tabulating system, accounting machine system, or unit-record system. The last term seems currently to be in highest favor.

Electronic computers

Charles Babbage. Turn your clock back briefly about one hundred and fifty years to the middle 1800's and meet another inventor, Charles Babbage, with some entirely new and advanced ideas on designing a computer. "I am going to construct a machine," wrote Babbage, "which will incorporate a memory unit system, an external memory unit, and conditional transfer. I am going to call this device an 'Analytical Engine.'" What Babbage described with startling accuracy is the modern computer.

Babbage was a mathematician of high repute, who spent his life and his fortune, as well as large sums of money from the British government, on the design of an automatic computer. The machine designed by Babbage was to have four basic parts. One part, consisting of the memory, was to be used to store the numerical data used in a calculation. A second part, consisting of gears and cog wheels on which digits were engraved, was to be used for computing. A third part, consisting of gears and levers, could move numbers back and forth between the memory and computing units. Finally, Babbage planned to use punched cards for getting information into and out of his machine. He planned to use the punched cards developed earlier by Joseph Jacquard for weaving patterns in rugs.

Babbage believed, moreover, that he could use cards to program his machine to handle computations automatically. He also seemed to have in mind the possibility of programming his machine to change from one series of steps to another when certain conditions were encountered. This is one of the most valuable abilities of today's automatic computers.

Babbage did not complete his machine, but he did leave to a new generation of inventors a great many detailed drawings and descriptions. Under tooling conditions existing then, the various parts of his machine simply could not be made to the exact specifications required. He was ahead of his time. Had he been successful, his machine would have been the first true digital computer. His work was largely forgotten until the

Chapter 2　　Development of data processing tools　　　　　　　　　　　　　　25

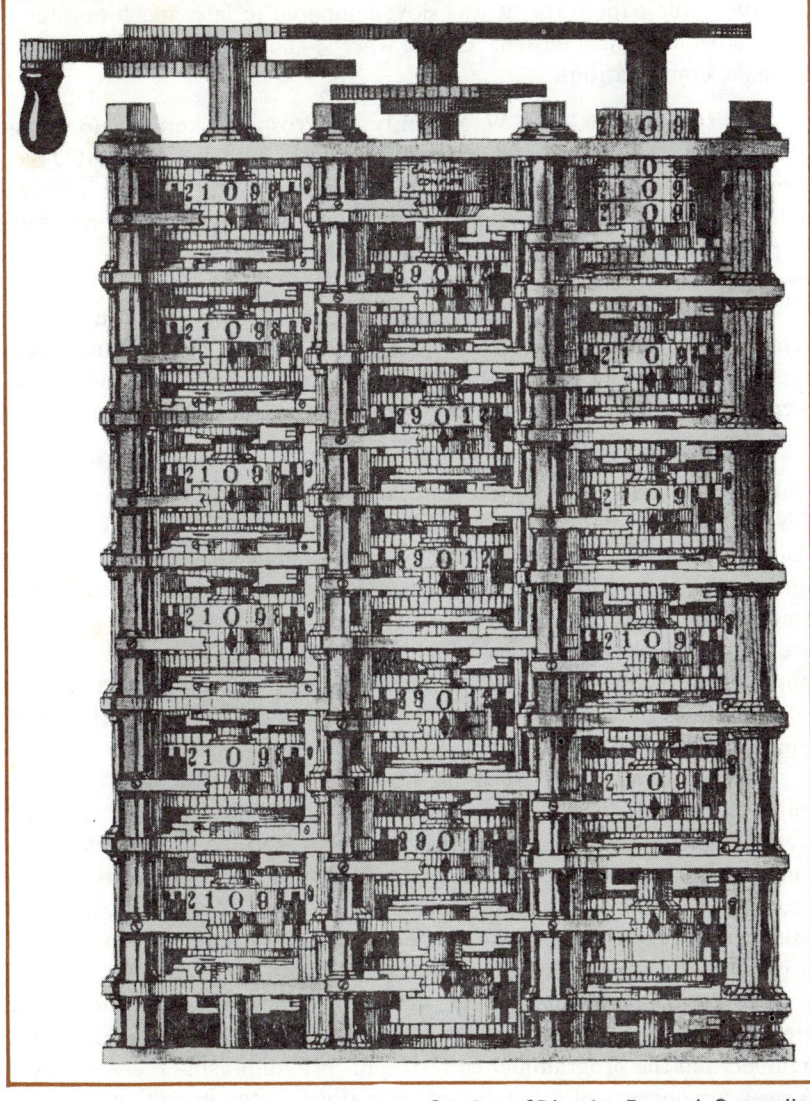

Figure 2-16. Charles Babbage's analytical "Difference Engine"

Courtesy of Planning Research Corporation

1940's, when new attempts were made to design and build a rapid, automatic computer.

Mark I computer. In 1944, Howard Aiken developed an automatic sequence-controlled calculator, the Mark I, generally regarded as the first successful general purpose digital computer. The Mark I obtained data from punched cards, made decimal calculations with the aid of counter wheels, switches, and other mechanical devices, and punched the results into a new set of cards. However, the sequence of calculations was controlled automatically by instructions punched into paper tape attached to the computer. While the computer processed data automatically through the use of the paper tape, it was slow compared to later machines due to its electromechanical design. Gears, wheels, and electric relays were used to make computations.

ENIAC. In 1946, John W. Mauchly and Prosper Eckert developed and tested the first truly *electronic* digital computer known as ENIAC (Electronic Numerical Integrator and Computer). It had no moving parts other than those used in feeding data into the computer or recording results in punched cards. Punched cards were used at both ends of the processing cycle.

A large number of vacuum tubes replaced the gears, wheels, and electric relays of the Mark I. Speed was thus gained because electric current can move faster than mechanical parts. The processing operations of ENIAC were regulated by a control panel in which instructions were wired by hand and attached to the computer.

EDVAC. At the time that Mauchly and Eckert were developing the ENIAC, J. von Neumann designed EDVAC (Electronic Discrete Variable Automatic Computer). It used binary arithmetic to make calculations internally. Most people are so accustomed to the decimal system, which employs ten digits from 0 to 9, that it is hard to accept the fact that there are other numbering systems. In binary arithmetic, which has a base-2 numbering system, only the 0 and 1 are needed. Each move from right to left multiplies the value of a number by two. Addition, subtraction, multiplication, and division are possible with the binary system.

EDVAC's chief claim to fame, however, is that it was the first computer to use the *stored program* principle. Instructions to process data were punched into cards and stored via the cards in the form of electronic impulses in the memory of the computer. This method of controlling the processing action of the computer was far faster and more flexible than using control panels or punched paper tape. The stored program principle is now used in all modern electronic computers.

In a stored program machine, certain common and basic operations are built into the circuitry of the computer. Each operation is given a number, and the programmer can write his program using these numbers. A program consists of a number of operations placed in sequential order. Moreover, the program is stored in the memory of the computer. When the program is executed, the computer proceeds automatically from one instruction to the next. The sequence of operations can be varied, however, as certain conditions arise. Some of the instructions may be repeated or skipped, or the transfer may be to a new set of instructions, depending upon the conditions set up in the program. This capability of the computer enables it to change the flow of its computation as it executes the program.

Developments since 1946. Since 1946, improvements in electronic computers have come at a rapid rate. New media have been developed for bringing information to computers. Punched cards are still used very widely, but new, faster devices include paper tape, magnetic tape, magnetic ink characters, and magnetic metal disks. The processed data may also be recorded on a wide range of devices, including cathode-ray tubes, which depict statistical data in the same way that a tube in a television set shows pictures.

Data can now be transmitted by special typewriter over telephone or telegraph wires to a centrally located computer. The computer processes the data and causes the results to be typed on the sender's typewriter. The results can also be punched into cards or be displayed on cathode-ray tube equipment located in the sender's office. This arrangement makes computer services available to almost everybody.

New units for the internal storage of data and instructions have been developed, thus greatly expanding the storage capacity of computers and making needed information available in a very small fraction of a second.

A wide range of programming languages has been developed. Some make it possible for programmers to write their instructions in a near-human system instead of the one used by the computer. Translating devices have been created to convert programs to the language of the computer, which has greatly simplified the work of the programmer.

Electronic computers were used in business for the first time in 1954. Because of the high premium placed on instantaneous information, obtainable exactly when and where it is needed, the computer is widely accepted. It is the most powerful tool yet devised by man for processing, storing, and retrieving information. In 1950, there were no more than fifteen computers in use in the United States. Today there are at least 48,000, and by 1975, the predictions are that there will be 85,000 computers at work in this country alone. Reports say that more than 3,000,000 people will be directly engaged in their operation.

Some misconceptions about computers

There is a mistaken belief that a computer is a very rapid adding machine. The computer is fast, all right, but the ability to handle computations is only a small part of the work it can do. Some of the ways in which it processes data will be explored in the chapters on the electronic computer. Basic principles and characteristics will be stressed. One of these is that the computer can manipulate electric current representing pieces of information. An adding machine, on the other hand, consists of wheels and dials that represent figures. Once this difference is grasped, much of the mystery surrounding the computer will vanish.

Computers are able to process very rapidly symbols representing data. Computers can store information and retrieve it when needed. With proper direction, they can make decisions similar to those made by man. Computers may be used in so many ways that only a small number of their applications can be covered in this book. Yet the student can distinguish enough common elements in these applications to make this journey into the Computer Age worthwhile.

Can computers think? Many people believe they can. This is a misconception. Computers can make decisions; but they make them on command, and not, as humans do, by instinct. If the data put into a machine are wrong, the computer will give the incorrect answer.

There is another widespread belief concerning the computer; namely, that a person must be a mathematical genius or an engineer to learn how a computer processes data. Wrong again! Many of the problems computers solve do not require any computations at all. Many require only the ability to calculate, add, and subtract. Most of the problems used in this book for illustrative purposes do not go beyond an understanding of elementary arithmetic.

SUMMARY

The computer is the most recent entry in a long list of inventions to help man with his computing tasks. The abacus marked the beginning; then came logarithms, invented by John Napier; and the slide rule, conceived by William Oughtred. Blaise Pascal invented the first successful adding machine, and this was followed by the Gottfried von Leibnitz machine, which, with patient coaxing, would not only add, but also subtract, multiply, and divide. The parts for his machine simply could not be made to the high precision required. Many years later, Charles Xavier Thomas invented a calculator that did what the von Leibnitz machine was supposed to do. Thomas' machine is said to be the ancestor of present-day desk calculators.

Herman Hollerith and James Powers developed an entirely new system of processing data by punched cards. Their efforts led to the development of the unit-record system, a system that is used widely today because it processes data automatically.

In 1946, John W. Mauchly and Prosper Eckert developed the first truly electronic digital computer, known as ENIAC. Since then, improvements and innovations have followed one another with amazing speed. The computer today is the most powerful and sophisticated tool ever devised by man for processing information.

REVIEW QUESTIONS

1. Who initiated punched card data processing? When?
2. In what contribution to data processing did each of the following men participate?
   a. Frank S. Baldwin
   b. Prosper Eckert
   c. Charles Babbage
   d. James Powers
3. Why was Herman Hollerith employed by the Census Bureau?

4. When was the first successful digital computer completed? By what name was it known?
5. What is the basic difference between the Mark I and the ENIAC computers?
6. What is the basic difference between the binary numbering system and the decimal numbering system? Which system do we normally use?
7. Which computer was the first to use the principle of a stored program?
8. When was an electronic computer first used commercially?
9. What are some of the improvements made on electronic computers since 1946?
10. Can computers think?

STUDY GUIDE 2

Complete Study Guide 2 by following the instructions in your STUDY GUIDES booklet.

PROJECT

Complete Project 2-1 by following the instructions in your PROJECTS booklet.

CHAPTER 3

MANUAL DATA PROCESSING

What is the origin of the data that processing systems handle? They come from a wide variety of sources. Information concerning students in a school, for example, comes from registration forms, grade reports, and other similar documents. Information regarding hours worked by an employee is derived from time tickets. Information on test scores is obtained from the scored tests. The data to be processed are referred to as *raw* or *original data*, and the documents on which the data appear are referred to as source documents. A *source document* is thus the document from which raw or original data are obtained.

DATA PROCESSING FRAMEWORK

The raw data are coded (classified) and enter the processing framework as input. The coded data are manipulated; that is, they undergo sorting, calculating, recording, communicating, and summarizing operations. The processed data emerge from this treatment as output in the form of checks, report cards, class schedules, and other reports or documents. The basic components of any data processing system are input, manipulation, output, and storage. Observe the diagram in Figure 3-1.

In the jargon of automation, the data that are recorded for processing are labeled as *input*. The forms on which these data are recorded are known as *input media*. The processed information is known as *output*. The forms on which the processed information appear are known as *output media*. In the discussions that follow, these terms are often used to describe data processing functions whether or not automated methods are used.

INPUT

Raw data (input) are originated and recorded on a form (input medium).

MANIPULATION

Raw data are processed (sorted, calculated, summarized).

OUTPUT

Processed data (output) are read out of the system on forms (output media, such as checks, statements, reports, report cards).

STORAGE

Processed data are stored.

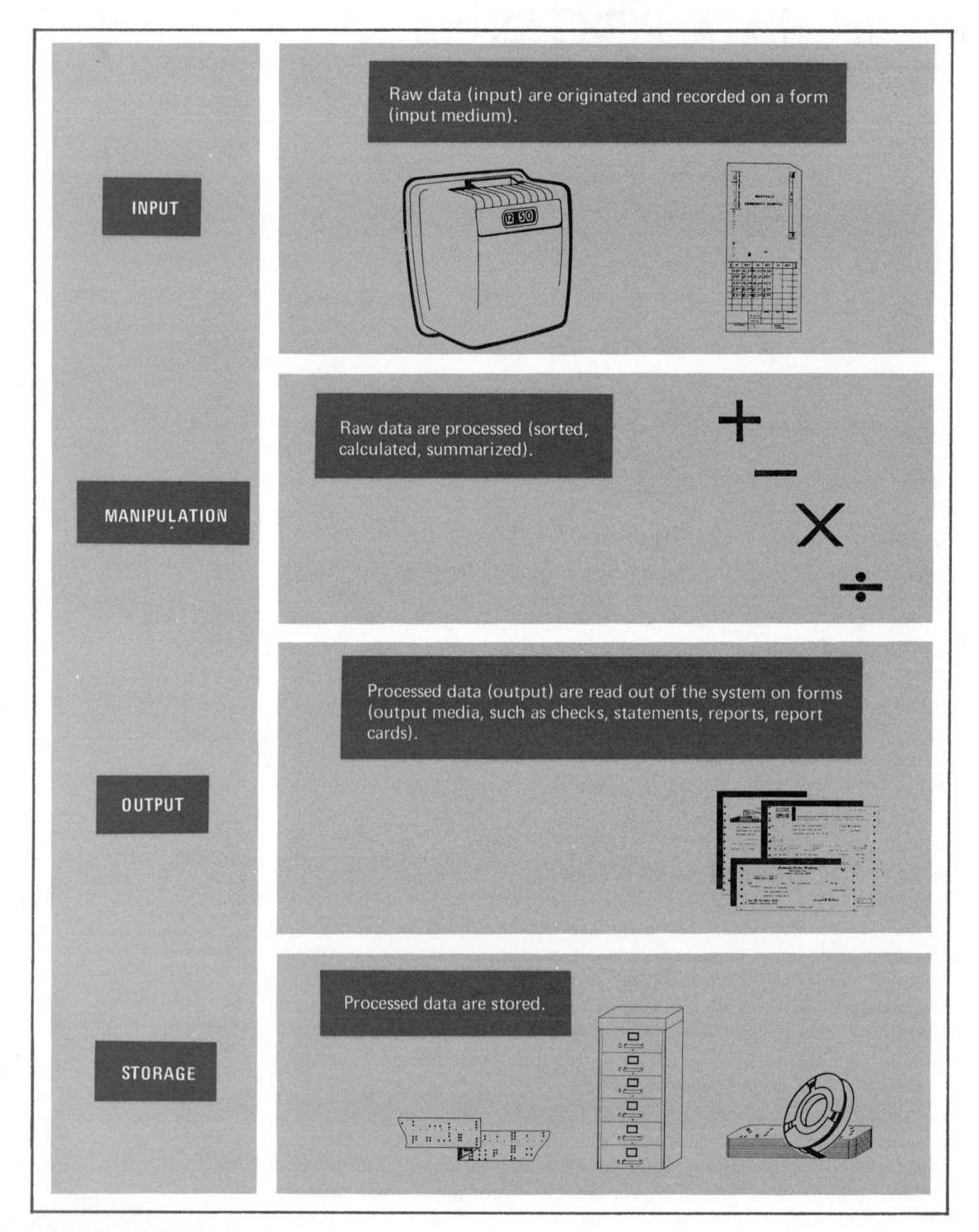

Figure 3-1. Data processing framework

Chapter 3　　Manual data processing

MANUAL DATA PROCESSING

The *manual method* of data processing is one in which the flow of a routine for handling a job consists of a number of fairly distinct steps, each of which is performed by some human effort, direction, and control. A typewriter, adding machine, calculator, or other device may assist the operator; but these machines are under the direct control of the operator. They do not change the basic character of the work involved in manual data processing.

In manual data processing, raw data, as input, enter the framework illustrated in Figure 3-1 and the data undergo manual sorting, recording, calculating, summarizing, and other operations. A number of office machines may assist the operator with these operations. Output emerges as useful information. While the framework within which data are processed is the same for all tasks, the routines set up vary from task to task. Some routines will include all of the data processing operations described in Chapter 1; some will include only a few. For example, the routine set up for processing a payroll includes sorting, recording, calculating, summarizing, and storing operations.

The steps outlined below are those included in a routine to process a payroll. Note the manner in which data flow through the framework illustrated in Figure 3-1. The routine begins with the time card as the source document. See Figure 3-2.

- Step 1: With a time clock, each employee of the company records on a time card his beginning and ending times of work for each day of employment. The time card is the source document.
- Step 2: Each week the cards are collected from the time card rack and the total hours worked by each employee for the week are calculated and recorded on his card.
- Step 3: The cards are sequenced in alphabetic order by employee names or in numeric order by employee numbers.
- Step 4: From the time cards, the employee names, their identifying numbers, and the number of hours worked are recorded in proper columns of the payroll register. In addition, the hourly rate of each employee and deductions for such items as group insurance premiums and withholding taxes are obtained from employment records and recorded in appropriate columns of the register.
- Step 5: The gross earnings for each employee are calculated by multiplying the hours worked by the rate of pay. The result is recorded in the earnings column of the register. Deductions are totaled and subtracted from earnings to arrive at net earnings, which are recorded in an appropriate column.
- Step 6: Summaries of earnings and deductions for each employee are prepared, and the employee's account is brought up to date.

Step 7: Paychecks and related reports, such as statements of earnings for employees, are prepared.

Step 8: The data are stored so that quarterly and other periodic payroll reports may be prepared.

Figure 3-2. Time card

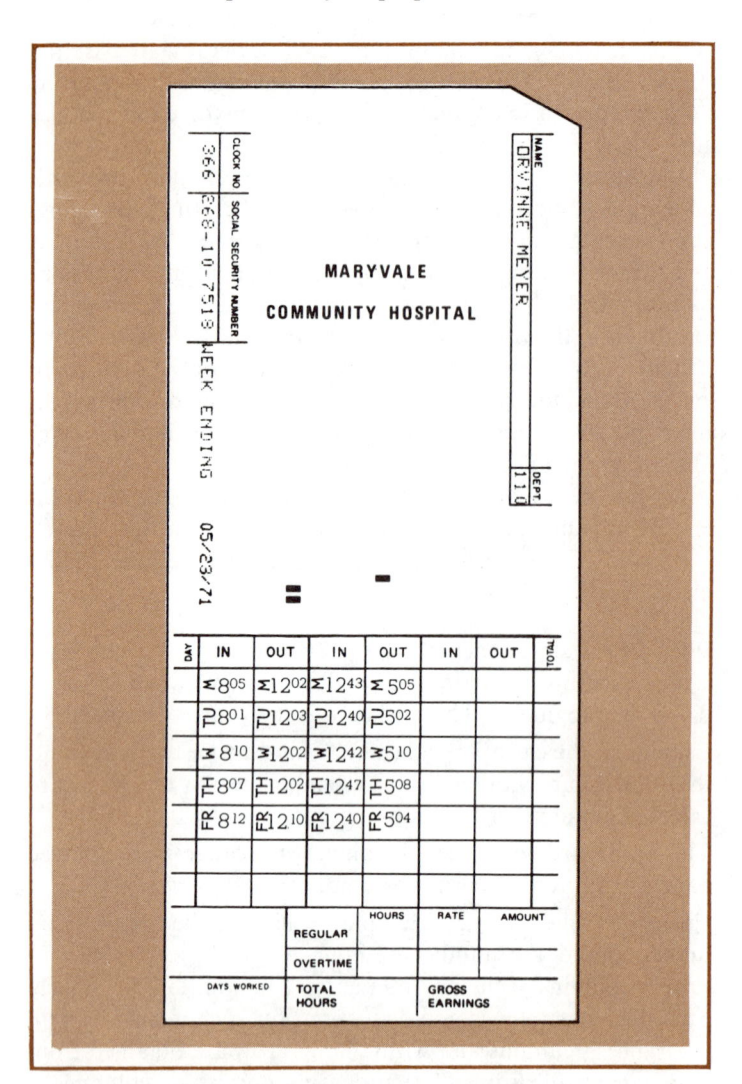

INSTRUCTIONS FOR PROCESSING DATA MANUALLY

Instructions are frequently written for the method to be used in processing data manually. These instructions are rarely written in the detailed, stylized form required when data are processed by the electronic computer method. The reason is that the writer of the directions assumes that the operator using a manual method will use intelligence in filling in the unwritten portions of a set of instructions. On the other hand, the electronic computer, with an I.Q. of zero, must be told in unerring detail what to do.

Chapter 3   Manual data processing   35

If directions were to be written for performing a job manually and they were as complete as those for handling the same job on an electronic computer, how would these directions look? The following detailed directions are those that might be written for keeping a club membership file up to date due to the addition of new members. On hand is a master file of 4- by 6-inch cards, arranged alphabetically according to the last name of the members. On hand also is a file of 4- by 6-inch cards of new members, also arranged alphabetically. Data for these cards were obtained from membership application forms. The new member cards are to be placed in the master file, and the entire file is to be arranged in alphabetic order. A typewritten report of the updated member file is to be prepared. The instructions would be as follows:

Step 1: Prepare a membership card for each new member from the approved application form.
Step 2: Arrange the new member cards in alphabetic order.
Step 3: Remove the first card from the new member file. Read the new member's name.
Step 4: Read the member's name on a card from the master file.
Step 5: Compare the two names. If the new member name is alphabetically ahead of the name in the master file, place the new member card in front of the master file card. If not, move to the next card in the master file and repeat, beginning with Step 4.
Step 6: Check to see if there are more new member cards to process. If there are, go back to Step 3 and repeat. When no new member cards remain to be processed, go to Step 7.
Step 7: Prepare a typewritten report of the updated member file.
Step 8: File the report.

Note the above routine for updating the file. Note, too, how the steps in this routine flow through the framework illustrated in Figure 3-1.

REVIEW QUESTIONS

1. Where are raw or original data obtained?
2. Define input; input media.
3. Define output; output media.
4. Why must instructions for electronic computers be detailed?
5. Are electronic computers involved in all data processing?
6. What are the components of a data processing framework?

SOME ASPECTS OF AUTOMATION APPLIED TO MANUAL DATA PROCESSING TASKS

Let us look at a number of data processing tasks in which some aspects of automation have long been employed. The processing methods used are chiefly manual, although they do contain certain automatic features.

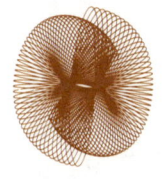

Carbon paper

The simplest and most widely used automatic device ever developed for processing data is carbon paper. When carbon paper is used, the original of a record is prepared manually and the copies are made automatically.

Window envelopes

When window envelopes are used, the address of the letter is usually typed manually. The address on the letter *automatically* appears in the window when the letter is folded and inserted into the envelope correctly. See Figure 3-3. No rewriting of the address on the envelope is necessary. A check for accuracy is not necessary, and the letter will always be placed in the correct envelope.

Snap-out carbon forms

When carbon copies of an invoice, for example, are made in sufficient quantity to serve as a shipping order, a packing slip, a customer's record of the order, an inventory record, and an accounts receivable record, we can say that many of the records needed in this transaction are made automatically. If the snap-out feature is used, no time is lost assembling and disassembling the forms and carbon paper. The forms are preassembled. They can be disassembled by snapping out (removing) the top or side portion of the forms to which are attached all the carbon sheets. Many documents are available in snap-out form.

Embossed metal plates

When names of customers or members of an organization are embossed on metal plates, this information can be recorded on a variety of documents without further rewriting. It can be said that the name and address information are recorded automatically. Therefore, embossed metal plates are essentially concerned with the recording process. See Figure 3-4.

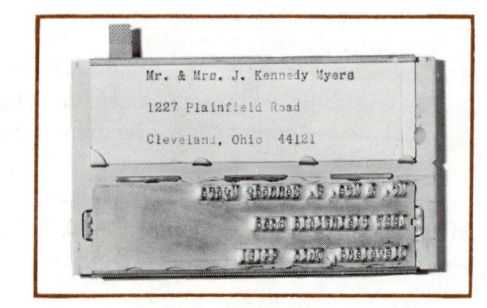

Figure 3-3. Window envelope

Figure 3-4. Embossed metal plate

Chapter 3   Manual data processing   37

The pegboard method

The *pegboard* method provides a means of recording identical information at the same time on forms of different size and design so that re-recording is not necessary. The pegboard is also referred to as a *writing board* or an *accounting board*. The forms used contain punched holes along the sides or the top edge. These forms are placed on pegs fastened to a board. The holes and pegs aid the operator in positioning the forms correctly, one over the other, so that information written on the original or top forms automatically appears in the correct space on the other copies. The correct spacing of data is accomplished by proper placement of the forms on the pegs. Recording of the data is done by hand with pen or pencil. A pegboard is illustrated in Figure 3-5.

Note that the pegboard method combines the advantages of a columnar register, in which the columns aid in assembling, sorting, and performing needed calculations with the special advantages provided by the pegboard in recording information on a variety of forms simultaneously. When a check is written by hand, the employee's number, his name, and the amount of the check are entered automatically on a line in the left-hand portion of the payroll journal and check register.

Figure 3-5. Pegboard

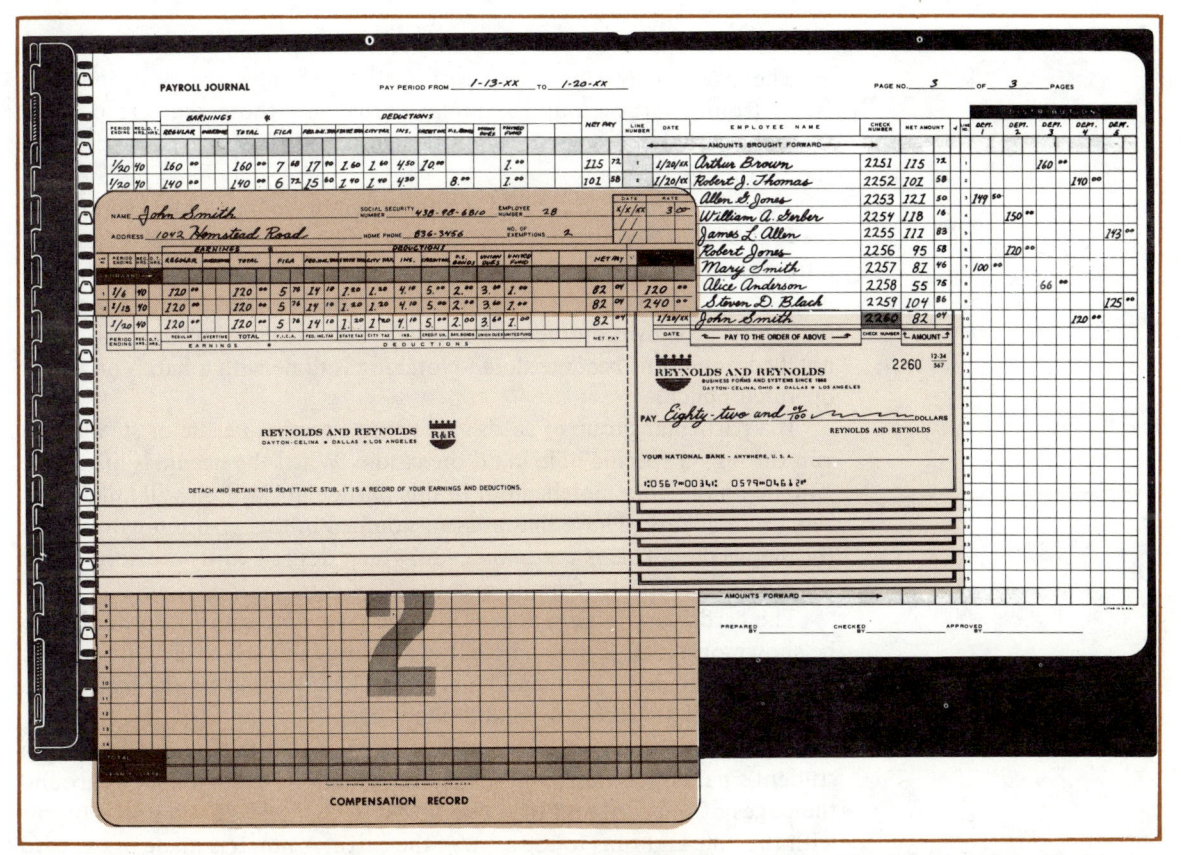

Courtesy of Post-Rite, a division of the Reynolds & Reynolds Company

A payroll journal and check register sheet is first placed on the pegboard. The employee's earning record is next dropped into place. Then the check with the attached employee's statement of earning and deductions is correctly positioned. The holes in the left edge of the employee's earning record and the pegs and scale on the pegboard aid the operator in aligning the forms so that entries are made on proper lines. Carbon paper is used between each form.

When the check, the employee's statement of earnings, and the deductions have been completed for a particular employee, these forms, plus the employee's earning record, are removed from the pegboard. Another set of forms is then placed in proper position. This procedure is followed until all paychecks are written, at which time the payroll journal and check register sheet are removed from the pegboard. Observe that the paychecks as well as the statements of earnings and deductions are prepared manually. The payroll journal, check register, and employee's earning record, however, are prepared automatically. The pegboard is used for many other similar office recording jobs.

Edge-notched cards

The *edge-notched* or *needle-sort* method enables the user to select (sort) from a large group of similar cards only those that are desired. Once the cards are prepared, very little manual effort is required to perform the sorting operation.

The *edge-notched cards* used in this system have holes punched around the four edges. Certain areas are blocked off on the cards to accommodate information *code fields*. The key to the information in each code field is usually printed on the card itself adjacent to the punched holes. The information to be shown on the card is notched in the edges of the card. The notched holes thus become slots. Notching is done with a hand- or a key-operated punch.

If a particular group of cards is desired, a sorting needle or steel rod is run through a specific hole in all the cards. When the needle is lifted, the cards with the holes notched out in this particular position will fall free or remain in a tray. Those that are not notched in this position will remain on the needle. This is the manner in which desired cards are sorted and selected automatically from a large stack of cards.

The cards vary in size, depending upon the amount of information to be shown on them. For example, the actual size of the card in Figure 3-6 is 8 by 10½ inches. Data can be typed or handwritten on the face of the cards to facilitate recognition and handling.

Figure 3-6 shows an edge-notched card that is used for recording a student's name, schedule, and related information. Note the holes around the edges of the card and the code fields on the card. Each notch begins with the hole and runs to the edge of the card. A notch is made in the card

Chapter 3   Manual data processing   39

to indicate the class in which the student is enrolled. In this illustration the student is a freshman; thus, the notch is made over the number "1" in the grade field which is the code indicating freshman.

A code number is assigned to represent the name, grade, district, and counselor. In Figure 3-6, the holes above the name, grade, district, and counselor field sections of the card have numeric values of 7, 4, 2, and 1. By using the holes in each group of four, singly or in combination, all the numbers from 0 to 9 may be designated. A two-digit number is indicated by notching the first digit in the (tens) section and the second digit in the (units) section.

The code representing the student's number is 1,249. This code is obtained by notching a 1 in the thousands section, a 2 in the hundreds section, a 4 in the tens section and a combination of 7 and 2 in the units section of the student name code field at the top of the card. A code representing the counselor for last year is number 21. This code is notched in the counselor field. Note that the number 1 is notched in the units section and the 2 is notched in the tens section.

Figure 3-6. Edge-notched card used as student enrollment card

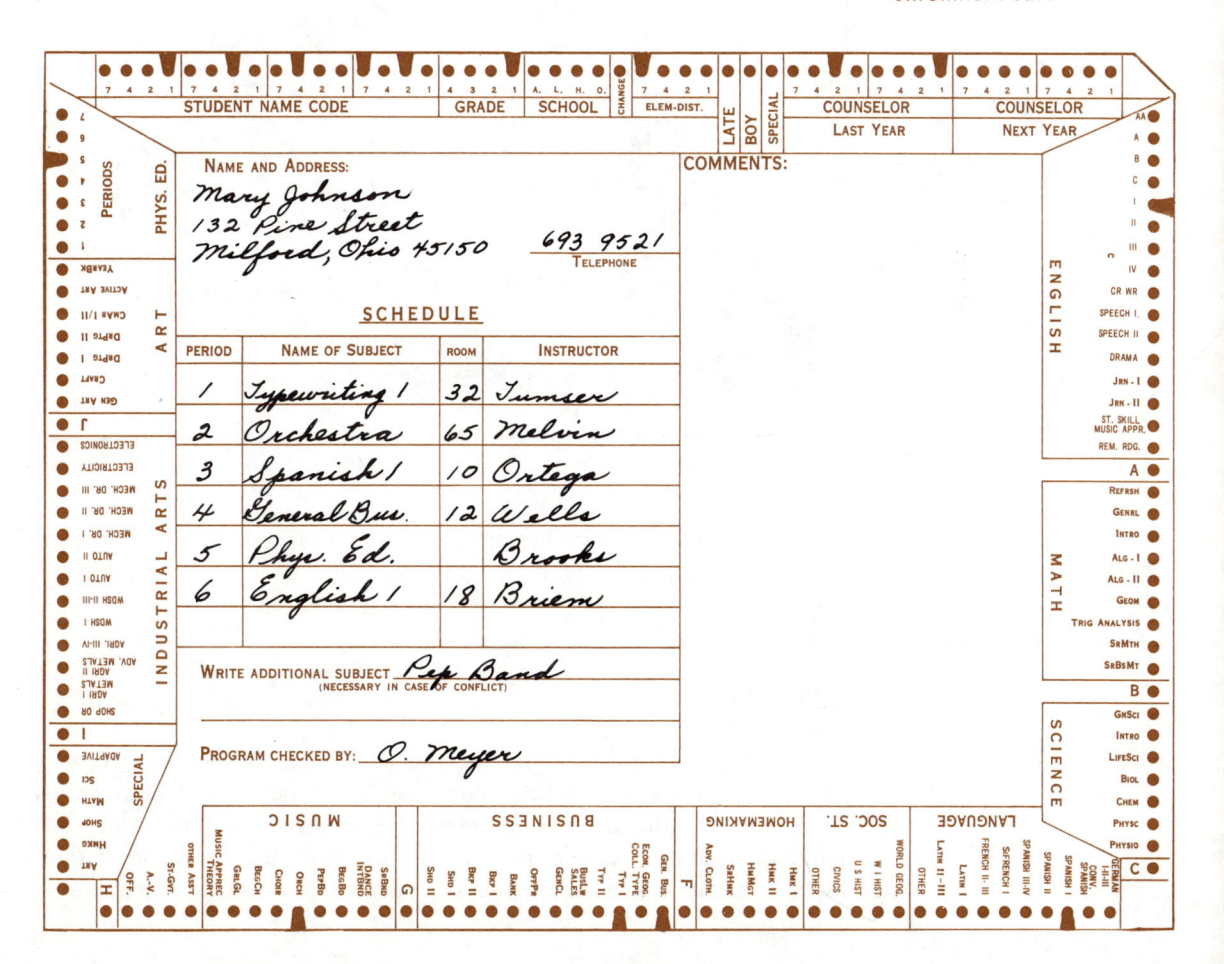

Assume that you desire to select from all students' cards the cards for freshmen who are enrolled in Typewriting I. First, the cards are aligned so that the edges are even. See Figure 3-7. Second, the needle is inserted in the hole above the Grade code 1, which represents freshmen. Third, the needle is lifted. The notched cards, which indicate freshmen, remain in the tray. The unnotched cards, which are for students in other grades, are lifted with the needle. Using only the cards for freshmen — those remaining in the tray — the operator inserts the needle in the proper Business code hole for Typing I. The notched cards representing Typing I will remain in the tray. All other cards, representing some other subject, will be lifted from the tray by the needle.

Figure 3-7. Sorting edge-notched cards by the needle-sort process

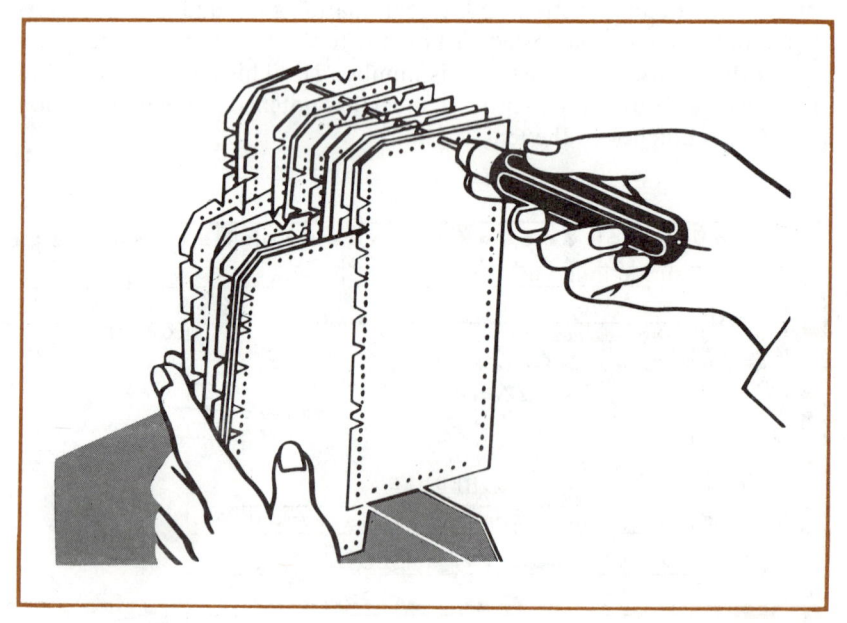

Courtesy of Litton Automated Business Systems

The edge-notched card has many other applications. It is used to sort checks, application forms, time cards, payroll records, and other similar data.

SUMMARY

Raw or original data appear on source documents and come from a wide variety of sources. Raw data enter the processing framework as input. They undergo processing and emerge in useful form as output. While the routines set up to handle tasks will vary, the framework within which data are processed remains the same: input⟶manipulation⟶output.

Chapter 3 Manual data processing

The manual method of data processing is one in which human effort directs and controls the various operations as well as the machines that may be used to assist the operator. In the manual method, data enter the framework as input and undergo recording, sorting, calculating, and other operations manually. Output emerges as useful information. The routines set up for handling a job may vary from task to task, but the framework within which data are processed is the same for all tasks.

In an effort to reduce the work of processing data manually, men have developed and used methods and devices that contain certain automatic features. Examples of these methods and devices are carbon paper, window envelopes, snap-out carbon forms, embossed metal plates, pegboards, and edge-notched cards.

REVIEW QUESTIONS

1. Name the data processing devices or methods discussed in this unit, in which some aspects of automation have been used in order to facilitate the handling of repetitive information.
2. What is the simplest and most widely used automatic device for recording data?
3. How is the pegboard helpful in the automatic preparation of a payroll summary sheet?
4. To what extent is the edge-notched-card or needle-sort process an automatic process?
5. What data processing operation does the edge-notched-card process facilitate?

STUDY GUIDE 3

Complete Study Guide 3 by following the instructions in your STUDY GUIDES booklet.

PROJECT

Complete Project 3-1 by following the instructions in your PROJECTS booklet.

CHAPTER 4

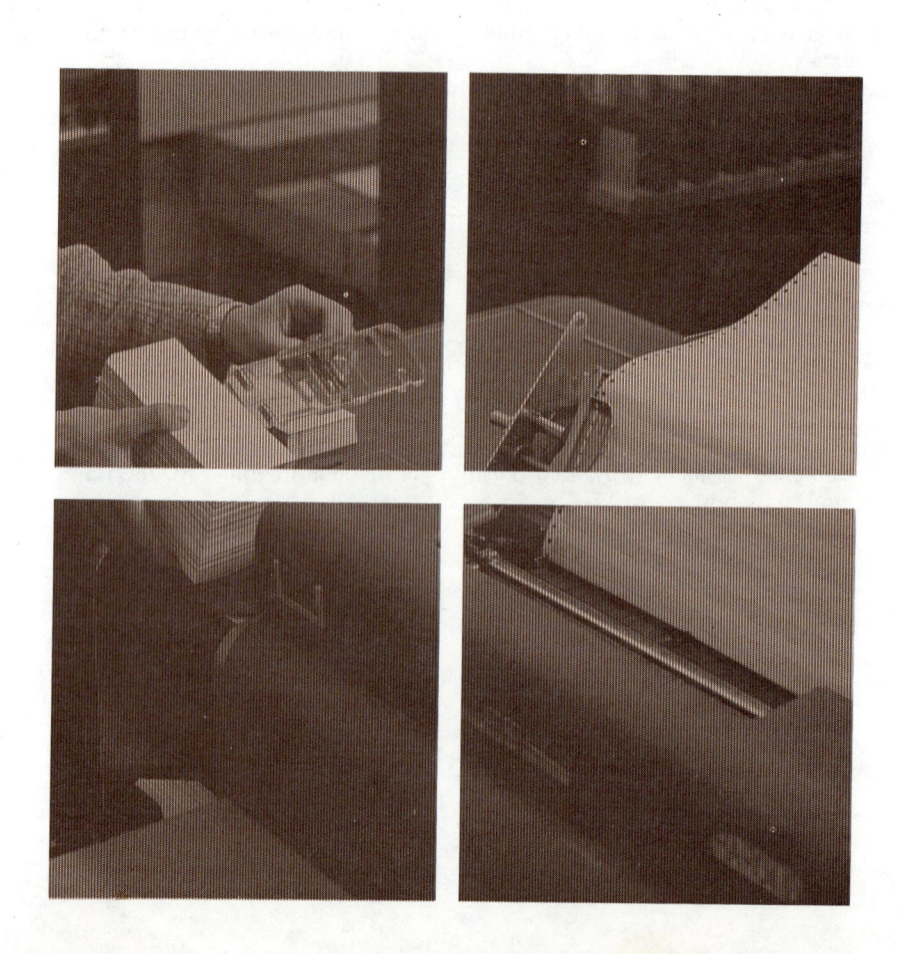

AUTOMATED DATA PROCESSING

What is automated data processing? *Automation* is a process in which work is done with a minimum of human effort and in which the process is largely self-regulating. *Automated data processing* may be defined, then, as a process, largely self-regulating, in which data are handled with a minimum of human effort and intervention. The process depends upon recording original information in such a way that further use can be made of it without subsequent manual rerecording.

Automation is a process, not a machine. Machines capable of handling data with very little human help are often used in the process. At the very heart of the process is an attempt to eliminate the drudgery that comes from the repetitive handling and rewriting of records countless times in order to make useful information available. The goal is to record the original data manually only once in such a way that the repeated use of figures and records will not require manual rerecording.

AUTOMATIC SYSTEMS OF DATA PROCESSING

From your readings thus far, you have probably discovered that there are two rather distinct "automatic" systems of processing data: (1) the unit-record, and (2) the electronic computer. Even though there are differences in the two systems, the general framework in which data are processed is essentially the same. Raw data are coded and enter the system as input. The data undergo sorting, recording, summarizing, calculating, and communicating activities and emerge as output in the form of finished products. Moreover, some of the machines and input and output media used in the unit-record system are also used in the electronic computer system. The card punch, verifier, sorter, and the punched cards are notable examples of this overlapping relationship.

UNIT-RECORD SYSTEM

The unit-record system may be defined as one in which data are recorded in code form in a punched card. The card is used in processing data throughout the system. All the unit-record machines can understand punched card language. Once recorded, the data may be sorted, computed, summarized, and rerecorded in a variety of ways to produce desired reports with a minimum of human help or intervention.

How the unit-record system works

In the discussion that follows, you will gain a general overview of the way the unit-record system works. In subsequent chapters, then, you will study details of the system in order to get a better understanding of it. The steps outlined below are those included in a routine to bring a club membership file up-to-date due to the addition of new members and to prepare a printed report of the updated file. The steps are illustrated in Figure 4-1.

Initially, the data are recorded in "human language" on source documents. *Human language* is a term used to refer to the language spoken and written by the persons processing the data, as contrasted to machine language, which is the only language intelligible to the machines processing the data. "Human language" in English-speaking countries, of course, would be English. The raw data on the source document may be either written or typed in human language. (Human language and machine language programming will be discussed in greater detail in Chapters 14 and 15.)

A source document, as you recall, is one from which basic or raw data are obtained. A source document containing information about new club members would be a membership application form. Generally, the form would contain the applicant's name, address, and telephone number. It might also include personal, school, and professional information about the applicant. Figure 4-2 illustrates such a form.

Some of the data on the source document are coded before they are punched into cards. That is, figures are assigned to some of the information. When the information is later punched into a card, the numbers will be used instead of full terms to represent the data.

Step 1: *The data are punched into cards*. Selected data from source documents are punched into cards. The punched holes are a code or a machine language that the machines in the system can comprehend. The

Chapter 4 Automated data processing   45

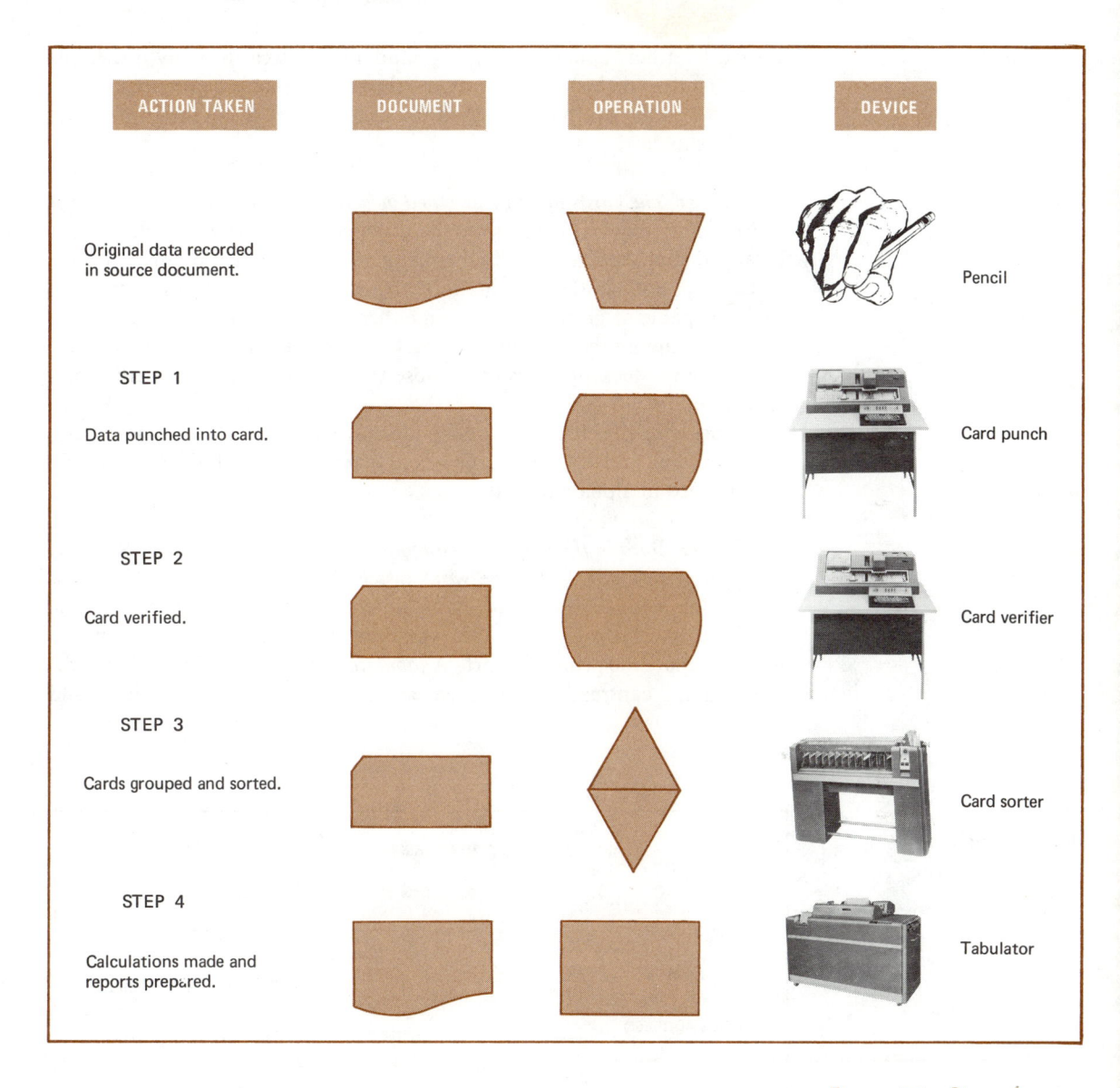

ACTION TAKEN	DOCUMENT	OPERATION	DEVICE
Original data recorded in source document.			Pencil
STEP 1 — Data punched into card.			Card punch
STEP 2 — Card verified.			Card verifier
STEP 3 — Cards grouped and sorted.			Card sorter
STEP 4 — Calculations made and reports prepared.			Tabulator

Figure 4-1. Steps for updating club membership with a unit-record system

machines can read and process electrically, through a sensing device, the information represented by the punched holes.

A key-operated card punch, usually shortened to *card punch* or *key punch*, is commonly used for punching the card holes. This is essentially a manual process, although, as we shall see later, some attempts have been made to make it automatic.

Step 2: *The punched cards must be verified*. The data punched into cards are proofread or verified. This is highly essential. The operator of the card verifier repunches the original data in the card. Only if the data are correctly punched in the cards can the reports that are prepared be correct. A *verifier* is a machine used for checking the accuracy of punched data in standard cards.

Step 3: The cards must be grouped or arranged in alphabetic or numeric order. The punched cards must be grouped and regrouped and usually arranged alphabetically or numerically to produce the reports desired. These steps are handled automatically by the sorter. A *sorter* is a machine that is capable of grouping cards on either an alphabetic or numeric basis and of arranging them in either alphabetic or numeric order. It can also select from a deck of cards only those that are needed to prepare a particular report.

In bringing the club membership file up-to-date, the cards of new members would be added to the cards of old members; and all the cards would be arranged in alphabetic order.

Step 4: Data in the cards are computed and printed. The type of report being prepared will determine what processing takes place at this point. In the club membership problem, a printed report of all members is to be prepared. Accordingly, the cards would be fed through a tabulator which would prepare the printed report. A *tabulator* is a machine that summarizes the data and can read the punched card codes, perform calculations, and

Figure 4-2. Application for membership

APPLICATION FOR MEMBERSHIP IN KENTWOOD CLUB

Date of Application_____

NAME IN FULL	Last Name	First Name	Initial	
RES. ADDRESS	Street	City	State	Zip
OFFICE ADDRESS	Street	City	State	Zip
TELEPHONE	Residence	Office	Extension	
OCCUPATION	Name of Firm	Type of Business	Position	
PERSONAL	Date of Birth	Place of Birth	Marital Status	
BANK REF.	Name of Bank	City	State	Zip
SPONSORS' NAMES (at least 3)			Action Taken	
			Date	

Chapter 4   Automated data processing 47

print the results. The following reports could be prepared if so desired by merely regrouping the cards and tabulating the desired information:

>   Report of members by age groups
>   Report of members by length of membership
>   Report of members by occupational groups
>   Report of marital status of members
>   Alphabetical list of members and their addresses

Moreover, if addition or subtraction operations were required, the tabulator could handle these tasks also.

Basic machines in the unit-record system

From the preceding discussion you may have discovered that the card punch, verifier, sorter, and tabulator are the basic pieces of equipment in the unit-record system. Additional machines are available, however, for high-volume work or specialized jobs. These machines will be described later. The punched card is the basic medium of communication. All machines in the system can interpret the punched holes in the cards.

Programming unit-record machines

Many of the machines in the unit-record system are programmed by detachable control panels. When these panels are wired correctly, they are attached to the machines. Figure 4-3 shows a control panel wired for a tabulator. Once attached, the control panels tell the machines what information to read from the punched cards and what to do with it. Each

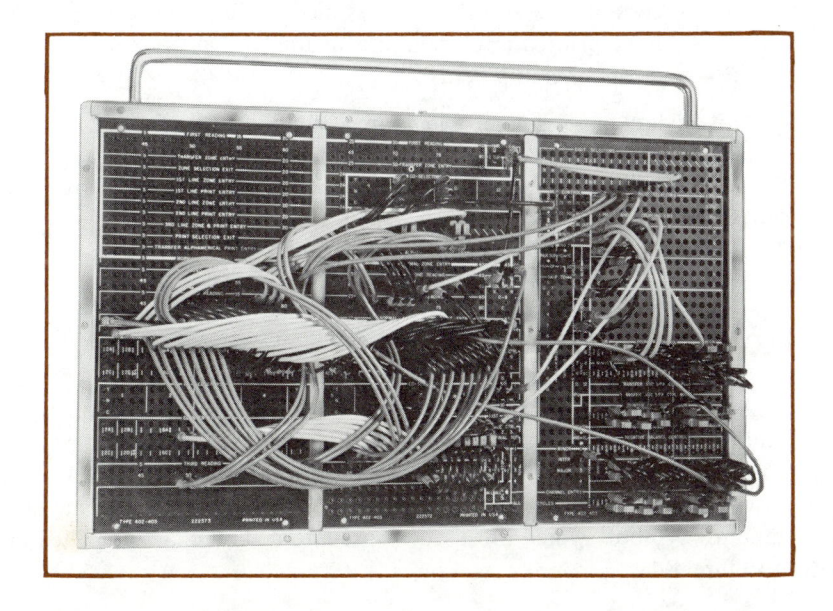

Figure 4-3. Control panel wired for a tabulator.

machine requires a different panel. The panel must be rewired when new types of reports are prepared. Control panels are discussed in more detail in a later chapter.

The only machines not programmed by control panels are the card punch, the verifier, and the sorter. The card punch and verifier are directed by the fingers and mind of the card punch operator. The sorter is programmed by a dial or crank.

SOLVING A PROBLEM BY THE UNIT-RECORD SYSTEM

Generally, the solution of a problem by the unit-record system requires the use of a number of machines. Each machine performs some part of the total job. The machines used and the job performed by each can be listed in a number of steps, just as the steps were listed when processing data manually. (See p. 35.)

Following is a routine for updating the master membership file:

Step 1: An application form is filled out by each applicant for membership.

Step 2: Punched cards are prepared from approved membership forms, using the card punch.

Step 3: The data punched in the cards are proofread, using a verifier.

Step 4: The new and old membership cards are arranged in alphabetic order, using a sorter.

Step 5: A report of the alphabetized names is printed, using a tabulator.

Step 6: One copy of the membership report is given to the membership committee. Another copy is filed. The punched cards, which have printed interpretations at the top, are retained and filed as membership cards.

Not all data processing problems are as simple as the one just described. Many of them encompass a number of machines, operations, and forms. For this reason, punched card data processing procedures are frequently shown in flow chart form.

FLOW CHARTS

A *flow chart* is a graphic representation of the sequence of operations required to carry out a data processing procedure, method, or system. Symbols are used to represent operations or equipment. A flow chart shows in sequential order the overall steps to be performed. Some of the standard symbols which are used to prepare a flow chart are illustrated in Figure 4-4.

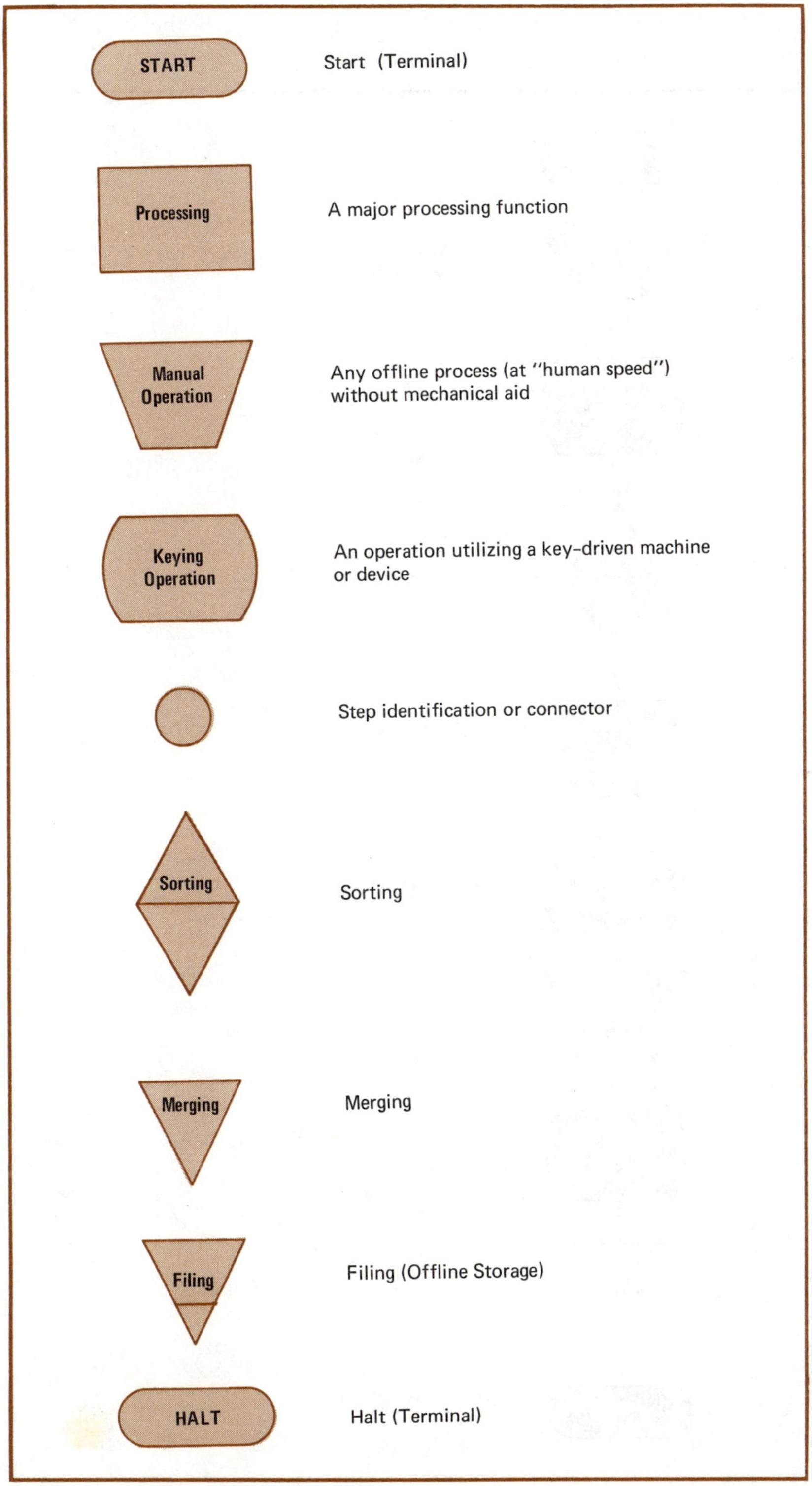

Chapter 4   Automated data processing

Figure 4-4. Flow charting symbols

START	Start (Terminal)
Processing	A major processing function
Manual Operation	Any offline process (at "human speed") without mechanical aid
Keying Operation	An operation utilizing a key-driven machine or device
○	Step identification or connector
Sorting	Sorting
Merging	Merging
Filing	Filing (Offline Storage)
HALT	Halt (Terminal)

The flow chart illustrated in Figure 4-5 illustrates the symbols and procedures for processing payroll data manually.

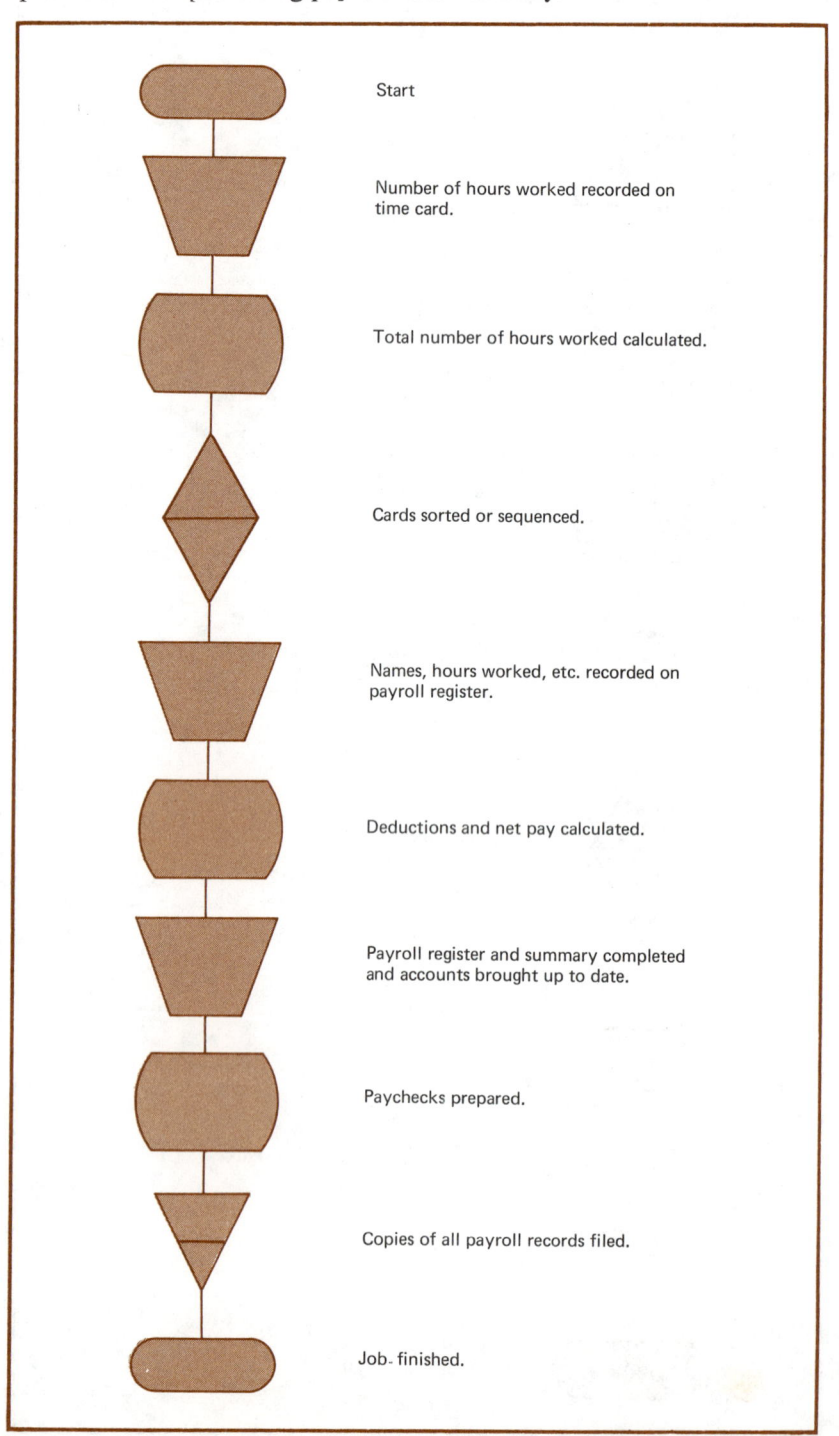

- Start
- Number of hours worked recorded on time card.
- Total number of hours worked calculated.
- Cards sorted or sequenced.
- Names, hours worked, etc. recorded on payroll register.
- Deductions and net pay calculated.
- Payroll register and summary completed and accounts brought up to date.
- Paychecks prepared.
- Copies of all payroll records filed.
- Job finished.

Figure 4-5. Flow chart for preparing a payroll manually

Chapter 4   Automated data processing

The flow chart illustrated in Figure 4-6 illustrates the symbols and procedures for updating a membership file using the unit-record system.

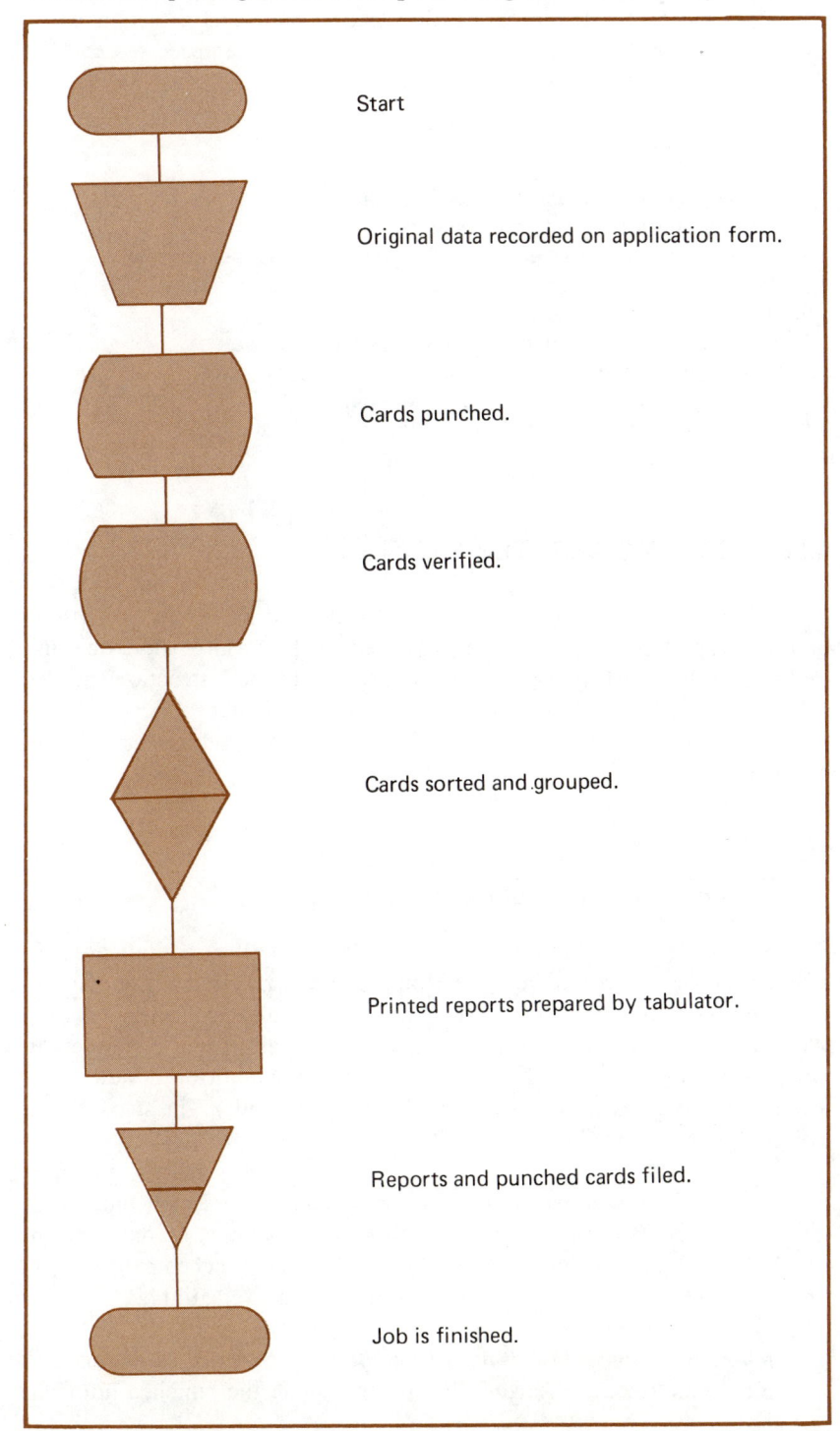

Start

Original data recorded on application form.

Cards punched.

Cards verified.

Cards sorted and grouped.

Printed reports prepared by tabulator.

Reports and punched cards filed.

Job is finished.

Figure 4-6. Flow chart for updating a club membership file using the unit-record system

A flow chart is like a roadmap. Through the use of the symbols and lines, the steps to be followed in the processing of a given set of data can be traced. To be able to prepare a flow chart, one must understand the symbols used in flow charting as well as the data to be processed and the action to be taken.

REVIEW QUESTIONS

1. Is "automation" a machine or a process?
2. What is automated data processing?
3. Name the two types of automated systems of processing data.
4. Define the unit-record system of processing data.
5. What is a source document?
6. Name the four basic machines in the unit-record system.
7. How is the tabulator programmed?
8. What is a flow chart? What is its function?
9. What is a verifier? What is its relation to the card punch?

ELECTRONIC COMPUTER SYSTEM

The *electronic computer system* may be defined as one in which both numeric and alphabetic data are processed in the form of electronic impulses. Both the information to be processed and the instructions needed to process it are stored in memory cells of the computer. Once recorded, the data may be manipulated in a variety of ways to produce desired solutions or reports with a minimum of human help or intervention. The system is largely self-regulating.

How the electronic computer system works

Even though there are fundamental differences in the way data are processed by the unit-record and electronic computer systems, the routines for handling a particular job are very much the same. Consider again the routine that would be followed, this time by an electronic computer, to bring a club membership file up to date, due to the addition of new members, and to prepare a printed report of the updated file. The steps in that routine are as follows:

Step 1: The data are recorded in input media. Selected data from source documents are punched into cards or paper tape, or recorded on other input media acceptable to the computer. The punched card is most widely used because of its economy, durability, and versatility.

Step 2: The punched cards must be verified. If punched cards are used as input media for the electronic computer system, the punched information should be verified for accuracy. This operation is commonly handled with the aid of a verifier.

Step 3: The cards must be grouped or sequenced. The punched cards are grouped and regrouped and arranged in alphabetic or numeric order as needed to produce the reports desired. Sorting and sequencing operations are generally handled by the sorter. Up to this point the steps in a routine to update membership cards and prepare an up-to-date printed list of members using the computer system are the same as those in the unit-record system. At this point, however, a change will be noted.

Step 4: A computer program is written. Detailed, step-by-step instructions are written for printing the updated file of members. These instructions may be written in one of several language systems developed for computers.

Step 5: The instructions are punched into cards or recorded on other media acceptable to the computer.

Step 6: The instructions are checked for accuracy. If punched cards are used, the verifier is generally used for this purpose.

Step 7: The step-by-step instructions are stored in the computer.

Step 8: The punched cards, containing the names and other important information concerning the members, are read by the computer. The names enter the computer as electronic signals. The electronic signals are sent to a printing device and converted into a printed report.

Step 9: The processed information is distributed and filed. One copy of the membership report is given to the membership committee. Another copy is filed. The punched cards, which have printed interpretations at the top, are retained and filed as membership cards.

Basic machines in the electronic computer system

From the foregoing discussion, you probably discovered that the card punch, verifier, and sorter are basic pieces of equipment in the electronic computer system, just as they are in the unit-record system. The punched card is common to both systems. The electronic computer system, however, is able to accept information from a number of additional media, such as punched paper tape, magnetic tape, and magnetic disks.

The central processing unit *is* the computer. The CPU can be equipped with a wide variety of input and output devices, which will be discussed in a later chapter.

PROGRAMMING THE COMPUTER

You already know that a computer processes data by programs that are written and stored in its memory. A number of languages have been developed for writing these programs. Anyone writing a program for solving a problem by a computer must write it in the language acceptable to that computer.

The program consists of a number of detailed steps which must be placed in correct order. Provision must be made in the program for returning to the first step and repeating the steps until all the cards containing data are processed. In the case of updating the membership file, the steps in the program would be repeated until all the cards containing the names of members had been "read" and the necessary information printed by the computer.

We shall assume that the computer can understand the English language. We shall also assume that the names of members are punched into cards on a card punch and that all cards are arranged in alphabetic order by a sorter. The following program would be written and stored in the computer to produce the updated membership file:

Step 1: Read a member's punched card.

Step 2: Move the member's name to print.

Step 3: Print the member's name.

Step 4: If the last card has not been read, go back to Step 1. If the last card has been read, continue to next step.

Step 5: Stop.

Note that the program requires the computer to repeat the Steps 1 through 4 until all the cards are processed, at which time the program tells the computer to go to Step 5, where it encounters an instruction to stop. Computers are capable of following directions of this type. As a matter of fact, the problem solved by these instructions is far simpler than most problems the computer is expected to solve. The computer can solve complex problems in which many decisions must be made either to follow one set of instructions or another.

SOME UNIQUE FEATURES OF THE ELECTRONIC COMPUTER SYSTEM

The computer can store both the data to be processed and the programs for processing the data. The programs are written in one of the languages acceptable to the computer. Each instruction in the program is punched into a card or recorded on other input media and stored in the memory of the computer. (Wired control panels are not used as they are in the unit-record system.) Computer instructions are followed in the order in which they have been stored, one following the other. However, the computer

Chapter 4   Automated data processing   55

is capable of changing from one set of instructions to another as certain conditions named in the program arise. When the last data card has been processed, for example, the computer changes to a new instruction which causes the machine to stop. This is a simple example of decision making on the part of the computer.

Computers are able to receive data from a number of input media, depending upon the computer attachments. The following are some of the examples of input media that may be used: punched cards, magnetic tape, punched paper tape, magnetic ink characters, magnetic disks, and console typewriters. Some computers can accept data from more than one medium. (The unit-record system is limited to input by punched cards.)

Data, such as the names of members, enter the computer and are immediately changed to electronic signals or pulses. In this form, data can be processed at very high speed. (In the unit-record system, data are generally processed by moving gears and cogwheels.) The data are processed and leave the computer as printed reports. However, at the same time, the processed data may be recorded in punched cards, on magnetic tape, or on some other output storage medium for which the computer has the proper attachments. Figure 4-7 illustrates a modern computer system.

Figure 4-7. An electronic computer system

Courtesy General Electric Corporation

COMMON ELEMENTS IN THE UNIT-RECORD AND COMPUTER SYSTEMS

You have discovered in your readings thus far that the two automated systems of processing data have a number of elements in common. Both systems are capable of "reading" data punched into cards. The recording of information in cards and the verification of this information is thus common to both systems. The sorting of cards before they are processed further is also common to both systems. These common operations will be explored in detail in Part 2, which follows.

SUMMARY

There are two distinct automatic systems of processing data: the unit-record system and the electronic computer system. The unit-record system is one in which data are recorded in code form in a card and then manipulated in a variety of ways to produce desired reports with a minimum of human help. In this system, data are processed by a number of machines, each of which is capable of one or two operations. The basic machines are the card punch, verifier, sorter, and tabulator. Additional machines are available for specialized jobs.

The card punch and the verifier are largely under the control of the operator, who manipulates a keyboard similar to that of a typewriter. Therefore, the skill most needed by a worker for preparing input in an automated office is the ability to operate a typewriter. Programming a sorter is handled by a dial or crank. All other machines in the system are programmed by detachable control panels, and each job requires an individual control panel for the machine. Because a number of machines are often used in a processing routine, flow charts are usually created to represent the flow of data through the different operations and machines.

The electronic computer system accepts data from various input media, including punched cards, and it manipulates the data to produce a variety of reports with a minimum of human help. The system is largely self-regulating. Data are processed as electronic signals or pulses, a feature that largely accounts for the computer's fantastic speed. The instructions for solving a problem are recorded on input media and stored in the memory of the computer. The computer executes instructions in sequence. It can change this sequence, however, as certain conditions arise in the data being processed.

The unit-record and electronic computer systems have some common elements. Both accept input data from punched cards. Both thus use the card punch machine, verifier, and sorter quite extensively. In both systems, all of the steps are not automatic. Automated data processing systems will never replace people. Data processed through both the unit-record and electronic computer systems always require human help.

Chapter 4   Automated data processing

REVIEW QUESTIONS

1. Define the electronic computer system of processing data.
2. What input media will electronic computer systems accept?
3. What three machines that are basic to the unit-record system are also basic to the electronic computer system?
4. What are some of the distinguishing features of the electronic computer system of processing data?
5. What elements do the two automated systems of processing data have in common?

STUDY GUIDE 4

Complete Study Guide 4 by following the instructions in your **STUDY GUIDES** booklet.

PROJECTS

Complete Projects 4-1 and 4-2 by following the instructions in your **PROJECTS** booklet.

PART 2

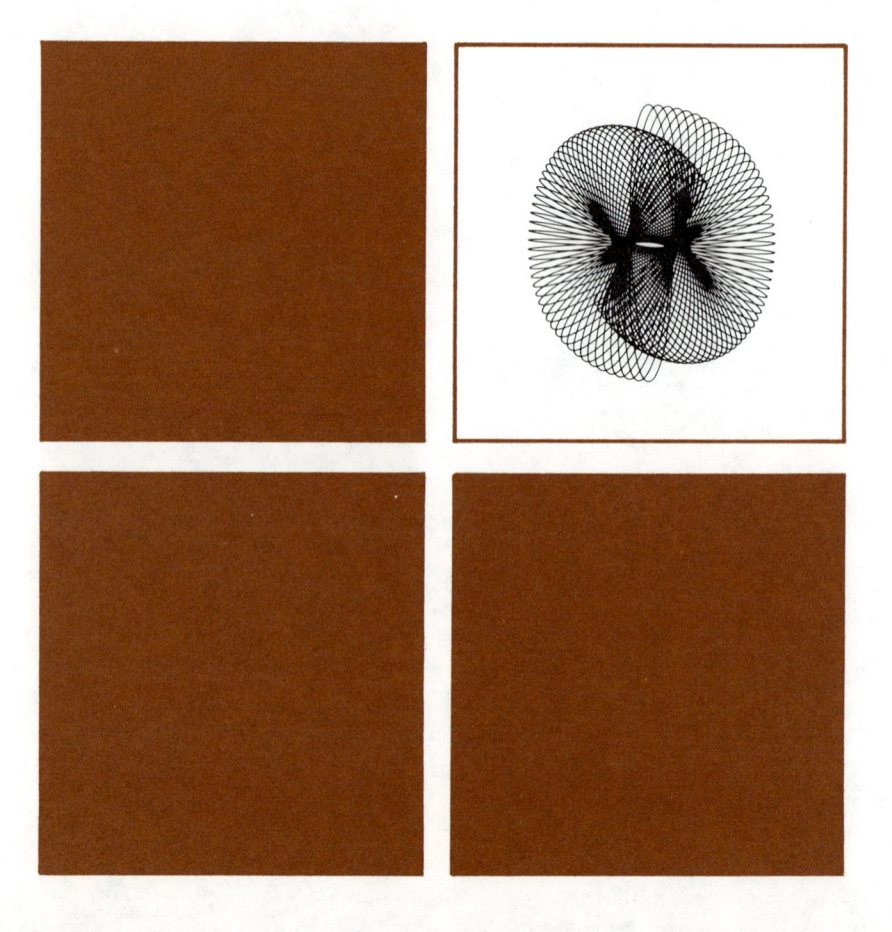

BASIC COMPONENTS OF AUTOMATED SYSTEMS

Chapter	5	THE PUNCHED CARD
Chapter	6	CARD PLANNING AND LAYOUT
Chapter	7	RECORDING INFORMATION IN CARDS
Chapter	8	SORTING AND CLASSIFYING DATA IN CARDS

CHAPTER 5

THE PUNCHED CARD

Generally, data originate in source documents, such as school enrollment forms, orders received for merchandise, membership application blanks, time tickets, and repair orders. The ideal data processing system would accept data directly from all these forms and supply needed reports automatically. For a number of reasons, this ideal system cannot be realized.

PROBLEMS ENCOUNTERED IN PROCESSING DATA

In the first place, source documents come in a wide variety of sizes and styles. Secondly, the methods used in communicating data vary greatly. Take, for example, the purchase orders received by a company for merchandise. Items may be ordered by letter, by postcard, by telegram, or over the telephone. Special order forms may be used by the purchaser. If forms are used, the needed information will almost certainly appear in different locations on each incoming form. If the orders are written, they may be handwritten or typewritten. They may be written in English or some other language.

The third obstacle encountered in processing source documents automatically is that several transactions may appear on the same form. This characteristic makes it impossible to group the forms by transaction type.

Some progress has been made in standardizing forms and written records, making automatic handling possible. Checks issued to the depositors of a bank are now of standard size. Information appears in uniform locations on all check forms supplied by a particular bank. Data essential to keeping a depositor's account in order appear in printed, block-type figures that can be "read" by machines. Each check represents an individual transaction. Sorting the checks by bank and the depositor's number and deducting the amounts of the checks from the depositor's account can thus be performed automatically.

NEED FOR STANDARDIZATION

Standardization is an important requirement for processing data automatically. The input medium must be of uniform size and shape.

Each transaction should be identified fully and recorded on a separate form. This requirement permits the forms to be grouped and tabulated according to the different categories of information included in the transaction. A separate card, for example, must be prepared for each subject for which a student enrolls. Each card must contain the name or number of the student, the name or number of the subject, the name of the teacher of the subject, the class period in which the subject is taught, and the date of enrollment. The cards may then be grouped according to subject number, class period, or teacher. The names of students may be listed according to the way in which the cards are grouped. By regrouping the cards after each tabulation, entirely different types of reports could be prepared, such as the following:

1. List of all students in a school
2. List of all students taught by a particular teacher
3. List of students enrolled before, on, or after a specific day
4. List of students studying a particular subject
5. List of students studying a particular subject during a specific period
6. List of subjects available at certain periods during the school day
7. List of all subjects available
8. List of all teachers
9. List of all teachers with subjects taught by each

All data must be recorded in uniform language and the language used must be "understood" by the various machines in a data processing system. Finally, the different pieces of information about transactions of a particular type must appear in uniform locations on the form. For example, if student numbers occupy the first four digit spaces at the left of an enrollment card, the student numbers must appear in the same location on all enrollment cards for the school. No machine is capable of identifying information on a form except in terms of the location of the information on the form.

Chapter 5   The punched card

STANDARD CARD

Formerly, an 80-column card was used with IBM systems; a 90-column card was used with UNIVAC systems. Both systems now use a standard 80-column card. The cards for both systems are identical in makeup and appearance. The 80-column card is thus the only one that will be described in the discussion that follows. The 90-column card will gradually become obsolete in the near future as the 90-column-card equipment is replaced by 80-column machines.

Size and shape of card

The 80-column card, which is oblong, measures 7⅜ inches by 3¼ inches. All cards are of uniform thickness. Strict adherence to standardized requirements must be observed if data appearing in the cards are to be processed accurately and quickly.

Recording columns

Examine the card in Figure 5-1. Note that it is divided into 80 vertical columns, commonly referred to as *card columns*. A scale at the bottom of the card and another near the top designate each of the 80 columns. A

Figure 5-1. Standard card

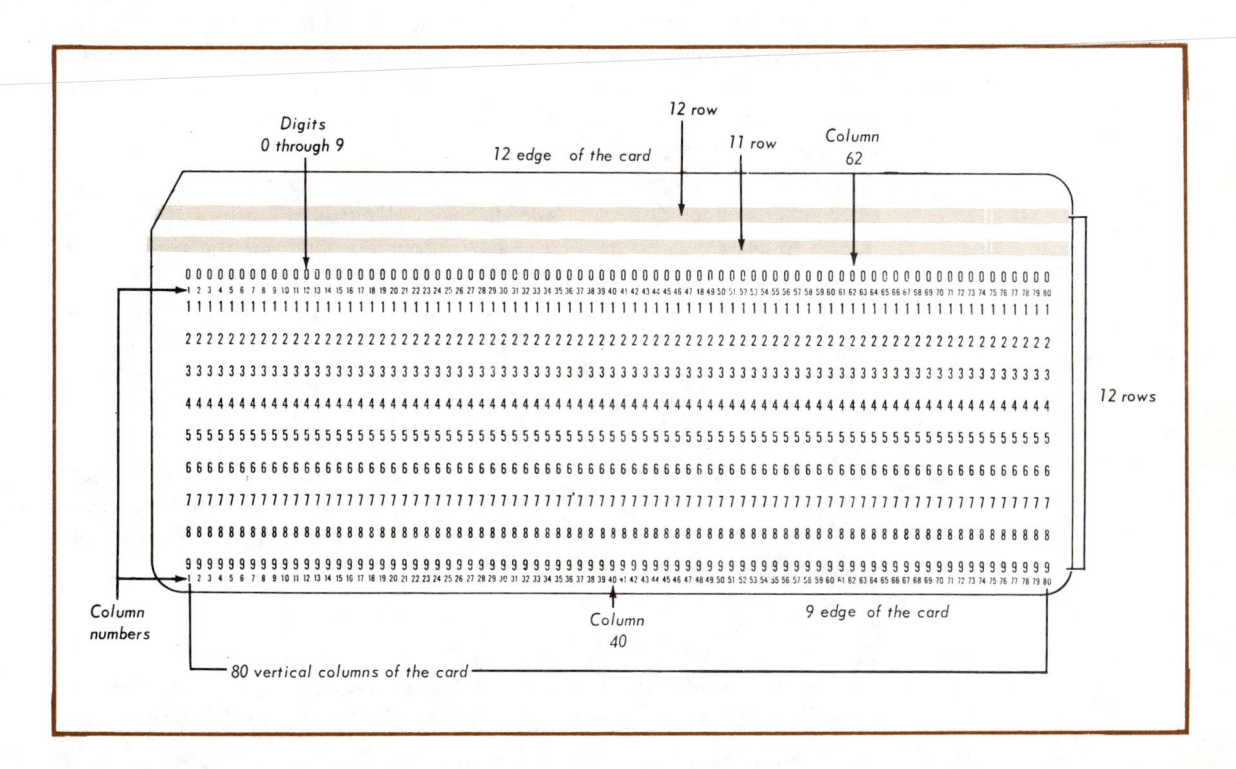

single figure, letter, or symbol may be recorded in each one of the 80 columns.

Observe that the digits 0 through 9 appear in each column and that the 12 and 11 positions, which appear at the top of the card, are not actually designated with numbers. Each vertical column is divided into 12 punching positions. Each horizontal line of punching positions across the card is referred to as a *row*. Each single digit, 0 through 9, may be punched into any one of the 80 columns. When a digit punch, 1 through 9, in any one of the columns is combined with a 12, 11, or Zero punch in the same column, a letter of the alphabet is recorded. The alphabetic code will be described later.

The top edge of the card is referred to as the *12 edge*; the bottom, as the *9 edge*. These designations are made to facilitate the feeding of cards into machines, as either edge may be fed first.

The 12 location on a card is also referred to as the *Y position*; the 11 location, as the *X position*. Punches in either of these two locations are referred to as *zone* punches. Punches in the 1 through 9 locations are referred to as *digit* punches. The Zero position may be either a zone punch or a digit punch. It is a zone punch when it is used in conjunction with another punch in the same column to represent a letter or special character. It is a digit punch when it stands alone in a column to represent zero.

Each column of the card will accommodate a punched hole, or holes, to represent a number, a letter, or a special character. Thus, the card can contain 80 and *only* 80 individual pieces of information. All 80-column cards are of the same size. Because of the limited number of columns on the card, information must often be condensed so that it will fit into the number of spaces available. One can use abbreviations or special numeric codes, in which figures and combinations of figures are used to represent alphabetic information.

Note that the upper left corner in the card in Figure 5-1 has been cut off. This has been done to make sure that all cards in a group are stacked in the same way. Either of the two upper corners and the right lower corner may be cut. Corner cuts may also be used for identification. Master cards may, for example, have the right upper corner cut, while detail cards have the left upper corner cut. Master and detail cards will be explained more fully later. Cards are available with either square or round corners. Cards with round corners do not bend or fray as easily as those with square corners.

Cards are available in a number of solid colors or with special stripes as an aid in identifying the different operations for which cards are used. Student enrollment cards may be one color, for example, and cards on which grades are reported may be another.

Numeric code

The card illustrated in Figure 5-2 is designed to show the digits 0 through 9 printed in each vertical column. The figure also shows the digits

Chapter 5   The punched card   65

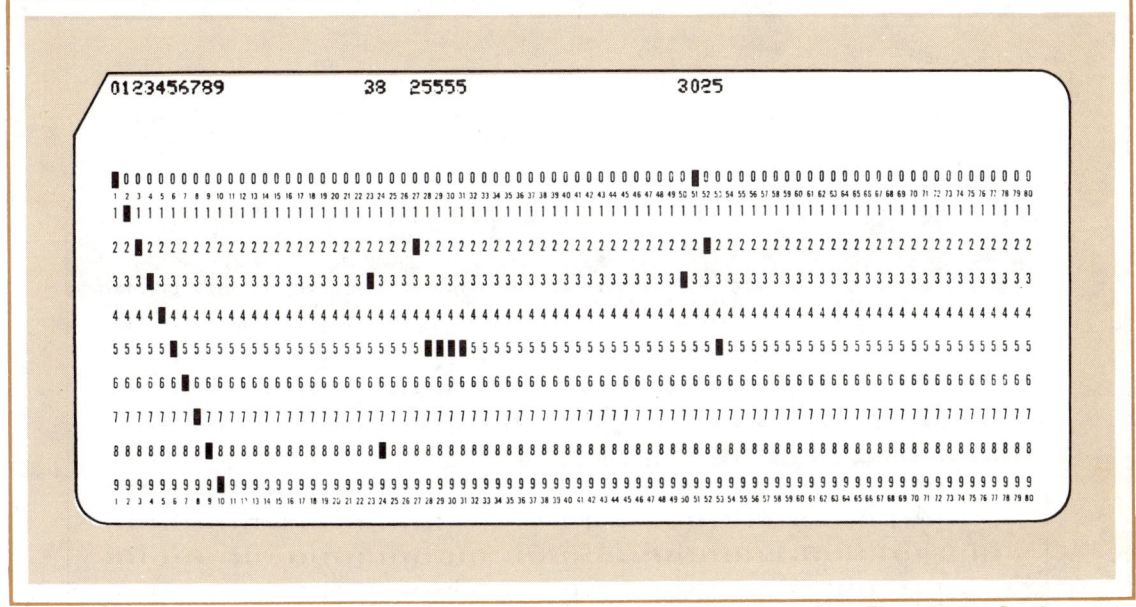

Figure 5-2. Card containing digit punches

0 through 9 punched in Columns 1 through 10. The interpretation of each punched hole is printed at the top of the card. A single digit can be punched in any one of the 80 columns on the card. For example, the Digit 2 in Column 27 could have been punched in any one of the 80 columns. It will be recognized as the Digit 2 by the machines designed to process information punched into cards.

When a two-digit number is to be recorded, two columns of the card must be used. A multidigit number must take up as many columns as there are digits in that number. For example, Number 38 appears in Columns 23 and 24 of Figure 5-2. One could not punch both of these digits in the same column; the processing machines would not interpret the information correctly.

Refer to Figure 5-2 again. What number is punched in Columns 27–31? In what columns is 3025 recorded?

Meanings assigned to figures

What do the figures in the various columns represent? They represent what one wants them to represent. There is no way of knowing what Number 3025 in Figure 5-2 means. It could mean the number of cars bought, sold, or on hand; it could mean $3,025 or $30.25. It could be the code name of a city or salesman. The number means nothing until one knows what it is intended to mean. What information is to be recorded in cards must be decided and meanings must be assigned to this information.

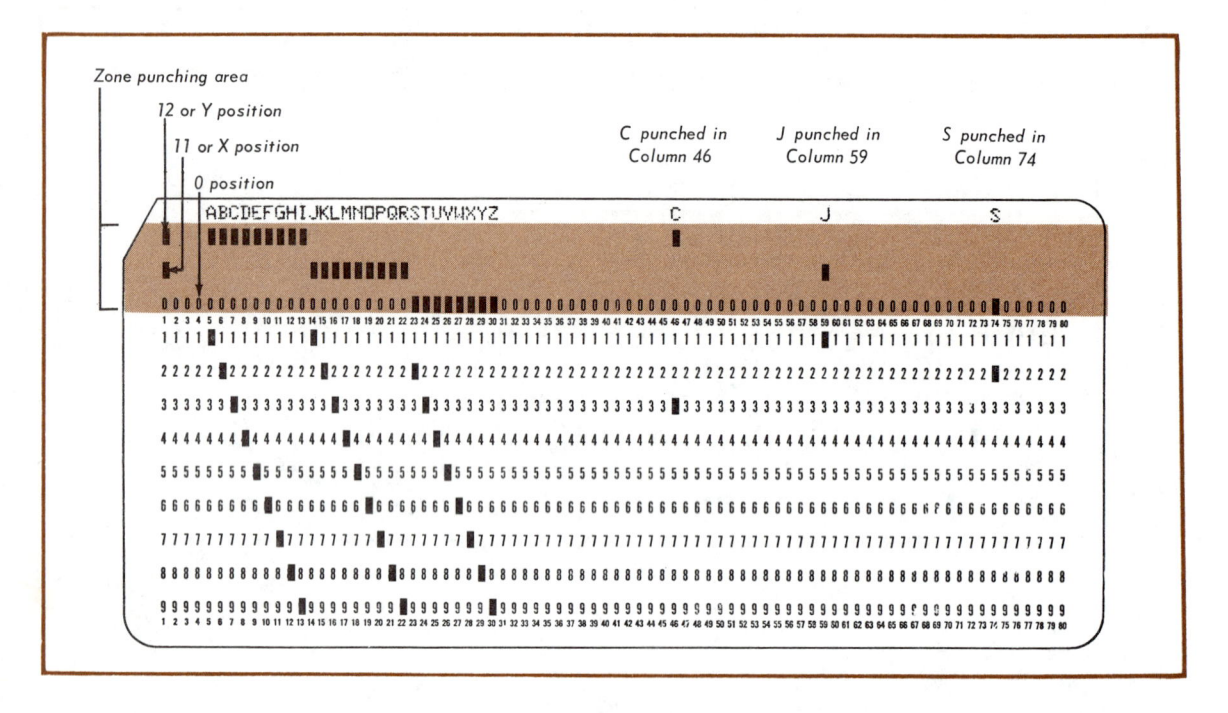

Figure 5-3. Card containing letters of the alphabet

Alphabetic code

Just as holes punched in a card represent various digits and numbers, punched holes may also represent the letters of the alphabet. Each letter of the alphabet is represented by two punches in any one column. One of the punches appears in the zone punching area of the card — the 12, 11, and 0 positions. The other punch appears in the digit punching area.

Figure 5-3 shows how all the letters of the alphabet are represented by punched holes in a card. The interpretation of the punches is shown at the top (12 edge) of the card. Any letter of the alphabet may be punched into any one of the 80 columns. However, only one letter may be represented in a column. The Letter A, for example, is represented by punches in the 12 and 1 rows; the letter Z, by punches in the 0 and 9 rows.

Observe that each of the first nine letters of the alphabet, A through I, is represented by a combination of a 12 punch and one of the digit punches 1 through 9. Each of the next nine letters, J through R, is represented by a combination of a punch in the 11 position and one of the digit punches 1 through 9. Each of the last eight letters, S through Z, is represented by a zero punch and one of the digit punches 2 through 9.

Code for special characters

In addition to the codes that have been devised to represent numbers and letters of the alphabet, codes have been developed to represent a few special characters such as (&#,$.-/@%*"?=!). The special characters are represented by one, two, and sometimes three punches in any one column

Chapter 5 The punched card   67

of the card. Figure 5-4 shows the punches that represent the different special characters.

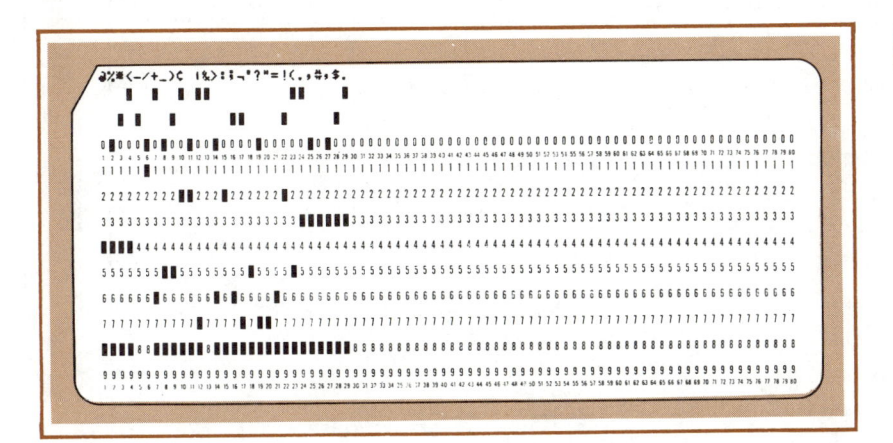

Figure 5-4. Card containing special characters

The card in Figure 5-5 contains the complete language of automation understood by the machines designed to process punched cards.

Figure 5-5. Card containing complete language of automation.

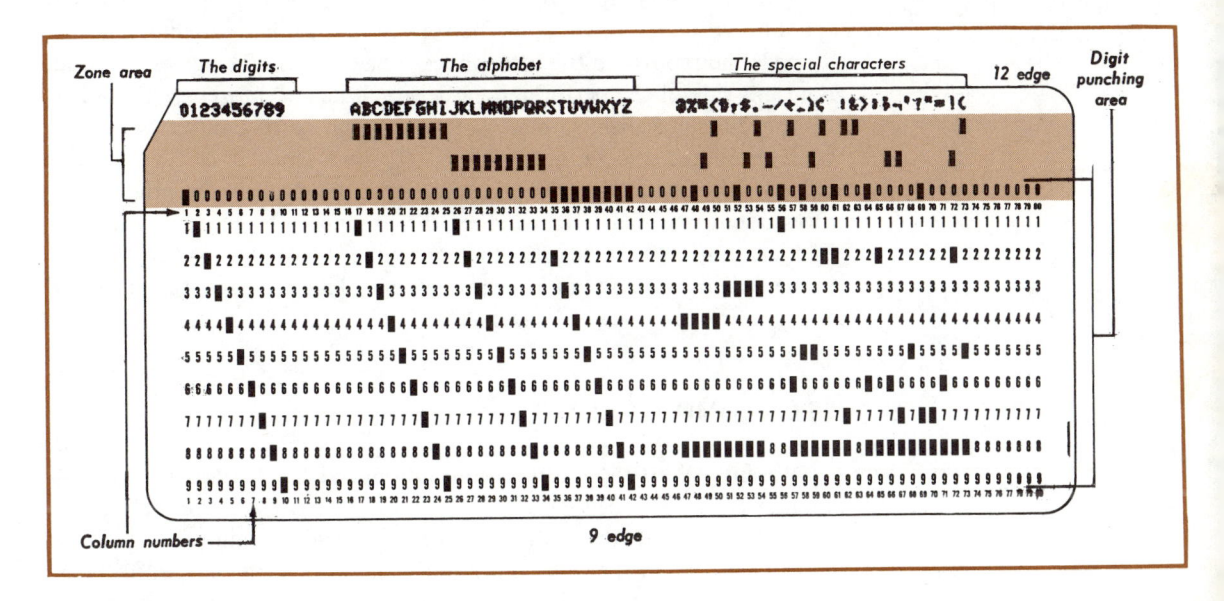

SHORT CARDS

Cards of varying sizes are available for specialized operations. Moreover, standard cards are available with perforations that make it possible to remove part of the card. The machines can be adapted to process the shorter card.

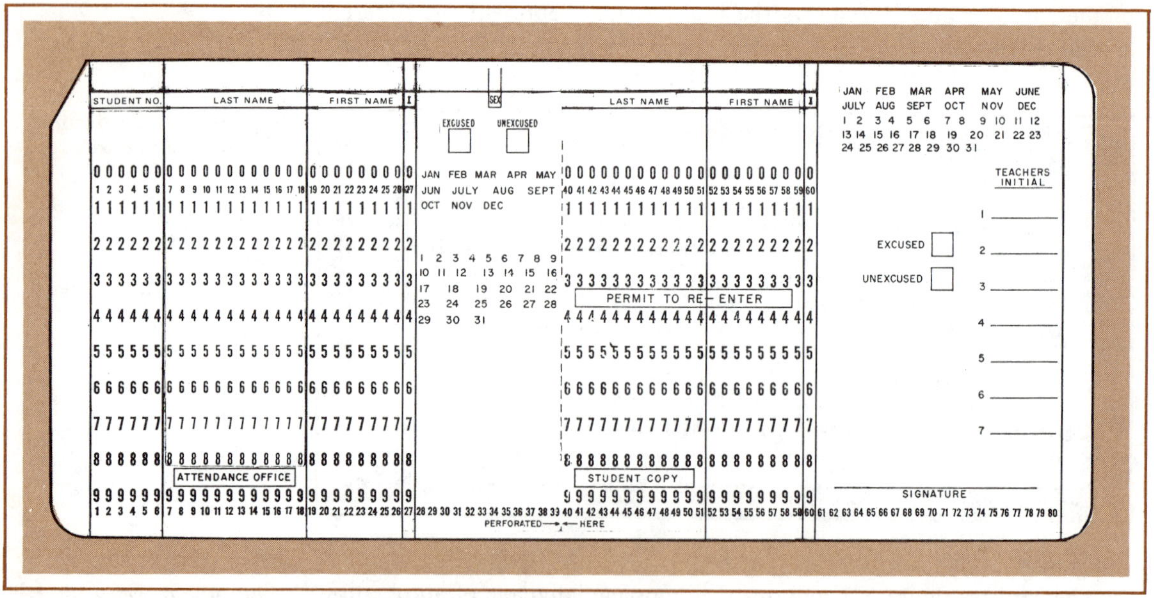

Figure 5-6. Student attendance card

The card illustrated in Figure 5-6 is one that is used in maintaining school attendance records. When a student returns to school after an absence, he reports to the attendance office. This office gives the student the right side of the perforated card, which has been prepared in advance by the data processing office. (The data processing office punches the student's name and number in the card and sends it to the attendance office.) The attendance office indicates on the card the months and days the student is absent and whether the absence is excused or unexcused. The left portion of the card, which contains 39 columns, is then sent back to the data processing office for processing. The student uses the right side as a reentry pass into his classes.

96-COLUMN CARD

Recently the IBM Corporation announced the development of a 96-column card. The new card is used with the System/3 computer, which has been designed for small businesses. The 96-column card uses round holes to represent the data. It can handle 20 percent more information, although it is one-third the size of the standard 80-column card.

SUMMARY

The punched card meets the requirements for processing data automatically. Punched cards are of uniform size. Each transaction is recorded on a separate card, permitting grouping and regrouping in order to

Chapter 5   The punched card

produce a variety of reports. Numeric and alphabetic codes consist of punched holes in the cards. These holes are interpreted by various processing machines. All data of a particular type must be predetermined as to location and number of card columns required. Once data are recorded in cards, therefore, all subsequent operations are largely automatic.

REVIEW QUESTIONS
1. What are the three obstacles encountered in processing source documents?
2. Why is standardization necessary in processing data by punched cards?
3. How many columns are there in a standard punched card? How many rows are there in a standard punched card?
4. How is the top edge of the card identified? The bottom edge?
5. Can a multiple-digit number (such as 123) be punched in a single column of a card? Explain.
6. How many card columns would be needed to record the number 1890?
7. How many card columns would be needed to record 1890A?
8. Why is it necessary to represent alphabetic characters with two punched holes in a card column?
9. What letter is represented by punches in the 11 and the 2 rows in the same column?
10. How many characters can be punched into a single card?

STUDY GUIDE 5

Complete Study Guide 5 by following the instructions in your STUDY GUIDES booklet.

PROJECTS

Complete Projects 5-1 and 5-2 by following the instructions in your PROJECTS booklet.

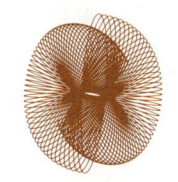

CHAPTER 6

CARD PLANNING AND LAYOUT

What kinds of data are punched into a card? The card may represent any data that can be expressed in figures, letters, or special characters. The possibilities are thus quite wide. The answer to the question lies in the kinds of data being processed and the necessity for various types of reports based on these data.

Examine Figure 6-1. It is a card that is punched with information about an individual customer. The card may be used to prepare monthly statements or sales reports. It may be used to record charges to a customer's account or for a number of other purposes. The firm using the card determines what information is required and the order in which the information will be punched into the card. Note that certain areas on the card are separated by vertical lines. Each area so designated is known as a field.

CARD FIELDS

The vertical column or group of consecutive columns set aside in a card to record a single fact is known as a *field*. The division of a card vertically into fields is an important characteristic. A card may contain many fields depending upon the particular types of information recorded. A field may vary in length from one column to many columns. The fields included on a card and the vertical columns assigned to each are determined in advance during the planning phase of data processing.

In Figure 6-1, the customer number is recorded in Columns 1–5, which constitute a card field. The customer number must appear in the same field

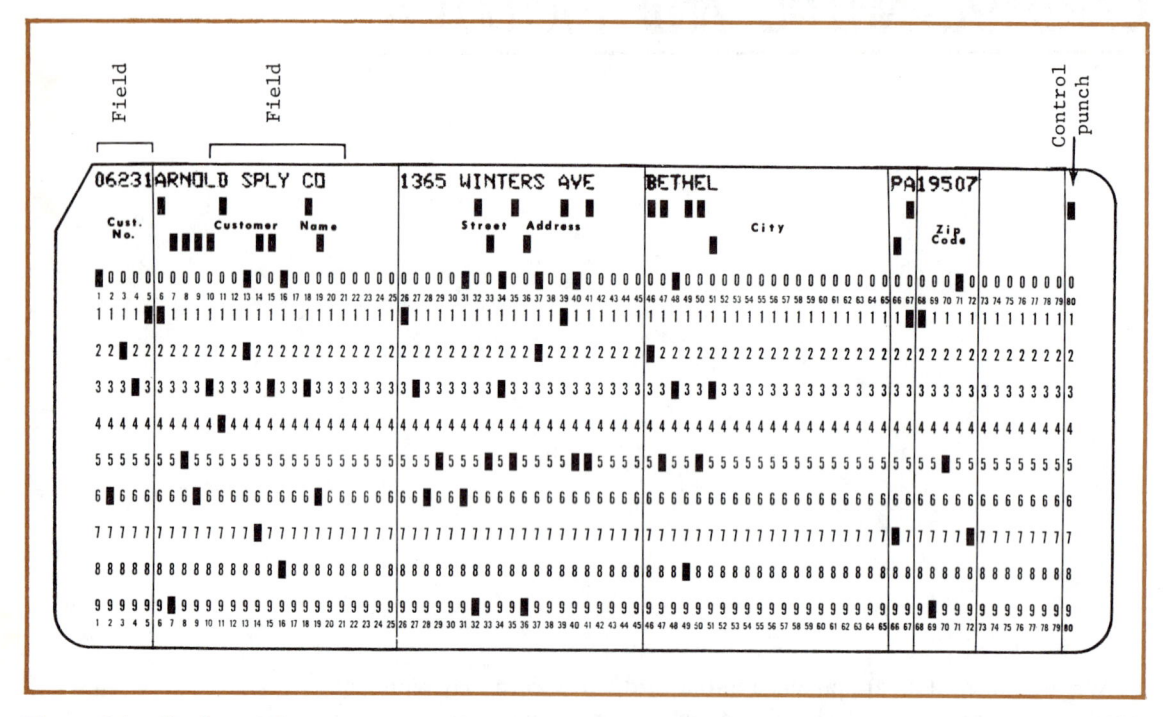

Figure 6-1. Card containing customer information

in all other cards prepared for processing similar information for a particular customer. The processing machines are completely dependent upon the uniform placement of information in cards relating to a particular type of transaction.

SIZE OF CARD FIELDS

Since the number of columns in which data may be recorded is limited to 80, care must be exercised in laying out card fields. No card column should be wasted by poor planning. One must be sure, however, to allow enough columns in a field to accommodate the largest name or number of digits anticipated for that field.

The planning of some fields will be relatively easy. When the date is expressed in figures, as it usually is in punched cards, six columns are needed; more will never be needed. *November 28, 1971* will be represented by *112871;* *April 15, 1971* will be represented by *041571;* and *June 3, 1971* will be represented by *060371.* Note that in each case, a six-column field is used. Note, too, that in each case, the code representing the month comes first, then the day of the month, and then the year. This practice also must be uniform. The machines used in processing data do not think. They work remarkably well when data are accurately and uniformly recorded.

Chapter 6   Card planning and layout

The planning of fields for invoice numbers and for numeric codes that represent names of states, names of salesmen, and names of customers should be equally easy. In planning card fields for recording quantities of an item of stock ordered or on hand, the amount of the sale, or the unit price, you may find that the job of estimating the number of necessary columns is not so easy. One must look at present practice and future prospects for an accurate answer. Careful planning of card fields is a demanding business. Once the fields are set, they must be adhered to until such time as the cards for a particular operation are revised.

PLANNING CARDS FOR RECORDING NUMERIC INFORMATION

Whenever possible, a number is used as a code to represent a classification normally identified by an alphabetic title. Such a code saves space, is easier to record, and takes less time to process. Account titles, for example, are frequently identified by number; so are names of states, names of students, names of courses, names of school departments, and names of customers.

Numeric fields must be right-justified. (The last digit in the field must be punched in the rightmost column in the field.) If fewer than the maximum number of columns planned for a numeric field are used, zeros must be added at the left to fill all the columns in the field. This is an important point to keep in mind because the machines are designed to process information in this manner. The zeros are punched into the card by the card punch operator. Some of the newer card punch machines will automatically punch the extra zeros needed in a field when the operator depresses a special key.* Note the zero recorded on the left in the unused column of the customer number field in the card in Figure 6-1.

The arrangement of fields on a card is of little consequence to the processing machines. They can read data placed anywhere on a card. If possible, however, the fields should appear in the same order as the information appears on the source document. This arrangement speeds up the card punching process because the operator is able to read and record the information in sequence.

Blank columns are not needed to separate the information recorded in one field from that recorded in an adjacent field. In the unit-record system, the spacing of data on a printed report is handled by the way in which the control panel is wired for the tabulator or one of the other unit-record machines, a topic that is discussed later in this book. In the electronic computer system the spacing is handled by the manner in which the computer program is written.

---

*Some new card punch machines have devices for suppressing the "leading zeros" so that they do not print at the top of the card, but the zeros are always punched into the card.

PLANNING CARDS FOR RECORDING ALPHABETIC INFORMATION

Fields for both types of information — numeric and alphabetic — may be planned in a single card. The alphabetic fields must be as carefully designed as are the numeric. All useful information should be recorded in the most economical way, using the least possible number of columns.

Zeros are not used in alphabetic fields to fill the unused columns because zeros are not alphabetic characters. Spaces or blank columns are used instead. Since alphabetic lists, addresses, and similar information are usually aligned on the left in printed reports, the alphabetic information in a card is normally aligned on the left also (left-justified). When the recorded alphabetic information requires fewer than the number of columns allowed for it in a field, the blank columns appear to the right of the alphabetic information. Note the customer name field in Figure 6-1.

Abbreviations are used to conserve space whenever possible and standard abbreviations need not be used. Except in those documents in which legal names are essential, such as payrolls, tax forms, and student enrollments, initials are commonly used for given names. When space is limited, the first and second initials may be run together.

Periods may be omitted after abbreviations. Commas are not used between the last and the given names or between cities and states.

UNIT-RECORD PRINCIPLE

A *unit record* is one in which all data concerning each item in a transaction is punched into one card. A punched card is a unit record; it represents only one transaction. However, each card contains all the information needed about the transaction.

Observe Figure 6-2. It is an invoice indicating that three individual items have been sold. Each item is a transaction; each requires a separate card. Each card contains the same type of information shown on the first one. See Figure 6-3.

By depressing a special duplicate key on the card punch machine, the operator can reproduce automatically the information appearing in one card that he wishes to duplicate in another card. Only the information that is different or variable must be punched manually into the second and succeeding cards. Note that the repeated or constant information in the cards in Figure 6-3 consists of the customer number, salesman's number,

Chapter 6   Card planning and layout   75

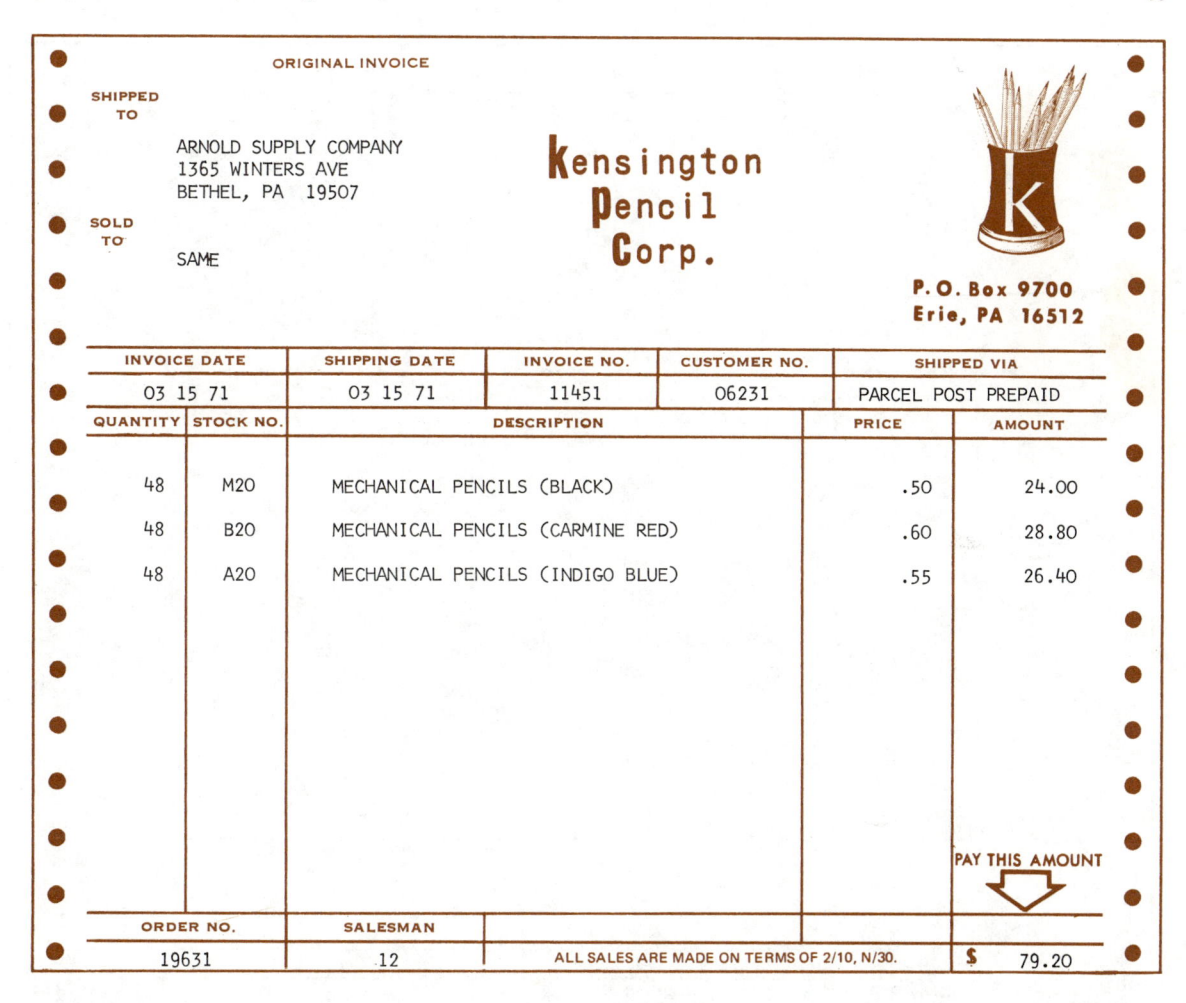

ORIGINAL INVOICE			

SHIPPED TO

ARNOLD SUPPLY COMPANY
1365 WINTERS AVE
BETHEL, PA 19507

SOLD TO

SAME

Kensington Pencil Corp.

P.O. Box 9700
Erie, PA 16512

INVOICE DATE	SHIPPING DATE	INVOICE NO.	CUSTOMER NO.	SHIPPED VIA
03 15 71	03 15 71	11451	06231	PARCEL POST PREPAID

QUANTITY	STOCK NO.	DESCRIPTION	PRICE	AMOUNT
48	M20	MECHANICAL PENCILS (BLACK)	.50	24.00
48	B20	MECHANICAL PENCILS (CARMINE RED)	.60	28.80
48	A20	MECHANICAL PENCILS (INDIGO BLUE)	.55	26.40

PAY THIS AMOUNT

ORDER NO.	SALESMAN			
19631	12	ALL SALES ARE MADE ON TERMS OF 2/10, N/30.	$	79.20

Figure 6-2. Invoice

date, and state number. The variable information consists of the quantity, stock number, unit price, and amount.

When invoice cards are prepared in the manner explained above, they can be grouped and regrouped to produce a variety of reports. The following report reproduced in partial form shows the sales of Stock Item G15 by Salesman 12. Dates of sales and their value are also shown.

SALES OF STOCK ITEM G15
BY SALESMAN 12

10 12 71	25	12 00	300 00
10 17 71	50	12 00	600 00
10 25 71	10	12 00	120 00

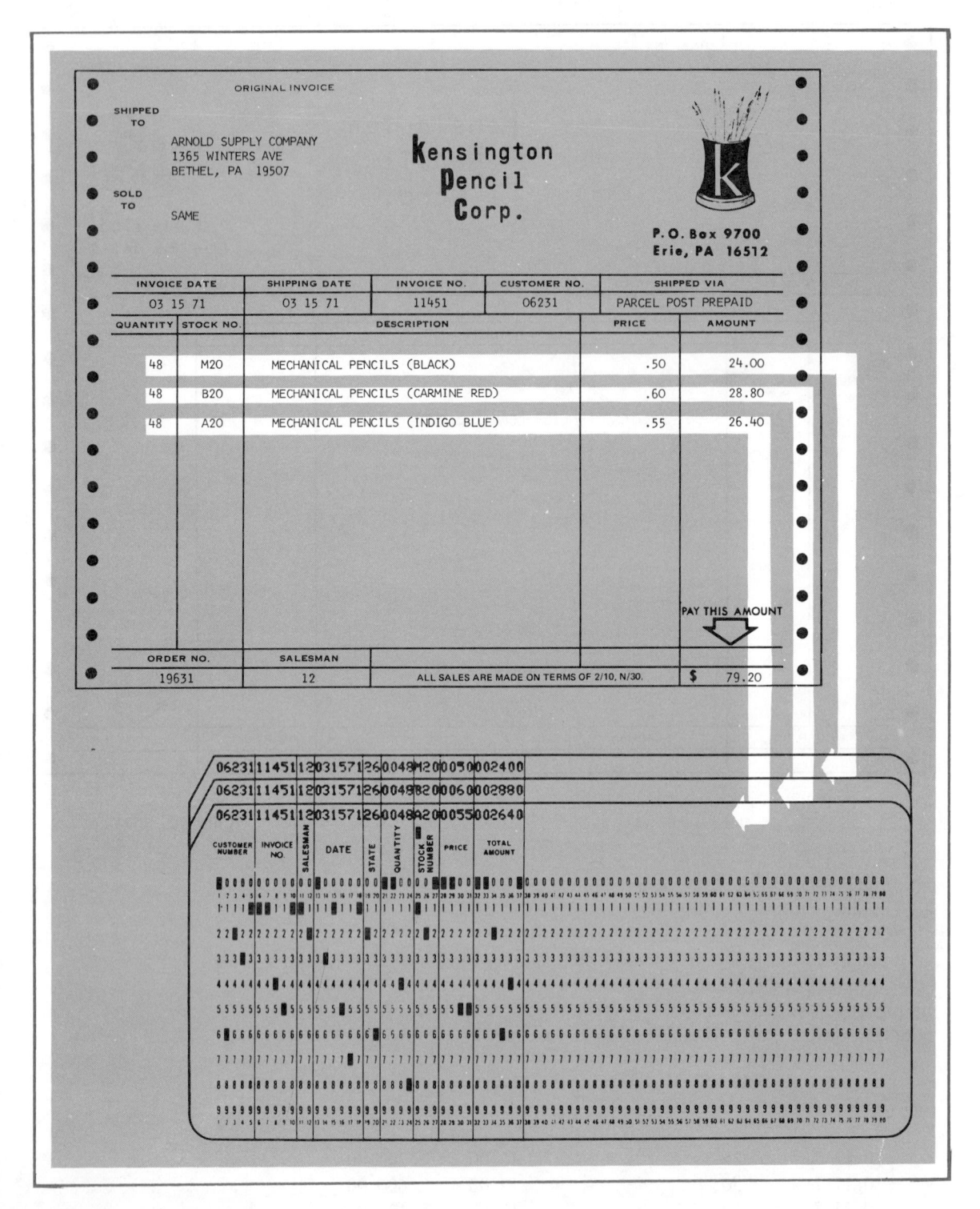

Figure 6-3. Sales detail card as unit record

Chapter 6   Card planning and layout

REVIEW QUESTIONS

1. Define the term *field* as it is used in recording information in a punched card.
2. If the numeric data recorded in a field take up fewer spaces than planned, what action must be taken?
3. Why must a particular field always appear in the same columns of a card?
4. Why are numeric codes often used in recording information in punched cards?
5. Whenever possible, why should card fields appear in the same order in which the information appears on a source document?
6. Are blank columns needed to separate card fields?
7. How is spacing of data on a printed report handled when the electronic computer system is used to process a punched card?
8. Why is the use of abbreviations encouraged in field planning?
9. Define a unit record.

Rarely are all the data needed in processing information included in one set of cards. You saw an example of this practice in the explanation of the unit-record principle. You recall that a separate card was prepared for each item listed in the invoice. A common classification of cards is one that labels them as *master*, *detail*, *summary*, and *balance*.

MASTER CARDS

A *master card* is one that contains fixed or constant information which applies to a group of cards. A master card for a customer, for example, includes such information as his account number, name, and address. A master card is illustrated in Figure 6-1, p. 72. It includes a customer's account number, his name, and his street, city, and state address. Some reports may be prepared from master cards. For example, an alphabetized list of customers for a particular state may be prepared. Cards for the particular state are first selected and then placed in alphabetic order. The customers' names are then printed by the tabulator or computer.

Master cards are frequently merged with detail, summary, or balance cards to produce reports which include information appearing in more than one type of card. For example, an invoice may be prepared by bringing together the master card and the detail cards for a particular sale to a customer. The master card contains the customer's number, name, and address. The sales detail cards may contain the customer's number, the date of sale, the invoice number of the sale, a description of items sold, and the price of each item. The invoice contains information from both types of cards. The customer's name and address are obtained from the master card. The details of the sale are obtained from the sales detail card. The merging of cards to prepare reports will be explained in a later chapter.

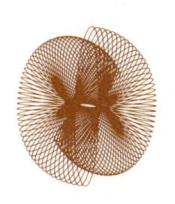

DETAIL CARDS

A *detail card* is one representing a single transaction and holding all the information pertaining to that transaction.

Sales detail cards

Sales detail cards are those prepared for each item listed in the body of a sales invoice. Such cards are illustrated in Figure 6-3. You will recall that a separate card must be prepared for each transaction listed in the body of a sales invoice. Data recorded in a sales detail card may consist of the customer's number, invoice number, date, quantity ordered, stock number of the item, description, unit price, and total amount. This type of detail card may also include the salesman's number, state number, branch number, or other pertinent information.

Payments detail cards

Another type of detail card used for processing data about customer accounts is a card that is used to process payments received on account. A payments detail card will include the customer's number, the date of payment, and the amount of payment received from the customer. See Figure 6-4.

The punch in Column 80 of the card is a control punch, which will be explained later in this chapter.

Figure 6-4. Payments detail card

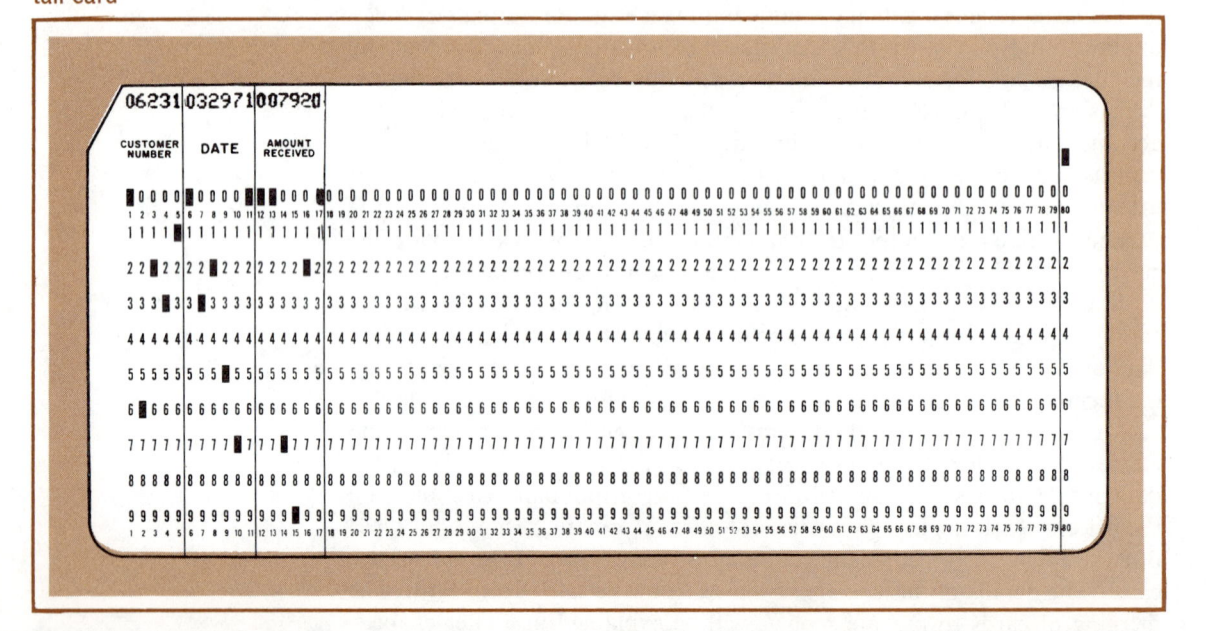

In large firms, two, three, or more detail cards may be designed, showing some or all of the foregoing information. For example, one card may be planned for the Sales Department, with only the salesman's number, code number of the item sold, and amount of the item sold. Still another detail card may be designed for the Accounting Department, showing the invoice number, date, and customer's number, as well as the quantity, description, stock number, and amount of the item sold. Reports and records can be prepared as needed from these cards, either singly or in combination with master cards.

SUMMARY CARDS

A *summary card* is one that summarizes the transactions of a group of similar detail cards. Several cards can then be replaced by one. The summary card is not concerned with the individual items sold — only with the total concerning the sale. A monthly report in dollar amounts of sales made to each customer may then be prepared from the summary cards. End-of-the-month reports may also be prepared, showing only the charges and invoice numbers for specific dates or only the payments received and dates of payment. A summary card for inventory can summarize all the items having a certain stock number that have been received within a definite period. Another summary card can summarize all the items having the same stock number that have been shipped during that period.

BALANCE CARDS

Balance cards, like summary cards, contain summarized information, usually for specific periods. The inventory summary card for receipts and the summary card for shipments may be merged and the amount calculated to show the balance of an item of stock on hand. This balance may then be recorded in a balance card.

A balance card can be planned to show a customer's name or number and the balance of his account at the end of a particular month. The balance card is then used as a starting point for a subsequent month. Much time is saved by this method, as detail cards do not have to be rerun in order to provide a continuing record of the customer's account. Master cards, sales detail cards, and payments detail cards can be merged to produce the statement of account for the customer. The balance card is then created, showing the new balance. See Figure 6-5. Note that the previous balance card furnishes the balance from the preceding month. The master card, sales detail cards, and payments detail card furnish the customer's name and address as well as the charges and payments for the current month. The new balance is then indicated on the statement, and a new balance card is made for use with the next statement of account.

A *balance card*, therefore, is intended to indicate the balance, for a specified period, of any type of account after the transactions for that period have been completed and calculated.

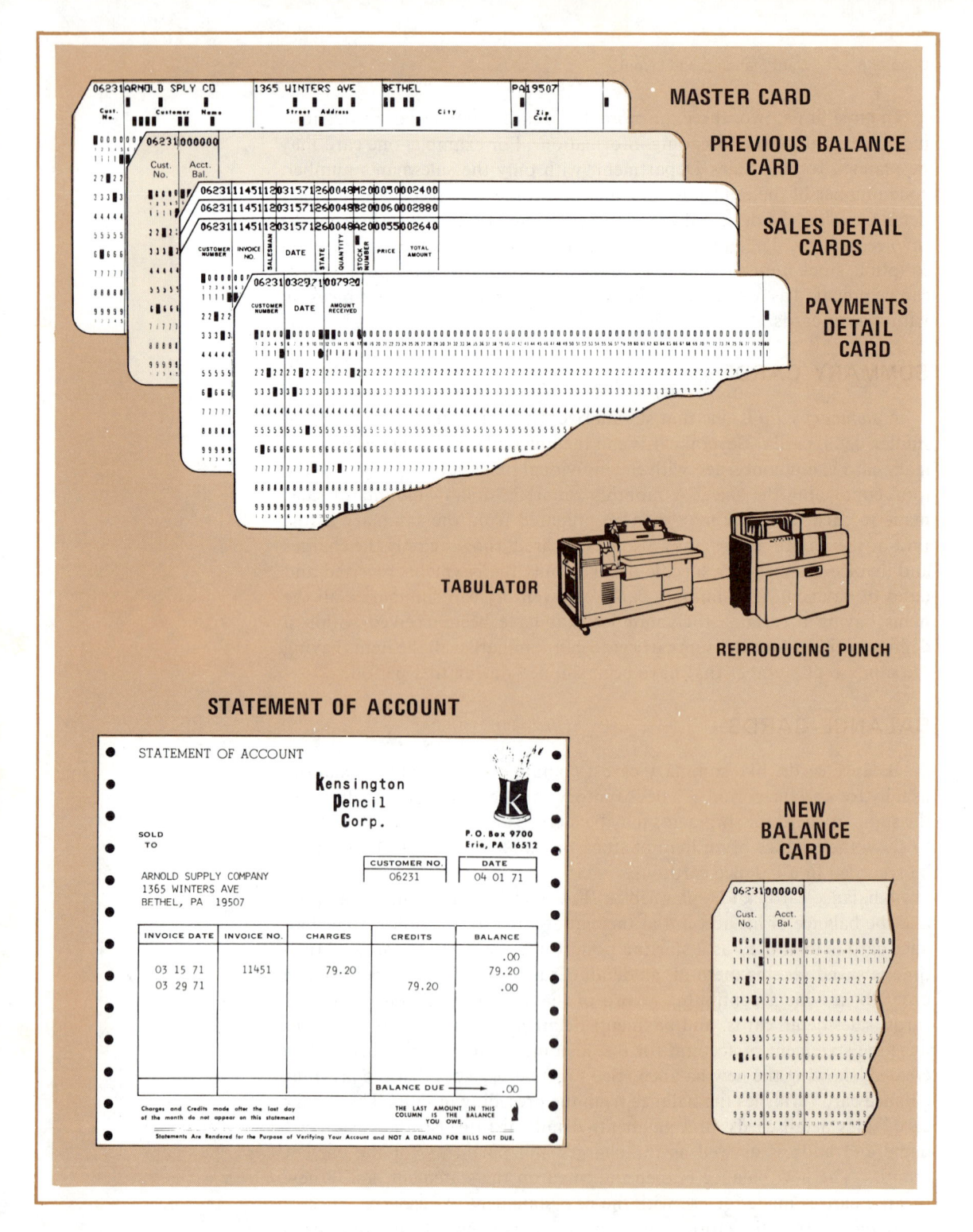

Figure 6-5. Statement of account with master, detail, and balance cards

Chapter 6   Card planning and layout

CONTROL PUNCHES IN CARDS

Control punches for cards processed by the unit-record system

Generally, holes in cards represent digits, letters of the alphabet, or special characters. In addition, however, a punch in a predetermined column (or several punches in several columns) may be used to instruct a machine in the unit-record system to perform a specific operation. A punch in Row 11 or Row 12 is commonly used as a control punch. For example, a control punch in a specific column may instruct a machine to add, subtract, or space data in a particular manner.

A control punch may be used to instruct the tabulator to print the name of a customer, his street address, and his city and state names in three lines instead of in one line as is usual in printing data from a single card. A punch may be used in a master card when preparing a statement on which the name and address of the customer appear in three lines. In Figure 6-1 note the punch in the 12 position of Column 80 of the master card. In Figure 6-4 the punch is in the 11 position of Column 80 of the payments detail card. A control punch enables the processing machines to distinguish the type of card and to space data properly provided the control panel is wired for this procedure. The control panel will be discussed in detail in Chapter 10.

A *control punch* is thus a specific code punched in a card to cause one of the data processing machines to perform a definite operation.

Control punches for cards processed by the electronic computer system

Control punches are also used in cards to direct some computers to perform specific operations. Computers can be programmed to produce statements and reports from master and detail cards. An 11 punch or a 12 punch in Column 80 of the master card can enable some computers to distinguish master cards from detail cards. Furthermore, a control punch above the units column of any quantity or amount field may cause some computers to record a negative value for the entire field. The return of a sale, for example, decreases the number of units sold and the amount of the sale. This information can be punched into a card, with 11 punches, for example, in the units column of each field. The 11 punches can cause the computer to subtract these amounts, even though the program itself includes a command to add the amounts.

PRINTED MATTER ON CARDS

Generally, printed headings appear at the top of card fields. Other information may be printed on the cards as well. The printed matter on a card means nothing to the machines that process the cards. All the machines can recognize is the punched holes. The printed information makes the cards more understandable to operators and to those who receive them in the form of checks or other business forms.

Since the printed matter on a card is meaningless to the processing machines, the printing can appear at any place. When a card is also a check, the printed matter is arranged in check form. The punched holes may or may not appear under the printed copy on the card.

See Figure 6-6, which is a punched card used as a receipt for cash fare paid as toll for a passenger car traveling through a tunnel between Norfolk and Hampton, Virginia.

Figure 6-7 is a punched card used as a monthly statement.

Figure 6-6. Punched card used as a receipt

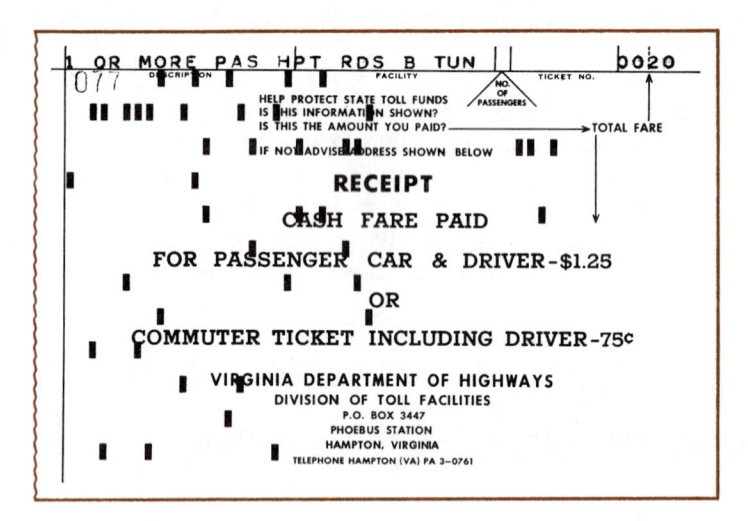

Figure 6-7. Punched card used as a statement

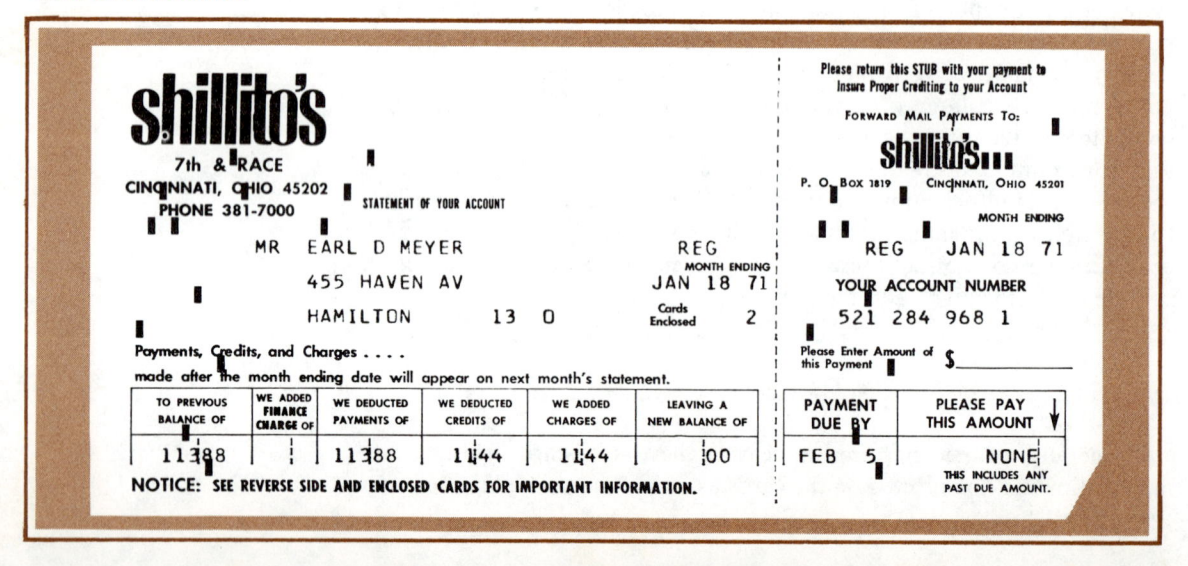

Cards used as business forms show amounts and other important matter in typed or printed form although there is numeric information punched in the holes. Further processing is thus made possible by automatic means. When the statement is returned with a payment, the punched card on which the statement appears is run through processing machines to make the necessary bookkeeping entries or to prepare reports. A great deal of rewriting of information by hand is avoided in this manner.

REVIEW QUESTIONS

1. Name the four types of punched cards.
2. What is the purpose of each of the four types of cards?
3. What is a control punch? Why is it useful?
4. Can the automated data processing machines read the printed matter appearing on a card?

PRINCIPLES OF CARD PLANNING AND LAYOUT

A summary is given here of the major points to be kept in mind as you plan the layout of a card to record both numeric and alphabetic data. Read these points carefully so that you can complete the projects on card layout at the end of this chapter.

1. The type of information to be recorded on the card must be determined. This step requires a knowledge of what papers and reports are to be prepared from the card.
2. The number of columns needed to record the selected information must be determined. Enough columns must be provided to take care of the longest group of letters or figures recorded in each field. Because of the limited number of columns available, only those columns needed to accommodate a field of information should be reserved.
3. Whenever possible, the fields should appear in the same order as the information on the source document. This arrangement speeds up the card punching process because the operator is able to read and record the information in sequence.
4. Once a field of some specified number of card columns is established for a particular recording job, the columns must not be used for other types of data. In addition, only the number of columns reserved for that specific field may be used.
5. A separate punched card (detail card) must be prepared for each transaction recorded in a source document. Each detail card must contain all the information that is essential to the transaction. For example, if a student enrollment form indicates that a student is taking five subjects, a separate class card must be prepared for each subject. Each card must contain the detailed information in identical fields.

6. Abbreviations may be used whenever possible, and standard abbreviations need not be used. In most billing and statement operations, initials may be used for given names; and the initials may be run together if last names are too long. In payrolls, tax forms, student enrollments, and other operations requiring legal names, the proper name should appear in the form filled out by the individual.
7. No periods are necessary at the end of abbreviations or initials. Commas are not essential between names of cities and states.
8. Whenever possible, a number should be used as a code to represent alphabetic information not used for mailing purposes.
9. No spaces need separate the data in one field from those in another. Needed spaces can be provided by the way in which the control panel is wired or the computer program is written.

ADVANTAGES OF RECORDING INFORMATION IN CARDS

The practice of recording information in punched cards offers a number of advantages. The five most important of these are as follows:

1. As an input medium, the card is versatile and durable. Once information is punched into it, the information is in permanent form and may be used repeatedly. Furthermore, it may be used in connection with other input media, such as paper tape and magnetic tape.
2. The card can accommodate printed or written matter and thus may be used as a check, an invoice, or some other business paper. Further processing of these papers is thus possible by automatic means.
3. Each card contains all the information describing a single transaction. All similar transactions can thus be grouped and processed according to a predetermined plan.
4. The card represents data that can be processed by a wide variety of automatic data processing machines. It is an input medium for both the unit-record and electronic computer system.
5. The punched data in a card can be verified for accuracy before processing takes place. An error detected can be corrected immediately.

The punched card has served long and faithfully as the workhorse of the data processing movement. Because of its advantages in handling data, there is little prospect that it will soon be made obsolete by other input media of more recent origin.

SUMMARY

The punched card may represent any data that can be expressed in figures, letters, or special characters. Once data have been recorded in cards, the cards may be used to prepare a variety of reports automatically. The laying out of fields for data is an important requirement in the planning phase of an operation. The fields must be large enough to accommodate all present and future information that may be punched in them. However, no card columns should be wasted by poor planning. Once designed, the fields must remain fixed.

The unit-record principle requires a separate card for each transaction. An individual card, therefore, must contain all the information necessary to describe a specific transaction.

Cards of four types — master, detail, summary, and balance — are commonly prepared and used as sources of data for the various reports needed by management. A master card contains fixed or indicative information for a group of cards. A detail card represents a single transaction, and the information it contains depends upon the reports that will be prepared from it. A summary card summarizes the transactions of a group of similar detail cards. A balance card shows the end-of-period balance of a particular account — information that can be used as a starting point for a subsequent period.

The several principles of card planning and layout should be used as guides in planning card fields for the different types of cards. Well-designed cards offer a number of advantages for recording information that is to be processed automatically. The cards are versatile and durable. They can be used as business documents. Each card contains all the information needed about a single transaction. In addition, the data are represented in a code familiar to data processing machines, and the coded information can be checked for accuracy before processing. Because of these advantages, the card has gained the distinction of being the workhorse of the data processing movement.

REVIEW QUESTIONS

1. What are the nine points to be remembered when planning the layout of a card?
2. How many detail cards must be punched to record data on an invoice listing seven separate sales items?
3. List the five most important advantages of recording information in punched cards.
4. The punched card has been utilized to process data since 1890. Is it likely to be made obsolete in the near future?

STUDY GUIDE 6

Complete Study Guide 6 by following the instructions in your STUDY GUIDES booklet.

PROJECTS

Complete Projects 6-1, 6-2, 6-3, 6-4, 6-5, and 6-6 by following the instructions in your PROJECTS booklet.

CHAPTER 7

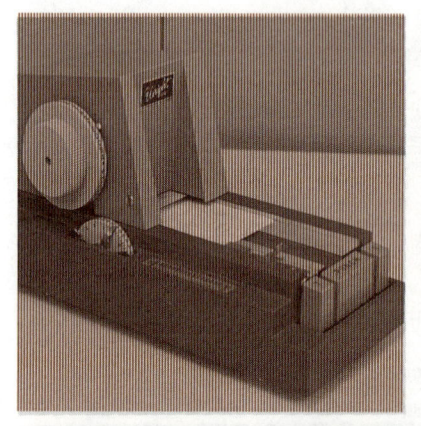

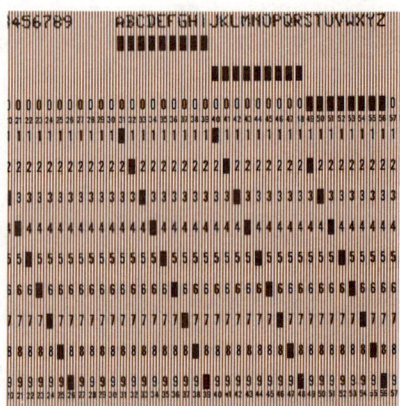

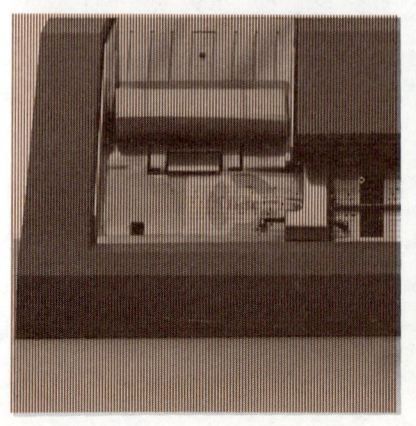

RECORDING INFORMATION IN CARDS

When a punched card is used as the input medium, the punching step usually follows the recording of data on the source document. The operator punching the card will find on the source document the data to be recorded. He will punch the data into the card in accordance with the way in which the card has been planned. Assume that a punched card is being used to process data relative to student enrollments. The data punched in the card would be taken from the application for enrollment, which, in this example, is the source document. One type of application for enrollment is illustrated in Figure 7-1. This form has been partially completed.

The data recorded on the application form are recorded manually. The relationship of the source document to a punched card is shown in Figure 7-2.

Once the card illustrated in Figure 7-2 has been punched, the card may be used to prepare a list of all freshmen, a list of all male freshmen, a list of all female freshmen, and other similar reports.

The various methods of recording input data in cards can be grouped under two main classifications: (1) the direct method of punching cards with a card punch machine, and (2) the indirect method.

DIRECT METHOD

In the direct method of recording information in a card, the holes are punched directly into the card itself. Each device or machine used in the direct method has only one function, and that is to punch holes in cards.

Basic components of automated systems   Part 2

Figure 7-1. Application for enrollment

> **APPLICATION FOR ENROLLMENT**
> **NORTH HIGH SCHOOL**
>
> Name _Price, Michelle Ann_ M ___ F ✓ Birthdate _9/2/53_
>   (Last)   (First)   (Middle)
> Address _455 Haven Ave., Garroway, Ohio_ Phone _893-8508_
> Name of Parent or Guardian _Thomas P. Price, M.D._
> Date of Enrollment _9/8/71_ Grade _12_
>
> | Subjects Requested | | Alternates | |
> |---|---|---|---|
> | Subject No. | Subject Name | Subject No. | Subject Name |
> | 024 | English IV | | |
> | 011 | Intro. to Data Proc. | 017 | Office Practice |
> | 104 | American History | | |
> | 105 | Problems of Dem. | 109 | Civics II |
> | 067 | Trigonometry | 066 | Solid Geometry |
> | 073 | Stage Band | 072 | Orchestra |
>
> **Department Codes**
>
> 00 Art   06 Mathematics
> 01 Business   07 Music
> 02 English   08 Physical Education
> 03 Home Economics 09 Science
> 04 Industrial Arts 10 Social Studies
> 05 Language
>
> Approved ✓ yes ___ no
>
> Counselor _Edward A. Parker_

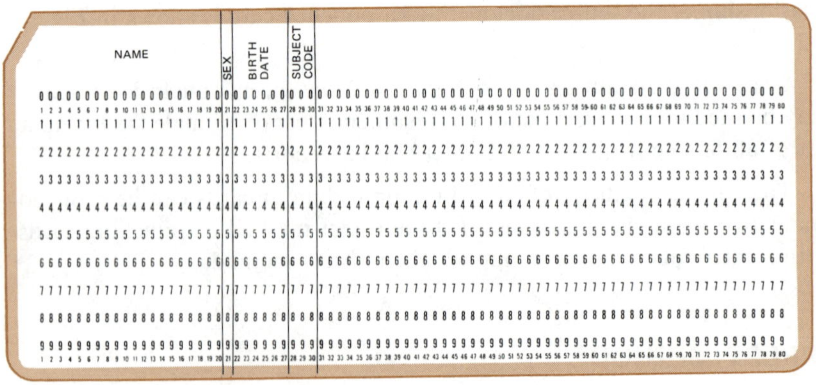

Figure 7-2. Punched card used for processing student enrollment data

Card punch machine

The most commonly known machine for direct card punching is the card punch, which is illustrated in Figure 7-3.

Chapter 7 Recording information in cards

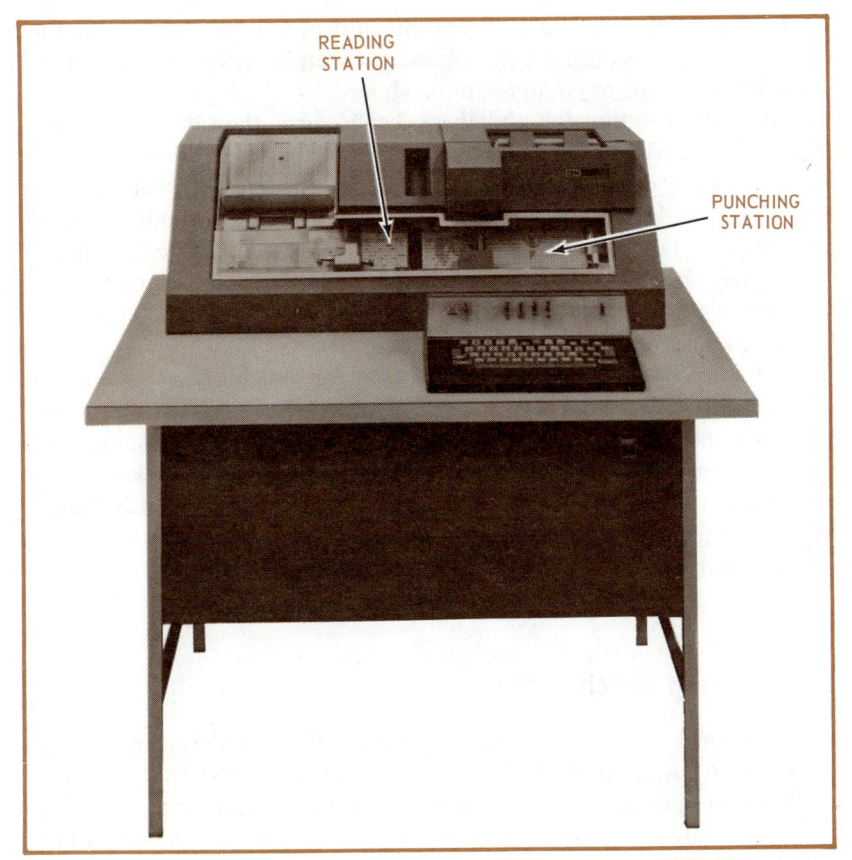

Figure 7-3. IBM 29 card punch machine

Courtesy of IBM Corporation

Figure 7-4. Keyboard for numeric card punch machine

Card punch machines are available with more than one type of keyboard. One keyboard is used for recording numeric data only. Figure 7-4 is an illustration of such a keyboard. Except for the arrangement of the keys, note that the keyboard resembles very closely the keyboard on a ten-key adding-listing machine.

Another type of keyboard found on card punch machines is one that can be used for recording both numeric and alphabetic data. Figure 7-5 illustrates this type of combination keyboard.

You will note that the alphabetic keyboard is the same as that of a standard typewriter. Observe the keys in the shaded area in Figure 7-5. These keys are controlled by the right hand and are used for punching both letters and numbers. For example, the U key will produce both U and Number 1. The letter is produced by depressing the indicated key; the number, by depressing the left shift key (NUMERIC) along with the indicated right-hand key. Note the keys that are used to punch the Digits 0 through 9. Note, too, the letters on these keys.

The combination keyboard can be used for punching both alphabetic and numeric information in a card. Generally, when numeric information alone is to be punched in a card, a card punch with the numeric keyboard is used. Regardless of the type of keyboard used, anyone who knows how to operate a typewriter and a ten-key adding-listing machine can usually operate either one of the two card punch machines described, after some training and practice.

Printing card punch

Card punch machines are available in a variety of models. Some models merely punch holes in the card. Other models will print at the top of the card the interpretation of the punch or punches made in each column of the card. Only upper case alphabetic symbols (capital letters) are printed. When a printing card punch is used, the printing and punching are done simultaneously. For those who desire to have the interpretation of the punches appear on the card, the printing card punch saves considerable time. This machine eliminates the necessity of using an interpreting machine to print the information punched in the card. The machine illustrated in Figure 7-3 is a printing card punch machine.

Portable card punch

In addition to the machines just illustrated and described, portable card punch machines may be used to punch data directly into cards. Because the portable card punch is small, it is used to punch data in cards when it would be difficult or impossible to have one of the larger punching machines available. A portable card punch machine is illustrated in Figure 7-6.

To use the portable card punch machine, the operator must adjust and operate the machine manually. The manual operation takes considerable time. Therefore, the use of the portable machine is restricted to the punching of limited amounts of data.

Chapter 7   Recording information in cards

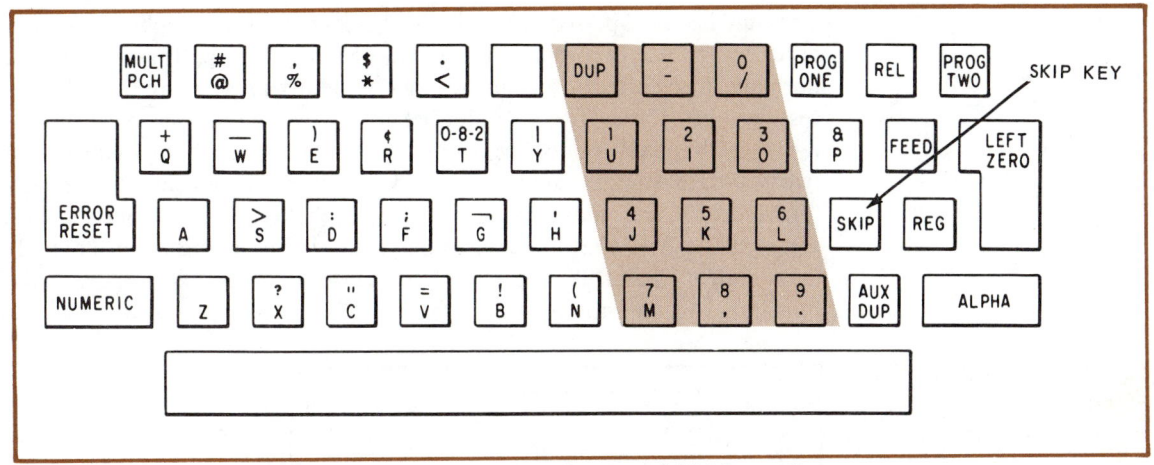

Courtesy of IBM Corporation

Figure 7-5. Keyboard of an IBM 29 card punch machine combining alphabetic and numeric keys

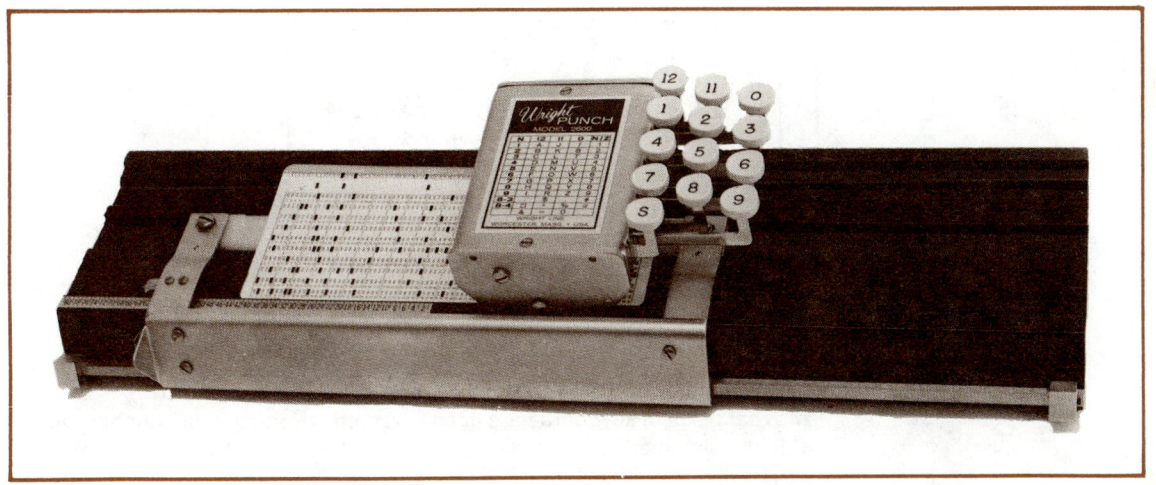

Courtesy of Wright Line, a division of Barry Wright Corporation

Figure 7-6. Portable card punch machine

Perforated card

A card has been designed in which the punching positions have been perforated. The perforated sections can be punched out of the card with a sharp pencil, stylus, or similar object. Perforated cards were designed to be used in instances when a card punch machine is not readily accessible.

The punches in a perforated card can be converted to punches in a standard card by use of a reproducer. Data recorded in a perforated card are normally transferred into punches in a standard card before further processing takes place. The reproducer handles this job automatically.

Note that each punching position of the perforated card consists of two standard card columns. To make meaningful punches in the perforated card, one must know both the alphabetic and numeric codes. Determining just what punches to make and then making them manually takes time. Therefore, the use of the perforated card is limited to the punching of small amounts of data.

Figure 7-7. Section of a perforated card

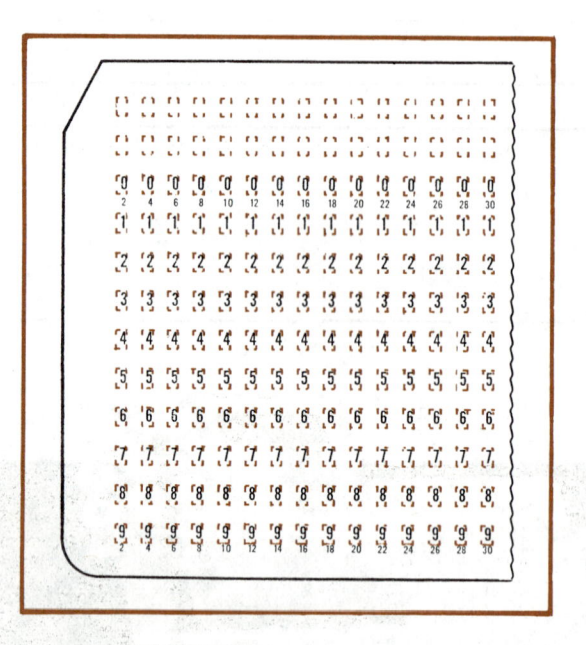

REVIEW QUESTIONS

1. How is information recorded in cards by the direct method?
2. What types of keyboards are used to record information in punched cards?
3. Is the alphabetic keyboard on a card punch machine the same as the standard typewriter keyboard?
4. Are both upper- and lower-case alphabetic symbols available on the card punch?
5. Why was the perforated card designed?

TIME-SAVING DEVICES

To save time in the punching process, manufacturers of card punching equipment have built into the machines several time-saving devices. In the main, these devices consist of a duplicate key, a skip key, a program card, and a special key for inserting zeros in the unused columns of a numeric field.

Chapter 7   Recording information in cards   93

Duplicate key

Generally, two locations, referred to as stations, are provided for placing cards in a card punch machine. One of these is the *punching station*; the other, the *reading station*. (See Figure 7-3, page 89.) Holes are punched into the card in the punching station as keys are operated. When the punching operation is complete, the card moves to the reading station. At the same time, a new card is fed into the punching station and data are punched in it manually. However, any data recorded in the first card that are to be repeated in the second card may be punched in the second card automatically by depressing a *duplicate key*. A sensing device, together with connecting cables, reads the information in the first card and punches it into the second. The location of a duplicate key (DUP) on one of the machines is shown in the shaded part of the keyboard in Figure 7-5, page 91. Automatic duplication of this type can also be handled by the use of a program card, a device that is explained in a later paragraph.

Skip key

A *skip key* is used to move quickly from one punching field to another. The skip key is similar to a tabulator key or bar on a typewriter. The location of the skip key (SKIP) on one of the machines is shown in the keyboard illustration in Figure 7-5, page 91. This key is operable only in conjunction with a program card, which is discussed in the next paragraph.

Program card

The *program card* automatically handles skipping, spacing, duplicating, and shifting from numeric to alphabetic positions. A separate program card must be prepared for each job. For example, one program card must be prepared for punching information in cards for invoices, another for punching information in cards for the payroll. When one of these cards is inserted into the program unit of a card punch machine, it handles the skipping, spacing, duplicating, and shifting operations automatically as payroll or invoice cards are prepared. Much of the operator's time is thus saved.

The operation of the card punch by means of a program card is very similar to the operation of an automatic clothes washer by means of its built-in control unit. In the clothes washer, the program is a rigid one. In the card punch, however, the program is flexible, as it can be changed each time the punching job is changed. A new program card for each new punching job is simply inserted on the program drum of the card punch.

A program card is illustrated in Figure 7-8. In design, it is identical to the cards used for recording data to be processed. The punches on the program card, however, cause the card punch to perform a number of steps or operations automatically. The punches and their functions are listed below.

Punches	Function
Blank (no punch)	A card column which is blank on the program card indicates the beginning of a field in which numeric data are to be punched on the card punch by the operator.
1	A punch in the Digit 1 position shifts the card-punch keyboard to the alphabetic position so that alphabetic characters will be recorded in the field.
0	A punch in the Zero position in the first column of a field on a program card starts the automatic duplication of data that appear in the same columns of a punched card inserted in the reading station of a card punch. These data are then punched on the card inserted in the punching station.
11	A punch in the 11 position in the first column of a field of a program card starts automatic skipping.
12	Punches in the 12 position designate the length, in card columns, of each field. Thus, for example, punches in the 12 position tell the card punch how many columns to skip or in how many columns data are to be duplicated.

In the program card in Figure 7-8, the following operations take place:

Columns 1–11: Data from the card in the reading station are punched into the card in the punching station.

Columns 12–24: Numeric data are punched into these columns by the operator.

Columns 25–40: These columns are skipped.

Columns 41–60: Data from the card in the reading station are punched into the card in the punching station.

Columns 61–80: These columns are skipped.

Some of the latest models of card punch machines are equipped to follow two separate programs punched in one program card. For example, one program may be used to control the spacing of data in a master card while the second program in the same program card may be used to control the spacing of data in a detail card. Refer to Figure 7-5 and note the keys for program control. The keys are labeled *program one* and *program two*.

Chapter 7   Recording information in cards   95

Figure 7-8. Program card

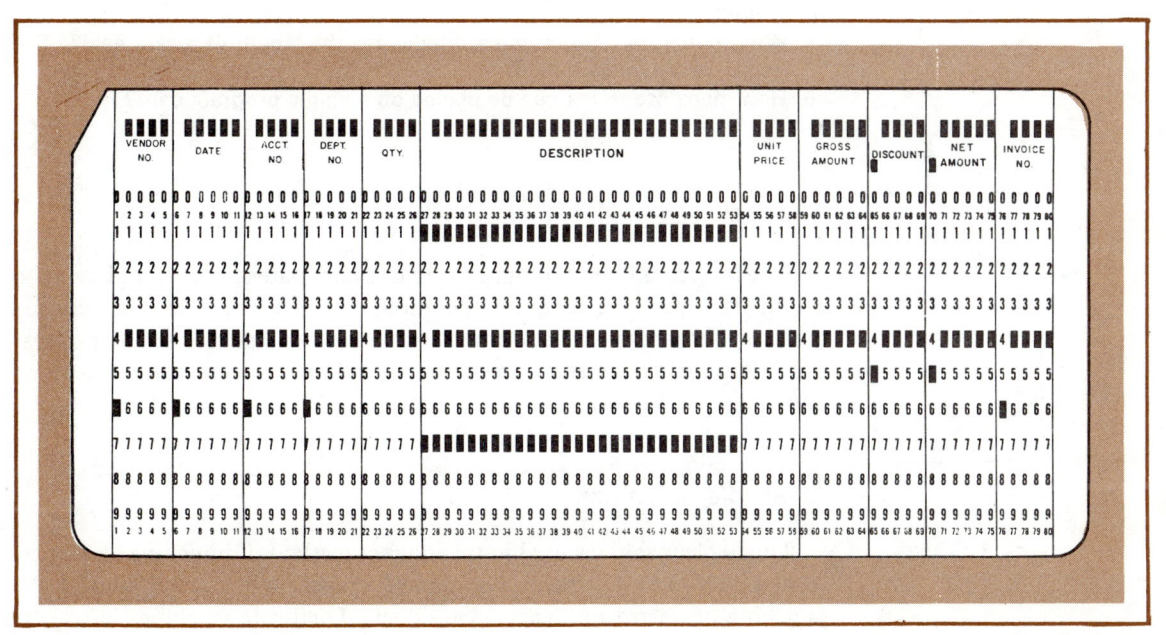

Figure 7-9. Program card with two programs

The card punch operator can switch from one program to the other by merely depressing a key. Figure 7-9 illustrates a program card with two programs punched in the card. Note that one program appears at the top of the card; the other program is punched near the middle of the card.

Left zero insertion

You have learned that zeros or spaces are placed in unused columns of a numeric field. Determining the number of zeros needed for a field and punching them in the appropriate columns is the responsibility of the card punch operator. The job can be very time consuming.

Some manufacturers of card punching equipment have equipped their machines with a special key which, when depressed, will automatically determine the number of zeros needed and punch the extra zeros. The location of the left zero key on one of the machines is shown in the keyboard illustration in Figure 7-5, page 91. This key works in conjunction with a program card placed in the machine.

REVIEW QUESTIONS

1. Name the four time-saving devices on card punch machines discussed in this section.
2. What are the functions of the reading and the punching stations on a card punch machine?
3. What operations will a program card handle?
4. Which key on the card punch machine is similar to the tabulator on a typewriter?
5. What punch in a program card indicates the length of a skip field? The length of a duplicate field?
6. How many programs can be placed on a single program card?

INDIRECT METHOD OF CARD PUNCHING

The indirect method of punching cards eliminates the need of having to punch the holes as a separate operation. Instead, the holes are punched indirectly, that is, in collaboration with or as the result of another operation. Several machines and methods of indirect punching are illustrated and explained below.

Dual-role machines

Dual-role machines used in the indirect method of punching cards perform a dual role: (1) the preparation of a business document, and (2) the punching of a card or a tape by-product. Dual-role machines have keyboards that are similar to that of a typewriter or those of common calculating machines. The machines are selective and will record in the card or tape for automatic processing only the desired information from the data appearing on the typed business document. The machines illustrated in Figures 7-10, 7-11, and 7-12 can prepare original documents and, at the same time, punch cards or tapes as by-products.

Chapter 7   Recording information in cards   97

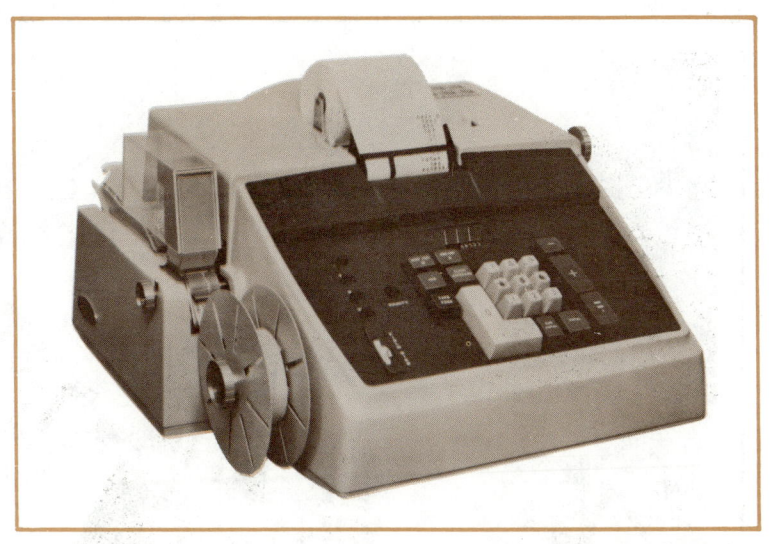

Figure 7-10. The ten-key adding machine has an attachment that punches data into paper tape.

Courtesy of Friden, Inc.

Figure 7-11. The Dura typewriter prepares business documents and punched tape simultaneously.

Reading device for tape or edge-punched cards

Punching device that punches paper tape; a device that punches edge-punched cards is also available

Courtesy of Dura Business Machines

Figure 7-12. The IBM 6430 prepares business documents and punched cards simultaneously.

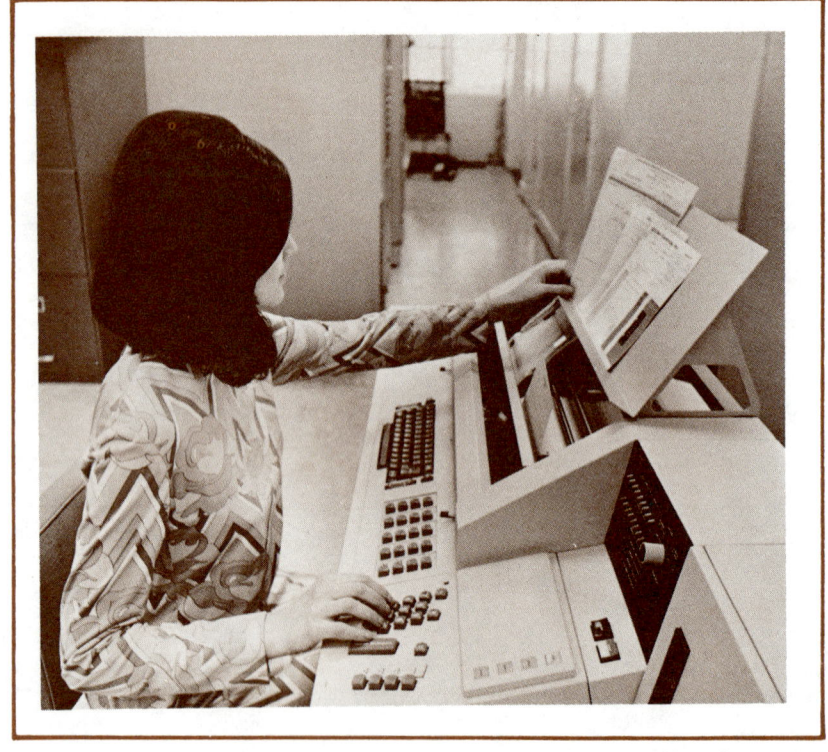

Courtesy of IBM Corporation

The *punched paper* tape prepared by some of the dual-role machines is similar to punched cards in that punched holes in the tape represent numbers, letters, and special characters. Paper tape is a continuous recording medium and can be used to record data of any length. Cards, on the other hand, are of fixed length and the recording of data in them is interrupted momentarily as new cards are fed into the card punch machine. Data that are punched in paper tape are converted to punched cards for processing by machines in the tabulating or computer systems. Converters are discussed later in this chapter.

The holes punched in paper tape appear in either real or imaginary channels running the length of the tape. Machines read the punches across, not down the length of the tape. Each horizontal row of punches represents one letter, digit or symbol. Because the holes appear in channels on the paper tape, the holes as codes are referred to as *channel* or binary codes. The size and shape of the holes and the code represented are not the same as those used with punched cards. Figure 7-13 is an illustration of punched paper tape with an interpretation of the holes punched in the tape. Accuracy of the tapes is determined by checking the typewritten letter or document of which the tape is a by-product.

Chapter 7   Recording information in cards   99

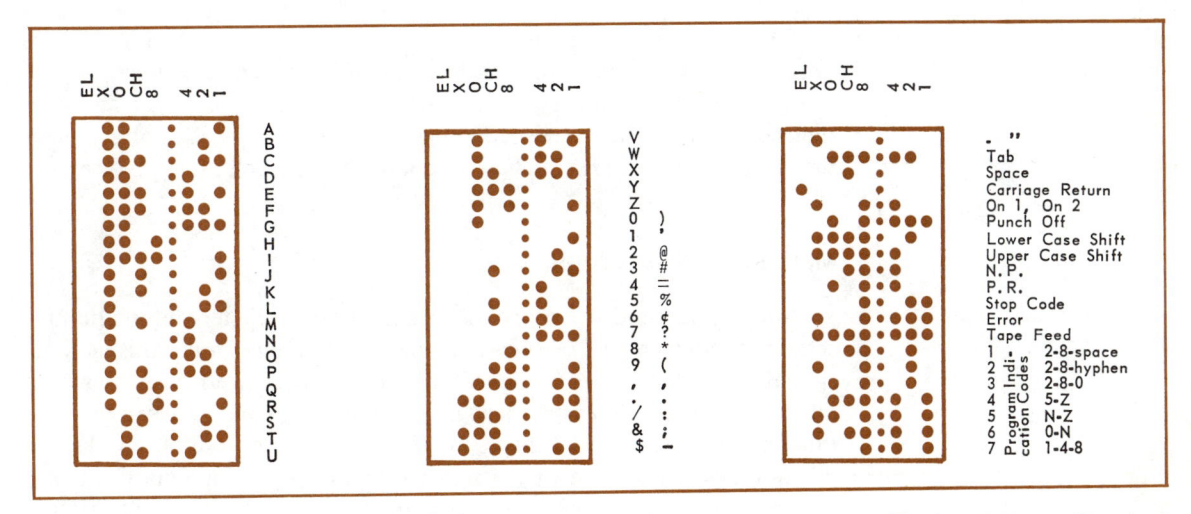

Figure 7-13. Punched paper tape

Invoices are often prepared on machines with tape-cutting and tape-reading attachments. The tape is punched as an invoice is typed. The data are then transferred from the tape to punched cards by a tape-to-card converter. The data in the cards are then processed as needed by unit-record machines.

Because a card is easier to file and handle and is also more durable than paper tape, a card somewhat similar to paper tape is sometimes used as a substitute for paper tape. This card is commonly referred to as an *edge-punched card*, an example of which is illustrated in Figure 7-14. The card gets its name from the fact that information is punched along the edge of the card. The same channel code used for recording information in paper tape is used for recording information in the card. An edge-punched card differs somewhat from a standard card. The edge-punched card is shorter and narrower. In addition, as already stated, channel code is used in an edge-punched card, whereas Hollerith code is used in the standard card.

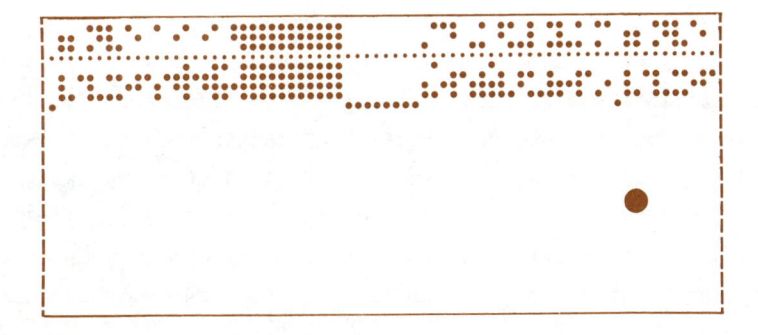

Figure 7-14. Edge-punched card

Because paper tape is not very durable, edge-punched cards are normally used to hold information of a more permanent nature. A customer's name and address, for example, can be punched in an edge-punched card. As the card is fed into a machine with a reading attachment, the data in the card are transferred to a document such as an invoice.

Mark-sensed recording

Another method of recording original data for later automatic processing is known as the *mark-sensed punching method*. Under this method, special cards have been designed for use by those who wish to record information with a graphite pencil. Graphite will conduct electricity and thus the marks can be used for processing data. Because the marks can be sensed electrically, this particular method of recording data is referred to as the mark-sensed method of recording. Figure 7-15 is an illustration of one card available for recording data by the mark-sensed method. The card illustrated is the same size as the standard card but it is somewhat different in design. The chief difference lies in the fact that the standard card contains 80 vertical columns; a card used in mark sensing contains only 27 vertical marking positions. These positions are shown at the bottom of the card by the scale immediately above the card column scale. The marks on the card rather than holes represent the data recorded. A single mark covers three regular card columns. Three columns are reserved for each mark because a handwritten mark may not be as precisely made and placed on the card as a hole punched into the card by a machine. A *mark-sensed card* is thus a special card, containing 27 vertical columns, designed to record information when used with a graphite pencil.

Figure 7-15. Mark-sensed card

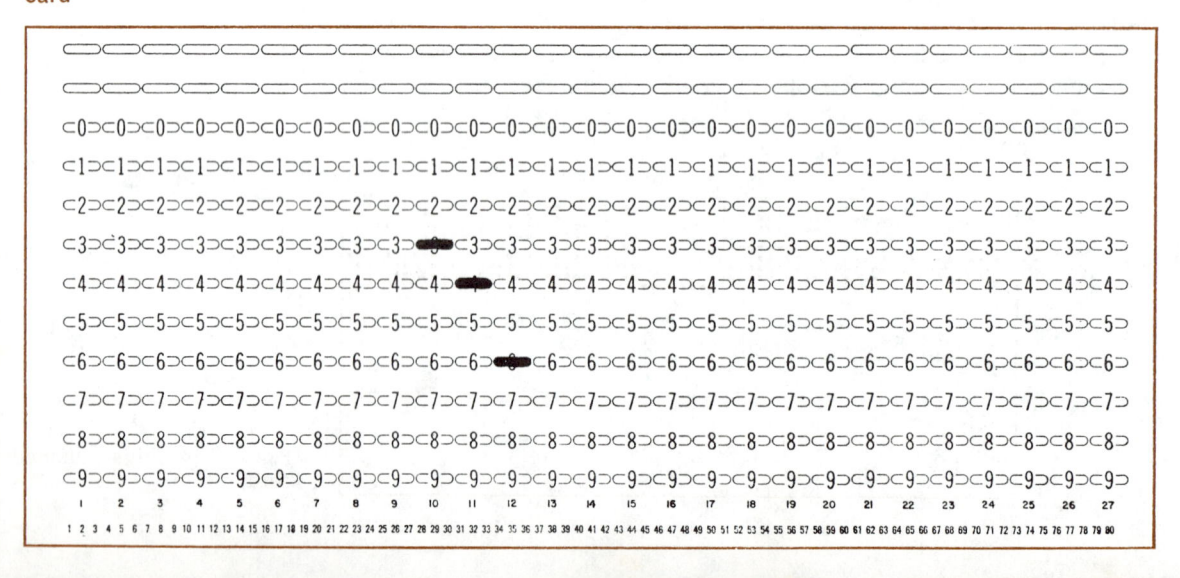

Chapter 7   Recording information in cards   101

Mark-sensed cards are similar to standard cards in that the digit positions are the same on both cards. Thus, a mark in the Digit 5 position in a column will be recognized as the Digit 5. In Figure 7-15, note the markings in Columns 10, 11, and 12 in which the Digits 3, 4, and 6 have been marked. Fields are planned for recording information in mark-sensed cards just as in standard cards. Mark-sensing is usually limited to recording numeric information. The numbers used normally contain only a few digits. It is possible to record alphabetic information in these cards, but the user must memorize the alphabetic code in order to record such information. For this reason, any alphabetic information is usually restricted to such items as stock numbers or other information containing a limited number of letters of the alphabet. Data recorded in a mark-sensed card are normally converted to a standard card for processing.

Input media reproducers and converters

Converter. A tape-to-card converter makes it possible for users of data processing systems automatically to convert data recorded in one medium to another. There are several advantages to this feature. Many common office machines, such as the typewriter, the 10-key adding-listing machine, and the billing machine, are equipped with special devices for recording data in punched tape. The by-product paper tape produced by the machine may be used to prepare punched cards. You learned earlier in this chapter that data punched in tape are normally converted to punched cards for further processing by the unit-record system. Figure 7-16 illustrates a tape-to-card converter.

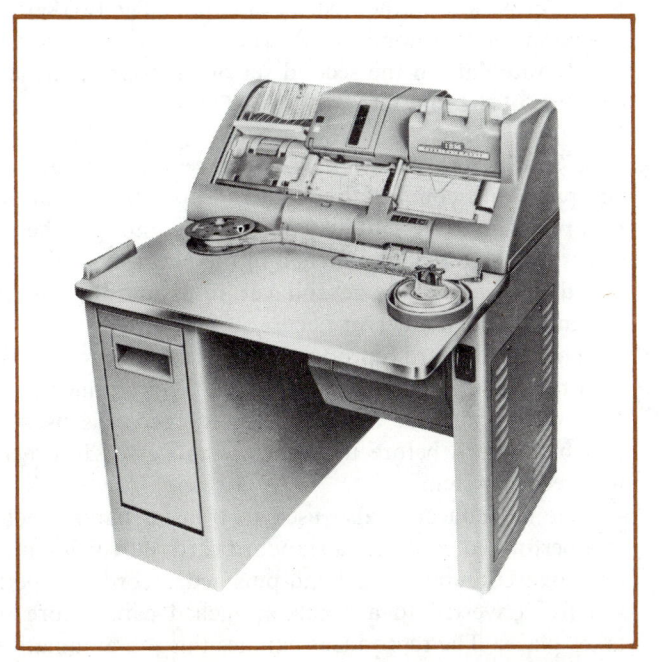

Figure 7-16. Tape-to-card converter

Courtesy of IBM Corporation

Reproducer. Users of punched cards can duplicate in one or more cards all or part of the data punched in the original card. The data can be duplicated by use of a special duplicate key on the card punch or by a program card. In addition to the foregoing methods, a card-to-card reproducer may be used.

A *reproducer* is a machine capable of punching information recorded in one card into as many additional cards as are needed. By using a comparison operation, the reproducer verifies the accuracy of the punches in the duplicate cards prepared by it. A card-to-card reproducer is illustrated in Figure 7-17.

The reproducer is capable of reproducing cards on a one-for-one basis or on a mass-production basis known as *gang punching.* Either process is accomplished through the use of a control panel, wired to give the reproducer a set of instructions for each job.

Reproducing cards on a one-for-one basis. The reproducer has two feed hoppers, as shown in Figure 7-17. The cards from which data are to be read are fed into one hopper; those in which the data are to be punched are fed into another. The control panel selects the specific data to be reproduced from one set of cards and causes the data to be punched in the other set. The data in any column or field in the first set of cards can be punched into any column or field in the second set.

For an example of the foregoing operation, assume that one set of punched cards contains a record of the number of hours worked by employees during a given period. Assume further that the hourly rate of each employee is punched into another set of cards and that you wish to enter this information on the first set of cards. The two sets of cards would be placed in the two hoppers. As the cards are fed into the reproducer, the hourly rate data in the second set of cards are punched into the desired columns of the first set.

Checking the accuracy of the reproduced data. The reproducer is equipped with comparing units to insure complete accuracy in reproduction punching. These units compare the data punched in the original set of cards with the data punched in the new set. If the punches in the two sets do not agree, the reproducer stops and an indicator points to the column in which an error occurs.

The card-to-card reproducer is also used to transfer data recorded on a card through the mark-sensed technique into punches in a standard card. You will recall that the mark-sensed record is usually converted to a punched record before the data are processed in other machines of the unit-record system.

The reproducer is also used to transfer hand-punched data recorded in a perforated card into a standard card, in which a punch is recorded in only one column. The hand-punched records on perforated cards are usually converted to a regular punched card before further processing takes place. The reproducer handles this job automatically.

Chapter 7   Recording information in cards   103

HOPPER

Figure 7-17. Reproducer

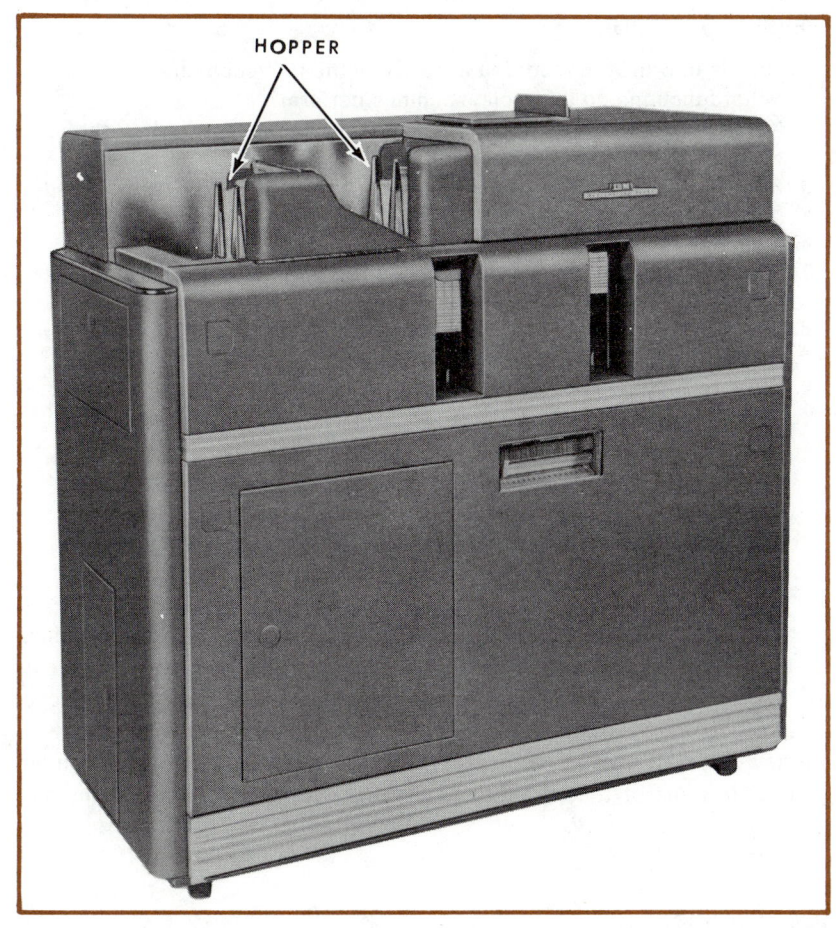

Courtesy of IBM Corporation

    The auxiliary equipment needed to reproduce cards or tapes or to convert from one medium to the other is of little consequence here. It should be noted, though, that duplicate copies may be reproduced by various methods. It is important for you to understand what purposes are served by these duplicate records.

Optical-scanning conversion

    Later in this book you will learn about optical scanners and optical mark page readers. An optical scanner reads printed material. An optical mark page reader reads marks made on sheets of paper. Normally, data read by these machines are converted by a converter to punched cards for further processing. Data recorded in a punched card by a converter are said to be recorded by the indirect method.

REVIEW QUESTIONS

1. How is information recorded in cards by the indirect method?
2. What functions do dual-role machines perform?
3. Name a major advantage of punched paper tape over punched cards.
4. How are data recorded in paper tape?
5. How do edge-punched cards differ from standard cards? Why are edge-punched cards used rather than punched paper tape?
6. Describe the mark-sensed punching method.
7. Why are fewer columns available on a mark-sensed card than on a standard card?
8. What is the function of a tape-to-card converter?
9. What is the purpose of a card reproducer?
10. What two methods of reproduction is the reproducer capable of performing?
11. How is the accuracy of reproduced data checked by the reproducer?

PROOFREADING AND CORRECTING ERRORS MADE IN CARD PUNCHING

The data punched in a card must be accurate or the card is worthless as an input medium. Inasmuch as the human element is involved in card punching, it is not reasonable to expect that cards will always be punched without error. Therefore, a number of methods are used to check the accuracy of data punched in cards. In the discussions that follow, you will note that some of the checking procedures require machinery, others do not.

Card verifier

Punched cards can be checked for accuracy by a *card verifier*, which is illustrated in Figure 7-18. This machine resembles the card punch in appearance. Cards punched on a printing card punch machine are not usually verified by proofreading them because the type is too difficult to read and visual verification is not as accurate as verification by machine.

The function of the verifier is to check rather than punch data into cards. The operator of the verifier feeds the punched cards into the machine. Using the same source documents from which the original cards were punched, the operator strikes the same keys on the verifier that have been or should have been struck when the cards were originally punched. As the keys of the verifying machine are struck, a metal plunger passes through (senses) the holes that were originally punched in the card. If the verifying operation detects a hole in the card that has been incorrectly punched, an error is indicated by a notch on the top of the incorrectly punched column. Note the notch at the top of the card indicating an error in Figure 7-19. A card containing an error usually is repunched on the card punching machine.

Chapter 7   Recording information in cards   105

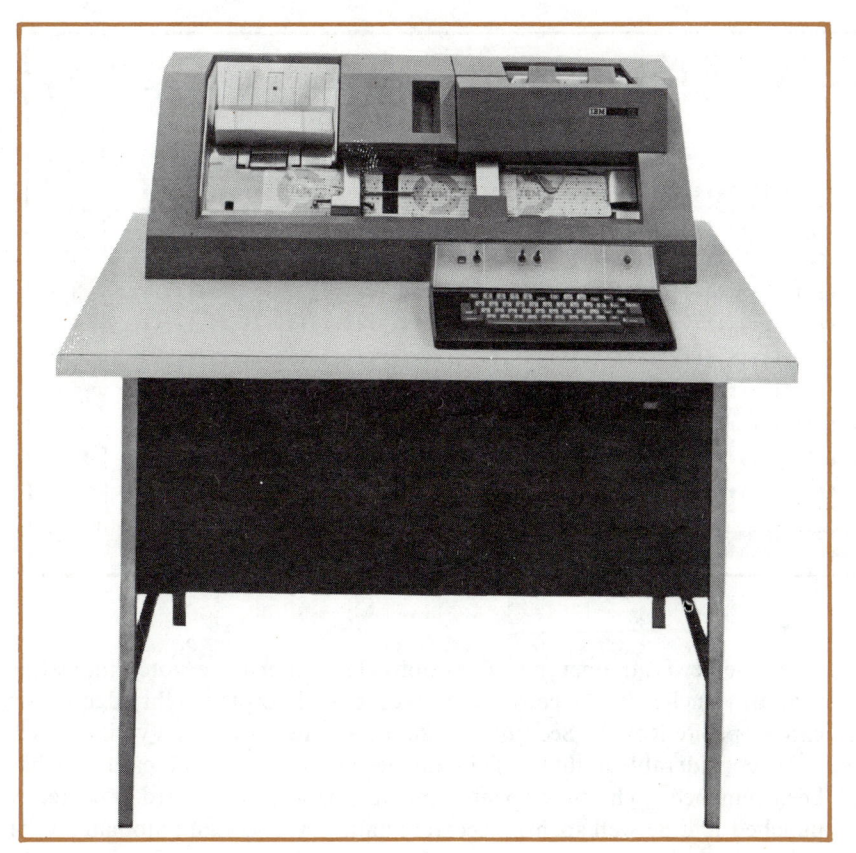

Figure 7-18. IBM 59 card verifier

Courtesy of IBM Corporation

Figure 7-19. Error-notched card

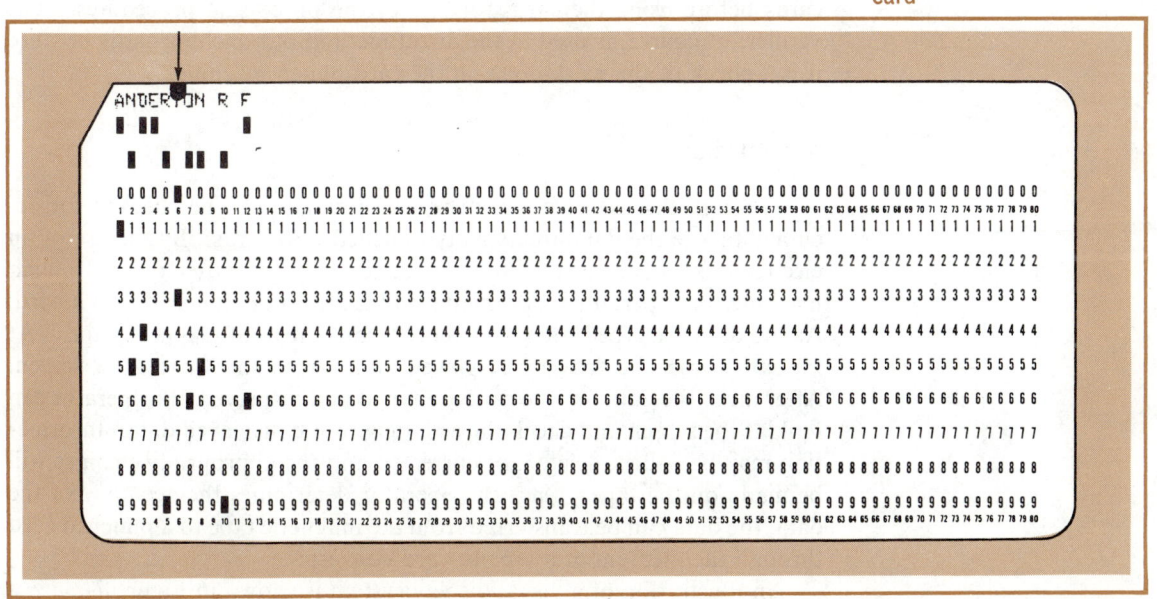

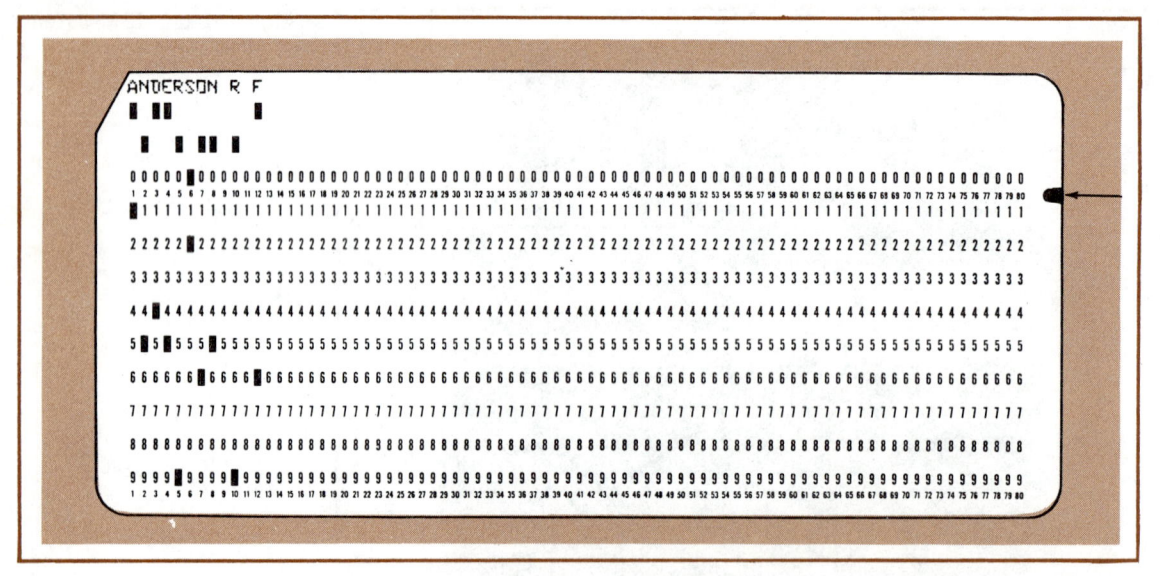

Figure 7-20. Verified card

If the verifying operation does not detect an error, a notch indicating that all punches in the card are correct is made on the right edge of the card opposite Row 1. See Figure 7-20 for an illustration of a verified card.

A considerable amount of time is needed to verify each card that has been punched. The time spent to make sure that each card is correctly punched is time well spent. Incorrect data that enter an automated data processing cycle create problems that are difficult if not impossible to overcome. It is much easier to check the accuracy of data punched in cards before using the cards for any of the processing procedures. The verifier, of course, is used in the direct method of punching cards because it is a check of the work done on the card punch machine.

Visual display

Through the use of visual display units, data can be checked for accuracy before the data are actually punched into cards. By the use of an electronic keyboard similar to that found on a typewriter or card punch machine, the operator types the data that are to be punched into a card. As the data are typed, they are recorded on a strip of magnetic tape. At the same time, the data are displayed on a screen similar to a TV screen. After all of the data for one card are typed and displayed, the operator can look at the screen and check the accuracy of the displayed data. Information may be added, deleted, or corrected and the appropriate changes will be made on the tape. Once the operator determines the accuracy of the data, the data can be transferred from the magnetic tape to a punched card through the medium of a tape-to-card converter.

An illustration of a visual display system is shown in Figure 7-21.

Chapter 7   Recording information in cards   107

Courtesy of Viatron Computer Systems

Figure 7-21. Visual display system (Viatron System 21)

Checking the print

If a printing card punch is used to punch a card, the printed interpretation at the top of the card may be read for accuracy. If an error is detected in the printed copy, the card has been punched incorrectly. Because the type is difficult to read, this method of proofreading is not commonly used and visual verification is not as accurate as verification by machine. If a card is punched by the indirect method of punching, the copy appearing on the document can be checked for accuracy. As is true of the printing card punch, an error in the copy on the document is an indication that the card is punched incorrectly. Cards incorrectly punched are corrected before being used for further processing.

Correction seals

Minor errors in a punched card that is to be used only once or twice are sometimes corrected with correction seals. The seals are small squares of tape, similar to scotch tape, that are placed over the incorrect punch or punches in the card. Correction seals are not usually used on cards that will be processed several times.

SUMMARY

Information from source documents is punched into cards, a machine-language medium, before processing takes place. Either the direct or indirect process may be used. In the direct method, a card punch machine is used. The card punch has a keyboard that is very similar to that found on a standard typewriter. Card punch machines come in a variety of models. Some punch only numeric data; some punch numeric and alphabetic data; some automatically print an interpretation of the punches at the top of the card; some are small and portable, requiring manual manipulation.

Standard card punch machines are equipped with a number of time-saving devices. These include a duplicate key for duplicating the punches in a card at the reading station into another card at the punching station. A skip key assists the operator in moving from one punching field to another. A program card prepared separately for each job handles skipping, spacing, repeating, and shifting from numeric to alphabetic positions automatically. The program card is of standard size. The punches in it control the operations listed above.

Some card punch machines are equipped with a special key which automatically determines and punches the number of zeros needed in the unused columns of a numeric field. The key works in conjunction with a properly prepared program card.

In the indirect method of punching, the cards are punched while some business document is being prepared. Only desired data are punched in the cards.

Cards are also available in which data may be recorded with a graphite pencil. Generally, the pencil marks are converted to punched holes by a reproducer. Once information has been recorded in a card by the punched card method or by use of a graphite pencil, the reproducer is capable of transferring the information to as many additional cards as are needed.

The verifier is commonly used to check the accuracy of data punched into cards. It is a device on which the holes punched in a card are tested for accuracy, punch by punch. If the verifying key strokes are the same as the original punches, no error is presumed to have been made.

If a printing card punch is used or if cards are punched while some document is being prepared, the printed copy may be proofread. If the document is accurate, it can be assumed that the punches in the cards are also accurate.

REVIEW QUESTIONS

1. Describe the method of utilizing a card verifier to check the accuracy of information punched into a card.
2. How are correctly punched cards identified by a verifier?
3. Why are cards punched on a printing card punch not usually verified by proofreading them, as is done when typewriting?
4. When are correction seals normally used?
5. What is the difference between the direct and the indirect methods of punching cards?

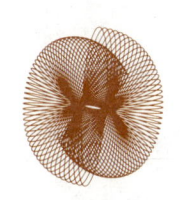

STUDY GUIDE

Complete Study Guide 7 by following the instructions in your **STUDY GUIDES** booklet.

PROJECTS

Complete Projects 7-1, 7-2, 7-3, and 7-4 by following the instructions in your **PROJECTS** booklet.

CHAPTER 8

SORTING AND CLASSIFYING DATA IN CARDS

After the information to be processed has been recorded in cards in a code understandable to the machines, processing can take place. Processing of data consists of recording, sorting, classifying, summarizing, calculating, communicating, and storing. Processing may include any one or all of these operations.

HOW MACHINES READ DATA

As a card is fed through one of the processing machines, each card column passes under a separate sensing device, usually a wire brush. If there is a punched hole in any column, the brush makes contact with a roller known as the *contact roller*. The roller emits an electrical impulse, which the machine is able to read and process as desired. If no hole appears in a column, the brush does not come in contact with the roller and no electrical impulse is created. Figure 8-1 shows a punched card as it passes through the electrical unit of a processing machine. The figure also shows how the electrical impulse is created.

The machine cycle is timed so that electrical impulses are generated at varied intervals as the card passes through the machine. Since punched holes appear in different vertical positions in the card, the impulses are made at different times in the cycle. The impulses then become *timed electrical impulses*. For instance, a punched hole in the 6 row on a card will create an impulse at a different time than a punched hole in the 8 row. If there is more than one hole in a column, two or more impulses are created. Each impulse is distinct to the machine. Each impulse is converted to the desired result. The impulses may be used to punch holes in

Figure 8-1. How an electrical impulse is created

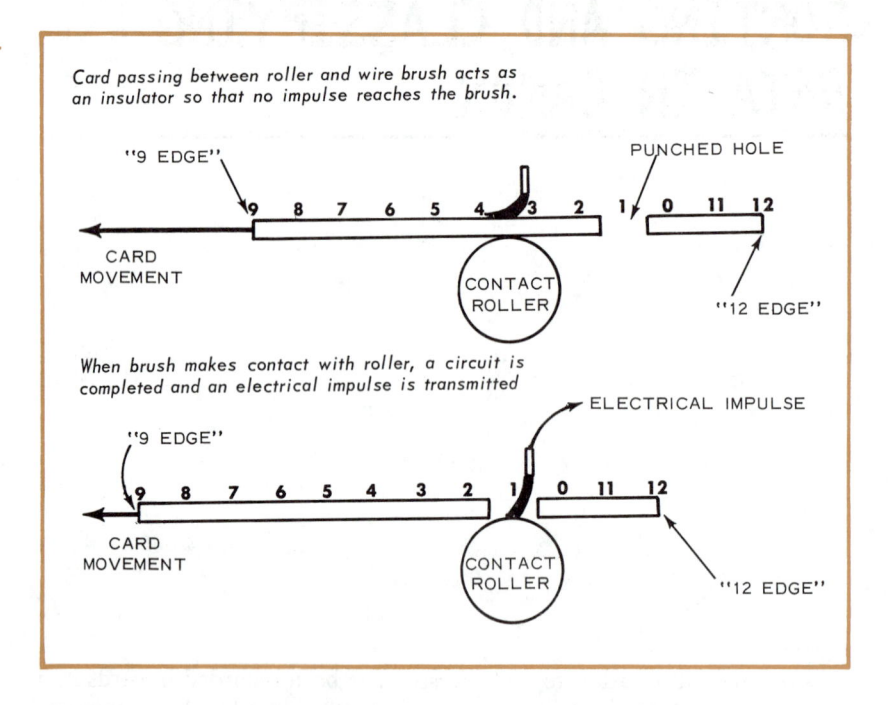

Card passing between roller and wire brush acts as an insulator so that no impulse reaches the brush.

When brush makes contact with roller, a circuit is completed and an electrical impulse is transmitted

another card, to sort cards and group them as desired, or to print lines of information.

The processing cycle of the punched card is as follows:

1. The card is fed into a processing machine, such as a sorter or tabulator.
2. Through timed electrical impulses, the processing machine reads the data punched in the card.
3. The impulses cause the processing machine to sort cards, tabulate and print forms, or make entries to accounts in understandable language.

Some of the newer processing machines are equipped with electronic beams (photoelectric cells) instead of brushes for sensing the holes in cards. This feature greatly increases the speed at which data punched in cards may be processed. The basic operating principles remain the same, however. In order to simplify the explanations, the wire brush will be used in this chapter to illustrate the concept of timed electrical impulses.

SORTING

After recording the data in cards, the cards may be used to prepare a wide variety of reports. For example, from a group of cards similar to the one illustrated in Figure 7-2, p. 88, a list can be prepared of all freshman

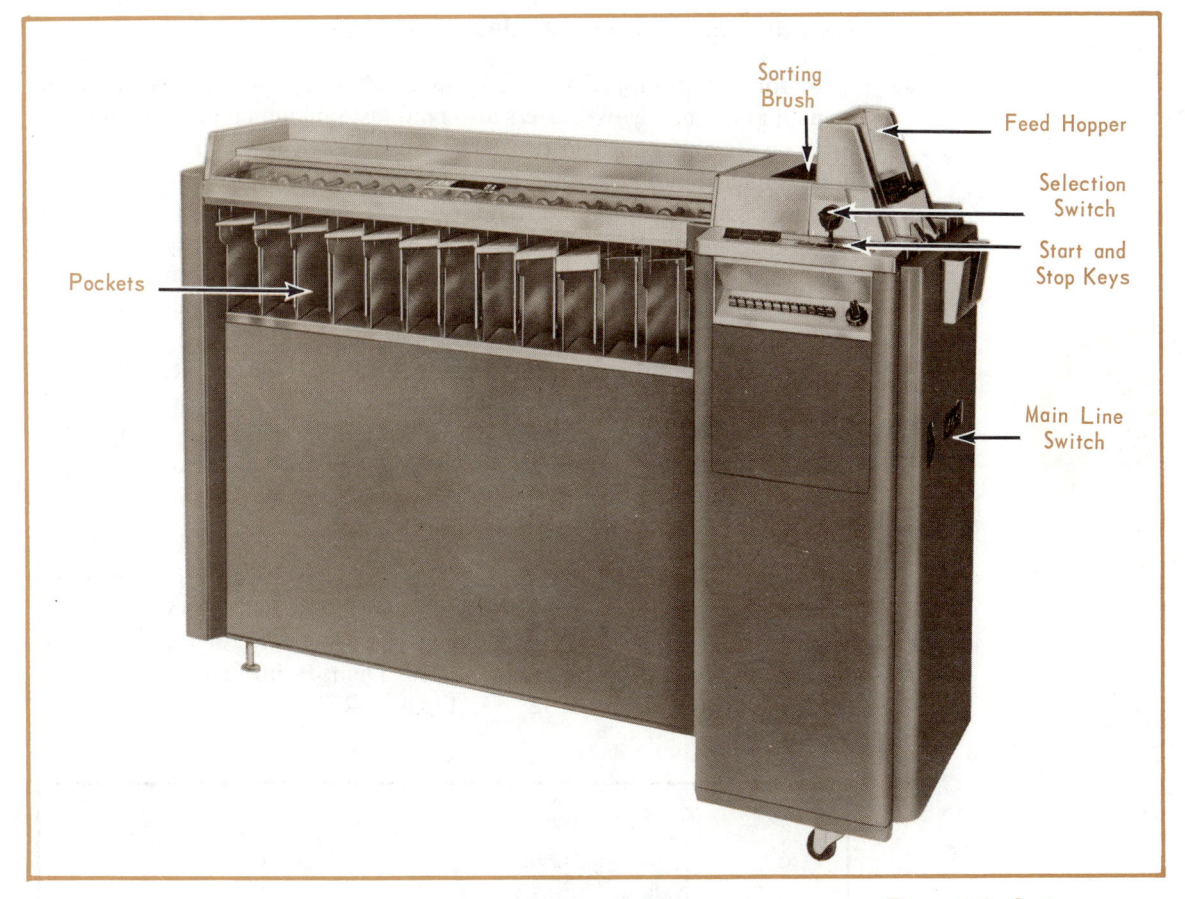

Chapter 8   Sorting and classifying data in cards   113

Figure 8-2. Sorter

students, all male students, all female students, or those enrolled in a particular subject. Before preparing a list of all female students, however, it is necessary to select from all of the cards only those containing the names of female students. From the selected cards, the list of female students can then be prepared. Arranging cards in groups or desired sequences can be done manually, but this process is very slow. A sorter can do the job much more quickly.

The *sorter* illustrated in Figure 8-2 is capable of handling three basic types of sorting or classifying jobs. These may be identified as sequencing, grouping, and selecting. Furthermore, any one of these jobs can be managed by the sorter on either a numeric or an alphabetic basis.

Sequencing is the process of arranging cards in either numeric or alphabetic order. *Grouping* is the process of arranging cards in groups according to the numbers or names punched into them. *Selecting* is the process of drawing out of a deck of cards only those that have a particular name or number in a designated field.

How the sorter processes data

A sorter is equipped with a sensing device that reads only one card column at a time. Most sorters also read just one punch in a column at a time; newer ones can read two. The sensing device, which interprets the holes punched in a card, may be set for any one of the 80 columns of the card by turning a crank or a dial located on the sorter. If the column for which the sensing device has been set contains a numeric punch, the card can be sorted with one pass through the machine. If the column for which the sensing device has been set contains an alphabetic character (two punches per column), the card must usually be passed through the machine twice to complete the sorting process. Generally, then, numeric data can be sorted more quickly than alphabetic data. Figure 8-3 is an illustration of a portion of the sorter showing how the sensing device, a sorting brush in this instance, is positioned for one column of the card. Note the selector handle.

The sorter illustrated in Figure 8-2 has 13 pockets or compartments into which the sorter cards drop. The first pocket (R) is for rejects — usually those cards not having a hole punched in the column on which sorting is taking place. The remaining 12 pockets are for the 12 vertical punching positions on the card — ten for Digits 0 through 9, and two for the Zone Positions 11 and 12. See Figure 8-4.

Figure 8-3. Sort brush and selector handle

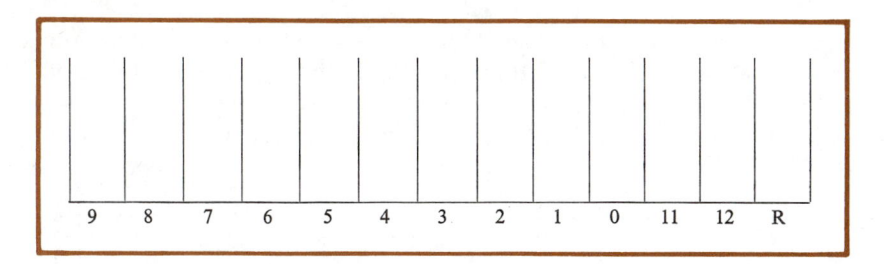

Figure 8-4. Pockets of the card sorter

Numeric code aids sorting

You will recall that a numeric punch can be sorted with only one pass through the machine. To save sorting time, abbreviated numeric codes are used to represent alphabetic data whenever possible. The Letter F is often used in manual operations to represent female. Writing the letter instead of the entire word saves time. The Letter F could be punched in a card and used in much the same manner. To save additional time in the sorting process, however, the Number 1 punched in a specific column of a card could be used as a substitute for the Letter F to represent a female.

Both the Number 1 and the Letter F are codes; however, the first can be sorted by most machines faster than the second. The person using the card must know what the Number 1 represents and in which column of the card it is punched. In the same manner, numeric codes may be assigned to represent the various class levels in your school. For example, the Number 1 may be used as a code to represent the freshman class; the Number 2, the sophomore class; the Number 3, the junior class; and the Number 4, the senior class. Here again, the user must know what the numbers represent and in which columns of the card they are punched.

Sequencing cards by number

Sequencing cards by number is the process of arranging the cards in numeric order. Assume that each student in your school is assigned a locker number and that these numbers extend from 1 through 500. Assume, further, that these numbers are punched in Columns 31, 32, and 33 of the cards and that the names of students to which the lockers have been assigned are punched in Columns 1–20. You wish to arrange these cards in numeric sequence according to locker numbers.

A three-digit numeric field must be passed through the sorter three times in order to arrange the cards in proper sequence. Sorting proceeds from right to left. The cards are sorted on the unit's digit; then the ten's digit; then the hundred's digit.

To sequence the cards on the sorter, you first place all the cards in the hopper *face down*, with the 9-edge forward. The sensing device is set to read the data punched into Column 33. As the cards pass through the

116　Basic components of automated systems　Part 2

sorter, all the cards with the Digit 0 in Column 33 will fall into Pocket 0; those with the Digit 1 will fall into Pocket 1; those with the Digit 2 will fall into Pocket 2; and this process will continue through Digit 9. See Figure 8-5 for an illustration of the way the cards appear after the first sort.

Figure 8-5. Cards sorted on unit's and ten's digits

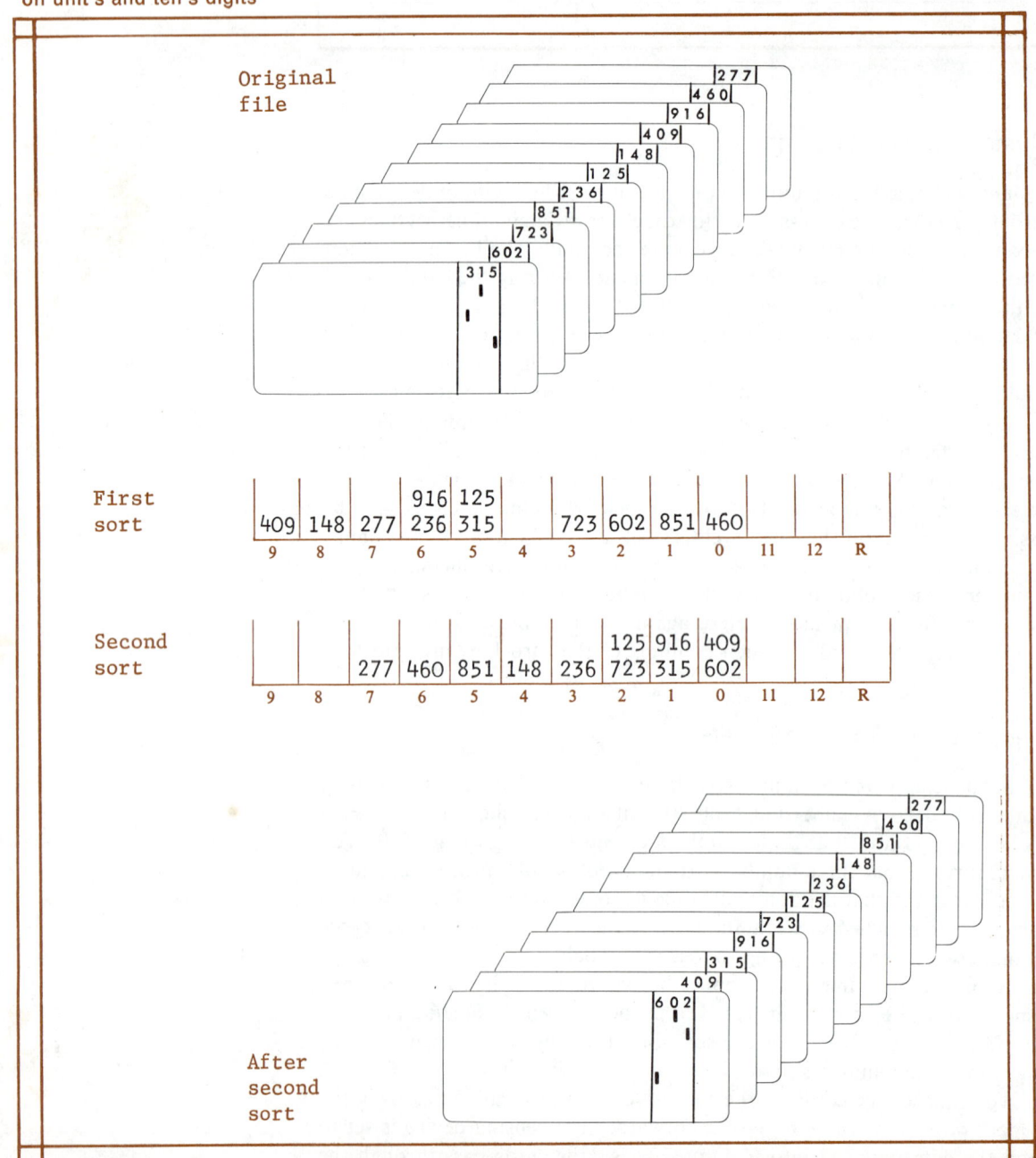

Chapter 8   Sorting and classifying data in cards

On the completion of the first sort, the cards are assembled and placed in the hopper again. The sensing device is set to read the data punched into Column 32. As the cards pass through the sorter, all the cards with the Digit 0 in Column 2 will fall into Pocket 0; those with the Digit 1 will fall into Pocket 1; and the process will be continued through Digit 9. See also Figure 8-5 for an illustration of the way the cards appear after the second sort.

On the completion of the third sort, the cards are removed from the pockets. See Figure 8-6 for an illustration of the way the cards will appear. Observe that they are now in numeric sequence.

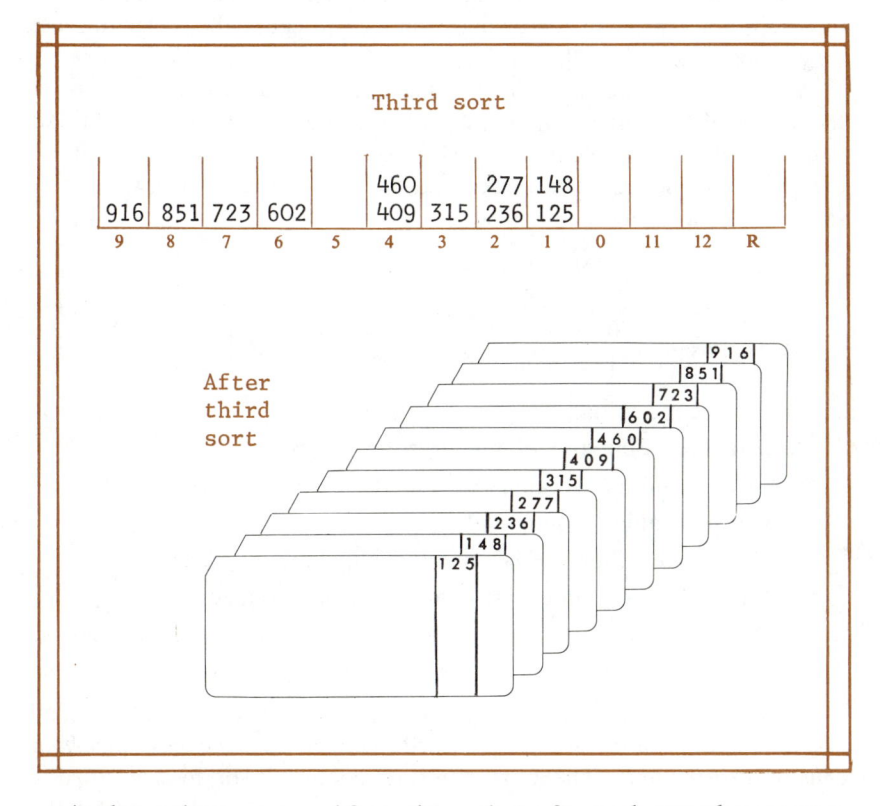

Figure 8-6. Cards sorted on hundred's digits

As the cards are removed from the pockets after each sort, the operator must be careful to remove them in exact order so that the cards from Pocket 1 are behind the cards from Pocket 0, and so on until the cards from Pocket 9 are at the bottom of the deck when looking at the front or face of the cards.

Arranging cards in alphabetic sequence

If alphabetic names are used instead of numbers, as explained in the foregoing discussion, the cards must usually pass through the sorter twice for each letter in the name or for each letter in the abbreviation of the name. Remember that there are two punches in each vertical column to represent a letter — one in the zone position and another in the digit position. In the sorting process, each punch is treated separately. The alphabetic sort can be used, and often is; however, it requires considerably more time than a numeric sort.

If you desire to arrange a deck of cards in alphabetic sequence, you will first sort on the numeric punch in a column and then on the zone punch in that column. As previously mentioned, sorting proceeds from right to left. Only the holes punched in Digits 1 through 9 are sensed in the first step. The cards are then fed through the sorter again on the same column. In this step, however, a switch or dial is moved to cause the sorter to sense only the zone punches (0, 11, 12).

When sorting cards in alphabetic sequence, in order to prepare a list of the names of the students in a school, one can usually sort on the initials and on the first four columns of the last name. This method will, with few exceptions, sequence the cards accurately. Note the manner in which this sequencing job would be handled:

```
        A N D E R S O N              H L
        ↓                             ↓
        0 0 0 0 0 0 0 0 1 1 1 1 1 1 1 1 1 2
Columns → 1 2 3 4 5 6 7 8 9 0 1 2 3 4 5 6 7 8 9 0
```

1. Sort second initial, Column 20, numeric.
2. Sort second initial, Column 20, zone.
3. Sort first initial, Column 19, numeric.
4. Sort first initial, Column 19, zone.
5. Sort fourth column of last name (E), Column 4, numeric.
6. Sort fourth column of last name (E), Column 4, zone.
7. Sort Columns 3, 2, and 1 on numeric and then zone punches, as noted above.

Only first and second initials of students are punched in the cards. Full first and second names are not recorded. *Observe that the least important column is sorted first.* The most important column is sorted last. Sorting progresses from right to left for the first and second initials; then for the first four letters of the last name. Figure 8-7 shows a group of cards arranged alphabetically.

Grouping cards

The sorter can group cards as desired. Assume, for example, that you desire to group cards according to classes: freshmen, sophomores, juniors, and seniors. The cards in Figure 8-7 include a class code for each student in Column 25. Freshmen are designated by 1; sophomores by 2; juniors by 3; and seniors by 4.

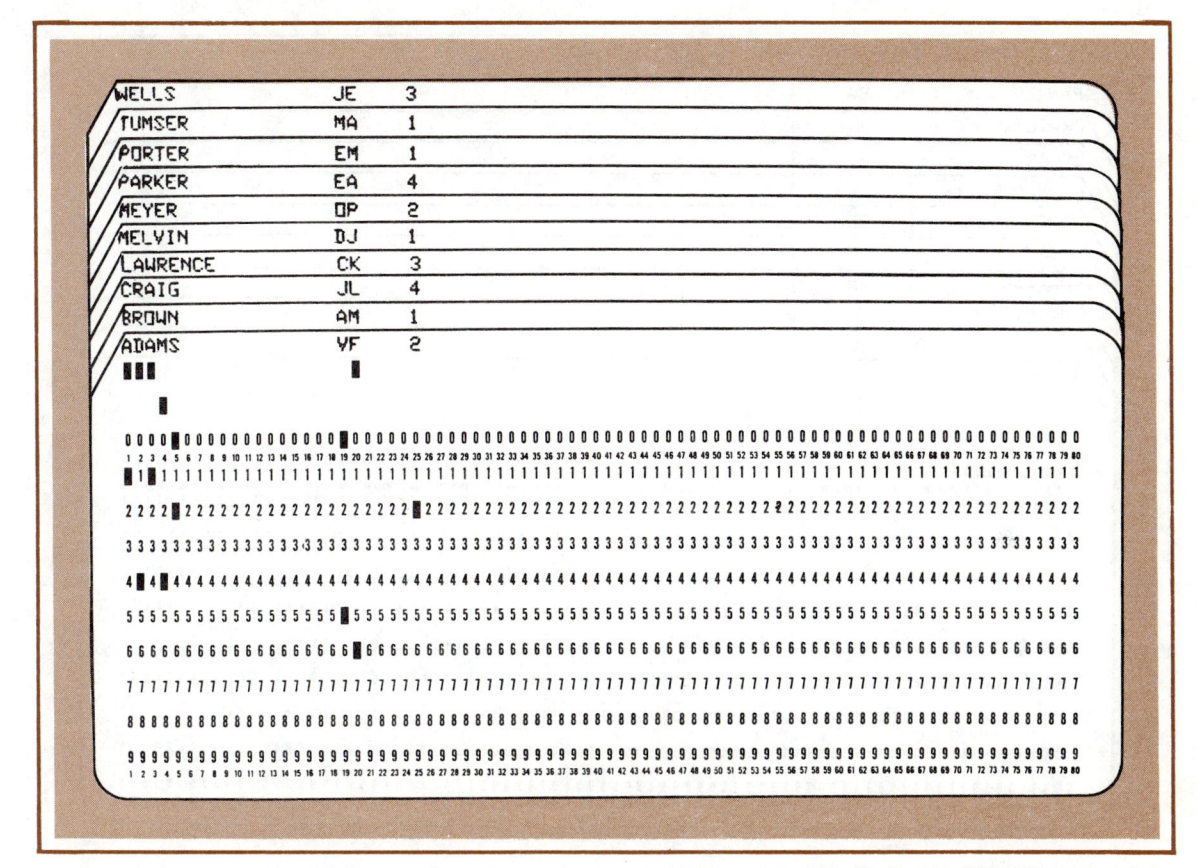

Chapter 8   Sorting and classifying data in cards   119

```
WELLS       JE   3
TUMSER      MA   1
PORTER      EM   1
PARKER      EA   4
MEYER       OP   2
MELVIN      DJ   1
LAWRENCE    CK   3
CRAIG       JL   4
BROWN       AM   1
ADAMS       YF   2
```

Figure 8-7. Punched cards arranged alphabetically

To group the cards by classes, all the cards are placed in the card hopper of the sorter, face down, with the 9 edge forward. The sensing device is set to read the data punched in Column 25. As the cards pass through the sorter, all the cards with the Number 1 punched in Column 25 will fall into Pocket 1; those with the Number 2 will fall into Pocket 2; those with the Number 3 will fall into Pocket 3; and those with the Number 4 will fall into Pocket 4. See Figure 8-8 for an illustration of the way the cards will appear after they are grouped.

If the students' names were in alphabetic sequence before the cards were grouped, each group of cards would be in alphabetic order. If not, they would be mixed. The sorter is not capable of grouping and sequencing cards in one operation.

Selecting cards

Selecting is a process whereby the cards containing a certain digit or a series of digits in a designated field are separated from the other cards in a deck. If you desire to select from a deck of cards only those for all freshman

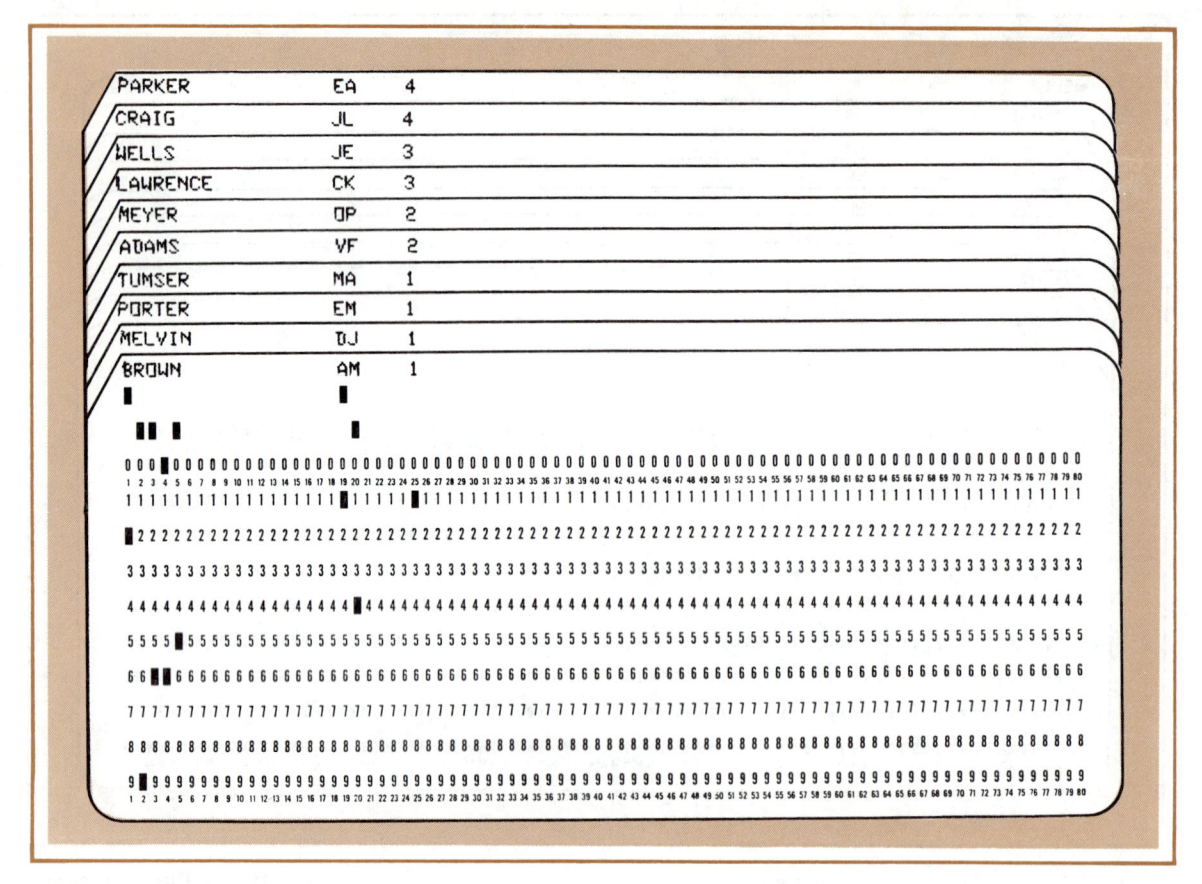

120   Basic components of automated systems   Part 2

Figure 8-8. Cards grouped by class number

students, the sorter can handle this job for you. For the cards in Figure 8-7, the sensing device must first be set on Column 25, the column in which class codes are punched: 1 for freshmen, 2 for sophomores, etc. The switches designating the 12 vertical positions on the card will be suppressed, except for the Digit 1.

All the cards are placed in the card hopper, face down, with the 9 edge forward. The cards for freshman students will drop into Pocket 1; all other cards will fall into the Reject Pocket. The cards for freshman students may be used to prepare such reports as are needed. See Figure 8-9.

Sorting shortcuts

Mention must be made here of the desirability of using numeric codes to identify alphabetic information. Not only may space be saved on the card, but also the job of sorting the cards is simplified.

When large numbers of cards must be sorted, a technique known as *block sorting* is sometimes used to release cards in groups for processing

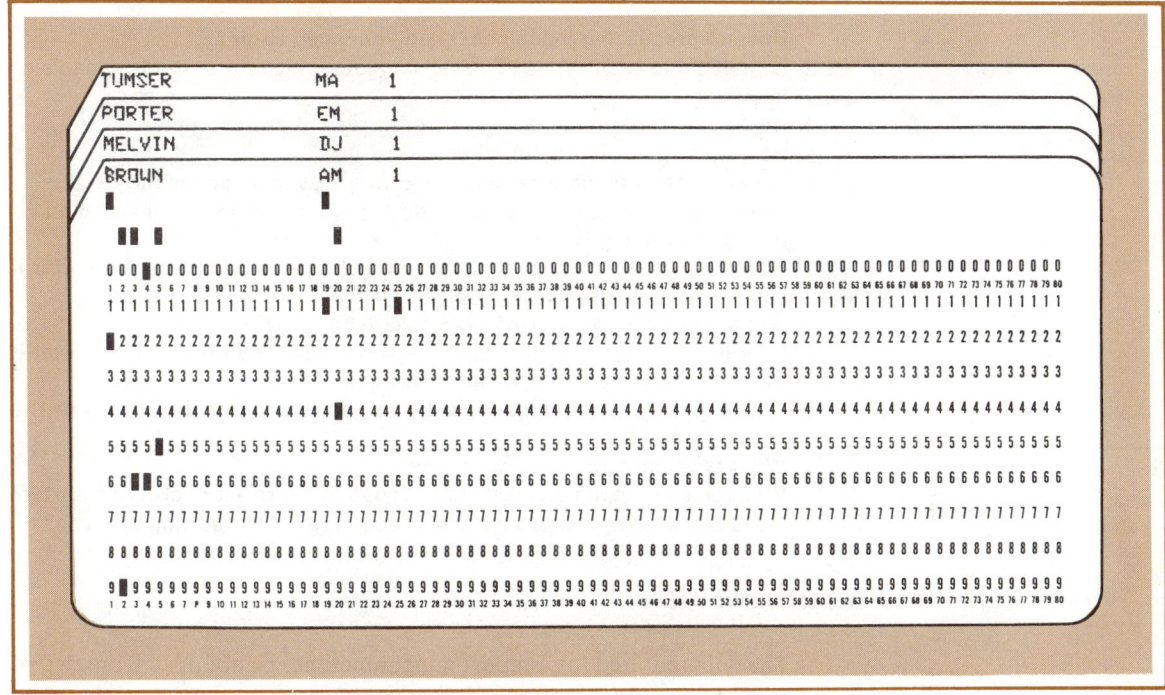

Chapter 8   Sorting and classifying data in cards

Figure 8-9. Selecting cards

by other units before all the cards are run through the sorter. Sorting time is not shortened. The overall time for processing the cards by the sorter and other units may be reduced considerably, however, because the other units may be employed as soon as the first block of cards has been sorted. Another advantage is that block sorting reduces re-sort time if errors are found, as only the incorrect group needs to be re-sorted.

In block sorting, the first sort is made on the high-order (leftmost) digit to break the total deck into subdecks. For example, if there are 9,000 cards to be sorted, the total deck can be divided into nine subdecks by sorting first on the leftmost digits of the four-digit field. The first sort will divide the original deck into subdecks as follows: 0001–0999, 1000–1999, 2000–2999, 3000–3999, 4000–4999, and similarly to the last card. Then each subdeck may be sorted separately in the normal manner — from right to left. As soon as the first subdeck, 0001–0999, is in order, this subdeck can be released for processing on another machine, such as the tabulator. The tabulator may prepare a printed report with cards 0001–0999 while the rest of the subdecks are being sorted. This procedure will permit handling the blocks (subdecks) in a manner that will permit continuous operation of the tabulator.

Block sorting thus enables several operators to work on a sorting job at one time and releases the first batch of sorted cards for processing by some other unit. By making more efficient use of time and equipment, block sorting reduces the overall time needed to produce a finished report when large numbers of cards must be sorted.

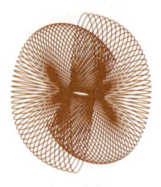

REVIEW QUESTIONS

1. How do processing machines "read" punched cards?
2. List the three basic types of classifying jobs which the sorter is capable of handling
3. How many card columns does a sorter read at any one time?
4. How many pockets are found on the sorter?
5. Why can numeric data be sorted more quickly than alphabetic data?
6. When sorting cards numerically, do you start with the left-hand digit or the right-hand digit? Why?
7. How many times must the cards usually be passed through the sorter if you are sorting a three-digit numeric field?
8. Are separate pockets provided for zone punches?
9. How many times must the cards usually be passed through the sorter if you are sorting a two-digit alphabetic field?
10. When sorting cards alphabetically, do you begin with the initials or the last name?
11. What is grouping?
12. What types of cards are likely to be found in the reject pocket of a sorter?
13. Does block sorting shorten the time required for the sorting process?

COLLATING

The data required for a report must sometimes be obtained from two or more card files. As a matter of fact, this procedure is the rule rather than the exception. The cards from the two files must be brought together and merged or matched before further processing is possible.

A *collator*, which is illustrated in Figure 8-10, is capable of performing several functions: (1) It can merge two decks of cards in numeric sequence; (2) it can match the cards from two files having the same numeric data

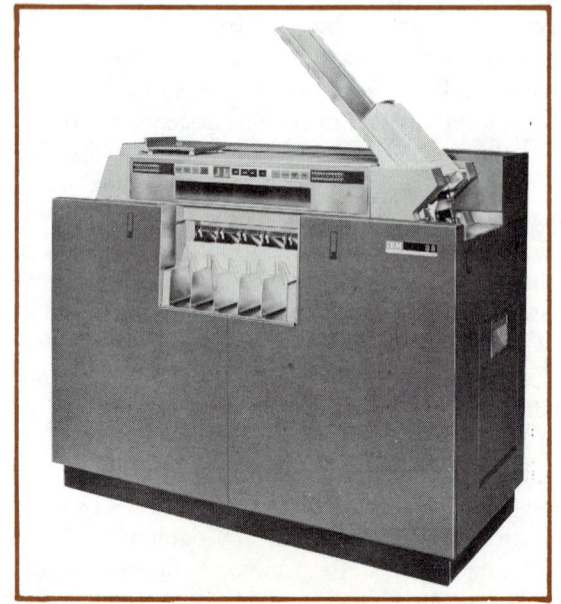

Figure 8-10. Card collator

Chapter 8   Sorting and classifying data in cards   123

punched in them in a particular field; (3) It can select from a deck of cards only those cards having a certain number or a series of numbers in a specified field; (4) It can check a file of cards to make sure that they are in sequential order. The collator is thus a very versatile machine. Even more surprising is the fact that it can combine some of these operations into a single, simultaneous one. The collator is programmed with a control panel.

Merging

In the *merging process*, two decks of cards arranged in sequential order are combined into one deck. The cards in the combined deck will also appear in sequence. This process is illustrated in Figure 8-11. The cards can be merged on a sorter but a collator can handle the job faster because

Figure 8-11.   Example of merging

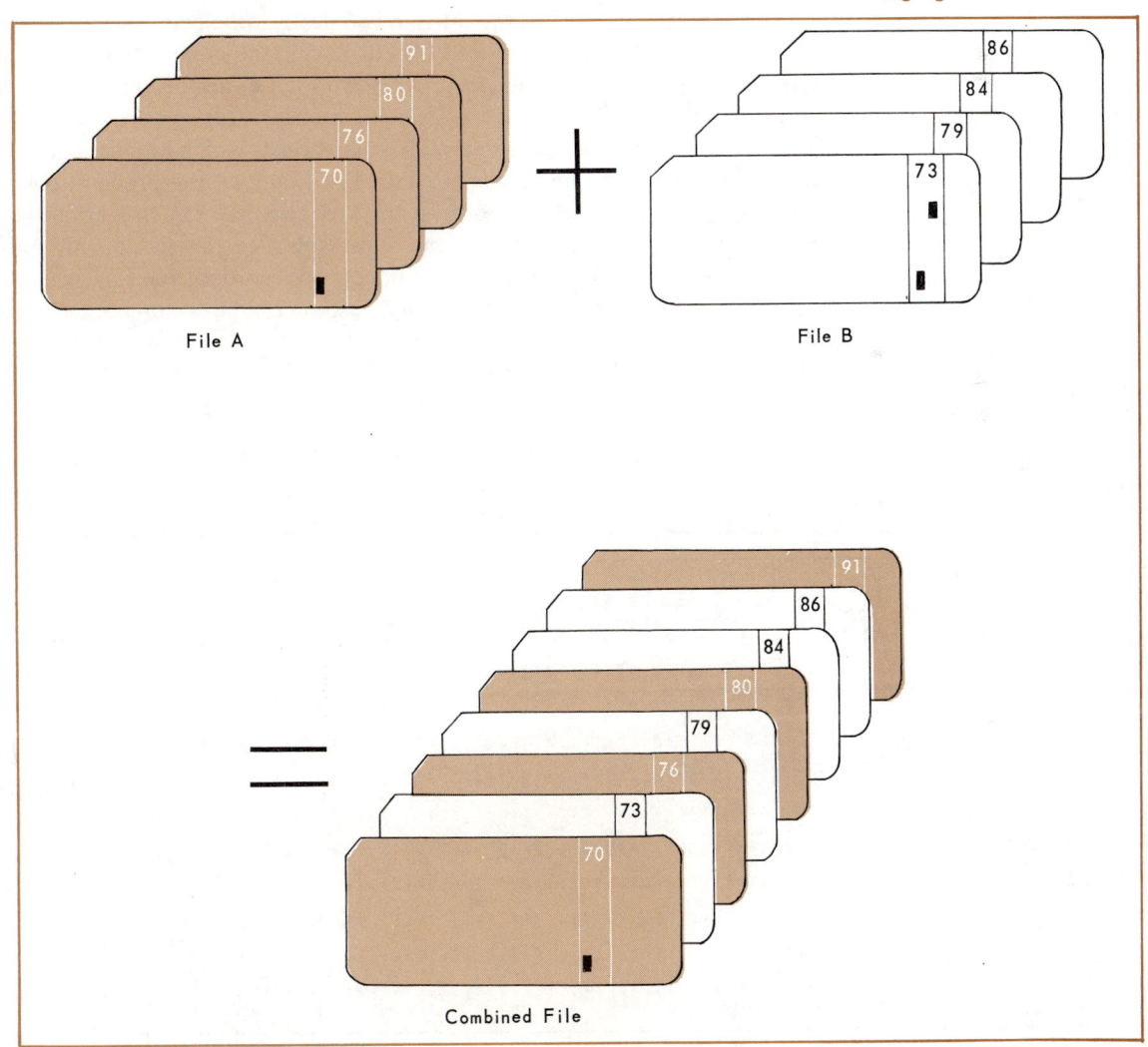

it works with two decks of cards at the same time and is able to compare an entire field in each card.

For an example of merging, assume that the master cards for customers appear in two decks. The cards in each file appear in sequential order by customer number. A master card is illustrated in Figure 8-12. A report is to be prepared listing all the customers in sequential order by customer number. Before the list can be prepared, the cards in the two decks must be brought together (merged). The collator can handle this operation. Each deck of cards is placed in a separate hopper on the collator. When the job is completed, the cards appear in numeric order in a single pocket.

Matching

In the *matching process*, the cards in two decks, which are each arranged in sequential order, are compared. Cards having the same data in a designated field are matched; matched cards are then either brought together (merged) or held in separate stacks. Unmatched cards in either deck are separated from the matched decks. Matched cards which are merged into one deck are said to be *match-merged*. For example, the preparation of monthly statements for customers may require the match-merging of (a) *master cards*, in which names and addresses of customers appear, with (b) *sales detail cards*, in which charges have been recorded, and (c) *payments detail cards*, in which receipts from each customer have been recorded. All three types of cards are required to prepare the customers' monthly statements, as was explained in Chapter 6.

Figure 8-12. Master card including customer's account number, name, and address

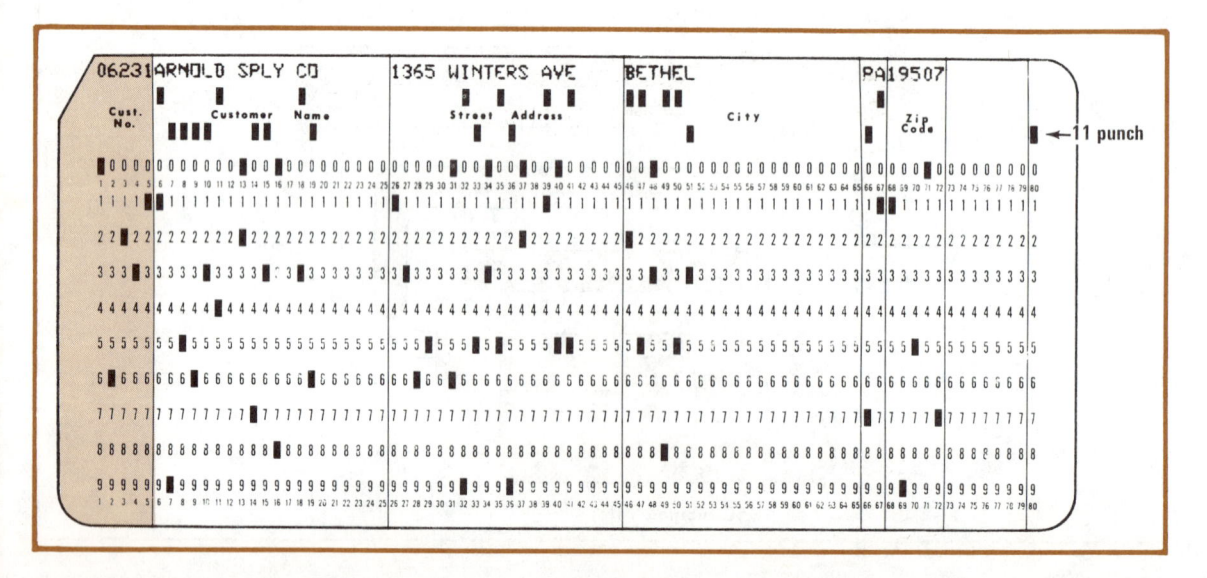

Chapter 8   Sorting and classifying data in cards   125

Figure 8-12 illustrates the type of information that might appear in a master card. This card contains the customer's account number, his name, and his complete address. This semipermanent information will be used regularly to produce reports. Figure 8-13 illustrates sales detail cards and a receipts detail card that would be match-merged with the master card.

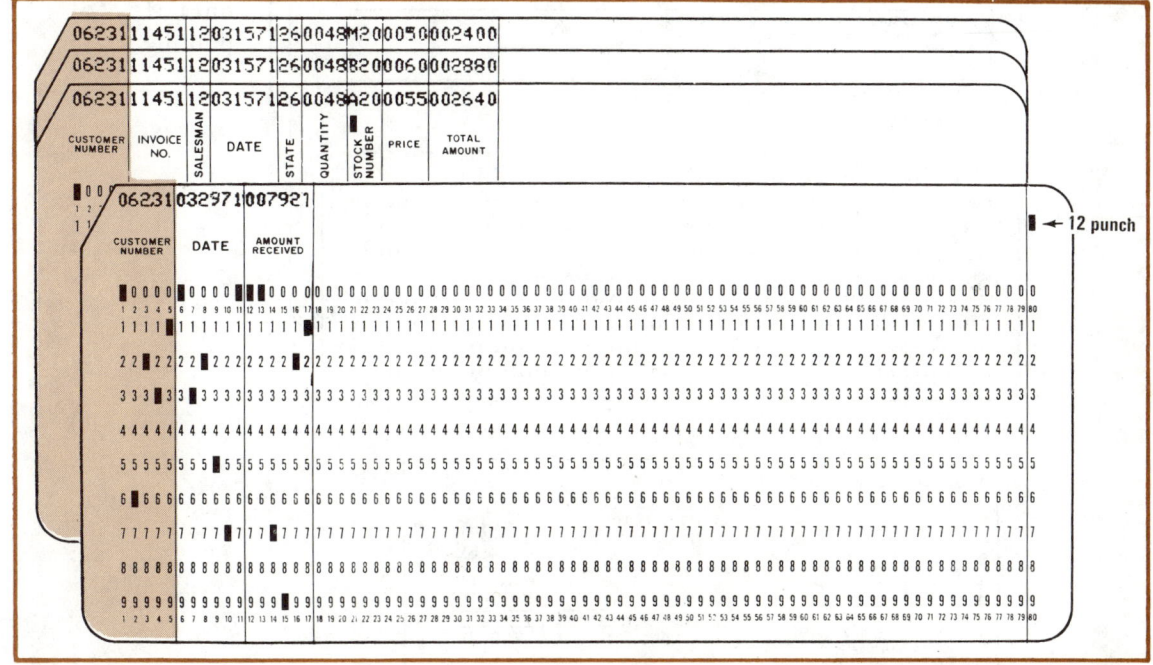

Figure 8-13. Sales and payments detail cards that would be merged with master card

There are often several detail cards for each master card. The master card would appear first; corresponding detail cards would follow it. The sales detail cards contain the customer's account number plus information relative to the sale of merchandise. The receipts detail cards contain the customer's account number plus information concerning payments made. Study the illustrations carefully and note that the customer's account number appears in the three sets of cards. The three sets of cards may thus be match-merged on the basis of these account numbers to produce the monthly statement shown in Figure 8-14. The master card provides the information appearing at the top of the statement; the detail cards provide the information recorded in the vertical columns. Balance cards were omitted from this illustration.

Keep in mind that the collator can match-merge cards by comparing entire fields of data in one operation, not column by column.

Basic components of automated systems — Part 2

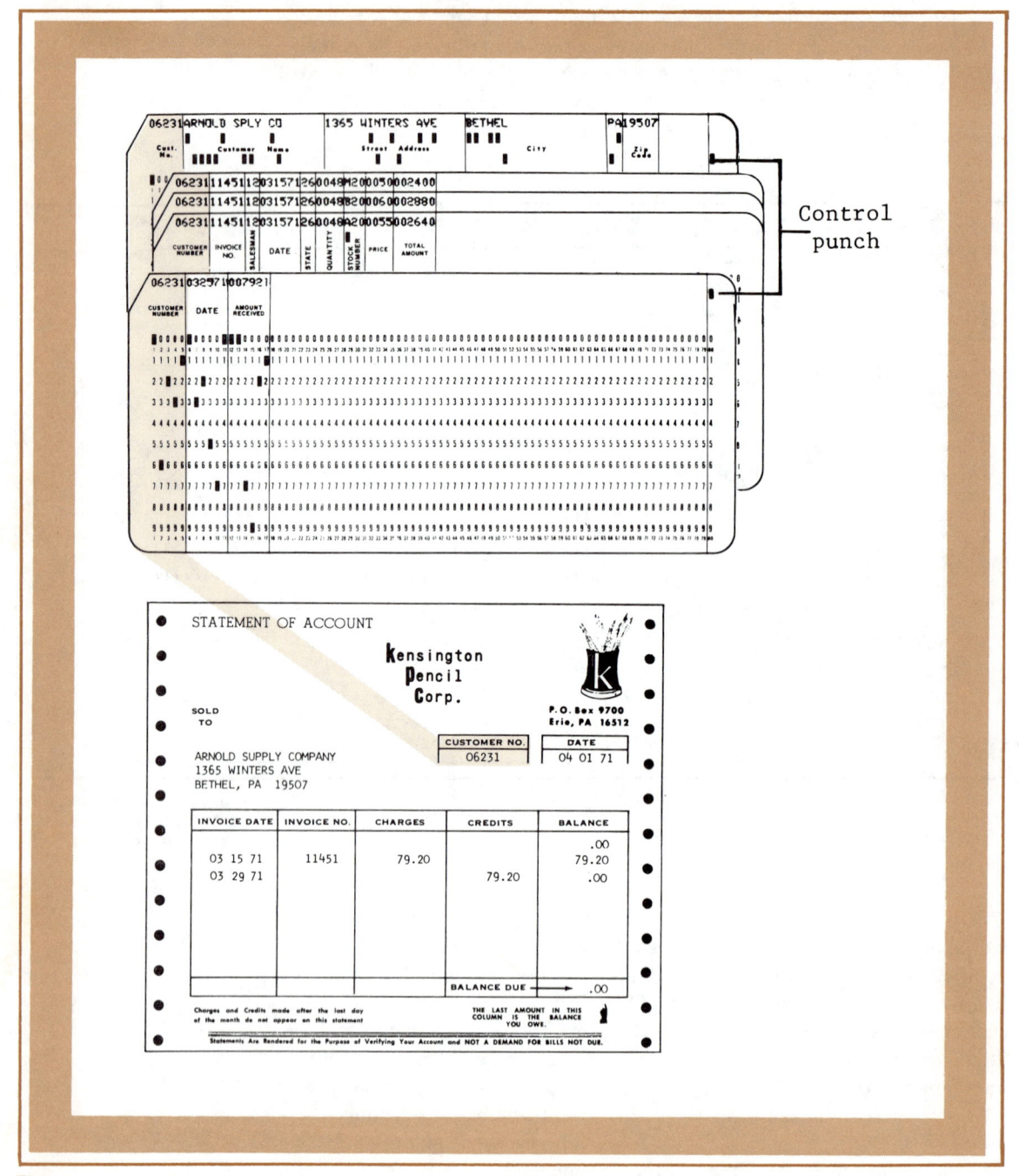

Figure 8-14. Statement produced by merged cards

In Figure 8-14 above, you will note that the sales detail and payments detail cards both use the same field for the customer's account number that is used in the master card. Since the same card columns are used for the customer's account field, the three types of cards can be matched to produce the monthly statement illustrated. The master card provides the information shown at the top of the statement. The detail cards provide the information in the vertical columns.

As mentioned briefly in Chapter 6, certain punches in a card are often used to control the action of processing machines and thus the punches are referred to as *control punches*. The X or 11 punch and the Y or 12 punch are often used as control punches. The X and the Y are used for identification purposes only. If a punch is made by an IBM 29 card punch machine in the 11 position on the card, the interpretation of the punch is not the Letter X. The interpretation of a punch in the 11 position is a hyphen (-). The interpretation of a punch in the 12 position is not the Letter Y. The interpretation of a punch in the 12 position is an ampersand (&). Because of the confusion caused by referring to control punches in the 11 and 12 positions of the cards as X and Y punches, the operators of machines in the automated data processing systems are more and more designating these punches as 11 and 12 punches.

To distinguish one type of card from another, identifying control punches may be placed in one column of any two of the three cards. In Figure 8-14, an 11 punch has been placed in Column 80 of the master card. This punch is not needed in matching the cards. It is needed in order to instruct the tabulating machine to arrange the customer's name and address in the order shown on the statement. The lack of a special identifying punch in the sales detail card instructs the machine to print the data on one line in specific columns as illustrated. The 12 punch in Column 80 of the payments detail card instructs the machine to print the data on one line in other columns. In this manner, the purchases are tabulated as charges to the customer's account and the payments are tabulated as credits.

It would be possible to place control punches in all three cards. Each punch would be used for a specific and different purpose, depending upon the wiring of the control panel. A 12, 11, or Zero zone punch might be used.

Selecting

In the selecting process, cards containing a certain number or a series of numbers in a designated field are separated from the other cards in a deck. For example, a card with the desired number, such as the class number, punched in a specified field, is placed in front of the deck. All cards with the same class number in the same field will then fall into one pocket of the collator. All other cards will fall into another pocket. The collator can also select all cards having numbers higher or lower than a given number in a specified field. For example, from a deck of cards all the cards may be selected for students who have a birthday on a certain date. On the other hand, all the cards may be selected for those who have a birthday before or after a given date.

Sequence checking

Sequence checking is the process of making sure that a deck of cards is in alphabetic or numeric order in a particular field of data. The collator is capable of making this check. This is an important step in the processing cycle of lengthy reports involving a great many cards. Consider the preparation of a report from a deck of 50,000 cards on the tabulator or computer. A card out of sequence might not be found until the report were almost complete. The cards would have to be rerun — at considerable expense. The error could have been eliminated by sequence checking the cards on the collator beforehand.

SUMMARY

The punched holes in a card represent a language that processing machines can understand. These holes are read electronically with the aid of sensing devices, usually wire brushes, or, in some of the newer machines, by photoelectric cells.

The sorter is a common processing machine. It can sequence cards numerically or alphabetically. It can group cards according to a specific classification. It can also select from a large number of cards only those that are needed for a particular report. The holes in a card are sensed in a single card column at a time. Sorting cards on a card field consisting of several columns thus requires the operator to run the cards through the sorter a number of times. The sorter illustrated in this chapter is programmed by a dial, which the operator turns to the column number on which sorting is to take place. The cards fall into pockets identified by the digit and zone punches in a card column, or into a reject pocket if there are no punches in a column on which the dial has been set.

Processing jobs requiring only the sequencing, selecting, or grouping of cards can be completed on the sorter. If calculations must be made or if printed reports are needed, processing will have to go beyond the sorter.

The collator is an advanced sorter. It can sequence and merge two decks of cards. It can check a file of cards to make sure they are in sequential order. It can match or match-merge cards from two files each having the same data punched in a particular field. It can also select from a deck of cards only those having certain data punched in a specified field. It is thus a versatile machine and is widely used in processing data automatically. The collator is programmed by a control panel that is wired manually and attached to it for each job on which it is used.

Chapter 8 Sorting and classifying data in cards

REVIEW QUESTIONS
1. Name the four functions of a collator.
2. What is merging?
3. Why can a collator merge two decks of cards into a single deck faster than a sorter can?
4. Give a reason why you might want to match-merge cards from two separate decks when you process data.
5. What three types of selection jobs can the collator perform?
6. Which machine is capable of performing the larger number of operations and the more complicated operations — the sorter or the collator?

STUDY GUIDE
Complete Study Guide 8 by following the instructions in your STUDY GUIDES booklet.

PROJECTS
Complete Projects 8-1 and 8-2 by following the instructions in your PROJECTS booklet.

PART 3

UNIT-RECORD SYSTEM

Chapter 9 PRINTING, CALCULATING, AND PREPARING REPORTS

Chapter 10 THE CONTROL PANEL

CHAPTER 9

PRINTING, CALCULATING, AND PREPARING REPORTS

The terminating steps of any data processing system consist of the making of calculations and the printing of data on forms or reports. When a punched card is used as the input medium, printing, calculating, and preparing of reports can be handled in a variety of ways and by various machines.

INTERPRETER

In Chapter 6, you learned that a printing card punch may be used to print on the top of the card an interpretation of the punches. Another machine, the *interpreter*, is available and may be used to print on the punched card the interpretations of the data already punched in it.

An interpreter differs from a printing card punch in that the interpreter can be wired to print in various locations on the punched card the interpretations of the punches in the card. A printing card punch, on the other hand, can print the interpretation only above the column in which the punch is made.

You will recall that a punched card is often used as a business form. Therefore, the interpretation of the data punched in the card must be printed on the card in the appropriate places in order to make the form meaningful. Simple printing jobs of this nature can be handled by the interpreter. More complicated printing jobs or jobs that involve mathematical calculations are handled by other machines. An interpreter is illustrated in Figure 9-1.

133

Figure 9-1. Interpreter

Courtesy of IBM Corporation

TABULATOR

A *tabulator* is a machine which reads information from one medium only — punched cards. By means of a control panel, it performs simple calculations of addition and subtraction and produces printed lists, tables, and totals on separate forms or on continuous paper. Actually, the tabulator is made up of three units — a reading unit, a printing unit, and a calculating unit. All three units are within the same machine; however, each performs a different function. Figure 9-2 illustrates a tabulator.

Reading unit

The *reading unit* senses the holes punched in the cards entering the tabulator and relays meaningful messages to the calculating and printing units in the form of timed electrical impulses. According to the wishes of the operator, all or just selected parts of the information recorded in a card may be read by the reading unit and then relayed to one of the other units.

Calculating unit

The *calculating unit* of the tabulator can add and subtract. The amounts in several fields of a card may be accumulated and totaled in one operation.

Chapter 9   Printing, calculating, and preparing reports

Figure 9-2. Tabulator

Courtesy of IBM Corporation

For example, a report can be prepared, showing the total sales for each salesperson, the total sales by department, and the total sales for each branch store. Furthermore, this report can be prepared in a single operation. If calculations are to be made, the numeric data will be relayed to the calculating unit from the reading unit.

Printing unit

The *printing unit* prints the alphabetic and numeric data punched in cards. This unit also prints the results of calculations performed in the calculating unit. The paper on which the printing unit prints may be plain or preprinted with business-form headings. One or more copies may be made simultaneously through the use of carbon paper. Continuous assembled forms are usually used to speed up the printing process. Tabulating machines print all the data in a single line simultaneously instead of serially, character by character. Thus, the printing process is very rapid.

Whereas standard punched cards contain information recorded in no more than 80 vertical columns, the printing unit provides a greater number of printing positions. One commonly used model has 120 such positions. The extra columns provide space for the separation of the copy in the various fields and for the insertion of dollar signs and other special characters. The separation of copy and the insertion of special characters is handled by the control panel that can be wired to accommodate a variety of jobs. The control panel is explained in Chapter 10.

Printing operations are of two types: *detail* and *group*. In the *detail printing* operation, information from every card entering the tabulator is printed on a line of the report being prepared. This operation is used when complete information about individual transactions is required. All or part of the information in each card may be printed. The control panel determines the arrangement in which information appears on the report. Amounts appearing in the various cards may be added or subtracted as the cards are fed through the tabulator, and the results of computations may be printed on the forms being prepared. Figure 9-3 illustrates an inventory report in which each receipt or issue of a particular stock item is listed separately. Each transaction appears on a line of the report. Observe, too, that the shipments listed are all for Part No. 5567. Another inventory report could be prepared for all the items of stock received on a certain date. The total could be accumulated by the tabulator and printed at the end of the report.

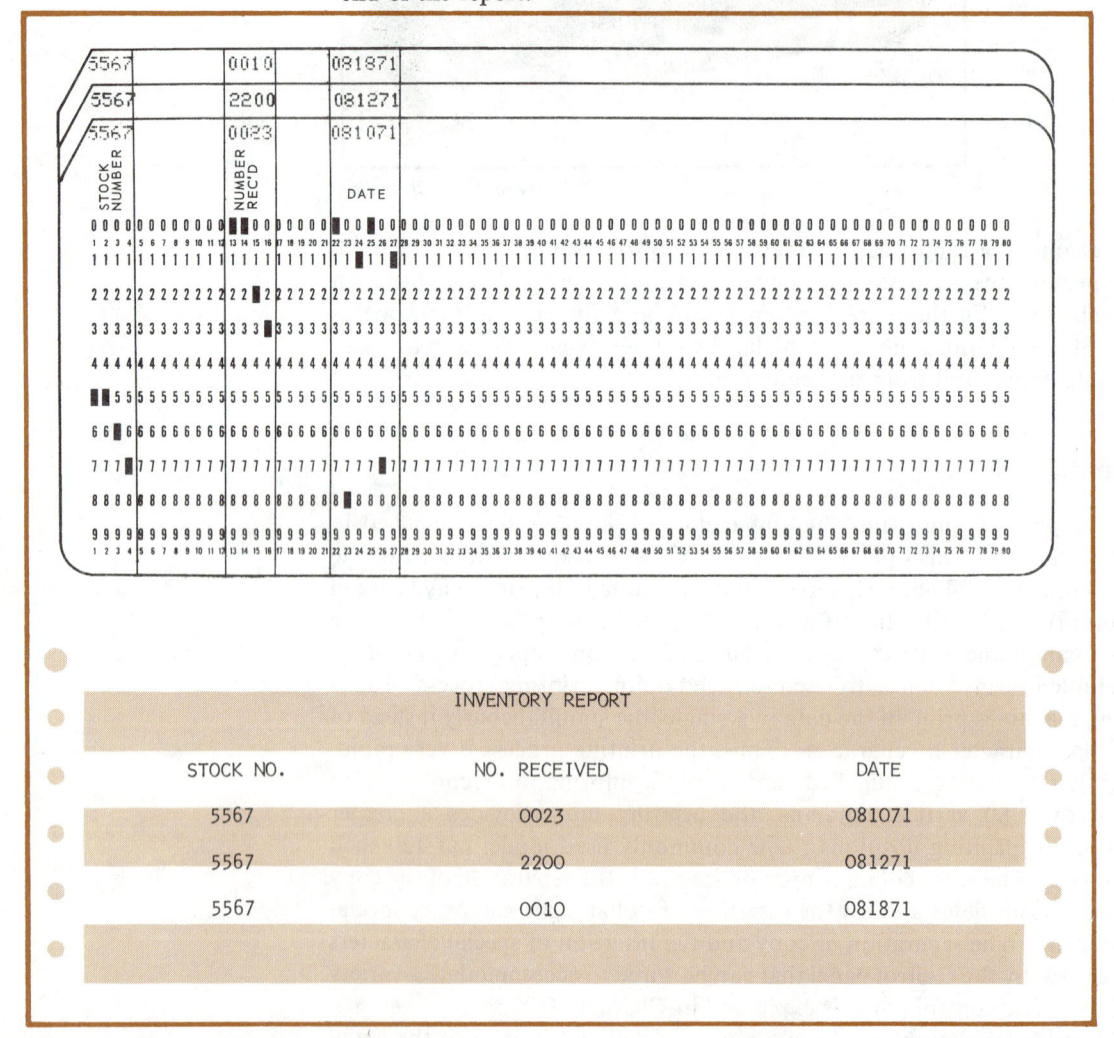

Figure 9-3. Inventory report listing each stock transaction (detail printing)

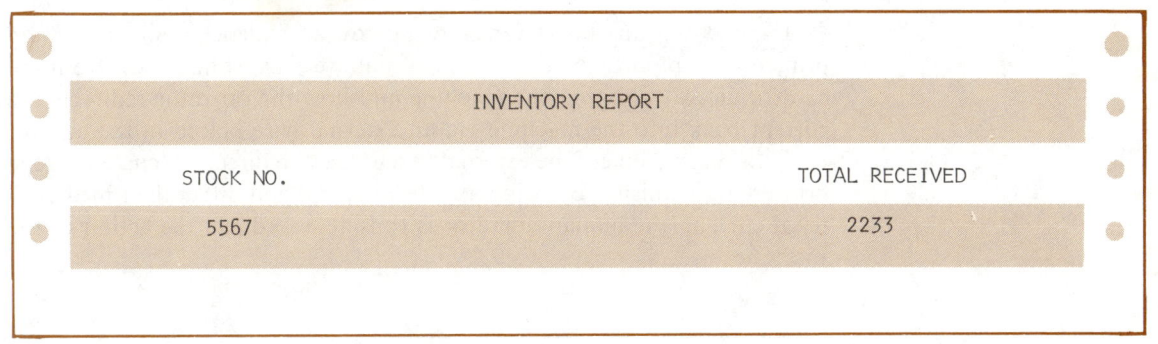

Chapter 9   Printing, calculating, and preparing reports

```
┌─────────────────────────────────────────────────────────────┐
│                                                             │
│         ┌─────────────────────────────────────────┐         │
│         │              INVENTORY REPORT           │         │
│         └─────────────────────────────────────────┘         │
│                                                             │
│             STOCK NO.                TOTAL RECEIVED         │
│         ┌─────────────────────────────────────────┐         │
│         │     5567                        2233    │         │
│         └─────────────────────────────────────────┘         │
│                                                             │
└─────────────────────────────────────────────────────────────┘
```

Figure 9-4. Inventory report in summary form (group printing)

In the *group printing* operation, the data from a group of cards relating to a number of similar transactions are summarized; and only the summary information is printed on the report. Figure 9-4 illustrates an inventory report using the group printing operation. Observe that it provides in summary form the same information provided in Figure 9-3.

Group printing on the tabulator is possible because the tabulator can distinguish one group of cards from another. As cards enter the tabulator, the data in a specified field of the cards are compared. All cards having the same part number pass through the tabulator, but no printing occurs. Only the amounts appearing on these cards enter the calculating unit, where computations are made. Each time a card passes through the reading unit, the part numbers are compared. When the comparison indicates that the last card of a group has entered the unit, the computations required for the report are completed and printed on the same line of the report occupied by the part number and name.

PRINTING ALPHABETIC DATA

The printing of alphabetic data by the tabulator is handled in a slightly different manner from the printing of numeric data to be calculated. Alphabetic data in a card are read by the reading unit which, as you know, is made up of reading brushes. From the reading unit, the data are transferred to the printing unit, which, in turn, prints the data on the form or report desired. There is no provision within the machine for storage of alphabetic data. Alphabetic data in the card are transferred via the electrical impulses created by the punched holes in the card, direct to the printing mechanism, which, in turn, prints the data. In other words, the timed impulses entering the tabulator from the card are used to select the desired letter or digit in the printing mechanism and to print this letter or digit. The tabulator cannot arrange data in alphabetic order. This job must be done by the sorter or collator before the tabulator is used.

Figure 9-5 is an illustration showing how alphabetic data in a card are printed on a report. Note the flow of data (electrical impulses) from the card to an exit point on the machine and how the operator redirects the current back into the machine via an external wire placed in the control panel of the machine. The external wire is used to direct the current to the printing mechanism. By being able to intercept and direct the timed electrical current, the human operator is thus able to direct the action of the machine.

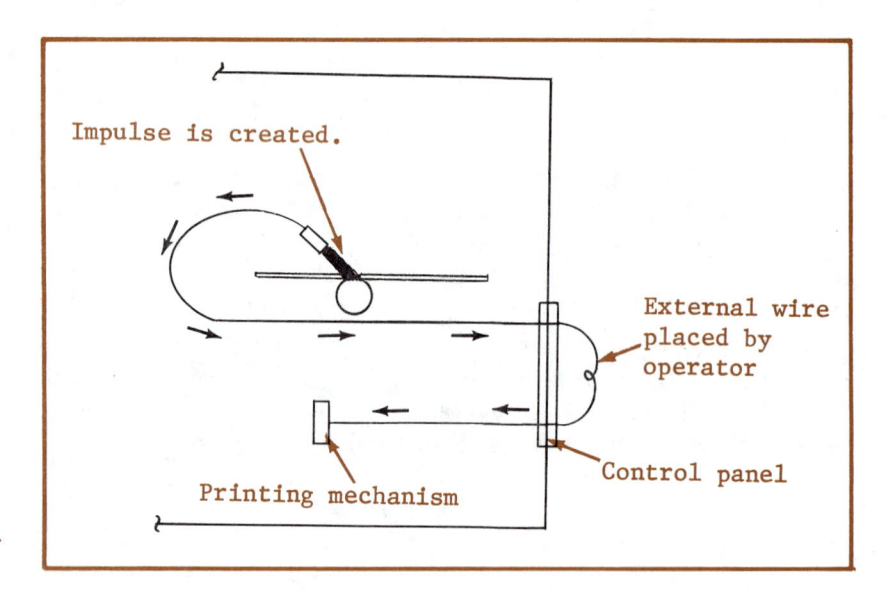

Figure 9-5. Printing alphabetic data

PRINTING NUMERIC DATA

Numeric data, as pointed out earlier, can be added or subtracted within the machine; the results of the calculations may be printed on a report. If calculations are to take place, the electrical impulses are first directed from the reading unit to calculating devices known as counters; and the results produced by the counters are then directed to the printing mechanism. The counters in a tabulator are similar to the counting mechanism found within a ten-key adding machine. Like the ten-key adding machine, provision is made within the counters of the tabulator for storage of accumulated totals. The totals may then be printed as desired.

Figure 9-6 shows how numeric data are directed from the reading unit to the counters and then to the printing mechanism. Numeric data that are not calculated are sent direct from the card to the printing unit.

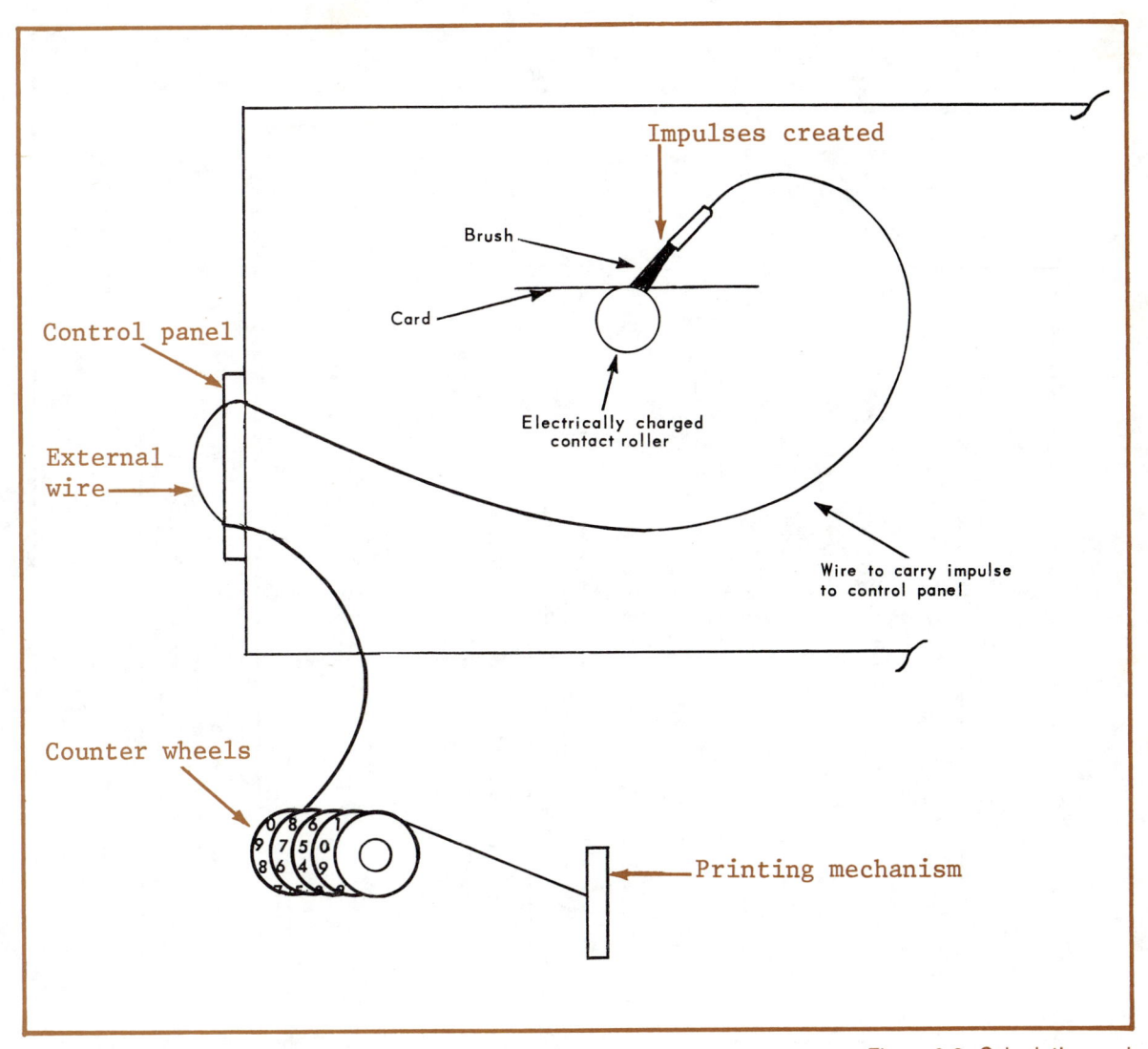

Chapter 9 Printing, calculating, and preparing reports

Figure 9-6. Calculating and printing numeric data

CARRIAGE CONTROL

As pointed out earlier, continuous assembled paper is usually used for printing. Small holes are punched on either side of the paper to allow sprocket wheels to keep the paper properly aligned and adjusted. Spacing of data on the paper is controlled by a control panel and paper tape. The tape is cut to coincide with the size of the form. Punches are then made in certain channels of the tape to control the vertical spacing of the data as desired. See Figure 9-7 for an example of matching a piece of tape to the size of the form.

Figure 9-7. Carriage tape cut and punched to control printing on a special form

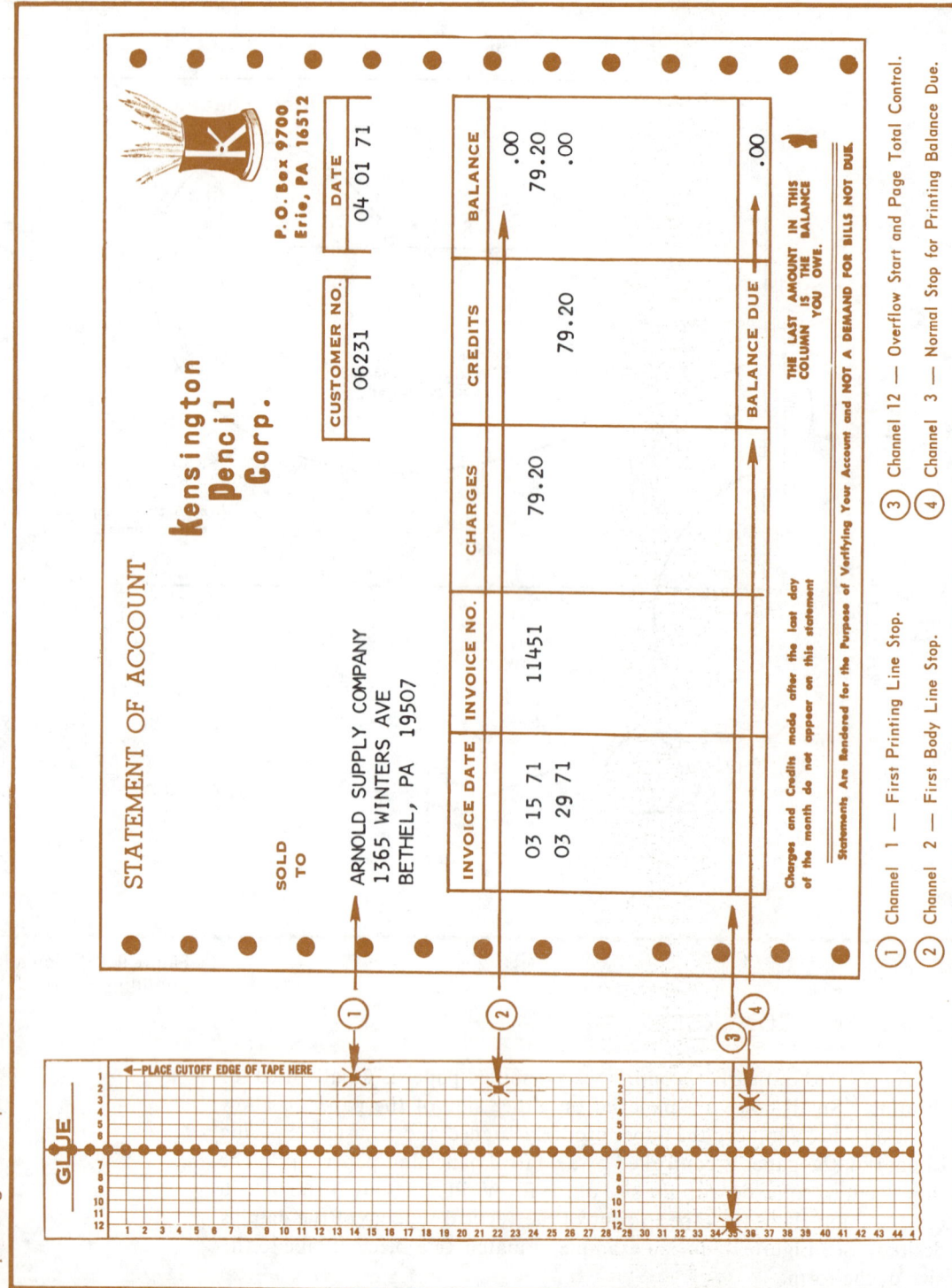

STATEMENT OF ACCOUNT

kensington
Pencil
Corp.

P.O. Box 9700
Erie, PA 16512

CUSTOMER NO.	DATE
06231	04 01 71

SOLD TO

ARNOLD SUPPLY COMPANY
1365 WINTERS AVE
BETHEL, PA 19507

INVOICE DATE	INVOICE NO.	CHARGES	CREDITS	BALANCE
				.00
03 15 71	11451	79.20		79.20
03 29 71			79.20	.00

BALANCE DUE → .00

THE LAST AMOUNT IN THIS COLUMN IS THE BALANCE YOU OWE.

Charges and Credits made after the last day of the month do not appear on this statement

Statements Are Rendered for the Purpose of Verifying Your Account and NOT A DEMAND FOR BILLS NOT DUE.

① Channel 1 — First Printing Line Stop.
② Channel 2 — First Body Line Stop.
③ Channel 12 — Overflow Start and Page Total Control.
④ Channel 3 — Normal Stop for Printing Balance Due.

Chapter 9   Printing, calculating, and preparing reports   141

Note the punches in the tape. Note, too, the explanation of each punch in the tape. Once it is properly cut, punched, and placed into position on the machine, the tape will handle spacing problems. The instructions in the punched tape and the control panel wiring are coordinated to produce forms with complex format requirements. By this method, for example, a customer's name and address may be printed in the appropriate space on an invoice or statement. The tape is used to control vertical spacing on the form. Horizontal spacing of data is controlled by the manner in which the control panel is wired. The report need not follow the sequence of data on the punched cards. Special headings may be printed on the form used, or the headings may be punched in cards and printed in accordance with the placement and spacing desired.

SUMMARY PUNCHING

Through the coordinated use of the tabulator and a reproducer (by direct connection), the data summarized within the tabulator may be punched into cards. For example, the total of charges to a particular customer for one month can be accumulated within the counters of the tabulating machine as each detail card representing a sale to that customer is passed through the tabulator. When all of the charges to the customer have been accumulated, the total charges can be printed on a report. At the same time, the total can be punched in a card if the tabulator is directly connected to a reproducing punch which is capable of punching holes in cards. The impulses used to direct the punching activity come from the tabulating machine.

CALCULATOR

The tabulator used in the tabulating and printing process is capable of either adding or subtracting the numeric data punched into cards and of printing subtotals and totals whenever required, as pointed out earlier. If more complicated calculations are required, involving multiplying and dividing, a special calculator must be used. A calculator, illustrated in Figure 9-8, is a device capable of performing arithmetic. Although some calculators are operated by electric current, one cannot speak of them as electronic computers — machines which will be explained in Part 4. Data requiring complicated computations are fed into the calculator via punched cards. The calculator performs the computations required and punches the results into punched cards.

The punch unit reads the information in the incoming cards and relays it to the calculating unit. The calculating unit performs the computations and the answers are relayed back to the punch unit, where they are punched

Figure 9-8. Calculator

Courtesy of IBM Corporation

into cards. Both units are controlled by control panels that are wired for the various jobs.

The usefulness of the calculator in handling a payroll is fairly evident. The card punch is used to punch into a card the employee's name, the number of hours worked, and his hourly rate. The card is then fed into the calculator, which multiplies the number of hours worked by the hourly rate, to obtain the total of the employee's wages. Deductions for taxes and other items are made next. This additional information is punched automatically by the calculator into a card. The card is then run through the tabulator, which prepares the employee's check. Some of the newer calculators are capable of printing information, in which case the information on the check in the foregoing example would be printed by the calculator. The need for a separate run through the tabulator would then be eliminated.

MULTI-FUNCTION CARD MACHINE

The IBM 2560 Multi-Function Card Machine combines the features of the card reader, card punch, collator, interpreter, and card document printer in a single unit. The Multi-Function Card Machine, which is illustrated in Figure 9-9, is designed for use with the IBM System/360 Model 20 Computer.

This multi-function feature permits collating, gangpunching, summary punching, calculating, printing, and classification of cards in one pass through the machine.

Chapter 9   Printing, calculating, and preparing reports   143

Courtesy of IBM Corporation

Figure 9-9. IBM 2560 Multi-Function Card Machine

CASE STUDY 1

At this point we can see how the unit-record system would be used to process data resulting in a printed report. Assume that a printed report is to be prepared, showing the names of contributors to a camp fund, the amount each has contributed, and the total contributions. The names are to be listed in alphabetic order. A revised (updated) report will be prepared each week.

The receipt in Figure 9-10 is the source document. It contains, among other information, the name of a contributor and the amount of his contribution.

The card in Figure 9-11 is the card that was planned to record the information on each contributor. Observe that the name of the contributor is punched in Columns 1 through 20. The first and second initials are punched into Columns 19 and 20. The amount contributed is punched in Columns 21 through 25.

Figure 9-10. Receipt for contribution to camp fund

TAFT HIGH SCHOOL

CONTRIBUTION RECEIPT

Name _Roger T. Benson_
Address _5109 Stearns Ave._
Tustin, CA 92680

Contribution Designation	Amount	
Camp Fund	15	00
Total Contribution	15	00

Received by _L. D. Taylor_

Figure 9-11. Card punched from data on receipt

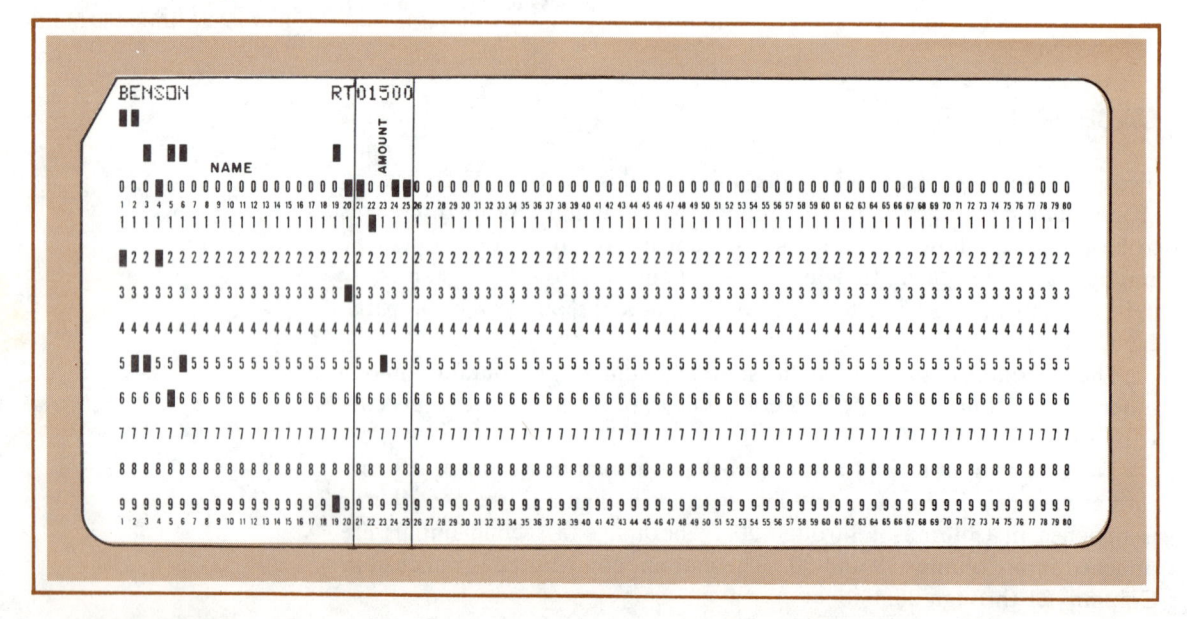

Chapter 9　　Printing, calculating, and preparing reports　　145

The flow chart to solve this problem appears in Figure 9-12. Observe the functions performed and the unit-record machine used in each step of the solution.

START — Terminal — Start or Halt

Receipts — Collect contribution receipts, which become source documents.

Card Punch — Punch one card for each source document.

Verifier — Check the accuracy of each punched card.

Sorter — Sequence cards in alphabetic order by family name.

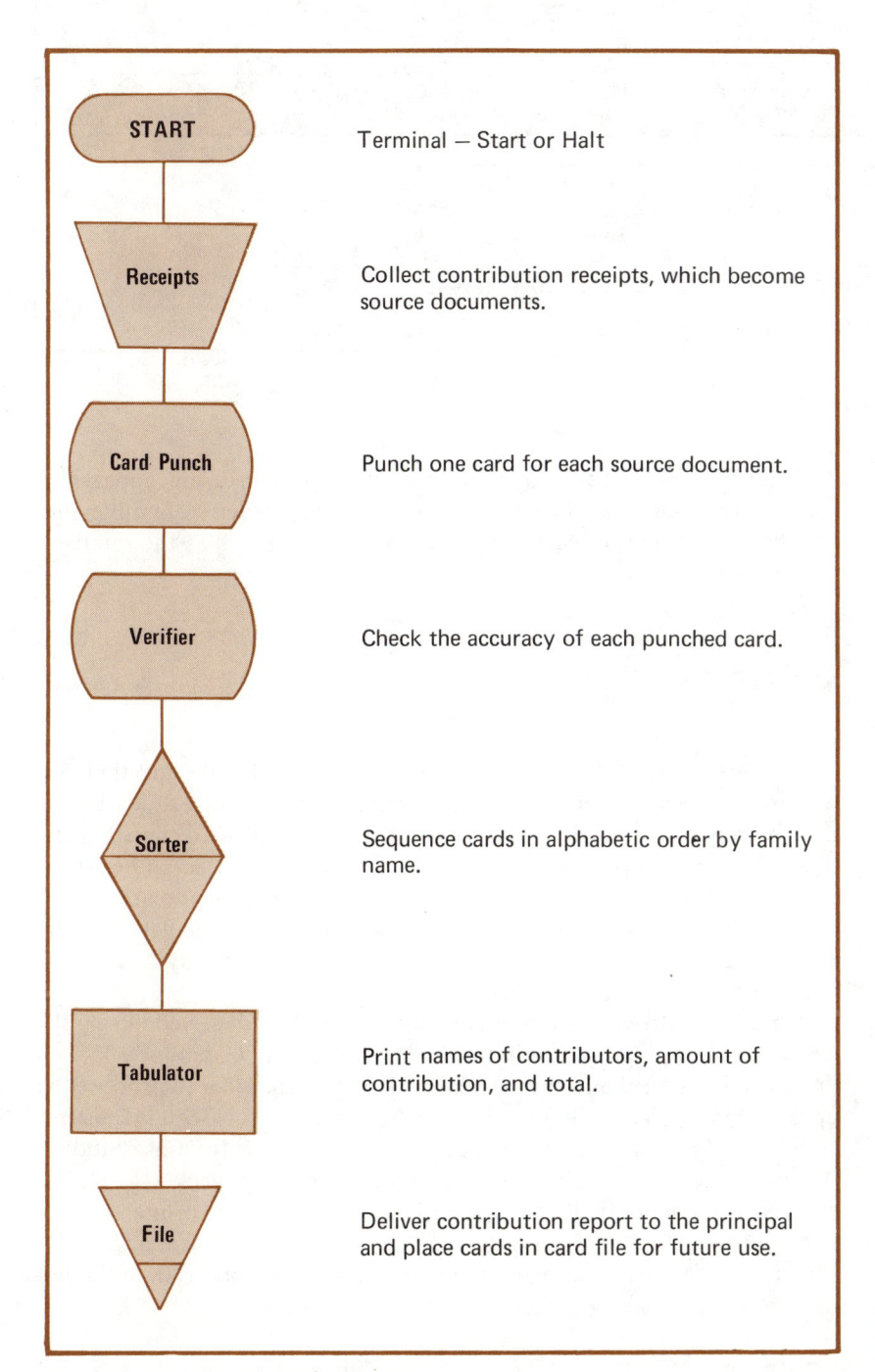

Tabulator — Print names of contributors, amount of contribution, and total.

File — Deliver contribution report to the principal and place cards in card file for future use.

Figure 9-12. Flow chart for Case Study 1

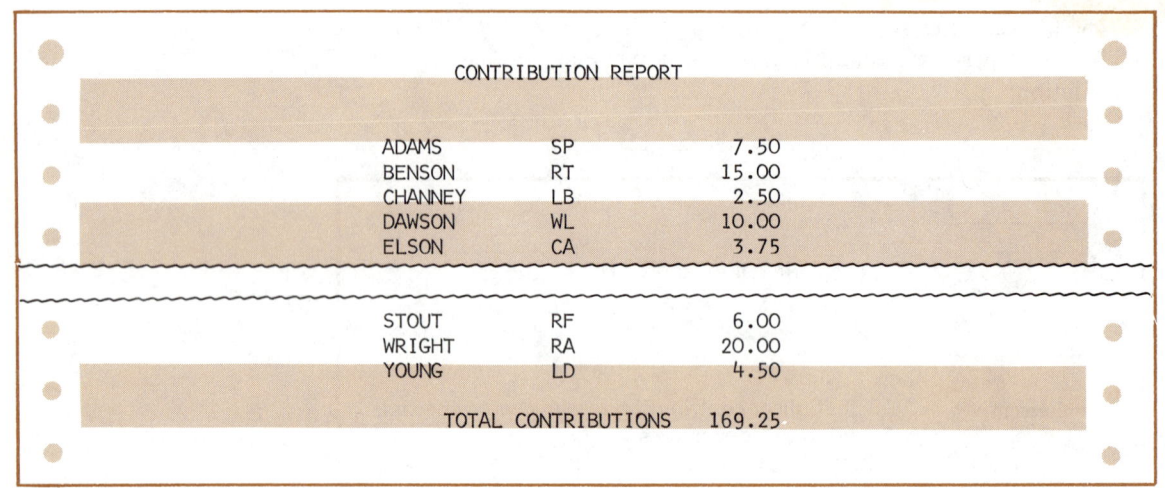

```
                    CONTRIBUTION REPORT

                    ADAMS        SP         7.50
                    BENSON       RT        15.00
                    CHANNEY      LB         2.50
                    DAWSON       WL        10.00
                    ELSON        CA         3.75
~~~~~~~~~~~~~~~~~~~~~~~~~~~~~~~~~~~~~~~~~~~~~~~~~~~
                    STOUT        RF         6.00
                    WRIGHT       RA        20.00
                    YOUNG        LD         4.50

                    TOTAL CONTRIBUTIONS   169.25
```

Figure 9-13. Partial contribution report

A portion of the final report prepared for this problem appears in Figure 9-13. Note that the names are in alphabetic order by family name and that the amount of each contribution is listed as well as the total.

CASE STUDY 2

Assume, for Case Study 2, that it is now one week later and that you wish to prepare an updated report of contributions from Case Study 1. The updated report of contributions will contain the names of all contributors: those listed on the previous report (Case Study 1) as well as those whose contributions have been received since the last report was prepared.

Case Study 2 will utilize the same forms (Figures 9-10 and 9-11) as were used in Case Study 1 because this is an extension of Case Study 1. The flow chart to solve this problem appears in Figure 9-14.

Observe that contribution receipts which have been received during the past week must be processed in the same manner as in Case Study 1; then they must be merged into the original deck of cards in order to produce the updated report. You will note that the flow chart for Case Study 2 has an additional step that does not appear in the flow chart for Case Study 1 (Figure 9-12). After alphabetic sequencing, the new deck of cards is merged with the original deck before the updated report is printed.

A portion of the updated report prepared for this problem appears in Figure 9-15. Note that all names remain in alphabetic order, even though new names have been inserted.

Chapter 9   Printing, calculating, and preparing reports   147

Figure 9-14. Flow chart for Case Study 2

START — Start.

New receipts — Collect contribution receipts which have been received during the past week.

Card Punch — Punch one card for each new source document.

Verifier — Check the accuracy of each new punched card.

Sorter — Sequence the new cards in alphabetic order by family name.

Collator — Merge the new deck of cards into the deck from which last week's contribution report was produced.

Tabulator — Print names of contributors, amount of contribution and total.

File — Deliver the new contribution report to the principal and place the cards in the card file for future use.

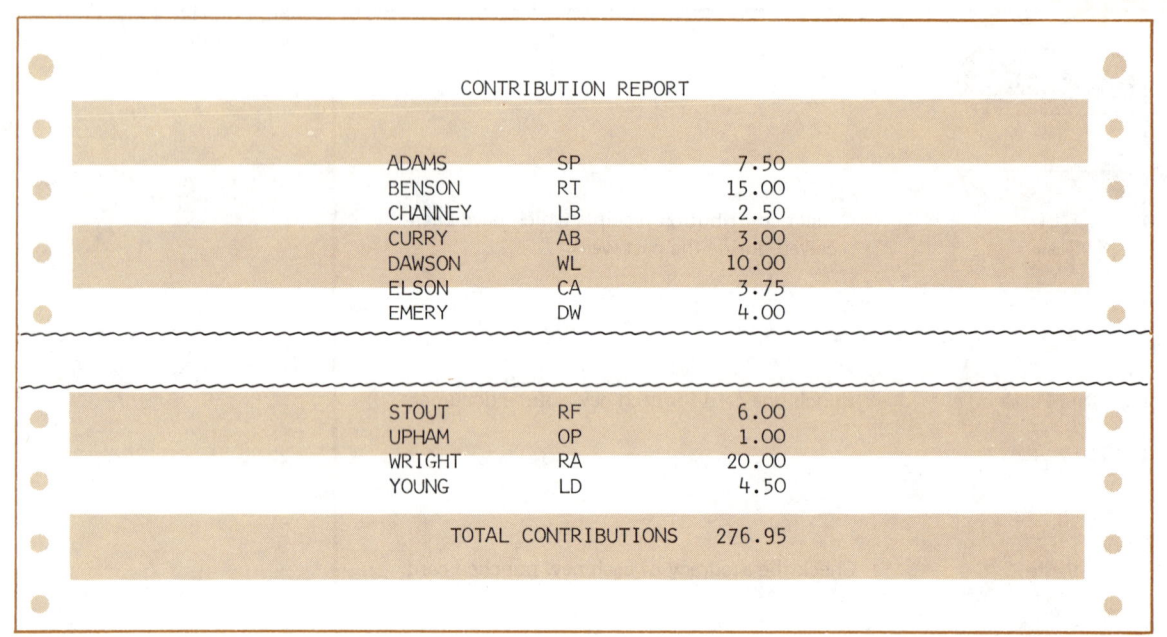

```
                    CONTRIBUTION REPORT


                    ADAMS         SP            7.50
                    BENSON        RT           15.00
                    CHANNEY       LB            2.50
                    CURRY         AB            3.00
                    DAWSON        WL           10.00
                    ELSON         CA            3.75
                    EMERY         DW            4.00


                    STOUT         RF            6.00
                    UPHAM         OP            1.00
                    WRIGHT        RA           20.00
                    YOUNG         LD            4.50

                    TOTAL CONTRIBUTIONS       276.95
```

Figure 9-15. Partial updated contribution report

SUMMARY

Printing and calculating functions may be handled in a variety of ways in the unit-record system. The interpreter is a printing machine. It prints on a card the information punched in that card. All or just part of the punched data can be recorded, and the printed data may be placed on the card as desired. A control panel must be wired and attached to the interpreter to program each printing job.

The tabulator contains reading, calculating, and printing units. The reading unit can sense the holes in all card fields or only those needed to produce a desired report. The calculating unit can add and subtract, and the amounts in several fields of a card can be accumulated and totaled in one operation. The printing unit prints alphabetic and numeric data punched in cards, as well as the results of calculations performed by the calculating unit.

The printing unit usually consists of a greater number of printing positions than there are columns in a card. This feature makes it possible to arrange data in columns and to add special signs and characters to the copy. The tabulator is also capable of summarizing information from a number of cards and of printing only the summary data. It can also print the data from each card, and usually the data in each card are printed on a single line of the report.

A tabulator is programmed by a control panel and by punched paper tape, which must be coordinated with the control panel. A variety of complicated forms may thus be prepared on the tabulator. The tabulator, when

Chapter 9   Printing, calculating, and preparing reports   149

it is attached to a reproducer, is also capable of punching summary information into cards. The impulses that are used to direct the punching activity come from the tabulator; the reproducer punches the holes.

When a processing job requires complicated calculations involving multiplication and division, a calculator is used. The calculator accepts data from punched cards, performs the required calculations with the aid of a control panel, and punches the results into the same card or a new set of punched cards. Some of the newer calculators are capable of handling limited printing operations.

REVIEW QUESTIONS

1. What are the terminating steps of any data processing system?
2. What is an interpreter?
3. How does the interpreter differ from a printing card punch?
4. What is a tabulator?
5. Name the three units of the tabulator.
6. What operations can the calculating unit of the tabulator perform?
7. How does the printing unit of the tabulator prepare more than one copy of processed material?
8. Why are more than 80 columns available on the printing unit when the standard punched card contains only 80 columns?
9. What is detail printing?
10. What is group printing?
11. How does the tabulator distinguish one group of cards from another in a group printing operation?
12. What operation can the tabulator perform on numeric data that it cannot perform on alphabetic data?
13. What are the calculating elements of the tabulator called?
14. What is the purpose of punched paper tape in the tabulating unit?
15. What is a calculator?
16. What is the **difference** between the calculating unit of the tabulator and the calculator itself?

STUDY GUIDE

Complete Study Guide 9 by following the instructions in your **STUDY GUIDES** booklet.

PROJECTS

Complete Projects 9-1, 9-2, and 9-3 by following the instructions in your **PROJECTS** booklet.

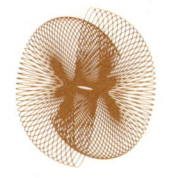

CHAPTER 10

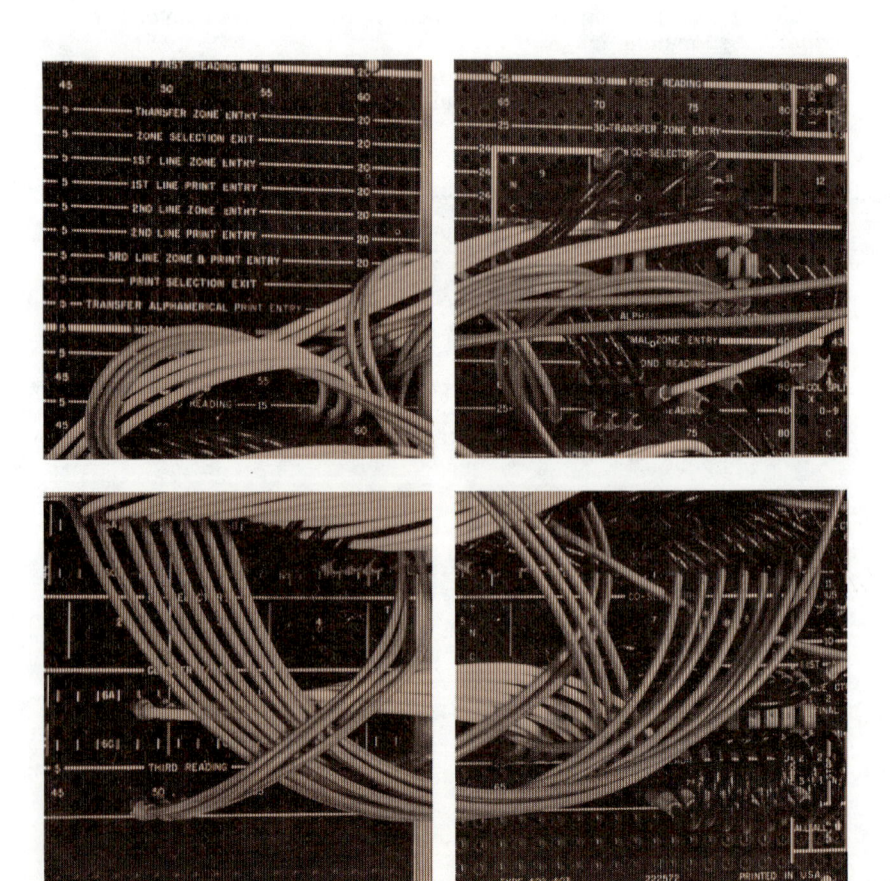

THE CONTROL PANEL

The operator controls the actions of many data processing machines in much the same manner as the actions of common household appliances are controlled — that is, by regulating the flow of electricity. For example, a common electric coffee percolator is directed to make coffee by plugging a cord into an electric outlet in the wall and into the coffee maker itself. The cord is the connecting link and is plugged into proper place by human action. The outlet in the wall is the source of electricity. The electricity is directed into the coffee maker by the person who uses the cord to make the proper connection. The electricity is directed to perform the action desired. Note how this is illustrated in Figure 10-1.

The electric current created within a machine as a result of the holes punched in a card is directed to exit points on a control panel. From these exit points, a human operator, by means of a wiring process, directs the current back into the machine through entrance points on the control panel. The point at which the operator wires the current back into the machine is significant because it is related to the function that the machine is to perform. By being able to intercept and redirect the current, the operator is able to control the action of the machine. The exit and entry points are holes or sockets into which wires can be inserted. Each of the holes or sockets through which an electrical impulse may be emitted or into which an impulse is sent is called a *hub*. The holes appear in a device or attachment known as a control panel. A *control panel* is a device, usually detachable, which employs removable wires to control the operation of punched card equipment. The control panel is used on most unit-record machines to carry out functions which are under the control of the operator. This panel is sometimes referred to as a *plugboard*, a *control board*, or a *wiring*

Figure 10-1. Controlling an electric coffee maker

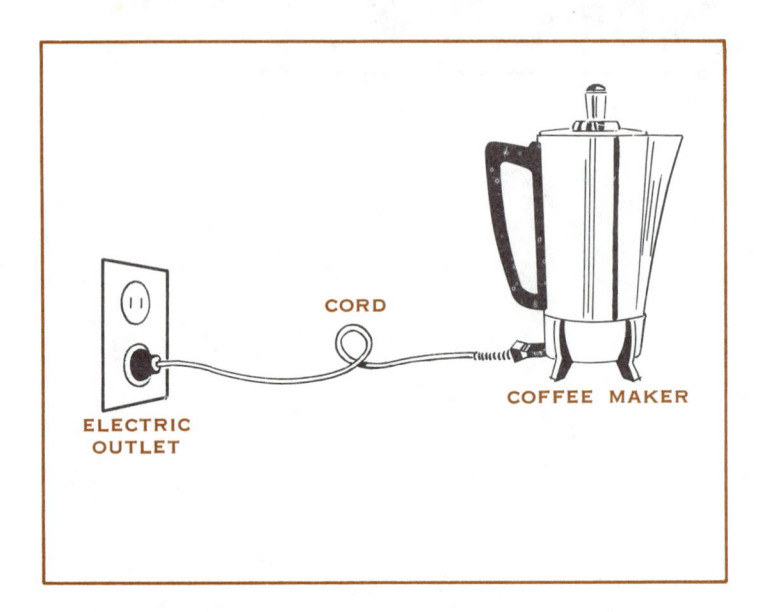

Figure 10-2. A control panel for the tabulator

board. A control panel for the tabulator is illustrated in Figure 10-2. The tabulator, interpreter, reproducer, collator, and calculator are examples of machines controlled by control panels. The control panel for each machine is designed to fit the needs of that particular machine.

Chapter 10   The control panel

The design of the control panel varies depending upon the machine to which it belongs. Wiring the control panel is a manual operation. The principle underlying this operation is very simple, for it consists of nothing more than the completion of an electric circuit. Plugging a coffee maker into the outlet on a wall or turning the ignition key in a car also involve the completion of electric circuits. The wiring of simple processing jobs can be an easy task. Jobs entailing complicated logical situations require technicians with high skill and a great deal of experience.

Control panels are usually detachable because each job requires a separately wired panel. It is easier to have several control panels wired permanently and to change a panel than to have one control panel which must be rewired constantly.

DIFFERENT TYPES OF HUBS

Exit hubs

All the hubs in the control panel do not necessarily perform the same function. One type of hub carries *out* of the machine electric impulses created *within* the machine as a result of the sensing of the holes punched in a card. There are certain hubs through which impulses are emitted. The socket on a control panel into which an electrical lead or plug wire may be connected in order to carry signals out of the machine is called an *exit hub*. The outflowing electrical impulses are created when the wire reading brush or electronic beam touches the contact roller through the holes punched in the cards. The reading brushes and contact roller were explained and illustrated in Chapter 8. Figure 10-3 shows how the impulse is carried from the reading brush to the exit hub of the control panel.

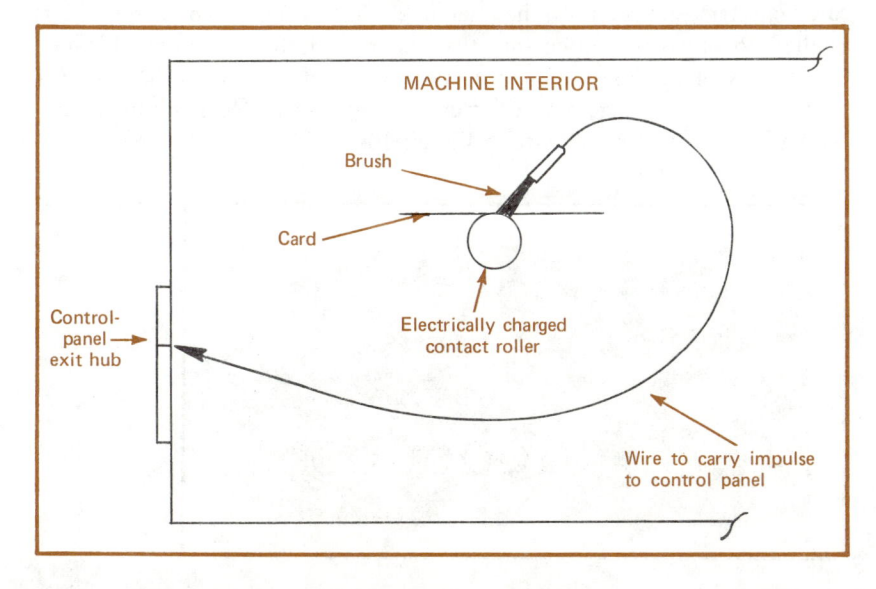

Figure 10-3. The electric impulse goes from reading brush to exit hub

Although more and more of the machines in the unit-record system are using electronic-beam sensing devices, in order to simplify the discussion in this text, the explanations will be concerned with reading brushes. The principle is basically the same.

You know that a standard card has 80 columns. In a processing machine, such as the interpreter, there are thus 80 reading brushes — one for each of the 80 columns of the card. There are also an equal number of exit hubs in the control panel to correspond to the reading brushes. This point is shown in a section of the control panel illustrated in Figure 10-4. The hubs illustrated are shown under a heading labeled "Reading Brushes" in order to aid the operator to distinguish them as exit hubs when he is wiring the control panel.

Figure 10-4. Section of a control panel showing exit hubs that correspond to the 80 reading brushes

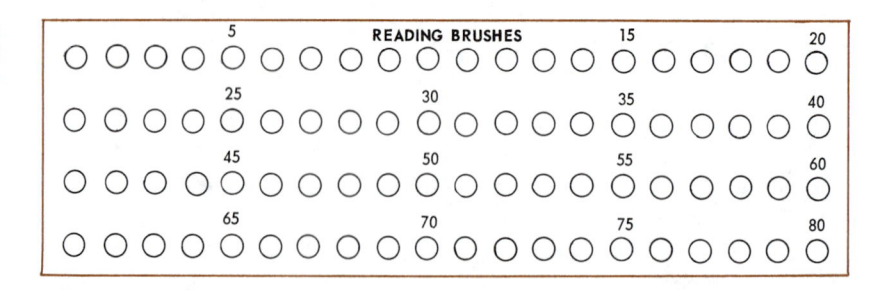

Entrance hubs

The electrical impulses directed to an exit hub are intercepted by plugging a wire into the exit hub. The impulses are directed back into the machine by plugging the other end of the wire into a socket called an *entrance hub*. An *entrance hub*, therefore, may be defined as a socket on a control panel into which an electrical lead or wire may be connected in order to carry electric signals into the machine. The term *control panel wire* is applied to any wire connecting two or more hubs in a control panel. Control panel wires are colored according to length to help the operator select one of appropriate size for connecting hubs. Note the hubs connected by a control panel wire in Figure 10-5.

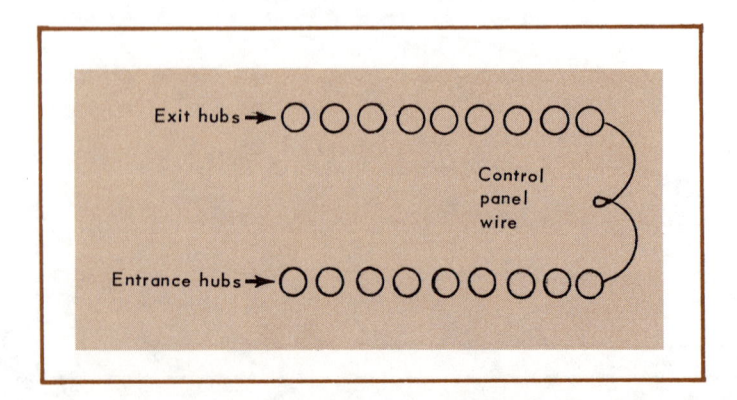

Figure 10-5. A control panel wire connecting hubs of a control panel

Common hubs

When two hubs on a control panel are connected in a straight line, they are said to be *in common*, as shown in (A) and (B) of Figure 10-6 below. Common hubs may be either exit or entry hubs. This feature enables an operator to connect two different exits to one entry, or to take one exit to two different entry hubs as shown in (C) and (D) below.

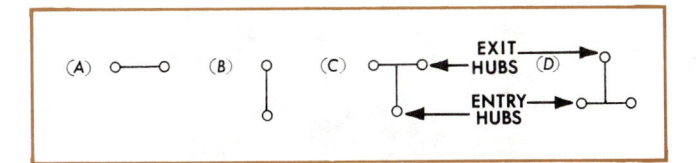

Figure 10-6. Common hubs

Interrelationship of the hubs

The control panel wire completes the electrical connection that directs the electric impulse to the area of the processing machine which performs the desired operations. The control panel is similar in principle to a telephone switchboard, and the function of the person who wires the panel is similar to that of a switchboard operator. An incoming call on the switchboard turns on a signal light that tells the operator on which line there is an incoming call. After the operator answers the call, she plugs a cord into a hub on the board that is internally connected to the desired extension. All the operator has done is complete the electric circuit. Similarly, the person who wires the control board merely completes an electric circuit to produce a desired result.

HOW THE IMPRINT IS MADE

Impulses directed back into a machine are sent there to perform specific tasks. In some machines, the current may be used to perform mathematical calculations. In other machines, the current may be used to print a record. For a simple illustration, assume that a printed record of data punched into cards is desired. The operator must use a control panel wire to connect the exit hub with an entrance hub, which is in turn connected to a printing device. This point was illustrated in Figure 10-5.

In the **IBM 548 Interpreter** used here for illustrative purposes, the printing mechanism is a typebar. The *typebar* is a mechanical device on which are located the digits, the letters of the alphabet, and some special symbols. A typebar similar to one found in an **IBM 548 interpreter** is illustrated in Figure 10-7. The printing mechanism used by other processing machines, such as the tabulator and the calculator, may vary slightly.

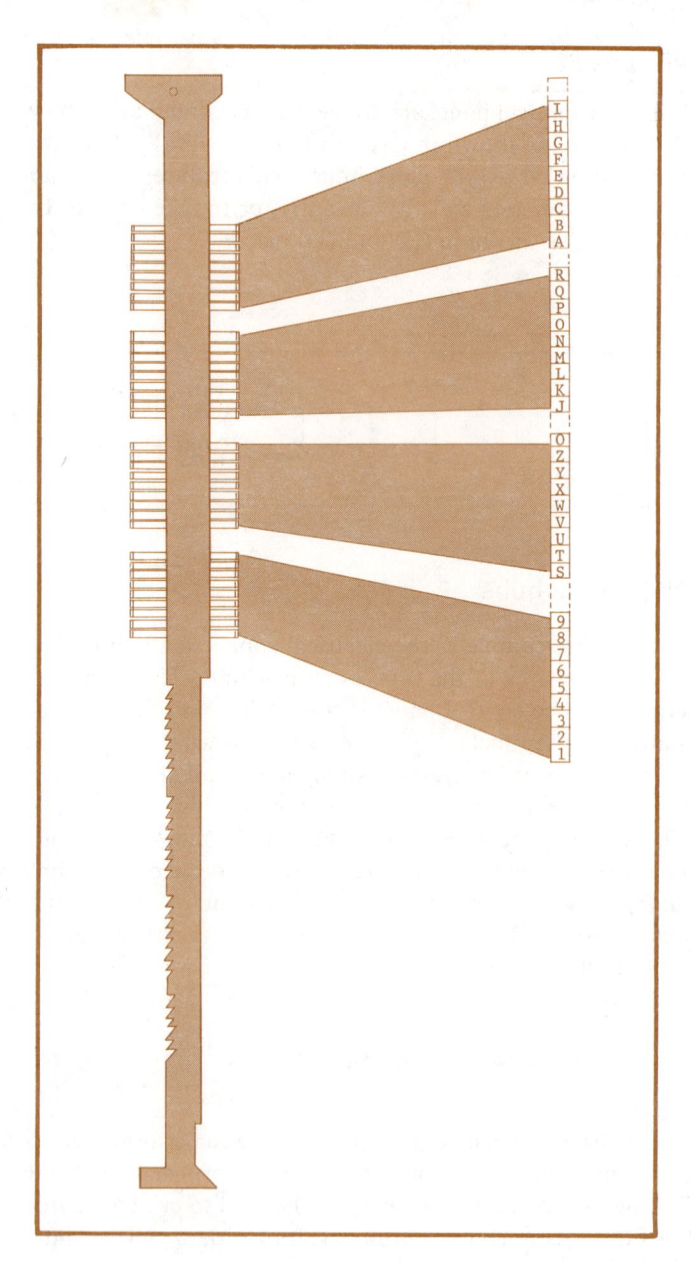

Figure 10-7. Typebar

A printing mechanism contains many typebars similar to the one illustrated in Figure 10-7. The number varies from 60 to 120 or more, depending upon the type of machine being used. According to the timed impulse received, the typebar positions itself before a platen similar to that found on a typewriter. Between the typebar and the platen is a ribbon. A small hammer strikes the key of the typebar, and the particular letter or digit makes an imprint on the paper. Figure 10-8 illustrates this action.

Chapter 10   The control panel   157

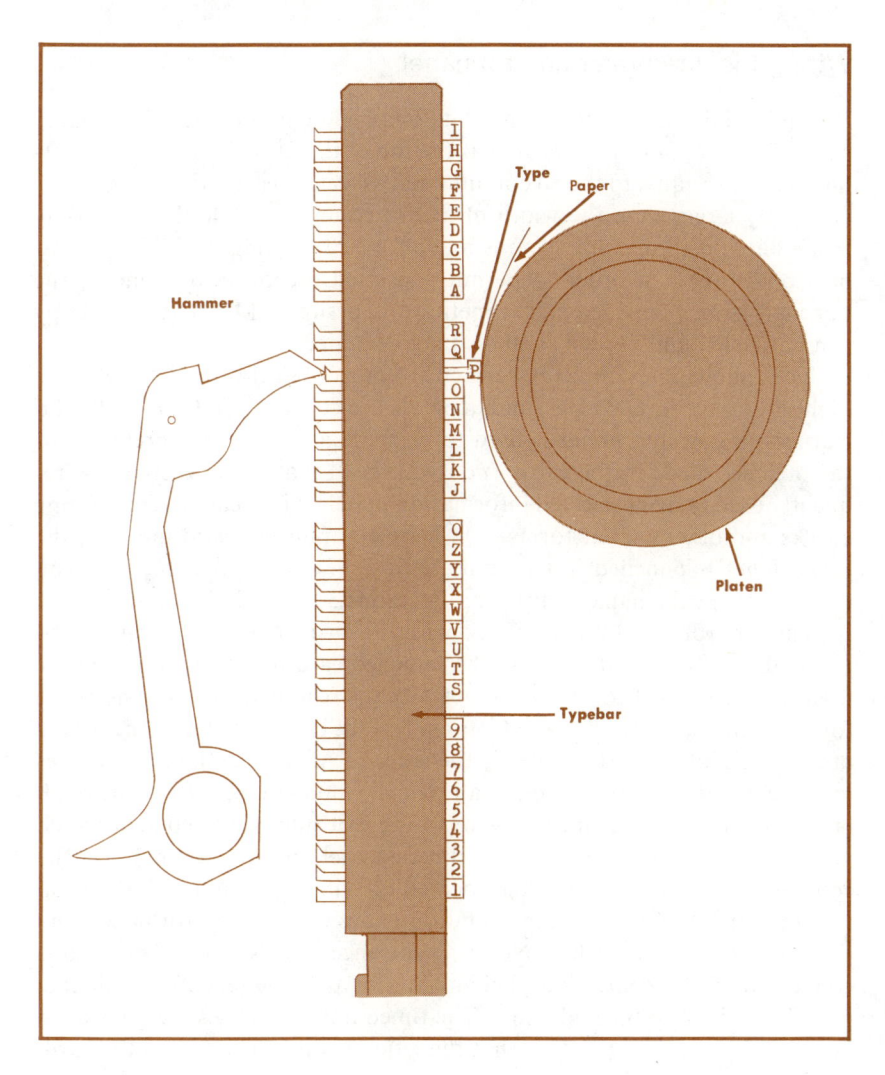

Figure 10-8. A letter or digit is printed

CONTROL PANEL FOR THE INTERPRETER

Up to this point, you have gained some understanding of the control panel and how it is used to control the inner action of some of the machines that make up the unit-record sytem of processing data. You will learn next, by means of a control panel diagram, how a control panel is wired to handle a relatively simple job. It is not the purpose of this introductory course to teach you how to become proficient in board wiring. A more comprehensive treatment of this subject is included in specialized courses. However, you can gain an understanding of the basic principles involved in board wiring.

Wiring the interpreter control panel

An IBM 548 interpreter prints data on two horizontal lines of 60 spaces each. The lines of print appear near the top of the card. Since the 60 printing spaces are equal to the 80 columns across a card, each printed character is slightly larger than the width of a card column. While there are only 80 reading positions, provision is made for 120 printing positions (in two horizontal lines) in order to permit a printed repetition of some of the punched items, provided such repetition is desired. Moreover, the copy can be spaced and needed symbols may be added.

The following example of wiring the control panel of an interpreter is highly simplified. Only the fundamentals are covered. In Chapter 9, you learned that an interpreter is used to print on a card an interpretation of the punches made in the card. You will recall that the interpreter is frequently used to print selected information punched into cards, representing checks and other similar forms. On hand is a punched card in which the name *Jones* is punched in Columns 5, 6, 7, 8, and 9. Assume that you desire to print the name in Printing Positions 30, 31, 32, 33, and 34.

The control panel must now be wired to print *Jones* in Printing Positions 30, 31, 32, 33, and 34. As the punched card is directed through the interpreter, the card comes in contact with the reading brushes. The brush for Column 5 reads the holes in Column 5 of the card and, due to the timing of the cycle, interprets the holes as the letter J. As the reading brush comes in contact with the contact roller, an electric impulse is sent from the reading brush through the internal wire to the exit hub of the control panel.

From this point, the current is directed back into the machine via the control panel wire to the typebar located in Printing Position 30, the position in which the printed interpretation is desired. A control panel wire connects reading brush hub No. 5 to entrance hub No. 30. This hub is connected to a typebar. The typebar contains all the letters of the alphabet plus the digits zero through nine. The timed impulse causes the typebar to be adjusted in such a position that the letter J will be printed on the card. Similarly, a wire is placed in the control panel to connect exit hub No. 6 to entrance hub No. 31. This wire carries the impulse for the letter O. Another wire is used to connect exit hub No. 7 to entrance hub No. 32. This wire carries the impulse for the letter N. The hubs for the remaining letters of the name are connected in a similar manner. When all letters are in position, an impulse is emitted that will cause the printing to take place on the card. Figure 10-9 shows a section of the control panel. It also shows how the panel would be wired to complete the simple job described.

Control panel diagram for the interpreter

Paper diagram forms of the hub layouts for control panels may be obtained for each of the processing machines in the unit-record system. The diagram forms are used to make pencil drawings showing how the wires

Chapter 10   The control panel

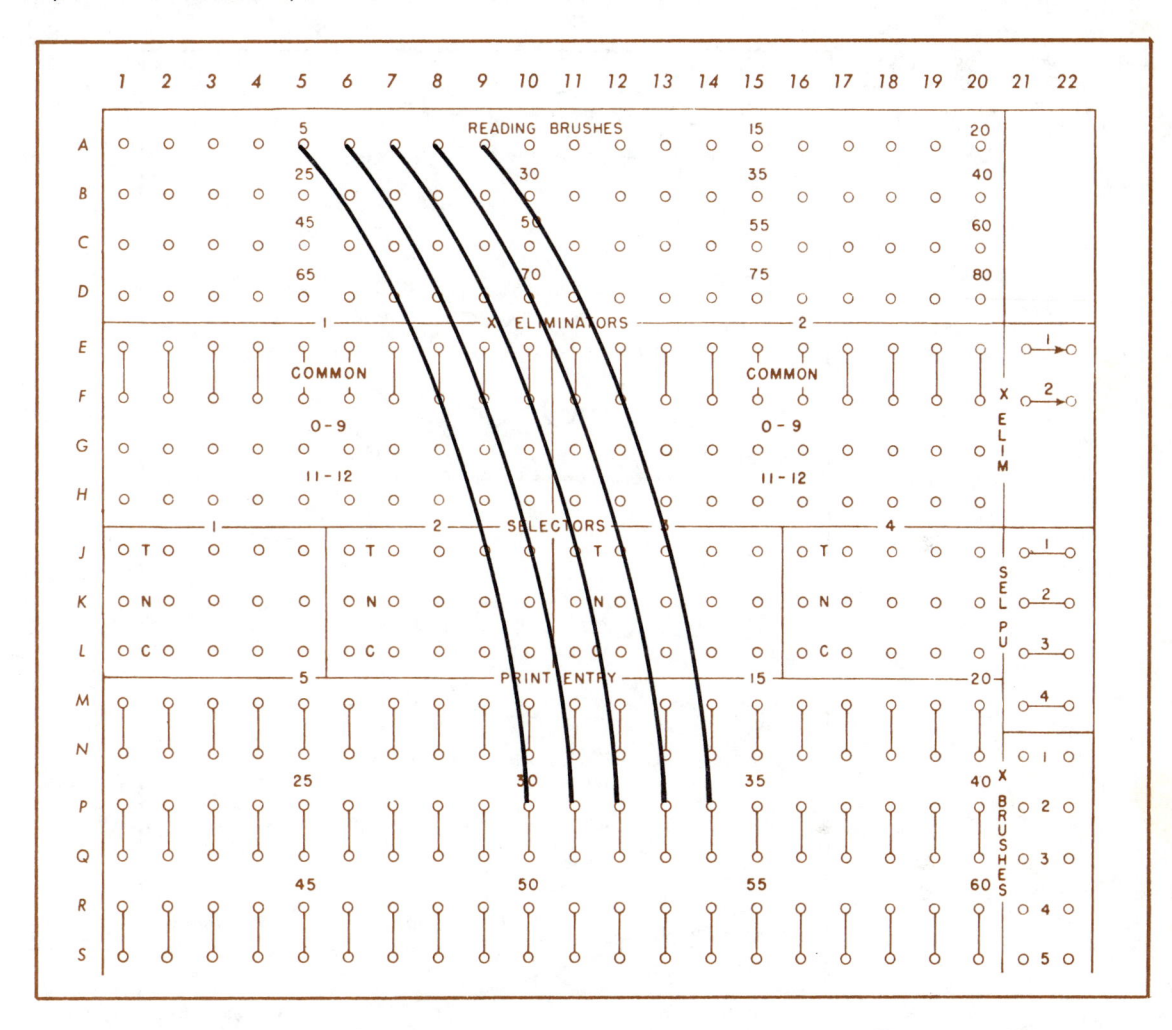

Figure 10-9. Wiring a control panel to handle a simple printing problem

should be placed in the panel for each job. Before the panel is wired, the diagrams are often prepared and checked for accuracy. A diagram may be retained as a permanent record of a particular control panel setup and would be useful should it be necessary to repeat the job at some later time.

Rules for preparing control panel diagrams

A few simple rules to be followed when preparing a control panel diagram are given below.

Rule 1. The hubs used for specific fields are connected with a horizontal line. See Figures 10 and 11.

Figure 10-10. Illustration of rules used in preparing control panel diagrams

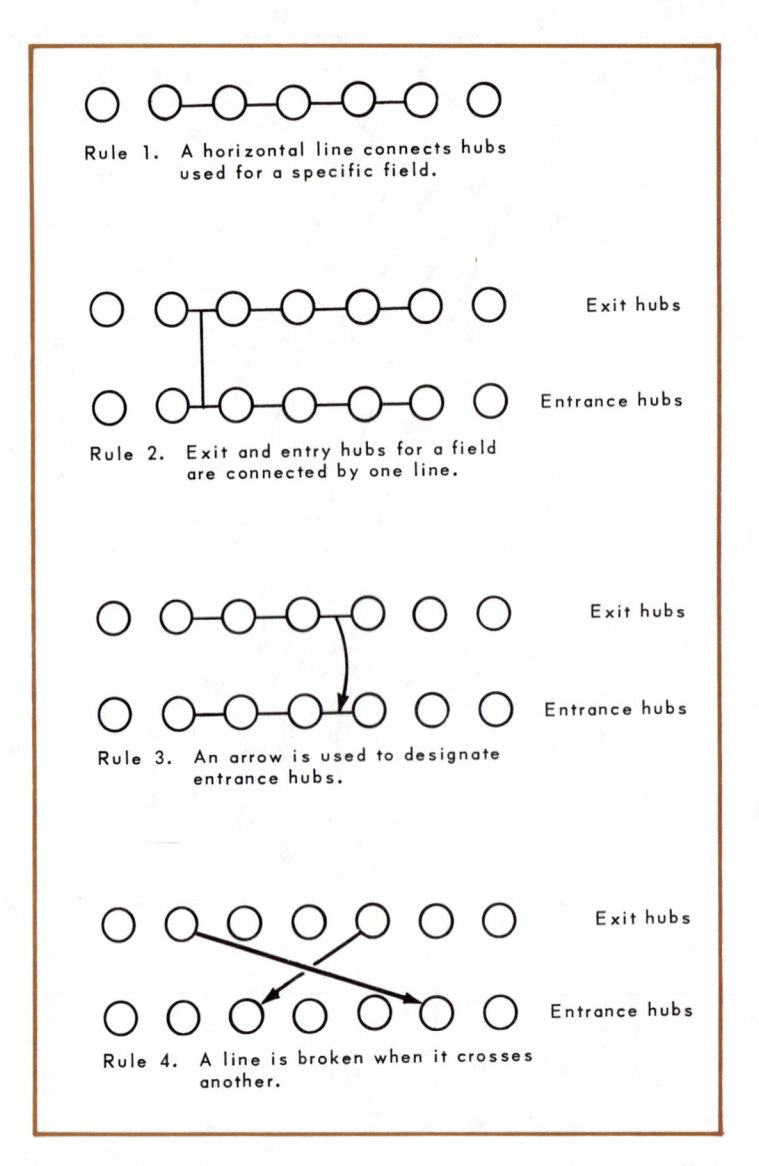

Rule 1. A horizontal line connects hubs used for a specific field.

Rule 2. Exit and entry hubs for a field are connected by one line.

Rule 3. An arrow is used to designate entrance hubs.

Rule 4. A line is broken when it crosses another.

    Rule 2. The exit and entry hubs used for a particular field are connected by a single line whenever possible. See Figure 10-11. This practice makes the diagram easier to read. It must be remembered that one wire must be used to connect each exit and entry hub in a field. A five-position field would require five wires in the control panel.

    Rule 3. Entrance hubs are distinguished from exit hubs by the use of an arrow pointing to the entrance hubs. See Figure 10-10.

    Rule 4. If it is necessary to cross lines on a diagram, one line is broken. This practice prevents the possibility of following the wrong line to the entrance hub. See Figure 10-10.

Chapter 10   The control panel

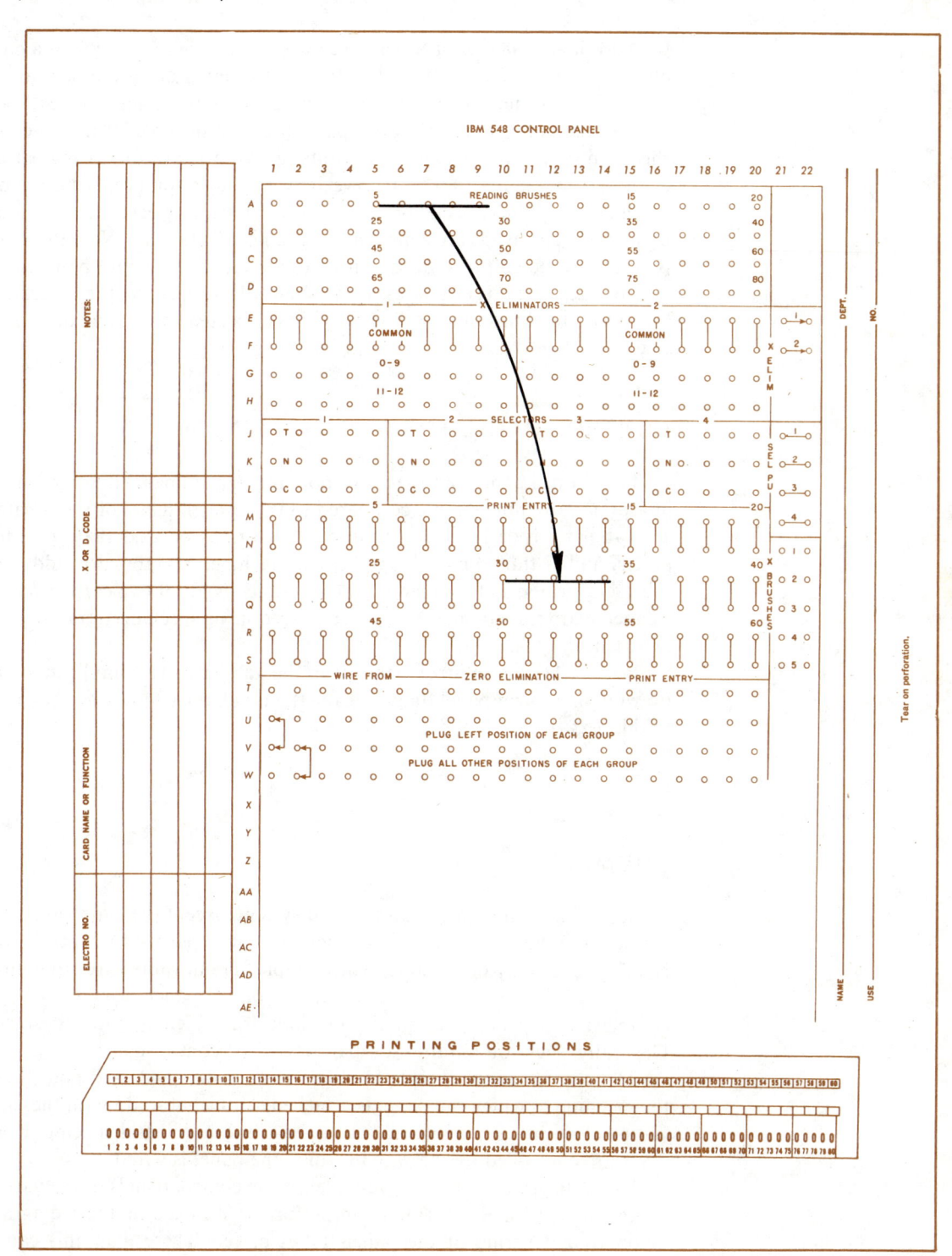

Figure 10-11. Control panel diagram for interpreter

Additional rules must be followed when preparing diagrams of a complicated nature. The brief explanation and simple rules given here are all that will be needed to complete the projects accompanying this textbook.

A diagram form of the control panel used for an IBM 548 interpreter is shown in Figure 10-11. The form contains a drawing of the wiring pattern described in Figure 10-9. Observe how the rules for preparing control panel diagrams have been applied. Instead of drawing each wire, the hubs used for specific fields are connected with a horizontal line. Note the arrow pointing to the entrance hubs. In real practice, there would be five individual wires, but it is not necessary to show all five wires on the diagram as long as all the hubs in a specific field are connected by a single horizontal line.

CONTROL PANEL FOR THE TABULATOR

The control panel and the corresponding control panel diagram of the interpreter are quite simple compared to the control panel of a tabulator. The tabulator is designed to handle a larger variety of tasks than the interpreter, and is thus a more complicated machine. A tabulator adds and subtracts, prints, and compares data in selected fields of two cards. Wiring a panel board for a tabulator is thus a job requiring specialized training and experience.

Because wiring control panels for the tabulator is complicated, the drawing of control panel diagrams for the tabulator will not be presented in this text.

SUMMARY

All the machines in the unit-record system, except the card punch, the verifier, and the sorter are programmed by control panels. A control panel is a device, usually detachable, which employs removable wires to control the operation of unit-record machines. Control panels vary in size and complexity, depending upon the machine for which they are designed. Generally, each job requires a separately wired control panel.

The control panel accepts impulses from a punched card and directs the machine to which the panel is attached as to what to do with these impulses. Printing, summarizing, calculating, and horizontal spacing operations are controlled by the way in which the panel is wired.

Paper diagram forms are available for the control panels of the various processing machines. Wiring patterns may be sketched on these diagrams before actual wiring of the panels takes place. These diagrams can be checked for accuracy before the panel is wired. Moreover, the diagrams may be retained for reuse as needed.

Chapter 10   The control panel

REVIEW QUESTIONS

1. How is the operation of a control panel similar to the operation of an electric coffee maker?
2. Why are control panels usually detachable?
3. What is a hub?
4. What is an exit hub? An entrance hub?
5. What are common hubs?
6. What is the function of a control panel wire?
7. Since each column in a card represents only a single character, how is it possible to have two lines of print on a single card?
8. Describe the internal operation of an interpreter.
9. Why is a paper diagram of the wiring of a control panel usually prepared and kept on file?
10. How are exit hubs indicated on a control panel diagram? How are entrance hubs identified?
11. Why is the control panel for the tabulator more complicated than the one for the interpreter?

STUDY GUIDE

Complete Study Guide 10 by following the instructions in your **STUDY GUIDES** booklet.

PROJECTS

Complete Projects 10-1 and 10-2 by following the instructions in your **PROJECTS** booklet.

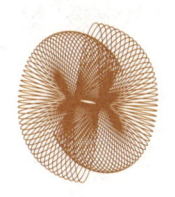

PART 4

THE ELECTRONIC COMPUTER SYSTEM

Chapter 11	THE ELECTRONIC COMPUTER
Chapter 12	LANGUAGE AND COMPUTING SYSTEMS
Chapter 13	INTERNAL STORAGE OF INFORMATION
Chapter 14	HUMAN LANGUAGE PROGRAMS AND BLOCK DIAGRAMS
Chapter 15	MACHINE LANGUAGE INSTRUCTIONS
Chapter 16	INTRODUCTION TO COBOL
Chapter 17	COBOL APPLICATIONS
Chapter 18	JOBS AND CAREERS IN AUTOMATED DATA PROCESSING

CHAPTER 11

THE ELECTRONIC COMPUTER

TYPES OF ELECTRONIC COMPUTERS

While the discussion in these chapters is concerned entirely with digital electronic computers, you should know that there are two basic types of computers: digital and analog.

The digital computer

A *digital computer* works with numbers or letters of the alphabet and special symbols that can be coded numerically. It solves problems electronically by counting, adding, subtracting, multiplying, and dividing. An adding machine is a digital device, as is a cash register. Numeric data can be stored in digital computers until a total or result is desired. The answer represents units of something that can be counted. Digital computers are widely used in processing business data and many kinds of engineering data. See Figure 11-1, which shows two typical digital computers.

The analog computer

An *analog computer* is a type of calculating machine that uses numbers to represent quantities that can be measured (such as voltages, resistances, or rotations). Therefore, the analog computer is actually a measuring device. By means of gauges, meters, and wheels, the analog computer can measure and process physical variables such as amounts of electric current, speed of sound, temperature, pressure, and velocity. The speedometer, by

168 The electronic computer system   Part 4

GE-410 *Courtesy of General Electric Co.*

IBM System/360 Model 85 *Courtesy of IBM Corporation*

Figure 11-1. Two typical digital computers

Chapter 11　The electronic computer　　　　　　　　　　　　　　　　　　　169

means of a rotating wire, measures the speed at which a car is moving. The needles on a meter can measure the amount of gas or electricity used in your home. The analog computer accepts these measures and processes them as directed. It is used primarily in scientific research.

The following comparison may be helpful in distinguishing between the two types of computers. A digital computer can count the number of light fixtures in a building. It is not concerned with the amount of light made available. An analog computer, on the other hand, measures the amount of light given off by each fixture and provides the answer in numeric form. Both process the data received, as directed by a program or formula.

Analog computers can accept data directly from gauges, meters, and other measuring devices. The data do not have to be converted to punched cards or other input media and entered into the computer. This feature makes the analog computer extremely fast and useful in such operations as controlling oil refineries, missile systems, and automatic pilot devices. See Figure 11-2, which shows an analog computer.

Figure 11-2. Analog computer (The Comcor 550)

Courtesy Astrodata, Inc.

GENERAL FEATURES OF DIGITAL COMPUTERS

Among the features that make an electronic computer different from the machines in the unit-record system are the flexibility with which the computer can be programmed when new problems must be solved, the blinding speed with which it processes data, and its built-in ability to follow and carry out in sequence the instructions stored in its memory unit. A computer can also change to a new set of instructions when certain conditions in the program have been met.

A different program is written for each new problem to be solved. The program is punched into cards or recorded on other input media and stored in the computer's memory. Data entering the computer are then processed in accordance with the stored program. The computer programs are often referred to as *software*. The computer and other processing machines are known as *hardware*.

All digital computers, regardless of size or make, have a central processing unit (CPU). This unit performs a variety of functions. It translates input data to the language system of the computer. It receives and stores instructions as well as the data to be processed. It transfers and edits stored data. It makes arithmetic computations. It makes decisions of logic. It directs the action of the input and output units. Moreover, a control device located in the central processing unit makes these functions work in harmony with one another.

In addition to the central processing unit, all computer systems are equipped with input and output (I/O) units. Most are also equipped with an external control unit and auxiliary storage devices.

CENTRAL PROCESSING UNIT (CPU)

The *central processing unit* (CPU) of the computer system consists of the internal storage, arithmetic-logic, and control components. The CPU is the heart of the electronic computer system.

Language translation

In all computers, the digits, letters of the alphabet, and symbols entering the central processing unit must be translated to the language system of the computer. Language translation is handled automatically by the central processing unit. For example, data punched into cards in Hollerith code are converted to electronic signals, which make up the language system of the computer. How does this language system work? To arrive at an answer to this question, you need only to understand that an electric light can be turned either on or off, that a switch can be either open or closed, or that a ring can be magnetized either clockwise or counter-clockwise. The language of the computer is thus based on a two-digit number system.

Chapter 11   The electronic computer   171

However, this system can represent all the digits, letters of the alphabet, and some special characters. In short, the digital computer has only two fingers on which it must do its counting. The two-digit language system is discussed in detail in the next chapter.

Internal storage

The internal storage component of the CPU is its memory. It is an integral part of, and under the direct control of, the computer. Depending upon their size, computers are capable of storing thousands of bits of information, each of which is almost instantly accessible.

The internal storage component can accept, hold, and release data as well as the instructions for processing these data. Data and instructions are stored as electronic impulses in specified locations in the memory unit. Each of these locations is identified by an address. Generally, addresses start with zero and extend to the highest number required. The locations are arranged in sequence, and any location may be reached in a fraction of a second. The data desired can be retrieved directly and used as many times as necessary.

Data are erased from memory only when an erase or clear instruction is executed or when new data are stored in memory locations in which data already appear. The new data will then replace the old.

The way in which data are stored in a computer is explained in detail in a later chapter.

Arithmetic-logic

All digital computers are equipped with an arithmetic-logic component, which adds, subtracts, divides, and multiplies numeric data as directed by the program. This unit also enables the CPU to make certain logical decisions in regard to the data it is processing. It can compare two numbers. It can determine whether the numbers are equal or which one is larger if they are unequal. It can also compare two names and determine whether they are the same or different names. Through its ability to compare two fields of data, the arithmetic-logic component can make many decisions.

As an example of this feature of the computer, assume that a company must send one of its employees to Spain quickly. The personnel director is asked to list the names of candidates who are single, under 40, and able to speak Spanish. Figure 11-3 shows how the computer would select the cards of employees who meet the conditions imposed.

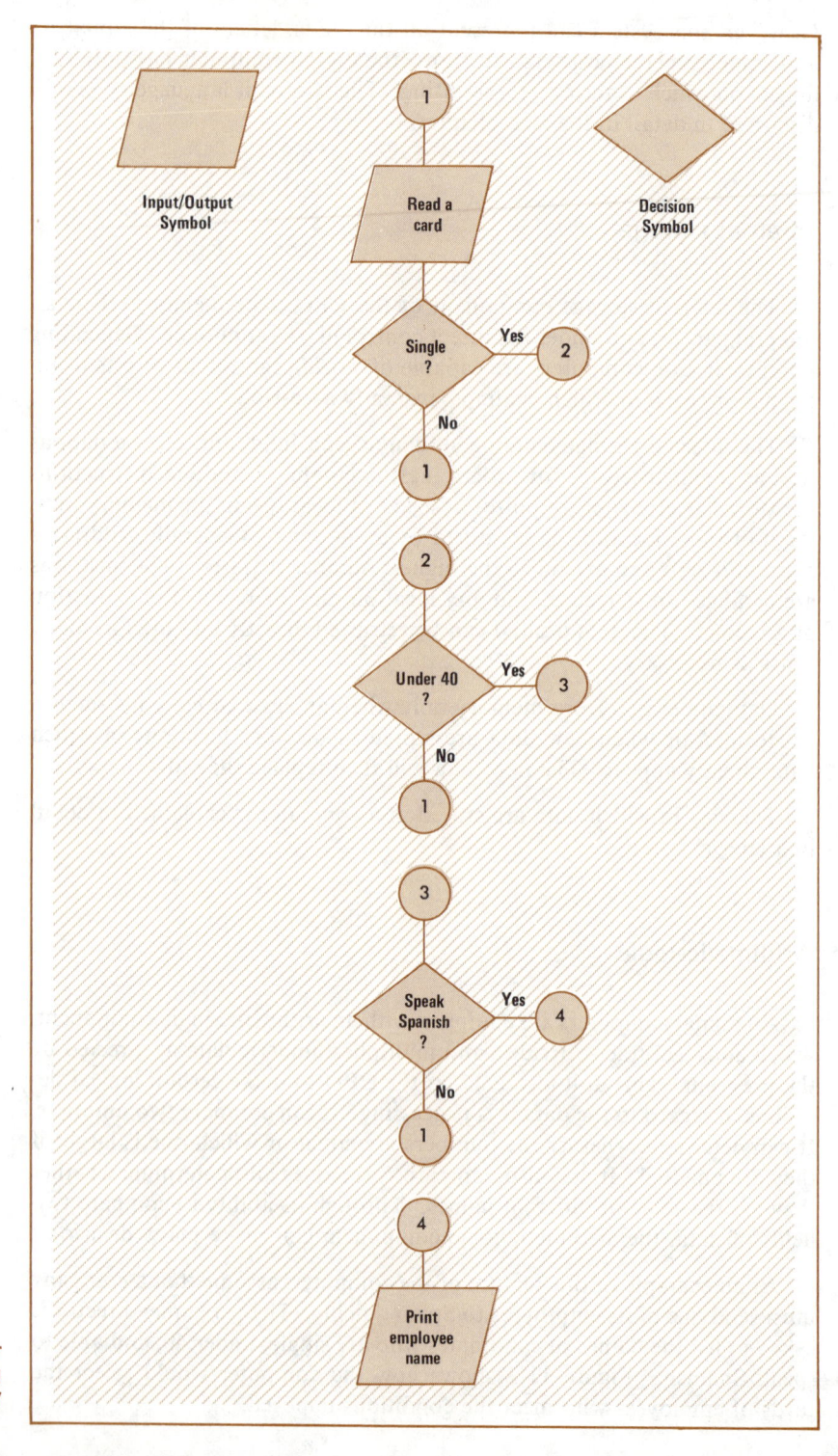

Figure 11-3. Flow chart for partial program indicating typical decisions made by a CPU

If a code number assigned to single employees in a punched card field equals the same number stored in the computer for comparison purposes, the computer will advance to the next instruction in the program. This instruction calls for the computer to compare a number stored in its memory with a number in a field of a punched card, which number represents the employee's age. If the comparison indicates that the employee is under 40, the computer advances to the next instruction, which calls for a comparison of code numbers regarding the employee's ability to speak Spanish.

The name of the employee whose card meets all three tests is then printed. The computer then repeats the above procedure until all cards have been processed. Any card failing one of the tests immediately causes the computer to cease further processing of the data on that particular card. Instead, the computer automatically proceeds to the next employee card in the deck. As a result, when all the employee cards are processed, the printed report contains only the names of those meeting the three tests established in the problem.

Note that the input-output symbol and the decision symbol are briefly introduced in the flow chart in Figure 11-3. These symbols are discussed in detail in Chapter 14. Figure 11-3 is only a partial illustration of the steps in a computer program.

Control

As you can see, the central processing unit is the heart of the entire electronic computer system. Because of the computer's unique electronic makeup, the electronic computer system is much faster and more flexible than any other data processing system developed up to this time.

So far, you have examined most of the vital organs of the central processing unit of a computer. One organ translates the data from the language of the input medium to the language of the computer. Other organs store data in memory, make calculations, and arrive at decisions on the basis of name or number comparisons. What gives life to these organs and makes them work in harmony with one another? The control component contains the master clock that provides this life-like element.

The *control component* regulates the various functions of the computer. It is here that the intricate timing system of the computer is located. It is here, too, that the instructions making up the programs are interpreted.

Examine Figure 11-4, which illustrates the central role played by the control component.

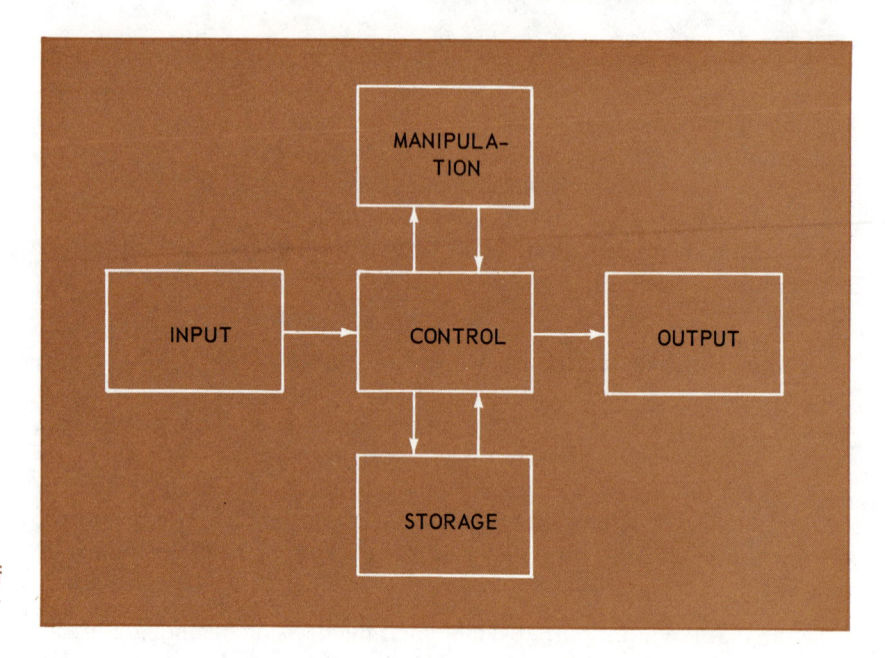

Figure 11-4. The flow of information in the electronic computer system

INPUT AND OUTPUT UNITS

All digital computers are equipped with one or more input and output units. These units, which are not considered as part of the CPU, bring raw data to the computer and take processed information from it.

Input unit

The *input unit* consists of one or more devices capable of receiving information and instructions needed to solve a problem. An input unit is able to receive data from the familiar punched card, magnetic or paper tape, an electric typewriter attached to the computer, or other input media acceptable to the computer. You are already familiar with punched cards. The other media will be described later in this chapter. After receiving the data, the input unit communicates the data to the CPU.

Output unit

After the problem has been solved and the processed data have been stored, the computer must reverse its opening procedure. It must now send the answer in the form of electronic impulses to the output unit. The *output unit* records or displays the processed information on the output media, which may be printed reports, punched cards, magnetic tape, or

Chapter 11   The electronic computer

some other medium compatible with the computer used. Output units vary from computer system to system. An output unit may be a high-speed printer, magnetic tape drive, card punch, cathode-ray tube, or one of the other visual or audio output devices in use.

Input/output units

Many of the input units can also be used as output devices as well. For example, the card read-punch unit illustrated in Figure 11-5 can read data punched into cards and transfer the data into the CPU for processing. After the data have been processed, if so desired, the results may be punched into a new set of cards. The CPU controls the action, but the card read-punch unit does the punching. The card read-punch unit is thus both an input and an output unit.

The magnetic-tape drive also illustrated in Figure 11-5 can be used to read data into the CPU for processing. Another magnetic tape drive unit can read the processed data out of the computer. Therefore, the magnetic-tape drive unit also may be used as either an input or an output device.

The high-speed line printer in Figure 11-5 cannot originate data. The information printed by it must come from the CPU. The printer, therefore, is an output unit only.

There are many other input/output devices in the electronic computer system, which will be discussed later in this chapter.

Figure 11-5. Some common computer input and output units

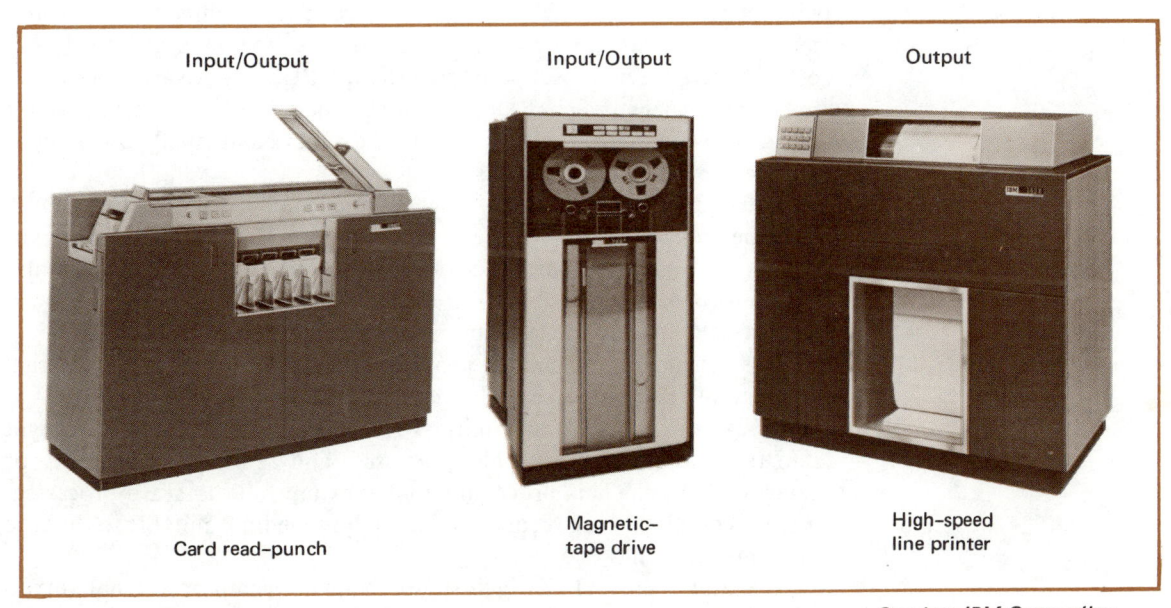

Input/Output — Card read-punch

Input/Output — Magnetic-tape drive

Output — High-speed line printer

Courtesy IBM Corporation

SUPPLEMENTARY STORAGE DEVICES

Auxiliary storage

Auxiliary storage devices supplement the internal storage or memory of the CPU. These auxiliary or "*on-line*" devices (consisting of magnetic disks, magnetic film, magnetic tape, or other input/output devices) are outside the central processing unit, but they are, nonetheless, connected to it. Data in auxiliary storage are thus under the control of the CPU and are accessible to it.

For example, a reel of magnetic tape that is connected to the computer by a magnetic-tape drive is said to be in auxiliary storage. When this particular reel is removed from the drive and filed, however, it is in external or "off-line" storage.

Auxiliary storage has a limited capacity but is often faster because some of the devices permit random access to data. *Random access* means that the computer can go directly to an item of information and retrieve it without examining all the data in a file.

External storage

External storage devices are completely independent of the central processing unit. However, the data are recorded in a form suitable to the computer. External storage devices may consist of punched cards and punched paper tape. Of course, when magnetic tape, magnetic disks, and other devices are no longer connected to the CPU, they are also considered to be in external storage. Random access to data in external storage is not possible. Data in external storage must be mounted manually on an input unit before they can be processed.

Auxiliary storage generally contains current operating data, such as customers' accounts, inventories, or subscription lists, which must be updated on a continuing basis. External storage generally contains information that is not used as often. For example, information about customers' accounts that are no longer active may be kept in external storage.

The instructions to solve a problem are usually stored in the internal memory of the computer. The data to be processed usually appear in auxiliary or external storage units. Portions of the data are then brought into the internal memory unit, processed, and returned to auxiliary or external storage. This procedure continues until all data are processed. The processed data are recorded on an output medium suitable to the type of computer being used.

Examine Figure 11-6, which shows the relationship of internal, auxiliary, and external storage components to the computer.

Chapter 11   The electronic computer

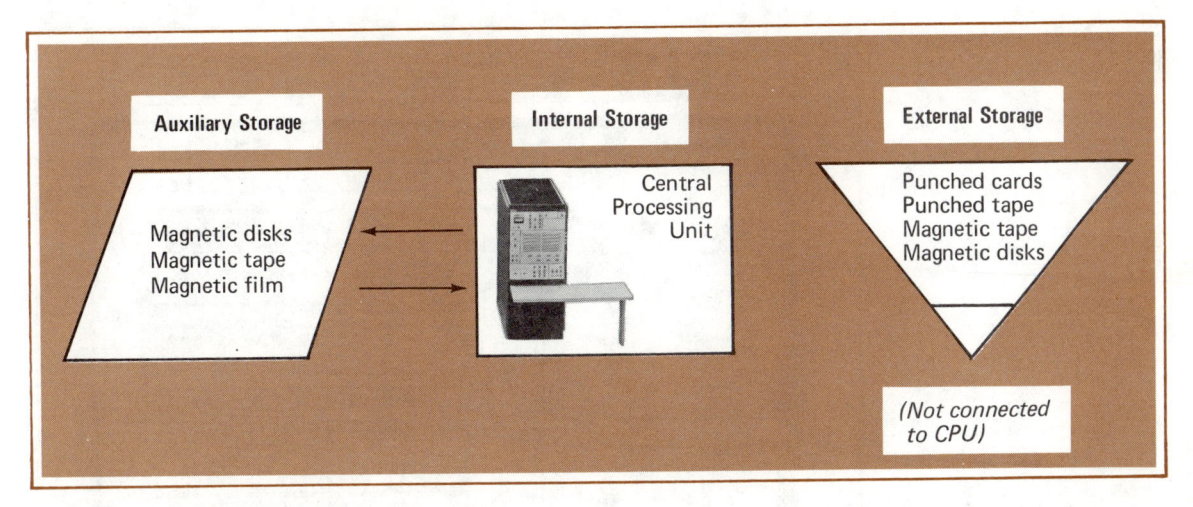

Figure 11-6. Relationship of internal, auxiliary, and external storage units of computer

EXTERNAL CONTROL UNIT

The internal control of computer operations is handled by the instructions that have been written to solve a problem and that have been stored in the internal memory of the CPU. However, external control of operations by an operator is also possible. An operator can control operations through the use of a *console* or *console inquiry station* with which computers are equipped. These are the glamour units of a computer because they are most often featured in printed illustrations. The console panel has flashing lights, buttons, and switches, which tell the operator how the computer is reacting to the data being processed and any difficulties it is encountering with the data or program.

Console

The *console*, such as the one shown on the IBM 360, Figure 11-7, is used to provide information to the operator about the performance of the system, to enter information into the system manually, to alter the data in storage when necessary, and to start and stop the computer. The operator also uses the console to test for computer failures and to track down any malfunctions. A console panel enables the operator to trace the movement of information throughout the system.

Console inquiry station

The *console inquiry station* extends the functions of the console. It may be part of the console or housed in a separate unit. Figure 11-8 shows it as a separate unit.

Figure 11-7. Console (IBM 360)

Courtesy of IBM Corporation

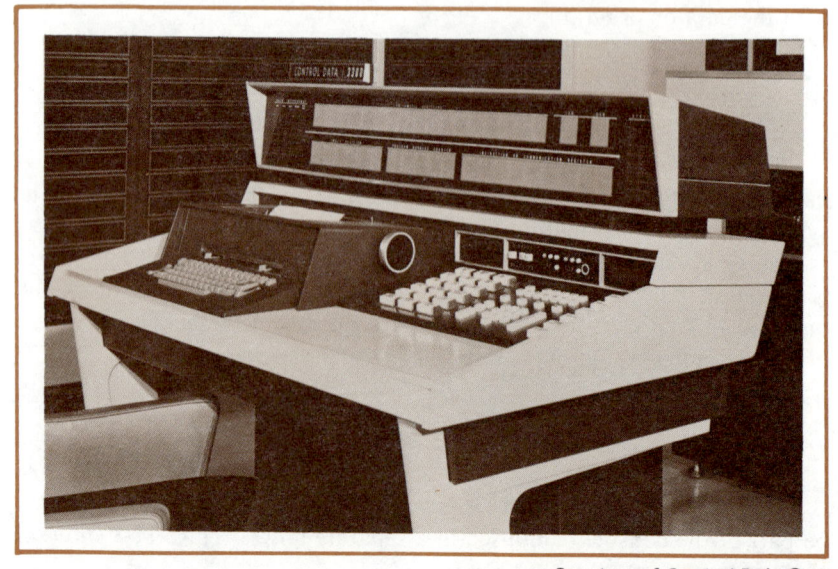

Figure 11-8. Console inquiry station

Courtesy of Control Data Corp.

The console inquiry station usually contains a built-in or auxiliary electric typewriter. With it, the operator can enter new data or instructions into the computer. He can also use it to request the computer to furnish certain types of information. The request must appear in the exact form required by the computer. The program stored in the computer can determine from the request what information is desired. The reply (requested information) will be typed out on the inquiry station typewriter.

PROCESSING PLAN OF THE ELECTRONIC COMPUTER SYSTEM

Figure 11-9 contains a flow chart depicting the plan followed by the electronic computer in processing data. The essential elements of this plan are as follows:

1. Information originates in source documents, such as time cards, enrollment forms, membership applications, invoices, and score sheets.
2. The data needed in solving problems is transcribed from source documents to punched cards, paper tape, magnetic tape, or other input media acceptable to the computer.
3. The data are checked for accuracy. (If punched cards are used, the cards are verified after punching.)
4. The punched cards are usually grouped and arranged in alphabetic or numeric sequence on a sorter or collator, as needed, to solve a particular problem.
5. Detailed instructions (the computer program) are written to solve a particular problem. These instructions are usually written, one instruction to a line on a program sheet, in the exact form required by the computer being used.
6. The instructions are rerecorded in punched cards or other media acceptable to the computer and the cards are verified.
7. The program instruction cards are read into the computer and stored in the CPU in the form of electronic impulses. The program instructions will be followed step-by-step as the computer carries out its work.
8. The program is tested by processing a sample of the data cards.
9. The data are "read" into the computer and translated to the language of the CPU, in which form they enter the internal memory unit.
10. The data are then processed (moved, used in calculations, compared) as directed by the computer program.
11. The processed data are directed out of internal storage and are translated from electronic impulses to the language of the output medium being used. A record of processed data is made.

180   The electronic computer system   Part 4

Source documents are collected.

Data are transcribed from source documents to punched cards, using card punch.

Punched cards are verified, using card verifier.

Punched cards are arranged in order, using sorter or collator.

Instructions are written for computer program, one instruction to a line.

Program instructions are punched into cards, using card punch.

Program instruction cards are verified, using card verifier.

Program instruction cards are read into computer.

Program is tested by processing sample of data cards.

Data cards are read into computer.

Data are processed by CPU.

Processed data are read out of computer in form desired.

Processed data cards are stored.

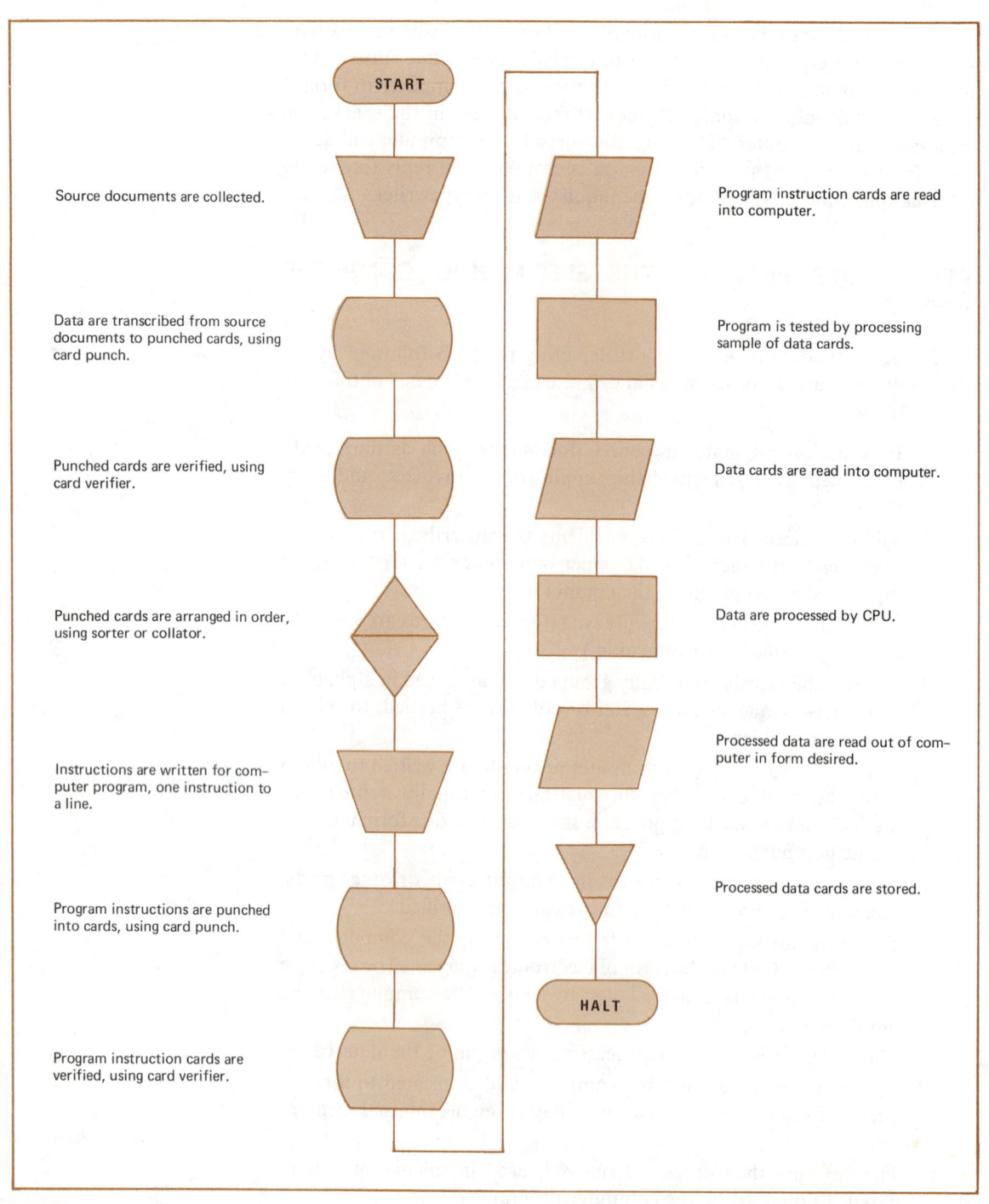

Figure 11-9. Steps followed in the electronic computer system when processing data

12. Processing continues until all information appearing on input media has passed through the foregoing plan and the program instructs the computer to halt. The data cards are stored.

REVIEW QUESTIONS

1. What is the function of an analog computer? A digital computer?
2. What features make an electronic digital computer system different from the unit-record system?
3. What functions are performed by the CPU?
4. How does the computer make logical decisions?
5. How are data erased from memory?
6. What functions are performed by the control component of a computer?
7. What is the function of the input unit? the output unit?
8. In what ways are external storage devices different from auxiliary storage devices?
9. What does the term "random access" mean?
10. How is internal control of the computer handled?
11. How is external control of the computer handled?
12. Briefly describe the steps included in processing data when an electronic digital computer is used.

INPUT AND OUTPUT MEDIA AND DEVICES

While the punched card has been the workhorse as an input medium for processing data automatically, other input media are available, some of which have been in use for quite some time. There is a continuous attempt on the part of engineers to find new and better ways of "feeding" data into a processing machine. The same efforts are being directed toward the development of output devices that make it easier for the user to utilize the output data produced by the machines.

Earlier in this book, you learned about the use of punched cards, punched paper tape, edge-punched cards, perforated cards, and mark-sensed cards as a means of communicating with automated machines. In this chapter, you will learn about additional devices now in use in the electronic computer system and especially about some of the recent advancements in this field.

Magnetic tape

An input, output, and storage medium commonly used with an electronic computer is magnetic tape. This tape is similar to that used in an ordinary tape recorder found in many homes and offices. The tape is coated with a magnetically sensitive substance. The data are then recorded on this tape as magnetized spots that create electrical impulses. Although

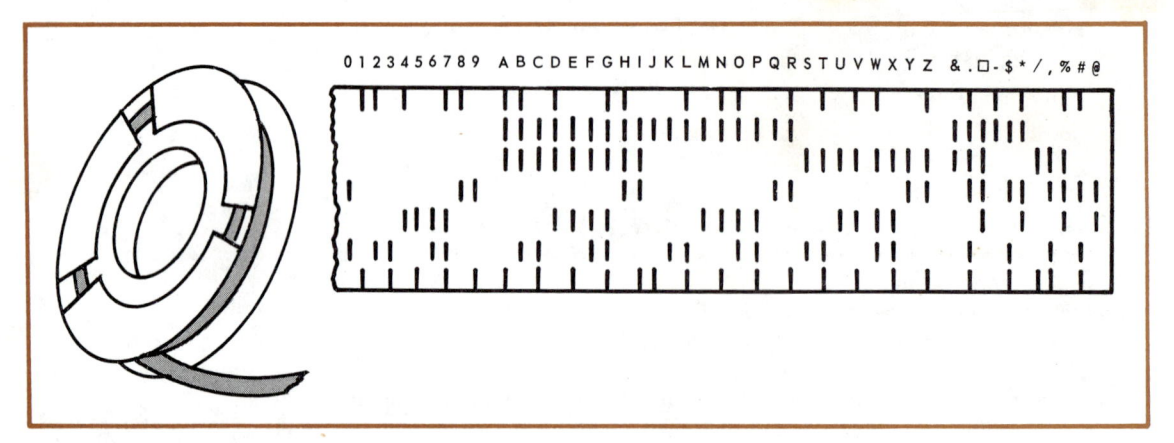

Figure 11-10. A visual representation of magnetic tape showing how the magnetized spots might appear

the magnetized spots on magnetic tape cannot be seen, Figure 11-10 shows how they might appear if visible. The use of magnetic tape for recording data and/or instructions is usually associated with average or large-scale computer systems.

The principal advantages of magnetic tape are the compactness with which data can be recorded and the speed with which the data can be processed. For example, it has been said that the information recorded in a stack of punched cards over 100 feet high and containing more than 14 million characters can be recorded in a single reel of magnetic tape. All this information can be read or reproduced in less than four and one-half minutes. Magnetic tape can be used over and over again for storing different information, whereas paper tape can be used only once. Although paper tape costs less than magnetic tape, the magnetic tape is more durable.

Recording information on magnetic tape. Information frequently enters the computer via punched cards or some other input medium. The processed output may then be rerecorded by the computer on magnetic tape. The information on the tape may later be used as input when further processing takes place.

Recent improvements in technology permit the direct recording of data on magnetic tape. A keyboard-to-tape machine, with a keyboard similar to that found on an electric typewriter or a card punch, is used for the purpose. Figure 11-11 illustrates a tape data recorder. (Sales orders phoned in by local salesmen are recorded on magnetic tape in tape cartridges in the open drawer.)

Proofreading magnetic tape and correcting errors. When data are punched in cards as the input medium and recorded in processed form on magnetic tape by the computer as output, the magnetic tape is not proofed. However, the data punched in the cards will have been checked on a verifier. This checking method was explained in an earlier chapter.

Chapter 11   The electronic computer   183

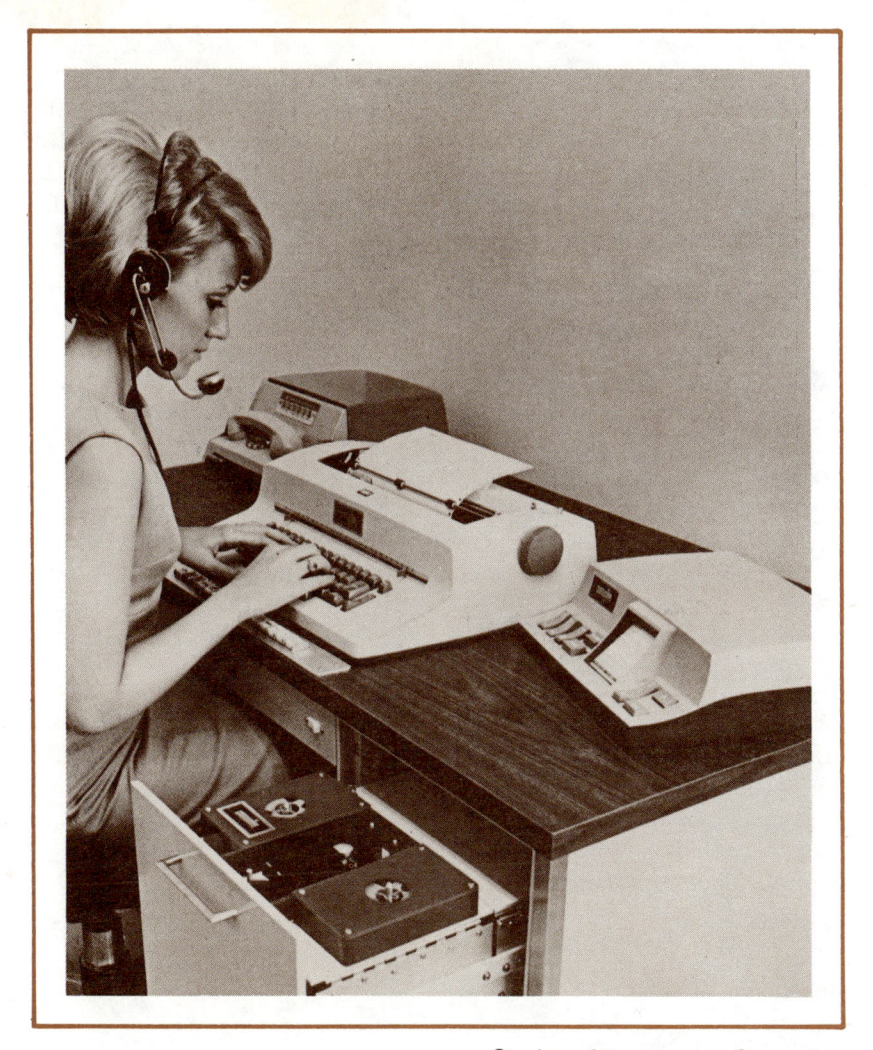

Figure 11-11. Magnetic tape data recorder

Courtesy of Communitype Corporation

The procedure for recording data directly on magnetic tape varies from machine to machine. Generally, however, the procedure is as follows:

(1) The operator keys the data from a source document into the tape-recording machine. The data are recorded in magnetic form in a buffer, which is an auxiliary storage device designed to hold the data temporarily. The buffer is attached to the tape-recording machine.

(2) After the data from a source document are recorded in the buffer, they are transferred on command to magnetic tape.

(3) When all source documents have been processed in the manner described above, the tape is reversed to the beginning entry and rerun. The information from the tape reenters the buffer.

(4) The operator keys the data into the buffer again from each source document. As each letter or digit is keyed, it is compared by the machine to the corresponding character stored in the buffer memory. Verification continues in this manner until an error is detected. When it is, the keyboard locks. The error may be corrected by merely striking the correct key at the point of the error. From the buffer, the verified data are transmitted to the magnetic tape.

Keying errors, if detected by the operator, may also be corrected immediately by backspacing and rekeying.

Information recorded in magnetic tape is of two types. One type contains the data to be read into the computer and stored there for later use. The other type contains the instructions that tell the computer what to do with the data it receives.

Data are recorded in parallel channels or tracks along the length of tape. Tapes having 7 or 9 channels are available. Seven-channel tape is illustrated in Figure 11-10. Letters of the alphabet, decimal numbers, punctuation marks, and special characters may be recorded on the tape.

Magnetic drums

Magnetic drums can be used as input, output, and storage media. Many early computers are still using the magnetic drum, which is a cylinder on which a series of bands or tracks appear on the outer surface. The bands are capable of being magnetized, and the magnetized surfaces can store electronic signals representing data. As the drum rotates at a constant rate, the data are either recorded or read by read-write heads.

Magnetic disks

Magnetic disks are also used for input, output, and storage. They operate in much the same way as magnetic drums. Disks are coated on both sides with a substance capable of being magnetized. Data are stored as magnetic spots on tracks on the disk. Read-write heads are mounted above each track to record or read data.

Magnetic ink characters

The use of magnetized spots on tape undoubtedly led to the development of magnetic ink characters. These numbers and symbols, which are of special design and are imprinted in magnetic ink, can be recognized and processed electronically by machines. Magnetic ink characters are unique in that they can be read by machines as well as by anyone familiar with the type used for printing the characters. A set of such figures is illustrated in Figure 11-12.

Chapter 11 The electronic computer

⑉⓪ ②⑥⓪ ⑪⓪③①⑤⑉ ①②⑨⑤⑪④③⑧⑦⑀

Figure 11-12. Figures designed for magnetic ink character reading

The figures, in addition to being printed in a distinctive style, are coated with a thick layer of a magnetic substance, thus making it possible for the machines to sense the figures electronically. Banks use these figures to process checks and deposit slips by computers. A magnetic ink character reader, illustrated in Figure 11-13, reads the data from the check or deposit slip and translates the data into computer code. The data can also be converted to punched cards or magnetic tape and read into the computer by these media. The chief advantage of using magnetic ink records is that they appear in readable human-language form and may thus be used on conventional business papers. In addition, they can be read into the computer with a minimum of human help.

Figure 11-13. Magnetic ink character reader (IBM 1259)

Courtesy IBM Corporation

Optical mark page reader

The *optical mark page reader* is a device capable of sensing marks made by regular pencil or pen on a specially designed form. The marks are not in human-language form. Actually, this optical scanning technique is similar to that used for mark-sensed cards, a process discussed in Chapter 7. In mark sensing, the marks are made on a card with a graphite pencil. Each mark is individually sensed. In optical scanning, using the optical-mark page reader, provision is made for far more marks than can be made on a card. Up to 1,000 marks can be made on an 8½- by 11-inch piece of paper.

Figure 11-14 shows one medium that is used. The form illustrated is a multiple-choice test form on which a student records the answers. Note that the fields are preplanned. Provision is made to record the student's name, identification number, and answer to each question. Note the boxes or spaces provided for the pencil or pen marks. These spaces are similar to the spaces provided on the mark-sensed card. The size and design of the form on which the marks are made are flexible and can be changed to take care of a special need. In Figure 11-14, ten spaces have been provided for recording the student number. Reading from the top to the bottom of the student number field, Number 0009425173 is recorded. Fifty questions in the test have been answered.

By scanning the page, an optical mark page reader interprets the marks and reads into the computer the data represented by the marks. Data can be fed into the computer directly by the optical scanning device. Most frequently, however, the data are converted to punched cards or magnetic tape and read into the computer by these media. An optical mark page reader is also illustrated in Figure 11-14. Instead of sensing each mark individually, as is done with the mark-sensed card, the optical mark page reader is equipped with photoelectric cells that scan the page and detect the marks, reading an entire row at a time. This technique provides a very flexible and rapid method of entering data into a computer.

Optical scanner

An *optical scanner* is a device that will read and transmit data from a page directly into a computer. The data to be read by an optical scanner are usually printed on the page in special type fonts similar to the special designs used for magnetic ink characters. The requirements of the special type fonts are determined by the individual scanner. Generally, the characters must appear in a certain area of the document. A scanner will read only what it has been programmed to read.

Scanners speed read photoelectrically numeric and alphabetic data and transmit the scanned data into the processing unit of the computer. Most scanners will read only those documents printed on paper of a certain weight. Generally, the paper must be white. Color of ink, smudges, paper creases, and other similar factors have a bearing on scanning efficiency.

Despite the rigid requirements referred to in the foregoing paragraph, scanners are being employed in increasing numbers by department stores to read price tickets and cash register tapes for billing and inventory control. They are also used for invoicing. In addition, more and more schools

Chapter 11   The electronic computer

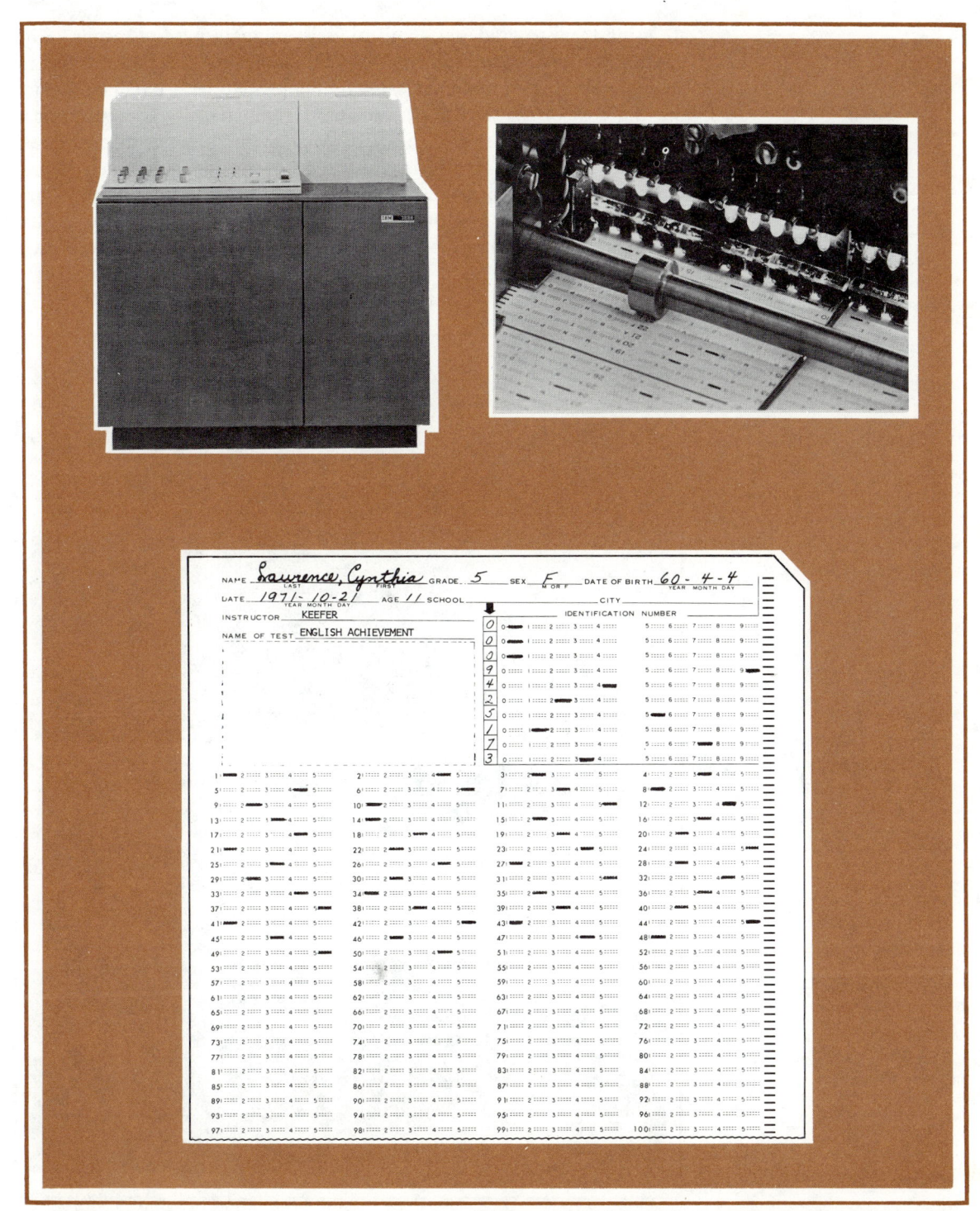

Courtesy of IBM Corporation

Figure 11-14. Optical mark page reader and forms

are using them to grade tests and to assist in analyzing test results. The Post Office Department is currently installing optical scanners to assist in sorting mail. If and when optical scanning procedures are refined further and the cost of the necessary specialized equipment is reduced, optical scanners may replace in part the preparation of input by punched cards or paper tape. Figure 11-15 is an illustration of an optical scanner. Magnetically coded merchandise tickets (top) and credit cards (bottom) are read, verified, and the information transmitted to J. C. Penney's Data Center in a fraction of a second over the TRADAR System point-of-sale terminals.

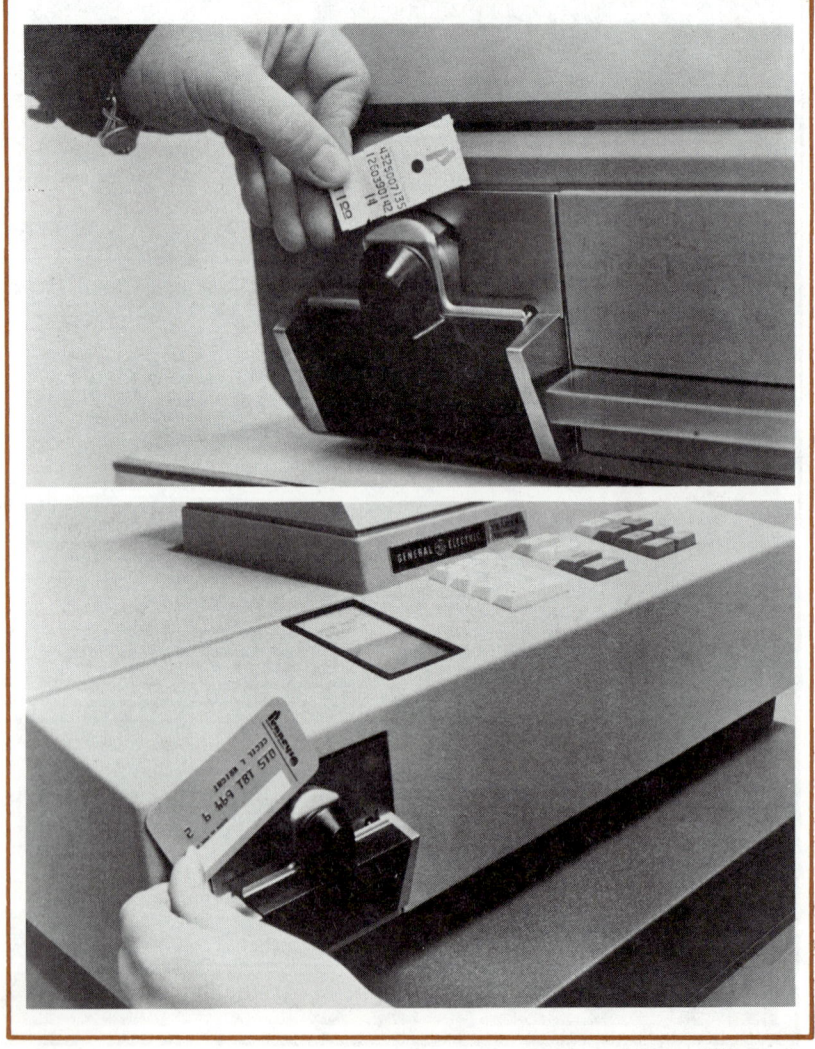

Figure 11-15. Optical scanning application

Courtesy of General Electric Co.

Optical scanners may read data from a variety of documents, including impressions made by gasoline credit cards and tapes prepared by cash registers and adding machines. In all cases, the scanner reads the data appearing in special type fonts on these documents. In the case of the gasoline credit card, the scanner reads the user's account number, in special type font, and the amount of each bill, after the amount has been imprinted in special type on the bill or has been punched into a card. In the cash register tape, a scanner can read the amount of each sale imprinted on the tape by the special fonts.

REVIEW QUESTIONS

1. What are the principle advantages of recording input data on magnetic tape?
2. In what way or ways does magnetic tape differ from punched paper tape?
3. Describe two ways of recording data on magnetic tape.
4. Describe two methods of checking the accuracy of data recorded on magnetic tape. How may errors on magnetic tape be corrected?
5. What is the chief advantage of using magnetic ink records?
6. Describe the procedure used by the optical mark page reader as an input medium.
7. Describe the procedure used by an optical scanner as an input medium.
8. Describe some of the ways in which optical scanners are used.

Direct input of handwritten numerals

A number of attempts are being made to enter handwritten information directly into a computer for storage or processing. One such attempt, known as Elastic Diaphragm Switch Technology (EDST), employs hundreds of tiny electrical switches combined in a complex assembly. As the operator writes on a card placed over the assembly, the pressure of his pen actuates the switches, causing the numerals he is writing to appear on a display panel. If the display is correct, the operator presses a button to transmit the data to the computer. If there is an error, the operator can correct it.

At present, the amount of information that may be entered into a computer by EDST is limited. However, the day may soon come when an unlimited number of handwritten characters, both alphabetic and numeric, will be acceptable input to computers.

Graph input and output units

In computer terminology, *graphic units* are those that represent data by use of pictures or graphs. With the arrival of graphic systems in computers, the concept of direct communication between man and machines has taken on new dimensions. Computer components have been developed that can process both graphic and alphameric information.

A complete graphic system will link to a computer various input-output units, such as film scanners, film records, and display units. This system will provide integrated graphic input, processing, and output. Information will be accepted in graphic form, converted to digital form for processing, and then stored. The system will convert the information from digital back to graphic form and display it on a television type screen or record it as required. See Figure 11-16 for typical input and output graph units.

IBM 2250 Graphic Display Unit

Eastman Kodak Rekordak Microstar

IBM 1627 Graph Plotter

Figure 11-16. Typical graphic units

Chapter 11 The electronic computer

Microfilm output units

A process recently developed for automated data handling is one in which an output unit takes information from a computer (or from computer-generated tapes) and records it directly on film for cartridge storage systems or aperture cards. Computer-processed information is converted to microfilm quickly and automatically.

Insurance companies, banks, utility organizations, and other firms that must store a large volume of computer-generated data can retrieve the information almost instantly when these data are recorded directly on microfilm cartridges or aperture cards. Typical applications are customer histories; account, payroll, and personnel records; transportation route and rate information; credit information; stock transfers; and inventory control.

An aperture card is illustrated in Figure 11-17. Information appears on the microfilm inset. The punched holes in the card provide a means of quick and automatic retrieval.

Figure 11-17. Aperture card

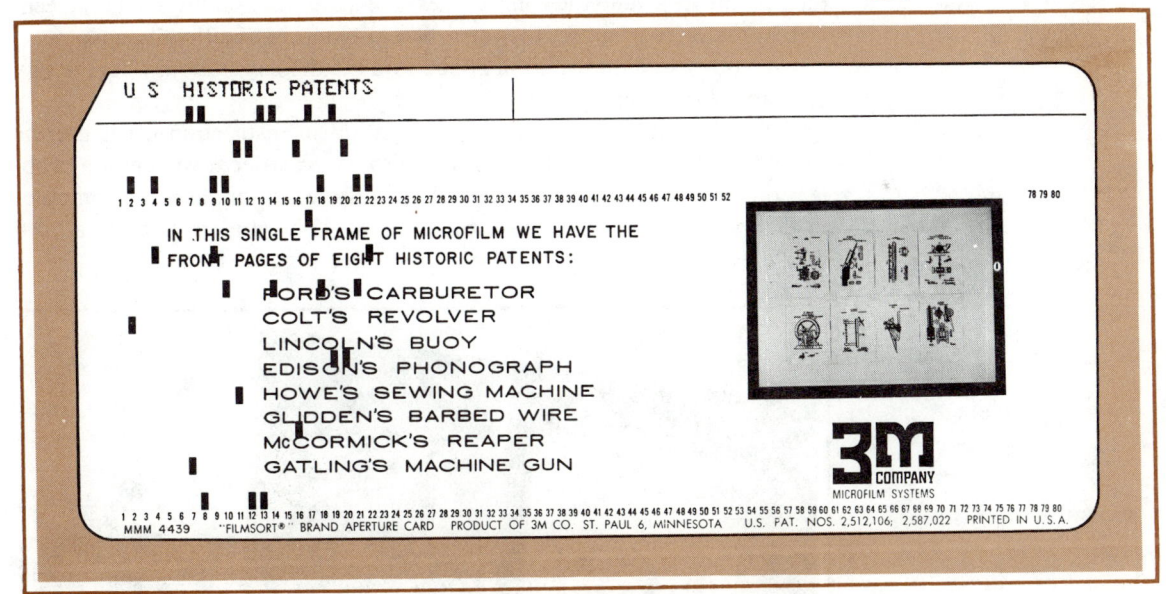

Courtesy of 3M Company

Cathode-ray tube input-output unit (CRT)

This unit consists of a console with a display station that has an electronic vacuum tube like the picture tube in a television set. The unit offers the user a rapid way of getting information into and out of a computer.

The complete unit has a keyboard, similar to that found on a typewriter or card punch, and a display screen, on which the data are viewed. The unit is also equipped with a buffer in which input information is stored temporarily before releasing it to the computer. In this way, the operator can proofread and correct the input before turning it over to the computer. An example of the way data are entered into this unit follows:

1. The system is made ready for data entry by keying in a special code identifying the user.
2. The program stored in the computer then forms a heading message on the display screen in order to identify the program.
3. The user then keys in the data on the console. The data enter the buffer and are displayed on the screen below the heading.
4. When the record is complete, the user presses an Enter Key; and the header and record are read into the computing system.

Should the operator of the console make an error and be aware of it, he can backspace and strike the correct key. When the computer detects an error (such as the form in which the data are recorded), the keyboard on the console locks and the computer explains the error on the display screen. The operator can correct the error before entering additional data.

The processed information appears on the display station, where it may be read by the user.

Schools that use the computer as an aid in instruction often use the cathode-ray tube for the input-output device. A student will enter a problem or inquiry into the computer via a console station, and the computer in turn will display the answer on the tube. The student is given an immediate visual response to the question. See Figure 11-18.

Figure 11-18. Student using terminal for computer-assisted instruction

Courtesy IBM Corporation

Through some recent developments, the computer can receive drawings and sketches. One of the ways in which sketches can be fed directly into a computer is through the use of a special grid. The grid consists of hundreds of wires that are connected to the internal workings of the computer. A piece of paper is placed over the grid. A special pen connected to the grid is used to make the desired sketch on the paper. As the sketch is made on the paper, the grid senses the position of the pen and sends impulses into the computer. The impulses may then be used to display the drawing on the cathode-ray tube.

Audio-response unit (ARP)

Man's effort to communicate with machines is ceaseless. You have learned that man is able to communicate with a machine by using punched cards, magnetic tape, magnetic ink characters, and other media. It is not surprising to see man now making some headway in an attempt to communicate with a machine verbally. A limited amount of success has been achieved in getting the machine to understand verbal input. Greater success has been achieved, however, in verbal output by a computer.

Audio-response units provide verbal replies to questions directed to the machine by means of various input devices, such as a special telephone or remote console combined with a listening device. Upon receipt of an inquiry, the computer selects the proper response from the vocabulary stored within its memory. The response is then transmitted verbally to the person making the inquiry. The vocabulary that can be stored within the machine on magnetic tape and then selected by the machine for verbal response is limited to a few words. What is important is that success in verbal communication has been achieved. It is predicted that great improvements will be made in audio-response units in the future. An audio-response unit is illustrated in Figure 11-19.

Remote consoles

Manufacturers have increased the speed and memory capacity to the point where it is possible for one computer to accommodate several different users on a time-sharing basis. *Time sharing* is an arrangement whereby more than one user shares the use of the same computer. Furthermore, the users can be located at different points and at some distance from the computer itself. In such instances, direct contact with the computer is achieved through a device known as a remote console. The remote console, therefore, eliminates the need for having a computer physically near and also reduces the cost of the computer to individual users by making time sharing possible.

The remote console is similar in appearance to an electric typewriter. The electronic keyboard of the console is connected by telephone or by wire direct to the computer and provides a means of communicating with

Figure 11-19. Audio-response unit (IBM 7770)

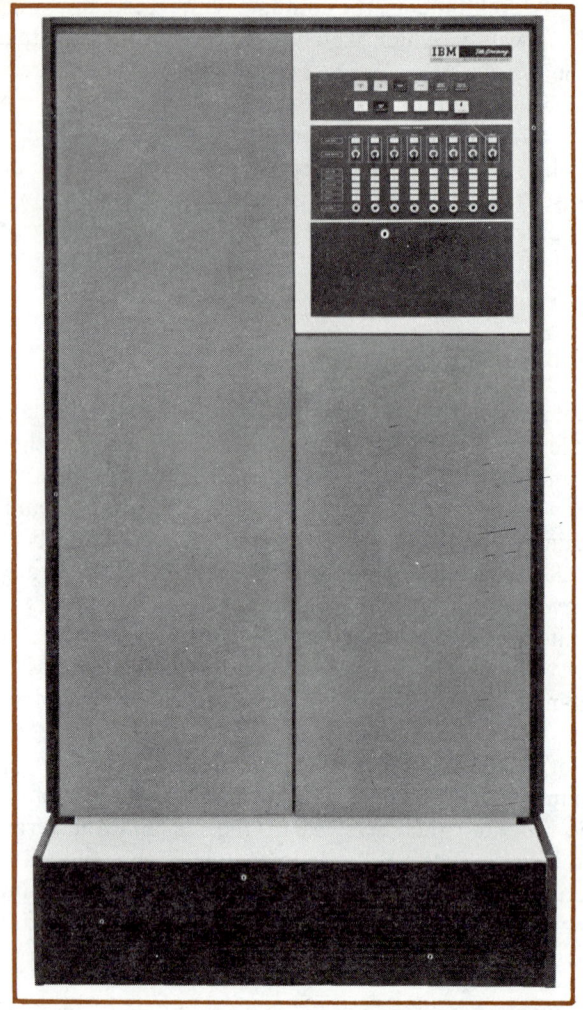

Courtesy IBM Corporation

the machine. See Figure 11-20 for the illustration of a remote console. If desired, a console can be equipped with a display tube, a unit which is capable of handling both input and output.

An example of the use of a centralized computer connected by several remote consoles is a school system comprised of several schools, each of which has access to the computer via a remote console or consoles located within the individual school. By this means, many students are provided the opportunity of sharing in the use of this marvelous machine.

Here is an explanation of how such a system works. The student identifies his station or location to the computer by typing an identifying number into the electronic keyboard on the console. The computer is able to identify each console connected to it. Upon proper identification, the user is signaled to feed his data into the machine. The data are processed, and the processed data are returned to the user via the remote console. If the

Chapter 11   The electronic computer   195

Courtesy of General Electric Co.

Figure 11-20. Remote control console

user makes a mistake and enters the wrong identifying number into the machine, the computer will respond by signaling that it does not recognize the user. If the computer is busy at the time the user gives his identifying number, the inquiry is momentarily stored in a buffer and the computer will respond just as soon as it is free, which normally is within a few seconds. Buffers are described on p. 197.

Printed output

A remote console is often used to produce processed data in printed form. Because the console is nothing more than an electric typewriter that is connected to the computer, the console can be used to print on paper whatever output is desired. The output can be numeric or alphabetic information. An operator must make certain that paper is inserted in the remote console before the printing operation starts. Spacing of the data on the paper is handled through the program stored in the computer.

When a remote console is used to produce printed output, the speed of output is limited because only one character at a time is printed. Furthermore, the mechanical parts on the typewriter cannot move at high speeds.

Whenever large quantities of printed output are desired, high-speed printers are used. High-speed printers are equipped with wheels, cylinders, or chains, on which are contained letters, digits, and special characters. Because each letter and digit appears in several places on the chain, more than one character can be printed at a time. Some of the faster models now in use can print up to 240,000 characters per minute.

The IBM 3211 impact printer, Figure 11-21, is capable of firing out words and numbers at the incredible rate of 2000 lines a minute. This printer is part of the IBM System/370, which is illustrated in Figure 11-22.

Figure 11-21. IBM 3211 impact printer

Courtesy of IBM Corporation

Figure 11-22. IBM System/370, Model 165

Courtesy of IBM Corporation

Buffers

While buffers are not classified as either input or output media, they are discussed briefly in this chapter because they are closely related to these media. Buffers are auxiliary storage devices that hold data in magnetic form on a temporary basis. In some cases, buffers facilitate the proofreading of data; for example, the proofreading of data recorded on magnetic tape by a magnetic tape data recorder. This use of buffers was explained earlier in connection with the discussion of proofreading magnetic tape and correcting errors.

In other cases, buffers facilitate the transfer of data to a computer. This is especially true when a computer is being used on a time-sharing basis by a number of users. Input, arriving while the computer is processing data from a program of another time-sharing user, is temporarily stored in magnetic form in a buffer memory. When the computer is ready for the input, this input is electronically transferred to the computer from the buffer. A computer may be equipped with several such buffers to accommodate simultaneous input from more than one user.

Consider also the fact that the CPU is capable of processing data so much faster than the input units can read the data into the computer from cards or tape. The CPU can also process data faster than the data can be read out of the output units on printed forms, magnetic tape, or other output media. The input and output devices operate mechanically, while the CPU operates electronically at much higher speeds than mechanical devices. Therefore, the CPU is forced to wait until these mechanical operations are completed. To take care of this time lag, buffers are sometimes attached to input and output devices. Data from input cards, for example, are stored in buffers attached to the card read-punch unit. Data from many cards can be stored in a single buffer. These data are then transferred to the computer at electronic speeds. Moreover, output that is to be printed can first be recorded in a buffer at electronic speeds. This information can then be transferred from the buffer to the printer at a rate at which the printer can handle it.

SUMMARY

There are two types of electronic computers: digital and analog. A digital computer counts. It uses numbers rather than physical variables such as temperature and velocity. It manipulates these variables in accordance with a program or mathematical formula.

A digital computer processes data in accordance with a program that has been recorded on input media and stored in its memory. It follows in sequence the instructions included in a program; but it can also branch to a new set of instructions when certain, specified conditions have been met. It works at very high speeds.

All digital computers have a central processing unit (CPU), which translates input data to the language system of the computer, receives and stores instructions as well as the data to be processed, transfers and edits stored data, makes arithmetic computations and decisions of logic, and directs the action of the input and output units. In addition, the CPU includes a control device that makes these functions work in harmony with one another.

All digital computers are equipped with one or more input and output units, which bring new data to and processed information from the CPU. These units may be capable of accommodating a variety of media, such as punched cards, punched paper tape, magnetic tape, magnetic ink characters, electric typewriters, cathode-ray tubes, graph plotters, optical scanners, or audio-response devices.

Auxiliary storage devices supplement the internal storage units of a computer. While these devices are outside the CPU, they are connected to it and are under its control. External storage devices are completely separated from and independent of the CPU. The data are recorded in a form suitable to the computer, however.

External control of the computer is possible through the use of a console or console inquiry station. These devices make it possible for the operator to enter information into the computer manually, to alter the data stored in the computer, to start and stop the computer, to track down failures, and to perform other necessary functions.

A number of input and output media have been developed to bring raw data to, and processed data from, computers. The punched card is a common form. Another commonly used input and output medium for electronic computers is magnetic tape. Data are recorded on this tape as invisible magnetized spots. The principal advantages of magnetic tape are the compactness with which data can be recorded and the speed with which information can be brought to and from the computer.

The computer is also capable of accepting information that has been printed on forms in magnetic ink. Usually, the printed characters are of special design. A magnetic ink character reader can read the data directly into the computer. Some magnetic ink character readers can also record the data in punched cards or on magnetic tape. The punched cards and magnetic tape may then be used as input media.

An optical mark page reader is capable of sensing marks made by regular pencil or pen on specially designed forms. This device interprets the marks and reads the data into the computer or records the information in punched cards or on magnetic tape. An optical scanner is capable of reading printed alphabetic and numeric data directly into a computer. Generally, the printed characters must be of special design.

Computer components that can process graphic information have also been developed. The information is accepted in graphic form, converted to digital form for processing, and reconverted to graphic form when the processed information leaves the computer. Some progress has also been made in developing an input device that can interpret handwritten information and relay it to the computer for storage or processing.

Computer input and output may also appear in graphic or descriptive form on a cathode-ray tube. Components have been developed that permit the computer to understand verbal questions and to provide verbal responses to the questions. As yet, the computer's vocabulary is quite limited.

Computers are also available that can process the information of several different users on a time-sharing basis. The users may be located some distance from the computer. Contact is made with the computer by one of the users by using a remote console, connected to a computer by telephone lines. The user transmits his problem to the computer via the console, The processed information is then received by him on the console.

Buffers are often used with input/output devices. Buffers are auxiliary storage devices that hold data in magnetic form on a temporary basis. In some cases, these devices facilitate the proofreading of data; for example. the proofreading of data recorded on magnetic tape by a magnetic tape data recorder. Buffers also facilitate the transfer of data to a computer when the computer is being used on a time-sharing basis. When used in connection with input and output of data, a buffer will permit the CPU to work at top speed.

REVIEW QUESTIONS

1. May handwritten numerals and letters of the alphabet be used as computer input?
2. Are computers capable of accepting input in graphic form?
3. When cathode-ray tubes are used as an output medium, how is the processed information displayed?
4. When cathode-ray tubes are used as an input medium, how are the data to be processed recorded?
5. What success has so far been achieved in communicating verbally with the computer?
6. Describe the procedure followed in communicating with a computer by remote consoles. What are the advantages of using remote consoles?
7. Describe some of the ways in which buffers are used to facilitate the processing of data by computers.
8. Why can the CPU process data so much faster than input/output units can handle it?

STUDY GUIDE

Complete Study Guide 11 by following the instructions in your **STUDY GUIDES** booklet.

PROJECT

Complete Project 11-1 by following the instructions in your **PROJECTS** booklet.

CHAPTER 12

LANGUAGE AND COMPUTING SYSTEMS

BINARY CODE

It is possible for one to operate an electronic computer without having any knowledge of the inner mechanism of the machine, just as it is possible to operate a typewriter or an adding machine without understanding the printing mechanisms of either. However, many students have found that a knowledge of the coding systems used by modern computers is fascinating. The discussions in this chapter will give a brief explanation of some of the codes most widely used with modern-day digital computers.

You have learned in an earlier chapter that the electronic computer is able to store the data being processed as well as the instructions for processing that data. Information is represented in almost all digital computers by positive and negative charges of electric current. If a magnetic core is magnetized in one direction, there will be a pulse; if the core is magnetized in the opposite direction, there will be no pulse.

The *magnetic cores* are tiny, doughnut-shaped rings, connected by wires. Each magnetic core is an information-storage position, capable of holding one *bit* (*bi*nary dig*it*) of information. The internal storage of information will be discussed in detail in Chapter 13. However, for a general understanding of the language systems of a computer, it is only necessary to understand that a computer is limited to a two-digit numbering system because the electronic circuits inside a computer can exist in only two possible states ("on" and "off"). This two-digit numbering system is known as the *binary code*, which is a system in which numbers are built on a base of 2.

Even though you may be familiar with other numbering systems, most of us are so accustomed to the decimal system, in which numbers are built on a base of 10, that we find it difficult to accept the fact that other systems are available. The number of hours in a day, for example, is counted by 12's (the duodecimal system), and the number of minutes in an hour by 60's (the sexagesimal system).

BINARY CODE FOR DIGITS

In the decimal system, employing ten digits from 0 to 9, the value of a digit increases 10 times with each move of one space to the left. This is another way of saying that the number increases by the power of 10.

In the binary system, the value of a digit increases 2 times with each move of one space to the left. The number thus increases by the power of 2.

In pencil and paper figuring, the binary system uses only two digits: 1 and 0. The other digits, 2 through 9, are never used. In a computer, the 1 represents a circuit turned on; the 0 represents a circuit turned off. Study the following table. Note that a digit doubles its value each time it moves one place to the left.

Decimal Digit	*Binary Notation*
1	0001
2	0010
4	0100
8	1000

Next, note how the other digits are expressed. The table below shows the on and off combinations for all the digits 0 through 9. Each horizontal row of four binary digits represents four core storage positions.

Decimal Digit	*Binary Notation*
0	0000
1	0001
2	0010
3 (2 + 1)	0011
4	0100
5 (4 + 1)	0101
6 (4 + 2)	0110
7 (4 + 2 + 1)	0111
8	1000
9 (8 + 1)	1001

Chapter 12 Language and computing systems

Each position represents a binary digit in core storage. Each row of four horizontal cores illustrated represents one unit of numeric information in the computer.

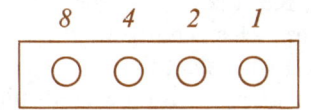

```
  8   4   2   1
  O   O   O   O
```

Observe that four core positions are needed in a single storage unit (cell) in the computer to represent all the digits: 0–9. Each core is capable of being turned on or off. It follows that the storage capacity of the computer is determined by the number of the on and off cores that are present.

The foregoing example shows how the digits 0 through 9 are represented. Storage of letters of the alphabet will be explained in Chapter 13.

Often the question is asked: "Is information lost when the computer is turned off?" The answer is "No." It is the direction of magnetism in the cores that is important. Therefore, when the computer is turned on again, a core is magnetized exactly as it was originally.

PURE BINARY

Higher numbers may be expressed in binary by extending the digits to the left, just as higher numbers are expressed in the decimal system. Observe the examples in the table below:

Decimal Digit	Binary Notation
1	00000001
2	00000010
4	00000100
8	00001000
16	00010000
32	00100000
64	01000000
128	10000000
66	01000010 (64 + 2)
40	00101000 (32 + 8)
45	00101101 (32 + 8 + 4 + 1)

The above method of expressing binary numbers is referred to as the *pure binary* system.

Arithmetic computations in pure binary

Arithmetic computations can be performed as easily with the binary system as they can with the decimal system. The same basic rules are observed. Note, however, that addition in the binary system results in frequent "carries." In binary, whenever the total exceeds one, there is a carry to the next column. You will recall that in the decimal system there is a carry to the next column when the total exceeds nine.

Addition in binary. Four basic rules must be kept in mind in adding binary numbers. These rules are as follows:

1. $0 + 0 = 0$
2. $0 + 1 = 1$
3. $1 + 1 = 0$, with a 1 carry
4. $1 + 1 + 1 = 1$, with a 1 carry

Observe how these rules are applied in the following example in which the numbers 3 and 5 are added:

Binary	*Decimal Number Equivalent*
0011	3
+0101	+5
1000	8

Subtraction in binary. Subtraction in binary is equally simple. These basic rules must be kept in mind:

1. $0 - 0 = 0$
2. $1 - 0 = 1$
3. $1 - 1 = 0$
4. $0 - 1 = 1$, with 1 borrowed from the adjacent left column.

Observe how these rules are applied in the following example in which 6 is subtracted from 10:

Binary	*Decimal Number Equivalent*
1010	10
−0110	−6
0100	4

In working a binary problem, you may need to borrow a quantity from the next left-hand position, just as you would in the decimal system. This is true in the above problem. The 1 cannot be subtracted from the 0 in the third position, so the 1 in the fourth position is borrowed. Remember, the 1 you borrowed from the fourth position has a value of 8. This 1 is being moved into the third position, where the value is only 4. Therefore, when borrowing from the fourth position, you have borrowed one 8 or *two* 4's (1+ 1 in the third position). After subtracting 1 from 1 + 1, there is still a 1 remaining. This is the reason for the rule, "0 − 1 = 1 with 1 borrowed from the adjacent left column."

	Binary				*Decimal Number Equivalent*
	0	1+1			
	1	0	1	0	10
	0	1	1	0	−6
	0	1	0	0	4
Values:	8	4	2	1	

Multiplication in binary. In multiplying two binary numbers, the following rules apply:

1. $0 \times 0 = 0$
2. $0 \times 1 = 0$
3. $1 \times 1 = 1$

Observe how these rules are applied in the following example in which 4 is multiplied by 3:

Binary	*Decimal Number Equivalent*
0100	4
×0011	×3
0100	12
0100	
0000	
0000	
0001100	

Division in binary. In dividing one binary number by another, one must merely keep in mind the rules already expressed for multiplication and subtraction. These rules are not restated here. Observe, though, how they are applied in the following example in which 25 is divided by 5:

Binary	*Decimal Number Equivalent*
101	5
101)11001	5)25
101	25
0010	0
000	
00101	
101	
00000	

BINARY-CODED DECIMAL (BCD)

Another method, somewhat easier to use, combines the binary and decimal systems and is known as the *binary-coded decimal* (BCD) system. Provision is made for expressing each decimal digit, 0 through 9, by four binary digits. Four binary digits are used in the binary-coded decimal system instead of three or some other number because four places are required to express the highest decimal digit, 9: 1001.

A move to the left from one group of four binary digits to the next group of four increases the value expressed in the group 10 times, just as it does in the decimal system. Thus, the term *binary-coded decimal* is an appropriate one. Observe the following example:

Thousands	*Hundreds*	*Tens*	*Units*	
	0010	0101	1000	*Binary Coded Decimal*
	2	5	8	**Decimal Equivalent = 258**
0111	0010	0110	1001	*Binary Coded Decimal*
7	2	6	9	**Decimal Equivalent = 7,269**

In pure binary the two numbers would be expressed as follows:

$$100000010 = 258$$
$$1110001100101 = 7,269$$

The advantage of using the binary-coded decimal system is readily apparent from a study of the foregoing examples.

Arithmetic computations in binary-coded decimal

Arithmetic computations can also be performed with the binary-coded decimal system. Addition is illustrated in the example that follows. The rules of binary addition are applied.

Binary Coded Decimal			*Decimal Equivalent*
Hundreds	Tens	Units	
0010	0101	0100	254
+0101	0010	0011	+523
0111	0111	0111	777

In our decimal numeric arithmetic system, we add only up to 9 in a single column. If the sum of a column is over 9, there is always a carry to the next high-order (leftmost) column. In the BCD system, the computer also will add a carry from one group of four cores to the next high-order group of four cores. However, there is a discrepancy between the highest number that can be accumulated in a column in our arithmetic system and the highest number that can be accumulated electronically in four cores of a computer. If all four cores in a group are turned on they will equal

8 + 4 + 2 + 1, or 15. The computer will not carry unless *all four cores in a group are turned on.* Therefore, whenever a number in a group of four cores *exceeds* 9, the computer will automatically add the *factor of 6* to this group of cores. The 6 represents the difference between the largest amount that can be accumulated in an ordinary column in our decimal numeric arithmetic system, 9, and the largest amount that can be accumulated electronically in binary form in four cores of a computer, 15. Observe the following example:

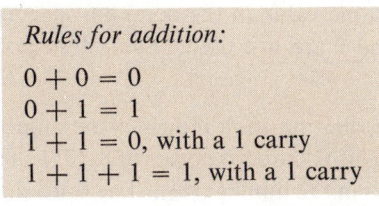

Rules for addition:
0 + 0 = 0
0 + 1 = 1
1 + 1 = 0, with a 1 carry
1 + 1 + 1 = 1, with a 1 carry

```
                        Decimal
  Tens      Units    Equivalents
  0011      1000         38
 +0100      0110        +46
  ----      ----        ---
  0111      1110    ←—   The answer in the units cores is 14.
 +0000      0110    ←—   The factor of 6 must be added because
  ----      ----         the sum exceeds 9.
  1000      0100         84
   ↑
   8         4    ———— Note the carryover to the tens position.
```

Adding the factor of 6 is the computer's method of automatically compensating for the difference in the bases of the two arithmetic systems.

REVIEW QUESTIONS

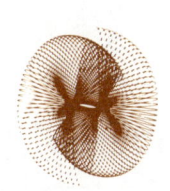

1. What is the binary numbering system?
2. Which digits are utilized in the binary system?
3. Why is the binary system essential to computer operations?
4. What decimal number does the binary notation 1010 represent?
5. What is the binary-coded decimal system? Why are groups of four digits utilized in this system?
6. Name the four basic rules for binary addition.
7. What are the decimal and binary answers to the following problem? 0010
   +0110
8. Name the four basic rules for binary subtraction.
9. What are the decimal and binary answers to the following problem? 1001
   −0101
10. Name the three basic rules for binary multiplication.
11. Which binary rules must be kept in mind in order to perform division in binary?
12. Why must you add the factor of 6 in some computations when working with the binary-coded decimal system?

OCTAL NUMBERING SYSTEM

Once you learn that the binary system, with a base of 2, can be used to count and perform arithmetic calculations, you can speculate that other systems have been devised which are equally useful. One such system contains eight digits — 0, 1, 2, 3, 4, 5, 6, and 7 — and is known as the *octal system*. It is built on a base of 8.

The Digits 0 through 7 have the same value in the octal and decimal systems. In the octal system, the 8 and 9 are not used. Each digit position is expressed as a power of 8.

Reading from right to left, the first digit position indicates the number of units, 0 through 7, in the number. This is the zero power of 8, (8^0). The second digit indicates the number of 8's in the number (8^1). The third digit indicates the number of 64's in the number (8^2). The next digit indicates the number of 512's (8^3), and so on. Observe the examples in Figure 12-1 in which sample numbers are included.

Decimal		Pure Binary							Octal		
10^1	10^0	2^6	2^5	2^4	2^3	2^2	2^1	2^0	8^2	8^1	8^0
10	1	64	32	16	8	4	2	1	64	8	1
	0							0			0
	1							1			1
	2						1	0			2
	3						1	1			3
	4					1	0	0			4
	5					1	0	1			5
	6					1	1	0			6
	7					1	1	1			7
	8				1	0	0	0		1	0
1	2				1	1	0	0		1	4
2	4			1	1	0	0	0		3	0
3	0			1	1	1	1	0		3	6
3	6		1	0	0	1	0	0		4	4
6	4	1	0	0	0	0	0	0	1	0	0

Figure 12-1. Comparison of decimal, pure binary, and octal systems

BINARY-CODED OCTAL SYSTEM

Computers using octal arithmetic must convert data to the *binary-coded octal* system, a combination of the octal and binary forms. There is a carry in octal numbering when digits exceed 7. Since 7 can be expressed in binary in three core positions (7 = 4 + 2 + 1), only three positions are needed. Observe the following example, in which the number 66 is expressed in four systems:

Decimal		6	6	
Binary-coded decimal		0110 (10's)	0110 (units)	60 + 6 = 66
Octal	1 (64's)	0 (8's)	2 (units)	64 + 2 = 66
Binary-coded octal	001 (64's)	000 (8's)	010 (units)	64 + 2 = 66

In the foregoing example, Number 66 is expressed in decimal, binary-coded decimal, octal, and binary-coded octal forms. Digits may be represented and calculations can be made by the computer in either one of the two binary-coded systems.

HEXADECIMAL NUMBERING SYSTEM

The *hexadecimal numbering system* is built on a base of 16. Each move of one position to the left multiplies the number 16 times. Sixteen single-digit symbols are needed to represent the 16 number values. Since the decimal system provides only 10 single-digit symbols, 0–9, how is this problem handled? Hexadecimal takes care of this problem by adding six additional one-digit symbols. The letters A, B, C, D, E, and F have been chosen for this purpose, though any other six letters or symbols could have been used. A complete list of hexadecimal digits thus consists of 0, 1, 2, 3, 4, 5, 6, 7, 8, 9, A, B, C, D, E, and F. Remember that the letters stand for 10, 11, 12, 13, 14, and 15.

Reading from right to left, the first digit position indicates the number of units, 0 through 15, in the number. The second digit indicates the number of 16's in the number. The third digit indicates the number of 256's in the number, and so on. Observe the examples in Figure 12-2, in which sample numbers are included.

Decimal				Hexadecimal			
10^3	10^2	10^1	10^0	16^3	16^2	16^1	16^0
1000	100	10	1	4096	256	16	1
			0				0
			1				1
			2				2
			3				3
			9				9
		1	0				A
		1	1				B
		1	2				C
		1	3				D
		1	4				E
		1	5				F
		1	6			1	0
		1	7			1	1
		2	0			1	4
		2	6			1	A
		2	7			1	B
		2	8			1	C
		3	1			1	F
		3	2			2	0
		4	2			2	A
		4	3			2	B
	2	9	0		1	2	2
	3	8	0		1	7	C
4	1	6	0	1	0	4	0

Figure 12-2. Selected decimal numbers with hexadecimal equivalents

BINARY-CODED HEXADECIMAL SYSTEM

Some of the newer computers, including IBM's 360, use the *binary-coded hexadecimal system*. As computer concepts have been refined, more information is being stored in less space. Binary coding (base 2) with its string of 0's and 1's is not economical to print and becomes confusing to read when the numbers are very large. Although BCD (binary-coded decimal) is easier to read than pure binary, only the decimal digits 0 through 9 can be stored in each group of four cores in BCD. Therefore, six number values are "wasted" (10 through 15). By using the hexadecimal system of arithmetic, with its base of 16 and by converting the data to the binary-coded hexadecimal system, there is more efficient use of storage space.

Chapter 12 Language and computing systems

To convert pure binary notation to binary-coded hexadecimal, it is only necessary to count the pure binary digits from right to left, marking off the binary digits in groups of four. An example follows:

$$0010|1111|0001|0010 = 0010\ 1111\ 0001\ 0010$$
$$2F12$$

Each group of four binary digits should be read as one unit, then replaced by the corresponding hexadecimal symbol, as above. You will note that in the binary-coded hexadecimal system, the value of a number is increased by 16 when a move is made to the left from one group of four binary digits to the next group.

Below are a few comparisons of numbers in decimal, binary-coded hexadecimal, and binary-coded decimal notations. Note that the larger the number, the more storage space is saved by the use of the binary-coded hexadecimal notation.

Decimal	Binary-Coded Hexadecimal			Binary-Coded Decimal			
	(256's)	(16's)	(Units)	(1000's)	(100's)	(10's)	(Units)
10			1010			0001	0000
26		0001	1010			0010	0110
33		0010	0001			0011	0011
3840	1111	0000	0000	0011	1000	0100	0000
	3 groups of cores			*4 groups of cores*			

Below is an example showing how a five-digit decimal number would be represented in only four groups of computer cores by use of the binary-coded hexadecimal notation:

Decimal	1	2	0	5	0
Binary-coded decimal	0001	0010	0000	0101	0000
Hexadecimal		2	F	1	2
Binary-coded hexadecimal		0010	1111	0001	0010

In the foregoing example, the number 12,050 is expressed in decimal, binary-coded decimal, hexadecimal, and binary-coded hexadecimal forms. Calculations can be performed and amounts can be stored in the computer in the binary-coded hexadecimal system just as they were in the binary-coded decimal system. Note the more efficient use of storage when the binary-coded hexadecimal system is used.

Some computers use the pure binary system; some, the binary-coded decimal, the binary-coded octal, or the binary-coded hexadecimal systems. Some computers use other numbering systems; but even in these, the binary system comes into play. The binary-coded decimal system is currently the most often used.

Information enters the computer as digits and letters of the alphabet punched into cards or paper tape or recorded on some other input medium.

The computer automatically translates this information into electronic signals. Data are moved around, used in calculations, and stored as signals based on the binary code. Finally, when the information is processed, the electronic signals are translated into records that may be seen or heard and that are understandable to humans. Usually the translation is in the form of printed records; but it can be in the form of visual and graphic displays or limited audio responses. At the same time that the computer is producing this translated output, the processed information can also be recorded in punched cards, on magnetic tape, or on other output media. Keep in mind that all of this action is handled automatically by the computer.

SUMMARY

Information is represented in almost all digital computers by magnetized cores. Since only two states are possible, on or off, computers are limited to the use of a two-digit numbering system known as the binary code. In this code, the value of a digit increases two times with each move of one space to the left.

In pencil and paper figuring by binary, only two digits are used: 1 and 0. Calculations can be made by the binary system as readily as they can be made by the decimal system.

Numbers can be expressed in pure binary or in binary-coded decimal. In pure binary, each move to the left increases the number two times. In the binary-coded decimal system, each digit is expressed by four binary digits. A move to the left within this group increases the value of a number by two. A move to the left from one group of four binary digits to the next group, however, increases the value of a number 10 times.

Information enters the computer as *coded* decimal digits. The computer automatically translates this information into electronic signals, based on the binary system. When the information is processed, the output is translated from electronic signals into displays or records understandable to the user. At the same time, the output unit produces for storage the magnetic tapes, disks, punched cards, or other devices from which the data may be retrieved for further processing at another time.

The decimal system uses a base of 10 to express numeric values; that is, each move to the left multiplies the value of the number by 10. The **binary** system uses a base of 2, the octal system uses a base of 8, and the hexadecimal system uses a base of 16. The binary-coded octal and hexadecimal systems are used in some computers. However, the binary-coded decimal system is currently the most often used.

A thorough understanding of the coding system used in any computer is not necessary for successful operation of that computer. However, the material concerning the various coding systems is fascinating and challenging, and is presented as part of the entire data processing picture.

Chapter 12　　Language and computing systems

REVIEW QUESTIONS

1. What base is used in the octal numbering system?
2. Which digits are utilized in the octal system?
3. How many positions are needed in each group when using the binary-coded octal system?
4. What base is represented by the hexadecimal numbering system?
5. Which digits are used in the hexadecimal system?
6. In the hexadecimal system, what decimal number does "E" represent?
7. Why does the binary-coded hexadecimal system provide an economical use of storage?
8. Name the four commonly used numbering systems for computers.
9. In the binary-coded decimal system, how many times is the value of a number increased by a move to the left from one group of four binary digits to the next group?
10. In the binary-coded hexadecimal systems, how many times is the value of a number increased by a move to the left from one group of four binary digits to the next group?

STUDY GUIDE

Complete Study Guide 12 by following the instructions in your **STUDY GUIDES** booklet.

PROJECT

Complete Project 12-1 by following the instructions in your **PROJECTS** booklet.

CHAPTER 13

INTERNAL STORAGE OF INFORMATION

HOW THE COMPUTER USES THE BINARY CODE

Up to this point, the binary code has been explained primarily as a pencil-and-paper digit expressing and figuring system. While binary arithmetic may seem complicated to you, the computer is able to handle it with ease. As explained earlier, processing of binary code is possible because the electronic circuits inside the computers can exist in only two possible states. The current can be on or off.

The magnetic, doughnut-shaped cores used in the circuits of the computer memory can be magnetized in one direction or in the opposite direction. Thus, in the computer the Digits 1 and 0 are not even used; they are replaced by magnetized positive or negative signals. These signals, however, express digits and make computations in much the same way that you did with pencil and paper. The signals can even be used to express letters of the alphabet so that the computer can also process alphabetic information.

As mentioned before, not only is the computer capable of storing and processing data in the form of electronic signals, but it is also capable of storing the program used to process the data. The program is also stored in the form of electronic signals. The data and program are stored in the memory of the computer. There are a number of devices available for internal storing of the data to be processed and the instructions for processing them, but only the magnetic core system of internal storage will be explained in detail in this chapter.

MAGNETIC CORE MEMORY SYSTEM

The *memory* is that part of a computer that stores the program and data being processed. The memory consists of cores and wires. The *magnetic cores* are tiny, doughnut-shaped rings, capable of being magnetized either negatively or positively. Two wires intersect each core at right angles. Any particular core or group of cores can be magnetized one way or the other in a few millionths of a second; and unless deliberately changed, the cores can retain their magnetism indefinitely.

The cores are placed on intersecting wires at regular intervals. When current is sent through the wires, the cores become magnetized. The direction of the current determines the magnetic state of the cores (positive or negative). Because of the arrangement of the wires, any particular core or combination of cores can be magnetized in one direction or the other. A core magnetized in one direction represents 1 as a binary digit. A core magnetized in the opposite direction represents 0 as a binary digit. Four cores connected by wires are needed to express all the digits 0 through 9 just as four binary digits are also needed to express the digits 0 through 9. Observe this close relationship in Figure 13-1.

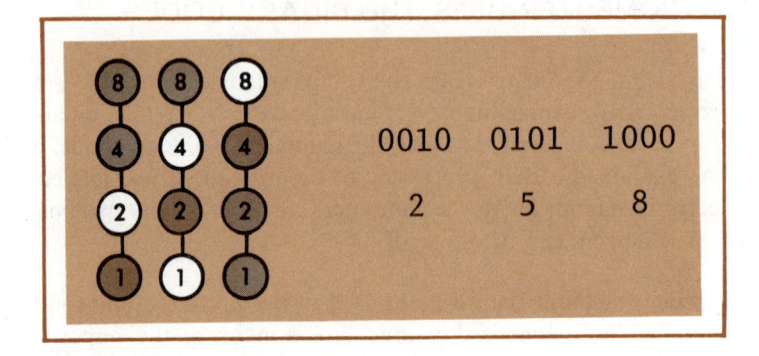

Figure 13-1. Magnetic cores storing binary digits in computers

MAGNETIC CORE PLANE

An electronic computer consists of many magnetic cores. The cores appear at each intersection of wires in a magnetic core plane. A *magnetic core plane*, which is similar in appearance to a window screen, is a grid of many fine wires running horizontally, intersecting at right angles. See Figure 13-2.

When the planes are stacked one over the other with the cores connected by vertical wires, groups of cores are formed similar to the three groups in Figure 13-1. Each group is capable of storing a binary digit. The binary digits can be expressed by using a stack of four planes. Additional planes must be added to the stack, however, when letters of the alphabet are to be stored in addition to numeric digits, and when special jobs must be handled.

Chapter 13 Internal storage of information

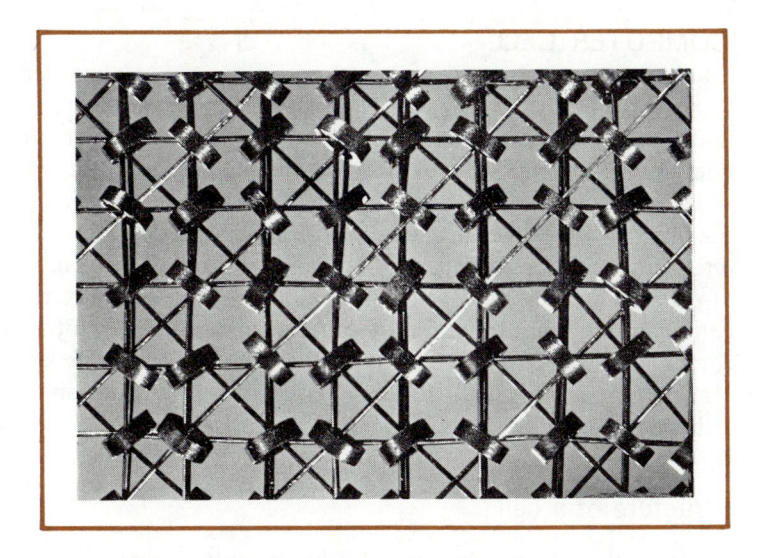

Figure 13-2. Magnetic core plane

Observe Figure 13-3. It shows a stack of eight magnetic core planes. Note the cores in the four planes that store the binary digits to express figures. They are the planes identified by 1, 2, 4, and 8. The cores in the remaining planes will be explained later.

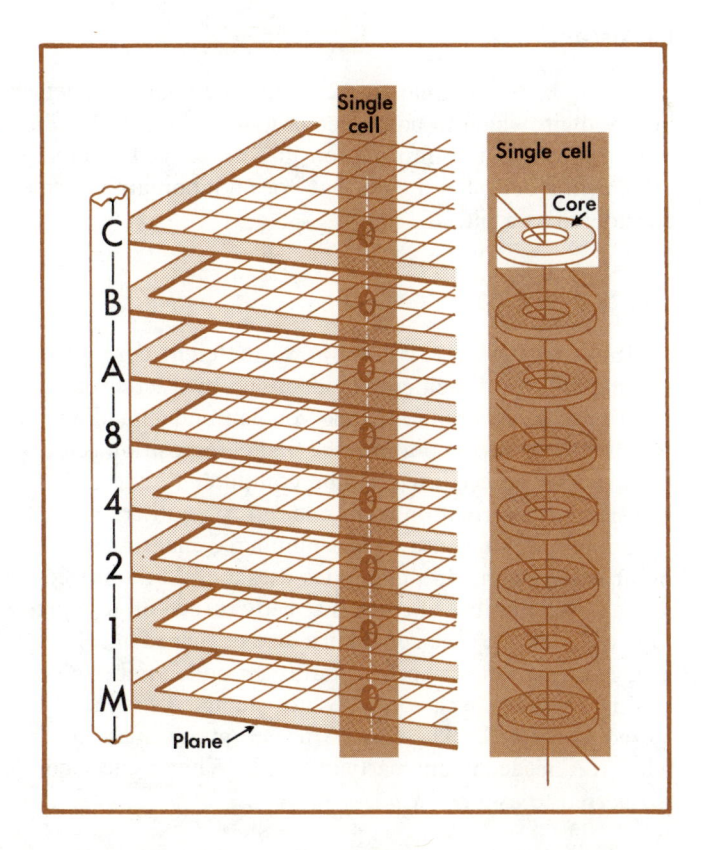

Figure 13-3. Stack of magnetic core planes

COMPUTER CELL

Observe Figure 13-3 again. Note that the eight planes are so arranged that all the intersections are in exact vertical alignment. Note the dotted line running through the cores located at the junctions of the wires in each of the eight planes. Any eight intersections that are in vertical alignment, together with the eight magnetic cores, make up a cell. A *cell* comprises one storage unit in a computer. A computer normally contains many sets of planes, and thus many cells. Each cell is capable of holding, in varying combinations, eight on and off electrical signals. Through these varying combinations of on and off signals, all the digits and all the letters of the alphabet are represented. Each cell is capable of storing only one digit, letter, or symbol.

Structure of a cell

While the cells illustrated in this book contain eight cores, some computers have fewer than this number. Some computers process only numeric data and do not require eight cores. We shall be concerned in this chapter, however, with eight-core cells similar to the one illustrated in Figure 13-4.

Cores and bits

As explained in Chapter 12, each core when magnetized represents a binary digit, which in computer jargon is shortened to bit (*bi*nary dig*it*). A *bit* represents the information in a core. A bit (binary digit) may be present in a core, but a core that does not contain information cannot be considered as a bit.

Parity check core

Refer to Figure 13-4. It shows the eight core positions of a cell in schematic form. Each core is identified by a letter or a figure. Keep the identity of each core in mind so you can understand how a cell functions. Reading from top to bottom, the first core position is identified by the letter C. This core is used by the computer to check its own accuracy in transferring information from one cell to another.

Some computers use an odd-numbered checking system; some an even-numbered system. If a computer uses an odd-numbered checking system and an even number of cores is already turned on to represent a particular digit or letter, the check core must also be turned on. Thus, when the check core is turned on, the cell contains an odd number of cores magnetized positively. The check core does not change the value of the digit or letter stored in the cell. The core is turned on automatically by the computer when it is needed in any particular cell. When a check core is turned on, it is referred to as a *check bit*.

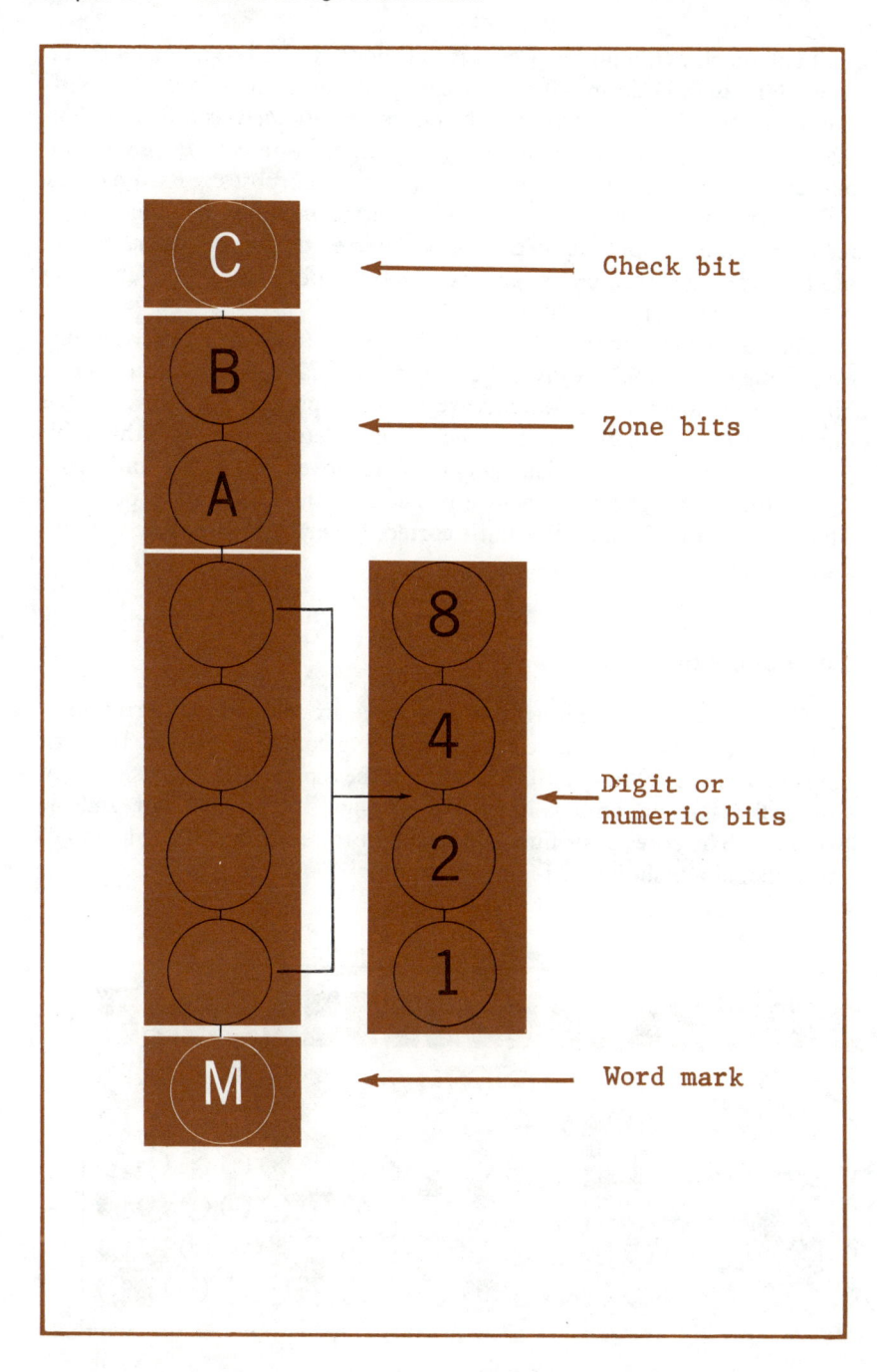

Chapter 13   Internal storage of information   219

Figure 13-4. Structure of eight-core cell with cores identified.

← Check bit

← Zone bits

← Digit or numeric bits

← Word mark

When a computer uses an even-numbered checking system, the procedure just described would be reversed, but the outcome would be the same. All cells with an odd number of cores turned on would automatically have the check core turned on also. All cells containing data would thus have an even number of cores magnetized positively.

In all displays of computer cells in this book, it shall be assumed that a computer with an odd-numbered checking system is being used. This self-checking operation is known as parity check. *Parity check* is thus a method by which a computer checks on its own accuracy in transferring data from one cell to another for storage or processing purposes. Parity check catches errors of transmission only. An error made by an operator in recording data in input media cannot be detected by the computer. Errors of this type can only be caught by careful proofreading and checking before data enter the computer.

The computer counts all "on" cores in a cell (including the check bit) every time the computer moves the contents of that cell. If the number of bits is odd in number, the contents are moved as planned. If, however, the number of bits is even in number, the computer stops. It knows that a bit (or bits) in the cell, from which data are being moved, has accidentally been lost or that a short or malfunction has caused an extra core to be "on." The operator of the computer must correct the error before the computer will continue.

Zone cores or bits

The cores identified by the letters B and A are frequently referred to as *zone cores* or *zone bits*. These cores are used in combination with the digit cores in a cell to represent all the letters of the alphabet as well as some of the special signs or symbols like the dollar sign, the percent sign, and the diagonal. The cores that must be turned on to represent all the letters of the alphabet are shown in Figure 13-5.

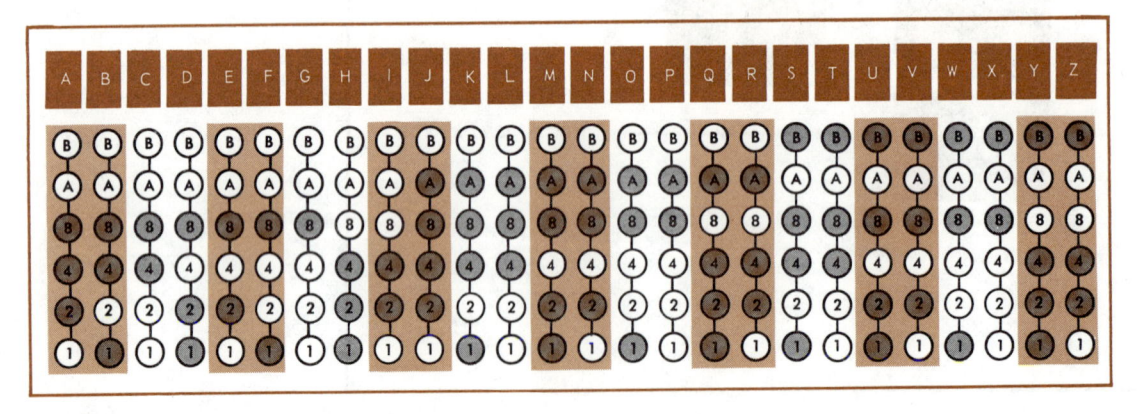

Figure 13-5. Binary code for letters of the alphabet

Refer to the foregoing figure. Note that the Letter A is represented in the computer by having the B, A, and 1 cores turned on. The Letter S is represented by having the A and 2 cores turned on.

Digit cores or bits

Refer to Figure 13-4 again. Observe the four cores capable of representing any one of the digits 0 through 9. You learned in Chapter 12 that various combinations of on and off electronic signals or pulses in these cores are used to represent figures.

Word mark core or bit

The eighth core position in Figure 13-4, identified by the Letter M, indicates the presence or absence of a word mark. If the core is turned on, a word mark appears. A *word mark* tells the computer that it has reached the end of a word.

A *word* in computer language is a single character or a group of characters representing a unit of information. For example, *347* is a word if it represents a unit of value. *JET* is another word. The name of a customer is another. The code number of a department, such as 6, for example, is also a word. A computer word and a punched card field are similar.

The position at the extreme left of a word is referred to as its *high-order position*. The position at the right is referred to as its *low-order* position. For example:

high-order position ⟶ 347 ⟵ low-order position
high-order position ⟶ JET ⟵ low-order position

We shall be referring frequently in subsequent discussions to the high- and low-order positions of computer words. It is important to be able to distinguish between the two positions.

Fixed word length. Some computers store and process data in fixed word lengths. A *fixed word length computer* is one in which each unit of information is stored and processed in a fixed or predetermined number of cells. Computers vary in the fixed number of cells assigned to each word — 14 cells, 16 cells, 20 cells, and similar fixed patterns. However, any one fixed word length computer will always use the same number of cells per word.

Only one word can be stored in each group of cells assigned to fixed word length storage. If a word requiring only 4 cells is stored in a fixed word length of 16 cells, 12 of the cells in this group will not be used.

Variable word length. In variable word length computers, the storage space assigned to each word depends upon the length of the word. One cell is made available for each character in the word. A word may thus consist of one cell or many cells. The chief advantage of this method is that better use is made of internal core storage space.

When a variable word length computer is used — and these are in the majority — some method must be devised to make each word in the computer distinct. This is the function of the word mark. A *word mark* is a core turned on in a computer cell to signal the end of a word to the computer. In Figure 13-6, these cores are the ones at the bottom, identified by the Letter M. Observe that 347 and JET are each identified as a word.

Figure 13-6. Storage cells with cores turned on to represent digits, letters, parity check, and word marks

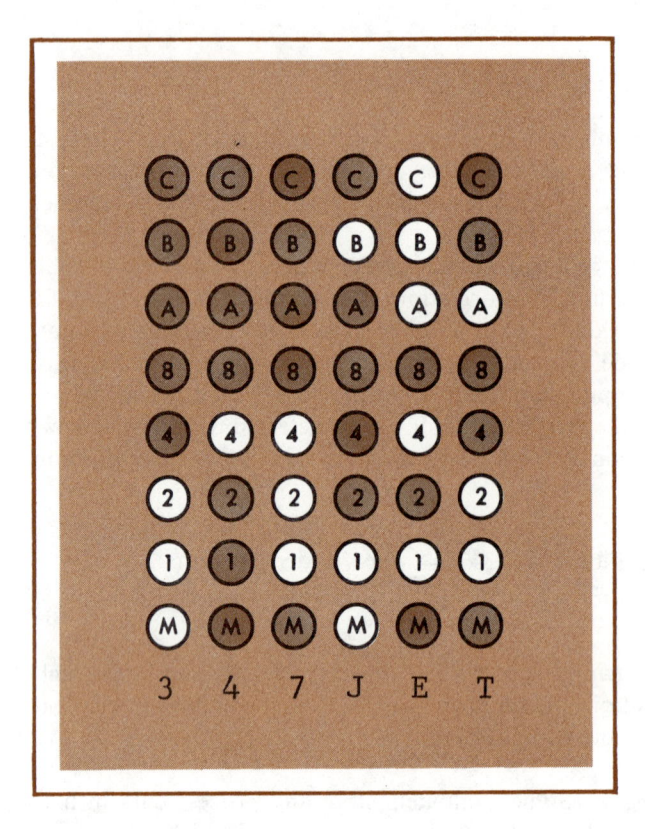

Observe also that a word mark is turned on in the high-order position of each word. A computer stores, moves, or reads data words from right to left. It stops when it encounters a word mark. This is the way in which the computer identifies a unit of information.

The word mark is not a character in itself; it does not change the letter or digit in a cell any more than does the presence of a check bit in a cell. The word mark is counted as a bit, however, insofar as parity check is concerned. Note the parity check bits added in Figure 13-6. In every case, the bits in a cell equal an odd number, and word mark bits are included in the count.

For the time being, you may assume that an instruction written into the program causes word marks to be set in cells requiring them. The word marks remain until they are cleared by a clear instruction. When data are moved from one location to another, word marks are generally not moved.

Chapter 13   Internal storage of information

For that reason, word marks must be reestablished in the new locations by program instructions.

In visual displays of words in cells or in computer programs, a word mark is often shown symbolically by underlining the character with which it is associated. The use of the symbol is merely an aid in writing the program. It is not part of the program punched into a card. Note the location of the word mark in the two examples that follow:

Word mark in high-order position   3̲4187   Student number

Word mark in high-order position   A̲TLANTA   Name of city

When the programmer directs a variable word length computer to a specific word in storage, he directs it to the low-order cell of that word; for example, to the "7" in the word 3̲4187. The computer starts with the low-order position and senses the data in each cell, moving from right to left, one cell at a time, until the cell containing the word mark is reached. The character stored in that cell is included in the word also. The computer does with this word whatever the program instructs it to do. For example, the word might be moved, added to another word, or printed.

Each computer cell has an address. Units of information are stored or reached by using the address of the low-order cell of the group of cells in which the information is stored.

REVIEW QUESTIONS

1. What is a magnetic core?
2. Under what condition is a core said to be "on"? "off"?
3. What is a magnetic core plane? Where are the magnetic cores located on a magnetic core plane?
4. What is a computer cell?
5. How much information can be stored in a single cell?
6. Name, from top to bottom, the core positions in an 8-plane cell.
7. What is the purpose of the parity check bit?
8. How is the parity check core turned on?
9. What is the purpose of the word mark?
10. How many cells would be needed to store each of the following words? In which cell in each word would the word mark be set?
    a. 1984
    b. 359Q472
    c. CHICAGO
11. Describe fixed word length storage. Variable word length storage.
12. What is the primary advantage of variable word length?
13. In which direction does a computer read data words?
14. Is the word mark bit counted in the parity check?

ADDRESSES OF WORDS IN COMPUTERS

Since data words are stored, moved around in the memory of the computer, and processed in specific cells of a computer, some way must be found of identifying and finding them. This is done by a system of numbers. Each cell in a computer has an address, starting with 000 and extending to the last cell. The cell number is called an address because the number assigned to each cell of storage is very similar to the address assigned to each house on a street. A computer word is stored or reached by addressing its low-order (rightmost) position. Each cell in a group of cells in which a word is stored does not have to be addressed, just the low-order cell of that group.

Observe the example in Figure 13-7.

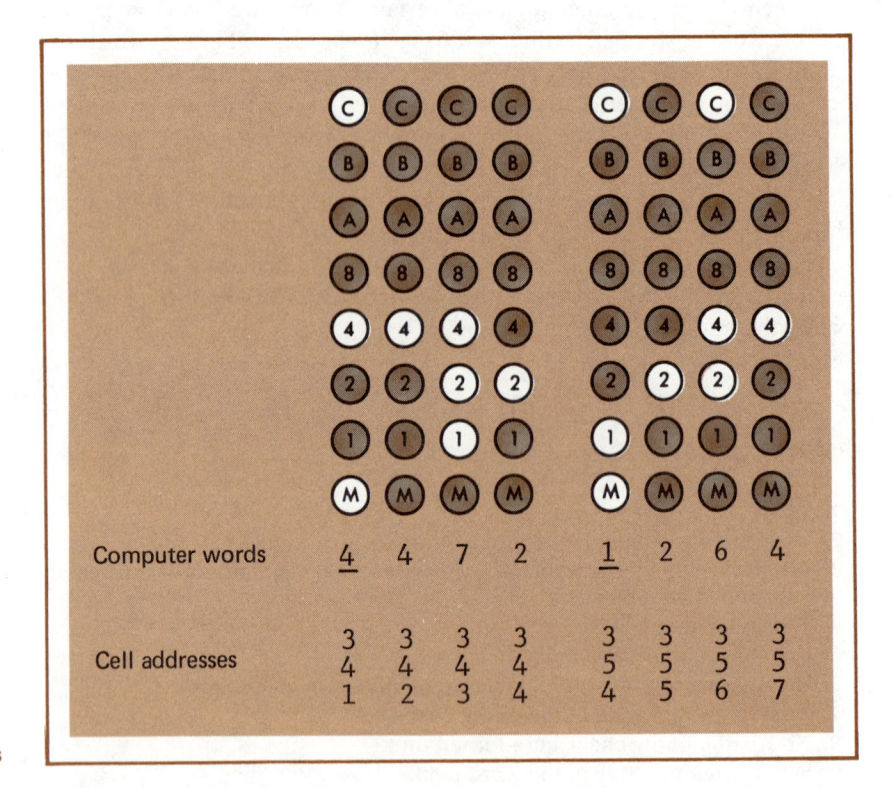

Figure 13-7. Cell addresses

Note that each cell has an address. Each computer word in this example consists of four cells. The first word, 4472, would be stored or moved in the computer by addressing Cell 344; the second word, 1264, by addressing Cell 357. Thus, if you wanted the computer to add the first word to the second, you would instruct it as follows: Add 344 to 357. The sum would be stored in the cells addressed by 357.

Observe the condition of the cores in the various cells when the add instruction has been executed in Figure 13-8. The data in the four cells at

Chapter 13   Internal storage of information   225

the left remain even though they have been duplicated and added to the four cells at the right. Data are cleared from cells only when they have been cleared by a clear instruction or when they have been replaced by new data, as was the case in the four cells at the right in the foregoing example. $4472 + 1264 = 5736$. The 4472 remains in the cells addressed by 344, but the total, 5736, is stored in the cells addressed by 357, thus replacing the previous cell contents, 1264, seen on the right in Figure 13-7.

Computer words   4   4   7   2   5   7   3   6

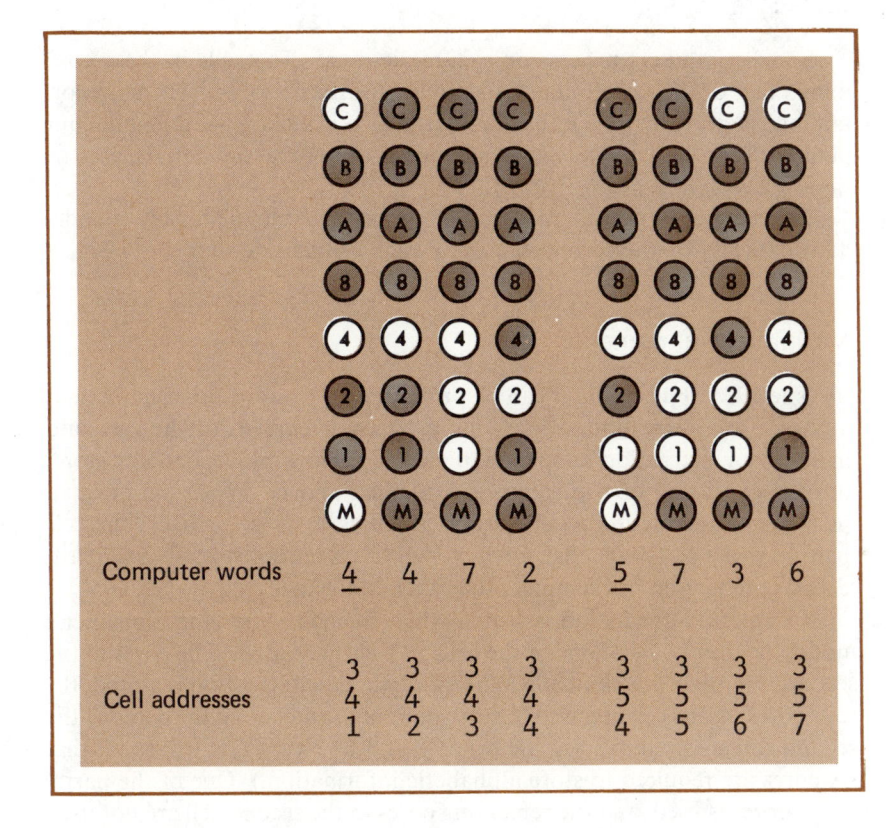

Cell addresses   3   3   3   3   3   3   3   3
                  4   4   4   4   5   5   5   5
                  1   2   3   4   4   5   6   7

Figure 13-8. Addition of data in cells

If you wished to move the first word to a new location in storage — for instance, Cells 665, 666, 667, and 668 — you would instruct the computer as follows:

　　　　　　　Set Word Mark in　　665
　　　　　　　Move　　　　　　　　344   to   668

A word mark is set in the new location to identify the word, consisting of four cells. In the Move instruction, the low-order cell of each location is addressed.

It can be noted at this point that the address of a cell and its content are entirely different. The address identifies the cell; the content refers to the digit or letter stored in it. In writing instructions for the computer, cell addresses are used rather than the data stored in the cells.

CELL ARRANGEMENTS IN COMPUTERS

In the discussion thus far, we have described a cell consisting of eight cores. This number is found in many computers. A variety of other arrangements are used, however, and these are touched on briefly here.

Five-core cells

Some computers process only numeric data. The cells in these computers can obviously eliminate the zone (A and B) cores. The core containing the word mark can be eliminated also if a fixed word length computer is used. Note the way in which numeric data are stored in the illustration of five-core cells in Figure 13-9.

Note the presence of the check bit in certain cells. This bit is added automatically by the computer to give each cell an odd number of bits.

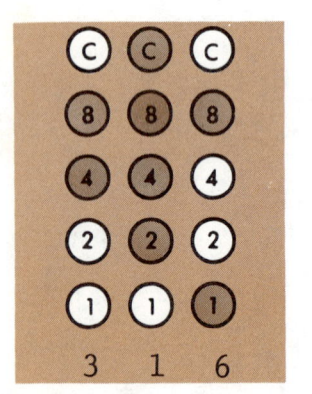

Figure 13-9. Five-core storage cells

Variable arrangements

The IBM 360 computer can be programmed to store either numeric or alphameric information. When the program prepared for the computer includes an instruction to operate in packed decimal mode, data are stored in cells consisting of five cores, as explained above. When the program includes an instruction to operate in alphameric mode or pack, the cells pair up to act as single cells. Each pair then has ten cores. Only one parity check core is used in each pair; the other is not used.

If numeric information is stored when the computer is in alphameric mode, the four cores of one of the cells in a pair are used. The cores in the second cell are not used at all. When alphabetic information is stored, the four cores of one cell are used to store digit bits, and two of the cores of the second cell are used to store the zone (A and B) bits. (You will recall that six cores are required to store alphabetic information.) One of the parity check cores is used, and the remaining cores in the second cell are not used at all; or, if used, they perform a number of special functions.

The IBM 360 can also be programmed to store numeric information in pure binary. When this arrangement is used, a number of cells are combined to give each resulting cell a large number of cores, a necessary requirement in the pure binary system.

MAGNETIC THIN FILM

Magnetic thin film can also store electronic signals representing data. This device consists of thin layers of glass or plastic, on which are mounted sections of metallic spots connected by very thin wires. The sections form planes of memory cores that are capable of being magnetized to represent digits, letters of the alphabet, or other characters in core storage.

Chapter 13　　Internal storage of information

SUMMARY

Data are stored and processed in the internal memory of the computer in the form of electronic signals. The internal memory can appear in several forms. A commonly used form is one in which cells are used. Each cell is made up of a predetermined number of cores that are capable of being magnetized positively or negatively. The magnetic state of the cores in a cell determines what character is being represented in the cell.

The number of cores per cell varies from computer to computer. Some computers have cells with eight cores. Six of the cores are used to represent the digits 0 through 9 and the letters of the alphabet. One core is the check-bit core, which the computer uses to detect the loss of information that has been stored in it. The remaining core identifies the length of a unit of information in a variable word length computer. Such a core is not needed in fixed word length computers.

In a variable word length computer, each unit of information occupies only as many cells as are allotted. The number varies from one unit of information to the next. In a fixed word length computer, each unit of information occupies a predetermined number of cells, even though all of the cells may not be needed.

Each computer cell has an address. Units of information are stored or reached by using the address of the low-order cell of the group of cells in which the information is stored.

REVIEW QUESTIONS

1. What is a computer address? Why is it called an address?
2. Which cell in a data word is addressed: high-order or low-order?
3. Is the address of a cell related to its contents?
4. Can each cell in the computer be addressed?
5. When data contained in one group of cells are moved to another group, do the data also remain in the cells from which the move has been made?
6. Under what conditions can a five-core cell be used rather than an eight-core cell? Which cores are omitted in a five-core cell?

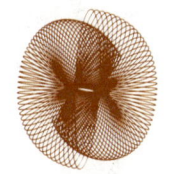

STUDY GUIDE

Complete Study Guide 13 by following the instructions in your STUDY GUIDES booklet.

PROJECT

Complete Project 13-1 by following the instructions in your PROJECTS booklet.

CHAPTER 14

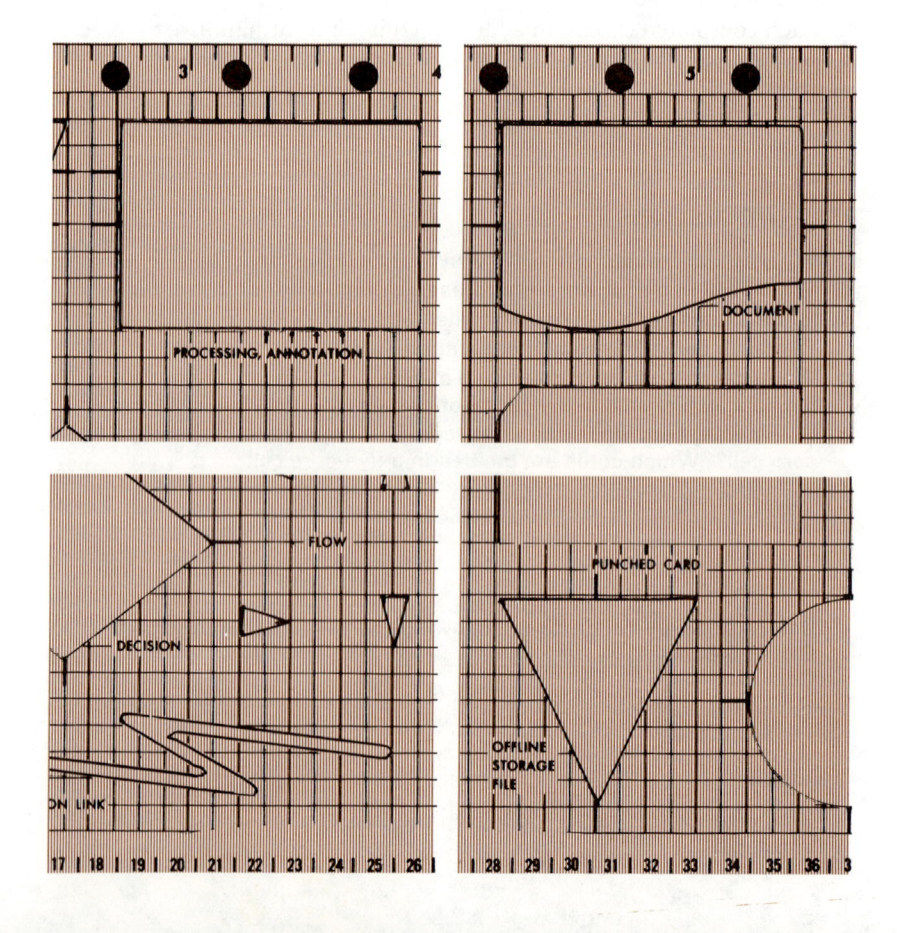

HUMAN LANGUAGE PROGRAMS AND BLOCK DIAGRAMS

Electronic computers are programmed by instructions which are written to solve a specific problem. These instructions are punched into cards, one instruction per card, or recorded on some other input medium acceptable to the computer. The instructions are then stored in binary code in the computer as electronic impulses. When the data needed to solve a problem are fed into the computer, the stored program takes over. No panel board is wired to solve the problem, as was the case with some of the machines in the unit-record system. A *program* thus is the complete plan for solving a problem on a computer; or more specifically, it is the complete set of instructions needed to solve a problem. A *computer instruction* tells in code form what action is to be taken on what data. The code form is one that can be stored in and understood by the computer.

IMPORTANCE OF PROGRAMMING

An obvious fact stands out. Program writing plays an important part in processing data by the computer. The program must be logically written and clearly defined, giving the computer step-by-step directions on the course to be followed. Even the simplest problem usually requires a number of detailed instructions that must be written and stored in the computer before processing can take place. A complex problem requires a great many detailed instructions, arranged in logical order.

In its advanced form, programming is an art that requires a thorough understanding of the business in which one is employed as well as an intimate knowledge of the computer being used. The programmer must also know how to write his programs in the language system that can be used by his computer.

Since this introductory course stresses basic concepts, you will not be expected to acquire the programming skill possessed by the experienced programmer. However, you will learn how to write some simple programs in computer language systems so that you may sample the different kinds of commands the computer can carry out. By writing these programs, you will also learn what decisions the computer can make and how it makes them.

WAYS IN WHICH PROGRAMS MAY BE WRITTEN

Computer programs may be written in four different ways, as follows:

1. They can be written in human language (English).
2. They can be written in the form of block diagrams.
3. They can be written in machine language — the basic language of the computer.
4. They can be written in one of the synthetic languages, such as COBOL or FORTRAN, especially developed for computers.

There are many methods for writing computer programs. Some require a complicated knowledge of the inner workings of the computer. Other methods require only a basic knowledge of the console of the computer and of the input-output devices being used. The computer programmer is usually trained to write a program in a synthetic language such as SPS, COBOL, or FORTRAN. As computer technology has become more complicated, it has been necessary for the computer manufacturers to develop translator-type programs that can translate a synthetic language into the machine-language binary code of the computer. Thus, it is not necessary for the programmer to understand principles of physics and electronics that cause the computer to function. These various manufacturer-supplied translator programs are often referred to as assembly programs, processor programs, and compilers. They will be discussed in detail in later chapters. *These programs comprise the software* in the electronic computer system, while *the computer and other processing machines are known as hardware*.

Generally, a program is written in both block diagram form and one of the synthetic languages. A block diagram is usually made before the program is written. A *block diagram* is a detailed flow chart showing what is to be done at each step of the solution of a computer problem. The block diagram acts as a check against the same program written in another form. If a program is written in human language, it must be coded later in a form acceptable to the computer before it can be stored and used to process data.

The discussion in this chapter is limited to an explanation of writing programs in English and in block diagram form. How programs are written in machine language and COBOL are topics handled in later chapters.

SOME BASIC FACTS ABOUT THE COMPUTER

In Chapter 2 you learned about the Mark I, the ENIAC, and the EDVAC. These were first-generation computers, using vacuum tubes for their memory circuitry. The first-generation computers needed special air-conditioning systems for cooling. Data were processed in milliseconds (thousandths of a second). By today's standards, these machines are obsolete. They were soon replaced by the second-generation equipment.

Advancing to the second-generation equipment, you will find that the magnetic cores are used for storage. (These magnetic cores have been explained in previous chapters of this text.) Internal operating speeds have increased; the core storage capacity has become greater; and the data can be processed in microseconds (millionths of a second). Many of these second-generation computers use the BCD (binary-coded decimal) configuration for storing data. (See Chapter 12.) The air-conditioning systems are smaller or not needed. The second-generation computers are still widely used, but they are being replaced gradually by the third-generation computers, such as the IBM 360.

In the third-generation computers, the magnetic cores are much smaller and are often arranged in the hexadecimal configuration. (See Chapter 12.) Circuit size has been reduced further, and data are processed in nanoseconds (billionths of a second).

To make the instructions in this chapter as simple as possible, they will be written for a small, second-generation computer, which is similar to those used in many offices. Just as it is necessary to learn addition and subtraction before a student can learn to multiply or divide, so it is also necessary to learn the basic facts about simple computers before advancing to more complicated machines. The basic fundamentals of programming can be understood more easily when applied to a simple computer such as the IBM 1401, which is not identical to other computers but is a typical second-generation computer. In order to simplify explanations, only certain areas of this computer will be used.

Later chapters in this text will be concerned with programs for the IBM 360 and other more complicated third-generation computers.

Cell make-up

The computer discussed in this chapter stores and processes both numeric and alphabetic information in the binary-coded decimal system. It uses an odd-numbered parity checking system, and it stores and processes data in variable word lengths.

Each storage cell in this computer contains eight cores. The computer may have 1,400 to 16,000 cells depending on the model being used. A data word consisting of JONES would appear as in Figure 14-1 when stored in Cells 401–405 of the computer.

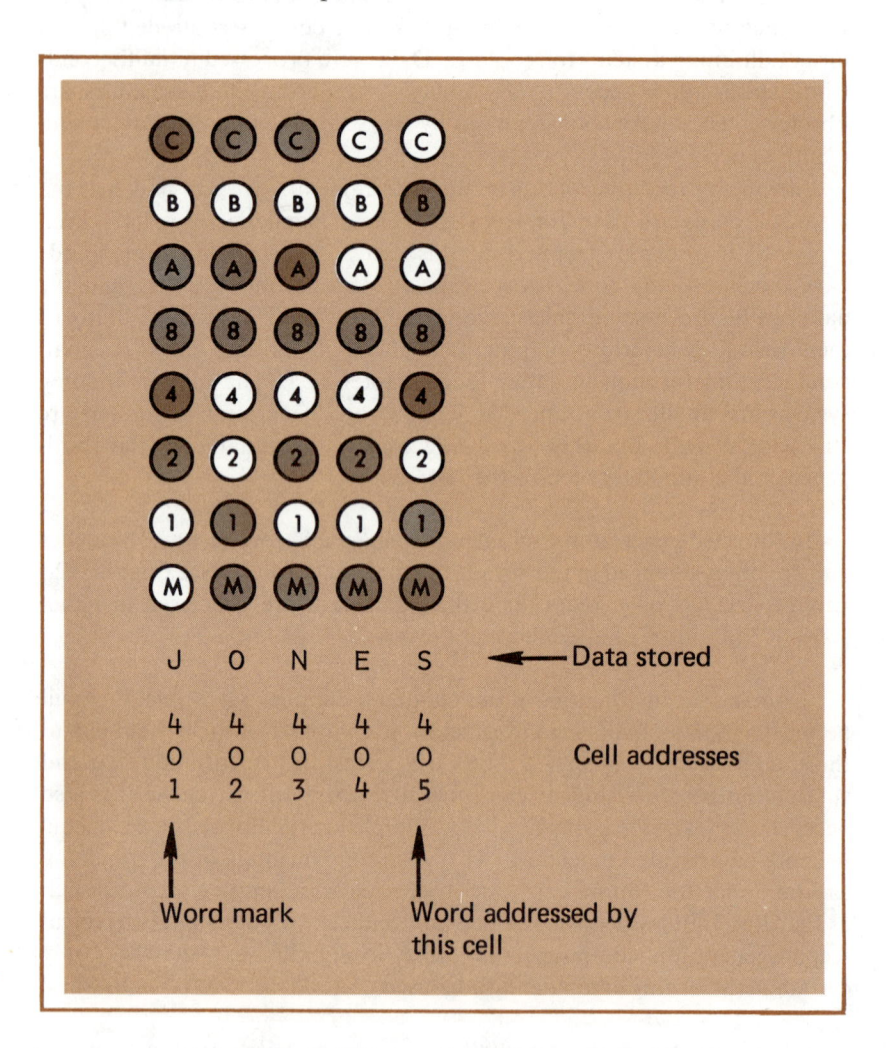

Figure 14-1. Storage of data

A word mark is turned on in Cell 401 to identify the length of the word. Observe too that the parity check bit is added in Cells 404 and 405 to give each cell an odd number of cores turned on. The word JONES would be stored or moved by addressing Cell 405. Each cell, reading from right to left, is filled with data or sensed until the word mark is reached. Finally, note that each cell is addressed by a three-digit number; for example, 405.

Word marks must be turned on by instructions written into the program. Parity check cores are turned on automatically by the computer.

You may ask at this point, "Why are three-cell addresses used if the computer has 1,400 to 16,000 cells?" There is a complicated code of digit and letter combinations for writing programs with cell addresses exceeding 999. This text teaches basic fundamentals only and is not concerned with advanced programming concepts. Therefore, the cell addresses used for teaching purposes will not exceed 999, and the code will be omitted from the discussion.

Standard read, punch, and print areas

Read area. When a read instruction is given, the data in the 80 columns of a punched card are transferred to the memory cells of the CPU. The data enter the first 80 cells of the computer, Cells 001–080, which are referred to as the *read area*. Data from Card Column 1 enter Cell 001; data from Card Column 2 enter Cell 002; and this procedure is continued until data from Card Column 80 enter Cell 080. The new data coming into the 80 cells of the read area erase data stored there previously. This means that each time a new card is read, all the data from the 80 columns of the preceding card will be erased, because it is not possible for a computer to read only part of a card. If there are no data in some of the columns of a punched card, the matching cells in the read area of the computer will be cleared to represent blanks. See Figure 14-2.

Translation from the Hollerith code used in the card to the binary code used in the computer is automatic.

Punch area. Data that are to be punched into a new card by the computer must first be moved by an instruction into the punch area of the CPU, which consists of Cells 101–180. Observe that there are just 80 cells in this area — the same as the number of columns in a card. When a punch instruction is given, the data that have been moved into the punch area are punched into a card. A character that has been moved to Cell 101 is punched into Card Column 1, and the character that has been moved to Cell 102 is punched into Card Column 2. The data in the other cells are punched into corresponding card columns. If some cells do not contain data, no holes are punched into those corresponding card columns. The characters are punched simultaneously.

Print area. The print area of a computer always contains more cells than there are columns in a punched card in order that the data on the printed report may be spaced out for easy reading. The number of cells varies with the model of printer being used for output. In this chapter, in order to simplify the programs, it will be assumed that the print area contains only 99 cells. These cells are 201–299.

234   The electronic computer system   Part 4

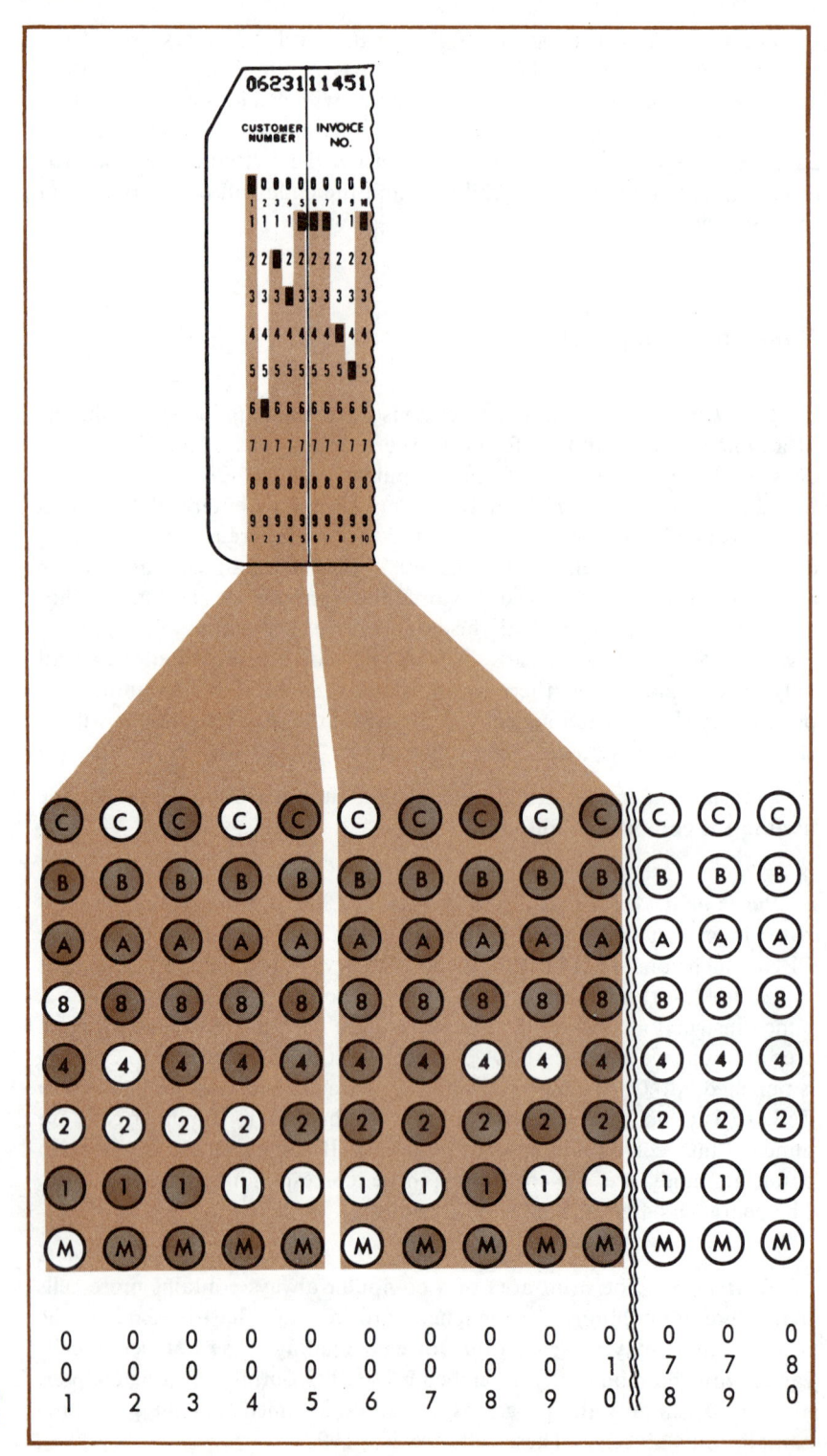

Figure 14-2. Data in punched card stored in read area of computer

By way of review, the three reserved storage areas in the computer discussed in this chapter are as follows:

```
Read Area   —  Cells 001–080
Punch Area  —  Cells 101–180
Print Area  —  Cells 201–299
```

Other areas. The read, punch, and print areas are the only reserved areas in the computer being discussed. All other cells may be used for computing, accumulating totals, and storing data. Remember, also, that a number of cells will be needed to store the program that has been written to solve a particular problem. A program can be stored in any group of cells; but, for obvious reasons, it would not be stored in the areas reserved for reading, punching, and printing.

Clearance of reserved storage areas

Before attempting to use a ten-key adding machine to solve certain problems, the operator of the machine must make certain that all previous data are cleared from the machine. In other words, the machine is made ready to receive new data. The same procedure is followed when an electronic computer is used to handle a specific job. Any previously stored data in the machine must be cleared before new data are entered. Otherwise, the results produced may be incorrect.

All reserved areas of the computer that will be used for processing data must be cleared by instructions before a new program is processed. Data and word marks from a previous program will remain in the computer until they are cleared. You have already learned that each time a new data card is read into the read area of memory, all the data from the 80 columns of the preceding card are erased; so you may ask, "Why should the read area be cleared?" The answer to this question is that the programmer sets word marks in the read area for each new program. These word marks remain for the entire program and are not cleared each time a new data card is read. Only the data are cleared. Therefore, the read area, as well as the other reserved areas of memory, must be cleared at the beginning of a new program. After the first clearance, the read area is self-clearing when the data from each new data card are received. Therefore, a clear instruction is not necessary after each data card is read. Although the read area is self-clearing, the punch and print areas must be cleared after the data from each card are processed.

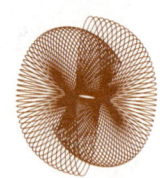

REVIEW QUESTIONS

1. Define a computer program.
2. Name the four ways in which programs may be written.
3. What is software? What is hardware?
4. What is a block diagram?
5. For which generation computer were the programs in this chapter written?
6. Discuss the cell organization of the computer described in this chapter as to number of cores in an individual cell, parity check, code used for storing and processing data, and type of word lengths.
7. Which cells are designated as the read area? Which cells are designated as the punch area?
8. Which cells are designated as the print area in this text?
9. Why should storage areas be cleared before data are placed in them?
10. Why is it unnecessary to clear the read area of memory after each data card is read?

WRITING PROGRAMS IN ENGLISH

The instructions for any computer may be written in English. In this form, they can be arranged in the logical sequence of a program. Of course, the computer could not be expected to accept the instructions in this form because each computer has a language of its own. Whatever information you want to tell the machine must be written in, or translated into, the language the computer uses.

In the preliminary stages of learning programming, however, there are some advantages in writing instructions in English. Attention can then be given to the detailed, logical sequence in which the instructions must be prepared. At the same time, you will not become distracted by the peculiarities of a computer language system. After the problem is defined and instructions are written in English to solve it, each instruction must be rewritten or coded in the language system of the computer. *Coding* is the process of writing instructions in a language acceptable to the computer. A description follows of some of the basic instructions that computers can understand and carry out.

Instructions for clearing storage

You will recall that all areas of the computer needed for processing the data to solve a particular problem must be cleared by program instructions. Those given here in English need no further explanation:

    Clear the read area   — Cells 001–080

    Clear the punch area — Cells 101–180

    Clear the print area   — Cells 201–299

    Clear a work area   — Cells 601–699

The foregoing instructions could, of course, have been shortened somewhat as follows:

>Clear Cells 001–080.
>
>Clear Cells 101–180.
>
>Clear Cells 201–299.
>
>Clear Cells 601–699.

Note that Cells 601–699 have been selected for a work area. The instruction to clear a work area is an example of a typical instruction for clearing storage. *Work areas* are areas in which totals may be accumulated or computations made and may be set up anywhere in the computer, other than in the areas reserved for reading, punching, and printing.

Instructions for setting word marks

Since the computer discussed in this chapter uses variable word lengths, word marks must be set by program instructions in order to identify each unit of information being processed. Because each field in a punched card consists of a unit of information, it can be quickly determined in which cells in the read area the word marks should be set. They should be set in cells that correspond to the left column of each card field. Observe Figure 14-3. The card is one of many similar cards that will be processed to produce a printed list of all students enrolled in a school. The list will also

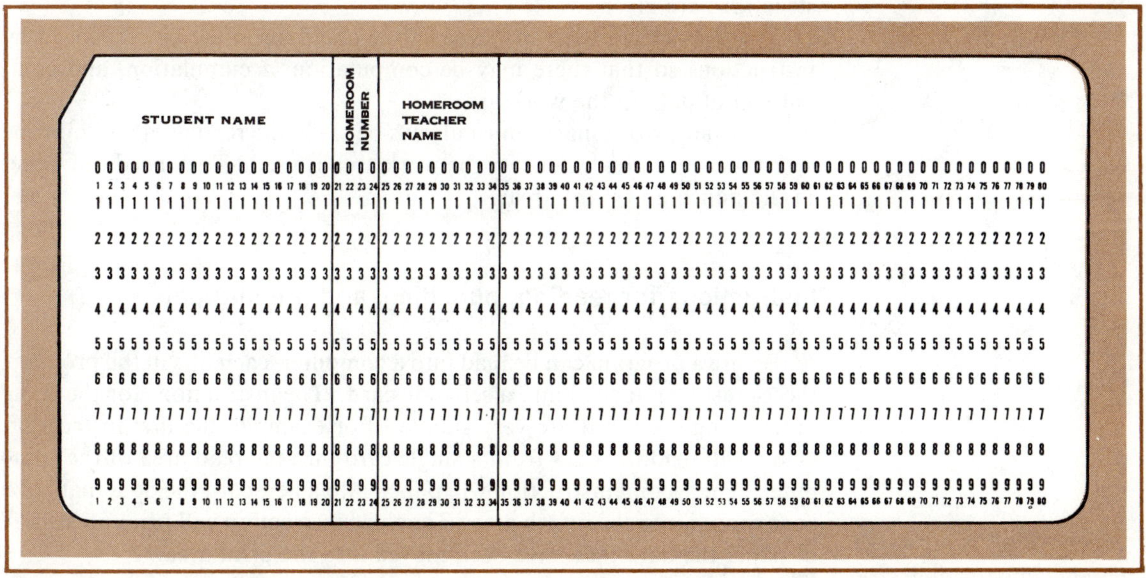

Figure 14-3. Punched card showing location of fields for names of students, homeroom numbers, and names of homeroom teachers

show each student's homeroom number and the homeroom teacher's name.

The first field, consisting of the student's name, includes Columns 1–20. The second field, consisting of the homeroom number, includes Columns 21–24. The third field, containing the homeroom teacher's name, includes Columns 25–34. The instructions to set word marks for these fields follow:

Set a word mark to identify student's name, Cell 001.

Set a word mark to identify homeroom number, Cell 021.

Set a word mark to identify homeroom teacher's name, Cell 025.

As word marks are always turned on in the leftmost cell of a field, the foregoing instructions could be shortened as follows:

>Set word mark in Cell 001.
>
>Set word mark in Cell 021.
>
>Set word mark in Cell 025.

In the discussion on p. 235 you were told that an instruction to clear storage in the read area is necessary only at the beginning of a program. This clear instruction erases the word marks set for a previous program. After the read area is cleared, the programmer is able to set new word marks in the read area for the current program. Although each new data card read into the read area will erase the data from the previous cards, the word marks will remain during the entire program. It is not necessary to set word marks in the punch and print areas because separate words are not addressed in punch and print instructions. Whatever data are moved into certain storage locations in the punch and print areas by a move instruction will be punched and printed when the punch and print instructions are given.

Word marks in the work area of the computer must be turned on by instructions so that there may be computation, accumulation, and comparison of data in the work area.

In review, word marks must always be set in the read area and must be set in the work area whenever the work area is used. They need not be set in the punch and print areas.

Instructions for reading, punching, and printing data

Before a program can be read into a computer, each line in the program sheet must be punched into a separate card. The instructions for the computer being discussed are very simple. For example, the first instruction below will read the data from a single card into the read area of the computer. The second instruction will punch into a new card the data that have been moved into the punch area. The third instruction will print on a sheet of paper the data that have been moved into the print area.

Read a card.

Punch data into a card.

Print the data.

If desired, these instructions could be shortened as follows:

Read.

Punch.

Print.

Move instructions

Assuming that we wanted to move the three data words, the student's name, his homeroom number, and his homeroom teacher's name, from the read area to the print area, we could write the following instructions:

Move student's name from the read area to the punch area.

Move student's homeroom number from the read area to the punch area.

Move the homeroom teacher's name from the read area to the punch area.

Observe that a separate move instruction is required for each data word. The following instructions are somewhat shorter and just as good in getting the job done:

Move contents of Cells 001–020 to Cells 101–120.

Move contents of Cells 021–024 to Cells 121–124.

Move contents of Cells 025–034 to Cells 125–134.

Or even better, because they are shorter, the following instructions would also suffice:

Move 020 to 120.

Move 024 to 124.

Move 034 to 134.

Even though the foregoing short instructions are in modified English form, they are very close to the language acceptable to the computer. Two new concepts have been introduced in these instructions that should be examined here. One is that in computer instructions, the data, as such, are not named. Instead, the cells in which the data are stored are named. For example: Move 020 to 120. This instruction really means to move the student's name from the read area to the punch area.

The other concept is that only the rightmost or low-order cell of a group of cells in which data are stored needs to be named. Cell 020 is the rightmost cell of those used to store the student's name in the read area.

Cell 120 is the rightmost cell of those used to store his name in the punch area. The name, however, occupies Cells 001–020 in the read area and Cells 101–120 in the punch area. The entire name can be moved into the punch area by giving only the two addresses: Move 020 to 120. You will remember that the computer senses the data from right to left. Therefore, it will move all the data beginning at Cell 020 and proceed leftward until a word mark is reached.

If a list were to be printed, using the names of the students, their homeroom numbers, and the names of their homeroom teachers, the list would probably not be spaced exactly as the data would appear on the card. The columns on the printed report would be evenly spaced, with margins on both sides. Provision for the spacing in the print area would be made in the move instruction. For example, if there were to be ten spaces in the left-hand margin, the move instruction would *not* say:

Move 020 to 220.

The move instruction *would* read:

Move 020 to 2<u>30</u>.

If the left-hand column were to contain 16 spaces, the move instruction would read:

Move 020 to 23<u>6</u>.

Cell 236 is the rightmost cell of those used to store the name in the print area. The name occupies 001–020 in the read area and would be moved to 217–236 in the print area. This instruction would allow for a left-hand margin of 16 blank spaces (201–216).

Sequence

A *sequence* is a series of steps or instructions in a program that the computer will perform without interruption. A computer follows instructions in sequential order. It will branch to a new set of instructions or repeat a sequence, depending upon the conditions met in solving a problem and the instructions written to handle those conditions.

Branch instruction

If you want the computer to list the information appearing on all the cards in the deck, you need an instruction to bring the computer back to the read instruction after the data in a preceding card have been printed A different program need not be written for each separate card. Instead, one program can process all the cards in the deck. What is needed is a branch instruction, and the one that follows will suffice:

Branch to the read instruction to process another card.

Figure 14-4 will help you visualize the action of the computer when the branch instruction is added. Each card in the deck will be processed by the same instructions, beginning with the READ instruction and ending with the CLEAR THE PRINT AREA instruction. The BRANCH instruction, which will follow the CLEAR PRINT instruction, will direct the computer to repeat the instructions until all the cards are processed. *Branching* is a computer term indicating that a series or sequence of steps in the program has been completed and is to be repeated or changed to a new instruction or set of instructions:

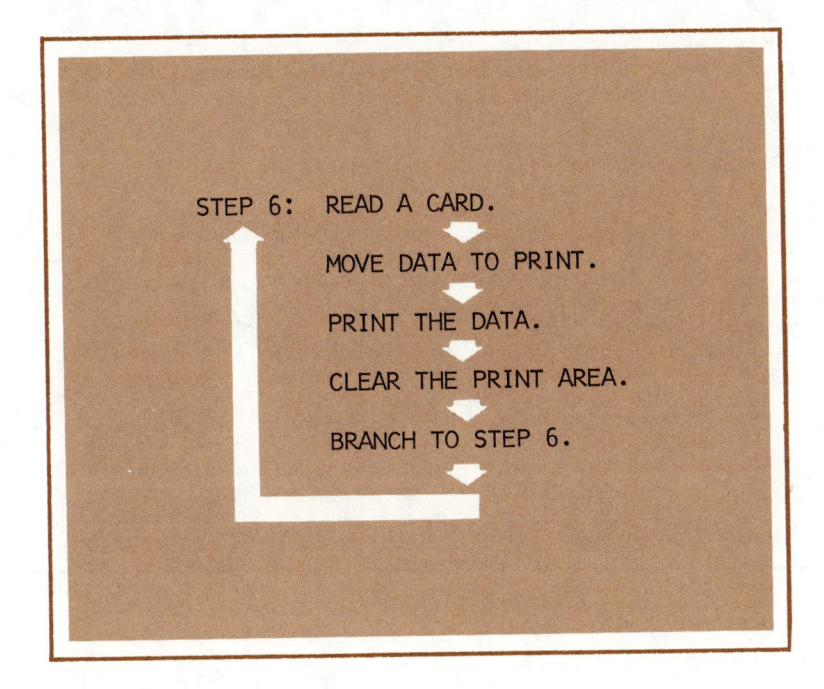

```
STEP 6:   READ A CARD.
          MOVE DATA TO PRINT.
          PRINT THE DATA.
          CLEAR THE PRINT AREA.
          BRANCH TO STEP 6.
```

Figure 14-4. Branch to repeat the sequence of instructions

Writing a program for problem 1

You now have had a sufficient number of instructions to write the program to solve a simple problem. For this problem, assume that you have a deck of cards on hand similar to the card illustrated in Figure 14-3 on p. 237. You are to write a program to prepare a printed report showing the names of students, their homeroom numbers, and the names of their homeroom teachers. The three items of information will be evenly spaced across a 99-space line. The program is to process the deck, card by card, until all the cards are processed. The program to solve this problem appears in Figure 14-5.

The abbreviated instructions are included in the foregoing problem. All of these instructions have been explained in the material just covered. Step 12 tells the computer to branch back to Step 6 to read the data from another card into storage and to repeat the steps in the program. The computer will then continue to repeat Steps 6 through 12 until the last card

INSTRUCTION	EXPLANATION
STEP 1. CLEAR CELLS 001-080	CLEAR READ AREA
STEP 2. CLEAR CELLS 201-299	CLEAR PRINT AREA
STEP 3. SET A WORD MARK IN CELL 001	IDENTIFY STUDENT'S NAME
STEP 4. SET A WORD MARK IN CELL 021	IDENTIFY HOMEROOM NUMBER
STEP 5. SET A WORD MARK IN CELL 025	IDENTIFY HOMEROOM TEACHER'S NAME
STEP 6. READ A CARD	READ PUNCHED DATA INTO COMPUTER
STEP 7. MOVE 020 TO 236	MOVE STUDENT'S NAME TO PRINT
STEP 8. MOVE 024 TO 256	MOVE HOMEROOM NUMBER TO PRINT
STEP 9. MOVE 034 TO 282	MOVE HOMEROOM TEACHER'S NAME TO PRINT
STEP 10. PRINT THE DATA	PRINT THE DATA
STEP 11. CLEAR CELLS 201-299	CLEAR THE PRINT AREA
STEP 12. BRANCH TO STEP 6	BRANCH TO BEGINNING OF LOOP TO PROCESS ANOTHER CARD

Figure 14-5. Program for Problem 1

finally has been read. Steps 6 through 12, together with the branch back to Step 6, would constitute a *loop*, which may be defined as the repetition of a group of instructions until certain conditions are reached — in this case, until all the cards in the deck are processed.

WRITING PROGRAMS IN BLOCK DIAGRAMS

Generally, the instructions for a computer are first written in block diagram form. A *block diagram* is very similar to a flow chart. Actually, a block diagram can be looked upon as a detailed flow chart, showing what is to be done by the computer at each stage in the solution of a problem. The term, block diagram, is especially associated with electronic computers. It gives the programmer an opportunity to visualize the order in which instructions occur as well as the relationship of one part of the program to another. The terms "block" and "symbol" are used interchangeably.

Basic block diagram symbols

Figure 14-6 shows the symbols that are commonly used in block diagramming. Basically, these symbols represent six types of action. The arrowheads indicate the direction followed by the computer in executing the instructions. The blocks or symbols that make up a particular sequence are connected by *flow lines*. The general direction of the flow is from top to bottom and from left to right. Whenever the direction of the flow is reversed, an arrowhead <u>must</u> be used. However, the use of arrowheads on every flow line is optional. The blocks are prepared with the aid of a template with which the blocks can be drawn quickly and accurately.

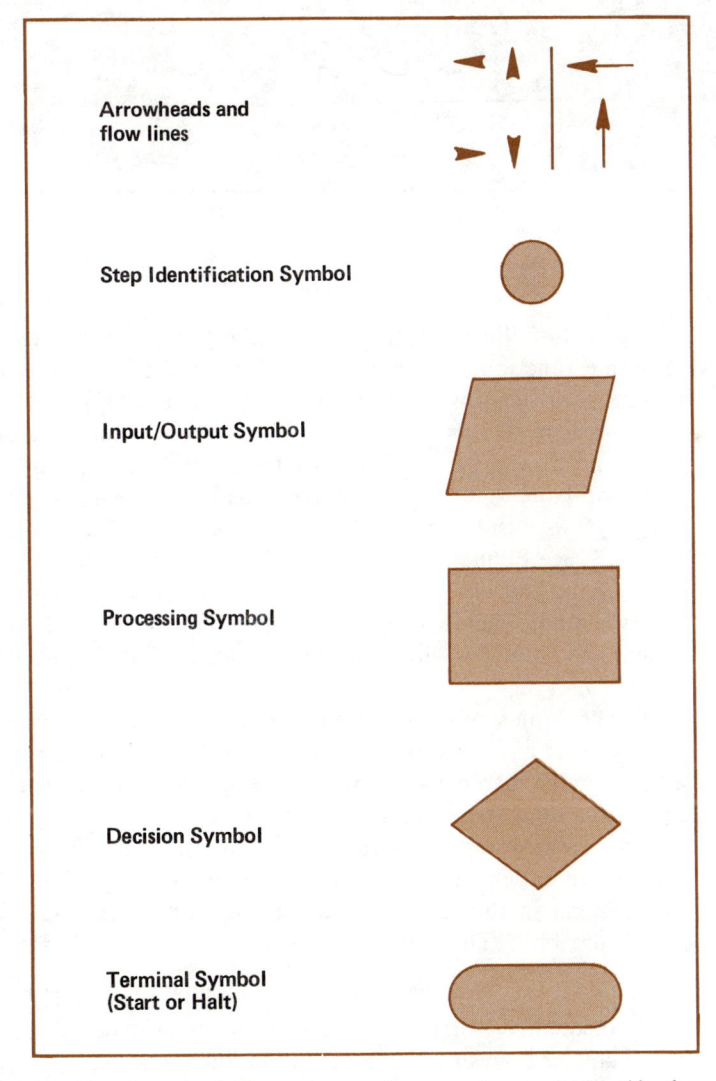

Figure 14-6. Basic symbols used in block diagramming

- Arrowheads and flow lines
- Step Identification Symbol
- Input/Output Symbol
- Processing Symbol
- Decision Symbol
- Terminal Symbol (Start or Halt)

The step identification symbol may be used to number and identify the introduction of a step or sequence of steps in a computer program.

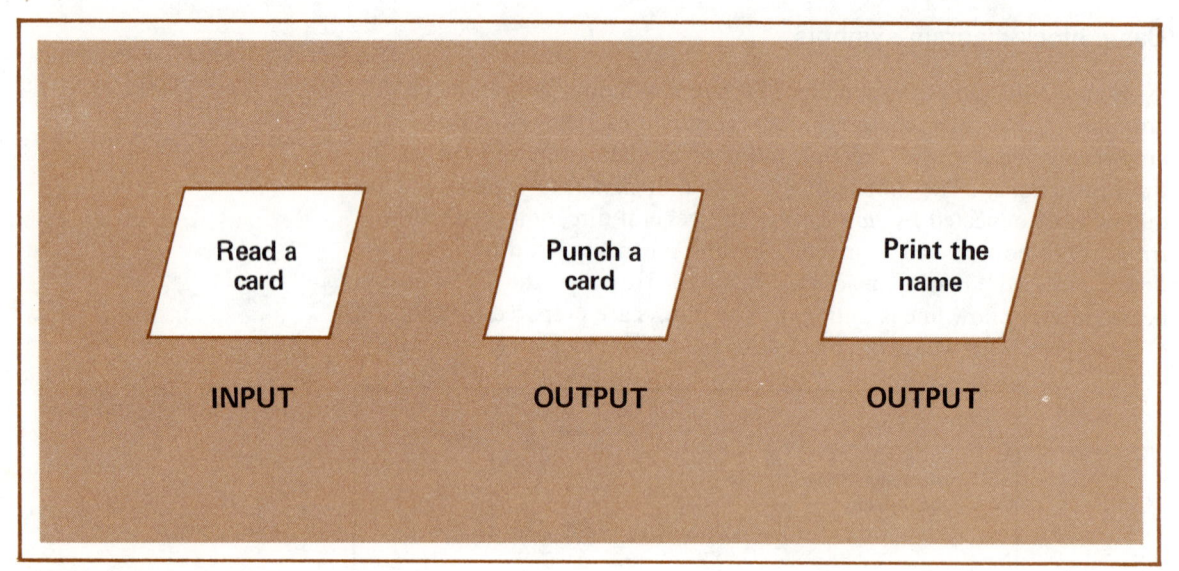

[Figure: Three parallelogram shapes labeled "Read a card" (INPUT), "Punch a card" (OUTPUT), and "Print the name" (OUTPUT)]

Figure 14-7. Input and output symbols

Figure 14-7 illustrates the symbol used to represent either an input or an output function. One function is distinguished from the other by the notations written inside the blocks. Observe in Figure 14-7 how the notations help to identify the functions of the input and output symbols.

The processing symbol identifies the processing steps in the computer program. Note that the programmer may designate move instructions by using arrows inside the processing blocks instead of using the word "Move." See Figure 14-8.

Since the amount of space within the blocks is very limited, the notations written inside blocks must be brief. Signs such as the arrow are used to keep the notations short and still provide clear directions on the action to be taken.

The decision symbol is used to indicate a point in the program at which the computer will perform a test of some kind. The results of the decision will determine the next step to be taken in the program. A computer can compare a digit in a program instruction to see if it is equal to another digit read into storage via a data card. For example, if the code number of sophomore students were 2, the computer could search for a 2 in the specific column in the card designating the code number for sophomores. See Figure 14-9. The computer is able to test for three conditions:

1. Equality — whether one number is equal to another number.
2. Inequality — if the numbers are unequal, whether one number is greater than or less than the other number.
3. The presence of data remaining to be processed — in this case, whether the last card has been read.

Chapter 14   Human language programs and block diagrams   245

The decision blocks in Figure 14-9 contain notations which indicate the types of decisions to be made. A decision block always requires a yes or no answer. The answer, of course, will determine the next step to be taken in the program.

The symbol used to represent a decision-making function.

Block	Meaning
Clear print area	This block means that the print area is to be cleared.
Move amount to print	This block means that an amount is to be moved to the print area.
Amount ⟶ print	This block also means that an amount is to be moved to the print area. (Note use of the arrow.)
Print	This block means that all the data in the print area should be printed.

2 in 29? — Yes / No
Digit 2 in Column 29?

B < A — Yes / No
B is less than A

B > A — Yes / No
B is greater than A

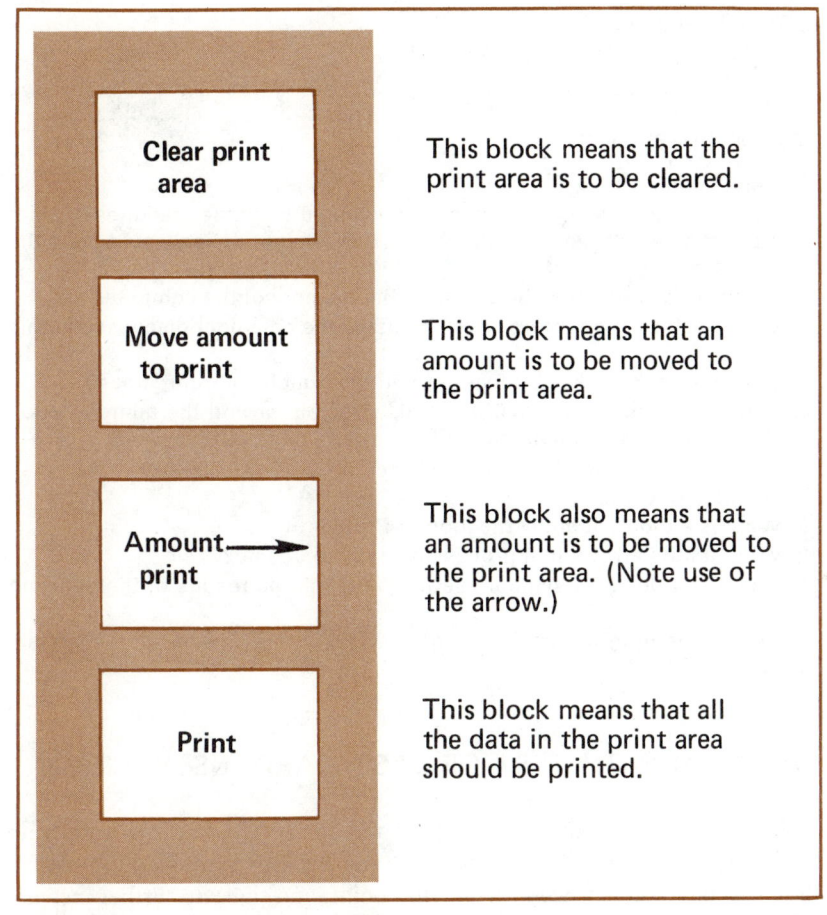

Last card? — Yes / No
Has last card been processed?

Figure 14-8. Processing symbols

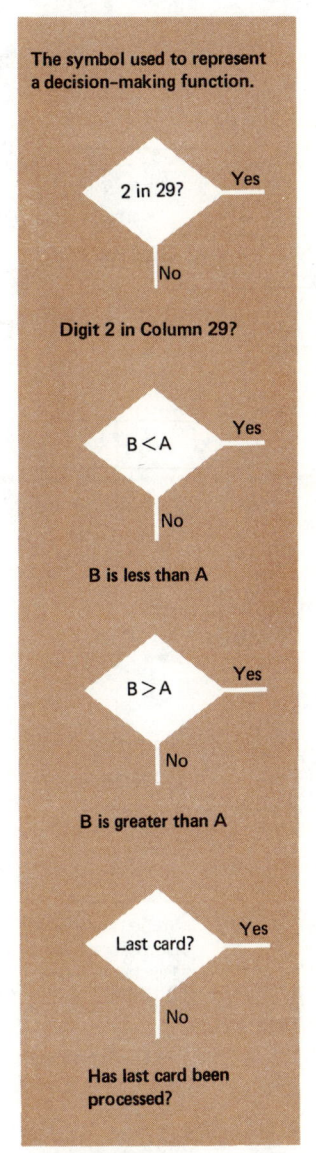

Figure 14-9. Decision-making symbols

Preparing a block diagram for problem 1

Figure 14-10 shows the block diagram that was prepared for Problem 1. The detailed English language instructions to solve this problem appear on p. 242. You will recall that the problem required the programmer to prepare a printed report showing the names of students, their homeroom numbers, and the names of their homeroom teachers.

Observe, first of all, the direction in which the program flows. Note the steps that are repeated until all the cards are processed. A branch occurs, without fail, to the first instruction in the series set up to process the cards.

While the program illustrated in Figure 14-5 could be used to produce the report desired, it is only a partial program because no provision is made in it for testing for the last card and halting when the last card has been processed. New instructions will be included in Problem 2 for handling these functions.

REVIEW QUESTIONS

1. Define coding.
2. Using cell addresses, what instruction would clear the read area? What instruction would clear the punch area? What instruction would clear the print area?
3. Where may work areas be set up in the memory of the computer?
4. Why must word marks be set when using the computer discussed in this chapter?
5. Why are word marks not necessary in the punch and print areas?
6. In the instruction, "Move 020 to 220," are you moving the numeric value (20) or the data that happens to be located in Cell 020?
7. Define a sequence of instructions.
8. Define branching.
9. What is a loop? Identify the loop in Problem 1.
10. What do the arrows in a processing symbol denote?
11. When is a decision symbol used? What will the results of the decision determine?
12. Why is the program for Problem 1, p. 242, in this chapter an incomplete program?

PROGRAM WITH TEST OF LAST CARD INSTRUCTION

The program for solving Problem 1 will cause the computer to operate in a loop from Step 6 through Step 12 and back to Step 6 again until all the cards have been processed. At that point, and since no further instructions are given, the operator of the computer would have to stop the computer manually.

Test of last card and halt instructions

Through a built-in sensing device, the computer can detect the presence of cards to be read. When all the cards are read, the sensing device informs the internal memory of the machine that there are no more cards to be processed. At that point, an alternate instruction or set of instructions may be brought into play. The steps followed in such an operation are listed in Figure 14-11.

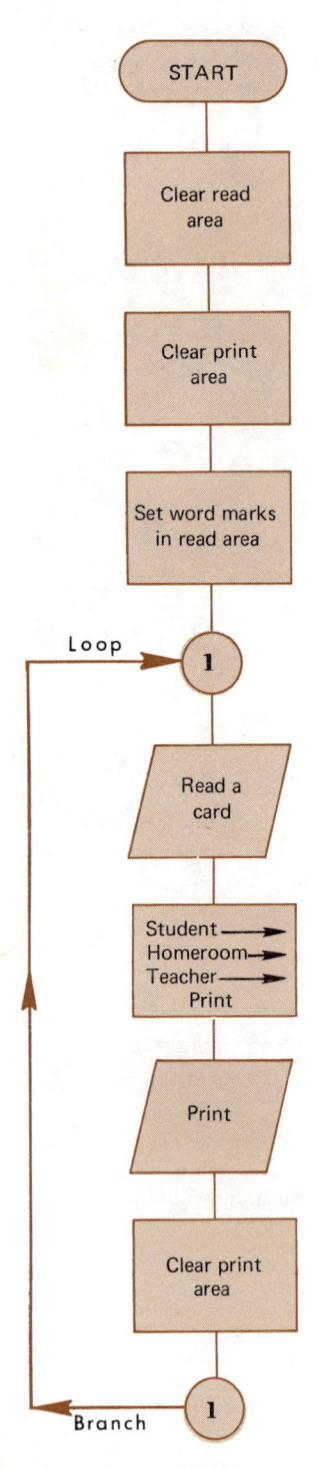

Figure 14-10. Block diagram for Problem 1

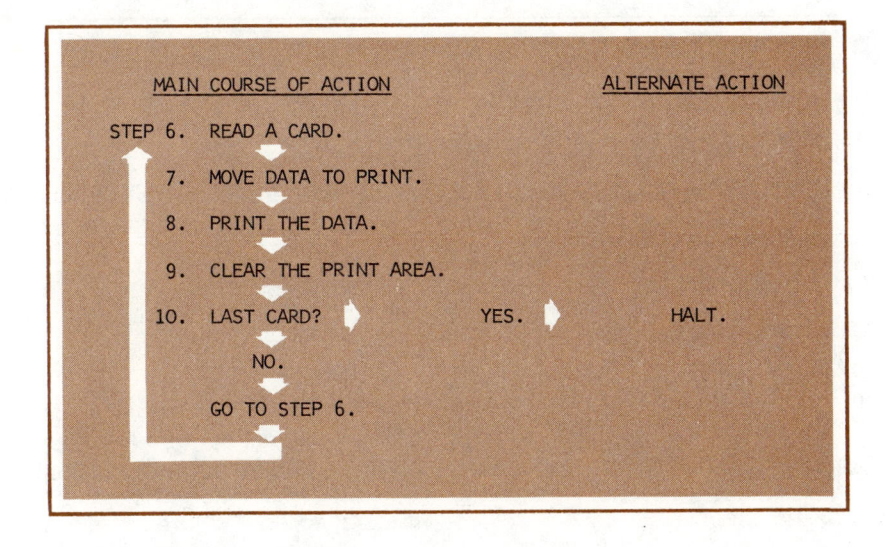

Chapter 14 Human language programs and block diagrams

```
        MAIN COURSE OF ACTION              ALTERNATE ACTION
STEP 6.  READ A CARD.
     7.  MOVE DATA TO PRINT.
     8.  PRINT THE DATA.
     9.  CLEAR THE PRINT AREA.
    10.  LAST CARD?            YES.             HALT.
         NO.
         GO TO STEP 6.
```

Figure 14-11. Last card test

Note the main and alternate courses of action. The computer will continue to repeat the steps in the main course of action until all cards have been read. Note that the decision must be made each time on the last card. When the last card has finally been read, the computer will branch to the alternate course of action if proper instructions are written into the program. The alternate course is usually the final instruction or sequence in the program. The following instruction will cause the computer to test for the last card and then either repeat the steps in the program or stop.

If last card, branch to Halt instruction.

If not last card, branch to instruction to repeat program.

Halt.

Problem 2 restated

Recall that you have a deck of cards on hand similar to the card illustrated in Figure 14-3. You are to write a program to prepare a printed report showing the names of students, their homeroom numbers, and the names of their homeroom teachers. The three items of information will be evenly spaced across a 99-space line. The program will process all the cards in the deck. It will also include a last card test instruction in order to stop the computer automatically when all the cards are processed.

Writing a program for problem 2

The program for Problem 2 is very much the same as the program for Problem 1. The program for Problem 2, of course, will include a last card test instruction, which will cause the computer to stop when the last card has been processed.

STEP NO.	INSTRUCTION	EXPLANATION
1	CLEAR CELLS 001-080	CLEAR READ AREA
2	CLEAR CELLS 201-299	CLEAR PRINT AREA
3	SET A WORD MARK IN CELL 001	IDENTIFY STUDENT'S NAME
4	SET A WORD MARK IN CELL 021	IDENTIFY HOMEROOM NUMBER
5	SET A WORD MARK IN CELL 025	IDENTIFY HOMEROOM TEACHER'S NAME
6	READ A CARD	READ PUNCHED DATA INTO COMPUTER
7	MOVE 020 TO 236	MOVE STUDENT'S NAME TO PRINT
8	MOVE 024 TO 256	MOVE HOMEROOM NUMBER TO PRINT
9	MOVE 034 TO 282	MOVE HOMEROOM TEACHER'S NAME TO PRINT
10	PRINT THE DATA	PRINT DATA IN PRINT AREA
11	CLEAR CELLS 201-299	CLEAR PRINT AREA
12	IF LAST CARD, BRANCH TO STEP 14	LAST CARD TEST
13	IF NOT LAST CARD, BRANCH TO STEP 6	BRANCH TO BEGINNING OF LOOP TO PROCESS ANOTHER CARD
14	HALT	STOP WHEN ALL CARDS ARE PROCESSED

LOOP → (steps 6 through 13)

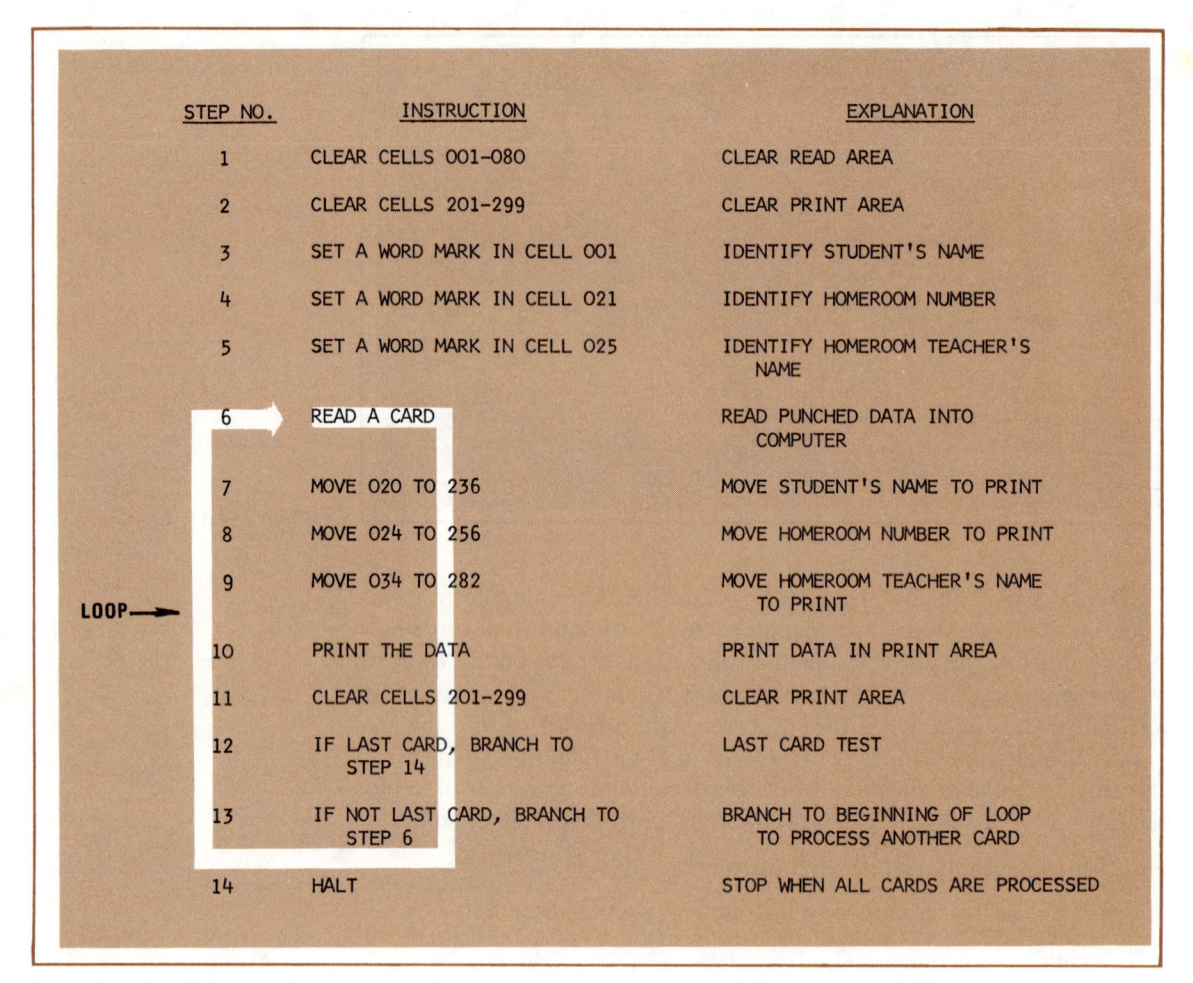

Figure 14-12. Program for Problem 2

Study Figure 14-12. Note that the first 11 steps are the same as those in the program for Problem 1. They need no further explanation. Step 12 asks the computer to test for the last card. If the last card has been processed, the instruction at Step 12 tells the computer to branch to Step 14, which is an instruction to halt. If the last card has not been processed, the computer automatically drops down to the next instruction Step 13, which is an instruction to branch to Step 6 to repeat the steps in the loop.

The instructions in the loop, Steps 6 through 13, will be applied to each card in the deck. The last card test will be made each time a card is processed. The branch to Step 14 will come only when all the cards in the deck have been processed.

Preparing a block diagram for problem 2

Figure 14-13 shows the block diagram prepared for the program for Problem 2. Observe the direction in which the program flows. Note the instructions that take care of the beginning "housekeeping" duties in this

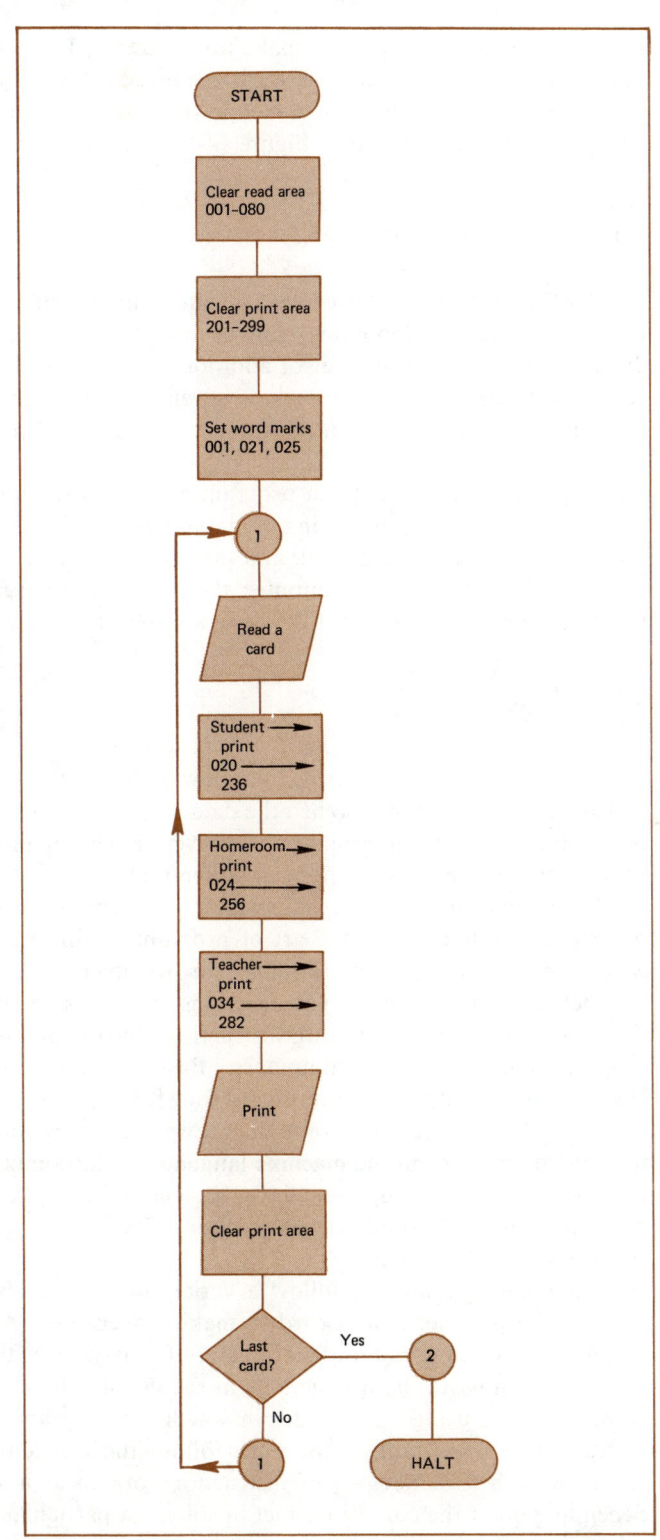

Chapter 14 Human language programs and block diagrams

Figure 14-13. Block diagram for Problem 2

program. Note the steps that make up the loop. These steps will be repeated again and again until there are no more cards to process. Note also the single instruction that is included in the windup of this program. The basic symbols are included in Figure 14-13. Can you identify them?

STORING INSTRUCTIONS

Most computers can execute a greater number of instructions than those given here. Computers can be instructed to multiply, subtract, divide, and conduct a number of additional operations. The instructions covered here are basic, but they have given you an insight into the way a computer works. With them, a number of additional problems may be solved.

Once the instructions for a program have been written in a language acceptable to the computer being used, these instructions are punched into cards, one instruction to a card, and then stored in the computer. As the data cards are fed into the computer, the stored program takes over. The CPU does with the data what the program tells it to do.

SUMMARY

A computer solves problems by following instructions that are written and stored in its memory. When the data needed to solve a problem enter the computer, the stored program takes over. Each step in a program must be correctly written. No detail can be omitted.

Computers vary in the form in which the instructions must be written. A basic understanding of the art of program writing may be gained by writing instructions in human language, by writing instructions in the form of block diagrams, by writing instructions in the basic language of a particular computer, or by writing instructions in one of the synthetic language systems devised for computers. Basic understandings are perhaps best gained by writing programs in all four forms.

In the days of the early computers it was necessary for a programmer to write instructions in the machine language of the computer being used. However, modern computers have become so complicated that their manufacturers will usually furnish translator-type programs that simplify the job of programming.

Computers are able to follow a variety of commands, from reading information punched into a card to making decisions. A problem to be solved by the computer must first be carefully analyzed by the programmer. He must then write the instructions in the detailed form required by the computer he is using. The order in which the programmer places these instructions is important. A computer follows the instructions in sequence. It will branch to a new set of instructions or repeat a sequence (loop) depending upon the conditions met in solving a particular problem.

Chapter 14   Human language programs and block diagrams

REVIEW QUESTIONS

1. How does the computer discussed in this chapter detect the presence of cards to be read?
2. Is the last card decision made to see if the last card has already been processed or if the last card is to be processed?
3. Is the last card test made each time a card is processed?
4. Name at least seven instructions discussed in this chapter that computers can execute.
5. How many program instructions may appear in a single punched card?

STUDY GUIDE

Complete Study Guide 14 by following the instructions in your **STUDY GUIDES** booklet.

PROJECTS

Complete Projects 14-1 and 14-2 by following the instructions in your **PROJECTS** booklet.

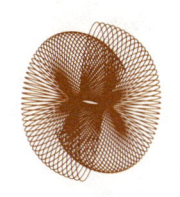

CHAPTER 15

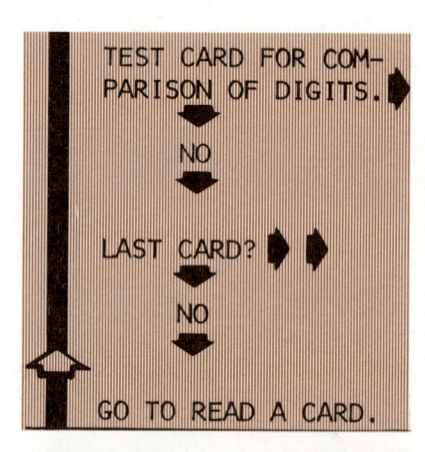

MACHINE LANGUAGE INSTRUCTIONS

Writing a computer program in English simplifies the writing process because the program is stated in terms that the reader easily understands. However, a program written in such a manner has little meaning to a computer. The computer does not understand the English language. Therefore, a program thus written must be coded in the language of the computer before the program can be understood or executed. The following discussion concerns the steps making up a machine language program.

Each model of a computer is built to understand a binary-based language that is unique to that machine. In other words, each computer has a machine language of its own. Usually that language consists of letters, digits, and special characters. A program written in this language is said to be a machine language program. A *machine language program* is one in which the instructions are written in a form that is intelligible to the internal circuitry of the computer. Such a program is sometimes referred to as "actual" or "absolute."

In the discussion that follows, you will learn about some of the digits, letters, and characters that will cause the second-generation computer discussed in Chapters 14 and 15 to carry out some of its functions. The machine language used is representative of other machine language systems and will provide a simplified basis for understanding other language instructions and programs.

INSTRUCTION FORMAT

Because the computer is such a precisely built machine, the various programs it uses must be written in an exacting manner. There must be a separate program for each problem, and in order to be meaningful, the instructions must be written in a prescribed format. *Instruction format* is the term given to the form in which computer instructions are written. The format may differ from computer to computer. Because all computers do not have the same internal circuitry, they do not all understand the same machine language. The format described in this chapter is for a small, second-generation computer.

A common form of writing instructions is one in which the instruction consists of four parts as noted below:

1. OPERATION CODE (tells what operation to perform)
2. A ADDRESS or OPERAND ⎫
3. B ADDRESS or OPERAND ⎭ (tells what is to be operated on)
4. d-CHARACTER (modifies or defines an operation code)

The general form of an instruction is as follows:

OPERATION CODE	A ADDRESS	B ADDRESS	d-CHARACTER
X	XXX	XXX	X

Operation code

Every instruction must have an operation code. The *operation code* tells the central processing unit of the computer what operation to perform (for example, to add, to punch, to print, or to move data). Without an operation code, an instruction is meaningless.

As in the case of data words, each program instruction is required to have a word mark in its high-order position. Therefore, the word mark for the instruction is always with the operation code because the operation code also is always in the high-order position. The word mark defines the length of an instruction. In the instructions illustrated in this chapter, the underscore is used with the operation codes to represent the presence of a word mark. The underscore itself is not a word mark.

A and B Addresses

A and B Addresses give the cell locations from which data to be processed may be obtained or in which results are to be placed. One or both of the addresses may be used depending upon the operation to be performed. If two amounts are to be added, for example, one amount will be designated by the A Address and the other by the B Address. The sum will be stored in the B Address. If an amount is to be moved from one location to another location, the A Address will give the location of the amount to be moved and the B Address will give the location to which it is to be moved.

Chapter 15   Machine language instructions   255

Keep in mind that cell addresses are used in machine language instructions rather than the actual data stored in these addresses.

The A Address also serves another function, and that is to give the location of an instruction when a branch must be made by the computer. Branching makes possible a choice of alternate steps from the normal, sequential routine. This is a special use of the A Address and should be remembered as such. When the A Address is used as the address of an instruction, it is frequently referred to as the I Address. The A and I Addresses thus occupy the same position in the format of an instruction.

d-Character

The d-Character, which is the last segment in the instruction, is a digit, letter of the alphabet, or special character that has a variety of functions. It is associated with the testing or decision-making ability of the computer. For example, the d-Character can be used as a test to see if two fields are equal, to see if the last card has been processed, or to see if the page on which output is being printed has been filled.

PROGRAM CHARTS

In addition to being written in a precise manner, instructions making up a computer program are normally written on special charts (sometimes called program sheets or coding sheets) prior to punching the instructions in a card. A program chart that is used for the writing of machine language instructions is illustrated in Figure 15-1. A program, which will be explained in detail later in this chapter, appears on the chart. The program chart is used to make it easier to code the program in the correct manner.

In Figure 15-1, notice the following characteristics of the program chart:

1. *Step No.:* The step number identifies each instruction. The step number need not be punched into a card. If it is punched into a card for identification purposes, the step number is not used by the computer. It is not part of the instruction.
2. *Inst. Address:* The instruction address column provides spaces for writing the address of the operation code of each instruction. The address of the operation code must be given with each instruction so that the CPU can locate the instruction. The address of the operation code of the first instruction usually follows the addresses of the cells reserved for printing. (To simplify the explanations in this chapter, the first instructions will begin at Cell 401 instead of immediately following the addresses of the cells reserved for printing.) Each cell can store only one character of a computer instruction. Instruction addresses are punched into program load cards. <u>The addresses are not part of the instruction</u>, however. They merely

PROGRAM CHART

Program: List of students, homeroom numbers, and teachers Programmer: Price Date: 10/12/71

Step No.	Inst. Address	OP	A/I d	B d	d	Remarks	Inst.	Data	Total
1	401	/	0 8 0			CLEAR READ AREA			
2	405	/	2 9 9			CLEAR PRINT AREA			
3	409	⊥	0 0 1	0 2 1		SET WORD MARKS FOR NAME, HOME ROOM NUMBER			
4	416	⊥	0 2 5			SET WORD MARK FOR TEACHER			
5	420	1				READ A CARD			
6	421	M	0 2 0	2 3 6		MOVE STUDENT NAME TO PRINT			
7	428	M	0 2 4	2 5 6		MOVE HOMEROOM NUMBER TO PRINT			
8	435	M	0 3 4	2 8 2		MOVE HOMEROOM TEACHER TO PRINT			
9	442	2				PRINT DATA			
10	443	/	2 9 9			CLEAR PRINT AREA			
11	447	B	4 5 6		A	BRANCH TO 456 (STEP 13) IF LAST CARD			
12	452	B	4 2 0			BRANCH TO 420 (STEP 5) IF NOT LAST CARD			
13	456	⊥				HALT			

Figure 15-1. Machine language program chart

indicate the location of each instruction. The instruction at Step 1 is located at Address 401–404; instruction at Step 2, at 405–408; and the instruction at Step 3 at 409–415. Four cells are needed to store the first instruction: /080. The operation code is stored in Cell 401. Each of the three digits in the A Address requires a cell. The operation code of the second instruction is located in Cell 405.

3. *OP:* The OP in the third column of the chart stands for the operation code of each instruction. An operation code describes the action to be taken. Remember that each operation code requires a word mark.

4. *A/I:* The A/I Column provides space for the address of the A data field. On occasion it is the address of the next instruction to be processed by the computer. In a test and branch operation, the A/I Address provides the location to which the computer will branch. There are branch instruction addresses in Steps 11 and 12 above.

Chapter 15 Machine language instructions

5. *B:* The B Column provides space for the address of the B data field, if there is one.
6. *d:* The column reserved for the d-Character provides space for the character that is required when a test is made to determine if the last card has been read. The d-Character is also used to make a number of other tests. Observe its use in Step 11 of the program.
7. *Remarks:* The space set aside on the program for remarks may be used to describe the action to be taken by each instruction. Notes written in this space are not punched into program cards; consequently, they are not stored in the computer. The remarks serve to remind the programmer what action is to be taken by each instruction.
8. *Effective No. of Characters:* The data written into the last three columns are used to estimate how much computer time will be used by each instruction. This information will not be determined in the program examples given in this book.

WRITING INSTRUCTIONS

Now that you have learned about instruction format and how a program sheet is used for the writing of an instruction, you are ready to write some commonly used instructions.

Clear storage instruction

The following instruction clears information from the storage positions of a computer. Clearance starts at the location specified by the A Address and continues to the *left* until the nearest hundreds position is reached. The hundreds position itself and all intervening data and word marks are cleared. The operation code for a clear storage instruction is a diagonal (/). When the instruction is written according to the format explained earlier in this chapter, the instruction will appear as follows:

OPERATION CODE	A ADDRESS	B ADDRESS	d-CHARACTER
/	699	(NOT NEEDED)	(NOT NEEDED)

In the foregoing example, cell locations 699, 698, 697, etc. through 600 are cleared. The instruction / 601 would clear cell locations 601 and 600. The instruction / 600 would clear only cell location 600. Since the clear instruction clears *word marks as well as data*, some way must be found to limit clearance operations. As a result, the computer is built to clear all positions from the one specified in the A address down to and including the nearest hundreds position. Thus, several instructions may be needed to clear desired locations.

In the previous chapter, it was explained that the number of printing positions used in the reserved print area will vary, depending upon the limitations of the output printing unit. Most printing units can print between 120 and 132 characters to a line. In order to simplify the clear instructions in this text, as mentioned in Chapter 14, it will be assumed that the print area contains only 99 cells. Thus, the student will be able to clear the print area with only one clear instruction. This practice would not be followed by a computer programmer but is used as a teaching device. The concept of clearing storage is taught without complicating the programs.

OPERATION CODE	A ADDRESS	B ADDRESS	d-CHARACTER
/	299	(NOT NEEDED)	(NOT NEEDED)

The above clear instruction will clear from Cell 299 down to and including Cell 200.

Keeping the foregoing in mind, what instructions would be needed to clear data and word marks from the (a) read, (b) punch, (c) print area used in this text, and (d) work area consisting of Cells 600–699 of the computer? The solutions follow:

	OPERATION CODE	A ADDRESS	B ADDRESS	d-CHARACTER
(A)	/	080	(NOT NEEDED)	(NOT NEEDED)
(B)	/	180	" "	" "
(C)	/	299	" "	" "
(D)	/	699	" "	" "

To erase any previous word marks that might be in the read area from a previous program, one must clear Cells 001 through 080 before beginning a program. Thereafter, no further clear orders need be written for the read area for the current program. The read area is self-clearing as each new card is read into the computer. Only data are cleared, however. The word marks set by the instructions for the current program are not disturbed in the self-clearing process. Remember that the read area is the only area that is self-clearing.

Figure 15-2 is an illustration of the foregoing instructions written on the program sheet.

Set word mark instruction

You will recall that a word mark must define each data word stored in a variable word length computer. The word mark is turned on in the high-order or leftmost position of the data word because the computer senses data words from right to left. The operation code for setting a word mark is a comma (,). The instruction to set word marks requires an operation code (comma) and both the A and B addresses if two word marks are

Chapter 15 Machine language instructions

needed or only the A Address if one word mark is needed. The A and B addresses should specify the cell addresses at which word marks are needed. The instructions should be repeated if more than two word marks need to be set. The d-Character is not needed in this instruction.

OPERATION CODE	A ADDRESS	B ADDRESS	d-CHARACTER
,	001	021	(NOT NEEDED)

In the preceding example, word marks would be set in Cells 001 and 021, which are located in the read area of the computer. If only one address had been used, only one word mark would be set.

Figure 15-3 is an illustration of the foregoing instruction written on a program sheet.

Figure 15-2. Instructions to clear storage

PROGRAM CHART

Program: _____ Programmer: _____ Date: _____

Step No.	Inst. Address	Instruction OP	A/I d	B d	d	Remarks	Effective No. of Characters Inst.	Data	Total
		/	0 8 0			CLEAR READ AREA			
		/	1 8 0			CLEAR PUNCH AREA			
		/	2 9 9			CLEAR PRINT AREA			
		/	6 9 9			CLEAR WORK AREA			

Figure 15-3. Instruction to set word marks

PROGRAM CHART

Program: _____ Programmer: _____ Date: _____

Step No.	Inst. Address	Instruction OP	A/I d	B d	d	Remarks	Effective No. of Characters Inst.	Data	Total
		,	0 0 1	0 2 1		SET WORD MARKS			

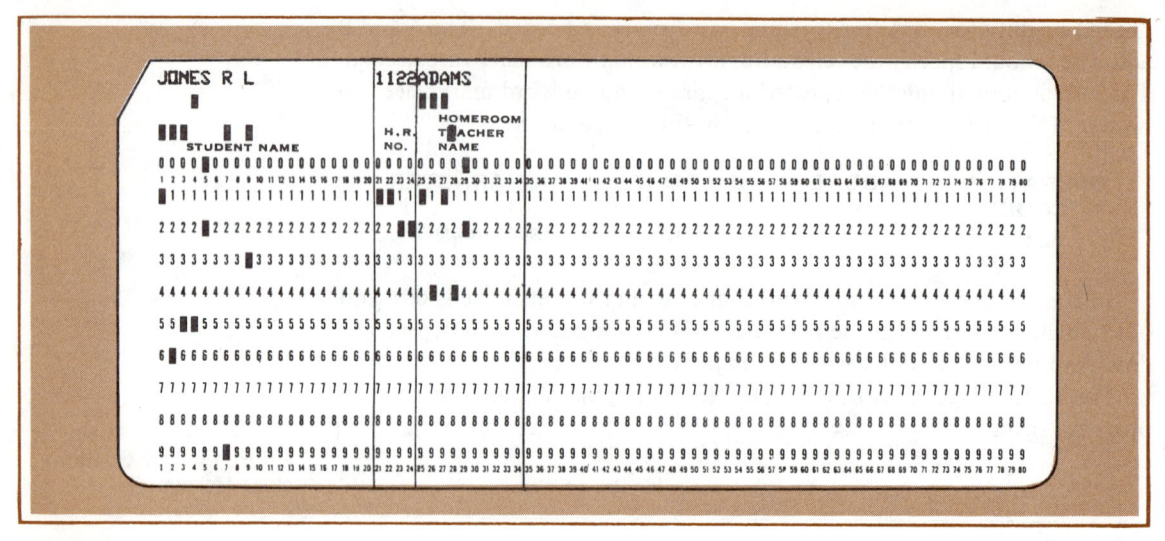

Figure 15-4. Card containing student data

Assume that you wanted to set word marks for the fields in the punched card illustrated in Figure 15-4 above.

The first field, consisting of the student's name, includes Columns 1–20. The second field, consisting of the homeroom number, includes Columns 21–24. The third field, consisting of the homeroom teacher's name, includes Columns 25–34. The instructions to set word marks for these fields follow:

OPERATION CODE	A ADDRESS	B ADDRESS	d-CHARACTER
,	001	021	(NOT NEEDED)
,	025		(NOT NEEDED)

Normally word marks are set before words are stored in the computer. Such is the case in the example shown above.

Each instruction is punched into a separate card. Each instruction must also have a word mark in the high-order position, which is always the operation code position. The word mark defines the length of the instruction. The underline is used in an instruction on a program chart as a symbol to indicate where the word mark is located. The underline is not part of the instruction.

When instructions are written in machine language and punched into cards, one needs to punch into each card the word mark for the instruction as well as the instruction itself.

Word marks are not needed in the punch and print areas because the separate words do not have to be addressed in punch and print instructions. Whatever data are stored in these entire areas will be punched or printed at the locations specified when the punch or print instruction is given. However, for the work areas of the CPU, a word mark must be turned on by instructions in order to have computation, accumulation, and comparison of data in a particular location.

Chapter 15   Machine language instructions   261

REVIEW QUESTIONS

1. What is a machine language program?
2. Do all computers understand the same machine language?
3. Define an "absolute" program.
4. What is the meaning of the term *instruction format*?
5. Name the four parts of the machine language instruction format used by the computer discussed in Chapters 14 and 15.
6. What is the purpose of the operation code?
7. Does the operation code always have a word mark associated with it?
8. What is the purpose of the A Address? The B Address?
9. What is the alternate name of the A Address?
10. For what part of an instruction is the address given? Why?
11. How many locations are required to store this instruction: /̲080? What does the underline under the / represent?
12. What is the meaning of the "I" in the term I Address?
13. What is the purpose of a program chart?
14. Name the eight subdivisions of the machine language program chart.
15. When writing a machine language program, what type of instruction usually appears first?
16. What is the maximum number of cells that can be cleared with a single instruction?
17. At what point does clearing stop?
18. Why is the read area cleared only at the beginning of a program? Are the word marks for a current program cleared when a new card is read?
19. What symbol is used as the operation code for clearing storage?
20. What symbol is used as the operation code for setting word marks?

Read instruction

This instruction reads the contents of an entire punched card into the memory of a computer. The 80 columns of data in a card are transmitted from the card to Cells 001 through 080, the cells reserved for data read into the CPU. Word marks stored in some of the cells by a previous instruction to define the data fields will not be disturbed. The A or the B Address and the d-Character are not needed in a read instruction because the read area (Cell locations 001–080) is a reserved area specified by the computer. The operation code for a read instruction is the digit one (1). A read instruction is illustrated below:

OPERATION CODE	A ADDRESS	B ADDRESS	d-CHARACTER
1̲	(NOT NEEDED)	(NOT NEEDED)	(NOT NEEDED)

As the card is read into the computer, the 80 columns of information, Columns 01–80, are read into the corresponding cell locations in computer memory, Cells 001–080. As previously explained, reading a new card into the read area of the computer automatically clears *all* cells from 001 through 080. The new data entering the cells in this area will erase the data stored there by a previous read command. The blank columns of a punched card record zeros or spaces, which erase data from all unused cells in the read area. Thus, data words in each field may vary in length; but when a new card is read into the machine, all previous data recorded there will be erased. The word marks set there previously remain, and they continue to remain there until removed by a clear instruction. Because this is true, word marks can be set in the read area at the beginning of a program and left there until a change is made in the length of the card fields.

Figure 15-5 is an illustration of a read instruction written on a program sheet. After the read instruction is completed, the data punched in the card will be stored in the read area of the computer. Figure 15-6 illustrates where the data are stored in the cells of the read area.

Move instruction

The move instruction will transfer data from one cell or group of cells specified by the A Address to another group of cells specified by the B Address. The operation code for a move instruction is the Letter M. Both the A and B addresses must be specified. A move instruction is illustrated below:

OPERATION CODE	A ADDRESS	B ADDRESS	d-CHARACTER
M	020	236	(NOT NEEDED)

In this instruction, the data stored at Address 020 in the read area will be moved to Address 236 in the print area. The A Address must specify the *low-order* (rightmost) cell from which data are being moved. The B Address must likewise specify the low-order cell to which the data are being moved. The data are moved one cell at a time from right to left until a word mark set by a previous instruction for the data found at the A Address is reached. The word mark is not destroyed or moved. A move instruction will cause data to be moved anywhere within the machine. That is, the data can be moved from the read area to the print area, from the read area to the punch area, and from the read area to some location within the machine for storage until needed at a later time. Each data word to be moved to a new location requires a separate instruction.

Assume, for example, that the data punched in the card illustrated in Figure 15-4 have been read into the read area. Assume further that you desire to move these data to the print area to be printed on a report. The three data words are the student's name, located in Cells 001–020; the homeroom number, located in Cells 021–024; and the name of the homeroom teacher, located in Cells 025–034. Three separate instructions are required to move these fields of data from the read area to the print area. The instructions that will carry out the job are illustrated in Figure 15-7.

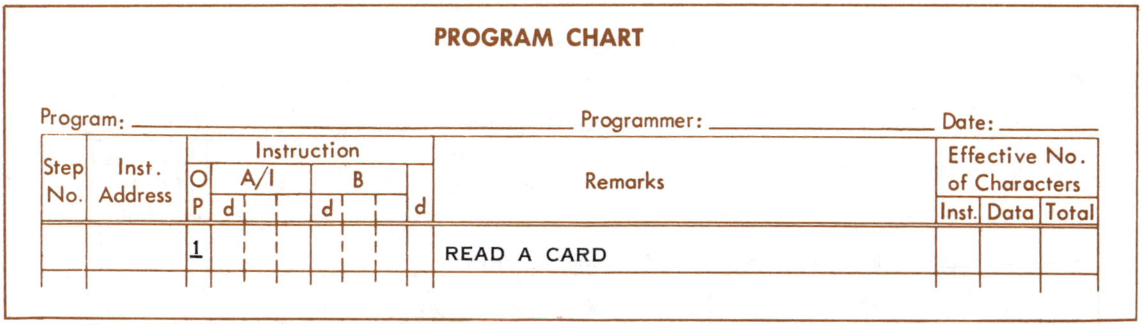

Chapter 15   Machine language instructions   263

PROGRAM CHART

Program: _____   Programmer: _____   Date: _____

Step No.	Inst. Address	OP	A/I d	B d	d	Remarks	Effective No. of Characters		
							Inst.	Data	Total
		1				READ A CARD			

Figure 15-5. Instruction to read a card

Figure 15-6. Data from card read into read area of computer

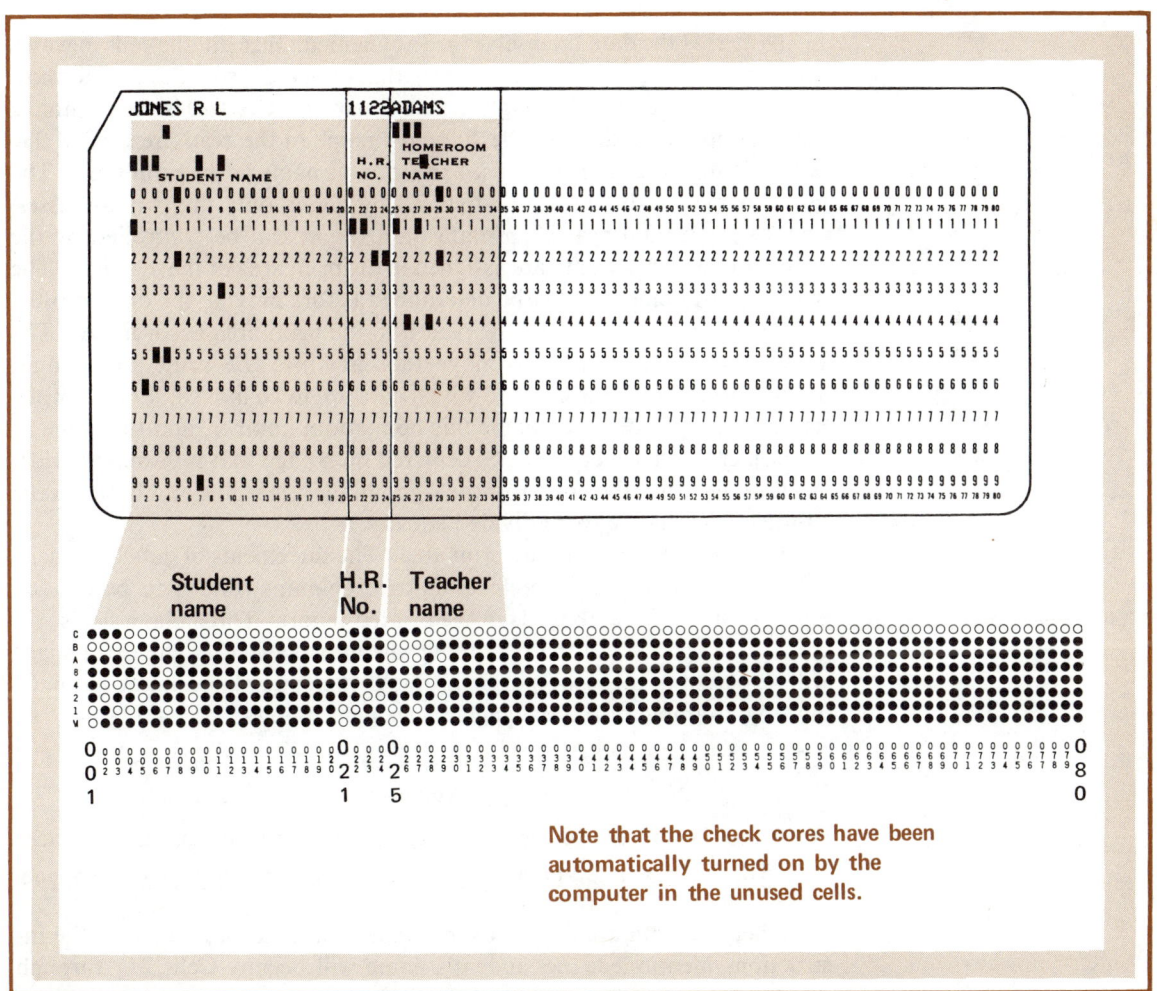

Note that the check cores have been automatically turned on by the computer in the unused cells.

PROGRAM CHART

Program: _____ Programmer: _____ Date: _____

Step No.	Inst. Address	Instruction O/P	A/I d	B d	d	Remarks	Effective No. of Characters Inst.	Data	Total
		M	0 2 0	2 3 6		MOVE NAME TO PRINT			
		M	0 2 4	2 5 6		MOVE HOMEROOM NUMBER TO PRINT			
		M	0 3 4	2 8 2		MOVE NAME OF HOMEROOM TEACHER TO PRINT			

Figure 15-7. Moving data to print

Note that the data themselves are not named. Instead, the cells in which data are stored are named. Note, too, that only the low-order or rightmost cell of a group of cells storing the data is named. Cell 020 is the rightmost cell of those used to store the student's name in the read area. Cell 236 is the rightmost cell of those used to store his name in the print area. The entire name can be moved and stored by giving only the two addresses.

The horizontal spacing of data on a report can be controlled by the manner in which the data are assigned in the print area of the machine. The spacing requirements must be determined before moving the data into the print area, and the data will be placed in the print area accordingly. The move instruction written to move the data into the print area should specify the appropriate cell into which data are to be moved. For example, assume that the student's name, his homeroom number, and the name of his homeroom teacher are to be centered on a page that is 99 spaces wide. Assume also that the spaces in the right and left margins and between the printed columns are to be divided equally.

There are 99 spaces in the print area. The three fields of data occupy 34 columns in the card. Therefore, 65 card columns remain to be divided equally into four blank fields in the printed report. Three blank fields will contain 16 spaces and the remaining one must have 17. The extra space will be placed in the right margin although it can be placed in the left margin. An example of the spacing arrangement follows:

	Student Name		*Homeroom Number*		*Homeroom Teacher*	
16 spaces	20 spaces	16 spaces	4 spaces	16 spaces	10 spaces	17 spaces
201–216	217–236	237–252	253–256	257–272	273–282	283–299

When the data are moved to the print area in accordance with the instructions mentioned, the student's name will occupy Cells 217 through

Chapter 15 Machine language instructions

236; the homeroom number will occupy Cells 253 through 256; and the homeroom teacher's name will occupy Cells 273 through 282. Figure 15-8 is an illustration showing how the data will appear in the cells of the print area. Upon execution of a print command, the data will be spaced properly on the page. The shaded areas indicate the columns on the card in which data have been recorded and the cells in the print area to which these data have been moved.

Figure 15-8. Data transferred from read area to print area

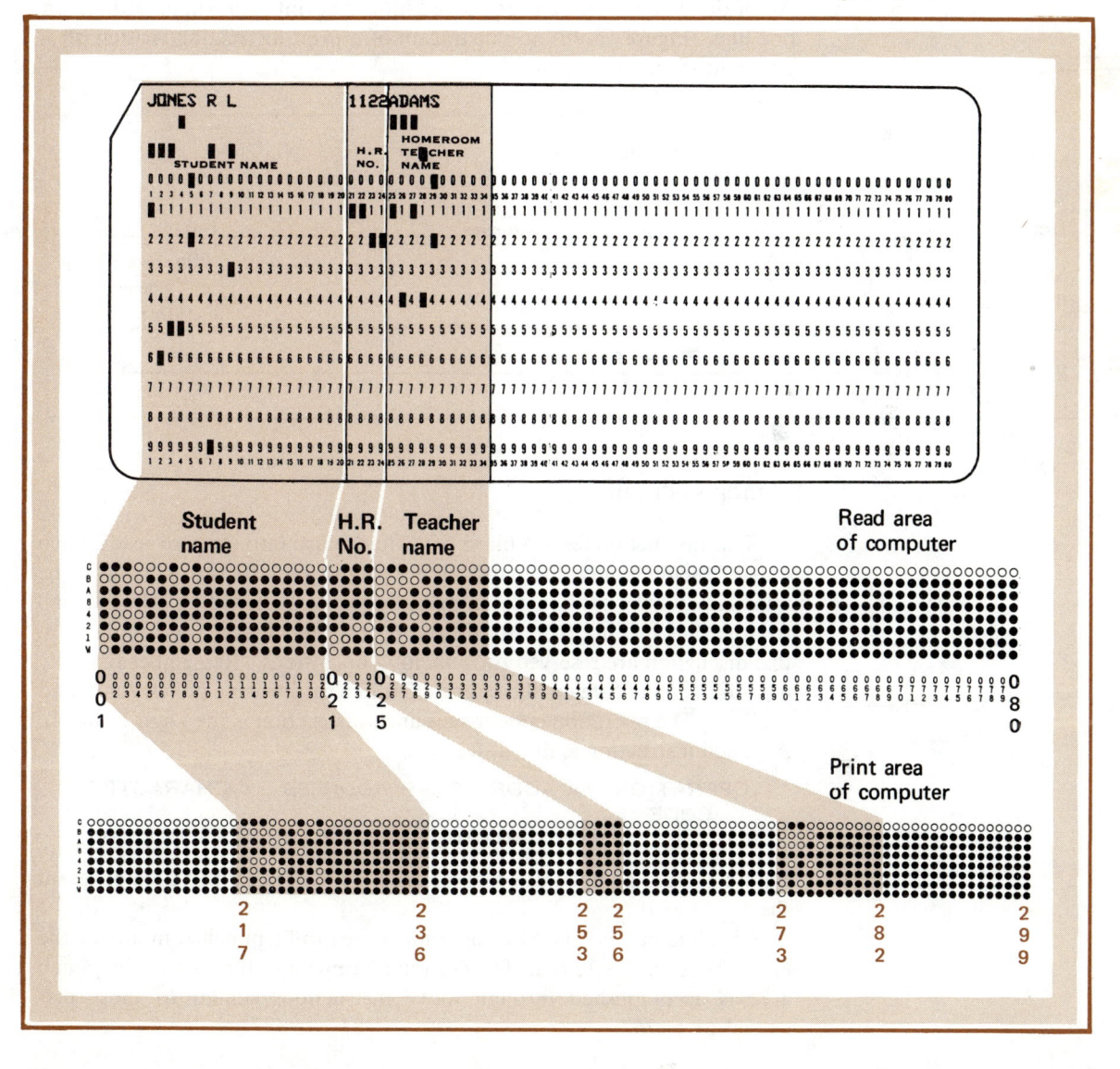

Print instruction

This instruction causes the printing of data that have been previously moved to the print area for storage. After the line is printed, the printer takes one automatic vertical space. You already know that cell addresses need not be given with the print instruction, as all data stored in the cells that make up the print area are printed. The operation code for a print instruction is the Digit Two (2). A print instruction is illustrated below:

OPERATION CODE	A ADDRESS	B ADDRESS	d-CHARACTER
2	(NOT NEEDED)	(NOT NEEDED)	(NOT NEEDED)

All of the data that have been moved into the print area will be printed on one line. Figure 15-9 is an illustration of a print instruction written on a program sheet.

PROGRAM CHART

Program: ______ Programmer: ______ Date: ______

Step No.	Inst. Address	Instruction OP	Instruction A/I d	Instruction B d	Instruction d	Remarks	Effective No. of Characters Inst.	Data	Total
		2				PRINT DATA			

Figure 15-9. A print instruction

Punch instruction

This instruction feeds a blank 80-column card into the card read-punch unit of the computer and causes the data in Cells 101 through 180 to be punched into the card. Only an operation code is needed. You will recall from earlier reading that Addresses 101 through 180 in the computer in this discussion are reserved for punching operations. Remember that any data in the punch area will be punched into a card when a punch command is given. The operation code for a punch instruction is the Digit Four (4). A punch instruction is illustrated below:

OPERATION CODE	A ADDRESS	B ADDRESS	d-CHARACTER
4	(NOT NEEDED)	(NOT NEEDED)	(NOT NEEDED)

Figure 15-10 is an illustration of a punch instruction written on a program sheet.

The data can be placed in the punch area to be punched in any of the 80 card columns required. The desired placement of the data in the punch area is accomplished through move instructions similar to those discussed on p. 262.

Chapter 15   Machine language instructions

Step No.	Inst. Address	Instruction O/P	A/I d	B d	d	Remarks	Effective No. of Characters Inst. Data Total
		4				PUNCH DATA	

Figure 15-10. A punch instruction

It can be noted here in review that a read, print, or punch instruction requires only an operation code.

Branch instruction

A computer reads instructions in succession unless instructed to do otherwise or until all instructions have been completed and the computer has been instructed to halt. If a particular job consists of a series of steps to be repeated over and over, it will not be necessary to write a complete set of instructions for each card involved in the job. Instead, the computer can be instructed to return to the first step of the series and to repeat each of the steps in the series. This is accomplished by writing an instruction telling the computer to branch back to the step that will cause it to read another card and process the new card in the same manner as the previous card or cards. You will remember that repeating the same sequence of instructions over and over until a particular job is completed is called looping. The repeated steps in the series are referred to as a loop. The loop will be repeated until certain conditions are reached. Then a branch instruction will cause the computer to go to a new step.

The operation code for a branch instruction is the Letter B. In addition to the operation code, the location of the instruction to which the computer is to branch must be given. The location is specified in the A/I Address. A branch instruction is illustrated below.

OPERATION CODE	A ADDRESS	B ADDRESS	d-CHARACTER
B	501	(NOT NEEDED)	(NOT NEEDED)

The foregoing instruction will cause the computer to branch unconditionally to Cell address 501 for its next instruction because 501 is the address specified in the A/I Address column. Any cell location can be specified in the A/I Address column. In this example, the computer will follow the instruction located at Address 501 and will continue to follow succeeding instructions until directed once again to branch or to halt.

PROGRAM CHART

Step No.	Inst. Address	Instruction OP	A/I d	B	d	Remarks	Effective No. of Characters Inst.	Data	Total
		B	5	0 1		BRANCH TO CELL 501 FOR NEXT INSTRUCTION			

Figure 15-11. An unconditional branch instruction

Figure 15-11 is an illustration of a branch instruction written on a program sheet. You will note that the d-Character is not needed for the unconditional branch because there is no decision making or test. An *unconditional branch* is an instruction that causes the computer to branch to another instruction regardless of conditions. An unconditional branch instruction is illustrated many times in the programs in this chapter. An unconditional branch instruction can be recognized because there is never a d-Character.

Test of last card instruction

The computer is equipped with an indicator which is turned on when the last card has been read. A sensing device within the machine is able to sense that no cards remain in the read hopper; and this sensing device turns on the indicator, signifying the absence of cards. The Letter A as a d-Character is the part of a computer instruction that tests the condition of the last card indicator. An example of an instruction to test for the last card is given below:

OPERATION CODE	A I ADDRESS	B ADDRESS	d-CHARACTER
B	XXX	(NOT NEEDED)	A

The test for the last card is always combined with a branch instruction. There is a reason for such a combination. If the last card has been processed, it is logical to direct the computer to branch to an instruction that will cause the machine to halt or change its course of action. This branch instruction, of course, is a *conditional branch instruction* because it is based on whether a certain test or condition has been met — in this case, whether the last card has been processed. If the last card has been processed, the computer will branch to the instruction located at Address 456 (Step 13), which directs the computer to halt. See Figure 15-12. If the last card *has not* been processed, the computer automatically moves to the *next* instruction and follows it. In Figure 15-12 the next instruction directs the computer to branch to Address 420 (Step 5) to read a new card and repeat the program.

Chapter 15   Machine language instructions

PROGRAM CHART

Step No.	Inst. Address	Instruction OP	d	A/I	d	B	d	Remarks	Effective No. of Characters Inst.	Data	Total
11	447	B		4 5 6			A	BRANCH TO 456 (STEP 13) IF LAST CARD			
12	452	B		4 2 0				BRANCH TO 420 (STEP 5) IF NOT LAST CARD			
13	456	.						HALT			

Program: _____   Programmer: _____   Date: _____

Figure 15-12. Test for last card, branch, and halt instructions

Halt instruction

When all of the cards have been processed, it is logical that the operator will want the computer to halt. The job is finished. The operation code for a halt instruction is a period (.). An example of a halt instruction is given below:

OPERATION   A ADDRESS   B ADDRESS   d-CHARACTER
CODE
  .   (NOT NEEDED)   (NOT NEEDED)   (NOT NEEDED)

Figure 15-12 is an illustration of the steps that will cause the computer to test for the last card and to repeat steps in the program or to halt.

Step 11 of Figure 15-12 asks the computer to test for the last card. If the last card has been processed, the instruction at Step 11 tells the computer to branch to Address 456 (Step 13), which contains an instruction to halt. As mentioned before, if the last card has not been processed, the computer automatically proceeds to the next instruction, Step 12, which creates a loop back to Step 5.

The instructions in the loop, Steps 5 through 11, will be applied to every card in the deck. The last card test will be made each time a card is processed until all the cards in the deck have been processed.

WRITING A PROGRAM

Statement of the problem (Problem 1)

Up to this point you have covered enough instructions to solve a simple problem. Assume that you have on hand a deck of cards similar to the card illustrated in Figure 15-4, p. 260. Assume also that you wish to write a program that will cause the computer to print a report listing the names of students, their homeroom numbers, and the names of their homeroom teachers. The three items of information are to be evenly spaced across the 99-space line. The computer is to process the deck card by card until all the cards are processed. When all cards are processed, the computer is to branch to a halt command and stop.

Program for Problem 1

The program to solve the foregoing problem appears in Figure 15-1. It is repeated here as Figure 15-13 for easy reference. The instructions in this program are those you have learned thus far. You will learn how to write additional instructions shortly.

Figure 15-13. A complete program, including last card test, branch, and halt instructions

PROGRAM CHART

Program: List of students, homeroom numbers, and teachers Programmer: Price Date: 10/12/71

Step No.	Inst. Address	Instruction								Remarks	Effective No. of Characters		
		OP	A/I			B			d		Inst.	Data	Total
			d			d							
1	401	/	0	8	0					CLEAR READ AREA			
2	405	/	2	9	9					CLEAR PRINT AREA			
3	409	,	0	0	1	0	2	1		SET WORD MARKS FOR NAME, HOMEROOM NUMBER			
4	416	,	0	2	5					SET WORD MARK FOR TEACHER			
5	420	1								READ A CARD			
6	421	M	0	2	0	2	3	6		MOVE STUDENT NAME TO PRINT			
7	428	M	0	2	4	2	5	6		MOVE HOMEROOM NUMBER TO PRINT			
8	435	M	0	3	4	2	8	2		MOVE HOMEROOM TEACHER TO PRINT			
9	442	2								PRINT DATA			
10	443	/	2	9	9					CLEAR PRINT AREA			
11	447	B	4	5	6				A	BRANCH TO 456 (STEP 13) IF LAST CARD			
12	452	B	4	2	0					BRANCH TO 420 (STEP 5) IF NOT LAST CARD			
13	456	.								HALT			

Chapter 15   Machine language instructions

In this chapter the instruction addresses will begin with Cell 401 instead of immediately following the print area. This method of programming will make the programs easier to write.

As you study Figure 15-13, note particularly the last card test, branch, and halt instructions. Note where they appear in the program. Follow the steps and observe the series of steps which make up a loop that will be repeated as long as cards remain to be processed. When the last card has been processed, the machine will branch to the step which will cause the computer to halt.

In Figure 15-13 you will see that the instruction address column contains the locations in which instructions are stored. The address given in each case is for the operation code of an instruction. The address of the operation code of the first instruction, for example, is 401; the address of the operation code of the second instruction is 405. Each location can store only one character. Four locations are thus needed for storing the first instruction although seven locations are needed for storing the third instruction.

Instruction addresses are punched into program load cards along with the instructions. The addresses are not part of the program, you will remember. Addresses merely indicate the location of each instruction.

The problem solved here by a machine language program is identical to the one solved by human language in Figure 14-12, p. 248. Turn to p. 248. Compare the human language and machine language programs. Point out a number of similarities. Point out also some of the chief differences.

Block diagram for problem 1

The block diagram for Problem 1 is identical to the one illustrated in Figure 14-13, p. 249. It is repeated here as Figure 15-14 for easy reference. Observe the flow of data through the loop in the diagram. Note the initial instructions to take care of the "get-ready" or "housekeeping" duties. Note also the block to which the computer branches when all the cards have been processed.

Printed report produced by program for problem 1

The report produced by the program for Problem 1 is reproduced in part in Figure 15-15. As each data card entered the computer, the data punched in it were read. The three items of information in the card were moved to the print area, one item at a time. Then the three items were printed as an entire line.

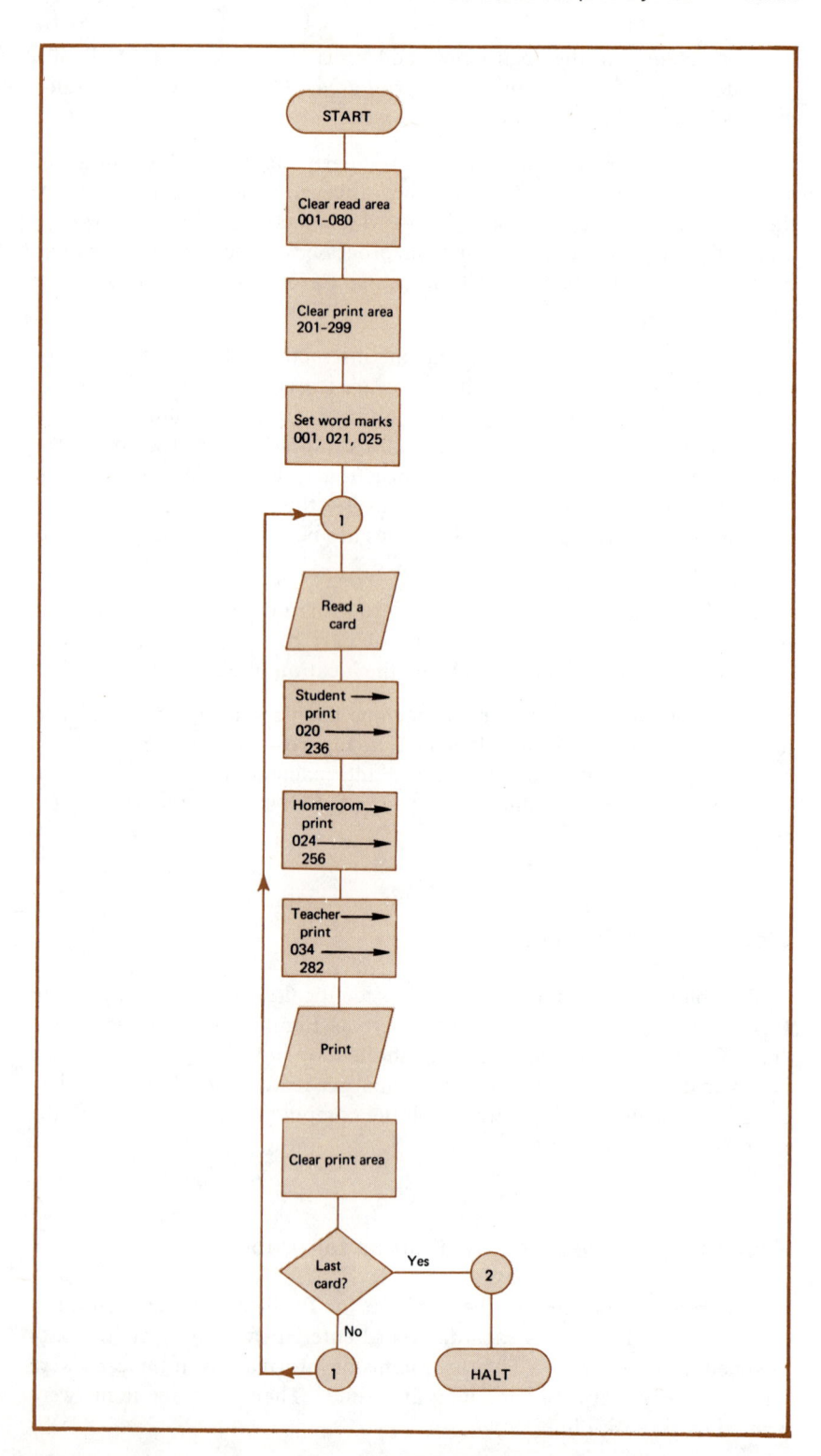

Figure 15-14. Block diagram for Problem 1, including last card test, decision, and halt blocks

```
        BRIEM JAMES              2249      KELLEY
        CALKINS CHESTER          2342      ZIMMERMAN
        CONDORODIS VICTORIA      2445      CUNNINGHAM
        DISTER ROBERT            1122      ADAMS
        FAIRBANKS MARY ALICE     2445      CUNNINGHAM
        FLANAGAN DENNIS          2342      ZIMMERMAN
        HENNINGER JOSEPH         2249      KELLEY
        JONES R L                1122      ADAMS

        MYERS BLAKE C            2342      ZIMMERMAN
        PARAGIN JACQUELINE       1945      MANTHEY
        PARKER VIRGINIA A        2445      CUNNINGHAM
        PEREZ MIGUEL             1122      ADAMS
        PHILLIPS MARY ELLEN      1945      MANTHEY
        PRICE THOMAS P           2342      ZIMMERMAN
        RHOLLANS ARTHUR          1122      ADAMS
        STAHLHEBER ELIZABETH     2445      CUNNINGHAM
```

Figure 15-15. Partial printed report produced by the program for Problem 1

REVIEW QUESTIONS

1. What is the operation code symbol for the read instruction?
2. Why are no A or B addresses needed for a read instruction?
3. What is the operation code symbol for the move instruction?
4. Why are two addresses needed for a move instruction?
5. In a move instruction, what information is specified by the A Address? by the B Address?
6. How is the horizontal spacing of data on a printed report controlled?
7. What symbol is used as the operation code for the print instruction? For the punch instruction?
8. Which storage locations are reserved for the punch area?
9. What is a loop?
10. What is the operation code symbol for a branch instruction?
11. What is the difference between a conditional and an unconditional branch instruction?
12. What is the instruction for testing for the last card?
13. Why is this test always combined with a branch instruction?
14. What happens if the last card has *not* been processed when the last card test has been applied?
15. What is the operation code for a halt instruction?

PROGRAM WITH AN ADD INSTRUCTION

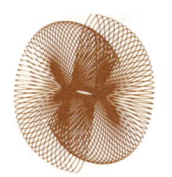

Computers are frequently required to add columns of figures and to produce a total. A computer is capable of accumulating a total in any of its cells. Even the smallest computer with a 1,400 cell capacity could accumulate totals from many columns of figures in the same program. In Chapter 14, you learned that a work area in the computer is usually set aside for the accumulation of totals. This work area should be established at addresses that will not interefere with the reserved read, punch, and print areas. The work area also should not interfere with locations in which the program will be stored.

In this chapter, as in Chapter 14, the program instruction storage area will be set up in cells beginning with the 401 series and the work area in cells beginning with the 601 series. A machine language programmer would not ordinarily waste core storage space by skipping many cells between the print area and the instruction storage area. However, by locating each starting area at an 01 position, the programming concepts will be easier to understand. Since the problems in this chapter require short programs, the cells from 401–599 will be ample for storing the program instructions. The programmer may assign a work area in any cell locations in the computer that do not conflict with the three reserved storage areas or the area he has assigned for storing instructions.

Two points must be made clear. The first of these is that work areas must be cleared before they can be used for the storage of totals or other data. Clearance commands should be included in the "get ready" instructions at the beginning of a program. The second point is that a word mark must be turned on in the leftmost cell of the computer cells designated for the accumulation of a total. Instructions for setting word marks in the work area should also be included in the "get ready" section at the beginning of the program. It will be necessary only to set word marks in the read area and the work area. Using the work area specified in this chapter, the word mark will be set in Cell 601. As you know, a work area should be addressed by the rightmost cell. The word mark should be turned on in the leftmost cell.

Since the total often takes more locations than the individual amounts being accumulated, the programmer must plan enough additional locations after he has determined the largest total that might be obtained. If a 4-digit total were accumulated, the work area would be addressed at Cell 604. If a 5-digit total were accumulated, the work area would be addressed at Cell 605. If a 6-digit total were accumulated, the work area would be addressed at Cell 606. In order to simplify the problems in this chapter, the totals will not require more cell locations than the individual amounts being accumulated.

Add instruction

An add instruction will cause the data located in one group of cells specified by the A Address to be added to another group of cells specified by the B Address.

OPERATION CODE	A ADDRESS	B ADDRESS	d-CHARACTER
A	635	606	(NOT NEEDED)

Chapter 15 Machine language instructions

The foregoing instruction will cause the amount stored in a group of cells identified as Address 635 to be added to an amount stored in a group of cells identified as Address 606. The total will be stored in the B Address cells, thus replacing the amount previously stored there. In Chapter 13, p. 225, it was explained that when the data in one area of a computer are moved (duplicated) into another area, the original data still remain in the first area. In the above example, the amount stored in the work area at Address 635 will be added to the amount stored in the work area at Address 606. The total will be stored at Address 606, but the original amount will also remain in Address 635.

In the preceding example, both amounts were stored in the work area of the computer. However, if a punched card were read into the computer and the amount stored in the read area at Address 035, this amount could be added to the total being accumulated in the work area at Address 606 with the following instruction:

OPERATION CODE	A ADDRESS	B ADDRESS	d-CHARACTER
A	035	606	(NOT NEEDED)

Again, the amount stored at the A Address would be added to the amount stored at the B Address and the total stored at the B Address. The original data would remain at the A Address. In this case, however, a clear instruction would not be necessary because the read area is self-clearing. The next card read into Cells 001–080 would automatically clear all data, including the amount stored previously at Cell 035.

The A and B addresses given above are used as examples only. Much more complicated problems can be solved by a computer, using many cells in memory other than those mentioned in these discussions.

Statement of the problem (Problem 2)

Assume, for example, that each student in the school has sold tickets to a music and sports festival. A card is punched for each student, containing his name in Columns 1–20. His classification, whether freshman, sophomore, junior, or senior, is punched in Column 24. The amount of money collected is punched in Columns 30–35. The sex, whether male or female, is punched in Column 40. In Column 24, freshmen are assigned Code No. 1; sophomores, Code No. 2; juniors, Code No. 3; and seniors, Code No. 4. In Column 40, female students are assigned Code No. 1 and male students, Code No. 2. The card in Figure 15-16 is typical of one of those in the deck.

For this problem, assume that you have a deck of cards similar to the one illustrated in Figure 15-16. A program is to be planned that will print each student's name and the amount of money he has collected from the sale of tickets to the festival. A total of these amounts is to be accumulated; and when all cards have been processed the total is to be printed under the amount column at the end of the report. Twenty spaces are to separate the two columns. The entire report is to be centered horizontally.

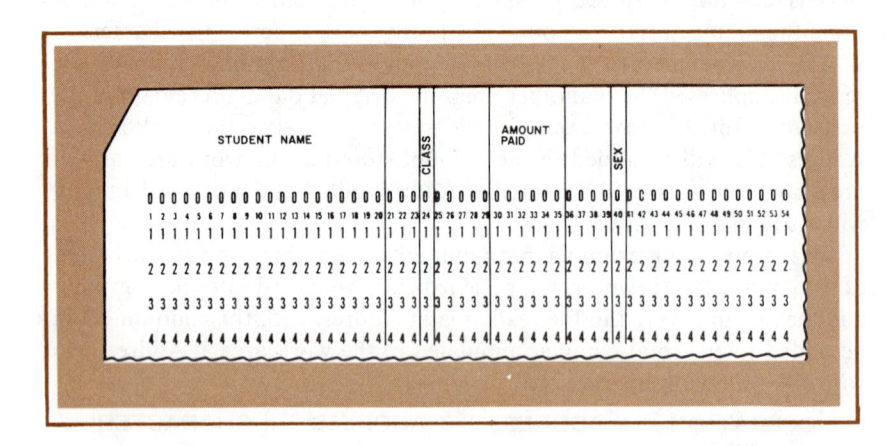

Figure 15-16. Sample data card for Problem 2

Block diagram for problem 2

The block diagram for Problem 2 appears in Figure 15-17. Observe the "get ready" or "housekeeping" instruction blocks. Observe also that an add block has been added, and that it calls for the accumulation of a total. The diagram indicates that when the last card has been read, the accumulated total should be moved to the print area and printed, as the first step in the windup series. Can you identify the steps or instructions that are included in the loop?

Program for problem 2

The program for Problem 2 appears in Figure 15-18. Observe the instructions in Steps 3 and 5. Step 3 clears that part of the 600 series cell locations to be used for a work area to accumulate the total. Step 5 turns on a word mark in the leftmost cell of the work area set aside for the total. The cells reserved for the total are thus 601–606. Refer to Figure 15-16. You will note that there are six columns in the punched card being used for input. It has been determined that the total in the work area will not exceed the number of columns in the card. The student sales will probably exceed $1,000.00 but will not exceed $9,999.99.

Observe Steps 7 and 8. Data are moved from the read area to the print area in such a way that 20 horizontal spaces will be allowed between the two columns, and the spaces in the left and right margins will be divided. Note the diagram below:

Left margin	*Student Name*	*Spaces between*	*Amount*	*Right margin*
26	20 ↓	20	6 ↓	27
	Address: 246		Address: 272	

Chapter 15   Machine language instructions

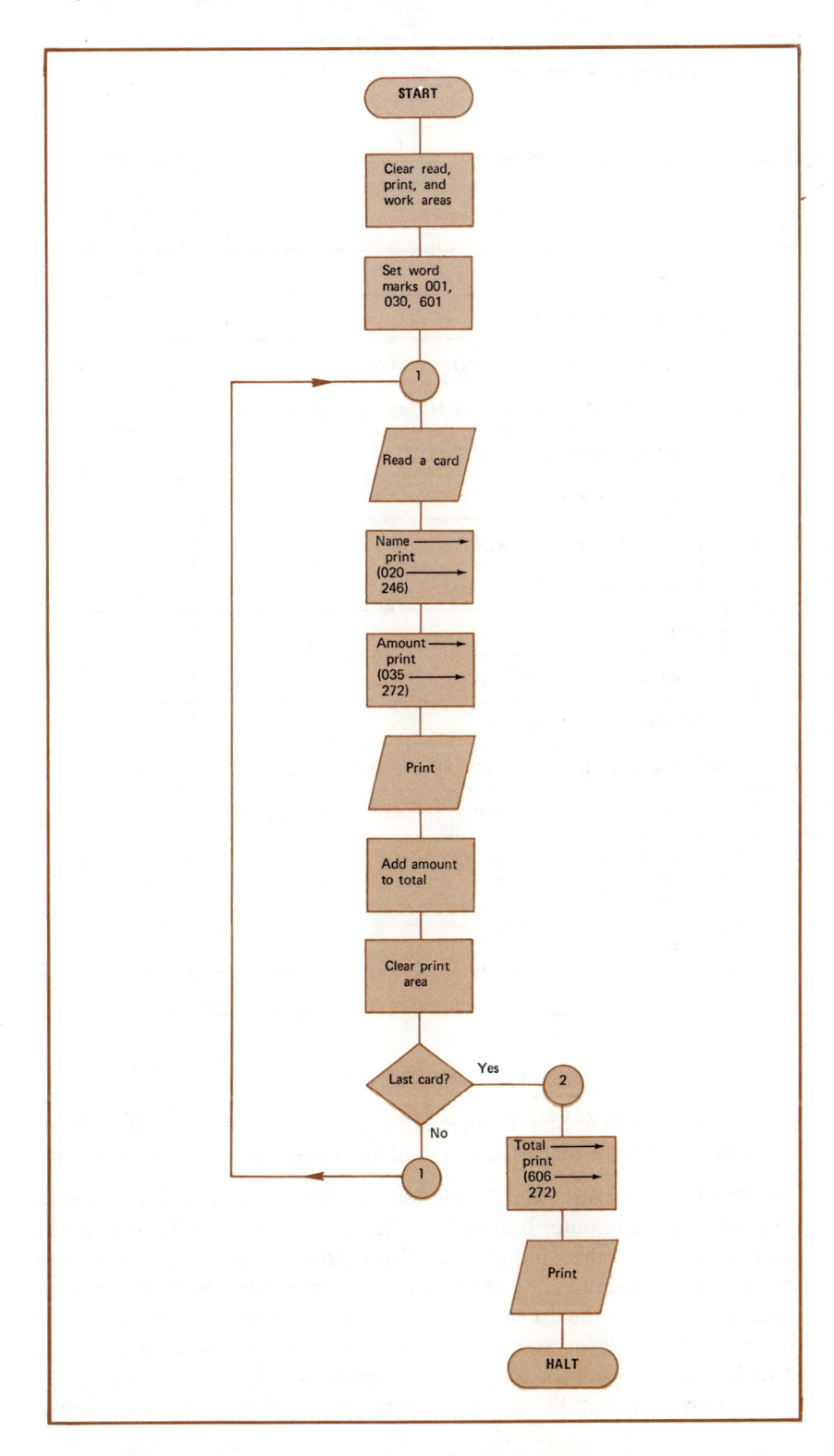

Figure 15-17. Block diagram for Problem 2

PROGRAM CHART

Program: Students and amounts Programmer: Hall Date: 10/05/71

Step No.	Inst. Address	OP	A/I d	A/I	A/I	B d	B	B	d	Remarks	Effective No. of Characters: Inst.	Data	Total
1	401	/	0	8	0					CLEAR READ AREA			
2	405	/	2	9	9					CLEAR PRINT AREA			
3	409	/	6	0	6					CLEAR WORK AREA FOR TOTAL			
4	413	,	0	0	1	0	3	0		SET WORD MARKS FOR NAME AND AMOUNT			
5	420	,	6	0	1					SET WORD MARK FOR TOTAL			
6	424	1								READ A CARD			
7	425	M	0	2	0	2	4	6		MOVE NAME TO PRINT			
8	432	M	0	3	5	2	7	2		MOVE AMOUNT TO PRINT			
9	439	2								PRINT			
10	440	A	0	3	5	6	0	6		ADD AMOUNT TO TOTAL			
11	447	/	2	9	9					CLEAR PRINT AREA			
12	451	B	4	6	0				A	BRANCH TO 460 (STEP 14) IF LAST CARD			
13	456	B	4	2	4					BRANCH TO 424 (STEP 6) IF NOT LAST CARD			
14	460	M	6	0	6	2	7	2		MOVE TOTAL TO PRINT			
15	467	2								PRINT			
16	468	.								HALT			

Figure 15-18. Program for Problem 2.

The instruction at Step 10 directs the computer to add an amount from a student card in the read area to a total being accumulated in a work area.

Step 12 is the instruction for the last card test. If the last card has been processed, the computer branches to Step 14, where it will encounter the first instruction in the windup series. This series instructs the computer to move the total accumulated at Cell 606 to the print area, to print the total, and to halt. Note the d-Character, the Letter A, included in the last card test at Step 12. If, at Step 12, the last card test indicates that the sense switch is not turned on, the computer automatically drops down to the next instruction, Step 13, which is an instruction to branch back to Step 6,

Chapter 15   Machine language instructions

the read instruction. As long as a card remains to be read at Step 12, the loop will be repeated (Steps 6 through 12). The windup sequence will not begin until the last card has been processed.

Printed report produced by program for Problem 2

The report prepared by the computer will contain the names of all students selling tickets and the amounts collected by each. It will also show the total amount collected. A portion of the printed report produced by the program is shown in Figure 15-19.

Figure 15-19. Partial printed report produced by the program for Problem 2

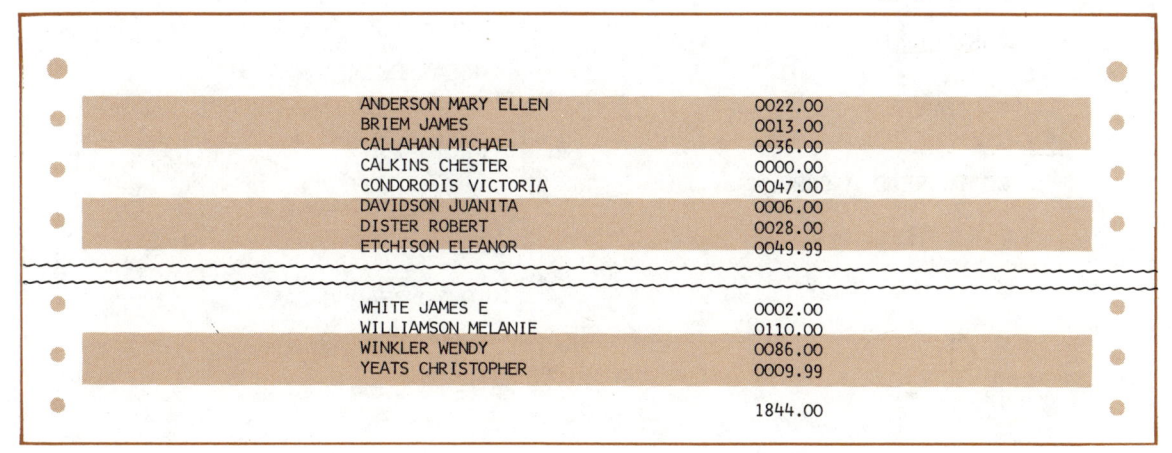

```
ANDERSON MARY ELLEN        0022.00
BRIEM JAMES                0013.00
CALLAHAN MICHAEL           0036.00
CALKINS CHESTER            0000.00
CONDORODIS VICTORIA        0047.00
DAVIDSON JUANITA           0006.00
DISTER ROBERT              0028.00
ETCHISON ELEANOR           0049.99

WHITE JAMES E              0002.00
WILLIAMSON MELANIE         0110.00
WINKLER WENDY              0086.00
YEATS CHRISTOPHER          0009.99
                           1844.00
```

PROGRAM WITH DECISION INSTRUCTION BASED ON DATA BEING PROCESSED

You have already written a program with a decision instruction. The last card test is such an instruction. In Problem 3, you will write an instruction for a decision based on the data being processed.

You learned in Chapter 14 that a computer can make decisions by comparing two fields of data. It can tell, for example, if two digits are the same or different. On the basis of this comparison, the computer can branch to a new set of instructions or proceed with those in the normal routine. A computer can make only one decision at a time, but it can make many consecutive decisions if the program is properly planned. A computer can only make these decisions if the program is logically constructed. Without a well-constructed program, the computer would not even be able to count, let alone make a decision.

The action followed by the computer in a decision-making operation based on a comparison of digits is illustrated in human language in Figure 15-20.

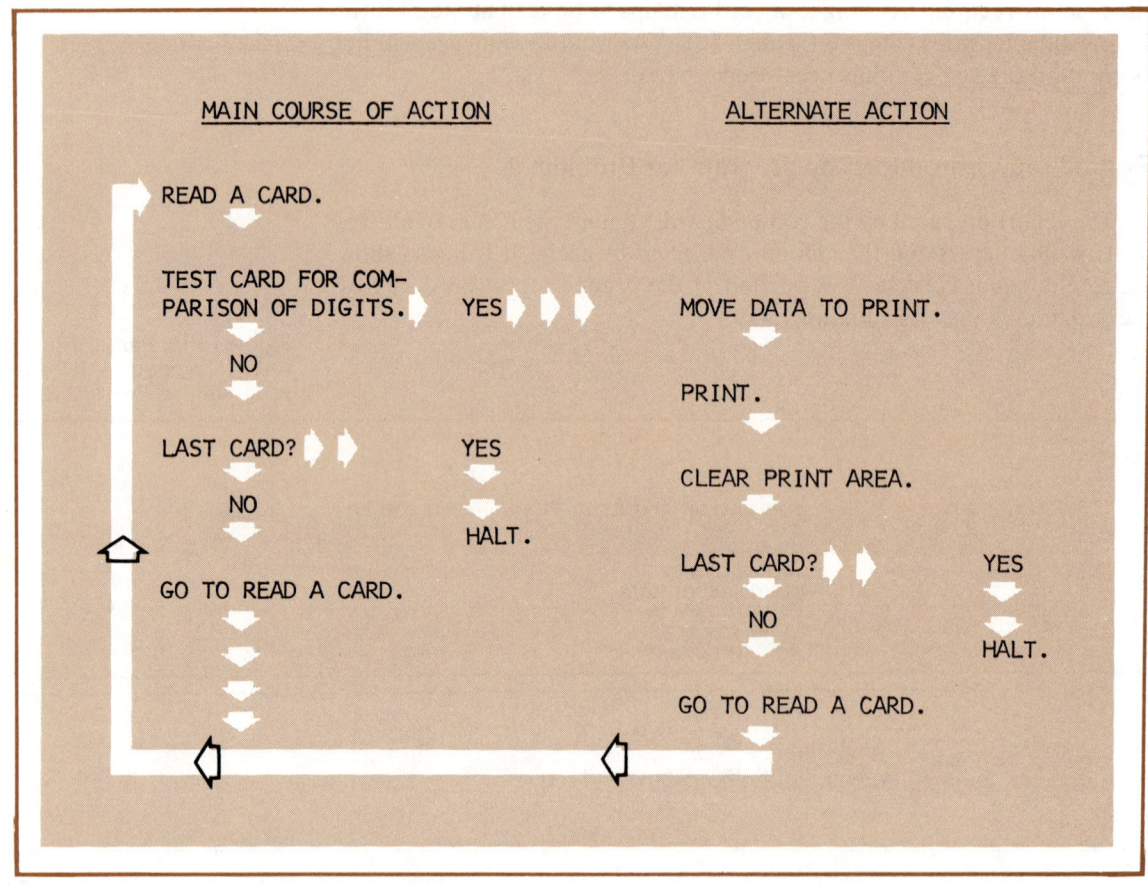

```
            MAIN COURSE OF ACTION                    ALTERNATE ACTION

         READ A CARD.

         TEST CARD FOR COM-
         PARISON OF DIGITS.      YES  ▶▶       MOVE DATA TO PRINT.
              NO
                                              PRINT.

         LAST CARD?  ▶▶          YES           CLEAR PRINT AREA.
              NO
                                  HALT.        LAST CARD?  ▶▶        YES
                                                   NO
         GO TO READ A CARD.                                           HALT.

                                               GO TO READ A CARD.
```

Figure 15-20. Decision based on digit comparison

A typical decision instruction appears below:

    If card is for male student, go to instruction to process card; if not, go to instruction to repeat sequence.

Only the cards in the deck for which two selected digits match will be processed. Those for which the digits are different will be ignored and will cause the computer to branch to the last card test instruction to see if another card remains to be processed. If another card remains, the computer will repeat the program.

Decision instruction

The machine language instruction which will cause the computer to compare two fields of data and to branch if the two fields are equal appears below:

OPERATION CODE	A ADDRESS	B ADDRESS	d-CHARACTER
B	440	040	2

Chapter 15   Machine language instructions

This instruction is shown on a program sheet in Figure 15-21.

PROGRAM CHART

Program: _____ Programmer: _____ Date: _____

Step No.	Inst. Address	Instruction O/P d	A/I d	B d	Remarks	Effective No. of Characters Inst. Data Total
7	428	B 4 4 0	0 4 0	2	BRANCH TO 440 (STEP 9) IF 2 IN 040	
8	436	B 4 6 6			BRANCH TO 466 (STEP 14) FOR LAST CARD TEST IF NO 2 IN 040	

Figure 15-21. A decision instruction

The first instruction in the figure compares the digit punched in Column 40 of the card and read into Location 040 with the Digit 2 appearing in the d-Character portion of the instruction. If the test is met, that is, if there is a 2 in Cell 040, the computer will branch to instructions beginning with 440 (Step 9), which direct the computer to move each male student's name and the amount collected to print, to print these items, and to add the amount collected to the total. Note that a comparison instruction is always combined with a branch instruction because the computer is making a decision. If the test is met, the computer branches to the address specified in the A/I Address column. If the test is not met, the computer proceeds to the next instruction in the program. You will remember that on p. 256 of this chapter you were told that a special function of the A/I Address is to give the location of an instruction when a branch is to be made. Step 7 tells the computer to branch to the A/I Address, Cell 440, if there is a 2 in Cell 040 (Column 40 of the data card being processed).

Statement of the problem (Problem 3)

Using cards that are similar to the one in Figure 15-16, a program will be written that will cause a computer to print a report that contains the following information:

The name of each male student.

The amount each male student has collected for tickets sold.

The total of all amounts collected by male students, to be printed at the end of the report under the amount column.

Twenty spaces are to separate the two columns, and the entire report is to be centered horizontally.

Block diagram for problem 3

Figure 15-22 shows the block diagram prepared for Problem 3. The detailed instructions to solve the problem appear on p. 284. The problem

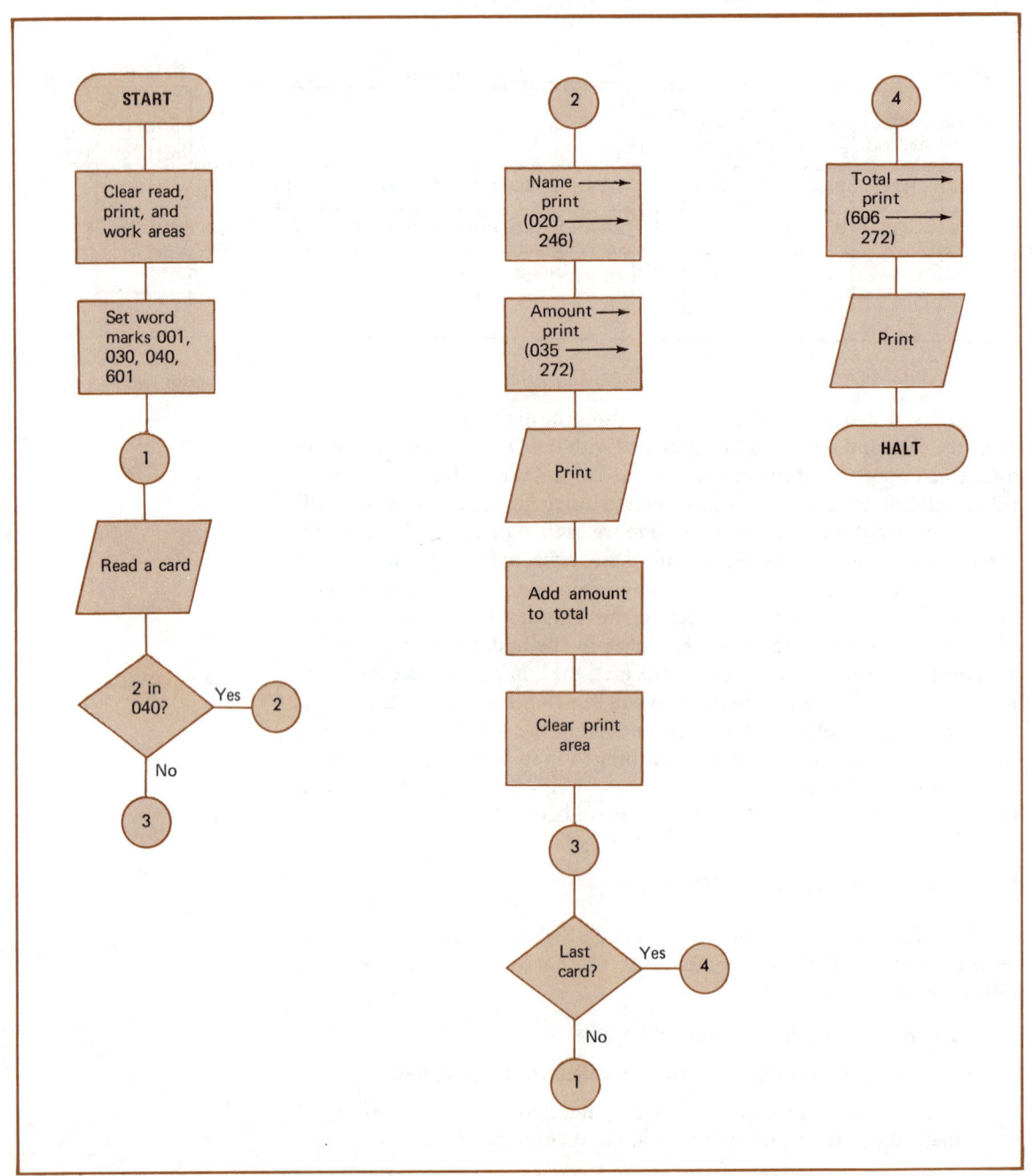

Figure 15-22. Block diagram for Problem 3

requires the programmer to plan instructions that will print a report listing only male students, the amount each has collected, and the total of these amounts.

Because of the difficulty of drawing loop and branch lines in Figure 15-22, step identifiers are used. The step identifiers merely specify the chronological order of the sequences and the points in a program at which the branches will be made.

If the first decision symbol indicates that there is a 2 in 040, the step identification symbol shows that a branch will be made to a series of instructions telling the computer to print the name of the student and the amount collected and then to add this amount to the total being accumulated. If there is not a 2 in 040 in the first decision block, the computer moves to the next instruction, which by its identification number indicates that a branch will be made to the last card test symbol.

Thus, while the loop and branch lines are missing in Figure 15-22 because of the complexity of the solution, the step identification symbols and numbers enable the programmer to observe the movement of data through his program.

Program for problem 3

The program for solving Problem 3 appears in Figure 15-23. Observe Step 7 of the program. After the card has been read into storage, the computer tests for a 2 in Cell 040. This test is called for by the Digit 2 in the d-Character portion of the instruction. This digit is punched into the card as part of the instruction and stored in the machine with the rest of the program. If the contents in the cells specified in the B Address are the same as the d-Character, the computer will branch to the instruction specified in the A Address. If there is a 2 in Cell 040, the computer will branch to the instructions beginning with Address 440 (Step 9).

These instructions cause the male student's name and the amount he has collected to be moved to the print area and to be printed. In addition, the amount he has collected will be added to the total that is being accumulated at Address 606 in the work area of computer memory.

If the test at Step 7 is not met — that is, if the card is not for a male student — the computer drops to the next instruction (Step 8), which is a branch to the last card test (Step 14). The last card test will tell the computer whether to loop back to Address 427 (Step 6), to read another card, or to branch to Address 475 (Step 16), where it will encounter the first instruction in the windup series.

In the windup series, the accumulated total will be moved to the print area, the total will be printed, and the computer will halt. The problem has been solved.

PROGRAM CHART

Program: Male students and amounts Programmer: Hall Date: 10/07/71

Step No.	Inst. Address	OP	A/I d			B d			d	Remarks	Effective No. of Characters Inst.	Data	Total
1	401	/	0	8	0					CLEAR READ AREA			
2	405	/	2	9	9					CLEAR PRINT AREA			
3	409	/	6	0	6					CLEAR WORK AREA FOR TOTAL			
4	413	,	0	0	1	0	3	0		SET WORD MARKS FOR NAME AND AMOUNT			
5	420	,	0	4	0	6	0	1		SET WORD MARKS FOR SEX AND TOTAL			
6	427	1								READ A CARD			
7	428	B	4	4	0	0	4	0	2	BRANCH TO 440 (STEP 9) IF 2 IN 040			
8	436	B	4	6	6					BRANCH TO 466 (STEP 14) FOR LAST CARD TEST IF			
										NO 2 IN 040			
9	440	M	0	2	0	2	4	6		MOVE NAME TO PRINT			
10	447	M	0	3	5	2	7	2		MOVE AMOUNT TO PRINT			
11	454	2								PRINT NAME AND AMOUNT			
12	455	A	0	3	5	6	0	6		ADD AMOUNT TO TOTAL			
13	462	/	2	9	9					CLEAR PRINT AREA			
14	466	B	4	7	5				A	BRANCH TO 475 (STEP 16) IF LAST CARD			
15	471	B	4	2	7					BRANCH TO 427 (STEP 6) IF NOT LAST CARD			
16	475	M	6	0	6	2	7	2		MOVE TOTAL TO PRINT			
17	482	2								PRINT TOTAL			
18	483	.								HALT			

Figure 15-23. Program for Problem 3

Problem 3 contains two decisions. The first test is for the sex of the student. The second test is to see if the last card has been processed. Review the block diagram in Figure 15-22 and compare it with the program in Figure 15-23 above. Note the relationship between the decisions in the two illustrations.

Chapter 15 Machine language instructions   285

Printed report produced by program for Problem 3

The partial report for Problem 3 is shown below.

Figure 15-24. Partial report for Problem 3

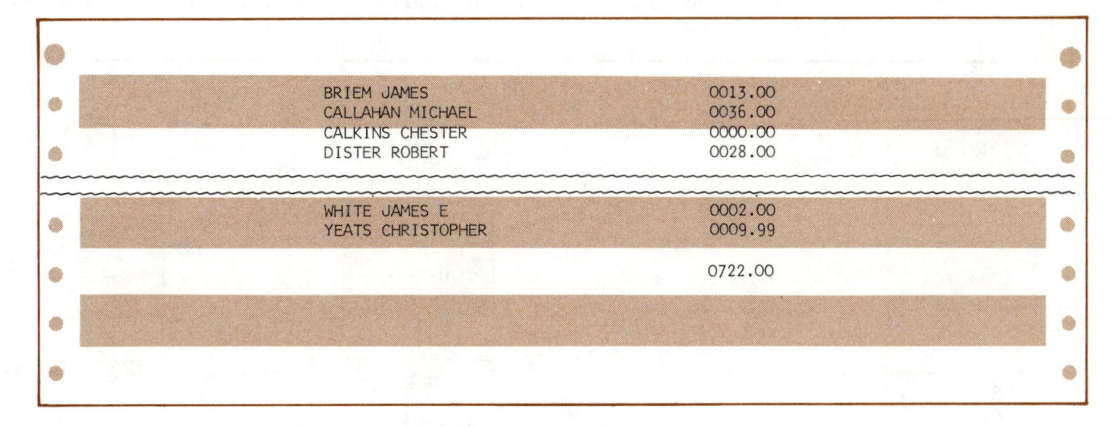

```
              BRIEM    JAMES              0013.00
              CALLAHAN MICHAEL            0036.00
              CALKINS  CHESTER            0000.00
              DISTER   ROBERT             0028.00

              WHITE    JAMES E            0002.00
              YEATS    CHRISTOPHER        0009.99

                                          0722.00
```

PROGRAM WITH MULTIPLE DECISION INSTRUCTIONS

Although a computer makes only one decision at a time, it can make several decisions, one following the other if necessary. Problem 3 required the computer to select cards for all male students. Problem 4 will require the computer to select cards for all female freshman students.

Statement of the problem (Problem 4)

For Problem 4, assume that a printed report is to be prepared, listing only female freshman students, the amount each has collected for tickets sold, and a total of these amounts. Only the cards in the deck that meet the two conditions are to be processed: those for female students who are also freshmen. The cards that fail either test will be ignored and the computer will move to the next instruction, which will be a branch instruction. The spacing directions are to be the same as for Problem 3.

Block diagram for problem 4

Figure 15-25 shows the block diagram prepared for Problem 4. You will note that step identifiers are used in this diagram just as they are in the block diagram for Problem 3, Figure 15-22. See if you can follow the flow of data through the computer by comparing the figures in the step identifiers.

Note especially how the data flow through the two decision symbols in the diagram. The first decision symbol tests for a 1 in 024. If this condition is met, the computer branches to the second decision symbol, which tests for a 1 in 040. If this condition is met, the computer will branch to a series of instructions, beginning with an instruction to move the student's name and the amount collected into the print area. The next instruction in the series will tell the computer to print this information and add the amount collected to the total being accumulated. When the last card test is met, the computer will move the total to the print area, print the total, and halt.

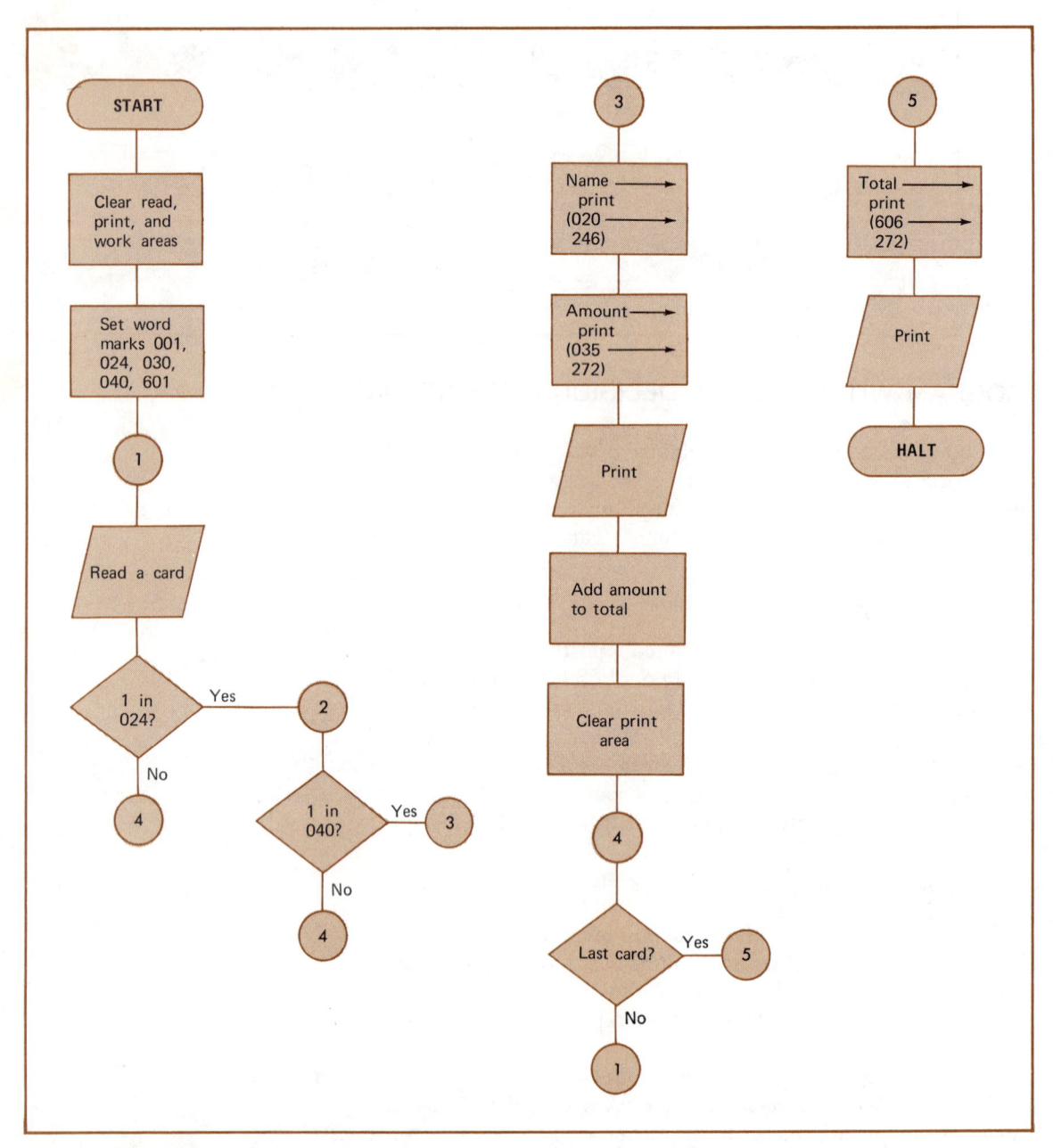

Figure 15-25. Block diagram for Problem 4

Chapter 15 Machine language instructions

Program for Problem 4

The program for Problem 4 in Figure 15-26 has three decisions. Step 8 tests for Digit 1 in Cell 024 (freshman student); Step 10, for Digit 1 in Cell 040 (code for female); and Step 17, for the last card.

PROGRAM CHART

Program: Female freshman students and amounts Programmer: Hall Date: 10/11/71

Step No.	Inst. Address	OP	A/I d	B d	d	Remarks	Inst.	Data	Total
1	401	/	0 8 0			CLEAR READ AREA			
2	405	/	2 9 9			CLEAR PRINT AREA			
3	409	/	6 0 6			CLEAR WORK AREA FOR TOTAL			
4	413	,	0 0 1	0 2 4		SET WORD MARKS FOR NAME AND CLASS			
5	420	,	0 3 0	0 4 0		SET WORD MARKS FOR AMOUNT AND SEX			
6	427	,	6 0 1			SET WORD MARKS IN WORK AREA FOR TOTAL			
7	431	1				READ A CARD			
8	432	B	4 4 4	0 2 4	1	BRANCH TO 444 (STEP 10) IF 1 IN 024			
9	440	B	4 8 2			BRANCH TO 482 (STEP 17) FOR LAST CARD TEST IF NO 1 IN 024			
10	444	B	4 5 6	0 4 0	1	BRANCH TO 456 (STEP 12) IF 1 IN 040			
11	452	B	4 8 2			BRANCH TO 482 (STEP 17) FOR LAST CARD TEST IF NO 1 IN 040			
12	456	M	0 2 0	2 4 6		MOVE NAME TO PRINT			
13	463	M	0 3 5	2 7 2		MOVE AMOUNT TO PRINT			
14	470	2				PRINT NAME AND AMOUNT			
15	471	A	0 3 5	6 0 6		ADD AMOUNT TO TOTAL			
16	478	/	2 9 9			CLEAR PRINT AREA			
17	482	B	4 9 1		A	BRANCH TO 491 (STEP 19) IF LAST CARD			
18	487	B	4 3 1			BRANCH TO 431 (STEP 7) IF NOT LAST CARD			
19	491	M	6 0 6	2 7 2		MOVE TOTAL TO PRINT			
20	498	2				PRINT TOTAL			
21	499	.				HALT			

Figure 15-26. Program for Problem 4

LOADING THE PROGRAM

Each of the instructions in the foregoing examples of programs must be punched into a separate program load card, which consists of two parts: (1) load instruction address, and (2) the load instruction (Operation Code, A Address, B Address, and d-Character).

| Instruction Addresses | Instructions to be Loaded |

Figure 15-27.   Program load card

When all program load cards are prepared, they are placed in the read hopper of the input unit of the computer and the load button is depressed. As each card is read, the load instructions punched into it are carried out, thus causing the instructions punched into the cards to be stored in the CPU at the designated addresses. The instructions remain there until they are replaced by other instructions or data or cleared by a clear instruction. The program processes data cards when (1) data cards are placed in the read hopper, and (2) the start button of the input reading unit is depressed. Depressing the start button causes the computer to branch to (begin execution with) Step 1 of the program. The purpose of the program load cards is to place the instructions for the program in the memory of the computer.

PROCESSING INSTRUCTION WORDS

Instructions for the computer used in this discussion are executed automatically from cell locations in ascending order unless this sequence is broken by a branch instruction in the program. The instructions are brought from storage to the control component for interpretation and execution. This is an automatic action on the part of the computer and one that need not be covered in an introductory text.

SUMMARY

A machine language program is one that is unique to a particular computer. The instructions described in this chapter are those unique to a small, second-generation computer. The instruction format for this computer consist of four parts: the Operation Code, which specifies the action to be taken; the A Address; the B Address; and the d-Character. The A and B addresses give the locations of data to be processed. The d-Character is associated with the decision-making ability of the computer.

The instructions given in machine language form in this chapter parallel those given in Chapter 14 in English language form. The clear instruction clears locations specified by the A Address down to and including the nearest hundreds position. A separate instruction must be written to clear each section of 100 locations or any part thereof. Word mark instructions turn on word mark cores at the addresses specified, to identify units of data or instructions.

Read, punch, and print instructions consist of operation codes only because the addresses of data undergoing these functions are predetermined by the computer and are considered as reserved storage areas. Move instructions must show in the A Address the location of the data to be moved. The B Address must give the location to which the data will be moved.

In an add instruction, data in the A Address are added to data in the B Address. The sum is stored in the B Address.

When data being processed have passed through the steps set up in the program, a last card test instruction must be written to see if additional similar data remain, and, if so, to branch to a repetition of the steps in the processing cycle (or loop). Instructions must also be written which will cause the computer to branch to a new set of steps if no more data remain to be processed. Provision must be made for both possibilities. In either case, the program must include the instructions specifying the cell address to which the computer will branch in order to carry out the next desired instruction. Thus, in a machine language program the location of the operation code of each instruction must be recorded. In recording instruction addresses, the programmer must remember that each digit of the instruction occupies a separate location, but the cell address specified in the operation code must be the high-order (leftmost cell). The word mark must be in the same location as the operation code.

REVIEW QUESTIONS

1. What is the operation code symbol for the add instruction?
2. In which address is the total stored?
3. How do you indicate to the computer in your program instructions that you want it to compare two items of data (if you are searching for a 2)? Use XXX for the addresses.
4. Why is the above comparison instruction always combined with a branch instruction?
5. Name the two parts of a program load card.
6. What is the purpose of a program load card?
7. How is the program loaded into the computer?
8. Which instructions consist of operation codes only?
9. Which addresses are needed for an add instruction? Where is the total stored? Is a d-Character necessary?
10. Which instructions require the use of the d-Character column?

STUDY GUIDE

Complete Study Guide 15 by following the instructions in your STUDY GUIDES booklet.

PROJECTS

Complete Projects 15-1, 15-2, and 15-3 by following the instructions in your PROJECTS booklet.

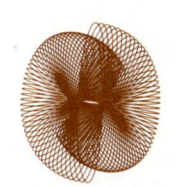

CHAPTER 16

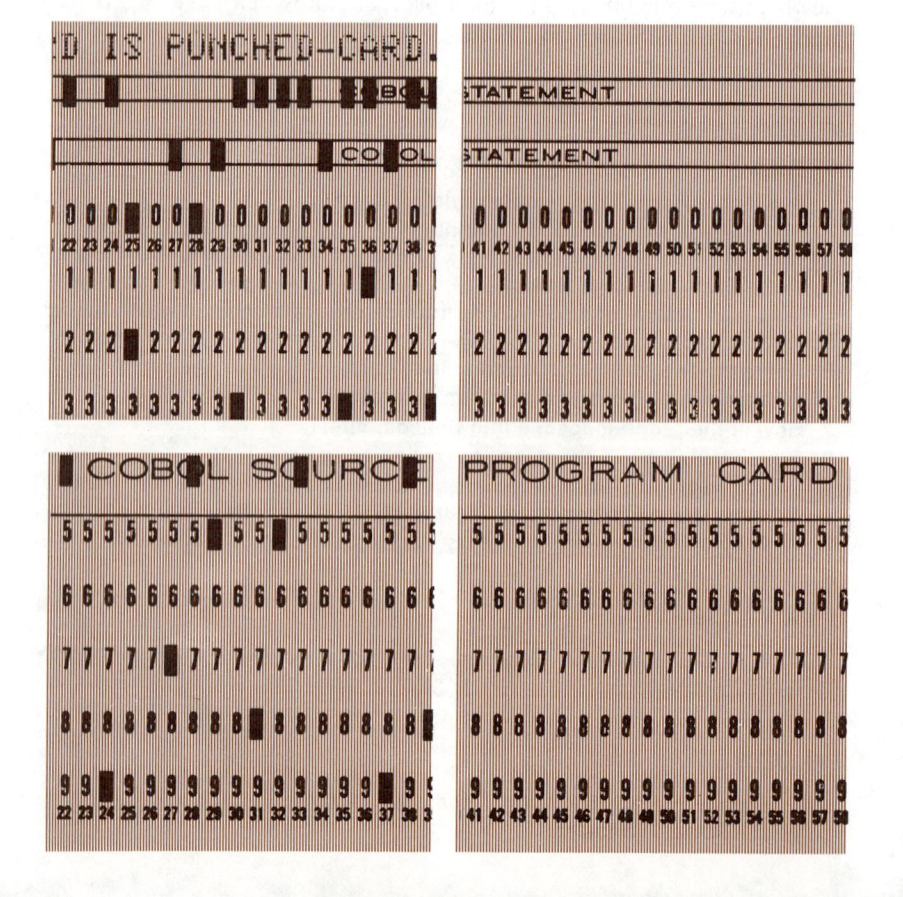

INTRODUCTION TO COBOL

Ever since the first computer was invented, programmers, computer manufacturers, and computer users have been trying to find ways to simplify programming. Their aim has been to develop a common programming language that is easy to understand and that can be used with many computers regardless of make or model. Numerous efforts have been made to develop a computer language that resembles human language.

In 1959, a programming language was developed that is very much like the English language. The name given to that programming language is *COBOL*, which is an abbreviation of the words *CO*mmon *B*usiness *O*riented *L*anguage. COBOL was developed by a commission representing the Federal Government, computer manufacturers, and private industry in general.

As a business-oriented programming language, COBOL is principally concerned with the creation and maintenance of files. The word FILE will be used many times in the discussion to follow. Any of the input/output media discussed earlier would be considered a file. However, in order to simplify the discussion in this text, a deck of punched cards related to a specific program will be referred to as a *FILE*. Also referred to as a *FILE* will be the printed report produced by the computer.

ADVANTAGES OF COBOL

In brief, COBOL language provides the following distinct advantages to the programmer:

1. The steps of the program can be stated in a near-English language. For example, the word ADD will command the computer to add numbers. The word MOVE will command the machine to move data from one location to another. The use of a near-English language makes it easier for the programmer to visualize the steps of the program in terms of the problem to be solved.
2. With COBOL, the cell addresses of data and instructions do not have to be specified as was the case in machine language. COBOL names are substituted for cell addresses. The job of assigning numeric cell addresses to the instructions and data is done by the compiler program. A compiler program will be explained in the discussion that follows.
3. Because the data are identified by name and because the processing steps are stated in a near-English language, the programmer is able to write the instructions in a language already familiar to him and to check the steps of the program for accuracy.
4. The compiler program does away with the need for writing instructions to set word marks. The compiler also can check to see that the COBOL program is written according to COBOL rules.
5. The COBOL language system can be used with any machine for which a COBOL compiler is available.

A program, written in a programming language that is to be translated into machine language before processing, is known as a *source program*. A COBOL program is a source program that must be translated into machine language before being processed by the computer. The translation process is handled by a *compiler* program furnished by the manufacturer of the computer. This compiler program is prepunched into a deck of standard cards, which are read into the computer. Each line of the COBOL source program is punched into a separate card, and the entire deck of cards making up the COBOL source program is then read into the computer. The compiler program decodes the COBOL cards, one at a time, and translates the COBOL source program into an *object* or machine language program acceptable to the computer. The points just listed make it obvious that writing a computer program using a near-English language such as COBOL should be easier than writing a program in machine language.

In review, a *compiler program* is one furnished by the manufacturer of the computer being used. The compiler translates a source program into machine language. The machine language program is frequently referred to as an *object program*.

PROBLEM USED AS AN EXAMPLE

In order to make COBOL language meaningful, the following problem will be used as an example throughout this chapter:

Chapter 16 Introduction to COBOL

1. On hand is a deck of punched cards containing the names of students, their homeroom numbers, and the names of their homeroom teachers.
2. The names of the students are punched in Columns 1–20.
3. The homeroom numbers are punched in Columns 21–24.
4. The names of the homeroom teachers are punched in Columns 25–34.
5. A program is to be written that will cause the computer to print a three-column report as follows:
   a. Names of students in the first column.
   b. Their homeroom numbers in the second column.
   c. Names of their homeroom teachers in the third column.
   d. Ten spaces are to appear between the columns. The entire list is to be centered horizontally on the output report, which will be printed on a 120-space printer.

One of the cards in this deck is illustrated in Figure 16-1. This problem is identical to the one described and solved in machine language as Problem 1, Chapter 15, on p. 270.

Figure 16-1. Sample data card

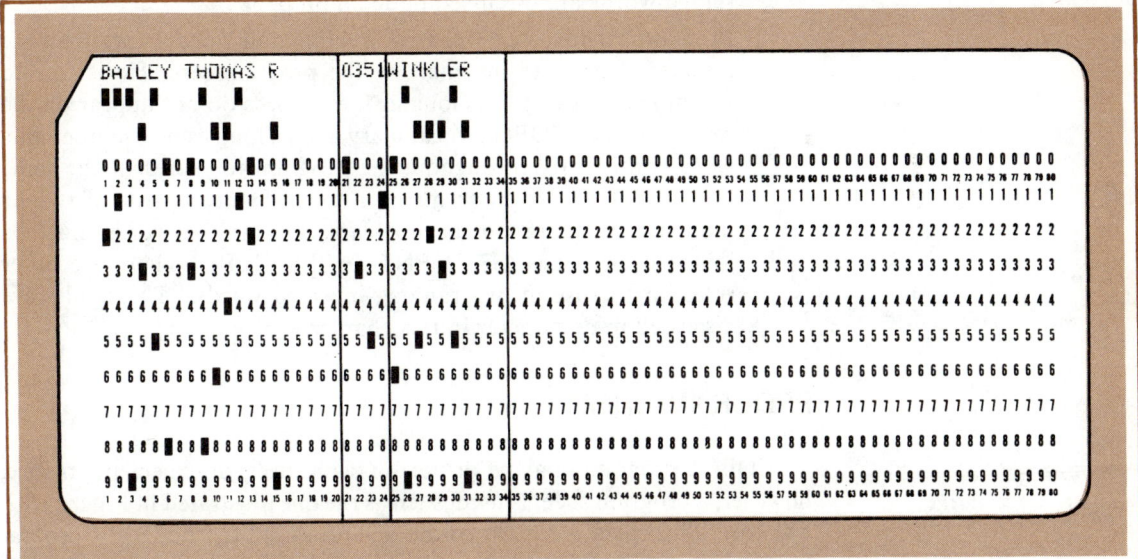

STRUCTURE OF A COBOL PROGRAM

As was true with a machine language program, a COBOL source program must be written in a precise manner and in accordance with a certain specified format. Otherwise, the compiler is unable to translate the COBOL program into an object or machine language program. Even though a near-English language is used in writing a COBOL program, certain words have specific meanings in COBOL, and these words must be used correctly. The discussion that follows will acquaint you with the two types of COBOL words and with the format rules to be followed in writing the computer commands of a program. Enough basic information will be given to enable you to write simple programs. COBOL language is being revised and updated constantly. The version of COBOL presented in this book is one that is used with many present-day computers. The language must be modified slightly to meet the requirements of the compilers developed for the different computers. The COBOL programs in Chapters 16 and 17 will work on some computers but not on all of them.

The words used in COBOL programs are of two types: those on a reserved list of COBOL words and those invented by the programmer.

(1) Reserved-list words. A partial list of COBOL reserved words may be found on p. 323. Certain words have a specific meaning to a COBOL compiler. The compiler reserves these words for special purposes. There are reserved words used in every program. The choice of words depends upon the problem to be solved, the program to be written to solve the problem, and the type of computer used. Some of the words must be used in all programs. The reserved words are discussed in detail on p. 322.

(2) Programmer-invented words. Generally, all words other than the reserved words are invented by the programmer. He is free to invent his own words as long as these words do not appear on the reserved list of COBOL vocabulary and as long as he uses the same word consistently throughout the program to represent the same item of data. If a programmer-invented name consists of two or more words, there can be no blank spaces; the words must be joined by hyphens (STUDENT-SALES-FILE). There are other rules for the use of programmer-invented words. These rules are discussed in detail later in this chapter.

PROGRAM SHEET

COBOL programs may be written on plain sheets of paper. In practice, however, a program sheet is used, such as the one illustrated in Figure 16-2. The form illustrated is similar to the one produced by the IBM Corporation for use with the IBM System/360 computer.

General characteristics

There are a few general characteristics that you should understand about the program sheet before observing how the statements of each division are written on it. Note that the sheet provides space for 80 columns of information to be punched into the COBOL source program cards. Information written in one of the numbered spaces will be punched into a corresponding column of the card.

Chapter 16   Introduction to COBOL

Figure 16-2. COBOL program sheet

In Figure 16-2, note the boxes in the upper left-hand corner of the page. These boxes are not numbered. The information written in these boxes will not be punched in a card. The information is provided on the sheet only for quick reference. Enlarged sections of the program sheet are shown below.

The box labeled "Identification" in the upper right-hand corner will contain information that will be punched into Columns 73–80. These spaces are for identifying the program if the programmer wishes to identify it. If he does, this name will be punched into cards. The box also provides a place to indicate the sheet and page number. This information is for quick reference.

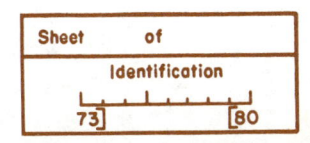

The page number that will be punched into cards is written in Columns 1–3 of the program sheet under SEQUENCE. Columns 4–6 are used to number the lines that make up the program. Column 7 is used for a hyphen to indicate a divided word. The hyphen is placed in Column 7 of the line on which the word is continued.

In Figure 16-2, Columns 8 through 72 will be used for writing the statements making up the program. No line in the program may extend beyond Column 72. Observe the Letters A and B appearing over Columns 8 and 12. Column 8 is referred to as the A-Margin and Column 12 as the B-Margin. You will learn how these columns are used as the various divisions and statements are explained and illustrated on the program sheets in this chapter.

PROGRAM DIVISIONS

A COBOL program consists of four divisions. These divisions and their titles *must* appear in every program in the following order:

IDENTIFICATION DIVISION, which gives the title of the program, the name of the programmer, and the date the program is written.

ENVIRONMENT DIVISION, which specifies the computer, the input/output devices, and input/output files.

DATA DIVISION, which describes the data files to be used as input before processing and the files and reports that will emerge as output after processing. (This division also specifies the WORKING-STORAGE SECTION reserved for constants and accumulating totals. However, for the brief program explained in this chapter, this section will be omitted.)

PROCEDURE DIVISION, which specifies the actual steps the computer is to follow in processing the data in order to achieve the desired results.

Each of the four divisions of a COBOL program may be written on a separate page, although this is a matter of preference.

REVIEW QUESTIONS

1. What does the term COBOL stand for?
2. What are the advantages of COBOL?
3. Can a computer process data directly from a COBOL program?
4. Define a source program. A compiler program. An object program.
5. What two types of words are used in COBOL programs?
6. How many spaces are provided in a COBOL program sheet for recording data? To what input medium do these spaces correspond?
7. What columns on a program sheet are used for recording the statements of a COBOL program?
8. What four divisions must be present in every COBOL program? In what order?

IDENTIFICATION DIVISION

This division includes the following information:

1. Name of the division: IDENTIFICATION DIVISION.
2. Title of the program.
3. Name of the programmer.
4. Date the program was written.

Example

The following example is for the problem defined on p. 293 and illustrates the foregoing information:

```
010  IDENTIFICATION DIVISION.
020  PROGRAM-ID.
030      'STUDENTS'.
040  AUTHOR.
050      WANOUS.
060  DATE-WRITTEN.
070      OCTOBER 2, 1971.
```

Figure 16-3. IDENTIFICATION DIVISION of COBOL program

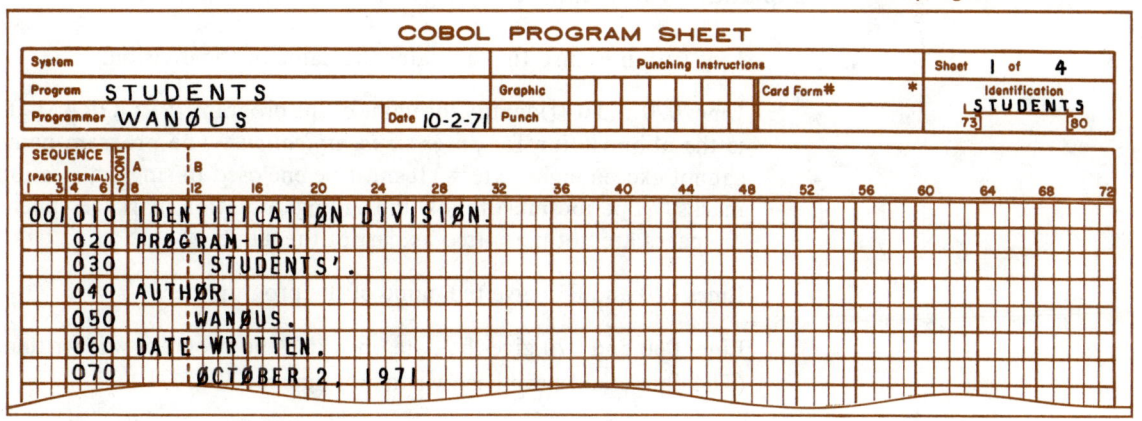

Each page in a COBOL program is always numbered in the upper right-hand corner. Figure 16-3 indicates that the IDENTIFICATION DIVISION is Sheet 1 of 4. The page number is also repeated in Columns 1–3. When the card punch operator punches the COBOL program card, the page and line numbers are punched into each card. Then if the program cards are accidentally dropped or separated, they can be reassembled easily. Some programmers write the page and line numbers together on each line of the program sheet. For example:

001	010
001	020
001	030
001	040

The page number in Columns 1–3 in this text will be written only on the first line of each new sheet, in order to make the programs simpler to write. In this case, if punched cards were being prepared, the card punch operator would still have to punch the page number into each card.

Each line in a COBOL program is normally numbered for convenient reference. In the above example, the line numbers could have been written in the usual manner (Line 1, Line 2, etc.); but the form used, Line 010, Line 020, etc., helps to avoid confusion if changes must be made in the program. The zero following the number allows for the insertion of additional lines when necessary. Therefore, Line 015 could be inserted between Lines 010 and 020 with no confusion.

Explanation of example

Line 010 in Figure 16-3 contains the name of the division.

Lines 020 and 030 identify the name of the program. PROGRAM-ID is the abbreviation for *program identification.* The program name cannot exceed eight letters. It must be enclosed in single quotation marks. A period must follow the ending quotation mark. Hyphens or spaces are not permitted as part of the name.

Lines 040 and 050 give the name of the programmer.

Lines 060 and 070 give the date on which the program was written. (The date could have been written in figures: 10/2/71.)

Observe that all items are written in capital letters. Each heading and each line of information is followed by a period. Some of the words are underlined. These underlined words are required by the compiler to appear in every program in the exact order given in the example. The underline itself is *not* part of the program. *The underline is used only as a teaching device* to identify the COBOL words required in a program. The alphabetic letters, O and Z in COBOL programs are written as Ø and Ƶ so that they cannot be confused with the Digits 0 and 2.

Format of statements in the IDENTIFICATION DIVISION

Observe Figure 16-3. Note the following characteristics about the statements appearing in the IDENTIFICATION DIVISION:

Line 010:
> The division name always appears first in a division. It starts at the A-Margin, Column 8, and ends with a period.

Lines 020, 040, and 060:
> The IDENTIFICATION DIVISION contains paragraphs. The paragraph names or headings in this division are required, as stated earlier. They are the words that have been underlined on p. 297. These paragraph headings start at the A-Margin and end with periods.

Line 030:
> The title used to identify the program is indented and starts at the B-Margin, Column 12, and ends with a period. (It is part of the paragraph PROGRAM-ID.)

Line 050:
> The author's name is indented and starts at the B-Margin, Column 12, and ends with a period. (It is part of the paragraph AUTHOR.)

Line 070:
> The date is indented and starts at the B-Margin, Column 12, and ends with a period. (It is part of the paragraph DATE-WRITTEN.)

ENVIRONMENT DIVISION

This division of a COBOL program must include the following information:

1. Name of the division: ENVIRONMENT DIVISION.
2. Names of the two sections in the division: CONFIGURATION SECTION and INPUT-OUTPUT SECTION.
3. Names of the source and object computers.
4. Name required by the COBOL program to identify the input and output files: FILE-CONTROL.
5. Name that the programmer assigns to the input file (data to be processed) and the name of the input medium to be used.
6. Name that the programmer assigns to the output file (data that have been processed) and the name of the output medium to be used.

Example

The following example of the ENVIRONMENT DIVISION is for the problem defined earlier. Recall that the underlined words are the COBOL words that are required by the program.

010 <u>ENVIRONMENT DIVISION</u>.
020 <u>CONFIGURATION SECTION</u>.
030 <u>SOURCE-COMPUTER</u>.
040   IBM-360.
050 <u>OBJECT-COMPUTER</u>.
060   IBM-360.
070 <u>INPUT-OUTPUT SECTION</u>.
080 <u>FILE-CONTROL</u>.
090   <u>SELECT</u> STUDENT-FILE, <u>ASSIGN</u> TO 'SYSIN' UNIT-RECORD.
100   <u>SELECT</u> PRINTED-REPORT-FILE, <u>ASSIGN</u> TO 'SYSOUT' UNIT-RECORD.

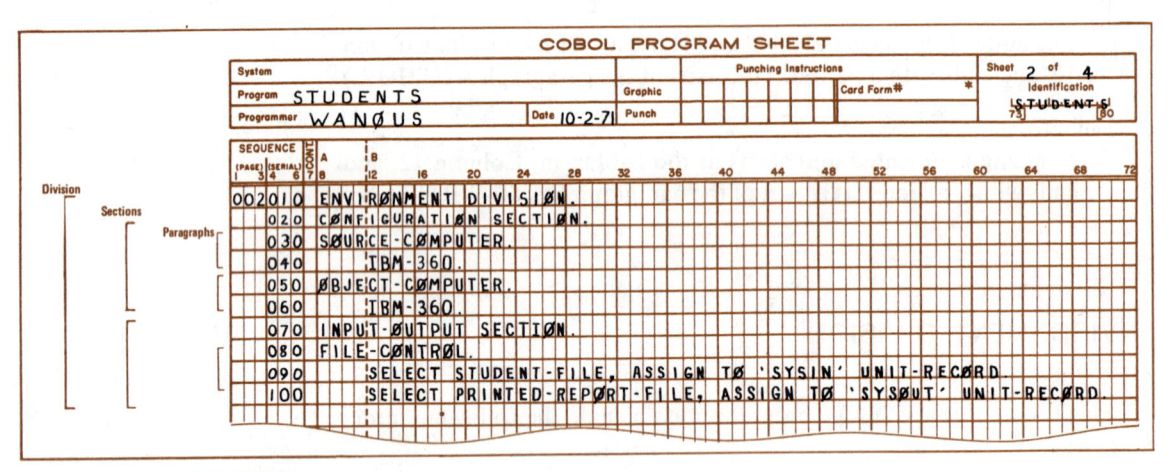

Figure 16-4. ENVIRONMENT DIVISION of COBOL program

Explanation of example

Line 010 in the foregoing example gives the name of the division.

Lines 020 and 070 give the names of the two required sections. These two section headings must appear in the ENVIRONMENT DIVISION of every COBOL program.

Lines 030 and 040 give the name of the computer that will translate the COBOL source program into a machine language object program.

Lines 050 and 060 give the name of the computer that will process the object program. The source and object computers often are the same computer.

Line 080 gives the paragraph heading for the input and output files: FILE-CONTROL. This heading is required in all COBOL programs immediately preceding the names of the input and output files.

Line 090 gives the name of the input file (cards containing data to be processed) and also indicates the input medium to be used. In the foregoing example, the *programmer has assigned the name* STUDENT-FILE to the input file. The name STUDENT-FILE refers to the entire deck of cards to be used as the input medium.

In COBOL, the name UNIT-RECORD is used to identify the punched card reader as the input device. The words SELECT and ASSIGN are required COBOL words in the statements under FILE-CONTROL.

'SYSIN' in single quotation marks is a COBOL reserved word that stands for *sys*tem *in*put. This word tells the compiler that STUDENT-FILE is the input. 'SYSIN' will appear in the FILE-CONTROL paragraph for all COBOL examples in this text.

Line 100 gives the name of the output file (PRINTED-REPORT-FILE) and also indicates which output device will be used (UNIT-RECORD, which is the printer). In the example, the *programmer has assigned the name* PRINTED-REPORT-FILE to the report containing output data. This name refers to the *entire report* which will be printed as output.

Note that in COBOL the name UNIT-RECORD may be used to identify the input device (card read-punch unit) or output device (printer).

'SYSOUT' in single quotation marks stands for *sys*tem *out*put. This term will appear in the COBOL programs in the FILE-CONTROL paragraphs at the point indicated.

Observe in the foregoing example that the only information furnished by the programmer in the ENVIRONMENT DIVISION is the name of the computer on which the program will be compiled (SOURCE-COMPUTER), the name of the computer on which the program will be run (OBJECT-COMPUTER), the names of the input and output data files, and the names identifying the input and output devices (UNIT-RECORD). All remaining information is prescribed by the COBOL language.

Format of statements in the ENVIRONMENT DIVISION

Observe Figure 16-4 once again. Note the following characteristics about the statements that appear in the ENVIRONMENT DIVISION.

Line 010:
　　Again, the division name comes first. It starts at the A-Margin and ends with a period.

Lines 020 and 070:
: Names of section headings start at the A-Margin and end with periods.

Lines 030 and 050:
: Names of paragraph headings that fall immediately under the section heading CONFIGURATION SECTION start at the A-Margin and end with periods.

Line 080:
: Name of paragraph heading that falls immediately under the section heading INPUT-OUTPUT SECTION starts at A-Margin and ends with a period.

Lines 040 and 060:
: The names of the source and object computers are indented under the proper paragraph headings. They start at the B-Margin and end with periods.

Lines 090 and 100:
: The statements that assign names to the input and output files, as well as the names of the input and output devices and media are started at the B-Margin, Column 12, under the appropriate paragraph heading FILE-CONTROL. These statements are followed by periods.

Commas may be used within lines to aid human reading, as they are in Lines 090 and 100 (SELECT STUDENT-FILE, ASSIGN TO 'SYSIN' UNIT-RECORD. SELECT PRINTED-REPORT-FILE, ASSIGN TO 'SYSOUT' UNIT-RECORD.). The commas may be omitted, however, because they have no effect on the object program. If commas are used, they must be followed by at least one space.

REVIEW QUESTIONS

1. What information does the IDENTIFICATION DIVISION contain?
2. What is the meaning of PROGRAM-ID?
3. At which margin does the division name begin? The paragraph name? The statements within the paragraph?
4. Is the period required after each statement in the IDENTIFICATION DIVISION?
5. What information does the ENVIRONMENT DIVISION contain?
6. Name the two sections that are included in the ENVIRONMENT DIVISION.
7. What paragraph name identifies the input and output files in the ENVIRONMENT DIVISION?
8. Who assigns the names to the input and output files?
9. Explain the meaning of this statement in the ENVIRONMENT DIVISION:
    SELECT EMPLOYEE-FILE, ASSIGN TO 'SYSIN' UNIT-RECORD.
10. Which of the words in the foregoing statement are required in a COBOL program?

DATA DIVISION

The major difference between machine language and COBOL is that in machine language programs the programmer uses the cell addresses when referring to the location of data. In COBOL the programmer uses names instead of numbers in order to describe these cells. When a computer command is written, such as GO TO STUDENT-NAME, the compiler will translate STUDENT-NAME into a specific numeric address. The programmer refers to each address by name instead of number.

For the foregoing reason, it is very important that the data files used as input should be described with the greatest accuracy. It is just as important that the output files and reports should be described exactly.

Files, records, and fields

In the DATA DIVISION, a clear distinction must be made between files, records, and fields. The following illustration, Figure 16-5, shows this distinction when punched cards are used as the input medium. An *input file* is a deck of punched cards. A *record* is a single punched card. A *field* is a division of a single card.

Figure 16-5. Input file, record, and field

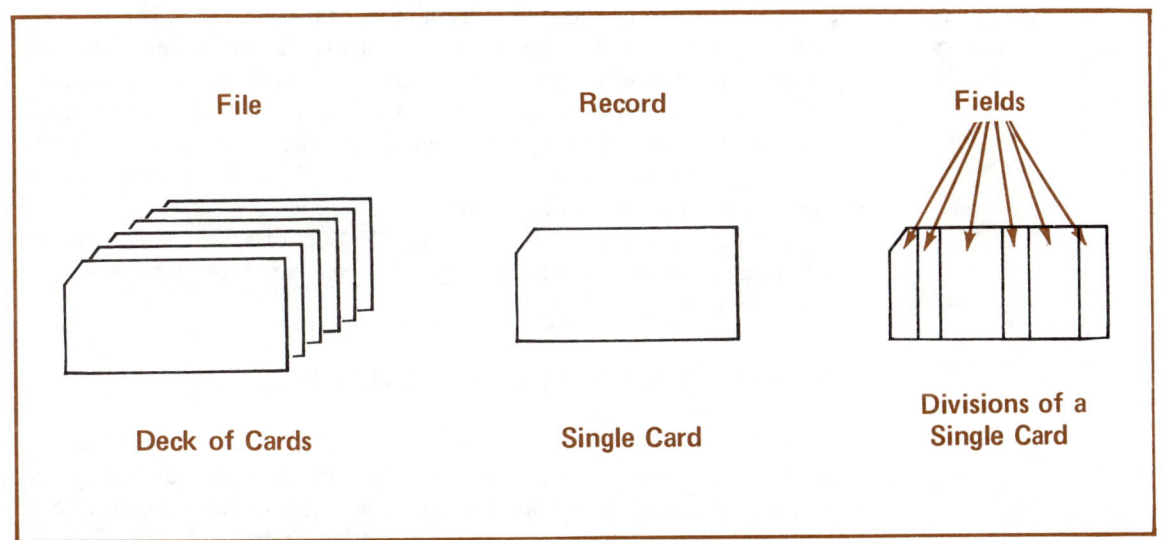

File — Deck of Cards

Record — Single Card

Fields — Divisions of a Single Card

A clear distinction must also be made between files, records, and fields when a printed report is used as the output medium. The following illustration, Figure 16-6, shows this distinction. An *output file* consists of a printed report containing processed information. A *record* is a single line on that file. A *field* is a specific item of information on that line.

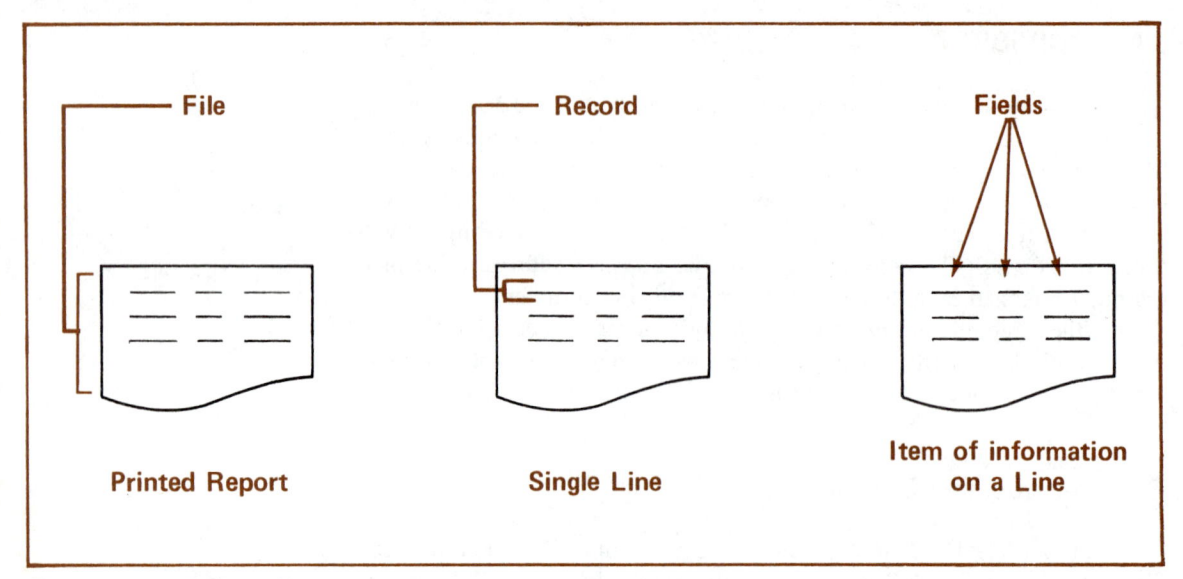

Figure 16-6. Output file, record, and field

Principal purpose of DATA DIVISION

The principal purpose of the DATA DIVISION is to describe the input file (PUNCHED-CARD in this text) with COBOL names in such an exact manner that the compiler will be able to translate the names into cell addresses that it will assign. The output file should be described with accuracy so that the compiler will be able to translate the names into cell addresses, to execute the computer commands, and to print the report exactly as desired. Although the step-by-step commands are given in the PROCEDURE DIVISION, if the DATA DIVISION is not written accurately, the program will not work.

For convenience, the DATA DIVISION is discussed in two parts: (1) Input Statements, and (2) Output Statements. Input statements are discussed first.

Input statements in the DATA DIVISION

As mentioned on p. 303, the *input file* consists of a deck of cards containing related information, which will be used by a particular program. A *record* is a single card within a file. A *field* is a specific column or columns on a card containing certain information or data.

Required input statements

The input portion of the DATA DIVISION of a COBOL program must include the following information:

1. Name of the division: DATA DIVISION. (See p. 307.)
2. Names of sections in the division: FILE SECTION. (WORKING-STORAGE SECTION, if needed).
3. Name that the programmer invents for each input file and several statements that will give the compiler information about the general characteristics of the input file. The name used in the DATA DIVISION for each file must be the same as that used in the ENVIRONMENT DIVISION. (In this chapter the input file has been specified as STUDENT-FILE. The output file is PRINTED-REPORT-FILE.) While compiler programs vary in the number and wording of explanatory statements needed, the following statements are usually included in all COBOL programs:
    a. A statement regarding the length of the recording mode. This statement tells the compiler whether the input record is of fixed, variable, or unspecified length. (The input record in this text is of fixed length since a punched card always contains 80 columns.)
    b. A statement regarding the length of the input record. (Of course, it contains 80 characters if a punched card is used.)
    c. A statement regarding the use of labels in the input record. Labels are used when magnetic tape serves as an input or output medium. These labels identify the beginning and ending of records on the tape. Labels are not necessary if punched cards are used. A statement about label records is required by the COBOL compiler even though no labels are used.
    d. Name the programmer invents for each record in the input file.
4. Restatement of the name that the programmer has invented for each record in the input file, and several statements which describe the fields on the record.
    a. Name that the programmer invents for each field of data on each record in the input file.
    b. A PICTURE clause to describe each input field of data. A PICTURE clause describes the number of characters in a field and the type of characters: alphabetic, numeric, or alphameric (mixed).
    PICTURE clauses will be discussed in detail later in this chapter.

Optional input statements

In addition, the following information may be included depending upon its use in the program.

1. Identification of the storage areas which will contain constants and data being accumulated, such as counts or totals. (This operation will be discussed in Chapter 17.)
2. Location of decimal points in numeric characters, when needed. (This operation is not covered in this book.)

Inventing names for input data

All input data referred to in the processing stage must be named in the DATA DIVISION. The names assigned to the various types of data to be processed must be invented by the programmer. Once invented in the DATA DIVISION, however, they must be referred to in exactly the same way every time they are used in the program. They cannot be misspelled, altered, or abbreviated.

Example

The following example is for the problem presented in this chapter. Recall that this problem calls for a printed report to be made from punched cards. The report will list the students in a school, their homeroom numbers, and the names of their homeroom teachers.

010 DATA DIVISION.

020 FILE SECTION.

030 FD STUDENT-FILE

040   RECORDING MODE IS F

050   RECORD CONTAINS 80 CHARACTERS

060   LABEL RECORDS ARE OMITTED

070   DATA RECORD IS PUNCHED-CARD.

Lines 030 – 070 make up a single unit of information and could be written continuously across the line with commas or spaces.

080 01 PUNCHED-CARD.

090   02 STUDENT-NAME   PICTURE A(20).

100   02 HOMEROOM-NUMBER   PICTURE 9(4).

110   02 HOMEROOM-TEACHER   PICTURE A(10).

120   02 FILLER   PICTURE X(46).

Explanation of example

Line 010 gives the name of the division: DATA DIVISION.

Line 020 gives the name of the section: FILE SECTION. (No WORKING-STORAGE SECTION is needed for this problem.)

Chapter 16   Introduction to COBOL

```
COBOL PROGRAM SHEET
System
Program STUDENTS
Programmer WANOUS          Date 10-2-71
Sheet 3 of 4
Identification STUDENTS

003010 DATA DIVISION.
   020 FILE SECTION.
   030 FD STUDENT-FILE
   040    RECORDING MODE IS F
   050    RECORD CONTAINS 80 CHARACTERS
   060    LABEL RECORDS ARE OMITTED
   070    DATA RECORD IS PUNCHED-CARD.
   080 01 PUNCHED-CARD.
   090    02 STUDENT-NAME              PICTURE A(20).
   100    02 HOMEROOM-NUMBER            PICTURE 9(4).
   110    02 HOMEROOM-TEACHER           PICTURE A(10).
   120    02 FILLER                     PICTURE X(46).
   130 FD PRINTED-REPORT-FILE
   140    RECORDING MODE IS F
   150    RECORD CONTAINS 120 CHARACTERS
   160    LABEL RECORDS ARE OMITTED
   170    DATA RECORD IS PRINTED-LINE.
   180 01 PRINTED-LINE.
   190    02 FILLER                     PICTURE X(33).
   200    02 STUDENT-NAME-PRINT         PICTURE A(20).
   210    02 FILLER                     PICTURE X(10).
   220    02 HOMEROOM-NUMBER-PRINT      PICTURE 9(4).
   230    02 FILLER                     PICTURE X(10).
   240    02 HOMEROOM-TEACHER-PRINT     PICTURE A(10).
   250    02 FILLER                     PICTURE X(33).
```

Figure 16-7. DATA DIVISION of COBOL program

Line 030 contains the FD, which stands for *File Description*. The file description line specifies the name which was assigned to the input file in the ENVIRONMENT DIVISION. In this problem, the name STUDENT-FILE was assigned to the card deck containing the input data.

Lines 040 through 070 contain the statements that give the compiler general information about the input file. The COBOL statements required vary from compiler to compiler. Some compilers do not require the first two statements at all.

Line 040 is a required COBOL statement which describes the recording mode of the input record. The input PUNCHED-CARD contains a *f*ixed number of columns; thus the statement RECORDING MODE IS F. (If magnetic tape or some other input medium is used, the RECORDING MODE or length might not be *f*ixed.)

Line 050 describes the length of the input records (80 characters).

Line 060 contains the required statement regarding the use of labels in the input records. None are used, as the statement indicates. (Labels are ordinarily used to identify magnetic tape or disk files.)

Line 070 contains the name assigned by the programmer to each record in the input file to be processed. In this problem, the name assigned to each record is PUNCHED-CARD.

Line 080 01 restates the name assigned to the data record (the card). In this problem, the name PUNCHED-CARD was assigned to the record. (The 01, which appears before the data record name, is a level number of the first order and will be explained later.)

Line 090 02 contains the name of the *first field* on the card, STUDENT-NAME (assigned by the programmer), and a description of the data. (The 02, which appears before the first field name, is a level number of the second order and will be explained later.)

Line 100 02 contains the name of the *second field* on the card, HOMEROOM-NUMBER, and a description of the data.

Line 110 02 contains the name of the *third field* on the card, HOMEROOM-TEACHER, and a description of the data.

Line 120 02 indicates that there are 46 unused columns on each data card. The word FILLER indicates spaces which are not used.

Note that the sum of the fields described in Lines 090 through 120 equals 80, which is the length of the data record, PUNCHED-CARD.

Level numbers

The DATA DIVISION does not contain paragraphs as do the other three divisions of a COBOL program. The DATA DIVISION contains level numbers instead. *Level numbers* perform the same function in a program that Roman and Arabic numerals do in an outline. Level numbers show the relationship of the data names in a program and are used in the DATA DIVISION only.

The division name and section names are always written at the A-Margin. Because the file is the broadest classification of data, it is assigned a special level indicator, FD, to place it at a primary level. The FD is also written at the A-Margin. The record is at the next level of importance, and it is always assigned the level number 01. All the record descriptions are divided into levels, depending upon their importance. Since the level 01 always refers to a record, the level 02 refers to a field within that record. The level 03 refers to an item within a field.

In the example of the program just illustrated, level number 01 designates PUNCHED-CARD as the record. Level 01 (PUNCHED-CARD) begins at the A-Margin. Level number 02 then designates the fields on the record (STUDENT-NAME, HOMEROOM-NUMBER, etc.). Level 02 begins at the B-Margin, Column 12. If a field were subdivided; for example, the STUDENT-NAME field into last name and first name, these subdivisions would be designated by Level 03 and would be indented to Column 16.

A similar use of level numbers will be made in designating the records and fields in the output portion of the DATA DIVISION.

PICTURE Clauses

No doubt you have already determined that PICTURE clauses in Lines 090 through 120 indicate the number of spaces used in each field. These clauses also tell the compiler what type of information is contained in each field. PICTURE clauses are used only in the DATA DIVISION and are used in both the input and output portions.

The Number 9 is used to indicate that a field is made up of numeric digits. The Letter A indicates that the field is made up of letters of the alphabet and spaces. The Letter X indicates that the field is composed of a combination of digits, special characters, letters of the alphabet, or blank spaces. If you will refer to the fields on the card in Figure 16-1, p. 293, the PICTURE clauses will become clear to you.

The identifying characters are summarized in the following table:

Character	Data Representation
9	Numeric digits
A	Letters of the alphabet with or without spaces
X	Combination of digits, letters of the alphabet, special characters, or spaces

Note that in Figure 16-7, all the PICTURE clauses begin at Column 48. The program was written in this manner in order to align all the PICTURE clauses on the program sheet, thus making the program easier to read. If the programmer decides to write the PICTURE clause immediately following the field name, he must allow at least one space between the field name and the PICTURE clause. Also, note that there is always one space between the word PICTURE and the remainder of the clause. There must be no intervening spaces in the descriptive portion of the PICTURE clause, such as A(20). The parentheses are required. The number inside the parentheses indicates the number of columns in the field. Note also that the PICTURE clause always ends with a period.

Format of statements in the DATA DIVISION

Refer again to Figure 16-7. Note the following characteristics about the statements in the DATA DIVISION. Only the statements presenting new problems will be discussed. Apply what you learned in the discussion on the format of statements in the previous divisions.

Line 010:
> The division name starts at the A-Margin and ends with a period.

Line 020:
> The section name (FILE SECTION) also starts at the A-Margin and ends with a period. In the problem in this chapter, there will only be a FILE SECTION, because the WORKING-STORAGE SECTION will not appear.

The five lines that follow contain the five required COBOL statements which name and describe the general nature of the *input* file. Only the last statement in the FD (Line 070) must end with a period.

Line 030:
> The FD (*File Description*) starts at the A-Margin. Note, however, that STUDENT-FILE, the name assigned to the input file, starts at the B-Margin.

Lines 040 through 070:
> The four statements describing the general nature of the input file, including the name assigned to the record within that file (PUNCHED-CARD) all start at the B-Margin. The period at the end of the statements (Line 070) is required. Some COBOL programmers insert commas or semicolons at the end of the descriptive statements, Lines 040–060. Since these commas or semicolons are not required, they will be omitted in this text in order to simplify the programs.

Line 080:
> The level number 01 has been assigned to the input record (PUNCHED-CARD). The 01 is written at the A-Margin. PUNCHED-CARD is written at the B-Margin and must be followed by a period. Note that the name of the input record is first mentioned in Line 070 and that it is restated on Line 080. The ending period is required by the COBOL compiler for the Level 01 statements in the DATA DIVISION, because the 01 statements name the records.

Lines 090 through 120:
> The level number of each field starts at the B-Margin. If there had been any Level 03 numbers in this program, they would have been started at Column 16, as mentioned before.
>
> Commas at the end of field names have been omitted, although their use is optional. Also optional is the placement of PICTURE clauses. These could follow the field names by only one space or be aligned as they are on the program sheet illustrated.
>
> Note that the codes, such as A(20), are written without intervening spaces. The parentheses are required. Note, also, that each PICTURE clause ends with a period, which is required.
>
> Line 120 describes the FILLER with the code X(46). This means that there are 46 spaces (blank columns) in the input record (the punched card illustrated in Figure 16-1, p. 293). The blank columns appear at the end of the card.

Note that the sum of the PICTURE clause fields (positions) equals 80, which is the *F*ixed length of the data record (PUNCHED-CARD).

Lines 130 through 250:

This part of the DATA DIVISION contains the statements relating to the output data and names. No new concepts are presented.

REVIEW QUESTIONS

1. Define a file, a record, and a field in reference to a deck of punched cards.
2. Define a file, a record, and a field in reference to a printed report.
3. What information must be included in the input portion of the DATA DIVISION?
4. For what types of information in the input portion of the DATA DIVISION must the programmer invent names?
5. Should the programmer-invented names remain the same in all divisions of a COBOL program?
6. Assume that you have a deck of cards in which have been punched customers' names and the amounts owed by them. Provide a name for the deck of cards, for a single card, and for each of the two fields on the card. Which is the file? The record? The field?
7. What is the meaning of the statement: LABEL RECORDS ARE OMITTED? Must the statement be included in a COBOL program?
8. Is the level number 01 associated with a file? A record? A field?
9. Is the level number 02 associated with a file? A record? A field?
10. Why are level numbers assigned to files in the DATA DIVISION?
11. Explain the following assignment of level numbers:
    ```
    01  PUNCHED-CARD.
        02  STUDENT-NAME
            03  LAST NAME
            03  FIRST NAME.
    ```
12. What are PICTURE clauses used to describe: Files? Records? Fields?
13. What format requirements must be observed in writing a PICTURE clause?
14. Explain the meaning of the following three statements in the input portion of the DATA DIVISION:
    ```
    01  PUNCHED-CARD.
        02  COURSE-NAME      PICTURE A(12).
        02  FILLER           PICTURE X(68).
    ```
15. What is the meaning of the Number 9 in a PICTURE clause? The Letter A? The Letter X?
16. What is the function of PICTURE clauses in the input portion of the DATA DIVISION?

Output statements in the DATA DIVISION

A discussion of the output statements of the DATA DIVISION follows. Actually, input and output statements appear together within the DATA

DIVISION. The discussion in this chapter is divided for ease in learning. It is important to remember that in the input portion of the DATA DIVISION a file is a deck of punched cards. In the output portion a file is a printed report. The input record is a single punched card. The output record is a single line on the printed report. The input field is a field on the punched card. The output field is a specific item on a line of the printed report.

The division name, section names, FD, and 01 level statements always begin at the A-Margin. The division name and the section name end with a period. The FD (*f*ile *d*escription) does not require a period until the end of the entire description on the line describing the data record (Lines 070 and 170 in Figure 16-7, p. 307).

A record is described at the 01 level. The 01 level statements require periods. A field is described at the 02 level. The periods appear at the end of the PICTURE clauses describing the fields. This much is review.

Names must be assigned to each output file, record, and field; and the names used must be different from those assigned to similar data in the input files, records, and fields.

Required output statements

The output portion of the DATA DIVISION of a COBOL program does not repeat the names of the division and the sections within the division, because this material has been covered in the input portion. The output portion of the DATA DIVISION must include the following information:

1. Name that the programmer invents for each output file produced as a result of his program and several statements describing the general nature of the output file. The name used here for each file must be the same as that used in the ENVIRONMENT DIVISION. These statements are similar to those that describe the general character of the input file, Lines 030 through 070.
2. Restatement of the name that the programmer has invented for each record in the output file and several statements which describe the fields on the record.

    These statements are similar to those that described the input records and fields, Lines 080 through 120, Figure 16-7, p. 307.

Inventing names for output data

All output data referred to in the program must be named in the DATA DIVISION. The names assigned to the various types of data being produced must be invented by the programmer. Once designated in the DATA DIVISION, however, they must be referred to in exactly the same way every time they are used in the program. They cannot be misspelled, altered, or abbreviated.

In contrast, however, names used in *different* COBOL programs have no relationship to one another (except for the words on the reserved word list) so there is no need for concern regarding words in different programs. Words invented *within* the same program to designate data and storage addresses must always be the same throughout the program, and they can be used with reference to only one item. Otherwise, the compiler becomes confused (just as you might if there were two or more students in your class with exactly the same name). If the same name is used for more than one item of data within a program, the compiler detects this error and the computer stops. The error must then be corrected before the COBOL program can be translated into an object program.

Distinguishing files, records, and fields

For emphasis, it must be restated that a clear distinction must be made between output files, records, and fields. The output file, which was designated as PRINTED-REPORT-FILE, is the entire completed report. A record, which will be designated as PRINTED-LINE, is a single line within this file. A field is a specific item of information on the record. You will recall that there are three items of information, or fields, on the output record: the name of the student, his homeroom number, and the name of his homeroom teacher. The names of the fields in the output record must be different from those assigned to fields in the input record. The names assigned to these output items are STUDENT-NAME-PRINT, HOMEROOM-NUMBER-PRINT, and HOMEROOM-TEACHER-PRINT.

Example

The following example of the output portion of the DATA DIVISION is for our problem. Recall that this problem calls for a printed report listing students in a school, their homeroom numbers, and the names of their homeroom teachers.

```
130 FD PRINTED-REPORT-FILE
140    RECORDING MODE is F
150    RECORD CONTAINS 120 CHARACTERS
160    LABEL RECORDS ARE OMITTED
170    DATA RECORD IS PRINTED-LINE.
180 01 PRINTED-LINE.
190    02 FILLER                      PICTURE X(33).
200    02 STUDENT-NAME-PRINT          PICTURE A(20).
210    02 FILLER                      PICTURE X(10).
220    02 HOMEROOM-NUMBER-PRINT       PICTURE 9(4).
230    02 FILLER                      PICTURE X(10).
240    02 HOMEROOM-TEACHER-PRINT      PICTURE A(10).
250    02 FILLER                      PICTURE X(33).
```

```
003 130    FD   PRINTED-REPORT-FILE
    140         RECORDING MODE IS F
    150         RECORD CONTAINS 120 CHARACTERS
    160         LABEL RECORDS ARE OMITTED
    170         DATA-RECORD IS PRINTED-LINE.
    180    01   PRINTED-LINE.
    190         02 FILLER                        PICTURE X(33).
    200         02 STUDENT-NAME-PRINT            PICTURE A(20).
    210         02 FILLER                        PICTURE X(10).
    220         02 HOMEROOM-NUMBER-PRINT         PICTURE 9(4).
    230         02 FILLER                        PICTURE X(10).
    240         02 HOMEROOM-TEACHER-PRINT        PICTURE A(10).
    250         02 FILLER                        PICTURE X(33).
```

Figure 16-8. Output portion of DATA DIVISION of COBOL program

Explanation of example

Lines 010 through 120 have already been illustrated and discussed in the input portion of the DATA DIVISION. This illustration has thus resumed with Line 130.

Line 130 is the name invented by the programmer to identify the output file in the DATA DIVISION. FD stands for *File Description* as in Line 030. This file name was designated in the ENVIRONMENT DIVISION. Line 130 corresponds to Line 030 of the input portion.

Lines 140 through 170 correspond to Lines 040 through 070 of the input portion of the DATA DIVISION.

Line 140 indicates that the output record is of fixed length. A printed report can accomodate only as many characters as are built into the printer; that is, 100, 120, or 132 characters. It is thus of fixed length.

Line 150 describes the length of the output record. The assumption is made that a 120-space printer is being used.

Line 160 states that no labels are used on the output record.

Line 170 contains the name invented by the programmer for the output record: PRINTED-LINE.

Lines 180 through 250 contain the names invented by the programmer for, and the description of, each field (column) being produced in the output record (line) of the output file (printed report).

Line 180 01 repeats the name of a record in the output file. This record is then subdivided into fields in the following lines:

Line 190 02 indicates that 33 spaces will appear in the left margin of the report. The reserved word FILLER is used with an alphameric PICTURE clause. This use of the word FILLER is one method by which output may be spaced horizontally.

Line 200 02 indicates that STUDENT-NAME-PRINT, which will appear in the first column of the printed report, will take 20 spaces and that it consists of alphabetic characters.

Line 210 02 indicates that 10 spaces will appear between the first and second columns of the report.

Line 220 02 indicates that HOMEROOM-NUMBER-PRINT, which will appear in the second column, will take 4 spaces and that it consists of numeric characters.

Line 230 02 indicates that 10 spaces will appear between the second and third columns.

Line 240 02 indicates that HOMEROOM-TEACHER-PRINT, which is to appear in the third column, will take 10 spaces and that it consists of alphabetic characters.

Line 250 02 indicates that 33 spaces will appear in the right margin.

Note that level numbers and PICTURE clauses are used in the output portion of the DATA DIVISION just as they were in the input portion. Note also that the sum of all PICTURE clause fields (positions) should equal 120, which is the *F*ixed length of the record (PRINTED-LINE).

REVIEW QUESTIONS

1. What information must be included in the output portion of the DATA DIVISION?
2. For what types of information in the output portion of the DATA DIVISION must the programmer invent names?
3. Assume that you intend to produce an output printed report showing customers' names in one column and the amounts owed by them in a second column. Provide a name for the report, for a single line in the report, and for each of the two fields in the report.
4. Can the names assigned in Question 3 above be the same as those assigned to the corresponding input data?
5. In the output portion of the DATA DIVISION, is the level number 01 associated with a file? A record? A field? Is the level number 02 associated with a file? A record? A field?
6. With which names in the output portion are PICTURE clauses used: Files? Records? Fields?
7. Explain the meaning of each of the following statements in the output portion of the DATA DIVISION:
   ```
   01   LINE-IN-PRINTED-REPORT.
        02   FILLER              PICTURE X(30).
        02   CITY                PICTURE A(15).
        02   FILLER              PICTURE X(38).
        02   POPULATION          PICTURE 9(7).
        02   FILLER              PICTURE X(30).
   ```
8. What is the capacity (in spaces) of the printer for Question 7?
9. Must the same names be assigned to the input and output files for a particular problem? To input and output records for a particular problem? To input and output fields for a particular problem?

PROCEDURE DIVISION

The PROCEDURE DIVISION is the fourth and final division in a COBOL program. The PROCEDURE DIVISION contains the logic of the computer program and specifies the actual step-by-step orders the computer will follow in processing the data cards.

Inventing paragraph names

Since COBOL is a near-English language, the sequences of the procedures can be broken up into paragraphs. The paragraphs, in turn, consist of statements or sentences. However, in the COBOL PROCEDURE DIVISION, instead of indenting the paragraph, it is given a name, which is called a *paragraph name*. In Figure 16-9, BEGINNING-OF-JOB, DETAIL-PROCESSING, and END-OF-JOB are paragraph names. The individual sentences will be discussed later in this chapter. Note that each paragraph name begins at the A-Margin and ends with a period. Observe also that each of the sentences in a paragraph begins at the B-Margin and ends with a period.

Now the advantage of COBOL over machine language becomes apparent. In the COBOL PROCEDURE DIVISION, the programmer can write an English-language order to go to any of these paragraph names. The compiler will take care of finding the proper cell addresses. Therefore, the use of names instead of numbers makes it easier to program in COBOL.

Required statements in PROCEDURE DIVISION

The PROCEDURE DIVISION includes the following information:

1. The name of the division: PROCEDURE DIVISION.
2. A paragraph name for the opening steps in the program.
3. The opening steps needed for "getting ready" the input and output files.
4. A statement that will clear the print area of the computer.
5. One or more paragraph names (depending on the problem) for the processing steps needed to solve the problem.
6. A list of the steps needed to solve the problem.
7. A paragraph name for the closing steps in the program.
8. The closing steps needed to end the program and stop the computer.

Chapter 16   Introduction to COBOL

Example

The following statements solve the problem used in this chapter:

```
010  PROCEDURE DIVISION.
020  BEGINNING-OF-JOB.
030      OPEN INPUT STUDENT-FILE.
040      OPEN OUTPUT PRINTED-REPORT-FILE.
050      MOVE SPACES TO PRINTED-LINE.
060  DETAIL-PROCESSING.
070      READ STUDENT-FILE, AT END GO TO END-OF-JOB.
080      MOVE STUDENT-NAME TO STUDENT-NAME-PRINT.
090      MOVE HOMEROOM-NUMBER TO HOMEROOM-NUMBER-PRINT.
100      MOVE HOMEROOM-TEACHER TO HOMEROOM-TEACHER-PRINT.
110      WRITE PRINTED-LINE.
120      MOVE SPACES TO PRINTED-LINE.
130      GO TO DETAIL-PROCESSING.
140  END-OF-JOB.
150      CLOSE STUDENT-FILE.
160      CLOSE PRINTED-REPORT-FILE.
170      STOP RUN.
```

Figure 16-9. PROCEDURE DIVISION of COBOL program

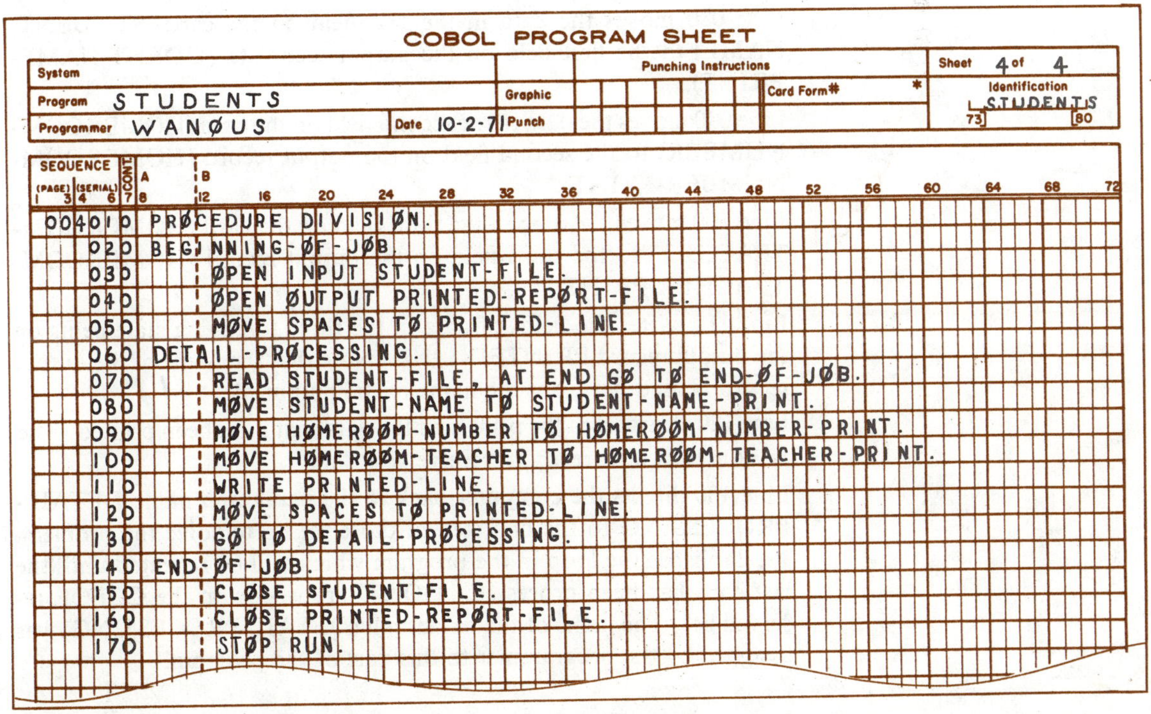

Explanation of example

Again, Line 010 gives the name of the division: PROCEDURE DIVISION.

Line 020 (BEGINNING-OF-JOB) is the paragraph name for the "get ready" or "housekeeping" steps of the program. A paragraph name is required in the program. The name of the paragraph is assigned by the programmer and may, therefore, be any name he desires to use so long as he keeps certain rules in mind.

Line 030 opens the input file. Line 040 opens the output file. These statements are essential. The names OPEN INPUT and OPEN OUTPUT are required statements. The names of the files are those that have been assigned to them by the programmer in the ENVIRONMENT DIVISION and described in the DATA DIVISION.

Line 050 clears the storage locations for printing by moving spaces (blanks) to all 120 spaces of the printed line.

Line 060 establishes a paragraph name (DETAIL-PROCESSING) for the processing steps needed to solve the problem. The paragraph name is required in the program because of the statement that appears on Line 130. The name of this paragraph is also invented by the programmer and can be anything he desires to make it.

Line 070 is the first step of those set up to solve the problem. It indicates that a card from the student file is to be read. It also indicates that after the last card has been processed, a branch is to be made to the paragraph name END-OF-JOB for the closing steps.

Line 080 moves the data in the first field on the card (STUDENT-NAME) to the first field on the output record (STUDENT-NAME-PRINT).

Line 090 moves the data in the second field on the card (HOMEROOM-NUMBER) to the second field on the output record (HOMEROOM-NUMBER-PRINT).

Line 100 moves the data in the third field on the card (HOMEROOM-TEACHER) to the third field on the output record (HOMEROOM-TEACHER-PRINT).

Line 110 writes the fields of data in the three foregoing statements on the output record PRINTED-LINE. Note that the name of the output record is used here, not the name of the output file.

Line 120 clears from the print area the data that have been printed. The print area is now ready to receive new data.

Line 130 directs the computer back to the paragraph name DETAIL-PROCESSING to the first step of those set up to solve the problem. It establishes the loop in the program which will be repeated until the last card has been processed. GO TO are words on the COBOL reserved list. The name of the paragraph (DETAIL-PROCESSING) was assigned by the programmer to this part of the program.

Line 140 establishes the paragraph name END-OF-JOB for the closing steps of the program. A paragraph name is required because of the statement that appears on Line 070. The paragraph name is also invented by the programmer and can be anything he desires to make it.

Line 150 closes the input file. Line 160 closes the output file. The word CLOSE is required in both statements. The words INPUT and OUTPUT are omitted because the two files were identified in Lines 030 and 040. The names of the files (STUDENT-FILE and PRINTED-REPORT-FILE) must be used, however.

Line 170 stops the run. The job is finished. The COBOL name STOP RUN is required and cannot be changed.

You can easily see that it is in the PROCEDURE DIVISION that the step-by-step directions for processing the data cards in the COBOL program are given. The entire concept is based upon the use of names for cell locations and the ability of the compiler to translate the source program into an object program. The paragraph name is used to identify the beginning of a new step or sequence of steps in the PROCEDURE DIVISION. The sentences comprise the individual steps in these sequences.

Format of statements in the PROCEDURE DIVISION

Refer again to Figure 16-9. The following requirements pertain to the statements in the PROCEDURE DIVISION:

Lines 010, 020, 060, and 140:
> The name of the division and the names of the paragraphs of the opening, processing, and closing steps of the program start at the A-Margin and end with a period.

Lines 030 and 040:
> The statements that open the input and output files start at the B-Margin and end with a period.

Line 050 is a statement that clears the print area. The statement begins at the B-Margin and ends with a period.

Lines 070 through 130:
> Each step of the program written to solve the problem starts at the B-Margin. Each statement is a sentence, so each statement ends with a period. If any one of these sentences is so long that it must be continued on additional lines, the continued statements will start at the B-Margin (Column 12) — or, if desired, the continuation can be indented to Column 16.

Lines 150 through 170:
> Each of the closing steps starts at the B-Margin. Each sentence, of course, ends in a period.

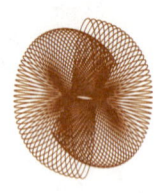

REVIEW QUESTIONS

1. What is the purpose of the PROCEDURE DIVISION?
2. How does the use of names make COBOL easier for the programmer than machine language?
3. What information is included in the PROCEDURE DIVISION of a COBOL program?
4. What statements are included under the paragraph name for the opening or "get ready" steps in a program?
5. Is the name of the paragraph for the opening steps in a program assigned by the programmer or required by COBOL?
6. Is the name of the paragraph for the processing steps in a program assigned by the programmer or required by COBOL?
7. Is the name of the paragraph for the closing steps in a program assigned by the programmer or required by COBOL?
8. What sentences are included under the paragraph for the closing steps in a program?
9. What are the paragraph names in Figure 16-9?
10. Define the action prescribed by the following processing steps.

    PROCESSING-STEPS.
       READ CITY-POPULATION-FILE, AT END GO TO NO-MORE-CARDS.
       MOVE CITY TO PRINTED-REPORT-CITY.
       MOVE POPULATION TO PRINTED-REPORT-POPULATION.
       WRITE LINE-IN-PRINTED-REPORT.
       GO TO PROCESSING-STEPS.

NAMES USED IN A COBOL PROGRAM

Each line of a COBOL source program is punched into a separate card. The computer reads each card, and the COBOL statements are translated to machine language statements by a compiler program, which is stored in the computer. From the machine language or object program, the computer then processes the data cards prepared for a problem. This much is repetition, but it may be needed to set the record straight concerning the significance of names.

It is obvious that the names used in a COBOL program are very important. These names are used instead of the cell addresses of the instructions and of the data being processed. In a machine language program an address is included for each instruction and for each item of data to be processed. The comparison of a partial machine language program and a partial COBOL program will make this relationship clear.

Chapter 16   Introduction to COBOL

In the following example, note how numeric addresses of instructions in the first program are assigned names in the second. Note, too, that numeric addresses of data in one program are assigned names in the other. The compiler translates the COBOL source program into a machine language object program. The machine language program, then, is the program that processes the data cards.

	Machine Language Program				*COBOL Program*
Instr/ Address	Op Code	A/I Add.	B Add.	d-Mod.	
401	B	423		A	DETAIL-PROCESSING. READ STUDENT-FILE; AT END, GO TO END-OF-JOB.
406	1				
407	M	020	220		MOVE STUDENT-NAME TO STUDENT-NAME-PRINT.
414	2				WRITE PRINTED-LINE.
415	B	401			GO TO DETAIL-PROCESSING.
419	.				END-OF-JOB.

Figure 16-10. Comparison of machine language and COBOL programs

At this point, COBOL may appear to be more difficult to understand and to use than machine language. It may seem that it would be easier to write a machine language program. It must be remembered, however, that the principles of machine language illustrated in this text have been purposely applied to second-generation computers, in order to make these concepts easier to understand. If a programmer were constructing a machine language program for one of the latest model computers, such as the IBM 360, it would be impossible to keep in mind the limitless core positions. In earlier chapters you were told that the IBM 360 uses a hexadecimal code. It would take much more time and knowledge to write a program in hexadecimal than in COBOL.

Reserved COBOL words

As stated before, certain English words designated by COBOL must be used in a COBOL program. Which words are used depends upon the problem being solved, the program written to solve it, and the versatility of the computer being used. The reserved words are designated by COBOL and must be used in a specified manner. These words appear in a partial list of reserved COBOL words in Figure 16-11.

If a PICTURE clause is needed in a program, for example, the name PICTURE must be used. If a card is to be read, the word READ must be used. SCAN will not do. If a line of data is to be printed, the word WRITE must be used. PRINT cannot be used. If a branch is to be made, the term GO TO is used. BRANCH TO or RETURN TO are not allowed because BRANCH and RETURN are not on the list of COBOL reserved words.

Required entries (Names)

Some required names must be used in every program. Examples are the names of the divisions and the names of the sections: ENVIRONMENT DIVISION, CONFIGURATION SECTION, and INPUT-OUTPUT SECTION. Additional examples are DATA DIVISION, FILE SECTION, WORKING-STORAGE SECTION, PROCEDURE DIVISION, SELECT, ASSIGN, and STOP RUN. In the examples of COBOL statements given earlier in this chapter, the names required in every program have been underlined. These names cannot be omitted or changed. Many of the required words appear in Figure 16-11, a partial list of COBOL reserved words.

Programmer-invented names

You have been told that certain COBOL reserved words are required in every program. With the exception of these reserved words, the programmer is free to invent names of his choice for data items and instructions in a COBOL program. Generally, he invents the names of the files, names of the records, and names of the fields of the data to be processed (STUDENT-FILE, PUNCHED-CARD, STUDENT-NAME, and HOMEROOM-NUMBER). In addition, he invents the names of processed files, records, and fields (PRINTED-REPORT-FILE, PRINTED-LINE, STUDENT-NAME-PRINT, and HOMEROOM-TEACHER-PRINT). He invents the names of the paragraphs in the PROCEDURE DIVISION (BEGINNING-OF-JOB, DETAIL-PROCESSING, and END-OF-JOB).

The names invented by the programmer must *not* appear on the reserved list. Since most of the names in the reserved list are not hyphened, the programmer is usually safe if he invents hyphened names. A hyphened name can consist of the words that appear individually in the reserved list. For example, CHECK and FILE appear in the reserved list. CHECK-FILE does not, and a programmer would be safe in inventing it.

ACCEPT	DE	INDEXED	PAGE	SENTENCE
ACCESS	DECIMAL-POINT	INDICATE	PAGE-COUNTER	SEQUENTIAL
ACTUAL	DECLARATIVES	INITIATE	PERFORM	SIZE
ADD	DEPENDING	INPUT	PF	SORT
ADVANCING	DESCENDING	INPUT-OUTPUT	PH	SOURCE
AFTER	DETAIL	INSTALLATION	PICTURE	SOURCE-
ALL	DIRECT	INTO	PLUS	COMPUTER
ALPHABETIC	DIRECT-ACCESS	INVALID	POSITIVE	SPACE
ALTER	DISPLAY	I-O	PRINT-SWITCH	SPACES
ALTERNATE	DISPLAY-ST	I-O-CONTROL	PROCEDURE	SPECIAL-NAMES
AND	DIVIDE	IS	PROCEED	STANDARD
APPLY	DIVISION		PROCESS	STOP
ARE		JUSTIFIED	PROCESSING	SUBTRACT
AREA	ELSE		PROGRAM-ID	SUM
AREAS	END	KEY	PROTECTION	SYMBOLIC
ASCENDING	ENDING			SYSIN
ASSIGN	ENTER	LABEL	QUOTE	SYSOUT
AT	ENTRY	LABELS	QUOTES	SYSPUNCH
AUTHOR	ENVIRONMENT	LAST		
	EQUAL	LEADING	RANDOM	TALLY
BEFORE	ERROR	LESS	RD	TALLYING
BEGINNING	EVERY	LINE	READ	TERMINATE
BLANK	EXAMINE	LINE-COUNTER	READY	THAN
BLOCK	EXHIBIT	LINES	RECORD	THEN
BY	EXIT	LINKAGE	RECORDING	THRU
		LOCK	RECORDS	TIMES
CALL	FD	LOW-VALUE	REDEFINES	TO
CF	FILE	LOW-VALUES	REEL	TRACE
CH	FILES		RELATIVE	TRACK-AREA
CHANGED	FILE-CONTROL	MODE	RELEASE	TRACKS
CHARACTERS	FILE-LIMIT	MORE-LABELS	REMARKS	TRANSFORM
CHECKING	FILLER	MOVE	REPLACING	TRY
CLOCK-UNITS	FINAL	MULTIPLY	REPORT	TYPE
CLOSE	FIRST		REPORTING	
COBOL	FOOTING	NAMED	REPORTS	UNIT
CODE	FOR	NEGATIVE	RERUN	UNIT-RECORD
COLUMN	FORM-OVERFLOW	NEXT	RESERVE	UNITS
COMMA	FROM	NO	RESET	UNTIL
COMPUTATIONAL		NOT	RESTRICTED	UPON
COMPUTATIONAL-1	GENERATE	NOTE	RETURN	USAGE
COMPUTATIONAL-2	GIVING	NUMERIC	REVERSED	USE
COMPUTATIONAL-3	GO		REWIND	USING
COMPUTE	GREATER	OBJECT-COMPUTER	REWRITE	UTILITY
CONFIGURATION	GROUP	OCCURS	RF'	
CONSOLE		OF	RH	VALUE
CONTAINS	HEADING	OH	RIGHT	VARYING
CONTROL	HIGH-VALUE	OMITTED	ROUNDED	
CONTROLS	HIGH-VALUES	ON	RUN	WHEN
COPY	HOLD	OPEN		WITH
CORRESPONDING		OR	SA	WORKING-
CREATING	IBM-360	ORGANIZATION	SAME	STORAGE
CYCLES	IDENTIFICATION	OTHERWISE	SD	WRITE
	IF	OUTPUT	SEARCH	WRITE-ONLY
DATA	IN	OV	SECTION	ZERO
DATE-COMPILED	INCLUDE	OVERFLOW	SECURITY	ZEROES
DATE-WRITTEN			SELECT	ZEROS

Figure 16-11. Partial list of reserved COBOL words

The names invented by the programmer can be anything at all. For END-OF-JOB the programmer could use COFFEE-BREAK or NO-END-IN-SIGHT, and the compiler would handle the translation accurately. What is important is that exactly the same name be used in a program each time it represents a particular heading, paragraph name, file, record, or field. The compiler always assigns the same cell address to the same name every time the name is used in the program.

While the names invented by the programmer may be selected by him, they should generally be meaningful to him and to anyone else reading the program. The language of a program is usually brief and highly stylized. In some cases, connecting words may be used by the programmer to improve the readability of his statements, but in the interest of brevity, these words are usually omitted. For example, CLOSE STUDENT-FILE could be written CLOSE THE STUDENT-FILE.

Rules for programmer-invented names

Certain rules must be observed by the programmer in inventing names for a COBOL program. These rules are as follows:

1. The same name must be used in a program each time it represents a particular heading, paragraph name, file, record, or field.
2. Names appearing in the COBOL reserved list may not be used in exactly the same way they appear on the list.
3. Letters of the alphabet, A through Z; digits, 0 through 9; and the hyphen may be used in inventing names, as long as the hyphen does not appear as the first or last character in the name.
4. Names invented by the programmer may consist of all alphabetic characters or a combination of alphabetic characters and figures. No name may consist of figures only or contain a space.

Study the following examples of programmer-invented names. Some meet the rules just stated; some do not.

Names		Comments
STUDENT NO	Wrong.	Space not permitted within name.
STUDENT-NO	Correct.	Meets all rules.
$-GROSS-PROFIT	Wrong.	Dollar sign not permitted.
-FILE-A23	Wrong.	Hyphen at beginning of name not permitted.
DATA	Wrong.	DATA is a COBOL reserved word.
GROSSPROFIT-	Wrong.	Hyphen at end of name not permitted.
314892	Wrong.	All figures not permitted.
STATION-XYZ-8	Correct.	Meets all the rules.
END-PROGRAM	Correct.	Meets all the rules.
END-OF-FILE	Wrong.	Name is a COBOL reserved word.

Chapter 16   Introduction to COBOL

PUNCTUATION RULES FOR COBOL

Punctuation marks appear in all COBOL programs. The following rules of punctuation must be observed at all times:

1. At least one space must appear between two successive words (except programmer-invented words, which may be hyphened).
2. A period, comma, or semicolon, when used, must immediately follow the word and must be followed in turn by at least one space.
3. Commas and semicolons are used for readability only and are never required in a statement.
4. Each division name, each section name, and each paragraph name must be ended with a period.
5. Each FD must end with a period after the last word in the last line of the file description.
6. Each statement or sentence in a paragraph must end with a period followed by a space.
7. Each field description must end with a period at the end of the PICTURE clause.

Several statements may be combined to form a sentence within the COBOL program. This is especially true in the PROCEDURE DIVISION. For example, you could write the following sequence of statements:

IF CLASSIFICATION IS EQUAL TO FRESHMAN-STUDENT, WRITE PRINTED-LINE. ADD ONE TO FRESHMAN-STUDENT-COUNT.

REVIEW QUESTIONS

1. In what ways does a COBOL program differ from a machine language program?
2. Does the computer process data directly from a COBOL program?
3. Give some examples of required names in a COBOL program. Must they be COBOL reserved words?
4. Give some examples of COBOL reserved words.
5. Give some examples of programmer-invented names.
6. Name the requirements that must be observed by the programmer in inventing and using names.
7. Which of the following names meet all the rules for inventing and using them in a COBOL program?

    CHECK   I-AM-TIRED
    IAMTIRED   FILE-422
    I AM TIRED   GO-TO WORK

8. What elements in a COBOL program must be followed by a period?
9. Are commas and semicolons needed in COBOL programs?
10. How many spaces must follow a period in a COBOL statement?

SUMMARY OF PROBLEM 1

The problem restated

1. On hand is a deck of cards containing the names of students, their homeroom numbers, and the names of their homeroom teachers.
2. Names of students are punched in Columns 1–20.
3. Homeroom numbers are punched in Columns 21–24.
4. Names of homeroom teachers are punched in Columns 25–34.
5. A program is to be written causing the computer to print a list of students, their homeroom numbers, and names of their homeroom teachers. There will be ten spaces between each of the three columns in the report. The entire list is to be centered horizontally on the output report, which will be printed on a 120-space printer.

The program

The complete program written to solve this problem is repeated in Figure 16-12. Each line of the program is punched into a separate card in the columns indicated on the program sheet.

Figure 16-12. Complete COBOL program for Problem 1

```
COBOL PROGRAM SHEET
System
Program    STUDENTS
Programmer WANØUS              Date 10-2-71
                                              Identification STUDENTS

001 010  IDENTIFICATIØN DIVISIØN.
    020  PRØGRAM-ID.
    030       'STUDENTS'.
    040  AUTHØR.
    050       WANØUS.
    060  DATE-WRITTEN.
    070       ØCTØBER 2, 1971.

002 010  ENVIRØNMENT DIVISIØN.
    020  CØNFIGURATIØN SECTIØN.
    030  SØURCE-CØMPUTER.
    040       IBM-360.
    050  ØBJECT-CØMPUTER.
    060       IBM-360.
    070  INPUT-ØUTPUT SECTIØN.
    080  FILE-CØNTRØL.
    090       SELECT STUDENT-FILE, ASSIGN TØ 'SYSIN' UNIT-RECØRD.
    100       SELECT PRINTED-REPØRT-FILE, ASSIGN TØ 'SYSØUT' UNIT-RECØRD.
```

Chapter 16   Introduction to COBOL

```
003010 DATA DIVISION.
   020    FILE SECTION.
   030    FD  STUDENT-FILE
   040        RECORDING MODE IS F
   050        RECORD CONTAINS 80 CHARACTERS
   060        LABEL RECORDS ARE OMITTED
   070        DATA RECORD IS PUNCHED-CARD.
   080    01  PUNCHED-CARD.
   090        02  STUDENT-NAME                PICTURE A(20).
   100        02  HOMEROOM-NUMBER             PICTURE 9(4).
   110        02  HOMEROOM-TEACHER            PICTURE A(10).
   120        02  FILLER                      PICTURE X(46).
   130    FD  PRINTED-REPORT-FILE
   140        RECORDING MODE IS F
   150        RECORD CONTAINS 120 CHARACTERS
   160        LABEL RECORDS ARE OMITTED
   170        DATA-RECORD IS PRINTED-LINE.
   180    01  PRINTED-LINE.
   190        02  FILLER                      PICTURE X(33).
   200        02  STUDENT-NAME-PRINT          PICTURE A(20).
   210        02  FILLER                      PICTURE X(10).
   220        02  HOMEROOM-NUMBER-PRINT       PICTURE 9(4).
   230        02  FILLER                      PICTURE X(10).
   240        02  HOMEROOM-TEACHER-PRINT      PICTURE A(10).
   250        02  FILLER                      PICTURE X(33).

004010 PROCEDURE DIVISION.
   020    BEGINNING-OF-JOB.
   030        OPEN INPUT STUDENT-FILE.
   040        OPEN OUTPUT PRINTED-REPORT-FILE.
   050        MOVE SPACES TO PRINTED-LINE.
   060    DETAIL-PROCESSING.
   070        READ STUDENT-FILE, AT END GO TO END-OF-JOB.
   080        MOVE STUDENT-NAME TO STUDENT-NAME-PRINT.
   090        MOVE HOMEROOM-NUMBER TO HOMEROOM-NUMBER-PRINT.
   100        MOVE HOMEROOM-TEACHER TO HOMEROOM-TEACHER-PRINT.
   110        WRITE PRINTED-LINE.
   120        MOVE SPACES TO PRINTED-LINE.
   130        GO TO DETAIL-PROCESSING.
   140    END-OF-JOB.
   150        CLOSE STUDENT-FILE.
   160        CLOSE PRINTED-REPORT-FILE.
   170        STOP RUN.
```

Figure 16-12. Complete COBOL program for Problem 1 (continued)

If you analyze this program, you will note that the commands are given in the PROCEDURE DIVISION for the computer to act on the data described in the DATA DIVISION. These data, in turn, are contained on FILES which are named in the ENVIRONMENT DIVISION, and these FILES are processed by hardware that is also named in the ENVIRONMENT DIVISION.

328 The electronic computer system Part 4

Two punched COBOL program cards are illustrated in Figure 16-13. The first card represents a single line from the DATA DIVISION. The second card represents a single line from the PROCEDURE DIVISION.

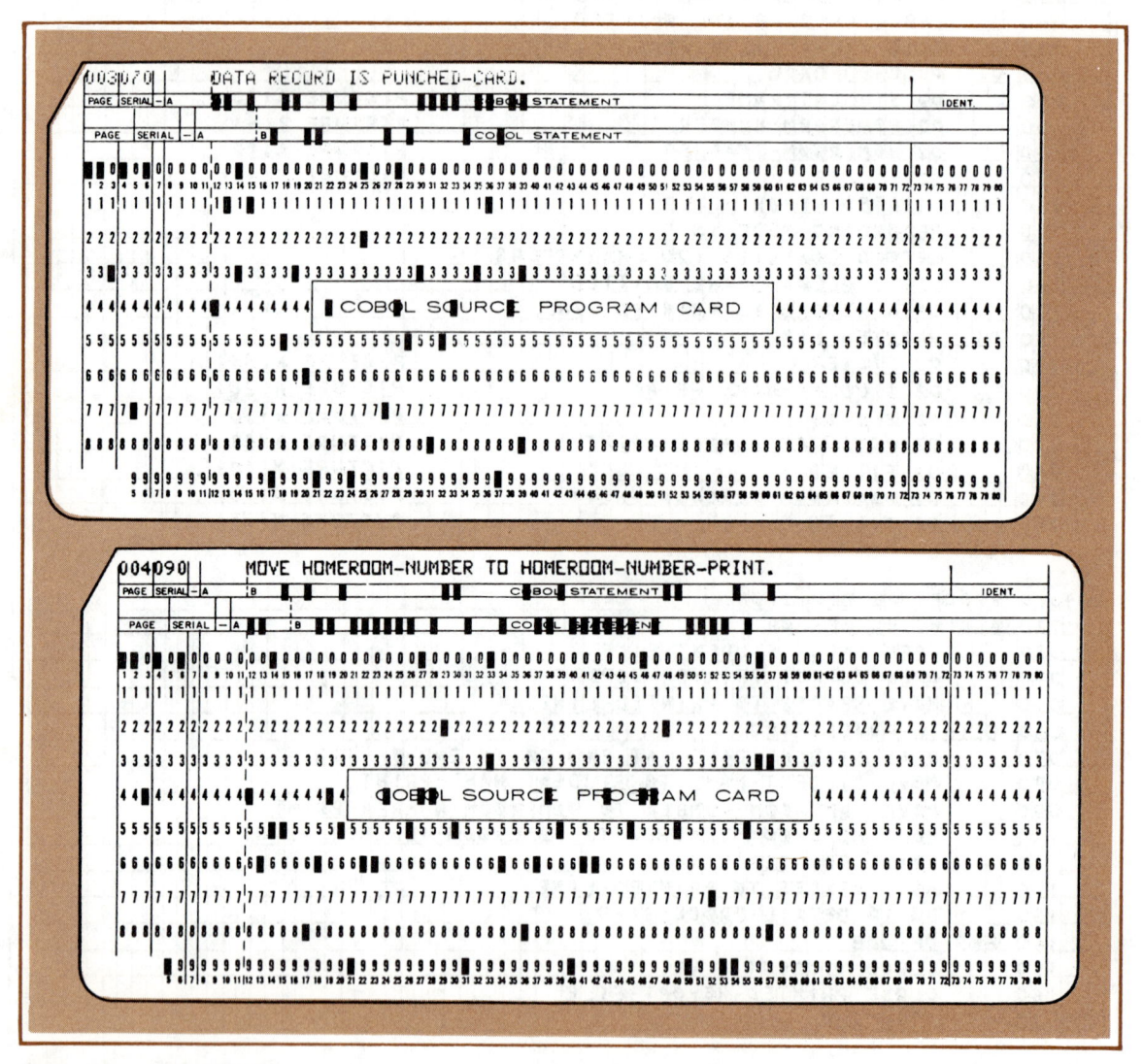

Figure 16-13. Sample COBOL program cards

The solution

The deck of punched cards comprising the compiler program is fed into the computer first. Next, the deck of COBOL program cards is fed into the machine. The compiler translates the COBOL program to machine langauge and prints a copy of the COBOL program at the same time.

Chapter 16   Introduction to COBOL

A deck of data cards, containing the names of students, homeroom numbers, and names of homeroom teachers, is then fed into the computer and processed under the direction of the COBOL program, which is now in machine language. The computer produces the printed report required in the problem. A part of the printed program is illustrated in Figure 16-14, and the printed report is illustrated in Figure 16-15.

Figure 16-14. Partial COBOL program as printed by the computer

```
001010 IDENTIFICATION DIVISION.
001020 PROGRAM-ID.
001030        'STUDENTS'.
001040 AUTHOR.
001050        WANOUS.
001060 DATE-WRITTEN.
001070        OCTOBER 2, 1971.
002010 ENVIRONMENT DIVISION.
002020 CONFIGURATION SECTION.
002030 SOURCE-COMPUTER.
002040        IBM-360.
002050 OBJECT-COMPUTER.
002060        IBM-360.
002070 INPUT-OUTPUT SECTION.
002080 FILE-CONTROL.
002090        SELECT STUDENT-FILE, ASSIGN TO 'SYSIN' UNIT-RECORD.
002100        SELECT PRINTED-REPORT-FILE, ASSIGN TO 'SYSOUT' UNIT-RECORD.
```

Figure 16-15. The printed report for Problem 1

```
BAILEY THOMAS R       0351    WINKLER
BENNETT JAMES         0351    WINKLER
BENSON ROGER L        0156    ZIMMERMAN
BLALOCK LOUISE        0363    JONES
BROWN HENRY L         0310    THOMAS
BUDNICK LYNETT        0119    BLALOCK
ERICKSON L W          0132    CARMICHAEL
FORRESTAL LYNN W      0211    ADAMS
GIBBS W E             0119    BLALOCK
HAMMACK FRANCIS       0210    HART
HANSEN MARY K         0211    ADAMS
HARRIS JOHN L         0363    JONES
HOLDER CHARLES        0363    JONES
HOWELL JACK E         0322    SMITH
ISSHIKI KOICHI        0322    SMITH
LOPP RICHARD T        0156    ZIMMERMAN
MITCHELL LOU          0363    JONES
MARTINO MARY L        0211    ADAMS
PERKINS WILLIAM       0322    SMITH
SHIPE THOMAS L        0300    JOHNSON
SPRING GENE R         0210    HART
TAYLOR MARY BETH      0211    ADAMS
TWISS JAMES L         0363    JONES
WASHINGTON CAROLYN    0132    CARMICHAEL
WILLIAMS ROGER        0211    ADAMS
WILLIAMSON MELANIE    0156    ZIMMERMAN
```

SUMMARY

COBOL is the name given to a symbolic language system for electronic computers. This system was developed by a committee representing the Federal Government, computer manufacturers, and private industry. The program statements in this system are written in a near-English form. Instruction addresses and the cell locations for data in storage are referred to by names instead of numbers. A COBOL program must be translated into machine language before the computer can process the program. The translation is handled by a compiler program obtained from the computer manufacturer. The compiler program is stored in the computer before the COBOL program is read into the machine.

A COBOL program consists of four divisions, which must appear in every program. The IDENTIFICATION DIVISION includes the name of the division, title of the program, name of the programmer, and the date the program was written. The ENVIRONMENT DIVISION includes the name of the division, names of sections in the division, names of the source and object computers, the name required to identify the input and output media and devices to be used, and the names the programmer assigns to the input and output files he will use in solving a problem.

The DATA DIVISION includes the name of the division and the names the programmer assigns to input and output files, records, and fields. Through PICTURE clauses the DATA DIVISION also indicates how data are arranged on input cards and how the processed data are to appear on output reports. The DATA DIVISION also may include a WORKING-STORAGE SECTION, in which the programmer assigns names to constants and storage locations for accumulating totals for a particular program. The WORKING-STORAGE SECTION is not used in the problem in this chapter.

In addition, level numbers are used in the DATA DIVISION to show the relationship of names assigned to records and fields in a program.

The PROCEDURE DIVISION includes the name of the division, paragraph names, and sentences (statements) relating to the opening, processing, and closing steps in a program. The PROCEDURE DIVISION specifies the actual steps the computer will follow in processing the data cards.

A COBOL program consists of some required names, some COBOL reserved words, and some names that are invented by the programmer. In inventing words, the programmer must be guided by a number of rules. The punctuation and format of his statements are also subject to strict regulation by COBOL. When names are used properly and when the statements of a program are punched in the proper columns of program cards, a COBOL compiler can translate the source program into an object program that a computer can use in processing data.

Chapter 16 Introduction to COBOL

REVIEW QUESTIONS

1. What is the purpose of the COBOL program to be written for Problem 1 of this chapter?
2. May more than one line of the program be punched into a data card?
3. Which deck of punched cards is fed into the computer first?
4. What is the second deck of cards to be fed into the computer?
5. What is the purpose of the compiler program?
6. After the first two decks of punched program cards are fed into the computer, what type of printed output is produced?
7. Which deck of cards is fed into the computer last?
8. Which one of the four divisions of a COBOL program actually gives the step-by-step directions for processing the data cards in the program?
9. What are the three types of names used in a COBOL program?
10. Why must COBOL rules be so strict?

STUDY GUIDE

Complete Study Guide 16 by following the instructions in your STUDY GUIDES booklet.

PROJECT

Complete Project 16-1 by following the instructions in your PROJECTS booklet.

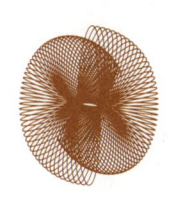

CHAPTER 17

COBOL APPLICATIONS

It should now be obvious why COBOL is frequently referred to as programming in a near-English computer language. An individual with little or no training in programming would be able to understand and follow the logic of the simple program written in Chapter 16. To the untrained, this program may seem like highly abbreviated "baby-talk," because many of the normally used words such as "the" and "and" have been omitted. This reference to "baby-talk" is closer to the truth than may be believed at first. Keep in mind that computers *cannot* think, make decisions, or function in any logical manner without some form of instruction. Therefore, computers are similar to babies in many ways.

Most programs required in actual business situations are more complicated than the one completed in Chapter 16; but all computer users, with very few exceptions, use programs to perform simple listing operations similar to those explained and illustrated in this text.

The knowledge gained about COBOL up to this point will become the foundation on which will be added more commands (verbs or operations) until there is a fairly complete understanding of the basic COBOL language.

So far, many of the required elements of a COBOL program have been explained. These elements will be continually reviewed as the solutions to the problems in this chapter are developed.

The next problem will be an extension of the COBOL program solved in Chapter 16, with slightly different input data. This problem is similar to the one that was block-diagrammed and solved in machine language in Chapter 15 (Figures 15–17 and 15–18). The block diagram and program are repeated here for easy reference.

PROGRAM CHART

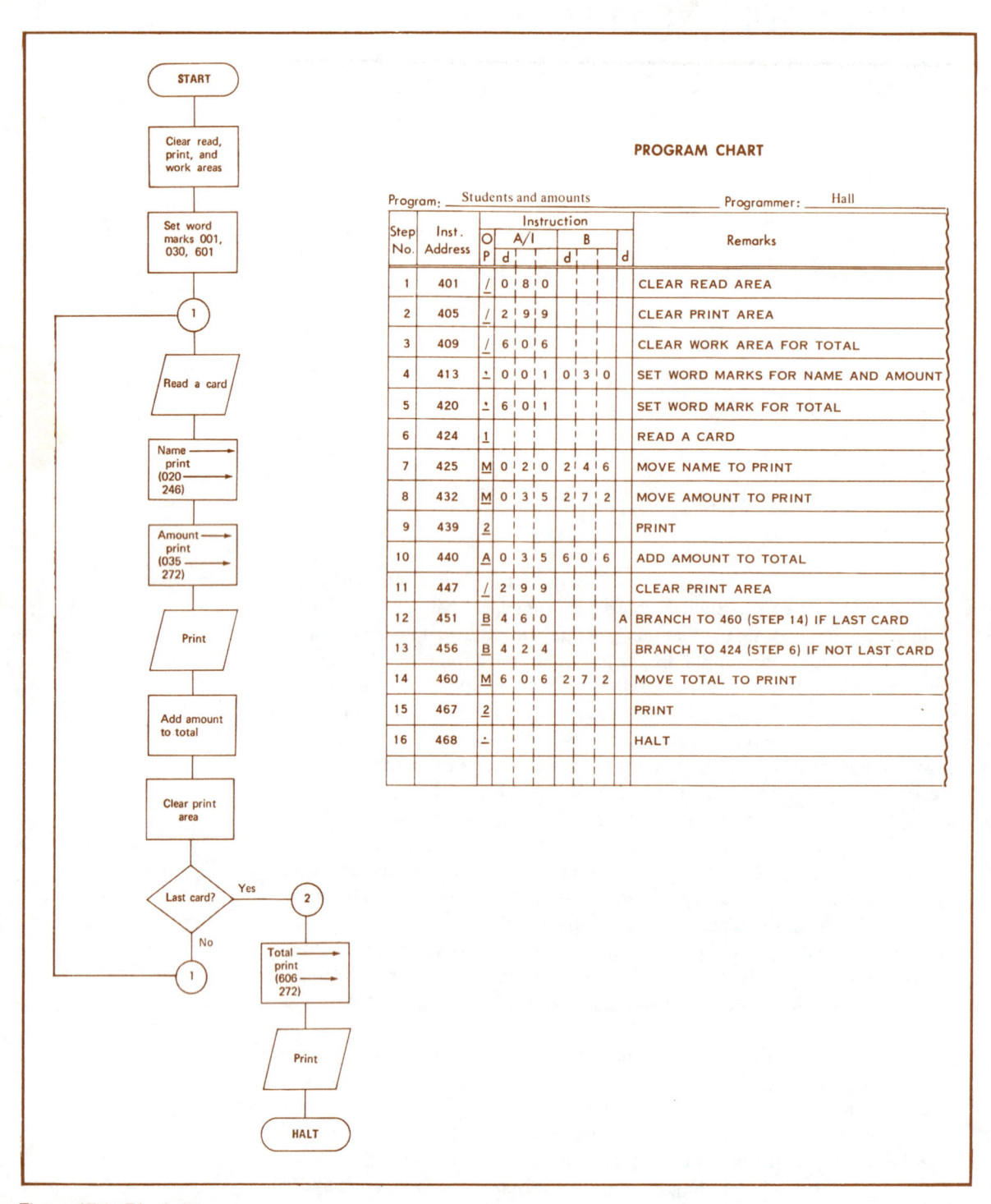

Program: __Students and amounts__   Programmer: __Hall__

Step No.	Inst. Address	O/P	A/I d		B d		d	Remarks
1	401	/	0 8 0					CLEAR READ AREA
2	405	/	2 9 9					CLEAR PRINT AREA
3	409	/	6 0 6					CLEAR WORK AREA FOR TOTAL
4	413	,	0 0 1		0 3 0			SET WORD MARKS FOR NAME AND AMOUNT
5	420	,	6 0 1					SET WORD MARK FOR TOTAL
6	424	1						READ A CARD
7	425	M	0 2 0		2 4 6			MOVE NAME TO PRINT
8	432	M	0 3 5		2 7 2			MOVE AMOUNT TO PRINT
9	439	2						PRINT
10	440	A	0 3 5		6 0 6			ADD AMOUNT TO TOTAL
11	447	/	2 9 9					CLEAR PRINT AREA
12	451	B	4 6 0				A	BRANCH TO 460 (STEP 14) IF LAST CARD
13	456	B	4 2 4					BRANCH TO 424 (STEP 6) IF NOT LAST CARD
14	460	M	6 0 6		2 7 2			MOVE TOTAL TO PRINT
15	467	2						PRINT
16	468	.						HALT

Figure 17-1. Block diagram and machine language program from Chapter 15

Chapter 17 COBOL applications

Although the block diagram repeated in Figure 17-1 was planned for use with a machine language program, the diagram is still significant to COBOL programmers. An important point to remember is this: the programming language may differ, but the basic logic for solving a problem will not.

Figure 17-2. Sample input cards for Chapter 17 problems

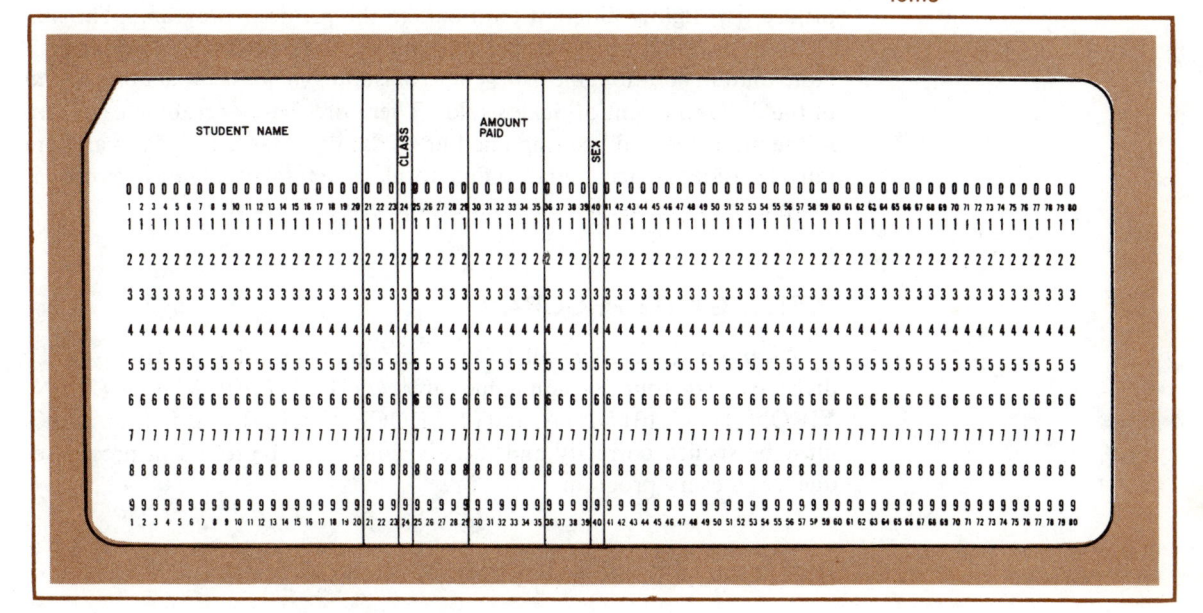

PROBLEM 1

1. The names of students are punched in Columns 1–20.
2. The class-code is punched in Column 24.
3. The sales amount is punched in Columns 30–35.
4. The sex-code is punched in Column 40.
5. A program is to be written that will cause the computer to print a two-column report.
    (a) The student name is to appear in the first column and the sales amount for each student in the second column.
    (b) The total of all sales amounts is to be printed at the end of the report following the last line of print.
    (c) Ten spaces are to appear between the two columns with the total amount under the Sales Amount column.
    (d) The report will be centered on a page 120 spaces wide.

In this problem the data cards are punched with blank columns between data fields, requiring a slightly different approach to planning the format for the data in the DATA DIVISION. FILLER areas will have to be identified between data fields in addition to the FILLER (unused) columns at the end of each card.

In Chapter 16, a COBOL program was written for printing a list of students, their homeroom numbers, and their homeroom teachers. The basic difference between the COBOL program in Chapter 16 and the program now being planned is that the computer will now be instructed to print a list slightly different than that in the previous program. The new COBOL program will list dollar amounts of student sales. See Figure 17-1. Note that, in addition, *the instructions must provide for accumulating a total* of the dollar amount of tickets sold. Therefore, besides reading each card in the input file and printing one line of data per card, each sales amount must be added to accumulate a final total. The total of all sales amounts is to appear as the last line of print on the printed report.

WRITING THE PROGRAM

As discussed earlier, all COBOL programs must have four specific divisions. The four division names are: (1) IDENTIFICATION, (2) ENVIRONMENT, (3) DATA, and (4) PROCEDURE. These division names must be spelled correctly and the divisions must be found in proper sequence in every program.

IDENTIFICATION DIVISION

The IDENTIFICATION DIVISION for the new program must be written first. Most of the entries in this division are required COBOL entries. Recall that the required entries are underlined. The underline is used only as a teaching device and is not part of the program. The required entries are as follows:

010 IDENTIFICATION DIVISION.

020 PROGRAM-ID.

040 AUTHOR.

060 DATE-WRITTEN.

Example

Once completed, the IDENTIFICATION DIVISION for the new program would look like this:

010 IDENTIFICATION DIVISION.

020 PROGRAM-ID.

030   'SALES1'.

Chapter 17　COBOL applications

040　AUTHOR.

050　　　WAGNER.

060　DATE-WRITTEN.

070　　　FEBRUARY 2, 1971.

Figure 17-3. IDENTIFICATION DIVISION of COBOL program

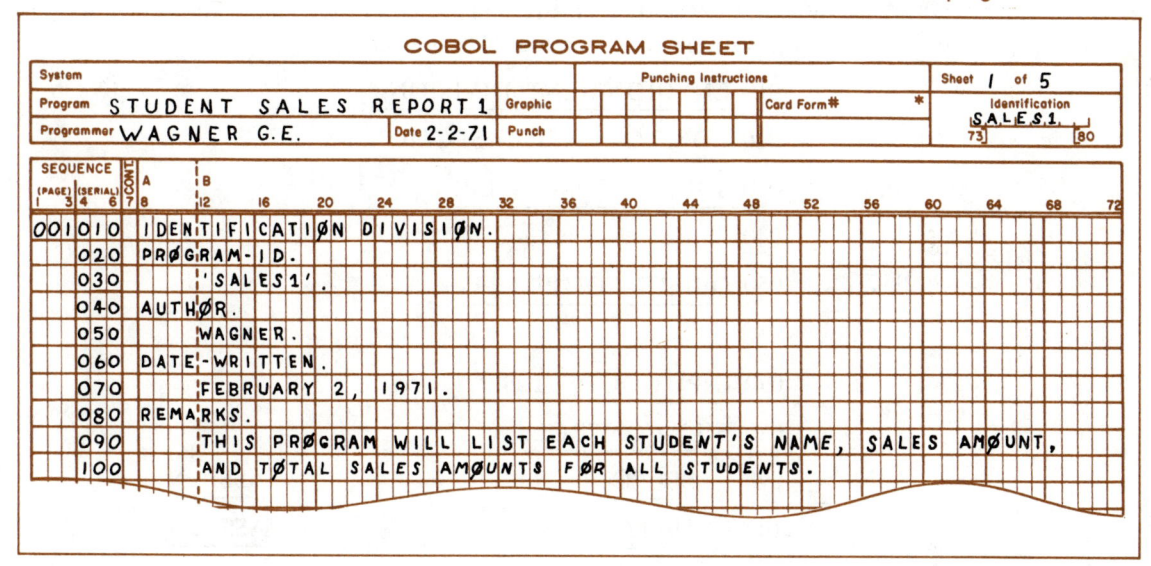

```
COBOL PROGRAM SHEET
System
Program    STUDENT  SALES  REPORT 1
Programmer WAGNER G.E.        Date 2-2-71
Sheet 1 of 5
Identification SALES 1

001010 IDENTIFICATIØN DIVISIØN.
   020 PRØGRAM-ID.
   030      'SALES1'.
   040 AUTHØR.
   050      WAGNER.
   060 DATE-WRITTEN.
   070      FEBRUARY 2, 1971.
   080 REMARKS.
   090      THIS PRØGRAM WILL LIST EACH STUDENT'S NAME, SALES AMØUNT,
   100      AND TØTAL SALES AMØUNTS FØR ALL STUDENTS.
```

Program identification

The PROGRAM-ID listed on Line 030 can be any name that does not exceed eight characters in length. This program name (Line 030), the author's name (Line 050), and the date (Line 070) are written in order to have positive identification of the type of program and the programmer. The foregoing information is advisable for clarity in later review of the program should a problem arise.

The eight-character-length limitation for the PROGRAM-ID creates some problems since the use of completely descriptive and meaningful names is limited. This limitation is required on the IBM 360 computer because the ID is also used as an identification label if the program is stored on tape and disk files. To compensate for this limitation, the REMARKS section can be used, and this allows the programmer to write anything he desires without restrictions.

In this program, therefore, the additional explanatory remarks (Lines 080, 090, and 100) are written and inserted after the date entry in the IDENTIFICATION DIVISION. Note that the paragraph name RE-

MARKS is written at the A-Margin and the actual explanation begins at the B-Margin. Figure 17-3 contains the completed IDENTIFICATION DIVISION after the remarks have been included.

ENVIRONMENT DIVISION

The ENVIRONMENT DIVISION appears next in a COBOL program and it, like the IDENTIFICATION DIVISION, has a large portion of the entries specified. The required entries are:

010 ENVIRONMENT DIVISION.

020 CONFIGURATION SECTION.

030 SOURCE-COMPUTER.

040

050 OBJECT-COMPUTER.

060

070 INPUT-OUTPUT SECTION.

080 FILE-CONTROL.

090   SELECT   ASSIGN   .

100   SELECT   ASSIGN   .

All that is left for you to do in this division is to fill in the computer models in Lines 040 and 060, provide your own file names, assign the input file to one of the computer units, and assign the output file to an output unit. The names of the files and of the input and output units are inserted in the blanks on Lines 090 and 100. The input file will be STUDENT-SALES-FILE, and the output file will be PRINTED-REPORT-FILE. In this problem, as in Chapter 16, the assignments will be made to UNIT-RECORD, which is the IBM name for the punched card input and printed output devices that you will be using. Like UNIT-RECORD, 'SYSIN' and 'SYSOUT' are names that may be used with the IBM 360 computer.

Example

The completed division would appear as follows:

010 ENVIRONMENT DIVISION.

020 CONFIGURATION SECTION.

030 SOURCE-COMPUTER.

040   IBM-360.

```
050 OBJECT-COMPUTER.
060     IBM-360.
070 INPUT-OUTPUT SECTION.
080 FILE-CONTROL.
090     SELECT STUDENT-SALES-FILE, ASSIGN TO 'SYSIN'
        UNIT-RECORD.
100     SELECT PRINTED-REPORT-FILE, ASSIGN TO 'SYS-
        OUT' UNIT-RECORD.
```

See Figure 17-4 for the ENVIRONMENT DIVISION as it would appear on a COBOL program sheet.

Figure 17-4. ENVIRONMENT DIVISION of COBOL program

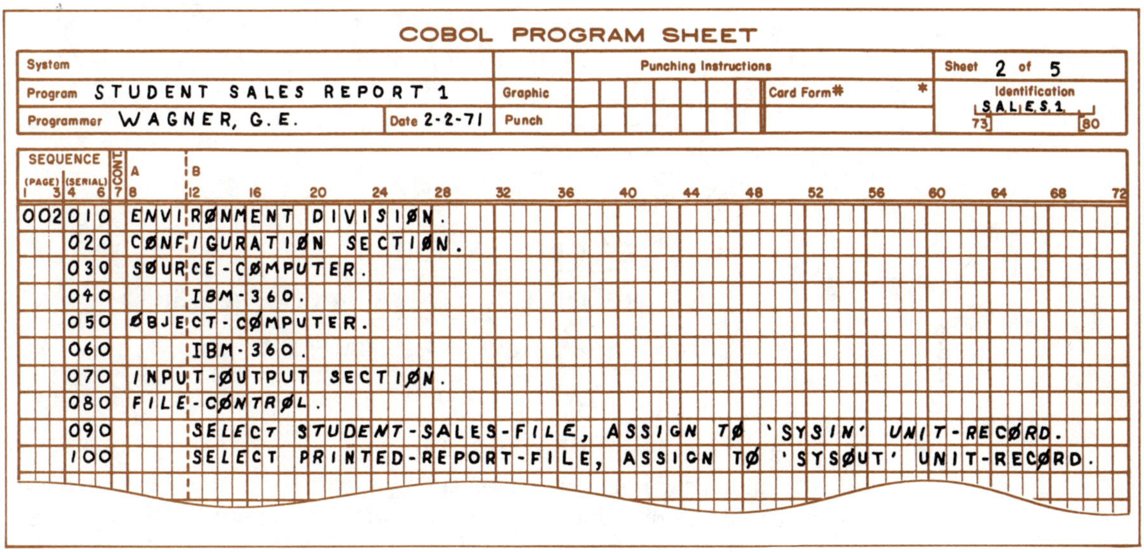
COBOL PROGRAM SHEET

System | Punching Instructions | Sheet 2 of 5
Program STUDENT SALES REPORT 1 | Graphic | Card Form # *
Programmer WAGNER, G.E. | Date 2-2-71 | Punch
Identification SALES1 (73–80)

```
002010 ENVIRONMENT DIVISION.
   020 CONFIGURATION SECTION.
   030 SOURCE-COMPUTER.
   040     IBM-360.
   050 OBJECT-COMPUTER.
   060     IBM-360.
   070 INPUT-OUTPUT SECTION.
   080 FILE-CONTROL.
   090     SELECT STUDENT-SALES-FILE, ASSIGN TO 'SYSIN' UNIT-RECORD.
   100     SELECT PRINTED-REPORT-FILE, ASSIGN TO 'SYSOUT' UNIT-RECORD.
```

DATA DIVISION

The third division in any COBOL program is the DATA DIVISION. This is the first division in which any great degree of difference appears from program to program. You will note that in Figure 17-5 the DATA DIVISION is written on two pages.

Page and line numbers

There are two ways to continue a division of a COBOL program from one page to the next. The line numbers may be continued in consecutive order. For example, the second page of the DATA DIVISION could begin with Line 260 instead of Line 010. However, in actual business situations the programmer does begin each page of a division with Line 010.

Many programs are quite long and may have more step numbers than could be fitted in the 3-column space (Columns 4–6) on the COBOL program sheet if the line numbers were continued in consecutive order. As long as each new *page* is numbered consecutively in Columns 1–3, the program cards can be kept in proper sequence. (For example, 004/010 would logically follow 003/010.) In this text the second page of the DATA DIVISION will begin with Line 010.

Required input statements

There are always certain required entries in the DATA DIVISION. The required entries for the input portion are as follows:

003/010 DATA DIVISION.
      020 FILE SECTION.
      030 FD
      040   RECORDING MODE IS F
      050   RECORD CONTAINS 80 CHARACTERS
      060   LABEL RECORD IS OMITTED
      070   DATA RECORD IS

The missing entries in the input portion are not nearly so obvious; so the rules for writing the input portion of the DATA DIVISION should be reviewed before proceeding. The following items must be included:

1. Name of the division: DATA DIVISION.
2. Names of sections in the division: FILE SECTION. (WORKING-STORAGE SECTION, if needed).
3. Name that the programmer invents for each input file. The name used in the DATA DIVISION for each file must be the same as the name used in the ENVIRONMENT DIVISION.
4. Name that the programmer invents for each record in the input file.
5. Name that the programmer invents for each field of data on each record in the input file.
6. A PICTURE clause to correspond to each input field of data.

   A PICTURE clause includes the following information:

   (a) Code classification of each field in the record: numeric, alphabetic, or alphameric (mixed).

(b) Number of characters in each field in the input record. The word PICTURE is a COBOL word that indicates that the code classification of each field and the number of characters in the field follow.

Optional input statements

In addition, the following information may or may not be included, depending upon its use in the program:

1. Identification of the storage areas that will contain constants and data being accumulated, such as counts or totals.

2. Location of decimal points, when needed, in numeric characters. (Decimal points will not be required in this chapter.)

Input file description

In Line 030 of the DATA DIVISION (Figure 17-5), a file name must be supplied by the programmer to complete the *File Description*. This name must be the same name that was assigned to the input file in the ENVIRONMENT DIVISION. By referring to Line 090 of the ENVIRONMENT DIVISION, note that the name STUDENT-SALES-FILE is used and must be inserted on Line 030 of the DATA DIVISION following the letters FD and a space.

Line 040 is required by the IBM 360 computer. You will remember that the Letter F (fixed) describes the fact that the punched card contains a fixed number of columns (80).

Line 050 is required to identify the length of each record in the file. (RECORD CONTAINS 80 CHARACTERS) This statement aids the computer in making the most efficient use of its memory.

In Line 060 the statement regarding the use of label records is required, although label records are not being used in this problem since the data are on punched cards rather than magnetic tape or disks.

In Line 070 the programmer is required to supply the name of the record that is found in the input file. The same record name, PUNCHED-CARD, will be used here as was used in our first COBOL program.

Now the program begins to take on a slightly different look from the one explained in Chapter 16, because the input cards are punched with different data fields and the data fields are separated by spaces. See Figure 17-5.

```
                        COBOL PROGRAM SHEET
System                              Punching Instructions         Sheet  3 of 5
Program  STUDENT SALES REPORT 1    Graphic │  │  │  │  Card Form# *  Identification
Programmer WAGNER, G.E.   Date 2-2-71  Punch                             SALES 1

003 010  DATA DIVISION.
    020  FILE SECTION.
    030  FD  STUDENT-SALES-FILE
    040      RECORDING MODE IS F
    050      RECORD CONTAINS 80 CHARACTERS
    060      LABEL RECORD IS OMITTED
    070      DATA RECORD IS PUNCHED-CARD.
    080  01  PUNCHED-CARD.
    090      02  STUDENT-NAME        PICTURE A(20).
    100      02  FILLER              PICTURE XXX.
    110      02  CLASS-CODE          PICTURE 9.
    120      02  FILLER              PICTURE X(5).
    130      02  SALES-AMT           PICTURE 9(6).
    140      02  FILLER              PICTURE X(4).
    150      02  SEX-CODE            PICTURE 9.
    160      02  FILLER              PICTURE X(40).
    170  FD  PRINTED-REPORT-FILE
    180      RECORDING MODE IS F
    190      RECORD CONTAINS 120 CHARACTERS
    200      LABEL RECORD IS OMITTED
    210      DATA RECORD IS PRINTED-LINE.
    220  01  PRINTED-LINE.
    230      02  FILLER              PICTURE X(42).
    240      02  STUDENT-NAME-PRINT  PICTURE A(20).
    250      02  FILLER              PICTURE X(10).
004 010      02  SALES-AMT-PRINT     PICTURE 9(6).
    020      02  FILLER              PICTURE X(42).
    030  WORKING-STORAGE SECTION.
    040  77  SALES-TOTAL             PICTURE 9(6).
```

Figure 17-5. DATA DIVISION of COBOL program

Each input record must be described in COBOL language in order to identify the nature and format of the data appearing within the record. Note that data names are invented and assigned to each field on the input record. The input data record would be described as follows:

080	01 PUNCHED-CARD.	
090	02 STUDENT-NAME	PICTURE A(20).
100	02 FILLER	PICTURE XXX.
110	02 CLASS-CODE	PICTURE 9.
120	02 FILLER	PICTURE X(5).
130	02 SALES-AMT	PICTURE 9(6).

140	02 FILLER	PICTURE X(4).
150	02 SEX-CODE	PICTURE 9.
160	02 FILLER	PICTURE X(40).

Filler statements

Unlike the first COBOL program, unused columns appear between the data fields on the input punched data card. (See Figure 17-2, p. 335.) The unused columns must be identified properly so that the computer will know how many columns to ignore before reading the next data field. These unused (blank) columns are identified by using the word FILLER. Refer to Lines 100, 120, 140, and 160 for the proper use of this COBOL word.

On Line 100, the PICTURE clause is PICTURE XXX. This means that the field will be programmed for a filler of three blank spaces. (Remember, the X is used for alphameric characters or for blanks.) Instead of using parentheses and writing the code as X(3)., the programmer wrote the X three times, thus saving a space. This practice is often followed with fields of less than four characters. Lines 110 and 150 could have the PICTURE statement written as 9(1), but the 9 by itself signifies one numeric digit. The PICTURE clause can be written on Line 130 as 999999 but 9(6). is shorter. The use of parentheses with the field length enclosed is considered a form of COBOL shorthand and this technique is used whenever programming time can be saved.

Output file description

Now that the input file has been described in detail, the output file must be described in the same manner. The required entries appear as follows:

170	FD	
180	RECORDING MODE IS F	
190	RECORD CONTAINS 120 CHARACTERS	
*200	LABEL RECORD IS OMITTED	
210	DATA RECORD IS	.

The output portion of the DATA DIVISION must include the following:

1. Name that the programmer invents for each output file. The name used in the DATA DIVISION for each file must be the same as the name used in the ENVIRONMENT DIVISION.

*NOTE: The label record may be referred to either in the singular or plural.

2. Name that the programmer invents for each record in the output file.
3. Name that the programmer invents for each field of data on each record in the output file.
4. A PICTURE clause to correspond to each output field of data.

The complete output description will appear as follows:

```
170      FD   PRINTED-REPORT-FILE
180           RECORDING MODE IS F
190           RECORD CONTAINS 120 CHARACTERS
200           LABEL RECORD IS OMITTED
210           DATA RECORD IS PRINTED-LINE.
220      01 PRINTED-LINE.
230         02 FILLER                PICTURE X(42).
240         02 STUDENT-NAME-PRINT    PICTURE A(20).
250         02 FILLER                PICTURE X(10).
004/010     02 SALES-AMT-PRINT       PICTURE 9(6).
020         02 FILLER                PICTURE X(42).
```

The preceding description of the output record causes the two columns of information, student name and sales amount, to be printed near the center of the 120-space line with a 42-space margin on each side of the report and 10 spaces between the two columns. (The class code and sex code on the input data card are not mentioned in the output portion of the DATA DIVISION because the printed list does not require class or sex identifications. Remember, the input portion of the DATA DIVISION describes the punched card in detail. The output portion describes only what the programmer wishes to appear on the printed report.)

Subdividing data items

Level numbers 01, 02, and 03 were discussed in the previous chapter. These level numbers indicate the relationship of the data items in the program and are required whenever a record is subdivided into fields.

In the DATA DIVISION of COBOL programs, there are two types of items:

1. *A group item* — an item that can be "broken down" or subdivided into smaller items. For example, a group item can be a proper name. It is possible to subdivide a proper name into the first, last, and

middle names. An address is a group item because it may be subdivided into a street address, city, state and zip code.
2. *An elementary item* — an item that cannot be subdivided any further. For example, a zip code can be considered an elementary item.

When a programmer is assigning level numbers, he organizes the facts as he would for any outline. For example, assume that a record consists of a student's name and homeroom number. The entire record will be referred to as PUNCHED-CARD. The levels might be arranged as follows:

01 PUNCHED-CARD.	(group item)
02 STUDENT-NAME	(group item)
03 LAST-NAME	(elementary item)
03 FIRST-NAME	(elementary item)
03 MIDDLE-INITIAL	(elementary item)
02 HOMEROOM-NUMBER	(elementary item)

The programmer is free to assign levels of 01 through 49, if necessary, for any of the group or elementary items. For the introductory type of programming to be done in this textbook, however, there will be no extensive subdividing of group items. In Figure 17-5, p. 342, you will note that the input and output records are not divided beyond the second level.

WORKING-STORAGE SECTION

One additional section is required in the DATA DIVISION for the completion of this problem: the WORKING-STORAGE SECTION. This section is used as a temporary storage area for computed results or other information developed during processing. The *WORKING-STORAGE SECTION*, therefore, is used to provide working areas in memory that are not part of the input and output files. A temporary storage area is needed to accumulate the total of all sales amounts. The temporary storage area is provided in the WORKING-STORAGE SECTION. This section in the program would appear as follows:

004/030 WORKING-STORAGE SECTION.
    040 77 SALES-TOTAL   PICTURE 9(6).

Entries for arithmetic computations in the WORKING-STORAGE SECTION are always assigned a level number of 77. The 77 is written at the A-Margin and is followed by the name assigned to the storage area. In the foregoing example, the work area is reserved for accumulating a total and the cell addresses are assigned the name SALES-TOTAL. The PICTURE clause indicates that this total will be numeric and that six positions are to be reserved for the total.

When items appear in the WORKING-STORAGE section at Level 77, they must always precede other items with different levels. This concept is followed in the WORKING-STORAGE SECTION of Figure 17-5, p. 342.

The DATA DIVISION is now complete. Figure 17-5 illustrates how it is written on COBOL program sheets.

PROCEDURE DIVISION

Now that the first three divisions have been written, you are ready to begin on the last division of the program. This is the division that provides the actual instructions to the computer regarding the procedure to be followed in the completion of the task at hand. This division is appropriately titled, PROCEDURE DIVISION. The required entries in the PROCEDURE DIVISION are:

010 PROCEDURE DIVISION.

030   OPEN INPUT

040   OPEN OUTPUT

190   CLOSE

200   CLOSE

210   STOP RUN.

You will note that the PROCEDURE DIVISION has very few required statements, because it contains the instructions to the computer. For this reason, the PROCEDURE DIVISION varies from program to program. The division name is always required as well as a statement or statements to open and close all files used by the program in processing the data and preparing the output. Before any data files can be processed, the input and output files must be opened. At the completion of the program these same files must be closed and the computer instructed to stop.

Example

The completed PROCEDURE DIVISION would appear as follows:

010 PROCEDURE DIVISION.

020 BEGINNING-OF-JOB.

030   OPEN INPUT STUDENT-SALES-FILE.

040   OPEN OUTPUT PRINTED-REPORT-FILE.

050   MOVE SPACES TO PRINTED-LINE.

060	MOVE ZEROS TO SALES-TOTAL.
070	DETAIL-PROCESSING.
080	READ STUDENT-SALES-FILE, AT END GO TO END-OF-JOB.
090	ADD SALES-AMT TO SALES-TOTAL.
100	MOVE STUDENT-NAME TO STUDENT-NAME-PRINT.
110	MOVE SALES-AMT TO SALES-AMT-PRINT.
120	WRITE PRINTED-LINE.
130	MOVE SPACES TO PRINTED-LINE.
140	GO TO DETAIL-PROCESSING.
150	END-OF-JOB.
160	MOVE SALES-TOTAL TO SALES-AMT-PRINT.
170	WRITE PRINTED-LINE.
180	CLOSE STUDENT-SALES-FILE.
190	CLOSE PRINTED-REPORT-FILE.
200	STOP RUN.

All names of data used in the PROCEDURE DIVISION have been previously described (defined) in the DATA DIVISION. It is extremely important not only that the same names be used but also that the names be spelled exactly the same. Once assigned, a name is permanently assigned to the same area of memory and to the same type of data for the duration of the program.

Looping in COBOL

All statements in the PROCEDURE DIVISION except paragraph names begin at the B-Margin. Paragraph names are desirable for clarity at the beginning of each new sequence or routine. This is the reason for including the first paragraph name (Line 020, BEGINNING-OF-JOB) in this program. However, paragraph names are *required* at the beginning of any sequence to which a branch will be made from the normal sequence in the program, thus creating a loop in the program. The normal sequence, of course, is the processing of each instruction or statement in the order in which it appears in the program. The normal sequence can be altered by using the GO TO statement and naming ("referencing") the paragraph name of the new sequence or routine to which the computer is to branch.

Figure 17-6 has the paragraph name DETAIL-PROCESSING on Line 070. On Line 140 the instruction is GO TO DETAIL-PROCESSING. This loop is repeated until the last card is read, when the computer will branch to the new procedure outlined on Line 150, END-OF-JOB. At this point, the question may be asked, "How does the computer know when to go to the end of the job?" On Line 080, it can be noted that the first step in the instructions for DETAIL-PROCESSING is an order to read the card and if the last card has been read the order is to go to the end of the job. (READ STUDENT-SALES-FILE, AT END GO TO END-OF-JOB.) A READ statement followed by an AT END statement is a *last card test* in COBOL. The last card test is discussed in greater detail on p. 353.

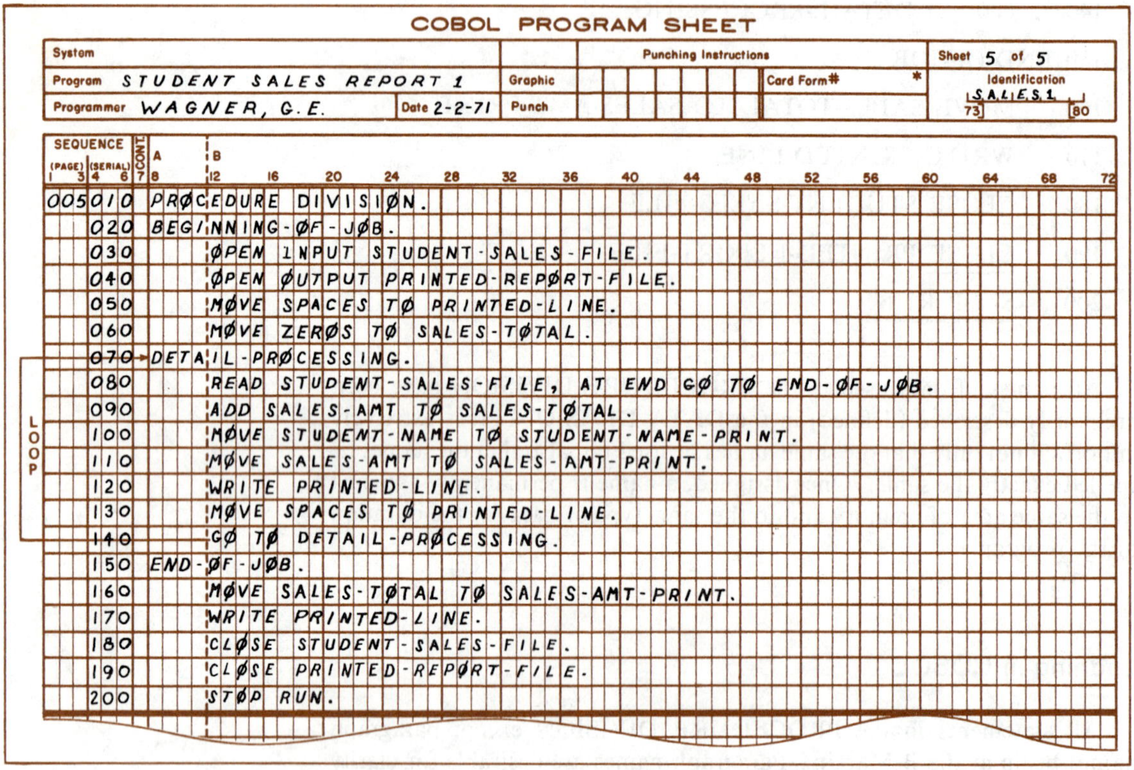

Figure 17-6. PROCEDURE DIVISION of COBOL program

```
COBOL PROGRAM SHEET
System
Program     STUDENT SALES REPORT 1
Programmer  WAGNER, G.E.         Date 2-2-71
Sheet 5 of 5
Identification S.A.L.E.S.1

005 010  PROCEDURE DIVISION.
    020  BEGINNING-OF-JOB.
    030      OPEN INPUT STUDENT-SALES-FILE.
    040      OPEN OUTPUT PRINTED-REPORT-FILE.
    050      MOVE SPACES TO PRINTED-LINE.
    060      MOVE ZEROS TO SALES-TOTAL.
    070  DETAIL-PROCESSING.
    080      READ STUDENT-SALES-FILE, AT END GO TO END-OF-JOB.
    090      ADD SALES-AMT TO SALES-TOTAL.
    100      MOVE STUDENT-NAME TO STUDENT-NAME-PRINT.
    110      MOVE SALES-AMT TO SALES-AMT-PRINT.
    120      WRITE PRINTED-LINE.
    130      MOVE SPACES TO PRINTED-LINE.
    140      GO TO DETAIL-PROCESSING.
    150  END-OF-JOB.
    160      MOVE SALES-TOTAL TO SALES-AMT-PRINT.
    170      WRITE PRINTED-LINE.
    180      CLOSE STUDENT-SALES-FILE.
    190      CLOSE PRINTED-REPORT-FILE.
    200      STOP RUN.
```

(Lines 070–140 bracketed as LOOP)

Clearing memory

The instructions on Lines 050 and 060 in the BEGINNING-OF-JOB paragraph clear areas of memory that will be used in this problem. These instructions are really instructions to clear storage. MOVE SPACES TO PRINTED-LINE will clear the print area and MOVE ZEROS TO SALES-TOTAL will clear the work area for accumulating a total. In machine

Chapter 17   COBOL applications   349

language, you will remember that it was also necessary to clear the read area of any previous word marks. In COBOL, however, the compiler program performs this function.

All print and working-storage areas should be cleared by the program before the computer is instructed to use these areas. This step is recommended for the same reason that an adding machine is cleared before using it. There may be information from a previous program in a particular area of memory that could cause mistakes if the old information were left in memory at the time of the running of the new program.

Memory is normally cleared in COBOL by moving either ZEROS or SPACES into it. In the case of a print area, spaces (blanks) should appear whenever there are no data to be printed, whereas zeros should appear in any areas in which totals will be accumulated. Zeros are considered to be numbers and can be added whereas spaces are considered alphameric characters in COBOL and, like the %, @, *, or $, the spaces cannot be added. Therefore, zeros should be used to clear areas for totals since addition will take place. Line 060 of Figure 17-6 indicates that zeros have been moved to SALES-TOTAL.

Management does not desire printed reports with zeros in all positions in which data are not printed. Thus, instead of zeros, blanks (spaces) are preferred between printed data to make the report easier to read. See Lines 050 and 130 of Figure 17-6. It is always good practice to clear the print area every time before moving new data into it (Line 130).

Addition

All of the other instructions (verbs) required in this program are familiar except one, ADD. The ADD verb, like the MOVE verb, follows the English language statement format as it would normally be used. ADD (something) TO (something). This statement takes the first value identified by the first name (something) and adds it to the second value, with the sum now replacing the second value. In machine language, the data from one cell address are added to the data in another cell address, and the results are stored in the second address. Again notice the similarity between COBOL and the machine language ADD instruction function.

Complete COBOL program for Problem 1

Now that the entire program for the student sales report has been completed, the program can be observed in its entirety. See Figure 17-7, pp. 350–351. This illustration shows the program written on COBOL programming sheets as the program would normally be written.

COBOL PROGRAM SHEET

System		Punching Instructions	Sheet of
Program STUDENT SALES REPORT 1	Graphic	Card Form # *	Identification SALES1 (73–80)
Programmer WAGNER G.E. Date 2-2-71	Punch		

```
001010 IDENTIFICATION DIVISION.
   020 PROGRAM-ID.
   030     'SALES1'.
   040 AUTHOR.
   050     WAGNER.
   060 DATE-WRITTEN.
   070     FEBRUARY 2, 1971.
   080 REMARKS.
   090     THIS PROGRAM WILL LIST EACH STUDENT'S NAME, SALES AMOUNT,
   100     AND TOTAL SALES AMOUNTS FOR ALL STUDENTS.

002010 ENVIRONMENT DIVISION.
   020 CONFIGURATION SECTION.
   030 SOURCE-COMPUTER.
   040     IBM-360.
   050 OBJECT-COMPUTER.
   060     IBM-360.
   070 INPUT-OUTPUT SECTION.
   080 FILE-CONTROL.
   090     SELECT STUDENT-SALES-FILE, ASSIGN TO 'SYSIN' UNIT-RECORD.
   100     SELECT PRINTED-REPORT-FILE, ASSIGN TO 'SYSOUT' UNIT-RECORD.

003010 DATA DIVISION.
   020 FILE SECTION.
   030 FD  STUDENT-SALES-FILE
   040     RECORDING MODE IS F
   050     RECORD CONTAINS 80 CHARACTERS
   060     LABEL RECORD IS OMITTED
   070     DATA RECORD IS PUNCHED-CARD.
   080 01  PUNCHED-CARD.
   090     02  STUDENT-NAME            PICTURE A(20).
   100     02  FILLER                  PICTURE XXX.
   110     02  CLASS-CODE              PICTURE 9.
   120     02  FILLER                  PICTURE X(5).
   130     02  SALES-AMT               PICTURE 9(6).
   140     02  FILLER                  PICTURE X(4).
   150     02  SEX-CODE                PICTURE 9.
   160     02  FILLER                  PICTURE X(40).
   170 FD  PRINTED-REPORT-FILE
   180     RECORDING MODE IS F
   190     RECORD CONTAINS 120 CHARACTERS
   200     LABEL RECORD IS OMITTED
   210     DATA RECORD IS PRINTED-LINE.
```

Figure 17-7. Complete COBOL program for Problem 1

Chapter 17 COBOL applications

```
    220  01  PRINTED-LINE.
    230      02  FILLER                  PICTURE X(42).
    240      02  STUDENT-NAME-PRINT      PICTURE A(20).
    250      02  FILLER                  PICTURE X(10).
004 010      02  SALES-AMT-PRINT         PICTURE 9(6).
    020      02  FILLER                  PICTURE X(42).
    030  WORKING-STORAGE SECTION.
    040  77  SALES-TOTAL                 PICTURE 9(6).

005 010  PROCEDURE DIVISION.
    020  BEGINNING-OF-JOB.
    030      OPEN INPUT STUDENT-SALES-FILE.
    040      OPEN OUTPUT PRINTED-REPORT-FILE.
    050      MOVE SPACES TO PRINTED-LINE.
    060      MOVE ZEROS TO SALES-TOTAL.
    070  DETAIL-PROCESSING.
    080      READ STUDENT-SALES-FILE, AT END GO TO END-OF-JOB.
    090      ADD SALES-AMT TO SALES-TOTAL.
    100      MOVE STUDENT-NAME TO STUDENT-NAME-PRINT.
    110      MOVE SALES-AMT TO SALES-AMT-PRINT.
    120      WRITE PRINTED-LINE.
    130      MOVE SPACES TO PRINTED-LINE.
    140      GO TO DETAIL-PROCESSING.
    150  END-OF-JOB.
    160      MOVE SALES-TOTAL TO SALES-AMT-PRINT.
    170      WRITE PRINTED-LINE.
    180      CLOSE STUDENT-SALES-FILE.
    190      CLOSE PRINTED-REPORT-FILE.
    200      STOP RUN.
```

Figure 17-7. Complete COBOL program for Problem 1 (continued)

Printed report for Problem 1

Figure 17-8 illustrates how the completed report would appear. The amount sold by each student is printed as a six-digit value, as described in the DATA DIVISION on 004/010.

Note, also, that the final total appears as the last print line of the report and in the same position as the individual amounts. This positioning was accomplished by the MOVE statement, Line 160 of the PROCEDURE DIVISION (MOVE SALES-TOTAL TO SALES-AMT-PRINT.). The total is moved to the print area named SALES-AMT-PRINT. This name is the same name associated with the print area used for each individual sales amount; therefore, the computer assumes that the total is to appear in the same column.

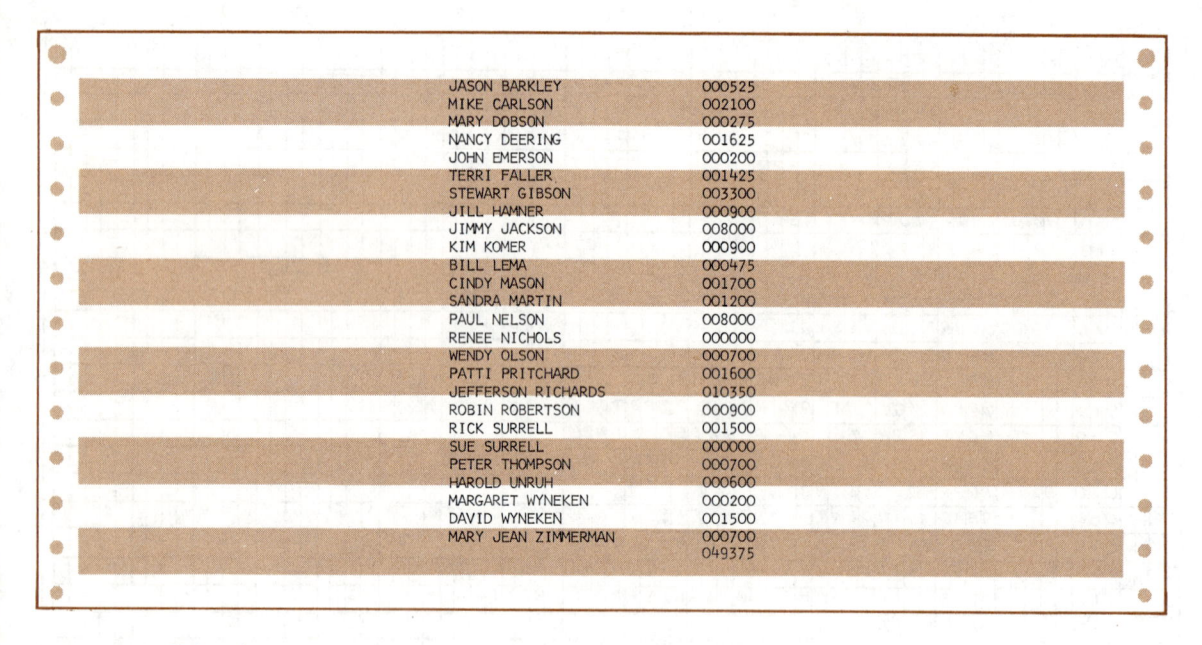

```
        JASON BARKLEY          000525
        MIKE CARLSON           002100
        MARY DOBSON            000275
        NANCY DEERING          001625
        JOHN EMERSON           000200
        TERRI FALLER           001425
        STEWART GIBSON         003300
        JILL HAMNER            000900
        JIMMY JACKSON          008000
        KIM KOMER              000900
        BILL LEMA              000475
        CINDY MASON            001700
        SANDRA MARTIN          001200
        PAUL NELSON            008000
        RENEE NICHOLS          000000
        WENDY OLSON            000700
        PATTI PRITCHARD        001600
        JEFFERSON RICHARDS     010350
        ROBIN ROBERTSON        000900
        RICK SURRELL           001500
        SUE SURRELL            000000
        PETER THOMPSON         000700
        HAROLD UNRUH           000600
        MARGARET WYNEKEN       000200
        DAVID WYNEKEN          001500
        MARY JEAN ZIMMERMAN    000700
                               049375
```

Figure 17-8. Printed report for Problem 1

REVIEW QUESTIONS

1. What is the maximum number of characters allowed in the PROGRAM-ID? How can the programmer give additional information in spite of this limitation?
2. What do the letters FD mean? In which division are they used?
3. Write the following PICTURE clause in another way:

    001   010   02   SALES-AMT   PICTURE   999999.

4. Describe how data are positioned in the print area to provide spaces between columns of information.
5. Explain the function of level numbers in the DATA DIVISION.
6. What is the difference between group and elementary items? Give an example of each.
7. When is the WORKING-STORAGE SECTION required?
8. What is the sequence of level numbers in the WORKING-STORAGE SECTION if 77 level numbers are present along with items of different levels?
9. What files must be opened in the PROCEDURE DIVISION before processing of data takes place?
10. Identify two reasons for using paragraph names in the PROCEDURE DIVISION.
11. What is the statement in COBOL that replaces a last card test (branch)?
12. Why should working-storage areas be cleared by the program prior to using the areas in question?
13. Why are zeros not recommended for clearing print areas?
14. Where does the result appear after the execution of a COBOL ADD instruction?

Chapter 17   COBOL applications

If you had trouble answering the REVIEW QUESTIONS, please review Chapter 16 and Chapter 17 up to this point before proceeding.

PROBLEM 2

The next two problems will be a modification of the problem just programmed. The entire program will not be rewritten. Only new and/or modified instructions will be written and new line numbers assigned for the steps that are new. It may be a good idea to mark the pages containing Figure 17-7 so that you can refer to them easily as needed in the following discussion.

1. The same input deck of cards as provided in Problem 1 is used. (See Figure 17-2, p. 335.)
2. A program is to be written that will cause the computer to print a two-column report.
   (a) This report is to contain a list of *male* students only. (The code for male is 2.)
   (b) The student name is to appear in the first column and the sales amount for each *male* student in the second column.
   (c) The total of all sales amounts is to be printed at the end of the report following the last line of print.
   (d) Ten spaces are to appear between the two columns with the total amount under the Sales Amount column.
   (e) The report will be centered on a page 120 spaces wide.

Figure 15-22 is reproduced on the next page as Figure 17-9. A comparison of this block diagram with Figure 17-1, p. 334, shows the relationship that exists between this new problem and Problem 1. Only a very minor change can be noted. This change primarily is the addition of another decision point to test for male students.

Last card test in COBOL

The last card test instruction is the same for Problem 2 as it was for Problem 1. The discussion is merely expanded here to give a clear understanding of the way in which this test works in COBOL and how it differs from the machine language last card test described in Chapter 15.

You were told on p. 348 that a READ statement followed by an AT END statement is a last card test in COBOL. This statement is true because the COBOL last card test is made immediately after the READ instruction.

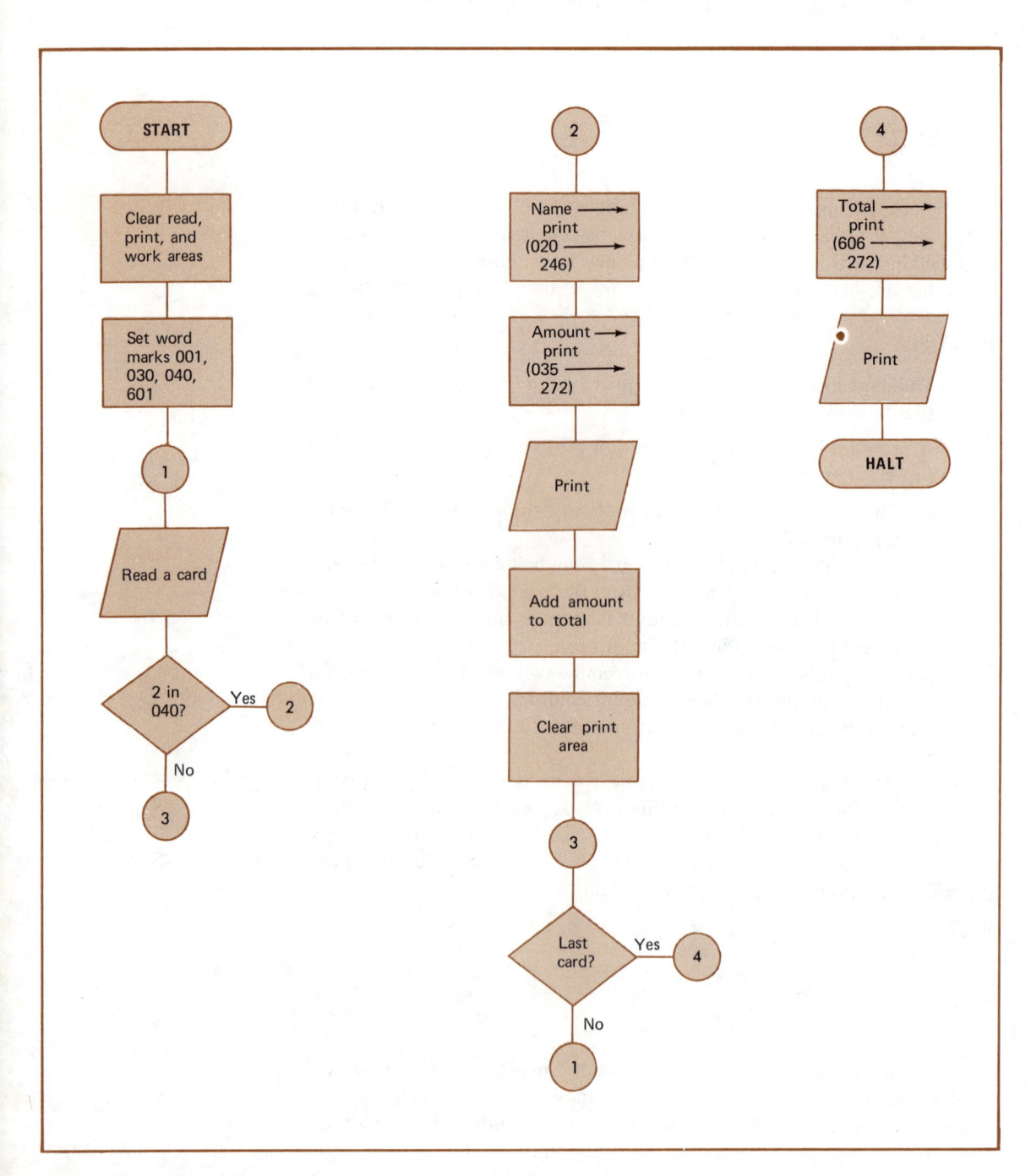

Figure 17-9. Block diagram for machine language program for Problem 2 (same as Figure 15-22, p. 282)

Chapter 17   COBOL applications

Figure 17-10. Block diagram for COBOL program for Problem 2

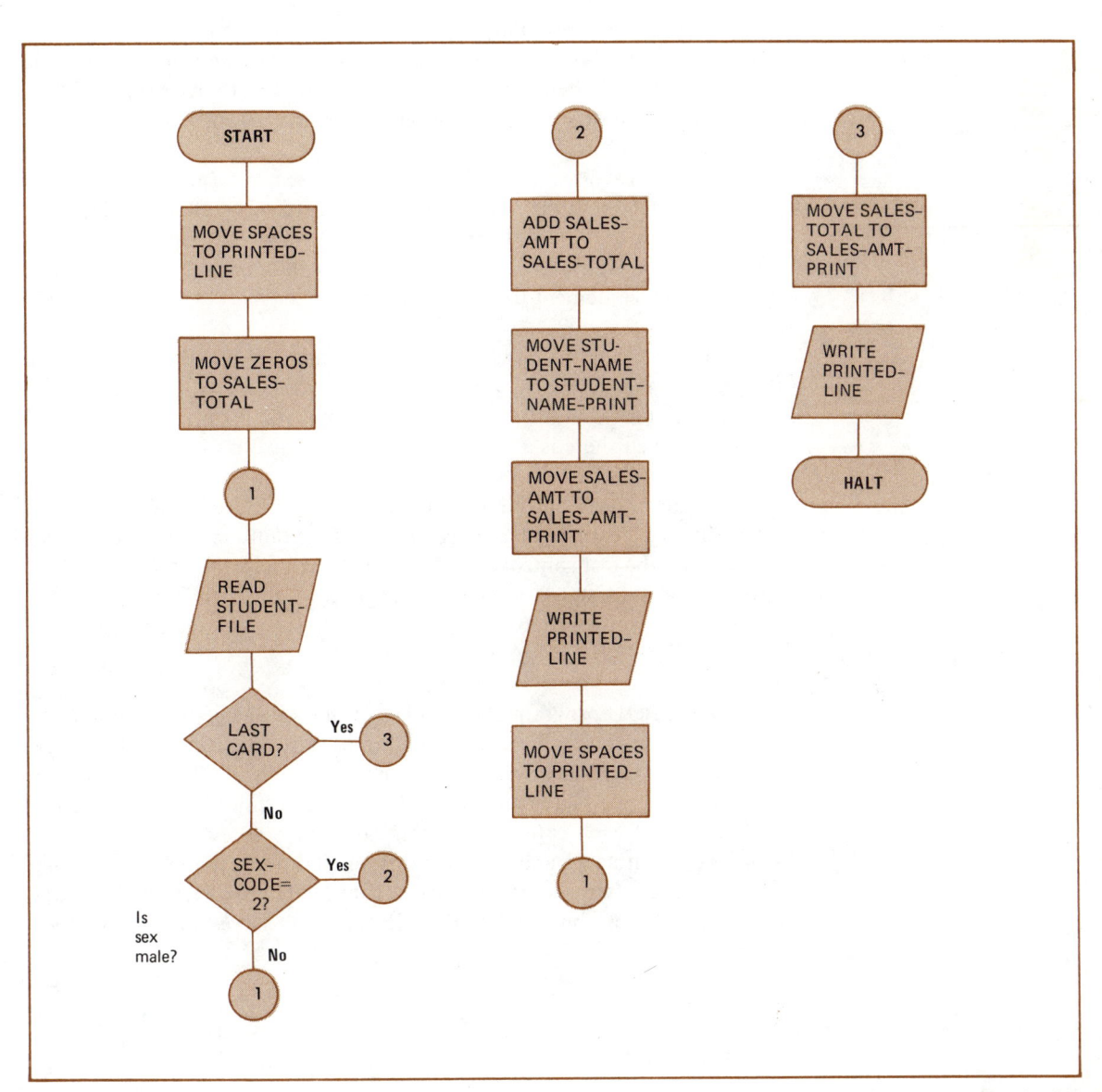

Figure 17-10 illustrates the block diagram for the COBOL program for Problem 2 in this chapter. Note that the last card test occurs much earlier than in the block diagram for the machine language program for the same problem (Figure 17-9). Instead of testing a last card sense switch <u>after</u> each card has been processed, the COBOL programmer places an additional coded *test control card* at the end of the input deck of data cards. This test control card may vary according to the type of computer used and according to the compiler program furnished by the computer manufacturer. The card could be punched with a /*, a //, the words END-OF-FILE, or one of many control punches or codes, depending upon the computer used. When the computer reads this test control card, a branch to the final step or steps of the program is made automatically.

If the last card test control code is not sensed in a data card, the computer will then continue to process the data card. Therefore, the last card test occurs in the COBOL block diagram immediately after the READ block. In the COBOL program, the READ statement is combined with the AT END statement to make a last card test.

In Figure 17-9, which is the block diagram for the machine language program, the last card test appears *after* the card has been *processed*. (The amount has been printed and added to the total and the print area has been cleared.) Then there is a test to see if the last card has been read.

In Figure 17-10, on the other hand, the last card test is made as soon as the punched card *enters the read area* of the computer. If the card does not contain the test control code for the last card test, the data card will be processed according to the COBOL program. If the card does contain the last card test control code, a branch is made to the final step or steps in the program.

The COBOL program for Problem 2 must instruct the computer to read every card in the file as before but must also cause information to be printed and added only if the card is for a male student. This identification of cards for male or female students can be determined by the punch in Column 40 of each card. The input cards have a sex code punched in Column 40, with a 1-punch representing female and a 2-punch representing male students. In machine language, a BRANCH instruction is used if the card meets the test, but in COBOL an IF statement serves the same purpose.

IF statements

"Decisions, decisions, decisions — how easy life would be without decisions!" is a comment heard frequently. Most computer programs, like life itself, involve decisions that must be made if the proper results are to be obtained.

In COBOL, the IF or condition statement is used to make certain tests and to direct further processing based upon the results of these tests. One of the easiest tests that can be made by an IF statement is the Relation Test.

Chapter 17   COBOL applications

Two values are compared in a relation test, and the result of this comparison will determine the next action (instruction) that is to be executed. The IF statement follows the English language logic. The program may say IF _____ IS NOT EQUAL TO _____ GO TO (some procedure-name).

Relation tests can be performed to test EQUAL, NOT EQUAL, GREATER THAN, LESS THAN, NOT GREATER THAN, and NOT LESS THAN.

Since Problem 2 requires a list of male students only, the sex code will be tested *before* doing any adding and printing. The card for each boy has a 2 punched in Column 40, so the IF statement will appear on Line 085 of the PROCEDURE DIVISION as follows:

080   READ STUDENT-SALES-FILE, AT END GO TO END-OF-JOB.

085   IF SEX-CODE IS NOT EQUAL TO 2 GO TO DETAIL-PROCESSING.

090   ADD SALES-AMT TO SALES-TOTAL.

In the machine language program, Column 40 was used to designate the student's sex, and the boys' cards were represented by a 2-punch. This is still the case because Column 40 has been given the COBOL name SEX-CODE in the DATA DIVISION.

As the READ instruction on Line 080 of the PROCEDURE DIVISION is executed, the digit representing student sex in Column 40 of the data card is stored in the computer memory in the area designated as SEX-CODE. Since all male students are represented by a 2-punch in this column, the actual value 2 can be used in the IF statement in the COBOL program as a factor for comparison. If the card is not a boy's card (does not have a 2 in Column 40), the program will branch to the paragraph named DETAIL-PROCESSING and continue execution.

At DETAIL-PROCESSING, the computer will read the next card and go through the test for the proper SEX-CODE again, repeating this loop over and over until the input deck of cards has been processed. If the card has a 2 in Column 40, the computer will continue to execute the program with the next statement following the IF statement.

The IF must always be written before the GO TO, because the computer follows instructions in logical order. If the programmer were to write GO TO first, the computer would go to the step mentioned and would never make the test. It would be as though the IF had never been written.

Options available with IF statements

The IF statement may be written in many ways because the programmer will have greater opportunity to use his own logic to accomplish the desired results. In the previous description of the IF statement, the condition NOT EQUAL is used as an example. EQUAL, GREATER THAN, LESS THAN, and NOT LESS THAN can be substituted if desired. The programmer tries to write the test that will create the fewest number of steps in the program.

Another method would be to use the EQUAL test but test for a SEX-CODE of 1.

    085   IF SEX-CODE IS EQUAL TO 1 GO TO DETAIL-PROCESSING.

In this statement a test is made for a 1-punch (female) in Column 40. If the punch in Column 40 equals a 1, the computer is instructed to go to the instructions headed DETAIL-PROCESSING and read another card. If the punch is not equal to a 1, therefore a 2 (male), the next instruction in the program will be executed — in this case, Line 090.

Revised program for Problem 2

The IF statement, once written, may be inserted into the program as statement number 085 of the PROCEDURE DIVISION. The remainder of the PROCEDURE DIVISION is unchanged. However, in the IDENTIFICATION DIVISION, the PROGRAM-ID (Line 030) and the REMARKS section, Lines 090 and 100, are revised if the title and description of the program are to be changed.

Line 030 of the IDENTIFICATION DIVISION in Problem 2 can be changed as follows:

    030   'SALES2'.

The REMARKS section can also be changed accordingly to:

080 REMARKS.

    090   THIS PROGRAM WILL LIST NAME AND SALES AMOUNT

    100   FOR MALES ONLY.

Once the above have been substituted for the corresponding statements in the program for Problem 1 (p. 350) and the IF statement has been added as Line 085 in the PROCEDURE DIVISION, the program for Problem 2 has been completed.

Chapter 17   COBOL applications

See Figure 17-11 for the revised IDENTIFICATION DIVISION and PROCEDURE DIVISION. Note that the Identification in the upper right-hand corner of the COBOL program sheets and the program name have been changed to reflect the new program. The ENVIRONMENT DIVISION and DATA DIVISION are not included in Figure 17-11 because the only changes are in the program name and identification.

```
COBOL PROGRAM SHEET                                    Sheet 1 of 5
System
Program    STUDENT SALES REPORT 2    Graphic              Identification
Programmer WAGNER, G.E.   Date 2-2-71  Punch              SALES2

001 010  IDENTIFICATION DIVISION.
    020  PROGRAM-ID.
    030      'SALES2'.
    040  AUTHOR.
    050      WAGNER.
    060  DATE WRITTEN.
    070      FEBRUARY 2, 1971.
    080  REMARKS.
    090      THIS PROGRAM WILL LIST NAME AND SALES AMOUNT
    100      FOR MALES ONLY.

005 010  PROCEDURE DIVISION.
    020  BEGINNING-OF-JOB.
    030      OPEN INPUT STUDENT-SALES-FILE.
    040      OPEN OUTPUT PRINTED-REPORT-FILE.
    050      MOVE SPACES TO PRINTED-LINE.
    060      MOVE ZEROS TO SALES-TOTAL.
    070  DETAIL-PROCESSING.
    080      READ STUDENT-SALES-FILE, AT END GO TO END-OF-JOB.
    085      IF SEX-CODE IS NOT EQUAL TO 2 GO TO DETAIL-PROCESSING.
    090      ADD SALES-AMT TO SALES-TOTAL.
    100      MOVE STUDENT-NAME TO STUDENT-NAME-PRINT.
    110      MOVE SALES-AMT TO SALES-AMT-PRINT.
    120      WRITE PRINTED-LINE.
    130      MOVE SPACES TO PRINTED-LINE.
    140      GO TO DETAIL-PROCESSING.
    150  END-OF-JOB.
    160      MOVE SALES-TOTAL TO SALE-AMT-PRINT.
    170      WRITE PRINTED-LINE.
    180      CLOSE STUDENT-SALES-FILE.
    190      CLOSE PRINTED-REPORT-FILE.
    200      STOP RUN.
```

Figure 17-11. Revised IDENTIFICATION and PROCEDURE DIVISIONS for Problem 2

Printed report for Problem 2

Using the same input cards that were used as data for Problem 1, the completed report for Problem 2 would contain only 12 entries (males only) plus the final total. See Figure 17-12.

```
JASON BARKLEY         000525
MIKE CARLSON          002100
JOHN EMERSON          000200
STEWART GIBSON        003300
JIMMY JACKSON         008000
BILL LEMA             000475
PAUL NELSON           008000
JEFFERSON RICHARDS    010350
RICK SURRELL          001500
PETER THOMPSON        000700
HAROLD UNRUH          000600
DAVID WYNEKEN         001500
                      037250
```

Figure 17-12. Printed report for Problem 2

REVIEW QUESTIONS

1. What is the reserved-list word in the COBOL conditional statement?
2. Assuming that the condition tested is not met, what instruction is executed next?
3. Identify six conditions that can be tested for with a conditional statement.
4. Why is it necessary to have so many different ways to write conditional statements?
5. Why is the IF statement written before the GO TO statement?

PROBLEM 3

1. The same input deck of cards provided in Problem 1 will be used. (See Figure 17-2.)
2. A program is to be written that will cause the computer to print a two-column report.
    (a) This report is to contain a list of only *freshman female students* and their sales.
    (b) The student name is to appear in the first column and the sales amount for each freshman female in the second column.
    (c) The total of all printed sales amounts is to be printed at the end of the report following the last line of print.

Chapter 17   COBOL applications

(d) Ten spaces are to appear between the two columns with the total amount under the Sales Amount column.
(e) The report is to be centered on a line 120 spaces wide.
(f) The report is to have a heading printed at the top of the report and centered.
(g) A double space is to appear between the heading and the first line of print.

This problem will require an additional IF statement, because two conditions must be met before a card can be listed. First, the SEX-CODE (Column 40) must be EQUAL to a 1, representing female; and second, the card must also be for a Freshman (1 in Column 24). Problem 3 also requires a printed heading with a space between the heading and the first line of print.

Constants and variables

Data in the memory of a computer can be of two types, constant and variable. Most of the data in our first two programs have been *variable*, because the data values could change each time a new card was read or each time another amount was added to the total. On the other hand, data *constants* are values that may be used over and over in a program but will never change. Constants are often used for comparisons in tests when making decisions, although there are other uses for constants as well.

Constants, like variables, must be placed into the memory of a computer before they can be used. As you know, the computer uses cell addresses to store or locate the correct data in memory. In machine language, an ADD instruction requires two addresses. Each address represents the location of one data field in memory. In COBOL, names are used to identify the numeric cell addresses. COBOL permits the programmer to use the actual value, if known, rather than an address or symbolic name to specify the location of the value to be used.

The actual value when used in a COBOL program is a constant. In Program 2, Line 085 of the PROCEDURE DIVISION, a Constant 2 was used in the IF statement. It was written as follows:

085   IF SEX-CODE IS NOT EQUAL TO 2 GO TO DETAIL-PROCESSING.

In this problem, all male students were represented by a 2 punched in Column 40 of the card (SEX-CODE). Since all male students have this 2 punched in Column 40 of the card, the Constant 2 can be used in the program as a test value for equality.

You will recall that when setting up the DATA DIVISION input description of PUNCHED-CARD, the programmer-invented word SEX-CODE was used to describe Column 40 of the card. If the number of spaces in the PICTURE clauses were counted, you would find that SEX-CODE is the name used to describe the cell address of the fortieth column in PUNCHED-CARD. (See Line 003/150, Figure 17-7, p. 350.) Refer now to the PROCEDURE DIVISION Line 085. The instruction card will read IF SEX-CODE IS NOT EQUAL TO 2 GO TO DETAIL-PROCESSING. When this instruction card is read into the CPU, the compiler program causes the 2 from the instruction to be compared automatically with the digit described in Column 40 of the data card. The constant (quantity used for comparison) will be 2. Instruction 085 in the PROCEDURE DIVISION thus sets up the Constant 2, and each data card read into the computer will be tested for a 2 in Column 40 (SEX-CODE).

Thus, it is possible to use an instruction in the PROCEDURE DIVISION of a COBOL program to set up a constant for comparison with a field in an input record. The constant serves the same purpose as the d-Character in the machine language branch instruction. See Figure 17-13.

Additional examples of constants in COBOL programs

The use of constants in COBOL is a technique that is very handy and simple to use with IF statements to test data in cards for specific conditions. In the statement on Line 086 below, the SALES-AMT field is checked to find any cards with exactly $25.00 in sales. Data in these cards will be processed according to the program.

086   IF SALES-AMT IS NOT EQUAL TO 2500 GO TO DETAIL-PROCESSING.

If a list were going to be made of all persons having sales of *more than* $25.00, the statement would read:

086   IF SALES-AMT IS GREATER THAN 2500 GO TO DETAIL-PROCESSING.

Since dollar signs and decimal points are normally not punched in cards, the test constant would be written as 2500 for both examples.

Constants can also be used in other instructions in the PROCEDURE DIVISION and are not limited in use to IF statements. Many reports require a count of all invoices, sales, employees, cards, etc. Counting is accomplished by adding 1 to a total each time. In this situation, 1 is constant and the Number 1 could be used in the ADD instruction as follows:

090   ADD 1 TO TOTAL.

The TOTAL must be described in the WORKING-STORAGE SECTION of the DATA DIVISION at Level 77.

Chapter 17 COBOL applications

DATA CARD

Column 40 is described as SEX-CODE.

DATA DIVISION OF COBOL PROGRAM

```
01  PUNCHED-CARD.
    02  STUDENT-NAME    PICTURE A(20).
    02  FILLER          PICTURE XXX.
    02  CLASS-CODE      PICTURE 9.
    02  FILLER          PICTURE X(5).
    02  SALES-AMT       PICTURE 9(6).
    02  FILLER          PICTURE X(4).
    02  SEX-CODE        PICTURE 9.
    02  FILLER          PICTURE X(40).
```

COBOL PROGRAM CARD

005085 IF SEX-CODE IS NOT EQUAL TO 2 GO TO DETAIL-PROCESSING.

Is there a 2 in Column 40?

PROCEDURE DIVISION

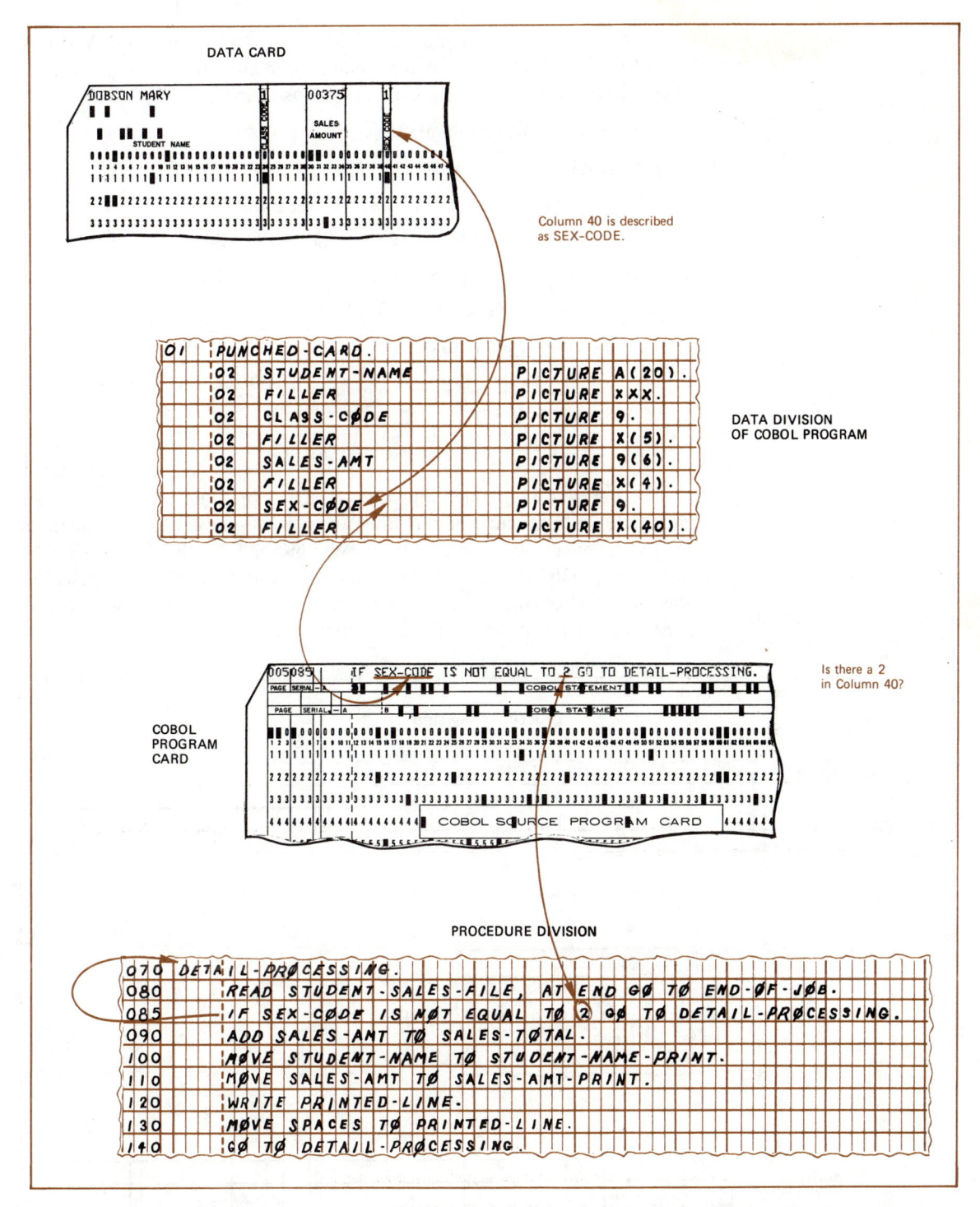

```
070  DETAIL-PROCESSING.
080  READ STUDENT-SALES-FILE, AT END GO TO END-OF-JOB.
085  IF SEX-CODE IS NOT EQUAL TO 2 GO TO DETAIL-PROCESSING.
090  ADD SALES-AMT TO SALES-TOTAL.
100  MOVE STUDENT-NAME TO STUDENT-NAME-PRINT.
110  MOVE SALES-AMT TO SALES-AMT-PRINT.
120  WRITE PRINTED-LINE.
130  MOVE SPACES TO PRINTED-LINE.
140  GO TO DETAIL-PROCESSING.
```

Figure 17-13. Constant established by IF statement

Assuming that you are required to write the PROCEDURE DIVISION for a COBOL program that will read and count all of the cards in a file, the PROCEDURE DIVISION would appear as follows:

010 PROCEDURE DIVISION.
020 BEGINNING-OF-JOB.
030   OPEN INPUT STUDENT-FILE.
040   OPEN OUTPUT PRINTED-REPORT-FILE.
050   MOVE SPACES TO PRINTED-LINE.
060   MOVE ZEROS TO TOTAL.
070 DETAIL-PROCESSING.
080   READ STUDENT-FILE, AT END GO TO END-OF-JOB.
090   ADD 1 TO TOTAL.
100   GO TO DETAIL-PROCESSING.

See Figure 17-14, which illustrates a partial program in which a count of female students could be accumulated in a 4-digit work area. Note that the work area has been defined in the WORKING-STORAGE SECTION at Level 77. Observe, also, that the add instruction in Line 090 comes after the cards are tested for the code for female students. As a result, only the cards for female students will be counted.

Figure 17-14. Constant established by ADD instruction

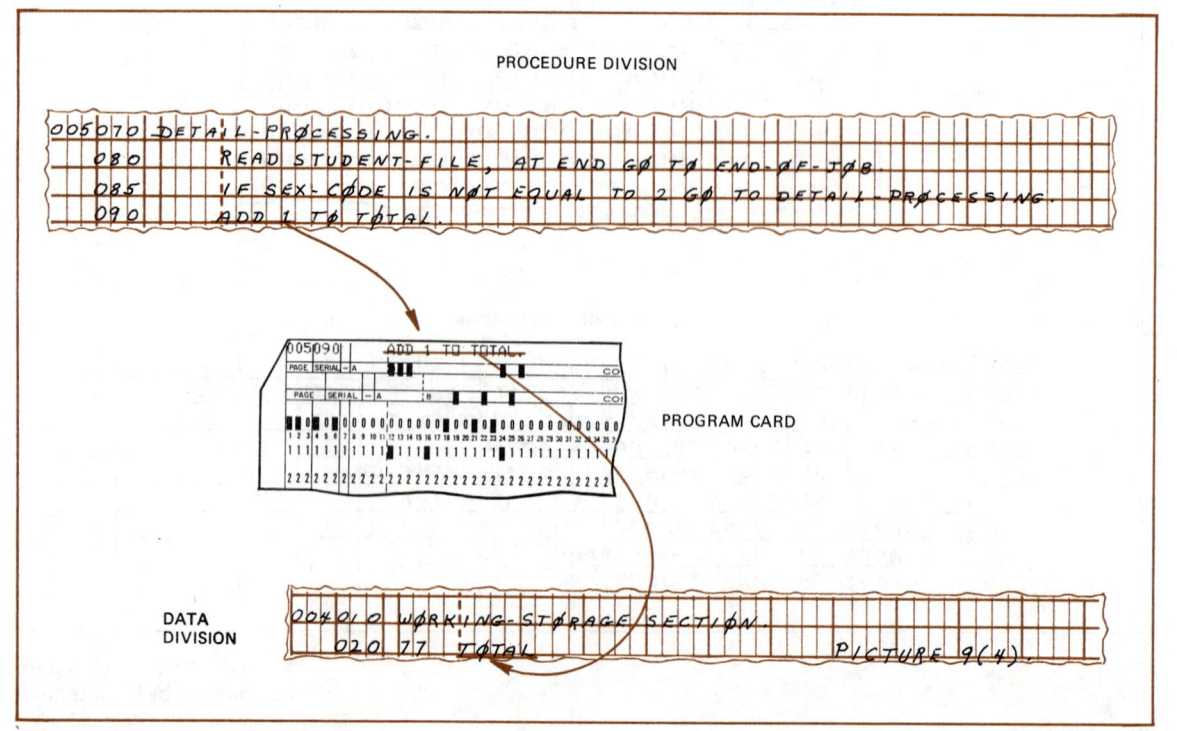

PROCEDURE DIVISION

```
005 070  DETAIL-PROCESSING.
    080      READ STUDENT-FILE, AT END GO TO END-OF-JOB.
    085      IF SEX-CODE IS NOT EQUAL TO 2 GO TO DETAIL-PROCESSING.
    090      ADD 1 TO TOTAL.
```

PROGRAM CARD
005 090 ADD 1 TO TOTAL.

DATA DIVISION
```
004 010  WORKING-STORAGE SECTION.
    020  77  TOTAL              PICTURE 9(4).
```

VALUE clauses

The VALUE clause is another method in COBOL that can be used to store constants in memory. The word VALUE is found on the COBOL reserved-word list. You will remember that a reserved word must be used in a specific manner. The use of the word VALUE has a special significance to the computer. This word can be used by the programmer to insert information into memory while he is compiling the program instead of repeatedly reading the information into memory as input each time the information is to be used. For example, a heading to appear at the top of each page of a printed report can be stored in the CPU as a constant.

Since constants can be used for printing headings, the report heading will be used here as an example of using a VALUE clause to print a heading. In the problem under discussion, the list of names in the printed report will be very short in order to simplify the problem. However, most printed computer reports consist of many pages. A continuous sheet of computer print-out is divided by perforated lines at regular intervals to form segments or pages. The program must provide for a heading to be printed at the top of each page for identification purposes. Since report headings are so often stored in the work area of the CPU, the report heading will be used here as an example for setting up nonnumeric constants in a COBOL program through the use of the VALUE clause. Since the heading 'SALES REPORT FOR FRESHMAN GIRLS' contains letters and spaces, the heading would be considered an alphabetic constant.

The report heading could be stored in the computer as a constant, using the word VALUE as follows:

070 02 REPORT-NAME   PICTURE A(31).
080   VALUE 'SALES REPORT FOR FRESHMAN GIRLS'.

Since the above entry will appear in the DATA DIVISION, the entry will have a level number followed by the data name. The A in the PICTURE clause refers to alphabetic characters, with or without spaces. The 31 inside the parentheses refers to the length of the data constant.

NOTE: All letters and spaces are counted in a VALUE clause of this type. The heading (actual constant to be stored) will be enclosed by single quotation marks. The single quotation marks are not counted in determining the length of the constant. The number of spaces set aside for the constant will be determined by counting all letters, special characters, numbers, and spaces within the single quotation marks.

As discussed earlier, the print line has a length of 120 positions. To be centered, the heading must have FILLER statements preceding and following it. By subtracting the heading length, 31 spaces, from 120 (the print-line length), 89 spaces remain to be divided between the two margins. There will be a FILLER of 44 spaces on the left of the heading and a FILLER of 45 spaces on the right.

The VALUE clause can also be used to clear areas of memory. Since this is a printed report to be read by someone else, the unused portions of the heading line should contain spaces. The word SPACES is used in the VALUE clauses (Lines 060 and 090) to describe the filler.

WORKING-STORAGE SECTION for Problem 3

The completed WORKING-STORAGE SECTION for this problem will be as follows:

```
030 WORKING-STORAGE SECTION.
040 77 SALES-TOTAL         PICTURE 9(6).
050 01 HEADING-LINE.
060    02 FILLER           PICTURE X(44) VALUE SPACES.
070    02 REPORT-NAME      PICTURE A(31)
080           VALUE 'SALES REPORT FOR FRESHMAN GIRLS'.
090    02 FILLER           PICTURE X(45) VALUE SPACES.
```

When a VALUE clause is used with a PICTURE clause, the period appears at the end of the VALUE clause.

The heading line entries (Lines 050–090) are included in the WORKING-STORAGE SECTION since the heading of the report has not been included in the input or output files of the DATA DIVISION.

HEADING-LINE is found at the 01 level in the WORKING-STORAGE SECTION of the DATA DIVISION. HEADING-LINE is the programmer-invented name assigned to the cell addresses of the output record. This name can be used by the programmer with a MOVE instruction to move the heading to the print area. The heading can then be printed at the top of the report with a WRITE instruction.

The 02 levels, as stated earlier, identify fields (sometimes referred to as items) within the record. In this case, the fields defined at the 02 level are the FILLERS and the REPORT-NAME.

Note also that the area reserved for computation (Line 040) has the Level 77 and is named first in the WORKING-STORAGE SECTION.

Example

The PROCEDURE DIVISION of this problem requires a few additional statements. These are illustrated and explained below:

```
070 HEADING-PRINT.
080    MOVE HEADING-LINE TO PRINTED-LINE.
```

090	WRITE PRINTED-LINE.
100	MOVE SPACES TO PRINTED-LINE.
110	WRITE PRINTED-LINE.
120	DETAIL-PROCESSING
130	READ STUDENT-SALES-FILE, AT END GO TO END-OF-JOB.
140	IF CLASS-CODE IS NOT EQUAL TO 1 GO TO DETAIL-PROCESSING.
150	IF SEX-CODE IS NOT EQUAL TO 1 GO TO DETAIL-PROCESSING.
160	ADD SALES-AMOUNT TO SALES-TOTAL.

Line 080 moves the HEADING-LINE to the print area, and Line 090 prints the heading. The next two lines are required in order to leave one blank line between the heading and the first line of print (the equivalent of a double space). This is accomplished by moving spaces to the printed line and then printing a line with only the spaces as data. The instruction at Line 100 clears the print area so that Line 110 will have nothing but spaces to write. Single spacing takes place automatically every time the computer executes a WRITE instruction; therefore, Line 110 performs the equivalent of double spacing by skipping one blank line.

Triple spacing could be achieved just as simply by repeating the instruction on Line 110, WRITE PRINTED-LINE. A total of two blank lines would be printed. The instruction at Line 100 clears the print area until new data are moved into this area. Each WRITE PRINTED-LINE instruction thereafter will cause another line to be skipped. Note that once the print area has been cleared it is not necessary to clear it each time for every WRITE instruction used for vertical spacing.

Line 140 is necessary to perform the extra test for CLASS-CODE. In this problem, Line 160 will never be executed unless an input data card satisfies both tests, female and freshman. If either condition is not met, the program directs the computer to the paragraph named DETAIL-PROCESSING, and a new data card is read.

Complete program for Problem 3

The complete program for Problem 3 is found in Figure 17-15, pp. 368–369. Note that it contains additional statements for preparing a sales report listing only freshman girls and for inserting an appropriate heading at the top of the page. A space will be skipped between the heading and the printed report.

COBOL PROGRAM SHEET

System			
Program: STUDENT SALES REPORT 3	Graphic	Card Form #	Sheet of
Programmer: WAGNER, G.E. Date 2-2-71	Punch		Identification SALES3 73 80

```
001010  IDENTIFICATION DIVISION.
    020  PROGRAM-ID.
    030      'SALES3'.
    040  AUTHOR.
    050      WAGNER.
    060  DATE-WRITTEN.
    070      FEBRUARY 2, 1971.
    080  REMARKS.
    090      THIS PROGRAM WILL LIST STUDENT NAME AND SALES AMOUNT FOR
    100      FRESHMAN GIRLS ONLY.

002010  ENVIRONMENT DIVISION.
    020  CONFIGURATION SECTION.
    030  SOURCE-COMPUTER.
    040      IBM-360.
    050  OBJECT-COMPUTER.
    060      IBM-360.
    070  INPUT-OUTPUT SECTION.
    080  FILE-CONTROL.
    090      SELECT STUDENT-SALES-FILE ASSIGN TO 'SYSIN' UNIT-RECORD.
    100      SELECT PRINTED-REPORT-FILE ASSIGN TO 'SYSOUT' UNIT-RECORD

003010  DATA DIVISION.
    020  FILE SECTION.
    030  FD  STUDENT-SALES-FILE
    040      RECORDING MODE IS F
    050      RECORD CONTAINS 80 CHARACTERS
    060      LABEL RECORD IS OMITTED
    070      DATA RECORD IS PUNCHED-CARD.
    080  01  PUNCHED-CARD.
    090      02  STUDENT-NAME     PICTURE A(20).
    100      02  FILLER           PICTURE XXX.
    110      02  CLASS-CODE       PICTURE 9.
    120      02  FILLER           PICTURE X(5).
    130      02  SALES-AMT        PICTURE 9(6).
    140      02  FILLER           PICTURE X(4).
    150      02  SEX-CODE         PICTURE 9.
    160      02  FILLER           PICTURE X(40).
    170  FD  PRINTED-REPORT-FILE
    180      RECORDING MODE IS F
    190      RECORD CONTAINS 120 CHARACTERS
    200      LABEL RECORD IS OMITTED
    210      DATA RECORD IS PRINTED-LINE.
```

Figure 17-15. Complete COBOL program for Problem 3

Chapter 17   COBOL applications

```
220 01 PRINTED-LINE.
230    02 FILLER                    PICTURE X(42).
240    02 STUDENT-NAME-PRINT        PICTURE A(20).
250    02 FILLER                    PICTURE X(10).
004010 02 SALES-AMT-PRINT           PICTURE 9(6).
020    02 FILLER                    PICTURE X(42).
030 WORKING-STORAGE SECTION.
040 77 SALES-TOTAL                  PICTURE 9(6).
050 01 HEADING-LINE.
060    02 FILLER                    PICTURE X(44) VALUE SPACES.
070    02 REPORT-NAME               PICTURE A(31)
080       VALUE 'SALES REPORT FOR FRESHMAN GIRLS'.
090    02 FILLER                    PICTURE X(45) VALUE SPACES.

005010 PROCEDURE DIVISION.
020 BEGINNING-OF-JOB.
030     OPEN INPUT STUDENT-SALES-FILE.
040     OPEN OUTPUT PRINTED-REPORT-FILE.
050     MOVE SPACES TO PRINTED-LINE.
060     MOVE ZEROS TO SALES-TOTAL.
070 HEADING-PRINT.
080     MOVE HEADING-LINE TO PRINTED-LINE.
090     WRITE PRINTED-LINE.
100     MOVE SPACES TO PRINTED-LINE.
110     WRITE PRINTED-LINE.
120 DETAIL-PROCESSING.
130     READ STUDENT-SALES-FILE, AT END GO TO END-OF-JOB.
140     IF CLASS-CODE IS NOT EQUAL TO 1 GO TO DETAIL-PROCESSING.
150     IF SEX-CODE IS NOT EQUAL TO 1 GO TO DETAIL-PROCESSING.
160     ADD SALES-AMOUNT TO SALES-TOTAL.
170     MOVE STUDENT-NAME TO STUDENT-NAME-PRINT.
180     MOVE SALES-AMT TO SALES-AMT-PRINT.
190     WRITE PRINTED-LINE.
200     MOVE SPACES TO PRINTED-LINE.
210     GO TO DETAIL-PROCESSING.
220 END-OF-JOB.
230     MOVE SALES-TOTAL TO SALES-AMT-PRINT.
240     WRITE PRINTED-LINE.
250     CLOSE STUDENT-SALES-FILE.
006010  CLOSE PRINTED-REPORT-FILE.
020     STOP RUN.
```

Figure 17-15. Complete COBOL program for Problem 3 (continued)

Printed report for Problem 3

A sample of the completed report for Problem 3 is illustrated on p. 370. You will note that the report has the centered heading, SALES REPORT FOR FRESHMAN GIRLS. A space has been skipped between the heading and the printed list.

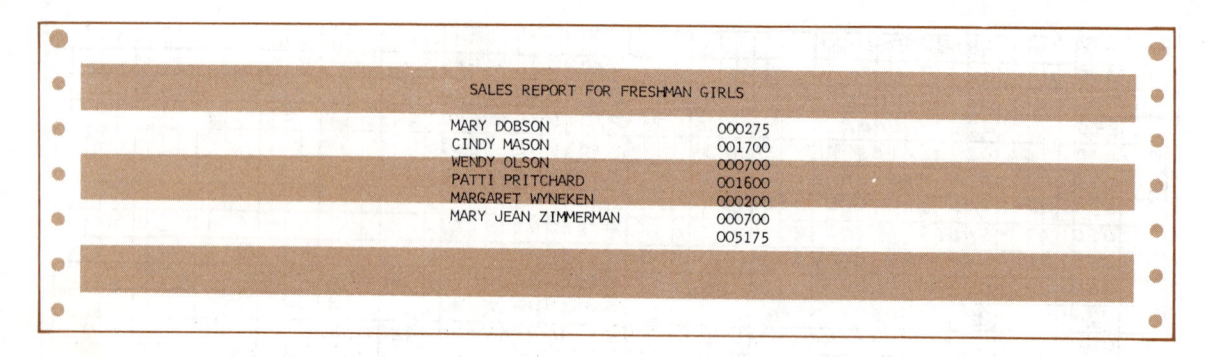

```
              SALES REPORT FOR FRESHMAN GIRLS
                   MARY DOBSON            000275
                   CINDY MASON            001700
                   WENDY OLSON            000700
                   PATTI PRITCHARD        001600
                   MARGARET WYNEKEN       000200
                   MARY JEAN ZIMMERMAN    000700
                                          005175
```

Figure 17-16. Printed report for Problem 3

SUMMARY

The tremendous acceptance of computers by governmental agencies, industry, and society as a whole has created many problems. One of these is a shortage of experienced, qualified machine language programmers. This shortage has led to the development of "higher" level languages such as COBOL.

COBOL has been developed to provide computer users with a uniform language that can be used on most medium-to-large-scale computers in operation today. It also is an attempt to provide man with a near-English language — one that requires less training than machine language in order to be used effectively.

All COBOL programs have four divisions. These division names must be spelled properly and must appear in the same sequence in every program. The four division names are: (1) IDENTIFICATION, (2) ENVIRONMENT, (3) DATA, and (4) PROCEDURE.

The IDENTIFICATION DIVISION is used to provide descriptive information about the program. This information can be used as a point of reference later and may include the program name (ID), the programmer's name, date written, and any other necessary remarks.

The ENVIRONMENT DIVISION includes all pertinent information relating to the hardware configuration (equipment) to be used. The manufacturer and model number of the computer or computers used as the SOURCE and OBJECT machines must be included. Input and output files are named.

Chapter 17   COBOL applications

The next division, DATA DIVISION, contains a detailed description of all input/output files used in the operation. The file description will describe every record, every field within each record, and the type of data (alphabetic, numeric, or alphameric) that is found in each position of the field.

In addition to describing input/output files, the DATA DIVISION is used to identify all WORKING-STORAGE areas of memory. A name is assigned to each area and the size and contents (VALUE) of each can be specified in the DATA DIVISION.

The WORKING-STORAGE SECTION provides working areas in memory that are not part of the input and output files. A temporary storage area is used for arithmetic computations and for accumulating totals. The temporary storage area may be defined at the 77 level in the WORKING-STORAGE SECTION.

The last division contains the instructions regarding the procedure to be followed and is properly entitled the PROCEDURE DIVISION. Although each statement must adhere to a preplanned format, this division is easier to read and understand than the first three. Each statement is executed in the sequence in which it appears in the program unless a conditional statement is reached. The word IF is the first word of a conditional statement. When a condition is met, based upon the IF statement, the computer can be directed to another section of the program by using a GO TO statement. If, on the other hand, the condition as stated is not met, the program will continue with the next consecutive statement.

The IF statement is used to make tests for relationship conditions such as EQUAL, NOT EQUAL, GREATER THAN, LESS THAN, NOT GREATER THAN, and NOT LESS THAN. The IF statement can also be used to establish a constant by causing each data card to be compared with a specific field described in the DATA DIVISION.

Headings and captions can be printed on the output reports as required. The heading may be set up as a record at the 01 level in the WORKING-STORAGE SECTION. A PICTURE clause and a VALUE clause are used to specify the exact copy desired. The PICTURE clause describes the number of characters and/or spaces in the field and whether the field is numeric, alphabetic, or alphameric. The VALUE clause specifies the actual words, spaces, or numbers in the heading.

The COBOL programming language described in the foregoing chapters is fairly standard as it is being used with most computers today. As was pointed out, specific rules must be followed in using the reserved COBOL words such as ADD, MOVE, and IF. These rules may vary slightly depending upon the make and model of the computer used. To aid programmers, manufacturers of computers normally provide a reference manual that spells out the rules a programmer must follow when writing programs for a particular machine.

COBOL is only one of many languages now being used with third-generation computers. Some languages are better suited than others for handling specific tasks. Regardless of the language used, it must be perfectly clear at this point that the writing of a computer program is an exacting task. To write a program, one must have a clear understanding of the problem to be solved and must state in a precise manner the steps to be followed in solving that problem. Although this text has offered experience in writing some simple programs, a considerable amount of time would have to be spent in additional study before a student could qualify as a competent programmer in a modern business office.

REVIEW QUESTIONS

1. Why were two IF statements required in Problem 3?

2. May a programmer use an IF statement in the PROCEDURE DIVISION to set up a constant to test for equality or inequality? Give an example statement assuming that if CLASS-CODE is not equal to 4, a new data card will be read.

3. In the above example, in what division must CLASS-CODE be described? In what portion of the division? In what record?

4. If the STUDENT-NAME is in Columns 1–20 of the data card, the CLASS-CODE in Column 21, and the rest of the card columns are blank, how would the programmer describe the record so that the compiler would be able to make the test for a 4 in CLASS-CODE? Use the proper level numbers and PICTURE clauses.

5. A total of students registered in a school could be accumulated with the following constant set up with an ADD instruction in the PROCEDURE DIVISION:

    095   ADD 1 TO TOTAL.

Assuming that a 4-digit area is to be defined in the WORKING-STORAGE SECTION of the PROCEDURE DIVISION for accumulating the total, what information is missing from the entry below?

    004 010   WORKING-STORAGE SECTION.
    020   ? TOTAL   PICTURE ? .

6. How is the length of a VALUE clause constant determined?

7. How are headings centered on a page?

8. How many spaces are required before and after the following heading if it is to be centered on a 120-space print line?

    'PROGRAMMED BY WAGNER'

9. What does an 01 level signify in the DATA DIVISION?

10. Why are spaces used to clear a print area?

Chapter 17   COBOL applications

11. How can double spacing be accomplished?
12. Which division in a COBOL program contains PICTURE clauses?
13. What type of statement will interrupt the normal sequence of execution of computer instructions? What is the first word in this statement?
14. What statement is always combined with the statement described in Question 13? Which of the two statements is always written first?
15. What is the last statement in the PROCEDURE DIVISION that ends a COBOL program?

STUDY GUIDE

Complete Study Guide 17 by following the instructions in your STUDY GUIDES booklet.

PROJECTS

Complete Projects 17-1 and 17-2 by following the instructions in your PROJECTS booklet.

CHAPTER 18

JOBS AND CAREERS IN AUTOMATED DATA PROCESSING

In 1950, there were no more than 15 electronic computers in use in the United States. Today, the figure has passed 48,000. By 1975, it has been estimated that there will be 85,000. More than three million people will be needed to operate them. Already, the computer is touching the lives of all people. The food they eat, the cars they drive, the clothes they wear, and the gas and electric power they use in large part are produced under the control of computers. Thousands of tasks are performed with incredible speed; still, the full impact of computers in education, space exploration, science, medicine, and business has hardly been felt.

Business and governmental agencies buy computers because computers are tools that can extend the ability to solve complex problems. A computer's value lies, not in displacing workers, but in expanding the value of every employee to himself and to his company or agency.

COMPUTERS AND YOU

Because computers influence the present and will dramatically shape the future, electronic data processing is perhaps the most exciting field the world has to offer young men and women today. It is a rapidly growing field and one of the most challenging and rewarding.

The electronic computer industry is moving ahead so rapidly that it needs many more trained young men and women than are now working in it. This condition will exist far into the future, making the industry very attractive for those who want to find careers in it. Moreover, the salaries for some of the occupations in this field rank among the highest offered in business.

SOMETHING FOR EVERYONE

There is a bright future in the electronic computer field for everyone, regardless of educational background. Interesting job and career opportunities exist at every level, from punching holes in cards to conducting scientific research. Now and in the future there will be a demand for craftsmen to construct computers, technicians to install and maintain them, engineers to design new computers, salesmen to sell them, scientists to discover new applications, and computer operators to turn raw data into useful information. This chapter will touch on the qualifications required of computer equipment operators and the career opportunities available.

OPERATORS OF COMPUTER EQUIPMENT

Generally, the operators of computer equipment are listed under the following occupations: card punch operator, unit-record equipment operator, computer operator, programmer, and systems analyst. In addition, supervisory jobs exist at each occupational level.

Card punch operator

Duties. A card punch operator is one who performs the following duties:

1. He operates an alphabetic and/or numeric card punch machine to record precoded or uncoded data.
2. He works from source material which may or may not be arranged for card punching.
3. He verifies his work or that of other operators on a verifying machine.
4. He prepares program cards for the card punch machine.

Education. Graduation from high school is required for employment as a card punch operator. Some companies employ graduates without office experience; some employ only those who have worked in an office for six months or more. Many companies have training programs for card punch operators; some send untrained employees to short training courses offered by the manufacturers of data processing equipment. Longer programs are offered in some high schools, private business schools, community colleges, and special automation schools.

Typewriting skill is invariably required for entrance to a training program. In some cases, a course in bookkeeping is also needed. A minimum typewriting speed of 40 words a minute with a high accuracy rating is usually sufficient to meet entrance requirements. More than specialized training on a card punch machine, employers generally stress the importance of typewriting, bookkeeping, and an introductory course in data processing, combined with a general education.

Chapter 18   Jobs and careers in data processing

Job opportunities and the future. There are many more openings for card punch operators than there are trained people to fill them. This is one of the reasons that many companies train their own operators. Studies conducted in a number of communities indicate that approximately 40 percent of the people employed in automated data processing operate card punch machines.

With the advent of optical scanners, magnetic tape, and other devices, the future for card punch operators has often been discussed. A national study reported in the June, 1969 issue of *Business Automation* indicates that punched cards account for nearly 85 percent of the computer input. The findings appear in the following table:

BASIC COMPUTER INPUT

Punched Cards	84.7%
Magnetic Tape	27.9
Paper Tape	9.5
Optical Scanners	3.9
Others	10.4

The table indicates that some companies use more than one input medium. It also indicates that punched cards remain in high favor in data processing.

Salaries and career advancement. The salaries for card punch operators, according to a national study reported in the June, 1970 issue of *Business Automation*, range from a low of $45 a week for a junior operator to a high of $225 for a lead operator. The average salary is $107 per week.

Card punch operators can move to jobs in which they will operate unit-record equipment. Additional training may be required in board wiring and bookkeeping. Essentially, however, these jobs are held by high school graduates who have gained on-the-job experience in operating the sorter, tabulator, collator, and other unit-record machines.

Unit-record equipment operator

Duties. A unit-record equipment operator performs the following duties:

1. He sets up and operates a variety of punched card equipment, including sorters, tabulators, reproducers, collators, and calculators.
2. He wires boards for routine jobs from diagrams prepared by other people.
3. He uses prewired boards on complex or repetitive jobs.
4. He locates and corrects difficulties encountered in operating the various machines.

Education. Graduation from high school is required for employment as a unit-record equipment operator. Very few companies employ high school graduates who have not obtained some experience on unit-record machines either in school or on the job. Some companies offer training programs to their employees. Training programs are also offered by manufacturers of data processing equipment, by some high schools, by some private business schools, by some community colleges, and by special automation schools. The ability to operate the different machines in the unit-record system can usually be acquired in a very short time. However, learning to wire panel boards for the machines takes more time.

Job opportunities and the future. Studies conducted in a number of communities indicate that approximately 12 percent of the people employed in automated data processing are operators of unit-record equipment. This is not a rapidly expanding occupational field, because the electronic computer is taking over many of the tasks formerly performed by unit-record machines. There are openings for operators, but these openings are not so difficult to fill as openings in some other occupations in data processing. This is evident in the table on p. 380. Some unit-record machines, such as sorters and possibly collators, are widely used in electronic computer systems. The need for operators for these machines should expand with the growth of computers.

Salaries and career advancement. The salaries for unit-record equipment operators range from a low of $58 to a high of $248 a week. The average salary is close to $123 a week. These figures come from the national study of 1970 referred to earlier.

Unit-record equipment operators can move to jobs in which they will operate electronic computers; some additional training is usually needed, however. As computers become more and more complicated, the training required to make this move will also increase.

Computer operator

Duties. A computer operator performs the following duties:

1. He operates computers, using established programs.
2. He prepares input data for entry.
3. He loads and unloads programs.
4. He manipulates control switches on the computer consoles.
5. He observes lights on consoles and other devices in the computer system, detecting processing and equipment errors and making normal adjustments.
6. He maintains operating records.

Education. High school graduation plus office experience is required. Many of those now entering this occupation were employed as unit-record equipment operators. They obtained training for the computer being used in their company by taking part in training programs offered by the manufacturer of the computer or by their company. Anyone entering this occupation must be prepared to attend training programs of this type as new advances are made in computer technology.

Computer operator training is also offered by community colleges, private business schools, and special automation institutes.

Job opportunities and the future. Computer operators are in demand because of the rapid advancement of computers in business and government. Most of the openings are for operators with training and experience with a particular type of computer. Openings in this field are not as difficult to fill as some of the other occupations in data processing. The table on p. 380 reveals this fact.

Salaries and career advancement. Figures made available by the 1970 national study cited earlier indicate that weekly salaries for computer operators range from a low of $58 a week for a junior operator to a high of $365 for a lead operator. The average weekly salary is close to $147.

The demand for computer operators will grow as new computers are installed. In addition, those in this field may advance to the occupation of programmer. This move requires additional education. Programmers must usually have training beyond a high school education.

Programmer

Duties. Several programmers are usually employed in a computer installation. They perform jobs at different levels. Frequently, they work in teams. The better trained and more experienced programmers handle jobs of a higher level than do those with less training and experience. Generally, a programmer performs the following duties:

1. He directs the coding of data to be recorded for input.
2. He analyzes the problems to be solved on the computer.
3. He prepares block diagrams.
4. He writes program instructions to solve those problems.
5. He codes program instructions in the language of the particular computer being used.
6. He prepares test data and debugs programs.
7. He documents the procedures used throughout a computer program.

Education. Programmers must have the ability to understand and analyze problems and arrange program instructions in logical order. They must be attentive to details. A two- to four-year college education is usually necessary. In addition to training in programming, training in mathematics and business is highly desirable for computer programmers in business establishments. Those interested in becoming programmers of scientific data would do well in college to stress mathematics, science, and engineering.

Most two- and four-year colleges offer preparatory courses for programmers. In addition, this training may be obtained in private business schools, automation institutes, and classes sponsored by the manufacturers of computers.

Many companies with computer installations have set up trainee sessions for those desiring to enter the programming field. Trainees earn while they learn. Those selected as trainees under this program must have some college training and high aptitude in problem-solving, logical reasoning, and mathematics.

Job opportunities and the future. Programmers are in great demand and estimates indicate that this demand will continue. Until recently, the position of programmer led all others as the most difficult to fill. It still stands high in this regard. The following table, taken from the national study reported in the June, 1968 issue of *Business Automation*, reveals some interesting findings.

POSITION MOST DIFFICULT TO FILL

Systems Analysts	47.1%
Programmers	45.2
Card Punch Operators	14.6
Computer Operators	11.0
Unit-Record Operators	4.5
Others	2.3
None	1.2

Some estimates show that by 1970 more than 200,000 programmers will be needed to man computers. There is quick placement of qualified candidates. The work is interesting and challenging, and the assignments are as varied as the many businesses now using computers.

Salaries and career advancement. The figures show that weekly salaries range from a low of $60 a week for a junior programmer to a high of $390 for a lead programmer. The average weekly salary for programmers is reported to be $200.

There is a brisk and continuing demand for programmers. Reports say that the demand will remain high. The salaries for programmers have been advancing rapidly; they will continue to advance. Programmers may advance to the job of systems analyst.

Systems analyst

Duties. A systems analyst must be familiar with all aspects of data processing. His goal is to improve management decision making by making available useful information. He performs the following duties:

1. He designs, installs, and implements computer information systems.
2. He studies existing operating procedures.
3. He analyzes a particular problem and prepares a flow chart which outlines the steps taken to process necessary data from source document to finished report.
4. He is concerned with machines, workers, forms, and layout. With these factors in mind, he sets up systems to produce the information a company needs for efficient operation.

Education. Graduation from a four-year college is usually required for this occupation. In addition, a number of years of experience as computer operator, programmer, or accountant is usually required.

College programs for those interested in entering this occupation should include courses in automated data processing, accounting, business management, mathematics, and systems analysis.

Many four-year colleges offer courses for preparing systems analysts. In addition, many companies have trainee programs for those who wish to enter this field.

Job opportunities and the future. As revealed by the table on p. 380, systems analysts are in great demand. Currently, this position is the most difficult to fill. Reports indicate that this situation will continue.

Salaries and career advancement. The figures show that weekly salaries range from a low of $80 for a junior systems analyst to a high of $519 for a lead analyst. The average weekly salary for analysts is about $248.

Systems analysts work closely with a number of company managers. Their natural avenues of promotion are to positions of office manager, controller, and manager of branch operations.

GETTING READY FOR A FUTURE IN AUTOMATED DATA PROCESSING

There are many steps one can take to prepare oneself for a successful career in data processing. It is necessary to learn how to study and to apply oneself to the solution of a variety of problems. Computers do not have minds, but the people who work with them must know how to use theirs. A student must learn how to express ideas clearly. These two qualities — knowing how to get facts and clear self-expression — are basic to progress in any field.

It is important to learn how to read. No problem can be solved if it cannot be understood. Mathematics and science courses should be taken. In addition, if a student plans to enter the technical and maintenance end of the computer business, drafting and shop courses should be included in school plans. Knowing how to read drawings, how to use one's hands, and how to work with tools and machines will prove very valuable in such a career.

If a student plans to enter the operating end of computers, such courses as typewriting, bookkeeping, accounting, office practice, business machines, and mathematics should be included in study plans. Knowing how to type, to understand business papers, to trace the course of data through a number of steps in a system, and to solve a variety of data processing problems will be extremely helpful in preparing for this career.

Many companies offer trainee programs. In these programs, an employee can become a part of the data processing system of a company and earn while learning. In this manner, all aspects of the total system will be seen to fit together to turn out the information needed by a company to operate efficiently. A variety of problems will be solved with the help and guidance of data processing specialists. The opportunities available to enter one of these trainee programs should be investigated by any interested student.

INTRODUCTORY COURSE IN AUTOMATED DATA PROCESSING

An introductory course in automated data processing has just been completed. The basic fundamentals concerning how data are processed manually, by the unit-record system, and by the electronic computer system have been learned. Many data processing problems have been solved; and, in so doing, one's problem solving ability has been sharpened. In addition, attention to details and logical thinking patterns have been developed while programming solutions to problems. How to speak and understand some of the basic language of computers has been learned. Thus, an important step has been taken in preparing for a career in electronic data processing.

SUMMARY

Electronic data processing is one of the most exciting fields open to young men and women today. It is growing rapidly; it is both challenging and rewarding. Many more young men and women are needed than are now in it or prepared to enter it. Reports show that this condition will continue far into the future.

Chapter 18   Jobs and careers in data processing

Interesting computer job and career opportunities are available at every level in both the technical and data processing areas. In data processing there are openings for card punch operators, unit-record equipment operators, computer operators, programmers, and systems analysts. One can enter this field as a high school graduate with little or no experience in data processing and move to the top job by learning the duties of each job and by acquiring the additional education that is needed for advancement.

Training programs are offered by high schools, private business colleges, community colleges, automation institutes, four-year colleges, manufacturers of computer equipment, and companies hiring data processing workers. Trainee programs have been set up by many companies with computer installations. In these programs, an employee can earn as he learns.

The salaries range from a low of $45 a week for a junior card punch operator to a high of $519 a week for a lead systems analyst. All indicators point to a bright future for those who seek careers in electronic data processing.

REVIEW QUESTIONS

1. Name the five occupations in data processing which have been discussed in this chapter.
2. Is a high school diploma necessary to obtain a job in electronic data processing? A college degree?
3. What high school courses are considered by employers to be important for card punch operators?
4. Name the general requirements for obtaining a job as a unit-record equipment operator.
5. What duties do computer operators perform? What are the educational requirements?
6. What duties do programmers perform?
7. What type of education must programmers usually possess?
8. In general terms, what is the job of the systems analyst?
9. Where can the necessary training for most jobs in data processing be obtained?
10. Name the major advantage of the trainee programs offered by many companies.
11. Discuss the knowledges which you have gained from this course.

STUDY GUIDE

Complete Study Guide 18 by following the instructions in your STUDY GUIDES booklet.

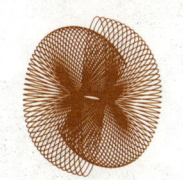

Courtesy of AMPEX CORPORATION

Computer equipment operators are copying data into the new AMPEX Video-file information system. The source document, placed under the black lid in front of the operator, is scanned by a television camera and recorded on video tape. With her right hand, the operator uses the keyboard to assign a digital address to the document, so it can be found again at any time.

GLOSSARY OF SPECIAL TERMS

Machine language addresses which give the cell locations from which data to be processed may be obtained or in which results may be placed. One or both addresses may be used, depending upon the operation to be performed. The A Address is also used to designate the address of the instruction to which a program is to branch when a sequence of steps is to be broken.	A AND B ADDRESSES
The first counting machine invented, consisting of a frame in which rods strung with beads are set. The beads represent digits and the rods represent places in multiples of ten.	ABACUS
A number designating a computer cell location in which information is stored.	ADDRESS
Field containing letters of the alphabet and spaces.	ALPHABETIC FIELD
Field containing a combination of letters of the alphabet, numbers, special symbols, and spaces.	ALPHAMERIC FIELD
Column 8 of the COBOL program sheet.	A-MARGIN
A calculating machine that uses numbers to represent quantities that can be measured (such as voltages, resistances, or rotations). By gauges, meters, and wheels, the analog computer can measure and process physical variables such as amounts of electric current, speed of sound, temperature, pressure, and velocity. Contrast with digital computer.	ANALOG COMPUTER
The part of the CPU that adds, subtracts, multiplies, and divides numeric data as directed by the program. It also enables the CPU to make certain logical decisions and comparisons.	ARITHMETIC-LOGIC COMPONENT
A device that provides verbal replies to questions that have been directed to the computer through a telephone input unit.	AUDIO-RESPONSE UNIT (ARP)

Glossary of special terms

AUTOMATED DATA PROCESSING	A process in which data are handled with a minimum of human effort. The process depends upon recording original information in such a way that further use can be made of it without later manual rerecording.
AUXILIARY STORAGE (also known as ON-LINE STORAGE)	Storage on devices attached to and directly under the control of the CPU. Auxiliary storage devices may consist of magnetic disks, magnetic film, magnetic tape, or other input/output devices that are outside the central processing unit but connected to it.
B ADDRESS	See A AND B ADDRESSES.
BALANCE CARD	A card similar to a summary card, showing the balance of an account at the end of a specified period. The balance card can be used as a starting point for a subsequent period.
BINARY CODE	The language of the computer, based on a two-digit numbering system, represented by two characters, 1 and 0.
BINARY-CODED DECIMAL SYSTEM (BCD)	A computer language based on a base of 10 combined with the binary-coded grouping of four core positions for units, 10's, 100's, etc. For example: the number 16 is represented as 0001 0110, whereas in pure binary 16 is represented as 10000.
BINARY-CODED HEXIDECIMAL SYSTEM	A computer language based on a base of 16 combined with the binary-coded grouping of four core positions for units, 16's, 256's, etc. This code is used in the IBM 360 and many other third-generation computers to make the best use of the core storage available in the computer memory.
BINARY-CODED OCTAL SYSTEM	A computer language based on a combination of the binary and the octal forms.
BINARY NOTATION	Term used to refer to the number system based on the "on" and "off" condition of the cores in a computer cell.
BLOCK DIAGRAM	Detailed flow chart showing what is to be done at each step of the solution of a computer problem.
BLOCK DIAGRAM SYMBOLS	Symbols used in a block diagram to represent basic instructions prepared for a computer.
BLOCK SORTING	A method used to process large numbers of cards by breaking the total deck into subdecks according to the high-order digit.
B-MARGIN	Column 12 of the COBOL program sheet.
BRANCHING	A computer term indicating that a series or sequence of steps in the program has been completed and is to be repeated or changed to a new instruction or set of instructions.
BUFFER	Auxiliary storage device designed to hold data in magnetic form on a temporary basis. In some cases buffers assist in the proofreading of data. In other cases buffers aid in transferring data to a computer when the computer is being used by more than one user on a time-sharing basis. Input that arrives while the CPU is processing data from one user is temporarily stored in the buffer memory and then transferred to the computer memory when the CPU is ready to accept the data.
CALCULATING	The mathematical process of computing. It usually results in the creation of new information.

Glossary of special terms

The unit of the tabulator that adds and subtracts the numeric data relayed to it from the reading unit.	CALCULATING UNIT OF TABULATOR
A machine that accepts numeric data from punched cards, performs arithmetic computations, and punches the results into punched cards. The calculator adds, subtracts, multiplies, and divides. Some of the newer calculators can print calculated information as well.	CALCULATOR — UNIT-RECORD SYSTEM
One of the 80 vertical arrangements of digits and zone positions in a standard card.	CARD COLUMN
A piece of office equipment which records data by punching holes in cards. Machines with two types of keyboard are available. One type records numeric data only; the other records alphabetic and numeric data.	CARD PUNCH MACHINE
A unit of the electronic computer system that reads information punched in cards into the CPU and also punches data that have been processed by the computer into a new set of cards.	CARD READ-PUNCH UNIT
A machine similar in appearance to a card punch machine. The verifier is used to check the accuracy of holes previously punched into a card on a card punch machine.	CARD VERIFIER
An electronic vacuum tube like the picture tube of a television set, containing a screen on which data may be displayed in graphic form.	CATHODE-RAY TUBE (CRT)
A cathode-ray tube display unit combined with a console inquiry station.	CATHODE RAY TUBE INPUT/OUTPUT UNIT
A storage unit in a computer.	CELL
The number, symbol, or name designating the location of a cell in which information is stored.	CELL ADDRESS
See CPU.	CENTRAL PROCESSING UNIT
A system of representing data in punched paper tape (or magnetically polarized spots on magnetic tape). The impressions are made in either imaginary or real channels that run the length of the tape.	CHANNEL CODE
A positively charged magnetic core that is used by the computer to check its own accuracy in transmitting data.	CHECK BIT
The systematic assigning of similar data into categories according to established rules.	CLASSIFYING (Coding)
A special programming language with which business data processing procedures may be written in a standard form. COBOL is a source language devised in order to write a program for any suitable computer for which a compiler exists.	COBOL (Common Business Oriented Language)
1. The process of writing instructions in a language acceptable to the computer. 2. Classifying similar types of data into categories according to established rules.	CODING

COLLATOR	A unit-record machine that can merge two decks of cards in sequence; can match cards from two files having the same data punched in a particular field; can select from a deck of cards only those cards having a certain number in a specific field; and can check a deck of cards to make sure that they are in sequential order.
COMMON HUBS	Two hubs on a control panel that are connected in a straight line.
COMMUNICATING	The process of transmitting information to the point of use.
COMPILER (also known as COMPILER PROGRAM)	A translating program that is furnished by the manufacturer of the computer. The compiler translates the source program, written by the programmer, into the object or machine language program that will be processed by the computer.
COMPUTER INSTRUCTION	An instruction that tells the CPU in code form what action is to be taken on what data. The instructions may be written in a source language or machine language. If instructions are punched in 80-column cards, each instruction is punched into a separate card.
CONDITIONAL BRANCH INSTRUCTION	An instruction that causes the computer to branch to another instruction if a certain test or condition has been met.
CONFIGURATION SECTION	The section of the ENVIRONMENT DIVISION of a COBOL program that specifies the names of the source and object computers.
CONSOLE	That part of the computer used to provide information to the operator about the performance of the system and to enter information into the system manually, to alter the data in storage when necessary, and to start and stop the computer.
CONSOLE INQUIRY STATION	Station, usually containing a built-in or auxiliary electric typewriter. The console inquiry station may be part of the computer console or be housed in a separate unit. With it, the operator can enter new data or instructions into a computer. He can also use it to request the computer to furnish information. The reply will be typed out on the inquiry station typewriter.
CONSTANT	1. A value that never changes. 2. Information stored in a computer in a fixed location and used as needed. For example, a constant may be an amount for which a test is made as each data card is processed.
CONTACT ROLLER	The roller in a processing machine that provides the electrical impulse needed to process the data represented by punched holes.
CONTROL COMPONENT	The component of the CPU that regulates and coordinates all the other components of the CPU. The control component is the master clock that controls the various functions of the computer and interprets the instructions that make up the program.
CONTROL PANEL — UNIT-RECORD SYSTEM (also known as PLUGBOARD, CONTROL BOARD, WIRING BOARD)	A device, usually detachable, which uses removable wires to control the operation of punched card equipment.

Glossary of special terms

A drawing on a special form, showing the hub layouts for a particular type of control panel. There are diagram forms available for each type of control panel produced.	**CONTROL PANEL DIAGRAM**
Any wire connecting two or more hubs in a control panel.	**CONTROL PANEL WIRE**
1. Punch used in a predetermined position to direct a data processing machine to perform certain operations or to alter a program in some manner. 2. A specific code punched in a card to cause a data processing machine to perform a definite operation.	**CONTROL PUNCH**
See MAGNETIC CORE.	**CORE**
A form of high-speed storage using magnetic cores.	**CORE STORAGE**
Small square of tape, placed over an incorrect punch in order to correct a minor error on a card that is to be used only once or twice.	**CORRECTION SEAL**
That part of the electronic computer system that consists of the internal storage, arithmetic-logic, and control components. The CPU receives and stores instructions, receives and stores data to be processed, transfers and edits data already stored, makes arithmetic computations, makes decisions of logic, and directs the action of the input and output units.	**CPU (also known as CENTRAL PROCESSING UNIT)**
Detailed or factual material of any kind.	**DATA**
The third of the four divisions in a **COBOL** program. This division describes the data files for input and output and also the WORKING-STORAGE SECTION reserved for constants and computations.	**DATA DIVISION**
Manipulation of factual matter of all kinds for the purpose of producing a desired answer or result. The term includes recording, classifying, sorting, calculating, summarizing, communicating, and storing of information, whether manual or by machine.	**DATA PROCESSING**
The last character in a machine language computer instruction. It is associated with the decision-making ability of the computer. Its function in the program is to ask the question, for example, if the last card has been processed or if the page on which output is being printed has been filled. It is also used to define an operation.	**D-CHARACTER**
A numeric system using ten digits represented by the symbols 0 through 9.	**DECIMAL SYSTEM**
A block diagram symbol used to identify a decision, test, or switching type operation that will determine the future action to be taken in a program.	**DECISION SYMBOL**
Punched card representing a single transaction and holding all information pertaining to that transaction. Detail cards are combined with a master card to produce a desired report.	**DETAIL CARD**
An operation in which information from each card entering the tabulator is printed on a line of the report being prepared. This operation is used when complete information about individual transactions is desired.	**DETAIL PRINTING — UNIT-RECORD SYSTEM**
A type of electronic computer that works with numbers or letters of the alphabet and special symbols that can be coded numerically. It solves problems electronically by counting, adding, subtracting, multiplying, and dividing. Coded data can be stored in the memory of the digital computer until a total or result is desired. A digital computer can store the instructions for processing the data as well as the data to be processed.	**DIGITAL COMPUTER**

Term	Definition
DIRECT METHOD	Recording of input data in cards by punching holes directly into the cards with a card punch machine.
DISK	See MAGNETIC DISK.
DUPLICATE KEY	Special key on a card punch machine used for automatically repeating in one card the punches previously made in another card.
EDGE-NOTCHED CARD (also known as NEEDLE-SORT CARD)	A card containing holes punched around the four edges. Certain areas are blocked off for information code fields. Information to be shown on the card is notched in the edges, causing the notches to become slots. Sorting is done with a needle.
EDGE-NOTCHED METHOD (also known as NEEDLE-SORT METHOD)	A method which makes it possible to select with a needle from a large group of similar cards only those cards that are desired because they have specific information.
EDGE-PUNCHED CARD	Card used for recording data in punched form. The data are punched in channel code in one edge of the card.
EDP	Electronic data processing
EDST	*E*lectric *D*iaphragm *S*witch *T*echnology.
EDVAC	*E*lectronic *D*iscrete *V*ariable *A*utomatic *C*omputer.
ELECTRONIC COMPUTER SYSTEM	System in which both numeric and alphabetic data are processed in the form of electronic impulses. Both the information to be processed and the instructions for processing are stored in memory cells of the computer. Work is performed with a minimum of human effort. The system is largely self-regulating.
ELEMENTARY ITEM (COBOL)	An item that cannot be subdivided any further. For example, a zip code can be considered an elementary item. Elementary items are described in the record descriptions in the DATA DIVISION of the COBOL program.
11 POSITION (also known as X POSITION)	The punching position immediately below the 12 position of the standard 80-column card.
ENIAC	*E*lectronic *N*umerical *I*ntegrator and *C*omputer.
ENTRANCE HUB	A socket on a control panel into which an electrical lead or wire may be connected in order to carry electric signals into the machine.
ENVIRONMENT DIVISION	The second of the four divisions in a COBOL program. This division specifies the computers used, the input and output files, and the input and output devices.
EXIT HUB	The socket on a control panel into which an electrical lead or plug wire may be connected in order to carry signals out of the machine.
EXTERNAL STORAGE (also known as OFF-LINE STORAGE)	Storage on devices not attached to or directly under the control of the CPU. When punched cards, punched paper tape, magnetic tape, magnetic disks, and other devices are no longer contained in an input or output unit connected to the CPU, they are said to be in external or *off-line* storage.
FD (File Description)	A description of an input or output file in the DATA DIVISION of a COBOL program, specifying the programmer-invented names for the input and output records and describing the character and length of these records.

Glossary of special terms

1. One vertical column or a set of vertical columns in an 80-column card consistently used for similar information. Example: Customer No. Field. 2. An area in a card or document used consistently for the same type of information. Example: Student No. Field in edge-notched card.	FIELD
When using punched cards, a division of a single punched card (RECORD) in a deck of punched cards (FILE) being used as input. On a printed report, a specific item of information on a line (RECORD) of the report (FILE) being produced as output.	FIELD (COBOL)
A collection of related records treated as a unit. When processing punched cards, a deck of punched cards related to a specific program is an input FILE. The printed report is the output FILE.	FILE (COBOL)
The term used to describe the unused spaces in the input and output record. The description, written in the DATA DIVISION, specifies the unused columns if a punched card is used as input and also the blank spaces in the margins and between items on the line of the output printed report.	FILLER (COBOL)
A term that refers to computers in which data are treated in units of a fixed number of cell positions (as contrasted with variable word length).	FIXED WORD LENGTH
A graphic representation of the sequence of operations required to carry out a data processing procedure, method, or system in which symbols are used to represent operations, data flow, and equipment.	FLOW CHART
A symbol used to represent the operations, data flow, or equipment for carrying out a data processing procedure.	FLOW CHART SYMBOL
In flow charting, a line representing a connecting path between symbols on a flow chart.	FLOW LINE
The process of reproducing all or part of the punches from one card into as many additional cards as are needed.	GANG PUNCHING
A statement used in the PROCEDURE DIVISION to direct the computer to branch to a step other than the next sequential step in a program.	GO TO STATEMENT (COBOL)
A device whereby information will be accepted in graphic form, converted to digital form for processing and storing, and then converted back to graphic form for display as required.	GRAPH INPUT AND OUTPUT UNIT
An item that can be "broken down" or subdivided into smaller items. For example, a group item can be a proper name. Group items are described in the record descriptions in the DATA DIVISION.	GROUP ITEM (COBOL)
An operation in which the data from a group of cards relating to a number of similar transactions are summarized and only the summary information is printed on the report.	GROUP PRINTING
Process of arranging punched cards in groups according to the numbers or names punched in them.	GROUPING
The flow charting symbol used to indicate the end of a program. The notation within the symbol will read HALT.	HALT SYMBOL (also known as TERMINAL SYMBOL)
The computer and other processing machines in the electronic computer system.	HARDWARE

HEXADECIMAL NUMBERING SYSTEM	A computer language based on a base of 16.
HIGH-ORDER POSITION	The position at the extreme left of a data word.
HIGH-SPEED LINE PRINTER	An output device that can print simultaneously one line of characters across a page (100 or more characters) as continuous paper advances line by line in one direction past type bars, a tape cylinder, or a chain that contains all characters in all positions.
HOLLERITH CODE	A system of representing data by rectangular holes punched in an 80-column card, invented by Herman Hollerith. In this system, each letter is identified by a punch in one of the three positions at the top of the card and by another punch in one of the numbered columns. Each number is identified by a punch in a column at a specific location.
HUB	A hole or socket in a control panel through which an electrical impulse may be emitted or into which an impulse may be sent.
HUMAN LANGUAGE	A term used to refer to the language spoken and written by the persons processing the data, as contrasted to machine language.
IDENTIFICATION DIVISION	The first of the four divisions in a COBOL program. This division gives the title of the program, the name of the programmer, and the date the program is written.
IF STATEMENT (COBOL)	A statement used to perform a test in COBOL. An IF statement combined with a GO TO statement will cause a branch to be made. IF and GO TO statements appear in the PROCEDURE DIVISION.
INDIRECT METHOD OF DATA PROCESSING	Recording input data in cards or tape as a by-product of the preparation of a business document.
INPUT	1. Data that are recorded for processing. 2. The process of transferring data into internal storage.
INPUT FILE (COBOL)	1. A collection of related records treated as a unit, recorded on a suitable input medium. 2. A deck of cards containing related information which will be used by a particular program.
INPUT MEDIA	The forms on which data are recorded for processing.
INPUT UNIT	That unit of an electronic computer system through which data are communicated to the system itself. The input unit will vary according to the input media used.
INPUT-OUTPUT SECTION	The section of the ENVIRONMENT DIVISION of a COBOL program that specifies the input and output files, the input and output media, and the input and output devices to be used for processing the data.
INPUT/OUTPUT SYMBOL	A block diagram symbol used to represent either an input or an output function. One function is distinguished from the other by notations written inside the blocks.
INSTRUCTION ADDRESS	The address at which the CPU can locate the instruction for each step in a program.

Glossary of special terms

The term given to the form in which computer instructions are written.	INSTRUCTION FORMAT
The memory of the CPU. It can accept, hold, and release data as well as the instructions for processing the data. Data and instructions are stored as electronic impulses in specified cell locations or addresses in the memory unit.	INTERNAL STORAGE COMPONENT
A machine that prints on a punched card the data already punched in the card	INTERPRETER
A block diagram symbol used to identify an operation using a key-driven device. Example: punching, verifying, or typing.	KEYING SYMBOL
See EDGE-NOTCHED CARD.	KEYSORT CARD
A sense switch that is turned on in some computers after the last card in an input deck of data cards has been processed. A test for the last card is written into the program. If the last card has been processed, the program will instruct the computer to branch to a new step or sequence of steps in the program.	LAST CARD SENSE SWITCH
A coded punched card placed at the end of an input deck of data cards. If the last card test code is not sensed by the CPU, the computer will continue to process the data card. If the last card code is sensed, the computer will branch to the next step or sequence of steps named in the PROCEDURE DIVISION.	LAST CARD TEST CONTROL CARD (COBOL)
A business form, retained by the seller as a permanent record, showing the amount of charges incurred, the payments made, and the balance due on an account.	LEDGER CARD
Numbers that perform the same function as Roman and Arabic numerals do in an outline. Level numbers appear in the DATA DIVISION only and explain the level of importance of the records, fields, and items in the fields.	LEVEL NUMBERS (COBOL)
The level number assigned in the WORKING-STORAGE SECTION of the DATA DIVISION of a COBOL program to the area reserved for arithmetic computations or for accumulating a total. The 77 is written at the A-Margin. Level 77 items must always precede other items in the description of the WORKING-STORAGE SECTION.	LEVEL 77
The repetition of a sequence of instructions in a routine until certain conditions are reached.	LOOP
The process of repeating instructions of a program until a certain condition is reached.	LOOPING
The position at the extreme right of a data word.	LOW-ORDER POSITION
1. A language for writing operation codes of instructions in single digit, letter, and character form. 2. Instructions written in a form intelligible to the internal circuitry of the computer. Sometimes called "actual" or "absolute."	MACHINE LANGUAGE
A small, doughnut-shaped metal ring, capable of being magnetized either negatively or positively.	MAGNETIC CORE
A group of magnetic cores arranged in a plane made up of many wires crossing one another at right angles. A magnetic core appears at each intersection of wires.	MAGNETIC CORE PLANE

MAGNETIC DISK	An input/output device that also serves as a storage medium. The disk is coated on both sides with a substance capable of being magnetized. Data are stored as magnetic spots on tracks on the disk, and read-write heads are mounted above each track to record or read the data.
MAGNETIC DRUM	An input/output device that also serves as a storage medium, on which a series of bands or tracks appear on the outer surface. These bands are capable of being magnetized and thus are able to store electronic signals representing data. As the drum rotates the data are either recorded or read by read-write heads.
MAGNETIC INK CHARACTER READER	A device that reads and processes information that has been printed or typed in magnetic ink in specially designed numbers and symbols.
MAGNETIC TAPE	An input, output, and storage medium in which data are recorded in the form of magnetized spots on the surface of magnetically sensitive coated tape.
MAGNETIC THIN FILM	Computer memory storage device consisting of thin layers of glass or plastic on which are mounted sections of metallic spots connected by very thin wires. The sections form planes of memory cores capable of being magnetized to represent digits, letters of the alphabet, or other characters in core storage.
MANUAL METHOD OF DATA PROCESSING	Method in which the flow of a routine for handling a job consists of a number of fairly distinct steps, each of which is performed by some human effort, direction, and control.
MANUAL OPERATION SYMBOL	A symbol used to identify any process performed at "human speed" without mechanical aid.
MARK-SENSED CARD	A special card, containing 27 vertical positions, designed to record information by using a graphite pencil. The card is read by special equipment which converts the pencil marks into punched holes.
MARK-SENSED PUNCHING METHOD	A method for detecting pencil marks entered in special positions on a card and automatically translating these marks into punched holes.
MASTER CARD	Card that contains fixed or constant information which applies to a group of cards, such as a customer's number, name, and address.
MATCHING	Process by which punched cards in two decks that have been arranged in sequential order are compared, matched according to the same information in a specific field, and then brought together (merged).
MEMORY	The same as STORAGE. A general term for a device into which data can be entered, held, and retrieved at a later time.
MERGING	Process by which two decks of punched cards, arranged in sequential order, are combined into one deck.
9 EDGE	A term used to refer to the bottom edge of a punched card.
NUMERIC FIELD (COBOL)	Field containing numbers and no spaces.
OBJECT PROGRAM	The machine language program into which the source program has been translated. This is the program that is intelligible to the inner circuitry of the computer.
OCTAL SYSTEM	A computer language based on a base of 8.
OFF-LINE STORAGE	See EXTERNAL STORAGE.
ON-LINE STORAGE	See AUXILIARY STORAGE.

Glossary of special terms

That part of the computer instruction that tells the CPU what operations to perform.	**OPERATION CODE**
A device capable of sensing marks made by regular pencil or pen on a specially designed form. It uses a technique similar to mark sensing.	**OPTICAL MARK PAGE READER**
A device that speed-reads photoelectrically the data from a page directly into a computer. Generally, characters must appear in a certain area of the document. The special type fonts needed are based upon the individual scanner being used.	**OPTICAL SCANNER**
Data to be processed.	**ORIGINAL DATA** (also known as **RAW DATA**)
1. Processed information. 2. The process of transferring data from internal storage to external storage.	**OUTPUT**
1. A collection of related records treated as a unit, recorded on a suitable output medium. 2. A printed report containing processed information.	**OUTPUT FILE (COBOL)**
Forms or devices on which processed information appear.	**OUTPUT MEDIA**
The unit in the electronic computer system that records or displays the processed information on the output media, which may be printed reports, magnetic tape, punched cards, or some other medium compatible with the computer used.	**OUTPUT UNIT**
1. Name of heading in the IDENTIFICATION, ENVIRONMENT, and PROCEDURE divisions of a COBOL program. The DATA DIVISION does not contain paragraph names. 2. Name of the heading in the PROCEDURE DIVISION to which the compiler can be directed *instead of to a cell address*, in order to carry out the COBOL program. Example: In the instruction GO TO DETAIL-PROCESSING, the paragraph name DETAIL-PROCESSING is used instead of a cell address.	**PARAGRAPH NAME (COBOL)**
A check that tests whether the number of magnetic cores turned on in a computer cell is odd or even.	**PARITY CHECK**
Detail card containing information relative to a customer's payment received on account. The card usually contains the customer's number, date of payment, and the amount of payment.	**PAYMENTS DETAIL CARD**
A board to which pegs are fastened. The board is used with special forms. The pegs keep the forms and any carbons in proper alignment for the recording of data.	**PEGBOARD** (also known as **WRITING BOARD** or **ACCOUNTING BOARD**)
Method that provides a means of manually recording identical information at the same time on forms of different size and design so that rerecording is not necessary.	**PEGBOARD METHOD**
Card in which the punching positions have been perforated so that the perforated sections may be punched out of the card with a sharp pencil, stylus, or similar object.	**PERFORATED CARD**
Term applied to a descriptive statement used only in the DATA DIVISION of a COBOL program to describe the fields in an input or output record. The clause is always preceded by the word PICTURE and followed by a space and a coded description as to whether the field is numeric, alphabetic, or alphameric and as to the length (number of characters) in the field.	**PICTURE CLAUSE**

PRINT AREA (COMPUTER)	The group of cells that are reserved for output that is to be printed on paper or some other business form.
PRINT ENTRY HUB	See ENTRANCE HUB.
PRINTING CARD PUNCH	A card punch machine that prints at the top of the card the interpretation of the punch or punches made in each column of the card.
PRINTING UNIT OF TABULATOR	The unit that prints the alphabetic and numeric data punched into cards and relayed to it by the reading unit. The printing unit also prints the results of calculations performed in the calculating unit.
PROCEDURE DIVISION	The fourth and last division in a COBOL program. This division specifies the actual steps the computer is to follow in processing the data.
PROCESSING SYMBOL	1. A block diagram symbol used to identify the processing activities that go on within the computer, such as arithmetic computations, movement of data, and comparison of data. A notation within the symbol indicates the type of process. 2. A flow charting symbol indicating a processing function causing change in value, form, or location of information.
PROCESSING UNIT (COMPUTER SYSTEM)	See CPU.
PROGRAM	1. A group of related routines to solve a given problem. 2. A complete set of instructions for solving a problem on a computer.
PROGRAM CARD (CARD PUNCH)	Punched card which automatically instructs the card punch machine to space, to repeat, or to shift from numeric to alphabetic positions.
PROGRAM CHART	The form on which the program for a computer is written.
PROGRAM LOAD CARD	A prepunched card for each instruction that tells the computer the address at which the instruction can be found and spells out the instruction itself.
PROGRAMMER	An operator or technician who plans the steps and order of the operations necessary to produce the desired report or document.
PROGRAMMER-INVENTED NAMES	Names the programmer may invent for a COBOL program for the files, records, fields, and paragraphs. The names must not appear on the COBOL reserved word list, must always be hyphened if two names are used together, and must never consist of all numbers.
PUNCH AREA (COMPUTER)	The group of cells that are reserved for output that is to be punched into cards.
PUNCHED CARD	1. A card punched with a pattern of holes to represent data to be processed. 2. A card that may be punched with holes to represent digits, letters, and special characters.
PUNCHED PAPER TAPE	A continuous paper tape recording medium, containing rows of punched holes that represent a code for letters, digits, and symbols.
PUNCHING STATION	The location on the card punch machine where cards are positioned for the punching process.
RANDOM ACCESS	The method by which some computers can go directly to an item of information and retrieve it without examining all the data in a file.

Glossary of special terms

The data to be processed (same as ORIGINAL DATA).	RAW DATA
The group of cells in the CPU that are reserved for receiving and holding information that is read into the computer from input media.	READ AREA (COMPUTER)
A wire brush that is part of the reading unit of some unit-record equipment. This brush makes contact with the contact roller through the holes in a punched card or tape, thus completing the circuit which creates timed electrical impulses.	READING BRUSH
The location on the card punch machine where cards are positioned for reading by a sensing device, for the purpose of duplicating data automatically in cards located in the punching station.	READING STATION
That part of the tabulator that senses the data recorded in the punched card and relays meaningful messages to the calculating and printing units.	READING UNIT OF TABULATOR
(When using punched cards) a single punched card in a deck of punched cards used as an input file. A single line in a report produced as an output file.	RECORD (COBOL)
The process of writing, rewriting, or reproducing data by hand or by machine.	RECORDING
Console inquiry station that is in direct contact with a computer but which does not have to be physically near to the computer. The console has a typewriter keyboard and may have a display tube.	REMOTE CONSOLE (also known as REMOTE CONTOOL CONSOLE and REMOTE DATA TERMINAL)
Machine capable of punching all or part of the information recorded in one card into as many additional cards as are needed.	REPRODUCER
COBOL names required in every program. These include division names, section names, and certain other words that the compiler program requires.	REQUIRED ENTRIES (COBOL)
A list of English words designated by COBOL that must be used only in a specified manner. These words have specific meanings to the compiler. Examples: READ, WRITE, GO TO.	RESERVED WORDS (COBOL)
Aligned at the right.	RIGHT-JUSTIFIED
One of the horizontal lines of punching positions on a punched card.	ROW (CARD)
Detail card prepared for a single item listed in the body of a sales invoice. A separate sales detail card is prepared for each transaction.	SALES DETAIL CARD
Process of separating from a deck of punched cards only those cards that have a particular name or number in a specific field.	SELECTING
A series of steps or instructions in a program that the computer will perform without interruption.	SEQUENCE
Process of arranging punched cards in alphabetic or numeric order.	SEQUENCING
A special key on a card punch machine, used to skip automatically from one punching field to another.	SKIP KEY
An instrument consisting of two rules divided into scales, arranged to slide on each other. The rules are moved either backward or forward until a selected number on one scale is made to coincide with a selected number on the other. The desired result is then read from a third scale. This instrument depends upon the use of logarithms.	SLIDE RULE

Term	Definition
SOFTWARE	The programs and routines used with a computer.
SOROBAN	Japanese counting device differing slightly from the abacus.
SORTER	A machine that sorts or classifies numeric or alphabetic data by sequencing, grouping, or selecting.
SORTING	The process of separating data into similar groups.
SOURCE DOCUMENT	The paper or form from which raw or original data are obtained.
SOURCE LANGUAGE	A synthetic language such as COBOL or FORTRAN, which is used to make it easier for a programmer to write a computer program. The source language is translated into machine language by a compiler or assembly program furnished by the manufacturer of the computer.
SOURCE PROGRAM	A synthetic program that must be translated into a machine language object program before processing by the computer.
STANDARD PUNCHED CARD (also known as 80-COLUMN CARD)	Card containing 80 vertical columns into which data may be punched. Each column is divided into ten digit positions, numbered 0 through 9. Above the Zero position in each column are two more punching positions, the 11 or X position and the 12 or Y position. The Zero, 11, and 12 positions are known as the zone positions of the card. With various combinations of punches in the digit and zone positions, it is possible to express alphabetic and numeric characters as well as many symbols.
START SYMBOL (also known as TERMINAL SYMBOL)	The flow charting symbol used to indicate the beginning of a program. The notation within the symbol will read START.
STATEMENT OF ACCOUNT	A business form that summarizes the charges to a customer's account, the payments made, and the balance due. This may be sent to the customer monthly or periodically.
STEP IDENTIFICATION SYMBOL	Symbol used in a flow chart or block diagram to number or identify the introduction of a step or sequence of steps in a computer program.
STORAGE	A general term for a device into which data can be entered, held, and retrieved at a later time.
STORAGE SYMBOL	Symbol used in flow charting to identify storage or filing of records.
STORING	The orderly filing of information so that it may be used when it is needed.
SUMMARIZING	The process of converting the processed data into a concise, usable form.
SUMMARY CARD	Card that summarizes the transactions of a group of similar detail cards.
SUMMARY PUNCHING	The summarization of data from detail cards and the punching of the summarized data into another or summary card.
TABULATOR	A unit-record machine, sometimes referred to as a printing or accounting machine, which performs the summarizing functions of reading, adding or subtracting, and printing.
TABULATING SYSTEM	See UNIT-RECORD SYSTEM.
TAPE-TO-CARD CONVERTER	A machine that automatically transfers information punched into paper tape (or recorded on magnetic tape) to a punched card.
TEMPLATE	A device that is used to draw symbols of different sizes and shapes for use in a block diagram or flow chart.

Glossary of special terms

The flow charting symbol used to indicate the beginning or end of a program. The notations within the symbol will read START or HALT.	TERMINAL SYMBOL
An arrangement whereby more than one user shares the same computer by use of remote consoles.	TIME SHARING
An impulse that is created at a certain time in a planned cycle.	TIMED ELECTRICAL IMPULSE
A term used to refer to the top edge of a punched card.	12 EDGE
The punching position nearest the top or 12 edge of the standard card.	12 POSITION (also known as Y POSITION)
A mechanical printing device on which are located the digits, the letters of the alphabet, and some special symbols.	TYPEBAR
An instruction that causes the computer to branch to another instruction regardless of conditions.	UNCONDITIONAL BRANCH
Record in which all data concerning each item in a transaction are punched into a separate card.	UNIT RECORD
Data processing system based on a unit record in which data concerning each item in a transaction are recorded in code form in a separate punched card.	UNIT-RECORD SYSTEM (also known as TABULATING SYSTEM)
A statement used with a PICTURE clause to attach a practical value to the PICTURE clause. The VALUE clause must agree with the description in the PICTURE clause. Example: PICTURE A(31) VALUE 'SALES REPORT FOR FRESHMAN GIRLS'.	VALUE CLAUSE OR STATEMENT
Data in storage that does not remain constant because the value may change each time a new record is read by the computer. Example: a total being accumulated.	VARIABLE DATA (COBOL)
A term that refers to a computer in which the number of cells addressed is not a fixed number but varies according to the length of the data or instruction. With a variable word length computer, it is necessary to use a word mark in the high-order position to signal the end of the word.	VARIABLE WORD LENGTH
A term in computer language to indicate a single character or group of characters that represent a unit of information.	WORD
A core that is turned on to indicate the end of a word to the computer.	WORD MARK
An area of the computer into which data are moved for computation and other types of processing necessary before moving into one of the output areas.	WORK AREA
Section of the DATA DIVISION of a COBOL program, describing the fields reserved for constants and computations.	WORKING-STORAGE
See 11 POSITION and 12 POSITION.	X AND Y POSITIONS
The top *printed* digit position of a standard 80-column card. A punch in this position represents the Digit Zero. When used in conjunction with another punched number, the Zero punch helps to represent a letter of the alphabet or a symbol.	ZERO POSITION
The cores used in combination with digit cores in a computer cell to represent the letters of the alphabet as well as some of the special signs and symbols.	ZONE CORES OR BITS
A punch in any one of the three top positions of 12, 11, or Zero in a standard punched card. A punch in one of these positions, together with a punch in the digit position, represents a letter of the alphabet or a special character.	ZONE PUNCH

INDEX

A

A Address, 254
   Operand, 254
Abacus, 13, *illustrated* 14
Absolute program, 253
Accounting board, 37
Accumulating total
   WORKING-STORAGE SECTION, 345, 346, 362, 366, 371
Add instruction, 273
ADD statement, 362
   Constant established by, *illustrated* 364
Adding machine, first mechanical, *illustrated* 17
Addition
   in binary, 204
   in COBOL, 349
   in computer cells, *illustrated* 225
Address, machine language instruction, 255
Addresses, words in computers, *illustrated* 224
A/I Address, 256
Aiken, Howard, 25
Alphabet, binary code for letters of, *illustrated* 220
Alphabetic
   code, 66
   data, tabulator, 138
   PICTURE clause, 309
   sequencing, 117, 118
   sorting, 117, 118
Alphameric PICTURE clause, 309
A-Margin, 296
Ampex Corporation, Videofile Information System, *illustrated* 384
Analog computer, 167, *illustrated* 169
Aperture card, *illustrated* 191
Application for enrollment, *illustrated* 88
Area
   print, 233
   program storage, 235
   punch, 233
   read, 233
   reserved storage, 235
Arithmetic computations
   in binary-coded decimal, 206
   in pure binary, 204
Arithmetic-logic, computer, 171
ARP, 193, *illustrated* 194
Astrodata, Inc. (Comcor 550) analog computer, *illustrated* 169
AT END statement, 321, 348, 353, 356
Audio-response unit (ARP) 193, *illustrated* 194
Automated data processing, 43
Automation, 43
   applied to manual data processing tasks, 35
Auxiliary storage, 176, *illustrated* 177

B

B Address, 254
   Column, 257
   Operand, 254
Babbage, Charles, 24,
   "Difference engine," *illustrated* 25
Balance cards, 79
Baldwin, Frank S., 19
BCD, 206
Binary
   addition, 204
   code, 201
      for alphabet, *illustrated* 220
      for digits, 202
   digits, 201
      stored in magnetic cores, *illustrated* 216
   numbering system, 26
   pure, 203
   subtraction, 204
Binary-coded
   decimal system (BCD), 206
      addition, 207
      arithmetic computations, 207
   hexadecimal system, 210, 211
   octal system, 209
Bit, 201, 218
   check, *illustrated* 219
   digit, *illustrated* 219
   word mark, *illustrated* 219, 220
   zone, 219, *illustrated* 220
      See also magnetic core.
Block, 242
Block diagram, 230, 242
   COBOL, 355
   human language problem
      preparing printed list, *illustrated* 246
      preparing printed report, including last card test, 248, *illustrated* 249
   machine language problem, *illustrated* 277, *illustrated* 334, *illustrated* 354
      including multiple decisions, 285, *illustrated* 286
      preparing printed list, *illustrated* 272
      preparing printed list and accumulating total, including two decisions, *illustrated* 282
   symbols, *illustrated* 243
Block sorting, 120
B-Margin, 296
Branch, *illustrated* 241, 246
Branch instruction 240, 267
Branching, 241
Brush, reading, *illustrated* 153
Buffers, 197
Burroughs Corp., first U.S. calculator, *illustrated* 20

C

Calculating, 7; *illustrated* 8
   and printing numeric data, tabulator, 139
   unit, tabulator, 134
Calculator, 141, *illustrated* 142
   Grant's 19
   Monroe International, Inc., 8
Carbon paper, 36
Card
   balance, 79
   collator, *illustrated* 122
   columns, 63
   containing
      complete language of automation, *illustrated* 67
      digit punches, *illustrated* 65
      letters of the alphabet, *illustrated* 67
      special characters, *illustrated* 67
   control punch in, 81
   detail, 78
   edge-notched, *illustrated* 39
   edge-punched, *illustrated* 99
   fields, 71, 72
   layout, 71

401

Card (continued)
  mark-sensed, *illustrated* 100
  master, 77
  payments detail, *illustrated* 78
  perforated, 91, *illustrated* 92
  planning, 71
  printed matter on, 82
  program, 93, *illustrated* 95
  receipt, *illustrated* 144
  row, 64
  sales detail, 78
  student attendance, *illustrated* 68
  summary, 79
Card punch, *illustrated* 23, *illustrated* 45, 88, *illustrated* 89,
  operator, 376, 377
  portable, 90, *illustrated* 91
  printing, 90, *illustrated* 89
Card punching
  direct method, 87
  indirect method, 96
Card read-punch, *illustrated* 175
Card verifier, *illustrated* 45, 46, 104, *illustrated* 105
Cards
  grouped by class number, 120
  recording alphabetic information, 74
  recording numeric information, 73
  sorted on hundred's digits, 117
  sorted on unit's and ten's digits, *illustrated* 116
Careers in data processing, 375
Carriage control, tabulator, 139
Carriage tape cut and punched to control printing on special form, *illustrated* 140
Cathode-ray tube, 191, *illustrated* 192
Cell
  addresses, *illustrated* 224
  arrangement in computers, 226
  computer, 218, *illustrated* 219, *illustrated* 222
  digit bits in, *illustrated* 216
  eight-core, *illustrated* 219
  five-core, *illustrated* 226
  storage in, *illustrated* 222
  structure of, 218
Central processing unit, see *CPU*.
Channel code, 98, *illustrated* 99
Chart, machine language program, 255, *illustrated* 256
Check bit, *illustrated* 219
Checking
  accuracy of reproduced data, 102
  print, 107
Classifying, 6
  data in cards, 111
Clause, PICTURE, 309
Clear storage instructions
  human language, 235, 236, 245
  machine language, 257

Clearance of reserved storage areas, 235, 236, 245
Clearing memory, COBOL, 348
Clearing print area, COBOL, 367
COBOL, 230, 291
  accumulating a total, 345
  clearing memory, 348
  constants and variables, 361
  DATA DIVISION, see DATA DIVISION.
  divisions, 296
  ENVIRONMENT DIVISION, see ENVIRONMENT DIVISION.
  file, 291
  file description, 308
  GO TO statement, 357
  IDENTIFICATION DIVISION, see IDENTIFICATION DIVISION.
  IF statement, 356, 357
  input field, 303
  input file, 301, 303
  input record, 303
  inventing names
    input data, 306
    output data, 312
    paragraphs, 316
  last card test, 348, 353, *illustrated* 355, 356
  level numbers, 308
  line numbers, 296, 339, 340
  looping, 347, *illustrated* 348
  names used in programs, 320
  output field, 304
  output file, 301, 304
  output record, 304
  page numbers, 295, 296, 339, 340
  PICTURE clause, 309
  Printed report, see Printed report, COBOL.
  program, *illustrated* 326, 327, *illustrated* 350, 351, *illustrated* 368, 369
  program, partial, as printed by computer, *illustrated* 329
  program cards, *illustrated* 328
  program divisions, 296
  program identification, 337
  program sheet, *illustrated* 295
  program structure, 293
  programmer-invented names, 294, 322
    rules for, 324
  punctuation rules for, 325
  relation test, 357
  required entries, 322
  reserved words, 294, *illustrated* 323
  source program cards, *illustrated* 328
  VALUE clause, 365
Code
  alphabetic, 66
  binary, 201. See also *binary code.*
  binary-coded decimal (BCD), 206
  binary-coded hexadecimal, 210

binary-coded octal, 209
channel, 98, *illustrated* 99
fields, edge-notched card, 38
numeric, 64
operation, 254
special characters, 66, *illustrated* 67
Coding, 6
  for computer, 236
Collating, 122
  symbol, *illustrated* 49
Collator, *illustrated* 122
Column, card, 63, 64
Common elements in unit-record and electronic computer systems, 56
Common hubs, *illustrated* 155
Communicating, 9
Communitype Corporation
  Magnetic tape data recorder, *illustrated* 183
Comparison of machine language and COBOL programs, 321
Compiler program, 292
Computer
  analog, 167, *illustrated* 169
  assisting in instruction, *illustrated* 192
  cell, 218
  decisions, 171
  digital, *illustrated* 55, 165, 167, *illustrated* 196, 226
  first-generation, 231
  fixed word length, 221
  instruction, 229
  operator, 378, 379
  programming, 54
  second-generation, 231
  third-generation, 231
  variable word length, 221
Conditional branch instruction, 268
Conditional statement, COBOL, see IF statement.
CONFIGURATION SECTION, 299
Console, IBM 360, *illustrated* 177, *illustrated*, 178
Console inquiry station, 177, *illustrated* 178
Console, remote, 193, *illustrated* 195
Constant, COBOL, 361, 362, *illustrated* 363, *illustrated* 364, 365
  established by IF statement, *illustrated* 363
  established by VALUE clause, 365
Contact roller, 111, *illustrated* 153
Control
  board, 151, *illustrated* 152
  card, 355
  carriage, tabulator, 139, 140
  component, 173
  electronic computer system, 173, *illustrated* 174
Control Data Corp., console inquiry station, *illustrated* 178

Index

Control panel, 151, *illustrated* 152, *illustrated* 154
    collator, 123
    interpreter, 157
    tabulator, *illustrated* 47, 162
Control panel diagram, interpreter 158, *illustrated* 161
    rules for preparing, 159, *illustrated* 160
Control panel wire, *illustrated* 154
Control punch, 81, 127
    for cards processed by the electronic computer system, 81
    for cards processed by the unit-record system, 81
Converter, 101
    tape-to-card, *illustrated* 101
Core
    magnetic, 201
    parity check, 218
    position, 202, 203
    storage, 201, 202
    storage, magnetic thin film, 226
    storage position, 202
Correction seals, 108
Counter wheels, tabulator, *illustrated* 139
CPU, 53, *illustrated* 170, *illustrated* 177
    decisions made by, 171, *illustrated* 172, 173
CRT, 191, *illustrated* 192

D

Data, 6
DATA DIVISION, 296, 303, *illustrated* 307, 339, *illustrated* 342
    elementary item, 345
    files, records, and fields, 303
    format of statements, 309
    group item, 344
    input statements, 304, 305
    inventing names for input data, 306
    inventing names for output data, 312
    Optional input statements, 341
    output portion, *illustrated* 314
    required input statements, 304, 340
    required output statements, 312
    subdividing data items, 344
    WORKING-STORAGE SECTION, 345
Data moved into read area of computer, 263
Data processing, 6
    framework, 31, *illustrated* 32
    history of, 13
    jobs and careers in, 375
        card punch operator, 376
        computer operator, 378
        programmer, 379
        systems analyst, 381
        unit-record equipment operator, 377
    manual, 31, 33
    salaries, 383
da Vinci, Leonardo, 15
d-Character, 244, 255
Decimal numbering system, 26
Decision
    based on digit comparison, *illustrated* 280
    instruction, 280
    symbol, 244, *illustrated* 245
Decisions, CPU, 171, *illustrated* 172, 173
    multiple, 285
Detail cards, 78
Detail printing, 135, *illustrated* 136
Diagram, block, 242
Digit cores, 221
Digit punches, 64
Digital computer, *illustrated* 55, 165, 167, *illustrated* 196, 226
Direct method of recording information in cards, 87
Disks, magnetic, 184
Double spacing, COBOL, 367
Dual-role machines, 96
Duplicate key, card punch, 74, 93, *illustrated* 91
Dura Business Machines, Dura typewriter, *illustrated* 97

E

Eastman Kodak, Rekordak Microstar, *illustrated* 190
Eckert, Prosper, 26, 28
Edge-notched card, 38, *illustrated* 39
    sorting by needle-sort process, *illustrated* 40
Edge-notched method, 38
Edge-punched card, *illustrated* 99
EDST, 189
Educational application, remote console, *illustrated* 192
EDVAC, 26, 231
80-column card, *illustrated* 67
Electric Diaphragm Switch Technology (EDST), 189
Electrical impulse, 111, *illustrated* 112, *illustrated* 153
Electronic computer, 1, 24, 43
Electronic computer system, *illustrated* 55, 167, *illustrated* 168
    basic machines in, 53
    input and output media, 181–199
    processing plan, 179
    steps followed when processing data, 52, 53, *illustrated* 180
    supplementary storage devices, 176
    unique features of, 54
Elementary item, 345
11 position, 64
Embossed metal plate, *illustrated* 36
ENIAC, 26, 28, 231
Entrance hub, 154
ENVIRONMENT DIVISION, 296, *illustrated* 300, 338, *illustrated* 339
    format of statements, 301
Equal condition, 358
Equality test, 371
Equality, testing for, COBOL, 357, 358
Error-notched card, *illustrated* 105
Exit hub, *illustrated* 153, *illustrated* 154
External control unit, electronic computer, 177, *illustrated* 178
External storage 176, *illustrated* 177

F

FD, 308, 310
Felt, Dorr Eugene, 19
Field
    card, 71
    COBOL, *illustrated* 303, 304
    code, edge-notched card, 38
File, COBOL, 291, *illustrated* 303, 304
File description, 310
FILE-CONTROL, 299
Files, records, and fields, 303
Filler, COBOL, 335, 336, 343, 365
First-generation computer, 231
Five-core storage cells, *illustrated* 226
Fixed word length, 221
Flow, information in electronic computer system, *illustrated* 174
Flow chart, 48
    for preparing payroll manually, *illustrated* 50
    for preparing printed report of contributions, unit-record system, *illustrated* 145
    for preparing updated printed report of contributions, unit-record system, 45
    steps followed in electronic computer system when processing data, *illustrated* 180

Flow chart (continued)
  symbols, *illustrated* 49
  typical decisions made by CPU, *illustrated* 172
Flow lines, *illustrated* 243
Format
  machine language instructions, 253
  statements in DATA DIVISION, 309
  statements in ENVIRONMENT DIVISION, 301
  statements in PROCEDURE DIVISION, 319
FORTRAN, 230
Friden, Inc., Ten-key adding machine with tape-punching attachment, *illustrated* 97

G

General Electric Corporation, GE-410
  digital computer, *illustrated* 168
  electronic computer system, *illustrated* 55
  remote console, *illustrated* 195
  TRADAR optical scanner, 188
GO TO statement, COBOL, 347, 357
Grant's calculator, 19
Graph
  input unit, 189
  output unit, 189
  plotter, IBM 1627, *illustrated* 190
Graphic display unit
  Eastman Kodak, Rekordak Microstar, *illustrated* 190
  IBM 2250, *illustrated* 190
Graphic units, 189, *illustrated* 190
GREATER THAN condition, 358
Group item, 344
Group printing, 135, *illustrated* 137
Grouping, 113
Grouping cards, 118

H

Halt instruction, 269, *illustrated* 247
Halt instruction, COBOL, 317, 319, 369
Halt symbol, *illustrated* 49, 243
Hardware, 170, 230
Heading, COBOL, 365
HEADING-LINE, in WORKING-STORAGE SECTION, 366, 371
Hexadecimal code, 209, *illustrated* 210
High-speed line printer, *illustrated* 175
Hodometer, *illustrated* 15
Hollerith, Herman, 20

Hollerith's punched card machine, *illustrated* 21
Hub
  common, 155
  entrance, 154
  exit, 153
Human language, 44
  decision instruction, *illustrated* 280
  programs and block diagrams, 229

I

I Address, 256
IBM Corporation, 21
  29 card punch machine, 23, *illustrated* 89
  29 card punch keyboard
  59 card verifier, *illustrated* 105
  083 card sorter, *illustrated* 113
  188 card collator, *illustrated* 122
  System/360 computer, 226, 231
    console, 176, *illustrated* 177
    Model 85, *illustrated* 168
  System/370, Model 165, *illustrated* 196
  402 tabulator, *illustrated* 135
  521 calculator, *illustrated* 142
  548 interpreter, *illustrated* 134
  548 interpreter typebar, *illustrated* 155
  1230 optical mark scoring reader, *illustrated* 187
  1259 magnetic ink character reader, *illustrated* 185
  1401 computer, 231
  1627 graph plotter, *illustrated* 190
  2250 graphic display unit, *illustrated* 190
  2560 multi-function card machine, 142, *illustrated* 143
  3211 impact printer, *illustrated* 196
  6400, *illustrated* 98
  7770 audio-response unit, *illustrated* 194
  card read-punch, *illustrated* 175
  high-speed line printer, *illustrated* 175
  magnetic tape drive, *illustrated* 175
  reproducer, *illustrated* 103
  tape-to-card converter, *illustrated* 101
IDENTIFICATION DIVISION, 296, 336, *illustrated* 337, *illustrated* 359
  format of statements in, 299
  sections of, 299
IF statement, COBOL, 356, 357, 358, 362, 371
  constant established by, *illustrated* 363
  options available with, 358
Impulse, electrical, 111

Indirect method of card punching, 96
Input, 31, 40
  buffer, 197
  electric typewriter, *illustrated* 178
  field, COBOL, 303
  file, COBOL, 301, 303
  file description, 341
  media, 31, 55, 181–194, 197
    cathode-ray tube (CRT) as, 191, *illustrated* 192
    graphic unit as, 189
    handwritten numerals as, 189
    magnetic disk as, 184
    magnetic drum as, 184
    magnetic ink characters as, 184
    magnetic tape as, 181, 197
    punched card as, 174, 181
    reproducers and converters, 101
  record, COBOL, 303
  statements
    DATA DIVISION, 304
    Optional, 341
    required, 340
  symbol, *illustrated* 244
  unit, graph, 189
  units, electronic computer system, 174, *illustrated* 175
Input/output media and devices, 181
INPUT-OUTPUT SECTION, 299
Input/output units, *illustrated* 175
Instruction
  add, 273
  branch, 240, *illustrated* 241, 267
  clear storage, 236, 245, 257, 259
  computer, 229
  computer-assisted, *illustrated* 192
  decision, 280
  format, 253
  halt, 269
  last card test, machine language, 268
  move, 236, 245, 262
  print, 236, 245, 266
  punch, 239, 266
  read, 239, 261, *illustrated* 263
  set word marks, 237, 258, *illustrated* 259
  storage of program, 250
Instruction address, machine language, 255
Instructions
  machine language, 253
  manual data processing, 34
Internal storage, digital computer, 171 215
Interpreter, 133; *illustrated* 134
  control panel diagram, 158, *illustrated* 161
Inventing names
  for input data, COBOL, 306
  for output data, COBOL, 312
Inventory report listing each stock transaction, *illustrated* 136

Index

Invoice, *illustrated* 75
Items
  elementary, 344
  group, 344
  subdividing data, 344

J

Jacquard, Joseph, 20
Jacquard's card, *illustrated* 20
Jobs in data processing, 375–383

K

Key
  duplicate 93, *illustrated* 91
  punch, 45
  skip, 93, *illustrated* 91
Keyboard
  IBM 29 card punch machine, alphabetic and numeric, *illustrated* 91
  Numeric card punch machine, *illustrated* 89
Keying symbol, *illustrated* 49
Key-operated card punch, 45

L

Language
  synthetic, 230
  translation, digital computer, 170
Last card sensing device, 246
Last card test
  COBOL 348, 353, *illustrated* 355
  control card, 355
  human language, 246, *illustrated* 247
  instruction, machine language, 268
Left zero insertion, 96
LESS THAN condition, 358
Level numbers, 308
Litton Automated Business Systems, sorting edge-notched cards by needle-sort process, 40
Loading program, 288
Logarithms, 16
Loop, 242, *illustrated* 248, *illustrated*, 280
Looping in COBOL, 347, *illustrated* 348
Low-order, 262

M

Machine language, 230
  block diagrams, *illustrated* 277, *illustrated* 282, *illustrated* 286
  instruction format, 253
  instructions, 253
    add, 273, 274, 275
    branch, 267, *illustrated* 268, 281
    clear storage, 257, 258, *illustrated* 259
    decision, *illustrated* 269, 279, *illustrated* 280, 281
    halt, *illustrated* 269
    last card test, 268
    move, 262, *illustrated* 263, *illustrated* 264, 265
    operation code, 254
    print, *illustrated* 266
    program
      including last card test, branch, and halt instructions, *illustrated* 270
      including multiple decisions, 285, *illustrated* 287
      printing list and accumulating total, *illustrated* 278
    program chart, 255, *illustrated* 256
    programs, *illustrated* 256, *illustrated* 270, *illustrated* 278, *illustrated* 284, *illustrated* 287, *illustrated* 334
    punch, 266, *illustrated* 267
    read, 261, *illustrated* 263
    set word marks, 258, *illustrated*, 260
    test and branch, 256
Magnetic core, 201
  memory system, 216
  plane, 216, *illustrated* 217
Magnetic cores storing binary digits in computers, *illustrated* 216
Magnetic disks, 184
Magnetic drums, 184
Magnetic ink character reader (IBM 1259), *illustrated* 185
Magnetic ink characters, 184, *illustrated* 185
Magnetic tape, 181, *illustrated* 182
  data recorder, *illustrated* 183
  direct recording of information on, 182
  drive, *illustrated* 175
  proofreading and correcting errors in direct recording, 182
Magnetic thin film, 226
Manipulation, 174
Manual data processing, 31, 33
Manual preparation of payroll, flowchart for, *illustrated* 50
Mark I computer, 25, 231
Mark-sensed card, *illustrated* 100

Mark-sensed recording, 100
Master card, 77, *illustrated* 124
Matching, 124
Match-merging, 124
Mauchly, John W., 26, 28
Media
  input, see Input media.
  output, see Output media.
Memory, computer, 171, 215
Merging, 123, *illustrated* 123
Merging of sales and payments detail cards with master card, *illustrated* 125
Microfilm output units, *illustrated* 191
Monroe, Jay R., 19
Morland, Samuel, 18
  adding machine, *illustrated* 18
Move instruction 239, 262, *illustrated* 264
MOVE statement, COBOL, 321, 349
Moving data to print, 264
Multi-Function Card Machine, 142, *illustrated* 143

N

Names
  Input data, COBOL, 306
  Output data, COBOL, 312
  used in COBOL program, 320
Nano-second, 1
Napier, John, 16, 28
Napier's Bones, *illustrated* 16
National Cash Register Co., accounting machine, 8
Needle-sort method, 38
9-edge, 64
96-column card, 63
NOT EQUAL condition, 358
NOT LESS THAN condition, 358
Numeric
  bit, *illustrated* 219
  code, 64, *illustrated* 65
  code aids sorting, 115
  data, processed by tabulator, 138
  PICTURE clauses, 309
  sorting of cards, 116, 117

O

Object program, 292
Octal numbering system, 208
Off-line storage, 176
On-line storage, 176
Operation code, 254

Optical
  mark page reader, 185, *illustrated* 187
  scanner, 186
  scanning, 185, 186, *illustrated* 188
  scanning conversion, 103
Optional input statements, COBOL, 305
Original data, 31
Oughtred, William, 16, 28
Output, 31, 40
  field, COBOL, *illustrated* 304
  file, COBOL, 301, *illustrated* 304
  file description, COBOL, 343
  media, 31, 55
    audio-response (ARP), 193, *illustrated* 194
    cathode-ray tube (CRT), 191, *illustrated* 192
    magnetic disk, 184
    magnetic drum, 184
    magnetic tape, 181
    microfilm, 191
    printed report, 195
    punched card, 174, 181
  portion of DATA DIVISION, *illustrated* 314
  printed, 195
  record, COBOL, *illustrated* 304
  symbol, *illustrated* 244
  units, 174, 175
    Audio-response (ARP), 193, *illustrated* 194
    Cathode-ray tube (CRT), 191, *illustrated* 192
    Electric typewriter, *illustrated* 178
    Graphic, 189, *illustrated* 190
    Remote console, 195

P

Panel, control, see Control panel.
Paragraph
  COBOL, *illustrated* 300
  names, 316
Parity check, *illustrated* 222
Pascal, Blaise, 17, 28
Payments detail card, *illustrated* 78, 124
Payroll summary sheet, *illustrated* 37, 38
Pegboard method, *illustrated* 37
Perforated card, 91, *illustrated* 92
PICTURE clauses, 309, 343, 371
Plane, magnetic core, *illustrated* 217
Planning cards for recording alphabetic information, 74
Planning cards for recording numeric information, 73

Planning Research Corporation
Babbage's "Difference Engine," *illustrated* 25
First mechanical adding machine, *illustrated* 17
Grant's calculator, *illustrated* 18
Hodometer, *illustrated* 15
Hollerith's punched card machine, *illustrated* 21
Jacquard's cards, 20, *illustrated* 19
Morland's adding machine, *illustrated* 18
Napier's bones, *illustrated* 16
Stonehenge, *illustrated* 15
von Leibnitz's calculator, *illustrated* 18, 28
Plugboard, 151, *illustrated* 152
Pockets of card sorter, *illustrated* 115
Portable card punch, 90
Post-Rite Division, Reynolds & Reynolds Company, pegboard, *illustrated* 37
Powers, James, 22
Powers' punching machine, *illustrated* 22
Print area, 233, *illustrated* 265
Print instructions, 239, *illustrated* 266
Printed
  heading, COBOL, 365, 366, 367, 371
  matter on cards, 81
  output, 195
  report
    COBOL, *illustrated* 329, *illustrated* 351, *illustrated* 360, *illustrated* 370
    contribution, partial, *illustrated* 146
    machine language, *illustrated* 273
    machine language with total accumulated, *illustrated* 279
    unit-record, 146, *illustrated* 148
Printing
  alphabetic data, tabulator, 137, *illustrated* 138
  card punch, 90
  numeric data, tabulator, 138, *illustrated* 139
  unit, tabulator, 135
PROCEDURE DIVISION, 296, *illustrated* 297, *illustrated* 317, 346, *illustrated* 359
  format of statements, 319
  inventing paragraph names, 316
Process
  collating, 122
  edge-notched, 38, *illustrated* 40
  grouping, 118
  matching, 124
  merging, 123
  off-line, 176
  on-line, 176
  selecting, 119, 127
  sequencing, 115
  sorting, 112

Processing instruction words, 288
Processing symbol, 244, *illustrated* 245
Program, 229
  card, 93, *illustrated* 95
    with two programs, *illustrated* 95
  cards, COBOL, *illustrated* 328
  cards, machine language, 288
  chart, 255
  compiler, 292
  divisions, COBOL, 296
  human language, *illustrated*, 242, 247, *illustrated* 248
  ID, 298, 337
  load card, machine language, 288
  machine language, 278
    multiple decision instructions included, 285, *illustrated* 287
    preparing a list and accumulating a total, two decisions included, *illustrated* 284
  object, 292
  sheet, COBOL, *illustrated* 295
  source, 292
  storage area, computer, 235
  test of last card included, 246
  translator, 230
Programmer-invented names, 294, 322, rules for inventing, 324
Programs, writing in English, 236
Proofreading and correcting errors made in card punching, 104
Proofreading magnetic tape, 182
Punch
  area, 233
  control, 127, *illustrated* 126
  instruction, 236, 266
Punched card, 61
  fields in, *illustrated* 237
  used for processing student enrollment data, *illustrated* 88
  used for receipt, *illustrated* 82
  used for statement, *illustrated* 82
  See also *Card*.
Punched cards, arranged alphabetically, *illustrated* 119
Punched paper tape, 98, *illustrated* 99
Punches, digit, 64
Punching, summary, 141
Punctuation rules for COBOL, 325
Pure binary system, 203

R

Random access, 176
Raw data, 31, 40
Read area of computer, 233
  data from punched card stored in, *illustrated* 234, 263, 265

Index

Read instructions, 239, 261
READ statement, COBOL, 321, 348, 353, 356
Reading brush, *illustrated* 153
Reading unit, tabulator, 134
Receipt used as source document, *illustrated* 144
Recording, 6
Recording information in cards, 87
Records, COBOL, *illustrated* 303, 304
Relation test, COBOL, 357
Remote console, 193
   educational application, 192
   space application, 195
Reproducer, 102, *illustrated* 103
   used with tabulator for summary punching, 141
Required entries, COBOL, 322
Required input statements, 304, 340
Required output statements, 312
Required statements, PROCEDURE DIVISION, 316
Reserved COBOL words, 294, 322, *illustrated* 323
Reserved storage areas, 235
Roller, contact, 111
Row, 64
Rules for preparing control panel diagrams, 159, *illustrated* 160, *illustrated* 161
Rules for programmer-invented names, 324

S

Salaries, data processing careers, 383
Sales
   application, optical scanning, 188
   detail card as unit record, *illustrated* 76, 78, 124, *illustrated* 125
   detail cards merged with payments detail card and master card, *illustrated* 125
Second-generation computer, 231
Sections, COBOL, *illustrated* 300
Selecting, 113, 119, 127
   cards, 119, 120, *illustrated* 121
Sequence, 240
   branch to repeat, *illustrated* 241
   checking, 128
Sequencing, 113
   alphabetically, 117, 118
   numerically, 115
Setting word marks, 238
Skip key, 93, *illustrated* 91
Skipping lines, COBOL, 367
Slide rule, 16, *illustrated* 17
Snap-out carbon forms, 36

Software, 170, *illustrated* 230
Soroban, 14
Sort brush and selector handle, *illustrated* 114
Sorter, *illustrated* 45, 46, *illustrated* 113
   pockets of, 115
   processing data, 114
Sorting, *illustrated* 7, 112
   data in cards, 111
   edge-notched cards by needle-sort process, *illustrated* 40
   numeric data, 114, 115
   shortcuts, 120
   symbol, *illustrated* 49
Source
   document, 31, *illustrated* 32, *illustrated* 144
   program, 292
SPS, 230
Standard card, *illustrated* 63, 71, see Card.
Start symbol, *illustrated* 49
Statement of account
   produced by merged cards, *illustrated* 126
   with tabulator tape, *illustrated* 140
Step identification symbol, *illustrated* 49, 243
Steps followed in electronic computer system when processing data, *illustrated* 180
Steps followed in unit-record system for updating club membership, 45
Stonehenge, *illustrated* 15
Storage
   auxiliary, 176, *illustrated* 177
   cells with cores turned on to represent digits, letters, parity check, and word marks, *illustrated* 222
   clearing, 236, 245
   data, *illustrated* 232
      in read area of computer, 234
   external, 176, *illustrated* 177
   instructions, 250
      clear, 236, 245
   internal, computer, 201, 202, 215
   magnetic disk, 184
   magnetic drum, 184
   magnetic tape, 183
   magnetic thin film, 226
   symbol, off-line, *illustrated* 49
Storing, 9
Structure of computer cell, 218
Student attendance card, 68
Subtraction in binary, 204
Summarizing, 8, *illustrated* 8
Summary cards, 79
Summary punching, 141
Sundstrand, David, 19
Sundstrand, Oscar, 19
Supplementary storage devices, electronic computer system, 176

Symbols, block diagram, *illustrated* 242–245
Synthetic language, 250
'SYSIN', 301
'SYSOUT', 301
System
   binary-coded decimal, 206, 207
   binary-coded hexadecimal, 210, 211
   binary-coded octal, 209
   decimal numbering, 26
   electronic computer, see Electronic computer system.
   hexadecimal numbering, 209
   magnetic core memory, 216
   manual, see Manual data processing.
   pure binary, 203
   unit-record, see Unit-record system.
Systems analyst, 381

T

Tabulator, *illustrated* 45, 46, 134, *illustrated* 135
   calculating unit, 134
   carriage control, 139
   carriage tape cut and punched to control punching on special form, *illustrated* 140
   control panel, *illustrated* 47, *illustrated* 152, 162
   detail printing, 135, *illustrated* 136
   group printing, 135, *illustrated* 137
   printing alphabetic data, 137, *illustrated* 138
   printing numeric data, 138, *illustrated* 139
   printing unit, 135
   programming, 148
   reading unit, 134
Tape
   magnetic, 181, 182
   punched paper, *illustrated* 99
Tape-to-card converter, *illustrated* 101
Ten-key adding machine with attachment for punching paper tape, *illustrated* 97
Terminal symbol (start and halt), *illustrated* 49, *illustrated* 243
Test
   control card, 355
   equality, 244, *illustrated* 245
      COBOL, 358
   inequality, 244, *illustrated* 245
Test, last card, 244, *illustrated* 245, *illustrated* 247, 268
      COBOL, 348, 353, *illustrated* 355, 356

Test, last card, branch, and halt instructions, *illustrated* 269
Test, last card and halt instructions, 246, *illustrated* 247
Third-generation computer, 231
Thomas, Charles Xavier, 18, 28
3M Company, aperture card, *illustrated* 191
Time card, *illustrated* 34
Time sharing, 193, 197
Timed electrical impulse, 111
Translator program, 230
Triple spacing, COBOL, 367
12 edge, 64
12 position, 64
Typebar, IBM 548 interpreter, *illustrated* 155

U

Unconditional branch instruction, 268
Unit
  input, see Input unit.
  output, see Output unit.
  tabulator
    calculating, 134
    reading, 134
    printing, 135
Unit record, 43, 74
  Sales detail card as, *illustrated* 76
Unit-record equipment operator, 377, 378
Unit-record system, 44, 74, 132, 162
  basic machines in, 47
  flow chart
    preparing printed report of contributions, *illustrated* 145
    updating club membership file, *illustrated* 51
    updating printed report of contributions, *illustrated* 147
  printed report, *illustrated* 146, *illustrated* 148

programming machines in, 47
steps in, 48, 51
steps for updating club membership, *illustrated*, 45
wiring control panel of interpreter, 158
Univac Division, Sperry Rand Corp., 22, Powers' punching machine, *illustrated* 22
Updated contribution report, partial, *illustrated* 148

V

VALUE clause used to describe report heading, 365, 371
Variable arrangements of cells in computers, 226
Variable word length, 221
Verified card, *illustrated* 106
Verifier, card, 46, 104, *illustrated* 105
Viatron Computer Systems, Viatron System 21 visual display system, *illustrated* 107
Visual display system, 106, *illustrated* 107
von Leibnitz calculator, *illustrated* 18
von Leibnitz, Gottfried, 18, 28

W

Window envelope, *illustrated* 36
Wire, control panel, 154
Wiring board, 151, *illustrated* 152
Wiring, interpreter control panel, 158, *illustrated* 159
Word
  length, 221
  mark core, 221

marks, instructions for setting, 237
read area, 238
work area, 238
WORKING-STORAGE SECTION, 345, 366, 371
  VALUE clause in, 366, 371
Wright Line Division, Barry Wright Corporation, portable card punch, *illustrated* 91

X

X position, 64
punch, 64

Y

Y position, 64
punch, 64

Z

Zero
  insertion, left, 96
  position, 64
  punch, 64
Zone
  bit or core, *illustrated* 219, 220
  punch, 64